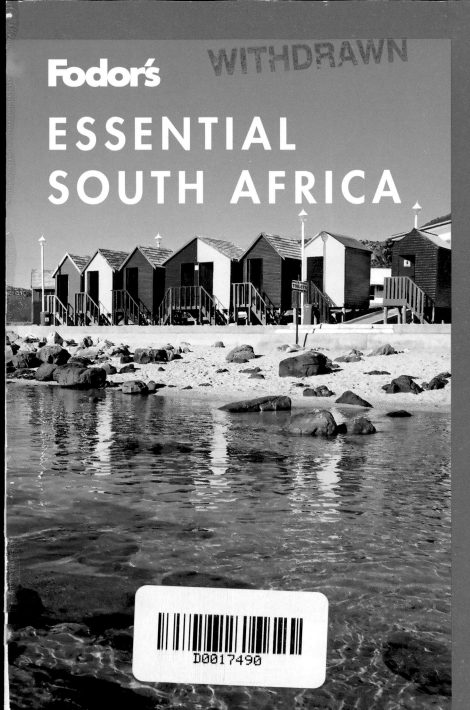

Fodor's

ESSENTIAL
SOUTH AFRICA

WELCOME TO SOUTH AFRICA

Everything about Africa that stirs the imagination is concentrated in its southernmost country. Lions freely roam vast game reserves such as Kruger National Park, vineyards stretch across the Cape Winelands, and mountains cascade into the sea along miles of beaches. In addition to dream safaris and romantic honeymoons, South Africa offers modern cities with thriving arts and dining scenes. South Africans are welcoming, and the country's emergence from a turbulent past provides a dramatic history lesson and the promise of something new every time you visit.

TOP REASONS TO GO

★ **Wildlife:** The "Big Five"—lion, elephant, rhino, leopard, Cape buffalo—and many more.

★ **Scenery:** Landscapes from the soaring Drakensberg Range to the endless Kalahari Desert.

★ **Cities:** Cape Town, Johannesburg, and Durban are among Africa's most vibrant places.

★ **Wine:** World-renowned viticulture, beautiful Cape Dutch architecture, and charming hotels.

★ **Beaches**: Surf, sand, endangered penguins, and abundant whale-watching from the shore.

★ **African Culture:** A diverse population (Zulu and Xhosa predominate) speaks 11 languages.

12
TOP EXPERIENCES

South Africa offers terrific experiences that should be on every traveler's list. Here are Fodor's top picks for a memorable trip.

1 Experience Cape Town and Table Mountain

South Africa's "Mother City" spreads magnificently around Table Mountain. Its popular Victoria & Albert Waterfront is a vibrant setting for many of the city's top hotels and restaurants. *(Ch. 2)*

2 Get to Know Nelson Mandela

See his grave in the Eastern Cape, the cell where he was imprisoned for 18 years on Robben Island, and the house where he lived in Soweto *(pictured)* until 1961. *(Ch. 8)*

3 Go Wine Tasting in the Cape Winelands

Known for Pinotage and Chenin Blanc varietals, as well as striking Cape Dutch architecture, South Africa's famous wineries are near Stellenbosch, Franschoek, and Parl. *(Ch. 3)*

4 Discover the Cradle of Humankind

The bones of our ancestors have been found in the complex of limestone caves that comprise this impressive World Heritage Site west of Johannesburg. *(Ch. 8)*

5 Drive Along the Scenic Garden Route

The 130-mile stretch of coast from Mossel Bay to Storms River has spectacular scenery and quaint towns, and it's one of the country's top draws for driving and hiking. *(Ch. 5)*

6 Learn the Secrets of the Kalahari Desert

The Northern Cape, the country's least-populated province, is home to the native San people and a vast, semi-arid savannah that stretches into Namibia and Botswana. *(Ch. 4)*

7 Go Whale-Watching

Hemanus harbors some of the world's best shoreside whale-watching. Southern right whales arrive here on their annual migration between June and November. *(Ch. 5)*

8 Hike the Drakensberg Mountains

The Zulu call this World Heritage Site the *uKhahlambra* ("Barrier of Spears"). It offers some of the most dramatic landscapes and best hiking in South Africa. *(Ch. 7)*

9 Spot the Big Five at Kruger National Park

Seeing lions, elephants, rhinos, leopards, and buffalo in their natural habitat is a breathtaking and humbling experience. *(Ch. 9)*

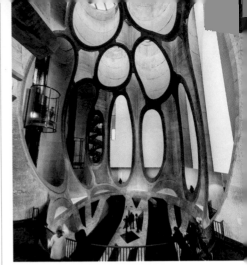

10 Explore the Southernmost Point in Africa

Just over 40 miles south of Cape Town, near the southernmost point of Africa, you can look out to the sea where the waters of the Atlantic meet the Indian Ocean. *(Ch. 2)*

11 See the Zeitz Museum of Contemporary Art

With cutting-edge architecture and a focus on telling the stories of African art in insightful new ways, the Zeitz MOCAA is one of the world's most influential art museums. *(Ch. 2)*

12 Sunbathe on Durban's Golden Mile

With more than 320 sunny days a year, this beachy playground on the Indian Ocean offers miles and miles of glistening sands, warm waters, and robust waves. *(Ch. 7)*

CONTENTS

CONTENTS

ABOUT THIS GUIDE

Top Picks		Hotels & Restaurants	
★	Fodor's Choice	🏨	Hotel
Listings		🛏	Number of rooms
✉	Address	🍽	Meal plans
📨	Branch address	🍴	Restaurant
☎	Telephone	✍	Reservations
📠	Fax	👔	Dress code
🌐	Website	💳	No credit cards
📧	E-mail	[$]	Price
🎫	Admission fee		
🕒	Open/closed times	**Other**	
[M]	Subway	⇨	See also
✣	Directions or Map coordinates	☞	Take note
		⛳	Golf facilities

Fodor's Recommendations

Everything in this guide is worth doing—we don't cover what isn't—but exceptional sights, hotels, and restaurants are recognized with additional accolades. **Fodor's Choice★** indicates our top recommendations. Care to nominate a new place? Visit Fodors.com/contact-us.

Trip Costs

We list prices wherever possible to help you budget well. Hotel and restaurant price categories from **$** to **$$$$** are noted alongside each recommendation. For hotels, we include the lowest cost of a standard double room in high season. For restaurants, we cite the average price of a main course at dinner or, if dinner isn't served, at lunch. For attractions, we always list adult admission fees; discounts are usually available for children, students, and senior citizens.

Hotels

Our local writers vet every hotel to recommend the best overnights in each price category, from budget to expensive. Unless otherwise specified, you can expect private bath, phone, and TV in your room. For expanded hotel reviews, visit Fodors.com.

Restaurants

Unless we state otherwise, restaurants are open for lunch and dinner daily. We mention dress code only when there's a specific requirement and reservations only when they're essential or not accepted. For expanded restaurant reviews, visit Fodors.com.

Credit Cards

The hotels and restaurants in this guide typically accept credit cards. If not, we'll say so.

EUGENE FODOR

Hungarian-born Eugene Fodor (1905–91) began his travel career as an interpreter on a French cruise ship. The experience inspired him to write *On the Continent* (1936), the first guidebook to receive annual updates and discuss a country's way of life as well as its sights. Fodor later joined the U.S. Army and worked for the OSS in World War II. After the war, he kept up his intelligence work while expanding his guidebook series. During the Cold War, many guides were written by fellow agents who understood the value of insider information. Today's guides continue Fodor's legacy by providing travelers with timely coverage, insider tips, and cultural context.

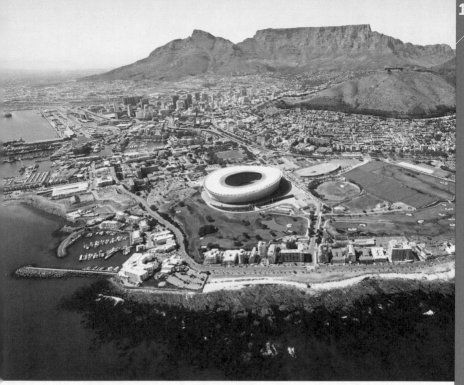

EXPERIENCE
SOUTH AFRICA

WHAT'S WHERE

1 Western Cape. Best known as home to Cape Town and the Cape Winelands, this province is a region of tranquil farms and popular beach resorts. The Overberg and Swartland areas have also become stellar wine regions. Whale-watching is guaranteed along the southern Cape coast.

2 Garden Route and the Little Karoo. The aptly named Garden Route is more than 100 miles of forested mountains, waterways, and beaches. The Little Karoo, through which threads the awesome R62, is separated from the coast by the Outeniqua Mountains, famous for their ostrich farms and the hugely impressive Cango Caves.

3 Northern Cape. South Africa's emerging tourist region offers seriously off-the-beaten-track adventures, including the spectacular Kgalagadi National Park. The Namaqualand spring flowers are a must-see, as is the country's last remaining wilderness, the rugged Richtersveld.

4 Eastern Cape. Birthplace of Nelson Mandela, this province of rolling green hills offers seaside family getaways on the Wild Coast, the country's lesser-publicized but fascinating battlefields, and

ZIMBABWE
Messina
Kruger
National
Park
Pietersburg
MPUMALANGA
MOZAMBIQUE
Pilanesberg
National Park
Sabi Sands
Game Reserve
Nelspruit
Cradle of
Humankind
6
PRETORIA
Soweto
Johannesburg
SWAZILAND
Mkuze
Game
Reserve
Tswalu
Kalahari
Reserve
Phinda
Private
Reserve
Itala Game Reserve
Thanda Game Reserve
Hluhluwe-
Umfolozi
Game Reserve
Ulundi
Drakensberg
Park
Bloemfontein
KWAZULU-NATAL
Richards Bay
LESOTHO
Pietermaritzburg
DRAKENSBERG MOUNTAINS
5
Durban
Margate
Umtata
EASTERN CAPE
East London
4
Grahamstown
Shamwari
Game Reserve
Port
Elizabeth

0   200 mi
0   200 km

EAN

the nation's premier elephant reserve, Addo Elephant National Park.

5 Durban and KwaZulu-Natal. Inland from Durban's bustling tropical port city are the battlefields where Boers, Britons, and Zulu fought to control the country. The province is also home to the dramatically beautiful Drakensberg Mountains, a sanctuary for hikers. Wildlife-viewing in the far north reserves rivals that at Kruger.

6 Johannesburg. This historic gold town orbited by the capital of Pretoria and the Soweto township is also an urban African powerhouse. See some of the world's oldest human fossils at the nearby Cradle of Humankind, and do not miss the sobering but excellent Apartheid Museum.

7 Mpumalanga and Kruger National Park. South Africa's premier wildlife destination is packed with epic battle and gold-rush history, not to mention any animal you might wish to see.

NEED TO KNOW

Pretoria

Atlantic Ocean

SOUTH AFRICA

Indian Ocean

AT A GLANCE

Capital: Pretoria, Cape Town, Bloemfontein

Population: 55,908,900

Currency: Rand (ZAR)

Money: ATMs common, credit cards widely accepted

Language: Afrikaans, English, Ndebele, Northern Sotho, Sotho, Swazi, Tswana, Tsonga, Venda, Xhosa, Zulu

Country Code: 27

Emergencies: 10111; 10177

Driving: On the left

Electricity: 220v and 230v/50 cycles; plugs have three round prongs

Time: GMT +2 (7 hours ahead of New York)

Documents: Up to 90 days with valid passport. Children under 18 must carry a birth certificate

Mobile Phones: GSM (900 and 1800 bands), UMTS (2100 band), LTE (1800 band)

Major Mobile Companies: Vodacom, MTN, Cell C

WEBSITES
⊕ www.southafrica.net

GETTING AROUND

✈ **Air Travel:** Johannesburg, Cape Town, and Durban have the main airports.

🚌 **Bus Travel:** Budget-minded travelers can use Baz Bus, which makes regular stops between Cape Town and Johannesburg.

🚗 **Car Travel:** Roads are good, and it's easy to drive between Johannesburg and Kruger, and from Cape Town through the Winelands and Garden Route.

🚆 **Train Travel:** Luxury trains run between Pretoria and Cape Town; regular trains take the same routes. Other trains are not considered safe for tourists.

PLAN YOUR BUDGET

	HOTEL ROOM	MEAL	ATTRACTIONS
Low Budget	R1,800	R350	National Gallery, R15
Mid-Budget	R4,000	R800	Theater ticket, R200
High Budget	R7,500	R1,500	Birding, R700

WAYS TO SAVE

Grab a bunny. One of the cheapest and most substantial take-out options is the bunny chow, a hollowed-out loaf of bread loaded with curried meat.

Self-cater. Cape Town and Johannesburg have huge selections of self-catering accommodation options with full kitchens that are usually much cheaper than hotels.

Get a bus pass. Many of the country's bus companies offer money-saving passes good for varying numbers of travel days.

Take a tour. A full-day ticket for City Sightseeing South Africa's Blue Mini Peninsula Tour takes you to 14 diverse stops for just R190 (less if bought online).

Hassle Factor	Medium. Direct flights operate from the United States, but it's a 17- to 18-hour trip. Connections are also possible through Europe, but they increase travel time substantially.
3 days	Explore Cape Town and Robben Island, where Nelson Mandela was imprisoned for 18 years.
1 week	Catch a flight to Kruger National Park. Drive along the Mpumalanga Panoramic Route to Johannesburg, where you'll tour for two days before heading to Cape Town.
2 weeks	Spend three days around Cape Town, then two in the Winelands. Take the Garden Route drive to Port Elizabeth and board a flight to a private reserve. Spend three days on safari before heading to Victoria Falls.

WHEN TO GO

High Season: From November through February. Though the bush is very hot in the summer, it's the best time to see young animals.

Low Season: May through August has unpredictable weather. Winter is the best time to go on safari—vegetation is sparse and water is scarce, so it's easier to spot game congregating around water holes.

Value Season: Cape Town's best weather is between February and March, and September and October are still great months to go on safari.

BIG EVENTS

January: Kaapse Klopse, also called Tweede Nuwe Jaar, sees some 13,000 minstrels take to the streets of Cape Town on January 2.

March-April: The fourth largest jazz festival in the world showcases international jazz and African music legends and discoveries alike. ⊕ www.capetownjazzfest.com

June–July: The 10-day National Arts Festival in Grahamstown is the oldest and largest of its kind in South Africa. ⊕ www.nationalartsfestival.co.za.

July: The popular Knysna Oyster Festival not only celebrates the oyster, but raises money for charity. ⊕ www.oysterfestival.co.za.

October: Bloemfontein's MACUFE, the Mangaung African Cultural Festival, showcases African music, theater, dance, fine art, and crafts. ⊕ www.macufe.co.za.

READ THIS

■ *My Traitor's Heart,* Rian Malan. The tale of an Afrikaner returning from exile to face violence preceding the fall of apartheid.

■ *July's People,* Nadine Gordimer. Written in 1981, this classic imagines a violent possible end to apartheid.

■ *The Heart of Redness,* Zakes Mda. A prophecy states that the British colonialists would be swept to sea if the Xhosa people killed their cattle.

WATCH THIS

■ *Tsotsi.* A grim look at the violent life of a Johannesburg teenage gang leader.

■ *Invictus.* Nelson Mandela uses rugby to unite a race-divided nation.

■ *Sarafina!* The 1976 Soweto uprising—as told through music.

EAT THIS

■ *Biltong:* air-dried meat, often made from venison

■ *Bobotie:* spiced ground meat and raisins, with egg-based topping

■ *Boerewors:* a beef, lamb, and/or pork sausage

■ *Bunny chow:* a bread loaf filled with curried meat

■ *Koeksister:* a doughnut, twisted and sweet, or egg-shaped and spicy

■ *Pap:* fluffy cornmeal porridge, similar to polenta

SOUTH AFRICA TODAY

The Rainbow Nation

Although massive progress has been made in terms of the intermingling of race groups and racial harmony in postapartheid South Africa, the so-called "Rainbow Nation" is still home to vast economic disparity and tensions.

The physical legacy of apartheid remains largely in place, with large shantytowns (called "townships") inhabited almost entirely by black South Africans; for many of the country's poor, things have not changed substantially since the 1990s. Black ownership of businesses has increased, but the wealth has often been transferred to a new black elite (former unionist leader Cyril Ramaphosa, for example). The tourism industry has begun evolving partnerships to improve the economic fortunes of rural communities and residents, who increasingly have shares in the lodges they work for. You'll find it's easier to meet South African blacks on an equal footing in Johannesburg than in Cape Town.

More than 80% of South Africans are Christians (the Protestant and Zion African Churches have the largest followings). About 3% follow other religions, including Islam, Hinduism, and Judaism. About 13% of the population claim no affiliation.

Performing Arts

Cape Town, Durban, and Johannesburg all have lively arts scenes. Annual festivals, such as the National Arts Festival in Grahamstown in late June and/or early July, are great places to experience innovative performing- and visual-arts trends in the country.

Singer/songwriter Johnny Clegg, Jazz musician Hugh Masekela, and a cappella group Ladysmith Black Mambazo put South Africa on the international map; however, they have been replaced by the likes of Afro-fusion band Freshlyground, singers like Thandiswa Mazwai and Simphiwe Dana, and alternative acts like Die Antwoord. There are many annual music festivals, mostly in the Western Cape, including Oppikoppi, Rocking the Daisies, and Splashy Fen.

Dance companies postapartheid have begun to use movement as a form of expression to explore the country's legacy. The dance form called Afro-fusion, named by Moving Into Dance Company's Sylvia Glasser, combines classic and traditional movements. Cape Town's Jazzart Dance Theatre, the oldest in the country, experiments with styles and expression.

Local theaters feature international as well as homegrown authors such as Athol Fugard, who often returns "home" from his residence in San Diego to direct his own works at the Fugard Theatre in Cape Town's District Six.

Literature

Most South African literature is published in English and Afrikaans, predominately because indigenous languages were not recognized and African experiences were not valued. Increasingly, however, works are being translated into other languages.

Fiction writers like Deon Meyer, Mike Nicholls, and Lauren Beukes have joined Nobel Prize winners Nadine Gordimer and J. M. Coetzee (who has also won the Booker Prize twice) in successfully flying the local literary flag in the international literary fiction market. The Franschhoek Literary Festival (May) and the Open Book Festival (in Cape Town in September) are both excellent opportunities to acquaint yourself with some of the country and continent's talent.

SOUTH AFRICA'S HISTORY

The First Known Inhabitants

Two-million-year-old hominid fossils of the earliest known prehuman ancestors were found in South Africa, at the Sterkfontein Caves, about an hour's drive from Johannesburg. This area is now known as the Cradle of Humankind. Meanwhile, the 2015 discovery of a previously unknown human relative, *Homo Naledi*, is likely to change the way scientists view human evolution.

Among the descendants of these prehistoric Africans were the San, Stone Age hunter-gatherers. From AD 200 to 400, people speaking various Bantu/Nguni languages moved into the area that is now South Africa's Eastern Cape and KwaZulu-Natal provinces, bringing with them Iron Age culture. Between AD 500 and the 1300s, the Khoikhoi—pastoralists and nomadic cattle herders—moved south and interacted, as well as clashed, with the San, as did a later group of farmers from the north. As the population increased, powerful kingdoms developed.

European Colonization

The Portuguese were the first to land in the Cape—in 1487—when pioneering a sea route to India, but it was the Dutch who decided to set up a refreshment station in 1652. Station commander Jan van Riebeeck later established a permanent settlement and imported a large number of slaves, mostly from the East Indies. The Cape Colony started to expand outward, and the Khoikhoi, who were living in the Cape, were no match for European weaponry. The colonial drive caused the Khoikhoi to lose most of their livestock, grazing areas, and population, and those who remained became marginalized servants. The Afrikaans language slowly evolved (in 1925 it became an official language) from the Dutch mother tongue, with words and sounds from the languages of other European settlers, slaves, and San and Khoikhoi servants thrown in.

Over the next 100 years, the Dutch pushed farther inland, often clashing with indigenous inhabitants. Official control seesawed between the Dutch and the British until the region was formally recognized by the 1815 Congress of Vienna as a British colony.

The Great Trek

The British government subsequently annexed the Cape Colony and outlawed slavery in 1834. The Boers, or Afrikaners, fled inland, setting up new communities and drawing up constitutions explicitly prohibiting racial equality in church and state.

Also known as the Voortrekkers (or pioneers), the Boers traveled into lands occupied by Bantu-speaking peoples, including the Zulu kingdom. Ruled by Shaka, the Zulus evolved during the 1820s into the most powerful black African kingdom in southern Africa and occupied most of what is now KwaZulu-Natal.

Between 1837 and 1838, Afrikaner farmer and businessman Piet Retief attempted to negotiate a land agreement with the Zulu king, Dingane. Deceit entered the frame, and the Zulus killed Retief and more than 500 Voortrekkers.

In retaliation, a Boer raiding party defeated the Zulus at the Battle of Blood River in 1838, establishing the short-lived Republic of Natalia. Also around that time, two Boer republics were established: the South African Republic (now Mpumalanga, North West, and Limpopo provinces) and the Orange Free State (now Free State).

Prosperity and Conflict

The discovery of diamonds in Kimberley in 1867 and then gold in 1886 outside Johannesburg changed South Africa's fortunes forever. The economic center moved from the British-controlled Cape to the Boer republics, and an agricultural society was transformed into an urbanized, industrial one.

Mining companies required a great deal of labor, supplied almost exclusively by black, male migrant workers, who by the 20th century were forced to live in single-sex hostels or compounds. Workers had to carry passes, and their movements were tightly controlled. The British, with financial interest in the mines, wanted to control the entire country and thus its mineral wealth. To this end, they took over Natalia and invaded Zulu territory. They next turned their attention to the two Boer republics.

To preempt an invasion by the British, the Boers declared war in 1899. The Anglo-Boer war (now called the South African War, as it involved all races) lasted until 1902. Britain's "scorched earth" policy meant farms were burned and women and children were put into concentration camps (the first of their kind). The Boers eventually surrendered, but bitterness toward the British remained. By 1910 the former British colonies were united as the Union of South Africa, and Afrikaners were appointed to government positions in an attempt to reconcile English and Afrikaans speakers.

Apartheid

In 1913, the Natives Land Act divided the country into black and white areas. Given less than 10% of land, many blacks were forced to become migrant workers on white-owned farms and mines. Black political leaders established the South African Native National Congress in 1912, a forerunner to the African National Congress (ANC), to protest against such measures.

During World War I, South Africa, as part of the British Empire, was at war with Germany, and invaded German South West Africa (later Namibia). White Afrikaners tried to exploit this opportunity to win back their country but failed. Between the World Wars, the country was ruled by an Afrikaner-dominated government. The ANC continued to peacefully protest, with little success.

Once World War II began, the Union voted to support the British by a small majority; many Afrikaners openly supported Nazi Germany. The National Party won the 1948 election on the platform of pro-apartheid policies, the cornerstone of which—the 1950 Population Registration Act—classified all South Africans according to race, and established the segregation of schools, universities, residential areas, and public facilities.

Opposition to Apartheid

The government introduced severe penalties for opposition to apartheid, and banned the ANC and Pan Africanist Congress (PAC)—a faction of the ANC, which went underground or into exile.

ANC leaders, Nelson Mandela among them, were arrested in 1952 and, after a lengthy detention and trial, sentenced to life imprisonment on Robben Island in 1964.

By the mid-1970s the antiapartheid struggle was revived, aided by condemnation from other countries, including South Africa's neighbors, who were no longer sympathetic to the white regime. In 1976 several thousand black African schoolchildren marched through the township of Soweto to protest Afrikaans becoming the language of instruction. During what became known as the Soweto Uprising, police opened fire on the crowds, killing between 200 and 500 people and injuring thousands. After this, the government was increasingly forced to rely on force to crush resistance and impose order; it never fully regained control.

By the 1980s, international condemnation of, and reaction to, apartheid had reached fever pitch: celebrities avoided South Africa, its sports teams were shunned abroad, and U.S. college students held rallies demanding that their universities divest their assets from the country. Despite this, the government continued to arrest South African journalists, students, and other opponents, detaining them without trial. Prominent apartheid opponents were killed in neighboring countries. However, sanctions, boycotts, strikes, and campaigns by the liberation organizations were damaging the economy, and business began to be badly affected.

The Dawn of Democracy

F. W. de Klerk became president of South Africa in December 1989, and in his first speech to Parliament two months after his election, he made the unexpected and astonishing announcement: Mandela and other political prisoners were to be released and the ANC and PAC were to be unbanned. Talks began between government and the liberation movements, although racial tensions remained. In 1994, South Africa had its first democratic election, and Mandela became president. It was a time of great joy and exultation for many, and South Africa rejoined the rest of the world on the political stage, resuming full participation in the United Nations and the Commonwealth, and sending its first racially integrated team to the Olympics.

A government-appointed panel called the Truth and Reconciliation Commission, headed by Desmond Tutu, an Anglican archbishop, began public hearings across the country to probe human-rights violations during the apartheid years. People could talk about their experiences, and the full extent of apartheid atrocities came to light; many considered this to be an important healing process.

Mandela was succeeded in 1999 by Thabo Mbeki, a Sussex (U.K.) university–educated intellectual who continued to guide the transformation process from a white-dominated, apartheid government to a democratic one.

The Present

In 2008, the populist Jacob Zuma became leader of the ANC, succeeding Mbeki as president in 2009. Although South Africans hoped that Zuma's populist utterances would translate into action to improve the lives of people, his administration has been hounded by scandal and corruption. Despite South Africa's modern economy, prosperous gold and diamond mines, and the export of raw materials, the country continues to face numerous problems, including an unskilled labor force, a threat to media freedom, failing infrastructure, violent crime, chronic unemployment, and the highest rate of HIV infection in the world. A symbol of Zuma's rule has been the 2015 "Fees Must Fall" Movement; a university student–led protest against tuition increases and the numerous broken promises affecting the country's majority black population.

IF YOU LIKE

Drop-Dead Luxury

Not into roughing it? No problem. Our favorite luxe properties will tempt you to defect from the real world and live like kings and queens.

Bushmans Kloof Wilderness Reserve, Western Cape. This Relais & Châteaux lodge is one of South Africa's gems. Set in a phenomenal, otherworldly mountain landscape, it offers beautiful views of nature, wildlife, and birdlife, as well as proximity to the country's finest collections of Bushman rock art found in the mountains.

Chitwa Chitwa, Sabi Sands Reserve. Family-owned and family-operated for more than 40 years, this luxurious private reserve sits across from the largest body of water in the area, and guarantees awesome animal sightings from just about every vantage point. For an extra dose of ultra pampering, Chitwa House comes with a private vehicle, guide, tracker, and chef.

Ellerman House. With a breathtaking location on the slopes of Lions Head overlooking Bantry Bay, this Edwardian mansion is all about understated service, fabulous art (the walls display one of the country's finest collections of South African fine art), and fine wine and cuisine. Families or groups wanting more privacy and their own staff should check out the private villas.

Leobo Private Reserve. Visitors to this private 20,000-acre reserve in the Waterberg Mountains will enjoy spectacular game sightings as well as total privacy and luxury in the exclusive-use chalets. Stargazers should consider the stunning Observatory private villa.

Tswalu Kalahari Reserve, Northern Cape. Big skies, superb accommodation, wonderful wildlife, and miles from anyone else—this, plus the fact that it's owned by the Oppenheimers, distinguishes it from most other game lodges. Tarkuni is the fabled family's own private home, and comes with its own chef and game-viewing vehicle.

Rubbing Shoulders with Locals

South Africa's rich cultural offerings run from the rhythms of Soweto to the jazz riffs of Cape Town's clubs. Crafts, drama, and dance combine to form the rich cultural mosaic of South Africa, where native beats mingle with European traditions.

Cape Town Stadium. For a soccer or rugby match or even a music concert, this is one of the country's best places to meet South Africans. In fact, any of the country's stadiums built for the FIFA 2010 World Cup are excellent.

Jazz Tours, Cape Town. Join like-eared aficionados for a tour that will show you the roots of jazz and expose you to some local ear candy.

Kirstenbosch National Botanical Gardens, Cape Town. The 1,304 acres feature indigenous southern African plants that captivate even the locals. Come for lawn picnics in the shadow of Table Mountain, and stay to listen to the Winter Concert Series.

Maboneng Precinct, Johannesburg. A creative hub and axis of Jo'burg's inner-city revitalization, this cluster of restaurants, shops, galleries, and a movie theater developed alongside sleek apartments and workspaces.

Market Theatre, Johannesburg. With its rich legacy, this is one of the country's renowned venues, and showcases new works. During the era of apartheid it was one of South Africa's few venues where all races could watch together.

Mzoli's. Party-loving carnivores will enjoy this open-air *braai* (barbecue) experience in the township of Gugulethu. Come on a Sunday afternoon to enjoy perfectly barbecued meat with a side of township dance party.

The Beach

South Africa's coastline stretches from tiny towns to desolate windswept acres, and most beach lovers can find exactly what they're after, be it a private cove or an endless stretch of sand.

Boulders Beach, Simon's Town, Cape Peninsula. The sparkling coves ringed by dramatic boulders are also home to a colony of seriously threatened African penguins. Share your spot in the sand with these curious creatures.

Camps Bay, Cape Town. A broad Atlantic beach backed by looming Table Mountain and a street full of umbrella-shaded cafés is the perfect place to watch a sunset or take a stroll. But it's a bit too cold for swimming.

Lookout Beach, Plettenberg Bay. Washed away (literally) a few years ago, it's back. South Africa's ultimate playtime beach has perfect bodysurfing waves, with dolphins often joining in, not to mention the most awesome, mountain-fringed setting.

Rocktail Bay, KwaZulu-Natal. If you're in the mood for pristine beaches, surf fishing, snorkeling, or sunbathing, then coming to the lodge nestled on the Maputaland Coastal Reserve will surely be the perfect beach getaway after your safari.

St. James, Cape Town. Just south of Kalk Bay's shops, St. James's colorful changing cabanas are photo icons. The gentle surf and nearby Dalebrook tidal pool are perfect for kids.

Second Beach, Port St Johns, Eastern Cape. Probably the country's most picture-perfect subtropical beach, fringed by bush and hills, this is for the adventurous—but it's so very worth it.

Getting Out of the Vehicle

Game drives are thrilling and often action packed, but sometimes, particularly if you are a second-time visitor to Africa and have ticked off your Big Five, you'll be interested in the more interactive aspect of safari, getting up close and personal with the African bush and its inhabitants.

Elephant Safaris. Whether people should ride elephants is the subject of debate, but if you prefer your wildlife a bit more tame, visit the Addo Elephant Sanctuary, where you'll meet some trained African elephants available for short rides, walks, petting, and feeding.

Rhino Tracking. Seeing a rhino on foot is quite a different experience from viewing one from a jeep. Depending on your level of interest, you can organize a walking safari within a special area of Kruger for several hours or several days. Along the way, the guide will point out interesting grasses and smaller animals.

Stargazing Safaris. Ask if your lodge has a guide trained in astronomy for a night safari of the Southern Hemisphere's sky. The west is best, but Sutherland in the Northern Cape may be a highlight.

Turtle-Watching. From St. Lucia to Kosi Bay, join a safari to look for loggerhead and leatherback turtles laying their eggs for a few months starting in October.

Walking Safaris. For some, feeling the grass on their legs and hearing the rustle under their feet is the best way to experience the land. Amble with trained guides for several hours to gain a new perspective on creatures large and small—you may spot the "little five" up close in many locations throughout the country.

Kid-Friendly Destinations

More and more families want their kids to share in safari or wilderness lodge experiences, and more lodges are catering to kids with programs designed especially for them. Always find out in advance which lodges welcome kids, as some still don't allow children under 12; most do not allow smaller children (under 6) on game drives. Try one of the malaria-free reserves to avoid the added worry of anti-malarial medication.

Crawford's Beach Lodge, Wild Coast. Perfect for families, this reasonably priced lodge on the Eastern Cape's gorgeous Wild Coast offers tons of activities from surfing to hiking to game drives at Inkwekwezi Private Game Reserve (5 miles away). An outdoor play area, games room, and holiday club (offered during South African school holidays) allow you to sit back and enjoy the view.

Jaci's Lodges, Madikwe. This could well be the original lodge to have made an art of child-friendly safaris. Jaci van Heterem celebrates children with jungle drives for the littlest adventurers and family drives for Mom and Dad, too.

Kariega Main Lodge, Eastern Cape. On the eastern end of the Garden Route, Kariega Private Reserve boasts the Big Five plus a plethora of activities when the little ones are not up to another game drive. A kids' play area, special daily activities, and babysitting are also on offer.

Phinda Reserve, KwaZulu-Natal. Staff are dedicated to entertaining children at this excellent game lodge. The kids even get to make pizzas in the kitchen.

Sabi Sabi Bush Lodge, Kruger National Park. The EleFun Centre at this luxury lodge in Kruger offers interactive, hands-on activities for two distinct age groups (4–8 and 9–12), all created to nurture your child's love of the wild.

Game-Viewing at Smaller Reserves

Kruger Park may well be the granddaddy of game-viewing in South Africa, but smaller reserves attract visitors seeking boutique accommodations, a special sense of place, or a particular type of game.

Kwandwe Private Game Reserve. Excellent, especially for nocturnal wildlife, this reserve is close to the Fish River valley near Grahamstown. Clean, modern lines take the place of animal skins and trophies in the lodge. Also a great option for families.

MalaMala, Mpumalanga. Retaining that genuine bushveld feel of bygone days, MalaMala, which adjoins Kruger National Park, is the largest privately owned Big Five game area in South Africa. The animal-viewing is unbeatable, probably because it was the first of the lodges in the Sabi Sands, and animals have learned historical familiarity.

Mattanu Private Game Reserve, Northern Cape. This small reserve—once a farm—was established in the early 1990s to breed rare and endangered antelope species from Zimbabwe. It has offered accommodations since 2006.

Phinda Reserve, KwaZulu-Natal. Seven ecosystems, superb, varied accommodations, and a wide variety of wildlife draw animal lovers to this luxurious retreat, which offers everything from glass-enclosed suites in the forest to a family lodge with a private butler and chef.

FLAVORS OF SOUTH AFRICA

South Africa's rich cultural legacy comes alive on the plate, in the array of flavors and tastes influenced by the mélange of people who have made South Africa their home, as well as in the global cuisine that has arrived with international chefs settling here in the past two decades. Local restaurants score well in global awards—including two listings in the top 50 restaurants in the world—and subscribe to the highest food-safety standards.

BBQ Traditions

South Africans love to *braai* (rhymes with rye)—that is, barbecue—at any opportunity. In townships, literally hundreds of people meet and socialize around an outdoor fire at recreational sites after purchasing meat from nearby butchers and drinks from a corner *shebeen* (neighborhood tavern). But it's in the homes of South Africans that the braai comes to life.

Boerewors (pronounced *boo*-rah-vors) or beef-and-pork sausage with heady doses of coriander seed, lamb chops, and chicken pieces are all braai staples. *Sosaties* (so- *sah*-teez), skewers of meat with fruit or vegetables, are also popular. Potatoes and sweet potatoes are often wrapped in foil and cooked among the coals. Rooster *Brood* (roosta-brewat) are sandwiches (typically onion and tomato) cooked on the fire to the perfect consistency: crisp on the outside, moist on the inside. A *potjie* (poy-kee) is a three-legged cast-iron pot as well as the name of the stew typically prepared in it: meat on the bone is layered with vegetables (potatoes, onions, garlic, dried beans) and cooked over low coals for hours. *Waterblommetjiebredie* (literally "flower stew") is a Western Cape speciality made from the blooms of a local flower.

During the grape harvest (March and April) a soft, sweet bread is made from the grape must. Called *mosbolletjies* (mohss-ball-eh-keys), it's irresistible if purchased fresh from the oven.

Indigenous South African Dishes

Pap (pronounced pup; also known as *samp*) is made from maize meal and cooked to varying consistencies—*krummel* (*kruh*-muhl) is dry and crumbly, whereas *stywe* (*stay*-ver) is like a stiff porridge. An African staple, it's served alongside stewed vegetables or meats and is extremely filling. The texture is like couscous, and the flavor is mild enough that it goes with everything. Other vegetables abundant in South African recipes include gem squash, butternut squash, pumpkin, green beans, tomatoes, and cabbage. You may also come across the following confusing terms: rocket (arugula), peppadew (a cross between a pepper and cherry tomato), and *mielies* (corn on the cob).

For dessert expect *malva* (muhl-vah) pudding, its sweet and sour notes created by pouring an apricot-jam-and-vinegar sauce over sponge cake. *Melktert* (melk-tet) is a thick custard typically dusted with cinnamon or nutmeg. *Koeksisters* (cook-sis-ter) is braided sweet dough boiled in cinnamon-spiced syrup (finger-shape coconut doughnuts available at Cape Malay restaurants or at carnivals are also called koeksisters).

Immigrant Influences

Despite the name, the cuisine of Cape Town's Malay community is not Malaysian, but instead mixes the flavors, spices, and preparations of Indonesia, India, Africa, and Europe. *Bobotie*, curried, chopped beef with raisins, topped with a savory custard mixture, most closely resembles English shepherd's pie—with a kick. *Bredie* is another way of saying stew and is often made with tomatoes. You'll find *samoosas* (samosas—pronounced sah- *moo*-sah here) at every corner café. *Rootis* (rotis—pronounced *root*-ee), a soft, griddled flatbread, when filled with curry-mince is called a *salomi* (pronounced sah- *low*-me). The Gatsby is a long hero roll packed with lettuce, tomatoes, french fries, and melted cheese; meat (usually sausage or steak) is added, and the whole thing topped with anything from mayonnaise to *peri-peri* (fiery Mozambican-style tomato-and-chili sauce). "Bunny chow," made famous in Durban by indentured Asian laborers who couldn't sit down to eat, is a half or quarter white-bread loaf that's hollowed out, filled with biryani, and capped by the leftover bread. Top your snacks with *chakalaka* (a spicy vegetable relish) or peri-peri, which is perfect with grilled seafood.

Beyond Beef

Biltong is a popular snack that's found just about everywhere from roadside stands to high-end markets. Types range from beef and ostrich to game (kudu is a favorite) and can be flavored with spices. "Wet" biltong is a moister version. *Frikkadels,* mini–lamb *rissoles* (small croquettes), are occasionally wrapped in cabbage leaves and flavored with nutmeg, reminiscent of Eastern European stuffed cabbage dishes or the little Greek meatballs called *keftedes.*

Many restaurants serve game such as ostrich and springbok but also wildebeest, impala, and kudu. Karoo lamb is some of the most delicious lamb you will ever eat, getting its flavor from the wild herbs the animals feed on in the arid Karoo region.

Succulent Seafood

As in the rest of the world, local fish stocks are under tremendous threat, and every decent seafood restaurant will have a sustainable-seafood guide (known as the SASI guide), explaining what on the menu is okay to eat. Rock lobster (also known as crayfish) is highly sought after, and closely resembles New England lobster. Costly perlemoen, or abalone, which is almost on the brink of extinction, is tough and best described as similar to calamari steak—only eat it if you know it's been farmed. Local fish include kingklip (a firm white fish), hake (a flaky, white fish called haddock once smoked), and snoek (pronounced snook), an oily fish with many long bones. Line-caught fish includes Cape salmon (also known as *geelbek*), which isn't salmon at all but is sure to be on the menu. You may come across kabeljou (*cabal*-yoh), also known as kob, a flaky and delicious fish. Tuna is also local, and often served seared or as sushi. West Coast oysters are another local favorite, and among the tastiest you will encounter.

Eating on Safari

Since most, if not all, of the ingredients must be flown in or grown locally in small quantities, you might expect meals to be limited. However, you'll usually have a choice of entrée options (two to three), and you'll be amazed at the delicious and innovative creations that come out of the kitchen. You'll also have plenty of opportunity to try new varieties of fish or game and South African wines. Breads and pastries are generally fresh baked, and any dietary concerns are catered to if possible. Don't be surprised if you gain a few pounds. It's not unheard of to eat six or seven times a day. Dining is a major pastime on safari. Stopping for coffee and rusks (rustic biscotti, which often include raisins and seed kernels) under an acacia tree, with wild animals surrounding you, is a morning game-drive highlight.

Taste at Your Own Risk

Odd-sounding treats are often presented on a township tour. Two of the most common are *smileys* (sheep's heads cooked in the fire) and *walkie-talkies*, which, appropriately are made from chicken heads and feet. You may also be offered Mopane worms, a tofulike, protein-rich staple that takes on the taste of other ingredients (it's typically cooked with tomatoes and onions). More Afrikaner than African, *skilpadjies* (skul-*pai*-keys) is calf liver covered by caul fat, and *poffaddertjies* (*pohf*-aader) is liver and kidneys stuffed into a sheep's intestine and cooked on the braai.

Wetting Your Whistle

South Africa's world-renowned wines generally offer great quality for lower prices than those in the United States and Europe. Pinotage, a cross between Pinot Noir and Cinsaut, is a native cultivar and widely available. Grassy or mineral-y Sauvignon Blanc is an excellent food wine, and the newer vineyards that receive ocean breezes (as in False Bay and closer to Agulhas and Elgin) are comparable to New Zealand's best. Local Cabernet Sauvignon, Shiraz, and Pinot Noir have been excelling in international competitions.

South Africans consume more beer than any other nation in Africa; this area was settled by the Dutch, Germans, and English, after all. South African Breweries (SAB Miller) became the world's second-largest brewer when it was bought by Miller of the United States, and controls most of the beer market here, with operations throughout Africa and throughout the world. Its most popular brew is Castle Lager. You'll also find Windhoek lager, a Namibian beer, and a rapidly increasing number of craft beers, mostly in Cape Town but also in Johannesburg and Durban. In fact, the first craft beers were made in the village of Nottingham Road, on KwaZulu-Natal's Midlands Meander. Hunters Gold and Savanna Dry are hard commercial ciders.

South Africans have created a variety of nectars from Muscadels (Muscatels) filled with intense fruits, to creamy liqueurs best served over ice under a full moon. Amarula, South Africa's unique creamy fruit liqueur with the elephant on the label, is popular. Some say it's similar to Bailey's Irish Cream. South Africa's brandy regularly beats cognacs in blind tastings.

With G&Ts long being a favored sundowner across Africa, it perhaps comes as no surprise that artisanal gin has become a craze in artisanally crazed Cape Town. Local gins like Inverroche, Musgrave, and Bloedlemoen are all wonderful, distilling their brews with combinations of classic and local botanicals.

Teetotalers might prefer to quaff *rooibos* (pronounced *roy*-boss), the unique South African red bush tea ("red espresso" is a wonderfully intense version of rooibos). Ginger beer, a carbonated soft drink, is another tasty option. Bos flavored ice teas and Appletiser (a carbonated fruit drink) are wildly successful exports. Top-quality local fruit includes the *naartjie* (*nah*-chee), an easy-peeling small citrus like a clementine, melons like *spanspek* (*spun*-speck) and pawpaw (papaya), grenadillas (passion fruit), avocado, mango, stone fruits, and figs.

GREAT ITINERARIES

SOUTH AFRICA IN 7 DAYS

With only one week, you can still enjoy the best of South Africa, including Johannesburg and Cape Town highlights, as well as a short safari.

3 Days: Kruger National Park

Spend your first afternoon recovering from your international flight by lazing at a luxury lodge, but take a short game drive if one is offered. Meals are all arranged for you, and bedtime is early.

Experience your first full safari on Day 2. A quick caffeine jolt at sunrise before setting out on a game drive (usually with a stop for morning coffee and snack) sets the tone for your stay—you'll love the sheer wildness. Return to the lodge for lunch and a rest during the midday heat. Depending on where you stay, you may be able to arrange for a massage or spa treatment during this time (it helps with the jet lag). After a hearty and proper afternoon tea of sweet and savory options, you're off in the vehicle again. Having sundowner drinks at sunset is an experience you'll never forget. After the evening drive, it's back to the lodge for cleanup, drinks, and dinner, where guests and guides share tales.

You'll fit in a morning game drive before departing the camp on Day 3. Head back to Johannesburg by car so you can stop at the sites along the Mpumalanga Panoramic Route through Blyde Canyon's breathtaking scenery, arriving in Johannesburg late in the day. Shoppers might select a small B&B or guesthouse in the thick of things (for example, the Melville, Parkhurst, or Maboneng neighborhoods); those looking for retail therapy will have the Rosebank shopping malls a short drive away. To experience life outside the cloistered environment and walk down a street or sit at a café, Melville is the bohemian choice, whereas the Maboneng Precinct tends toward chic shopping and eating.

Logistics: To make the most of your time, take a direct flight from O. R. Tambo Airport to a safari lodge at one of Kruger's fly-in reserves. International flights arrive in the early morning, making it easy to board the daily mid-morning South African Airlink flight to an airfield servicing one of the private reserves making up the Greater Kruger National Park, like Timbavati and Sabi Sands. Rent a car for your return trip.

1 Day: Johannesburg

Prearrange a township tour to Soweto to learn about the roots of apartheid and the way entrepreneurs are changing lives within the community. A tour of Alexandra township will be just as informative but off the beaten track. Be sure to stop at the Apartheid Museum for an excellent if sobering taste of the country's history. Catch a late-afternoon or early-evening flight to Cape Town, where you'll spend the next two nights.

Logistics: Arrange a township tour of your choice in advance; choose a company that offers a pickup at your hotel so you don't have to drive (return the rental car on arrival in Jo'burg and take a taxi to your hotel).

1 Day: Cape Town

A stay at the V&A Waterfront will allow you to walk to its many attractions, but if you prefer something more authentically Cape Town, try one of the numerous excellent guesthouses or boutique hotels in the CBD/Gardens/Tamboerskloof areas. Whichever you choose, dinner will feature Table Mountain looming behind you.

On the following morning, take the first boat to Robben Island to see where Nelson Mandela spent decades, and inhale that bracing, fresh sea air. When you return,

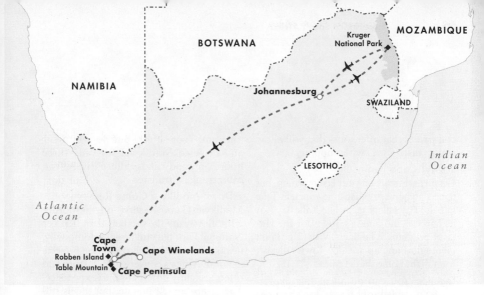

grab a taxi to the base of Table Mountain and ride up on the cable car for magnificent views. Walk a few miles on one of the trails to stretch your legs and enjoy the gorgeous fynbos plants. If you're a shopper, you could spend the rest of the afternoon browsing the shops in town (the area between Wale, Bree, Hout, and St Georges Mall is great) and then grab a snack in one of the numerous cafés in the same zone. The Cape Quarter in De Waterkant offers more chic shopping and cafés. Alternatively, you could rent a car to visit Kirstenbosch National Botanical Gardens to see magnificent protea plants—the national flower—and views (in summer there are concerts on the lawns). You may even have time to dip into some nearby wine-tasting rooms before heading to Camps Bay for sunset cocktails and a stroll along the beach before heading back to town for dinner.

Logistics: Your day in Cape Town will be busy and hectic; be sure to plan it in advance, and book a guided tour if possible to maximize your time.

1 Day: Cape Winelands
Head out early to the university town of Stellenbosch, less than an hour from Cape Town. Check out the historic downtown's Cape Dutch architecture before settling into a typical South African B&B (La Petit

Ferme in Franschhoek has standout views). Consider booking some spa time wherever you stay. Stop for some wine tastings at the excellent estates by Helshoogte Pass or Annandale Road, both of which areas also have wonderful lunching options (we love Tokara and Overture, depending on which area you choose).

Logistics: You don't have to rent a car to do this trip, nor do you have to spend a night in the Winelands; there are plenty of companies that offer tours that will allow you to taste wines with impunity.

1 Day: Cape Peninsula

Get an early start on your last morning, but there's no point in exhausting yourself. Take in False Bay village gems like Kalk Bay (for its harbor) and Simon's Town for the fantastic penguins at Boulders. Visit Cape Point before finishing up at Cape Town's airport for a flight home that evening.

Logistics: You can do all of this exploring on a guided tour if you don't want to drive yourself.

SOUTH AFRICA IN 10 DAYS

With 10 days you can spend the majority of your time on safari and finish up with highlights of the Cape.

2 Days: Johannesburg

Commence your journey with a didactic experience in the City of Gold. A variety of excellent accommodations and activities are a highlight in this place colloquially known as "Jozi" (or Jo'burg). Many new developments within the central business district, such as the Maboneng Precinct and Braamfontein, offer a great variety of local eateries and opportunities to walk the city streets, discovering the history and evolution of this rejuvenated South African icon. The museums and outdoor educational tours on offer—from paleo-anthropological interests to South Africa's more modern heritage, including the evolving Soweto and Alexandra townships and a gold-mining experience—are captured in this city. On Day 2, a trip to the Cradle of Humankind would also be worthwhile.

Logistics: Don't drive in Johannesburg. You can do all your local exploring on guided tours, which will maximize your

time and your safety. But do rent a car and drive to Madikwe. It's only three hours on good roads; alternatively, you can arrange a transfer.

2 Days: Madikwe Game Reserve

Madikwe Game Reserve on the border with Botswana is smaller than Kruger National Park but still large. Additionally, it was one of the largest relocation projects in South Africa's conservation history and offers a slightly different safari experience. The camps are all private, but this is still Big Five country and offers a wider variety of birdlife and varying accommodations options, all within a significant landscape. Spend the early afternoon of your arrival day visiting a community program just outside the reserve's gates, then relax and enjoy the still air and hot breeze of the middle of the day from a private balcony or a luxury lodge's plunge pool. Night drives may bring out the elusive leopard or lions feasting on a kill. Go on a morning safari on your second day before heading to Kruger that afternoon, with an overnight en route in Dullstroom, which is in misty-morning highland trout country with excellent accommodations and a beautiful change in landscape. The early part of the drive will give you views of contemporary African villages in the country's platinum-mining belt, as well as the distant Waterberg and Pilanesberg ranges, which add awesome vistas to the drive.

Logistics: It's a long trip to Kruger from Madikwe, so if you don't want to drive, you may want to return to Jo'burg and fly to Kruger so you can have three nights there.

3 Days: Kruger National Park

If you decided to stop over in Mbombela (Nelspruit) or elsewhere, rise early on Day 5, so you can meander through the scenic Blyde River canyon with views of the

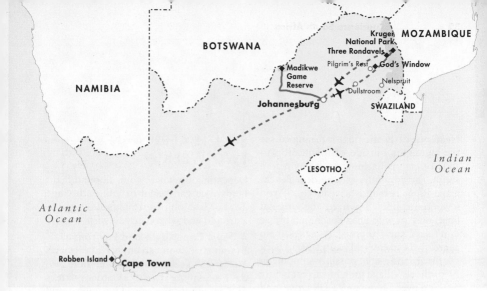

distant eastern Drakensberg Range. Consider visiting the Three Rondavels and God's Window, a lookout where you can see clear to Mozambique some days. Stop for lunch in quaint Pilgrim's Rest, a former mining town. Remember to get through Kruger's gates long before sundown (check times) so you can settle in and avoid the fines for driving after dark. Choose either a national park accommodation (there are some awesome locations) or a luxury lodge—which number in the hundreds and offer the options of spas, walking safaris, and local community interaction in addition to game drives—or split your stay.

On your first full day in Kruger, take an organized guided trip at a rest camp to get your bearings and learn how to spot game. Book a dinner at a *boma* under the stars or a stargazing safari for a memorable only-in-Africa experience. Your final day should be spent exploring the park in detail, viewing your favorite animals for as long as you wish.

Logistics: From Madikwe it's a seven-hour drive (without stops) to Mbombela (Nelspruit). It's only about two hours from Mbombela (Nelspruit) to Pilgrim's Rest, but leave plenty of time to watch the scenery, and stop frequently for the views. It's a long trip back to Jo'burg by car; rather,

> ## TIPS
>
> ■ Three nights inside a park or reserve allows you much more flexibility to relax and take in the experience. If you stay two nights at a game lodge, you'll have at most four drives.
>
> ■ You can split your stay between more than one lodge in Kruger, but the best plan is to base yourself in one place and visit others during the day.
>
> ■ This is a country laced with adventure, so don't be afraid to make an unexpected stop or just enjoy the countryside on the long drive from Madikwe.

drop your car off in Mbombela (Nelspruit) and fly back.

3 Days: Cape Town
After arriving in Cape Town and dropping your bags, you should have enough time for a stroll along the Mouille Point promenade or around the Waterfront harbor precinct (the excellent Watershed market is where to find great local buys and is open late), followed by a sundowner or a sunset cruise. If you choose sightseeing, book dinner at any excellent city restaurant (the V&A Waterfront by night lacks soul).

Head out early the next morning to see the highlights outside of town. Stop to shop or eat in charming Kalk Bay before seeing the penguins at Boulders Beach. Cape Point demands a visit, and if you have time, hike down to the original lighthouse or wild Diaz Beach (but please don't feed the baboons! It makes them aggressive and can end badly). Head back via the Atlantic side, possibly stopping in Noordhoek Village for a bite to eat before heading over Chapman's Peak Drive, and finishing your long day with a sundowner at Camps Bay or dinner at one of the many establishments across the road.

On your final day, weather permitting, plan to visit both Table Mountain and Robben Island. If the wind gets in the way, head to Kirstenbosch Botanical Gardens. Either way, lace up your hiking shoes and fit in enough walking before your lengthy flight home. There's no better place to do it.

Logistics: Whether driving or flying, make sure you get back to Johannesburg in time for an early-afternoon flight to Cape Town. For convenience, base yourself at a V&A Waterfront hotel in Cape Town, or if you want a more relaxing experience, get a hotel in Gardens or Camps Bay. If you don't want to rent a car in Cape Town, there are plenty of tour companies to show you the Cape Peninsula and the city. Most flights to the United States leave in the early evening, so you can have a full day of sightseeing before your departure.

SOUTH AFRICA IN TWO WEEKS

Depending on where your inbound flight lands, you can begin or end with Cape Town. Most long-haul flights allow you to start and end wherever you wish.

4 Days: Cape Town and Environs

In four days, you can enjoy Cape Town's attractions at a leisurely pace. Take two days to explore the city's outdoor spaces and fabulous markets. Live music and laid-back days are enjoyed in most open spaces in summer—including the almost legendary Kirstenbosch National Botanical Gardens on the backside of Table Mountain, and the Company's Garden in the city center—surrounded by museums and the antiapartheid political landmark, St. George's Cathedral.

On Day 3, get an early start and take a day-pack hike, allowing you to take in the scenery of Table Mountain and recharge, far away from a car. If you don't do Table Mountain, Lions Head is a good option if time is tight: both offer spectacular views. Lunch could be a leisurely picnic on the lawn of the Roundhouse in the Glen, right below Lions Head, overlooking Camps Bay. Then try a restaurant along trendy Bree Street for dinner. Use Day 4 to make a full loop of the Cape Peninsula, heading out of town through Hout Bay, over Chapman's Peak Drive (one of the world's most spectacular), then making for a walk along the boardwalk among the penguins at Boulders Beach. Be sure to stop at Cape Point for a walk around Cape Peninsula National Park. As you loop back up the False Bay coast, consider stopping for dinner at the Harbour House in charming Kalk Bay.

Logistics: If you don't want to drive yourself around Cape Town, then tours can

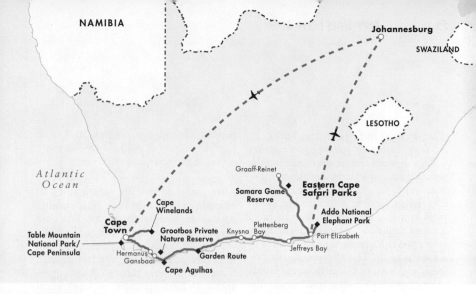

get you to all the same places. For a longer stay, pick a more relaxing location for your hotel than the V&A Waterfront. There are plenty of inviting guesthouses and B&Bs.

3 Days: The Garden Route via the Cape Winelands

Heading out from Cape Town on Day 5 you'll have plenty of time to linger over culinary tastings in Stellenbosch, dine on gourmet French food in Franschhoek, and stroll alongside Paarl's mix of Cape Dutch, Edwardian, Victorian, and art deco architecture lining the main street. With so many excellent guesthouses to choose from, part of the fun is deciding which fantasy accommodation suits you best (and in which town)—from tranquil lakeside to mountain or historic main street cottages in Stellenbosch, Paarl, or Franschhoek.

Begin Day 6 with a drive to Hermanus for lunch, where you can watch whales from the shore—or if your sea legs are up to it, try a little shark-cage diving around the corner in Gansbaai. Spend the night in remarkable accommodations at the gorgeous Grootbos Private Nature Reserve.

Next day, head for Africa's southernmost point, Cape Agulhas, also called the Cape of Storms, with its own standout vineyards and shipwreck history. Five

TIPS

■ You know it already, but don't cram in too much. If you have two weeks, savor what you do rather than rushing to your next appointment. Even if it's your first visit, you'll likely be back.

■ Read up on your next destination. There's a compelling history behind every place you visit.

■ Walk as much as you can. Moving slowly (not driving) allows you to take in this new experience.

minutes around the corner from the rocks is Stilbaai, with 30 km (19 miles) of empty sandy beaches, gentle surf, and seafood. Spend the night in Knysna or Plettenberg Bay. The former is packed with history, standout golf courses, forest, and water sports; the latter has some of the best swimming beaches in the country, framed by rugged mountain ranges and the ocean.

Logistics: Rent a car in Cape Town for the remainder of your trip. You could accomplish everything with guided tours, but it's nicer to go at your own pace.

5 Days: Eastern Cape Safari Parks

An early start from your accommodation will see you cruise past the turnoff to the surfing mecca of Jeffreys Bay as you make your way to the outskirts of Port Elizabeth. The remaining time is for winding down in sublime surroundings. Spend them between the Addo National Elephant Park, where you will overnight and are bound to see some of the best elephant activity on offer, and Samara Game Reserve, a little more than two hours inland outside the beautiful historic Karoo town of Graaff-Reinet. Samara is a remarkable reserve that has reclaimed old farming land and been restocked with indigenous game since it was purchased. It has a standout cheetah-monitoring program and employs locals. The privacy and accommodations are as good as it gets (and don't forget the resident rhino population).

Logistics: Spend two nights in Gorah Elephant Camp in Addo, and two more nights in Samara Game Reserve.

2 Days: Johannesburg

After your Eastern Cape safari, you'll be relaxed and ready to head to Johannesburg, Africa's shopping mecca, for two final days of exploring. Visit the Maboneng Precinct, see the city's exciting rejuvenation, watch some theater, and take a quad bike through Soweto or art tour through Alexandra—with both days accompanied by excellent food. It's a fine way to complete a fantastic trip to South Africa.

Logistics: It's a two-hour drive back to Port Elizabeth, where you board a flight to Johannesburg for two final nights. There, you can see everything on guided tours.

CAPE TOWN AND PENINSULA

Updated by
Lee Middleton

A favorite South African topic of debate is whether Cape Town really is part of Africa. That's how different it is, both from the rest of the country and the rest of the continent. And therein lies its attraction. South Africa's most urbane, sophisticated city sits in stark contrast to the South Africa north of the Hex River valley. Here, the traffic lights work pretty much consistently and good restaurants are commonplace. In fact, dining establishments in the so-called Mother City always dominate the country's "best of" lists.

What also distinguishes this city is its deep sense of history. Nowhere else in the country will you find structures dating back to the 17th century. South Africa as it is known today began here. Elegant Cape Dutch buildings abut ornate Victorian structures and imposing British monuments. In the predominantly Malay Bo-Kaap neighborhood, the call to prayer echoes through cobbled streets lined with houses painted in bright pastels, and the sweet tang of Malay curry wafts through the air. Flower sellers, newspaper hawkers, and numerous markets keep street life pulsing, and every lamppost advertises another festival, concert, or cultural happening. This is a relaxed city, packed with occasions and events.

What you'll ultimately recall about this city depends on your taste. It could be the Cape Winelands over *the* mountain, the Waterfront shopping (a consistent winner, given exchange rates favoring virtually any foreign currency), or Table Mountain itself. Thoroughly imposing, presiding over the city as it does, the mountain is dramatic, with a chain of "sister" mountains leading from the Table to Cape Point (roughly 68 km/42 miles south) cascading into the sea in dramatic visual fashion. Francis Drake wasn't exaggerating when he said this was "the fairest Cape we saw in the whole circumference of the earth," and he would have little cause to change his opinion today.

A visit to Cape Town is synonymous with a visit to the peninsula south of the city, and for good reason. With pristine white-sand beaches, hundreds of mountain trails, and numerous activities from surfing to paragliding to mountain biking, the accessibility, variety, and pure beauty of the great outdoors will keep nature lovers and outdoor adventurers occupied for hours, if not days. A week exploring just the city and peninsula is barely enough.

Often likened to San Francisco, Cape Town has two things that the former doesn't: Table Mountain and Africa. The mountain, or tabletop, is vital to Cape Town's identity. It dominates the city in a way that's difficult to comprehend until you visit. In the afternoon, when creeping fingers of clouds spill over Table Mountain and reach toward the city, the whole town seems to hold its breath—because in summer it brings frequent strong southeasterly winds. Meanwhile, for all of its

TOP REASONS TO GO

City Sophistication: Cape Town is a cosmopolitan city with a rich heritage that's proudly on display. It might be more laid-back than Johannesburg, but it has shaken off its sleepy, parochial air and now bristles with world-class shops and restaurants and cutting-edge art and design.

Table Mountain: Fantastic Table Mountain towers over Cape Town and dominates the whole peninsula. Exploring the mountain is a must; you can either take the cable car to the top or hike up various routes. It's not a particularly difficult climb, but having an athletic frame will help you pull and scramble up the odd steep bit, and there are easy routes, too.

Nature's Playground: Capetonians are proud of their city's stylish good looks and make the most of the mountain and beaches. In summer you'll find professionals shrugging off their suits as they head for the beach after work, surfboards, picnics, and sundowner drinks in tow. In winter they bundle up against the cold and go walking, mountain biking, or running in the city's countless green spaces.

Markets Galore: Cape Town's markets are the best in the country—informal, creative, funky, and with a good selection of both tacky and splendid African curios. The Old Biscuit Mill overflows with foodie delights and designer goods, and the Oranjezicht City Farm Market, now in a prime position at Granger Bay in the Waterfront, offers everything from artisanal meats to scrumptious prepared meals.

Historical Heritage: Cape Town is saturated with an extremely rich and fascinating history. At Robben Island you can stand in Nelson Mandela's old cell and learn about political and social banishment during apartheid, and the District Six Museum tells the poignant tale of the destruction of one of the country's most vibrant inner-city neighborhoods. The Castle of Good Hope—the first European building on the continent—is also a remarkable piece of history, with interiors of antique furniture and historic paintings.

bon-vivant European vibe, Cape Town also reflects the diversity, vitality, and spirit of Africa, with many West and Central Africans and Zimbabweans—many of them having fled from conflicts elsewhere—calling this city home.

ORIENTATION AND PLANNING

GETTING ORIENTED

Cape Town lies at the northern end of the Cape Peninsula, a 75-km (47-mile) tail of mountains that ends at the Cape of Good Hope. Drive 15 minutes out of town, and you may lose yourself in a stunning landscape of 18th-century Cape Dutch manors, historic wineries, and white-sand beaches backed by sheer mountains.

Everyone uses Table Mountain for orientation. Cape Town's aptly named heart, the City Bowl, fills the basin between the lower northern slopes of the mountain and the rim of a busy harbor. Though it's called interchangeably "City Centre" or "Cape Town Central," the City Bowl actually encompasses Cape Town Central as well as adjacent neighborhoods of Gardens and Bo-Kaap. Cape Town is compact, and neighborhood boundaries can be fluid, but navigation is generally not a problem.

Cape Town Central. Cape Town's central business district is bounded by Buitenkant Street to the east, Buitengracht Street to the west, the Company's Garden to the south, and the Foreshore to the north. Included in this district is the stand-out CT International Convention Centre (CTICC), the head offices of banks and big businesses, Parliament, the central railway and bus stations, some great architecture, and a good number of tourist attractions.

> ### CAPE TOWN ADDRESSES
>
> Street signs in Cape Town alternate between English and Afrikaans. For example, *Wale* is English and *Waal* is Afrikaans, but they mean the same thing. In Afrikaans you don't put a space between the name and the street. So an address could be Orange Street or Oranjestraat. Kaapstad is Afrikaans for Cape Town. Increasingly, streets are renamed after heroes of the struggle or with African-language names.

Woodstock. Once a working-class industrial area, this booming creative hub is minutes from the city center and boasts the country's top-rated restaurant and the city's trendiest weekend market.

Bo-Kaap. Gracing the lower slopes of Signal Hill, wedged between the hill, De Waterkant, and Cape Town Central, this small City Bowl neighborhood is the historic home of the city's Muslim population and remains so to this day. Its main thoroughfare is Wale Street.

Gardens. This mixed residential and commercial neighborhood offers a growing array of the city's top entertainment and shopping options. It begins at the southern end of the Company's Garden, stretching south toward the base of Table Mountain and Lion's Head. Most shops and restaurants are centered on Kloof Street.

Tamboerskloof. A popular area beneath Signal Hill, this lovely neighborhood is filled with coffee shops, restaurants, and boutiques down toward Kloof Road.

Oranjezicht. Right below the Table Mountain massif, this affluent area in the middle of the City Bowl is home to a few cafés, and De Waal Park.

V&A Waterfront. Once a seedy harbor, the V&A (Victoria & Alfred) Waterfront, often simply referred to as the Waterfront, is now one of South Africa's most popular tourist destinations. Nowadays, this highly commercial area between the bay and Table Mountain is filled with shopping, restaurants, bars, and upscale residential buildings. Cruises into Table Bay and Robben Island depart from here.

Green Point. The gay hot spot is home to the iconic Cape Town stadium and the neighboring Green Point Common.

Mouille Point. Cape Town's iconic lighthouse sits on the wonderful promenade lined with cafés and restaurants.

2

Sea Point. Mainly known for its glorious pedestrian walkway along the Atlantic (abutted by large grassy recreational areas), Sea Point was traditionally the heart of Cape Town's Jewish community, and now is also host to an increasingly good array of restaurants.

Clifton. Carved out of spectacular granite rock formations, this elite beachside residential area is home to some of the world's most beautiful city beaches.

Camps Bay. A wide, popular beach sits across the road from the city's trendiest café strip.

Table Mountain National Park. Running north–south through the Cape Peninsula from Cape Town, Table Mountain National Park's 220 square km (85 square miles) include Table Mountain itself, most of the high-lying land in the mountain chain that runs down the center of the peninsula from Table Mountain south, the Cape of Good Hope nature reserve at the peninsula's end, and the stunning scenery and beaches in between. The park is bordered by the Atlantic Ocean to the west and False Bay to the east.

Southern Suburbs. Southeast of the City Bowl and at the base of Table Mountain's "backside" are the mainly residential neighborhoods known collectively as the Southern Suburbs, where the fantastic Kirstenbosch National Botanical Gardens and some of the area's oldest wine estates can be found.

Cape Peninsula. The Cape Peninsula, much of which is included in Table Mountain National Park, extends for around 40 km (25 miles) from the city through to Cape Point. The peninsula's eastern border is False Bay, whose Indian Ocean waters are (relatively) warmer and calmer than those of the peninsula's wilder, emptier, and arguably more beautiful Atlantic side. A coastal road and railway line connects east-coast towns.

PLANNING

WHEN TO GO

Whatever activities you hope to accomplish in Cape Town, head up Table Mountain as soon as the wind isn't blowing. Cape Town wind is notorious, and the cable car can be closed for days on end when the gales blow. Summer (October–March) is the windiest time of the year, and from December to April winds can reach 60 km (37 miles) an hour. The winter months are not immune from wind, either—though it is much less of a problem. If you're planning to visit Robben Island during peak season, it's also wise to book well in advance. One of the best months to visit is April, when the heat and wind have abated and the Cape is bathed in warm autumnal hues. Winter rains can put off visitors, but this time of the year holds its own surprises: the countryside is a brilliant green, and without fail the best sunny and temperate days come between the rainy spells. Whales are seen in False Bay in spring (August to late September), when wildflowers are also in bloom.

EVENTS

Cape Minstrel Carnival. One of the oldest celebrations in Cape Town is the annual Cape Town Minstrel Carnival. The origins of this January festival date to the early colonial period, when this was the one day of the year that slaves were given time off. The tradition continued even after the emancipation of slaves, and today is celebrated by thousands of people in vibrant sequined costumes—complete with matching umbrellas—to sing *moppies* (pronounced a somewhat guttural *more peas,* they're vaudeville-style songs), accompanied by banjos, drums, and whistles. The celebration lasts one or two days.

Cape Town Carnival. Held in March along Green Point's pedestrian "Fan Walk," this parade of fantastical costumes, live music, and street party revelry celebrates creativity and the diverse communities making up the city. ⊠ *Green Point* ⊕ *www.capetowncarnival.com.*

Cape Town International Jazz Festival. Music, especially jazz and African music, was an extremely potent instrument for social change during the oppressive apartheid regime. South Africans remain passionate about music, and they celebrate their love of jazz with the Cape Town International Jazz Festival, usually held in late March or early April. Started in 1999, this event is arguably the best weekend of the year in Cape Town. There's an even mix of local and international stars, and past festivals have included the likes of Randy Crawford; Abdullah Ibrahim; Hugh Masekela; Ismael Lo; Earth, Wind & Fire; and Ladysmith Black Mambazo. ⊠ *Cape Town International Convention Centre, 1 Lower Long St., Convention Sq., Cape Town Central* ⊕ *www.capetownjazzfest.com.*

Design Indaba Festival. World Design Capital winner in 2014, Cape Town is the epicenter of all things design in South Africa. As such, this conference and festival held in February or March and sporting the tagline "a better world through creativity," is a great opportunity to hear and see how South African and African designers and artists approach the world of objects, in some cases to improve the world, and in others to simply make it more beautiful. A host of music and film events runs simultaneously, and yes, there are also lovely things to buy. ⊠ *Cape Town* 🕾 *021/465–9966* ⊕ *www.designindaba.com.*

Encounters Documentary Film Festival. This small but well-curated festival held in June or July showcases an always fascinating array of documentary films by a mix of South African, African, and international filmmakers. ⊠ *Cape Town* 🕾 *021/418–3310* ⊕ *www.encounters. co.za.*

FAMILY **Kirstenbosch Summer Sunset Concerts.** From late November to early April, enjoy the best in South African music, from African to classical to electronica, at outdoor concerts on Sundays at Kirstenbosch Summer Sunset Concerts. It's a Cape Town summer institution, not to be missed. ⊠ *Kirstenbosch National Botanic Gardens, Rhodes Ave., Newlands* 🕾 *021/799–8783* ⊕ *www.sanbi.org/news/kirstenbosch-summer-concerts-2016-2017* 🎫 *R125–R165.*

MCQP (*Mother City Queer Party*). A key event on Cape Town's party calendar is December's MCQP, which started in 1993. It's part Mardi Gras, part Gay Pride, and all enormous fancy-dress party. Each year is themed, and people go all-out to create and strut fantastic outfits. All are welcome! ⊠ *Cape Town* ⊕ *www.mcqp.co.za.*

GETTING HERE AND AROUND

AIR TRAVEL

Cape Town International Airport is about 19 km (12 miles) from the city center. It should take about 20 minutes to get from the airport to the city; during rush hour plan to double that. Private airport-transfer operators abound, and there is now public (MyCiti) bus service to and from the airport. All major car-rental companies have counters at Cape Town International, and driving to the City Bowl or V&A Waterfront is straightforward in daylight. If your flight arrives after dark, consider prearranging transportation through your hotel. There is a main tourist information desk as you approach the exit from either the domestic or international terminal. *For information about airlines that fly to Cape Town, see Air Travel in Travel Smart.*

Contacts Cape Town International Airport. ⊠ *Matroosfontein* ☎ *021/937– 1200, 086/727–7888 flight information* ⊕ *capetown-airport.co.za.*

AIRPORT TRANSFERS

Metered taxis and shuttle services (usually minivans) are based inside the domestic baggage hall and outside the international and domestic terminals and can also be phoned for airport drop-offs. Rates vary depending on the operator, number of passengers, destination, and time of arrival. The fare for one person to the city center is R350 in a metered taxi; a group of up to four will usually pay the same rate. A surcharge of up to R50 is sometimes levied from 10 pm until early morning, and some services charge more for arrivals than for departures to cover waiting time. MyCiti, a public bus, also serves the airport, and for R90.50 it's the cheapest way to or from the airport and City Centre.
■TIP➜ Reports of overcharging are common, so discuss the fare before entering any taxi.

Uber or Taxify users can hail a ride to or from the airport. When you exit the airport, follow signs to Parkade 1 and the Pick Up Zones (1 is closer, but 2 is only another minute away and less congested), which is where Uber drivers can pick you up.

BUS TRAVEL

Intercape Mainliner is the main option for Western Cape destinations; Greyhound, Translux/City-to-City, and Baz Bus (popular with back-packers) also provide service. Common routes from Cape Town include Johannesburg and Tshwane, Springbok, Windhoek, George, Port Elizabeth, and Durban. All the main bus companies operate from the bus terminal alongside the central train station on Adderley Street, and most have their offices there. *See Bus Travel in Travel Smart for details on intercity bus companies.*

Within Cape Town, MyCiti bus service now serves the entire city, including the Cape Flats. Buses run at regular 10-minute intervals during peak period (5 am–9 am) and at 20-minute intervals for the rest of the day. The service is perfect for tourists because you can catch a bus into town—a short ride—and from there walk the entire city. Or you can catch a connecting bus almost anywhere, including Hout Bay, the Waterfront, and Blouberg Beach. Only prepaid cards are accepted for MyCiti (get these at kiosks in every station and at some retailers). Timetables are found at each stop and can be scanned for easy reference. These buses run until 9 or 9:30 pm. The Backpacker Bus is also an economical way to get to or from the airport or Stellenbosch winelands.

Contacts MyCiti. ☎ *080/065–6463* ⊕ *myciti.org.za.*

CAR TRAVEL

Although many locals drive, tourists may find Uber, public transportation (MyCiti buses), or taxis a better option; save the rental car for when you are getting out of town. Cape Town's roads are excellent, but getting around can be a bit confusing. Signage is inconsistent, switching between Afrikaans and English, between different names for the same road (especially highways), and between different destinations on the same route. Sometimes the signs simply vanish. ■**TIP→ Cape Town is also littered with signs indicating "Cape Town" instead of "City Centre," as well as "Kaapstad," which is Afrikaans for Cape Town.** A good one-page map is essential and available from car-rental agencies and tourism information desks. Among the hazards are pedestrians running across highways, speeding vehicles, and minibus taxis. Roadblocks for document and DWI checks are also becoming more frequent.

Parking in the city center is a nightmare. There are simply not enough parking garages, longer-stay parking spaces are scarce, and most hotels charge a small fortune for parking. There are numerous pay-and-display (i.e., put a ticket in your windshield) and pay-on-exit parking lots around the city, but parking is strictly enforced. Prices range from R8 to R12 per half hour. For central attractions like Greenmarket Square, the Company's Garden, the South African National Gallery, and the Castle of Good Hope, look for a lot around the Grand Parade on Darling Street. Picbel Parking Garage on Strand Street and the Sanlam Golden Acre Parking Garage on Adderley Street offer covered parking, and Queen Victoria Street alongside the South African Museum (and Company's Garden) sometimes has a few spaces.

The main arteries leading out of the city are the N1, which bypasses the city's Northern Suburbs en route to Franschhoek and Paarl and, ultimately, Johannesburg; and the N2, which heads out past Khayelitsha and through Somerset West to the Overberg and the Garden Route before continuing on through the Eastern Cape to Durban and beyond. Branching off the N1, the N7 goes to Namibia. The M3 splits off from the N2 near Observatory, leading to the False Bay side of the peninsula via Claremont and Constantia; it's the main and quickest route to the beaches of Muizenberg, Kalk Bay, St. James, and Simon's Town. Rush hour sees bumper-to-bumper traffic on all major arteries into the city from 6 to 9, and out of the city from 4 to 6:30.

MOTORCYCLE AND SCOOTER TRAVEL

Renting a scooter or motorbike (motorcycle license and deposit required) is a good option within the city if you have a motorcycle license. Scooters can be rented from Scoot Dr. for R300–R500 per day, and far cheaper rates the longer you keep it.

Contacts Scoot Dr. ⊠ *Castle Mews, 16 Newmarket St., Foreshore* ☎ *021/418-5995* ⊕ *www.scootdr.com.*

TAXI TRAVEL

Until the arrival of Uber, Cape Town taxis were expensive and not necessarily easily hailed. This is still the case, so if you are going old-school, don't expect to see the throngs of cabs you find in London or New York. Know that you are unlikely to hail a cab in the street, and taxis rarely have roof lights to indicate availability. If you do flag an occupied cab, the driver may radio another car for you. Your best bet is to summon a taxi by phone or head to one of the major taxi stands, such as those at the V&A Waterfront, Greenmarket Square, or either end of Adderley Street (near the Slave Lodge and outside the train station). Expect to pay R60–R70 for a trip from the city center to the Waterfront (far less if using Uber or Taxify). In addition to the companies listed here, ask your hotel or guesthouse which company it recommends. Lodging establishments often have a relationship with particular companies and/or drivers, and this way you will be assured of safe, reliable service. If you have the app and a smartphone with data, Uber or Taxify rides are almost always the fastest, cheapest and best option.

Contacts Backpacker Bus. ☎ *082/809-9185* ⊕ *www.backpackerbus.co.za.* **Citi Hopper.** ☎ *021/936-3460* ⊕ *www.citihopper.co.za.* **Excite Taxis.** ☎ *021/448-4444* ⊕ *www.excitetaxis.co.za.* **Unicab.** ☎ *021/486-1600* ⊕ *www.unicab.co.za.*

TRAIN TRAVEL

Cape Town's train station is on Adderley Street, in City Centre, surrounded by lively rows of street vendors and a taxi stand. The station building received a complete revamp as part of the general infrastructure upgrade in 2010. The station services local, interprovincial, and the odd luxury lines (Blue Train and Rovos Rail).

Metrorail, Cape Town's commuter line, offers regular service but has issues with safety and is not recommended for most tourists.

National carrier Shosholoza Meyl runs the Trans-Karoo most days to Johannesburg. Shongololo Express runs multiday journey-tours, with its Good Hope train traveling from Cape Town through the Karoo, the Garden Route, Durban, the Drakensberg mountains and Kruger Park to Johannesburg over 15 days. And the luxurious Blue Train and Rovos Rail's *Pride of Africa* both have several departures per week for Tswhane. *For more information on all these services, see Train Travel in Travel Smart.*

SAFETY

There's no reason for paranoia in Cape Town, but there are a few things to look out for. Women and couples are strongly advised not to walk in isolated places after dark. If you want to walk somewhere in the evening, make sure you do so in a large group. Keep flashy jewelry and expensive cameras hidden, or better yet, at the hotel, much as you would in any unfamiliar city. It's difficult for any youthful-looking tourist to pass a street corner in the city's nightlife district without being offered drugs.

Watch your pockets at busy transportation hubs and on trains. It's better to sit in a crowded car; if you suddenly find yourself alone, move to another one. Public transportation collapses after dark. Unless you're at the Waterfront or in a large group, use Ubers or metered taxis.

Even though Table Mountain is in the middle of a major city, a hike to the top should be taken seriously: always bring water, sunscreen, and a warm layer—it's another world up there.

Drivers quickly discover that poor signage is a general issue in Cape Town.

TOUR OPTIONS

Countless companies offer guided tours of the city center, the peninsula, the Winelands, and any place else in the Cape (or beyond) that you might wish to visit. They differ in type of transportation used, focus, size, and guide quality. For comprehensive information on touring companies, head to one of the Cape Town Tourism offices or ask for recommendations at your hotel. Listings here are limited to more specialized tours.

BOAT TOURS

Boat tours are very popular, but the only ones that actually land on Robben Island are the ferries operated by the museum there.

Drumbeat Charters. Drumbeat Charters has been operating since 1989 and is based in the fishing village of Hout Bay, offering daily scenic cruises. Their big attraction is the Seals & the Shipwreck trip, where you'll visit Duiker Island, home of the Cape fur seals, and then travel farther along the Kabonkelberg Mountain range to Moari Bay to view the shipwreck of the *Bos 400*, which ran aground in 1994 during a Cape winter storm. ☎ *021/791–4441* ⊕ *www.drumbeatcharters.co.za.*

Simon's Town Boat Company. From whale-watching to trips to Seal Island or Cape Point, this company has you covered for False Bay water activities. ☎ *083/257–7760* ⊕ *www.boatcompany.co.za.*

Waterfront Charters. This operation seems to do everything connected to having fun on the water in Table Bay and the eastern seaboard, with trips on a range of boats, from yachts to large motor cruisers. A 1½-hour sunset cruise from the V&A Waterfront costs about R360 and includes a glass of bubbly. Cruise & Dine Packages cost R660 for dinner, R375 for lunch. Jet boat rides are R880 per hour. ☎ *021/418–3168* ⊕ *www.waterfrontcharters.co.za.*

BUS TOURS

Art Route Cape Town. Owned and operated by artist and art historian Talita Swart, Art Routes creates bespoke tours of Cape Town's exploding art scene for groups of any size (all in the comfort of a Mercedes with free Wi-Fi on board). From art galleries to artists' studios to the archives of national arts institutions, Art Routes guides provide you with a fascinating and inspiring insider overview of whichever aspect of local art interests you. ☎ *082/348–4380* ⊕ *www.artroute.capetown* 🖃 *Starting from R900 for half day; R1,200 for full day depending on group size.*

2

Cape Sidecar Adventures. Unique for Cape Town, this has seemingly captured a niche market, with vintage Chinese military motorcycles dating back to the early 1960s being used to see one of the most beautiful cities in the world. In fact the owner, who got the idea after owning one in Shanghai, believes it's one of three such operations on the planet. Great for children, too, the cycles chug stylishly and safely around some of the most beautiful roads and views on the planet in their designer gear—you actually get kitted out rather stylishly. There's a nice little coffee-bar in the shop afterward that offers an awesome collection of helmets (Batman's included) for sale. It's worth noting that although this operation is entirely legal, the Harley tours in the city could be jumping through some legal loopholes. ☎ *021/434–9855, 082/308–5483 mobile* ⊕ *www.sidecars.co.za.*

City Sightseeing. The hop-on/hop-off red City Sightseeing bus is a great way to familiarize yourself with Cape Town; a day ticket costs R170, and there are two routes to choose from. The Red Route runs through the city, and you can get on and off at major museums, the V&A Waterfront, Table Mountain Cableway, Two Oceans Aquarium, and other attractions. The Blue Route takes you farther afield—to Kirstenbosch National Botanic Gardens, Hout Bay, and Camps Bay, to name a few destinations. Tickets are available at the Waterfront outside the aquarium or on the bus. The newer Cape Explorer options offer full-day tours of Cape Point or the Winelands, and at R550 are an economical way to visit these popular destinations. ⊕ *www.citysightseeing.co.za.*

Coffeebeans Routes. Coffeebeans Routes's famous Jazz Safari ($130) takes small groups to meet key musicians of Cape Town's jazz scene in their homes for dinner, followed by a visit to nontouristy jazz clubs in the Cape Flats. If authenticity is what you're looking for, this is it. These tours show Cape Town as it is, with informed guides. Whether the Revolution Route, Cape Town Cuisine Route, or Theatre in the Backyard tour, these experiences are infused with an authentic element of storytelling. ☎ *021/813–9829* ⊕ *www.coffeebeansroutes.com.*

Friends of Dorothy. These tours are aimed at the gay market; among the offerings are the Ruby Slipper Tour (to the Cape Peninsula), Yellow Brick Road Tour (to the Cape Winelands), and Aunty Em's Tour (a country roads tour). Small groups—maximum of seven passengers—keep the service personal. The company is gay-owned and uses the services of gay guides and drivers. ☎ *021/531–0646, 083/555–6611 mobile* ⊕ *www.friendsofdorothytours.co.za.*

Kiff Kombi Tours. An alternative (and well priced) way to see the sights, this company uses VW vans (known locally as kombi) to take you on tours that include things like craft beer tastings and graffiti art stops. ☎ *072/213–3888* ⊕ *www.kiffkombitours.co.za.*

Maboneng Township Arts Experience. A wonderful way to visit the townships, these tours take you into the gallery homes of artists where you can see (and sometimes purchase) vibrant artwork, share a local meal, and learn about the history of the area, after which you will visit other important public art and architecture spots. ☎ *021/824–1773* ⊕ *www. maboneng.com.*

WALKING TOURS

Pamphlets for a self-guided walking tour of city-center attractions can be picked up at Cape Town Tourism.

Cape Town Free Walking Tours. Nielsen Tours offers free daily walking tours along several routes through the city. The City Walk, which provides a great and informative introduction to the historic city center, starts in the Company's Garden and heads down St. George's Mall towards the Fan Walk, ending in St. Andrew's Square. Private tours tailored to your interests can also be organized for a fee. ☎ *076/636–9007* ⊕ *www.nielsentours.co.za/capetown.*

Wanderlust – Cape Town on Foot Walking Tour. Owner Ursula Stevens leads walks through Cape Town, around the Cape of Good Hope, and up the West Coast—all guided by the seven books she has written on the areas full of interesting historical information. City walking tours last about 2½ hours and cover major historical attractions, architecture, and highlights of modern-day Cape Town. ☎ *021/462–4252* ⊕ *www.wanderlust.co.za.*

VISITOR INFORMATION

From October to March, the office in City Centre is open weekdays 8–6, Saturday 8:30–2, and Sunday 9–1; from April to September, it's open weekdays 8–5:30, Saturday 8:30–1, and Sunday 9–1. The branch at the Waterfront is open daily 9–7, and the airport branch is open 6–9 (Monday–Friday) and 8–8 on weekends.

Contacts Cape Town Tourism. ⊠ *The Pinnacle Bldg., Burg St. at Castle St., Cape Town Central* ☎ *021/487–6800* ⊕ *www.capetown.travel.*

EXPLORING

Cape Town has grown as a city in a way that few others in the world have. Take a good look at the street names. Strand and Waterkant streets (meaning "beach" and "waterside," respectively) are now far from the sea. However, when they were named, they were right on the beach. An enormous program of dumping rubble into the ocean extended the city by a good few square miles (thanks to the Dutch obsession with reclaiming land from the sea). Almost all the city on the seaward side of Strand and Waterkant is part of the reclaimed area of the city known as the Foreshore. If you look at old paintings of the city, you will see that originally waves lapped at the very walls of the castle, now more than half a mile from the ocean.

CAPE TOWN CENTRAL

In Cape Town's city center, moderately sized glass-and-steel office blocks soar over street vendors selling everything from seasonal fruit and flowers to clothes and cigarettes. Sandwiched in between these modern high-rises are historic buildings dating to the 1600s. There's an impressive collection of art deco buildings, and there is always something undergoing restoration. Don't try to navigate the center of Cape Town by car. It's small enough to walk, and on foot you can explore the

CLOSE UP

Cape History at a Glance

It's said that Cape Town owes its very existence to Table Mountain. The freshwater streams running off its slopes were what first prompted early explorers to anchor here. In 1652 Jan van Riebeeck and 90 Dutch settlers established a refreshment station for ships of the Dutch East India Company (VOC) on the long voyage east. The first European toehold in South Africa, Cape Town is still called the Mother City.

Those first Dutch settlers established their own farms, and 140 years later the settlement supported a population of 20,000 whites and 25,000 slaves brought from distant lands like Java, Madagascar, and Guinea. Its strategic position on the southern edge of Africa, however, meant that the colony never enjoyed any real stability. The British occupied the Cape twice, first in 1795 and then more permanently in 1806, bringing with them additional slaves from Ceylon, India, and the Philippines. Destroyed or assimilated in this colonial expansion were the indigenous Khoekhoen (previously called Khoikhoi and Hottentots), who once herded cattle and foraged along the coast.

Diamond and gold discoveries in central and northern South Africa in the late 1800s pulled focus away from Cape Town. However, in 1910, when the Union of South Africa was created, Cape Town was named the legislative capital, and it remains so today. The diamond and gold boom fueled rapid development in Cape Town and throughout the country.

The wounds of the 20th century are due to apartheid. Although apartheid ended in the 1990s, its legacy of underdevelopment remains, and Cape Town still remains divided along racial, economic, and physical lines. As you drive into town along the N2 from the airport, you can't miss the shacks built on shifting dunes as far as the eye can see—a sobering contrast to the first-world luxury of the city center on the other side of Table Mountain.

Khayelitsha is the main "black" township, attached to which are numerous squatter camps, more politely known as informal settlements. Well over 2 million people live in Khayelitsha today, most of whom originated in the underdeveloped Eastern Cape province, where work is scarce and the medical and educational facilities have all but collapsed. For these reasons relatives of Khayelitsha's inhabitants arrive almost daily.

Much of South Africa's rich and fascinating history is reflected in Cape Town. Most of the sites worth seeing are packed into a small area, which means you can see a lot in just a few hours. The District Six Museum tells the heartbreaking story of the apartheid-era demolition of one of Cape Town's most vibrant mixed-race neighborhoods, and the Bo-Kaap Museum tells the story of the city's Muslim community, who settled here after the abolition of slavery. The Castle of Good Hope, former seat of the British and Dutch governments and still the city's military headquarters, is the oldest colonial building still standing in South Africa. Mandela's tiny jail cell has been preserved on Robben Island, and you can learn about his banishment there as well as about the ecological significance of the island. For a taste of the city's long naval history, visit Simon's Town, where you can tour a retired submarine.

2

many galleries, coffee shops, and markets that appear on every corner. If your feet have had it, the MyCiti bus works a treat if you have a card.

TIMING AND PRECAUTIONS

If you are pressed for time, you can explore the city in a day, getting the lay of the land and a feel for the people of Cape Town while visiting or skipping sights as your interests dictate. However, if you'd like to linger in various museums and galleries, you could easily fill two or three days. Start at about 9, when most workers have finished their commute, and then stop for a long, leisurely lunch, finishing the tour in the late afternoon. If you have to head out of town on either the N1 or N2, be sure to depart before 4, when rush-hour congestion takes over.

Except for the top end of Long Street and around Heritage Square where there are lots of bars and cafés, the city center is very quiet at night, and you are advised not to wander the streets after dark. The last commuters leave around 6 (note that the city center can also be deserted on weekends). The biggest threat is being mugged for your cell phone, jewelry, or money. Fortunately many of the old city buildings are being converted into upscale apartments, thus rejuvenating the city center.

TOP ATTRACTIONS

FAMILY **Company's Garden.** One of Cape Town's best-kept secrets is also a great place to seek relief from a sweltering summer day if the beach is packed. These lush, landscaped gardens are are all that remain of a 43-acre tract laid out by Jan van Riebeeck in April 1652 to supply fresh vegetables to ships on their way to the Dutch East Indies. By 1700 free burghers were cultivating plenty of crops on their own land, and in time the VOC vegetable patch was transformed into a botanic garden. It remains a delightful haven in the city center, graced by fountains, exotic trees, rose gardens, and a pleasant outdoor café. At the bottom of the gardens, close to Government Avenue, look for an **old well** that used to provide water for the town's residents and the garden. The old water pump, engraved with the maker's name and the date 1842, has been overtaken by an oak tree and now juts out of the tree's trunk some 6 feet above the ground. A huge **statue of Cecil Rhodes,** the Cape's prime minister in the late 19th century, looms over the path that runs through the center of the gardens. He points to the north, and an inscription reads, "your hinterland is there," a reference to Rhodes's dream of extending the British Empire from the Cape to Cairo. Continue past the pond and toward the South African Museum, outside of which the **Delville Wood Monument** honors South Africans who died in the fight for Delville Wood during the great three-day Somme offensive of 1916. A self-guided walking brochure (R20) with detailed historical information about the gardens and nearby sights is sold at the shop next door to the small but informative visitors center, which are both by the restaurant. ✉ *Between Government Ave. and Queen Victoria St., Cape Town Central* ☎ *021/426–2157* ✉ *Free* ☉ *Visitors center closed weekends.*

2

NEED A
BREAK

Located in the leafy green of the gardens, the **Company's Garden Restaurant** (⊠ *15 Queen Victoria St., Cape Town Central* ☎ *021/423–2919*) serves a wide range of light meals, teatime favorites, and South African fare from morning to late afternoon. It's a gorgeous place to sit and watch the buzz of Cape Town's foot traffic passing you by, and also great for kids.

District Six Museum. Housed in the Buitenkant Methodist Church, this museum preserves the memory of one of Cape Town's most vibrant multicultural neighborhoods and of the district's destruction in one of the cruelest acts of the apartheid-era Nationalist government. District Six was proclaimed a white area in 1966, and existing residents were evicted from their homes, which were razed to make way for a white suburb. The people were forced to resettle in bleak outlying areas on the Cape Flats, and by the 1970s all the buildings here, except churches and mosques, had been demolished. Huge controversy accompanied the proposed redevelopment of the area, and only a small housing component, Zonnebloem, and the campus of the Cape Technicon have been built, leaving much of the ground still bare—a grim reminder of the past. There are pockets of redevelopment and plans to bring former residents back into the area and reestablish the suburb; however, the plans are beset by infighting, and the old swinging District Six will never be re-created. The museum consists of street signs, photographs, life stories of the people who lived there, and a huge map, where former residents can identify the sites of their homes and record their names. This map is being used to help sort out land claims. You can arrange in advance for a two-hour walking tour of the district with a former resident for a nominal amount. ⊠ *25 Buitenkant St., Cape Town Central* ☎ *021/466–7200* ⊕ *www.districtsix.co.za* ✆ *R30.*

Greenmarket Square. For more than a century this cobbled square served as a forum for public announcements, including the 1834 declaration abolishing slavery, which was read from the balcony of the Old Town House, overlooking the square. In the 19th century the square became a vegetable market as well as a popular watering hole, and you can still enjoy a drink at an open-air restaurant or hotel veranda while watching the crowds go by. Today the square has been re-cobbled, and the outdoor market sells predominantly African crafts from around the continent. It is also flanked by some of the best examples of art-deco architecture in South Africa. ⊠ *Greenmarket Sq., Burg St., between Longmarket and Hout Sts., Cape Town Central.*

NEED A
BREAK?

Dear Me. Just a few blocks from the bustle of Greenmarket Square, this airy comfortable café serves delicious breakfast and lunch fare. Lunches tend to have some Asian influences, but you can also expect a good array of salads, pastas, and sandwiches. ⊠ *165 Longmarket St., Cape Town Central* ☎ *021/422–4920* ⊕ *www.dearme.co.za* ☉ *Closed weekends.*

Slave Lodge. Built in 1679 by the Dutch East India Company to house slaves, convicts, and lunatics, it also housed the supreme court from 1815 to 1914. The lodge now holds a museum with a fascinating and sobering account of slavery in the Cape, as well as excellent and evocative temporary exhibits that generally examine more contemporary views on apartheid and human rights. The somewhat randomly curated

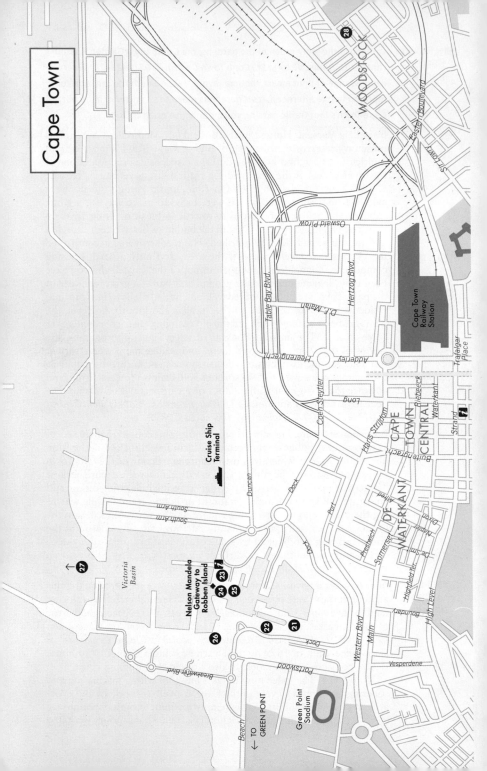

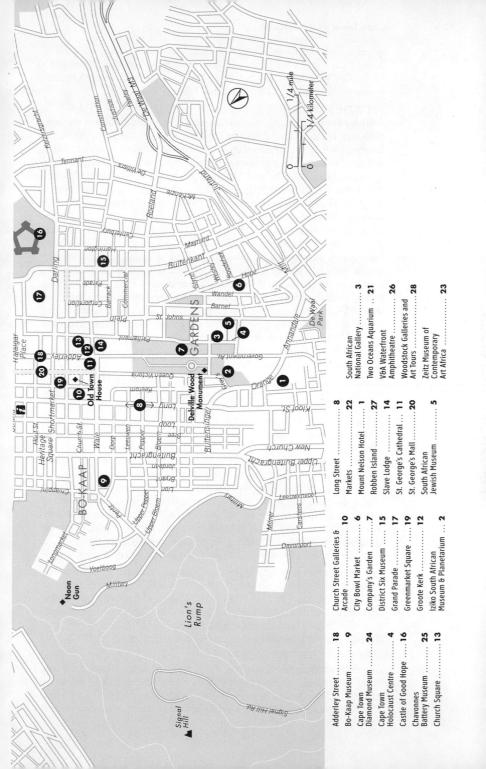

Noon Gun

Signal Hill

Lion's Rump

BO-KAAP

GARDENS

Delville Wood Monument

Old Town House

Castle of Good Hope

Adderley Street	18
Bo-Kaap Museum	9
Cape Town Diamond Museum	24
Cape Town Holocaust Centre	4
Castle of Good Hope	16
Chavonnes Battery Museum	25
Church Square	13
Church Street Galleries & Arcade	10
City Bowl Market	6
Company's Garden	7
District Six Museum	15
Grand Parade	17
Greenmarket Square	19
Groote Kerk	12
Iziko South African Museum & Planetarium	2
Long Street	8
Markets	22
Mount Nelson Hotel	1
Robben Island	27
Slave Lodge	14
St. George's Cathedral	11
St. George's Mall	20
South African Jewish Museum	5
South African National Gallery	3
Two Oceans Aquarium	21
V&A Waterfront Amphitheatre	26
Woodstock Galleries and Art Tours	28
Zeitz Museum of Contemporary Art Africa	23

1/4 mile
1/4 kilometer

upper galleries house exhibits of artifacts from the various groups popu-
lating the Cape, as well ceramics and an Egyptology collection. ✉ *49
Wale St., Cape Town Central* ☎ *021/481–3800* ⊕ *www.iziko.org.za/
museums/slave-lodge* 🖂 *R30* ☉ *Closed Sun.*

WORTH NOTING

Adderley Street. Originally named Heerengracht after a canal that once ran
the length of the avenue, this street has always been Cape Town's principal
thoroughfare. It was once the favored address of the city's leading families,
and its oak-shaded sidewalks served as a promenade for those who wanted
to see and be seen. By the mid-19th century the oaks had all been chopped
down and the canal covered, as Adderley became the main commercial
street. By 1908 it had become so busy that the city planners paved it with
wooden blocks in an attempt to dampen the noise of countless wagons,
carts, and hooves. Although there are a couple of glorious old buildings
dating to the early 1900s, and the beautiful Addereley Street Flower Market—one of the city's oldest markets, located in Trafalgar Place between
Strand and Darling streets—has hung on, Adderley Street in recent years
has lost most of its charm. Mostly you will find uninspiring office buildings
and sidewalks packed with street hawkers selling everything from fruits and
vegetables to cell phone covers and tea towels. City management is trying
to halt the urban decay, however, and there's evidence of regeneration. A
lot of old office buildings are now being converted to upscale apartments,
and beautiful old art-deco buildings are getting the spit and polish they so
desperately need. ✉ *Cape Town Central.*

Castle of Good Hope. Despite its name, the castle isn't the fairy-tale fantasy
type but rather a squat fortress that hunkers down as if to avoid shellfire.
Built between 1665 and 1676 by the Dutch East India Company (VOC)
to replace an earthen fort constructed in 1652 by Jan van Riebeeck, the
Dutch commander who settled Cape Town, it's the oldest building in
the country. Its pentagonal plan, with a diamond-shape bastion at each
corner, is typical of the Old Netherlands defense system adopted in the
early 17th century. The design was intended to allow covering fire for
every portion of the castle. As added protection, the whole fortification
was surrounded by a moat, and back in the day, the sea nearly washed up
against its walls. The castle served as both the VOC headquarters and the
official governor's residence, and still houses the regional headquarters of
the National Defence Force. Despite the bellicose origins of the castle, no
shot has ever been fired from its ramparts, except ceremonially.

You can wander around on your own or join one of the highly informative guided tours at no extra cost. Also worth seeing is the excellent
William Fehr Collection. Housed in the governor's residence, it consists
of antiques, artifacts, and paintings of early Cape Town and South
Africa. Politicians and corporates occasionally hold dinners in the grand
dining room. ✉ *1 Buitenkant St., Cape Town Central* ☎ *021/787–1249*
⊕ *www.castleofgoodhope.co.za* 🖂 *R30.*

Church Street Galleries & Arcade. The center of Cape Town's art and
antiques business, this pleasant block of Church Street is a pedestrian
mall filled with art galleries, antiques dealers, small cafés, and a few
excellent boutiques. Among the art galleries worth visiting are **AVA**

($\boxtimes$ *35 Church St.*), **World Art** ($\boxtimes$ *54 Church St.*), and **The Cape Gallery** ($\boxtimes$ *60 Church St.*). A daily antiques and flea market is also held here. ■**TIP→** Note that Church Street is (somewhat confusingly) not located directly off of Church Square and Groote Kerk (the church for which the street is named), but across Adderley Street. $\boxtimes$ *Church St., between Burg and Long Sts., Cape Town Central.*

2

Long Street. The section of Long between Orange and Strand streets is lined with magnificently restored Georgian and Victorian buildings. Wrought-iron balconies and fancy curlicues on these colorful houses evoke the French Quarter in New Orleans. In the 1960s, Long Street played host to bars, prostitutes, and sleazy hotels. Today antiques dealers, backpackers' lodges, the Pan-African Market, funky clothing outlets, and a plethora of cafes, bars, and restaurants make this one of the best browsing streets in the city; by night, it can live up to some of its older reputation. At the mountain end is the Long Street Baths, an indoor swimming pool and old Turkish *hammam* (steam bath). $\boxtimes$ *Long St., between Orange and Strand Sts., Cape Town Central.*

NEED A BREAK

Loaves on Long. The smells of freshly baking bread will immediately whet your appetite at this friendly café serving delicious breakfasts, lunches, and treats daily except Sunday. $\boxtimes$ *33 Long St., Cape Town Central* ☎ *021/422–3353* ⊕ *www.loavesonlong.co.za* ⊙ *Closed Sun.*

St. George's Cathedral. This stunning cathedral was once the religious seat of one of the most recognizable faces—and voices—in the fight against apartheid, Archbishop Desmond Tutu. In his position as the first black archbishop of Cape Town (he was elected in 1986), he vociferously denounced apartheid and relentlessly pressed for a democratic government. It was from these steps that he led a demonstration of more than 30,000 people and coined the phrase the Rainbow People to describe South Africans in all their glorious diversity. Tutu, long retired, and the cathedral continue in their active monitoring role today, holding marches and the new government to account. The Anglican cathedral was designed by Sir Herbert Baker in the Gothic Revival style; construction began in 1901, using sandstone from Table Mountain. The structure contains the largest stained-glass window in the country, some beautiful examples of late-Victorian stained glass, and a 1,000-year-old Coptic cross. If you want to hear the magnificent organ, go to the choral evensong at 6 on Sunday evening. $\boxtimes$ *5 Wale St., Cape Town Central* ☎ *021/424–7360* ⊕ *www.sgcathedral.co.za* ☐ *Free.*

St. George's Mall. This pedestrian-only promenade stretches about five blocks from St. George's Cathedral through the city center (passing Greenmarket Square) to the financial district. Shops and cafés line the mall, and street vendors hawk everything from T-shirts to African arts and crafts. Street performers and dancers gather daily to entertain crowds of locals and visitors, who rub shoulders on their way to and from work or while sightseeing. The very good "Earthfair" food market is held on the Cathedral end of the mall every Thursday from 11 to 3. $\boxtimes$ *Between Burg and Adderley Sts. from Wale St. to Thibault Sq., Cape Town Central.*

WOODSTOCK

Just a stone's throw northeast of city center, once-gritty Woodstock continues to be the recipient of massive if sometimes controversial regeneration efforts, and is now home to numerous galleries, shops, and restaurants, including the country's number-one-rated establishment, the Test Kitchen, and the famous Old Biscuit Mill Saturday market.

NEED A BREAK

The Kitchen. Put on the map by Michelle Obama in 2011, this beloved and quirky local deli located across the street from the Goodman and Stevenson galleries serves a spectacular variety of amazing salads, scrumptious "love sandwiches," and some excellent sweet treats. ⊠ *111 Sir Lowry Rd., Woodstock* ☎ *021/462–2201* ⊕ *www.lovethekitchen.co.za* ⊗ *Closed weekends.*

Fodor's Choice
★

Woodstock Galleries and Art Tours. Most of Cape Town's best-known galleries are clustered along a few blocks of Sir Lowry Road (⊠ *Main Rad.*) and a slightly longer stretch of Albert Road (⊠ *Lower Main Rd.*) in Woodstock. In fact, along with the renovation of **The Old Biscuit Mill** (⊠ *375 Albert Rd.*) and its celebrated Saturday market, the relocation of galleries like **Stevenson** (⊠ *160 Sir Lowry Rd.*) and **The Goodman Cape Town** (⊠ *176 Sir Lowry Rd.*) from the CBD in the early aughts were integral to the revitalization of this semi-industrial neighborhood. While wandering from gallery to gallery (**Whatiftheworld, blank projects,** and **Art It Is** are also worthwhile), art lovers can also enjoy the plethora of cafés and boutiques that have sprung up on Sir Lowry Road, and on the stretch of Albert Road between The Biscuit Mill and **The Woodstock Exchange** (⊠ *66 Albert Rd.*). While in the area keep an eye out for the remarkable street art—mostly in the form of graffiti murals—much of which predates the gallery invasion. To fully appreciate the latter, taking a tour like those offered by **Juma Mkwela** (⊕ *www.townshiptours.co.za/woodstock-creative*). ⊠ *Sir Lowry Rd. at Albert Rd., Woodstock.*

BO-KAAP

Bo-Kaap is the historic home of the city's Muslim population, brought from the East as slaves in the late 17th and early 18th century. The Auwal Mosque, the oldest mosque in South Africa, built in 1798, is also here. You'll know you're in the Bo-Kaap (Afrikaans for "on top of the Cape") when you hear the call of the muezzin from one of the many mosques in the area. You might even have to sidestep lights, cameras, and film stars, since the district is an oft-used setting for movies and magazine shoots—the brightly colored houses make a stunning backdrop. Although foreigners and locals have started buying in the area—real estate in the City Bowl is at a premium, and without gardens these properties are cheaper—it remains overtly traditional, so much so that a bar that opened up on the corner of Wale and Rose streets to attract tourists and new residents had to close because of local pressure from the Muslim community. Today the area remains strongly Muslim, and it's fascinating to wander the narrow, cobbled lanes past mosques and the largest collection of pre-1840 architecture in South Africa. The Bo-Kaap is also known as the Malay quarter, even though its inhabitants originated from all over, including the Indonesian archipelago, India, Turkey, and Madagascar.

TIMING AND PRECAUTIONS

There have been a few muggings in the Bo-Kaap, so to experience all that the area has to offer we recommend that you take a guided tour *(See Walking Tours, in Planning, at the beginning of the chapter)* or stick to Wale, Dorp, and Shortmarket streets.

TOP ATTRACTIONS

Bo-Kaap Museum. Most guided tours of the Malay quarter include a visit to this 18th-century home, which originally belonged to well-known Turkish scholar and prominent local Muslim leader, Abu Bakr Effendi. The museum showcases local Islamic heritage and culture, with highlights including "Who Built Cape Town?," "Mapping Bo-Kaap: History, memories and spaces," and the documentary "Viewing Bo-Kaap." ✉ *71 Wale St., Bo-Kaap* ☎ *021/481–3938* ⊕ *www.iziko.org.za/museums/bo-kaap-museum* 🎫 *R20* ⊙ *Closed Sun.*

GARDENS

An affluent city neighborhood, Gardens is populated largely by young professionals. Gardens has numerous restaurants, cafés, hotels, and shops, as well as many beautiful homes. Main thoroughfares like Kloof Street are packed with funky boutiques and are pleasant to stroll and explore. Once the beginning of central Cape Town's residential area heading from the Company's Garden up toward Table Mountain, Gardens has increasingly merged with "town" as the number of cafés and restaurants here has grown, making it a popular place both to stay and explore, day or night.

TIMING AND PRECAUTIONS

Unlike Cape Town Central, Gardens' commercial zone remains relatively lively into the evening. From where Kloof Street begins (at the end of Long Street) until it intersects with Camp Street, restaurants, cafés, and Cape Town's art-house cinema make the area lively and safe for walking until about 10 pm. Even after this, the main irritation for a tourist is likely only to be from beggars. In other areas take the usual precautions.

TOP ATTRACTIONS

FAMILY **Iziko South African Museum & Planetarium.** Founded in 1825, this natural history museum houses more than 1.5 million scientific specimens, but is most popular for its "Whale Well," where life-size casts of enormous marine mammals are suspended over a multi-storied chamber, which leads to displays of marine and terrestrial animals in the old diorama style. International photography exhibits are often on display upstairs, and there is an interesting if creepy section on the fossil remains of prehistoric "mammal-like" reptiles. In the adjoining planetarium, visitors can experience the thrills of a 360-degree multisensory, full-dome theater, where a variety of shows for children and adults play throughout the week. ✉ *25 Queen Victoria St., Gardens* ☎ *021/481–3800* ⊕ *www.iziko.org.za/museums/south-african-museum* 🎫 *Museum R30* ⊙ *Closed May 1 and Dec. 25.*

■ **Mount Nelson Hotel.** The Nellie, as it's known, was erected in 1899 to welcome the Prince of Wales on his visit to the Cape and today remains one of Cape Town's most fashionable and genteel social venues. Don't miss the legendary high tea. Served from 2:30 to 5:30, the pastry selection can tempt even the most jaded palate, and the savory treats make for a scrumptious meal. ⊠ *76 Orange St., Gardens* ☎ *021/483–1000* ⊕ *www.mountnelson.co.za.*

South African Jewish Museum. Housed in the Old Synagogue—South Africa's first synagogue, built in 1863—this museum sits in the same complex as the Cape Town Holocaust Centre and spans 150 years of South African Jewry. The themes of Memories (immigrant experiences), Reality (integration into South Africa), and Dreams (visions for the future) are conveyed with high-tech multimedia and interactive displays, models, and artifacts. The complex also includes the Great Synagogue (built in 1905), an active place of worship, a temporary gallery for changing exhibits, an auditorium, and a museum restaurant and shop. The museum also exhibits the extraordinary Isaac Kaplan collection of Japanese netsuke, considered among the world's finest. ⊠ *88 Hatfield St., Gardens* ☎ *021/465–1546* ⊕ *www.sajewishmuseum.co.za* ⊠ *R60* ⊘ *Closed Sat. and Jewish holidays.*

South African National Gallery. This museum houses a good collection of 19th- and 20th-century European art, but its most interesting exhibits are the South African works, many of which reflect the country's traumatic history. The gallery owns an enormous body of work, so exhibitions change regularly, but there's always something provocative—whether it's documentary photographs or a multimedia exhibit chronicling efforts to "disrupt" traditional boundaries. The museum would like to position itself as a leader of contemporary and traditional African art. Free guided tours on Tuesday and Thursday take about an hour. ⊠ *Government Ave., Gardens* ☎ *021/481–3970* ⊕ *www.iziko.org.za/museums/south-african-national-gallery* ⊠ *R30.*

WORTH NOTING

Cape Town Holocaust Centre. The center is both a memorial to the 6 million Jews and other victims who were killed during the Holocaust and an education center whose aim is to create a caring and just society in which human rights and diversity are valued. The permanent exhibit is excellent and very moving. A multimedia display, comprising photo panels, text, film footage, and music, creates a chilling reminder of the dangers of prejudice, racism, and discrimination. The center is next to the South African Jewish Museum. ⊠ *88 Hatfield St., Gardens* ☎ *021/462–5553* ⊕ *www.holocaust.org.za* ⊠ *Free* ⊘ *Closed Sat. and Jewish holidays.*

City Bowl Market. Experience real Cape Town local life every Thursday from 5 to 8 in this rented church hall space. With fresh produce, a wide variety of really good food, craft beers and wines, and even clothes and jewelry on sale, this is a vibey City Bowl social gathering. ⊠ *Red Harbour Church, 14 Hope St., Gardens* ☎ *073/270–8043* ⊕ *www.citybowlmarket.co.za* ⊘ *Closed Fri.–Wed.*

V&A WATERFRONT

The V&A (Victoria & Alfred) Waterfront is the culmination of a long-term project undertaken to breathe new life into the historical dockland of the city. Although some Capetonians deem the Waterfront too "mallish," it remains South Africa's most popular attraction—probably because of a combination of the ease and safety of being a pedestrian here, favorable currency exchange rates for North American and European visitors, and the ever-increasing number of truly worthwhile attractions and activities on offer. Hundreds of shops, movie theaters, restaurants, and bars share quarters in restored warehouses and dock buildings, all connected by pedestrian plazas and promenades. Newer developments like the excellent Watershed craft market and two fantastic food markets have made the V&A more of a locals destination. On top of this, the much-anticipated Zeitz Museum of Contemporary Art—Africa's first such institution—could be the final nail in the "mallish" coffin. Another major plus to the area is that it's clean, safe, and with massive under- and over-ground parking promenades, you can move about car-free.

TIMING AND PRECAUTIONS

You could see the area's major sights in half a day, but that won't give you much time for shopping, coffee stops, or lunch, or for all that the worthwhile aquarium has to offer. A more leisurely approach would be to set aside a whole day, at the end of which you could find a waterside restaurant or bar to enjoy a cold glass of wine or a cocktail. With its crowds of people, security cameras, and guards, this is one of the safest places to shop and hang out in the city. That said, you should still keep an eye on your belongings and be aware of pickpockets.

TOP ATTRACTIONS

Markets. Featuring more than 150 vendors selling the best of local design, arts, and crafts, the extremely worthwhile **Watershed Market** is located in a huge warehouse by the aquarium. Next door is the **V&A Food Market**, where you can find everything from sushi to biltong to curry, craft beer to gelato to handmade organic chocolate. Finally, every Saturday from 9 to 2, the **Oranjezicht City Farm Market** showcases the Cape's bounty in the form of organic produce, wonderful prepared foods, and scrumptious take-away treats (think dried meats, artisanal cheeses, fantastic pastries and the like), all with a great view of the sea. ⊠ *Victoria and Alfred Waterfront* ⊕ *www.waterfront.co.za.*

Fodor's Choice
★ **Robben Island.** Made famous by its most illustrious inhabitant, Nelson Mandela, this island, whose name is Dutch for "seals," has a long and sad history. At various times a prison, leper colony, mental institution, and military base, it is finally filling a positive, enlightening, and empowering role in its latest incarnation as a museum.

Declared a World Heritage site on December 1, 1997, Robben Island has become a symbol of the triumph of the human spirit. In 1997 around 90,000 made the pilgrimage; in 2006 more than 300,000 crossed the water to see where some of the greatest South Africans spent decades of their lives. Visiting the island is a sobering experience. The approximately four-hour tour begins at the Nelson Mandela Gateway to Robben

Island, an impressive embarkation center that doubles as a conference center. Changing exhibits display historic photos of prisoners and prison life. Next make the 45-minute journey across the water, remembering to watch Table Mountain recede in the distance and imagine what it must have been like to have just received a 20-year jail sentence. Boats leave three or four times a day, depending on season and weather.

Tours are organized by the Robben Island Museum (other operators that advertise Robben Island tours only take visitors on a boat trip *around* the island.) Most guides are former political prisoners, and during the two-hour tour, they will take you through the prison where you will see the cells where Mandela and other leaders were imprisoned. The tour also takes you to the lime quarry, Robert Sobukwe's place of confinement, and the leper church. Due to increased demand for tickets during peak season (December and January), make bookings at least three weeks in advance. Take sunglasses and a hat in summer. ■ **TIP→ You are advised to tip your guide only if you feel that the tour has been informative.** ✉ *Nelson Mandela Gateway, Victoria and Alfred Waterfront* ☎ *021/413–4200* ⊕ *www.robben-island.org.za* ✉ *R320.*

FAMILY
Fodor's Choice
★
Two Oceans Aquarium. This aquarium is widely considered one of the finest in the world. Stunning displays reveal the regional marine life of the warmer Indian Ocean and the icy Atlantic. It's a hands-on place, with a touch pool for children, opportunities to interact with penguins, and (for certified divers only) to dive in the vast, five-story ocean exhibit with shoals of fish, huge turtles, and sting rays, or the new shark exhibit, where you might share the water with large ragged-tooth sharks (*Carcharias taurus*) and enjoy a legal adrenaline rush (for an additional fee, of course). If you don't fancy getting wet, you can still watch daily feedings in either the ocean, penguin, or shark exhibits. But there's more to the aquarium than just snapping jaws. Look for the trippy jellyfish display, the Knysna seahorses, and the alien-like spider crabs. ✉ *Dock Rd., Victoria and Alfred Waterfront* ☎ *021/418–3823* ⊕ *www.aquarium.co.za* ✉ *R160.*

Fodor's Choice
★
Zeitz Museum of Contemporary Art Africa. Opened in September 2017, this museum is the first major museum dedicated to contemporary art from Africa and its diaspora on the African continent. Inhabiting the massively renovated historic Grain Silo in what is now called the Silo District of the V&A Waterfront, the museum itself is a work of art, reimagined by designer Thomas Heatherwick. ✉ *Silo District, Victoria and Alfred Waterfront* ⊕ *www.zeitzmocaa.museum* ✉ *R180* ☉ *Closed Tues.*

WORTH NOTING

Cape Town Diamond Museum. This small museum attached to the Shimansky boutique tells the fascinating history of the little stones that played such a big role in South Africa's history. The 45-minute tour covers a time line of 3 billion years, mostly focusing on how the local industry developed in the 19th and early 20th centuries, and ending in a showroom where polishers are busy "brillianteering" stones that are available for purchase. ✉ *Level 1, The Clocktower Waterfront, Victoria and Alfred Waterfront* ☎ *021/421–2488* ⊕ *www.capetowndiamondmuseum.org* ✉ *R50.*

**NEED A
BREAK?**

Willoughby's. For what many would argue is Cape Town's best sushi, head to Willoughby's, which is in the V&A's shopping mall, with seating both inside and out. But this is all about the food—there are no views. ⊠ *Victoria Wharf, Shop 6132, Victoria and Alfred Waterfront* ☏ *021/418–6115.*

V&A Waterfront Amphitheatre. If the scattered benches looking out at the harbor activity are full, this open-air space is a good spot to eat your take-way lunch—if there's no performance on. This popular outdoor space mounts performances ranging from concerts by the Cape Town Philharmonic Orchestra to gigs by jazz and rock bands and even Turkish minstrels. (Check the Waterfront's website or its branch of the tourism office for a schedule of events.) The amphitheater stands on the site where, in 1860, a teenage Prince Alfred inaugurated the construction of a breakwater to protect ships in the harbor from devastating northwesterly winds. ⊠ *Near Market Sq., Victoria and Alfred Waterfront* ☏ *021/408–7600 for schedule* ⊕ *www.waterfront.co.za.*

SEA POINT

Defined largely by the incredibly popular pedestrian promenade that stretches from Sea Point's southern edge and carries on to Mouille Point and Granger Bay in the Waterfront, this is one of the few middle-income residential areas in Cape Town that is actually on the sea. About 10 km (6 miles) long, **The Sea Point Promenade** is populated by a constant slew of walkers, runners, and cyclists. To one side of the promenade, grassy lawns buffer pedestrians from the street, making them a popular spot for picnics, pick-up soccer games, and people-watching. To the other side, a few city beaches (none recommended for swimming) offer stunning urban views of the wild Atlantic Ocean. Sea Point is also home to the **Sea Point Pavilion**, where you will find what may be the world's most stunningly located public swimming pool. Surrounded by views of Lion's Head and the Atlantic Ocean, the only downside to this amazing saltwater pool is that it isn't heated (and it can get very busy during school holidays). Previously considered a dead zone dining-wise, this has changed in recent years, and the area is home to numerous inexpensive (though largely unremarkable) options, as well as a few real winners, and the fantastic **Mojo Market,** where you can find literally dozens of great dining and drinking options, as well as some fabulous boutiquey shopping.

TABLE MOUNTAIN NATIONAL PARK

Nowhere else in the world does an area of such spectacular beauty and rich biodiversity exist almost entirely within a metropolitan area. Large swaths of the Cape Peninsula are devoted to this spectacular 220-square-km (85-square-mile) park, which is home to countless hiking trails and gorgeous beaches, as well as two world-renowned landmarks: the eponymous Table Mountain and the legendary Cape of Good Hope. Although several parts of the park are within the boundaries of Cape Town, others are in the Cape Peninsula (*see Cape Peninsula*). The park requires entrance payments only at three points: the Cape

Point nature reserve, Boulders Beach, and Silvermine Nature Reserve. The rest of the park is open and free for all to enjoy.

TIMING AND PRECAUTIONS

It would be easy for nature lovers to spend days in the park. Most visitors spend about three hours going up Table Mountain by cable car, and another half day visiting Cape Point. For the fit, hiking up Table Mountain (and taking the cable car down) is a far more rewarding way to experience the mountain, but requires decent weather and at least half a day. To experience the wild beauty of Cape Point, a full day is recommended to visit the point lighthouse (either walking or by funicular), walk to the Cape of Good Hope, and explore the gorgeous empty beaches around Olifantsbos or Platboom. Within Cape Point, the main safety issue is baboons: they are dangerous and should not be messed with. Do not feed them. In other parts of the park (e.g., hiking trails around the city bowl, Camps Bay, Hout Bay, the Southern Suburbs, Muizenberg, and Silvermine Nature Reserve) remember that much of the park is bordered by city neighborhoods, and muggings can occur in isolated areas. Don't walk alone, and don't carry valuables if you can avoid it. Finally, when hiking on the Table Mountain, be aware that dramatic weather changes can (and probably will) occur, so regardless of conditions when you set out, always carry extra layers of clothing, water, a hat, and sunscreen.

TOP ATTRACTIONS

Fodor'sChoice
★
Hoerikwaggo Trail. A great way to get acquainted with Table Mountain and all its moods is to hike part of the Hoerikwaggo Trail, which opened in 2006. The trail follows the spine of the mountains that run the length of the peninsula, linking four lovely tented camps from the Table Mountain lower cable station all the way to the Cape Point lighthouse. The camps are located at Orangekloof, Silvermine, Slangkop, and Smitswinkel. Hikes can be guided and portered, but you'll still have to organize your own food (which will be delivered to your camp). Experienced hikers can also go it alone, but even with a map the trails can be confusing in places, and not taking a guide is not recommended. Built on wooden platforms, the tented camps have beds, hot showers, kitchens, and *braais* (barbecues). You can opt for as many nights at any of the tented camps as you like; the adventurous can take on the whole trail (four nights). ⚠ **At the time of writing the Silvermine camp was closed due to fire damage.** ⊠ *Table Mountain National Park* ☎ *021/422–1601* ⊕ *www.sanparks.org/parks/table_mountain* ⊠ *R670 per tent per night.*

Fodor'sChoice
★
Table Mountain. Table Mountain truly is one of southern Africa's most beautiful and impressive natural wonders. The views from its summit are awe inspiring. The mountain rises more than 3,500 feet above the city, and its distinctive flat top is visible to sailors 65 km (40 miles) out to sea. Climbing up the step-like Plattekloof Gorge—the most popular route up—will take two to three hours, depending on your fitness level. There is no water along the route; you *must* take at least 2 liters (½ gallon) of water per person. Table Mountain can be dangerous if you're not familiar with the terrain. Many paths that look like good routes down the mountain end in treacherous cliffs. ⚠ **Do not underestimate**

Table Mountain National Park and Southern Suburbs

TO ROBBEN ISLAND ↑

Table Bay

PARDEN EILAND

N1

Green Point

See Point

Signal Hill

FORESHORE

Bantry Bay

CAPE TOWN

OBSERVATORY

Irma Stern Museum

Clifton

Lion's Head

Devil's Peak

M3

N2

Table Mountain Aerial Cableway

Bakoven

ROSEBANK

12 Apostles

Table Mountain

Maclear's Beacon

RONDEBOSCH

NEWLANDS

CLAREMONT

M6

Table Mountain National Park

Kirstenbosch National Botanical Gardens

BISHOPSCOURT

KENILWORTH

Rhodes

WYNBERG

Llandudno

Constantia Glen

CONSTANTIA

PLUMSTEAD

World of Birds

Main

Groot Constantia

Hoerikwaggo Trail

HOUT BAY

Buitenverwachting

M4

Hout Bay

TOKAI

M3

Duiker Island

Hout Bay

M42

RETREAT

M6

Chapman's Peak Drive

Silvermine

M5

Noordhoek

▲ *Chapman's Peak*

Silvermine Nature Reserve

M6

M64

Muizenberg

Sun Valley

M65

Kommetjie Main

Fish Hoek

Kommetjie

Ocean View

M6

False Bay

Soet Water

Hoerikwaggo Trail

Wildland

Dido Valley

M65

Simon's Town

Scarborough

Mt. Pleasant

INDIAN OCEAN

Perdekloof

M4

Plateau

Table Mountain National Park

M65

Cape of Good Hope

A T L A N T I C   O C E A N

Cape Point

0 — 2 miles

0 — 2 kilometers

this mountain: every year local and foreign visitors to the mountain get lost, some falling off ledges, with fatal consequences. It may be in the middle of a city, but it is not a genteel town park. Because of occasional muggings near the Rhodes Memorial (east) of the mountain, it's unwise to walk alone on that side. It's recommended that you travel in a group or, better yet, with a guide. If you want to do the climb on your own, wear sturdy shoes or hiking boots; always take warm clothes, including a windbreaker or fleece; travel with a mobile phone; and let someone know of your plans. Consult the staff at a Cape Town Tourism office for more guidelines. Another (much easier) way to reach the summit is to take the cable car, which affords fantastic views. Cable cars (R135 one way) depart from the Lower Cable Station, which lies on the slope of Table Mountain near its western end; the station is a long way from the city on foot, so save your hiking energy for the mountain, and take a taxi or the MyCiti bus to get here. ⊠ *Tafelberg Rd., Table Mountain National Park* ☎ *021/712–0527* ⊕ *www.sanparks.org/parks/table_mountain.*

NEED A BREAK

During the warm summer months—and on the many good winter days—Capetonians are fond of taking picnic baskets up the mountain. The best time to picnic is after 5, as some say sipping a glass of chilled Cape wine while watching the sun set from Table Mountain is one of life's great joys. If you fail to bring your own provisions, the large self-service restaurant at the top of Table Mountain is called, quite simply, the **Table Mountain Cafe** and serves reasonable hot breakfasts, sandwiches, buffet-style meals, and local wine. The adjoining **Wifi Lounge** dishes up a spectacular view along with free Wi-Fi, nonalcoholic beverages, beer, bubbly, and bar snacks.

Table Mountain Aerial Cableway. This is a slick operation. Two large, wheelchair-friendly revolving cars that provide spectacular views take three to five minutes to reach the summit. The Lower Cable Station lies on the slope of Table Mountain near its western end. Save your walking energy for the mountain, and take a taxi or MyCiti bus to get to the station.

Operating times vary from month to month according to season, daylight hours, and weather. To avoid disappointment, phone ahead for exact times. You can't prebook for the cable car, but in the ever-expanding peak season (December–April), if you arrive at 10 am you could wait for an hour. Several tour operators include a trip up the mountain in their schedules. ■TIP➔ Lines to purchase tickets for the cable car can be crazy in season, so book online to speed things up.

⚠ The cable car stops operating in strong wind conditions (common in summer), so be sure to factor in that possibility, especially if relying on it to get back down after a tiring hike up. ⊠ *Tafelberg Rd., Table Mountain National Park* ☎ *021/424–8181* ⊕ *www.tablemountain.net* 🚡 *R255 round-trip.*

WORTH NOTING

Lion's Head and Signal Hill. The prominent peak to the right of Table Mountain is Lion's Head, a favorite hiking spot for locals. The hike takes about 1½ hours (each way), with 360-degree views of the city unfolding as you spiral up the "lion" as well as from the top. The trail is gorgeous and well marked; unfortunately its charms have made it so popular that

CLOSE UP

The Wilds of Table Mountain

Despite being virtually surrounded by the city, Table Mountain is a remarkably unspoiled wilderness. Most of the Cape Peninsula's 2,200 species of flora—about as many plant species as there are in all of North America and Europe combined—are found on the mountain. This includes magnificent examples of Cape Town's wild indigenous flowers known as *fynbos*, Afrikaans for "fine bush," a reference to the tiny leaves characteristic of these heathlike plants. The best time to see the mountain in bloom is between September and March, although you're sure to find flowers throughout the year.

Long gone are the days when Cape lions, zebras, and hyenas roamed the mountain, but you can still glimpse *grysbokke* (small antelopes), baboons, and the rabbitlike *dassie* (rhymes with fussy). Although these creatures, also called rock hyraxes, look like oversize guinea pigs, this is where the similarities end; the dassie's closest relative is the elephant. They congregate in large numbers near the Upper Cable Station, where they've learned to beg for food. Over the years a diet of junk food has seriously compromised their health. ■TIP➜ **Do not feed the dassies, no matter how endearing they look.**

on nice days you can find yourself in a hiker-jam. That said, it's a great hike, and though easier than climbing Table Mountain, the last quarter will earn you a post-hike beer or *malva* pudding (a baked sponge cake sauced with orange juice, apricot jam, and vinegar). As always, don't hike alone, and keep alert, especially as sunset approaches. For those less inclined to sweat, Signal Hill is the smaller flat-topped hill extending from the northern lower slopes of Lion's Head, also sometimes called the "Lion's Rump." Once the location for signal flags communicating weather warnings to ships visiting the bay, Signal Hill is also the home of the Noon Gun, still operated by the South African Navy and South African Astronomical Observatory. Both Lion's Head and Signal Hill are accessed by Signal Hill Road, which ends at the Signal Hill parking lot. The lot has spectacular views of Sea Point and Table Bay. ⚠ **Be careful especially after hours and/or if it's deserted. There have been incidents of violent crime.** ✉ *Signal Hill Rd., Table Mountain National Park.*

SOUTHERN SUBURBS

HOUT BAY

About 25-minutes' drive from Cape Town Central, this once-quiet fishing village on the Atlantic coast is the gateway to Chapman's Peak Drive. Those basing themselves here will want a car to get around, but proximity to various Atlantic beaches (Hout Bay Beach itself is not great), the Constantia wine estates, the peninsula, and the city—plus relatively good-value accommodations—are the draw. The drive along Chapman's Peak, which winds its way down to Nordhoek, is a must, and Hout Bay's quay-side fish-and-chips right at the farthest point of the harbor, and its all-weekend market are good value. If you're getting hungry, head to Snoekies (pronounced like cookies) right on the water, at the southern end of the little harbor. Snoek is a barracuda-like fish that is eaten smoked when given its traditional Malay treatment. Try the more touristy Mariners Wharf if the former is full. Friday to Sunday sees the bustling **Bay Harbour Market**, a weekly social event for locals by night where you will also get all your original gifts for home. You'll also find craft beers, music, and good food. The market is open all day on weekends, but it gets very full.

TOP ATTRACTIONS

Chapman's Peak Drive. Rock slides and unstable cliff faces mean this fantastically scenic drive can often be closed for maintenance, as it was for the greater part of 2008–2009. Work began on the drive in 1910, when it was considered an impossibility. Charl Marais, a mining surveyor, wasn't deterred by the task and set about surveying a route by sending a worker ahead of him to chop out footholds and create rudimentary platforms for his theodolite. There are stories of him hanging on to the side of the cliff by ropes and nearly losing his life on a number of occasions. His tenacity paid off, and with the help of 700 convicts, a road was chipped and blasted out of the rock. Chapman's Peak Drive officially opened in 1922 with views rivaling those of California's Pacific Route 1 to Big Sur. When open, you can access the drive from both Noordhoek and Hout Bay. The toll-gate installed on the drive has been the source of huge local controversy—but you as a tourist won't notice a thing (apart from the fee). Also, this is part of the route for the Cape Argus, the world's largest timed bicycle race—with about 35,000 entries every year from around the globe. ⊠ *Hout Bay* ⟁ *From Hout Bay to Noordhoek* ☎ *021/791–8222* ⊕ *www.chapmanspeakdrive.co.za* ⊠ *R45 toll for cars each way.*

WORTH NOTING

FAMILY **World of Birds.** Here you can walk through aviaries housing more than 400 species of indigenous and exotic birds, including eagles, vultures, penguins, and flamingos. With neither bars nor nets separating you from most of the birds, you can get some pretty good photographs; however, the big raptors are (wisely) kept behind fences. Kids will love the "monkey jungle," where a few dozen highly inquisitive squirrel monkeys roam freely, often lighting on your shoulders or back. ⊠ *Valley Rd., Hout Bay* ☎ *021/790–2730* ⊕ *www.worldofbirds.org.za* ⊠ *R95.*

CONSTANTIA

The most upmarket of the so-called Southern Suburbs, this primarily residential zone is home to several of the Cape's oldest wine estates, as well as some of the city's best dining options. It's about a half-hour drive from Cape Town Central, so you'll need wheels to get around. If you don't have time for the Cape Winelands but still want to experience the Cape's stellar wines, Constantia's many excellent estates are a lovely compromise.

TOP ATTRACTIONS

Groot Constantia. The town of Constantia takes its name from the wine estate established here in 1685 by Simon van der Stel, one of the first Dutch governors of the Cape. After his death in 1712 the land was subdivided, with the heart of the estate preserved at Groot

Constantia. The enormous complex, which enjoys the status of a national monument, is by far the most commercial and touristy of the wineries (the tasting room includes a shop, small gallery, free Wi-Fi, and branch of Constantia Valley Tourism). Van der Stel's magnificent homestead, the oldest in the Cape, lies at the center of Groot Constantia. It's built in traditional Cape Dutch style, with thick, whitewashed walls, a thatch roof, small-paned windows, and ornate gables. The house is a museum furnished with exquisite period pieces. The old "Cloete" wine cellar sits behind the manor house and serves as an additional tasting room. Built in 1791, it is most famous for its own ornate gable, which contains a sculpture designed by Anton Anreith. The sculpture, depicting fertility, is regarded as one of the most important in the country.

In the 19th century the sweet wines of Groot Constantia were highly regarded in Europe, but today Groot Constantia is known for its award-winning Chardonnay (voted best in the world in 2013) and splendid red wines. The best of the latter is the excellent Bordeaux-style Gouverneurs Reserve, made mostly from Cabernet Sauvignon grapes with smaller amounts of Merlot and Cabernet Franc. The Pinotage is consistently good, too, reaching its velvety prime in about five years. The estate operates two restaurants: the homey Jonkershuis and Simon's, which serve both sophisticated meals as well as deli-style offerings and picnics, which you can enjoy on the surrounding lawns. ⊠ *Off Constantia Rd., Constantia* ☎ *021/794–5128 winery, 021/795–5149 museum, 021/794–6255 Jonkershuis, 021/794–1143 Simon's* ⊕ *www. grootconstantia.co.za* ⊠ *Museum R30; tasting R75; museum, wine tour, and tasting R95.*

WORTH NOTING

Buitenverwachting. Once part of Dutch governor Simon van der Stel's original Constantia farm, Buitenverwachting (meaning "beyond expectation" and roughly pronounced "Bait-in-fur-WAGH-ting") boasts one of the most gorgeous bucolic settings imaginable. An oak-lined avenue leads past fields of horses and over a small stream until passing the Cape Dutch homestead and eventually arriving at the small modern cellar. Acres of vines spread up hillsides flanked by more towering oaks and the rocky crags of Constantiaberg Mountain. Buitenverwachting's wine is just as good as the view. The biggest seller is the flagship red, "Christine," a Bordeaux-style blend of mostly Cabernet Franc and Merlot. The winery's eponymous restaurant is also excellent and enjoys fabulous views of the vineyards. ⊠ *Off Klein Constantia Rd., Constantia* ☎ *021/794–5190* ⊕ *www.buitenverwachting.com* ⊠ *R50* ⊗ *Closed Sun.*

NEED A BREAK?

Buitenverwachting Coffee BloC. This delightful coffee shop serves excellent freshly baked pastries and cakes, as well as very good breakfasts and light lunches. Coffee is roasted on-site, and numerous seating options inside and out mean you can find a cozy, shady, or sunny nook depending on mood and whim. ⊠ *Buitenverwachting Wine Estate, off Klein Constantia Rd., Constantia* ☎ *021/794–5190* ⊕ *www.buitenverwachting.com/coffeebloc.php* ⊗ *Closed Sun.*

Constantia Glen. Yet another award-winning wine estate, this one enjoys sweeping open views of the Constantia winelands just below the Constantia Nek roundabout. A huge "tasting room" spread across four different areas including a beautiful covered veranda, glassed-in conservatory space, and cozy lounge space offers wine tastings with a small menu of delicious light fare, cheese platters, and the like. A wine-and-chocolate pairing is also available. ⊠ *Constantia Main Rd., Constantia* ☎ *021/795–5639* ⊕ *www.constantiaglen.com* ☜ *R50.*

ROSEBANK

Lying largely in the shadow and protection of Table Mountain, this southern suburb is known for its leafy, affluent charm. Home to the University of Cape Town (UCT), it also boasts attractions like UCT's Baxter Theatre *(See Nightlife and Performing Arts)*, and the Irma Stern Museum.

TOP ATTRACTIONS

Irma Stern Museum. This small but wonderful museum is dedicated to the works and art collection of Irma Stern (1894–1966), one of South Africa's greatest painters. The museum is administered by the University of Cape Town and occupies the Firs, the artist's home for 38 years. She is best known for African studies, particularly her paintings of indigenous people inspired by trips to the Congo and Zanzibar. Her collection of African artifacts, including priceless Congolese stools and carvings, is superb. ⊠ *Cecil Rd., Rosebank* ☎ *021/685–5686* ⊕ *www.irmastern.co.za* ☜ *R20* ⊙ *Closed Sun. and Mon.*

NEWLANDS

This leafy residential suburb is home to most of Cape Town's best private schools and is known as the entry for the Newlands Forest, a part of Table Mountain National Park.

TOP ATTRACTIONS

FAMILY

Fodor's Choice

★

Kirstenbosch National Botanical Gardens. Spectacular in each season, this renowned botanical garden was established in 1913, and was the first in the world to conserve and showcase a country's indigenous flora. With its magnificent setting extending up the eastern slopes of Table Mountain and overlooking the city and distant Hottentots Holland Mountains, these gardens are truly a national treasure. In addition to thousands of out-of-town visitors, Capetonians flock here on weekends to laze on the grassy lawns, picnicking and reading newspapers while the kids run riot. Walking trails meander through the plantings, which are limited to species indigenous to southern Africa. Naturally the fynbos biome—the hardy, thin-leaved plants that proliferate in the Cape—is heavily featured, and you will find plenty of proteas, ericas, and restios (reeds). Garden highlights include the Tree Canopy Walkway, a large cycad garden, the Bird Bath (a beautiful stone pool built around a crystal-clear spring), the fragrance garden (which is wheelchair-friendly and has a tapping rail), and the Sculpture Garden. Free 90-minute guided tours take place daily except Sunday. Those who have difficulty walking can enjoy a comprehensive tour lasting one hour (R70, hourly 9–3) in seven-person (excluding the driver) golf carts. Concerts featuring the best of South African entertainment—from classical music to township jazz to indie rock—are held on summer Sundays at 5 (be sure to arrive early to get a spot), and the Galileo Outdoor Cinema screens movies on Wednesdays an hour after sunset. A visitor center by the nursery houses a restaurant, bookstore, and coffee shop. There are also several trails taking you to the top of Table Mountain, from which point you can hike to the cable car station. Unfortunately, muggings have become increasingly more common in the gardens' isolated areas, and women are advised not to walk alone in the upper reaches of the park far from general activity. ⊠ *Rhodes Dr., Newlands* ☎ *021/799–8783* ⊕ *www.sanbi.org* ⊠ *R60.*

CAPE PENINSULA

The peninsula is a massive treat for any Cape Town visitor, and a round-trip drive that takes in both the False Bay coastline and the Atlantic Ocean may be one of your most memorable experiences. Among the highlights of the False Bay coast are the quaint fishing village of Kalk Bay and the penguins at Boulders Beach; both are must-visits, the former for the great food, bars, and shops in a historic village right on the sea, and the latter for the privilege of walking among the threatened African (jackass) penguins that call the national park's protected beach home. Cape Point and the Cape of Good Hope nature reserve are 15 minutes farther on at the tip of the peninsula, and few fail to fall in love with the area's wind-swept beauty. The wilder and more rugged Atlantic coastline is one of the most stunning in the world. Highlights include a drive along the Misty Cliffs between Scarborough and Witsands, and horseback riding down Noordhoek beach. You might even consider spending a night or two in one of the many B&Bs that dot the coast, or even inside the Cape Point nature reserve at one of the cottages on Olifantsbos Beach.

TIMING AND PRECAUTIONS

Distances on the peninsula are not that great, so it's certainly possible to drive the roughly 120-km (75-mile) loop in a day, visiting a few sights of interest to you. It's equally possible, and far more rewarding, to spend three days here, either moving slowly around the peninsula and staying in a different guesthouse each night or returning to a central spot in the Southern Suburbs or town at the end of each day. Just remember, however, that during peak season (generally mid-November–late-January) and holidays, traffic—particularly along the M3 getting in or out of Cape Town, and then again between Muizenberg and Kalk Bay—can keep you gridlocked for many frustrating hours. Although touring the peninsula poses no obvious danger, you are advised not to park or walk alone in isolated areas. And watch out for baboons at Cape Point. If you're carrying food, they invite themselves to lunch and can be highly aggressive—the result of human folly.

ATLANTIC COAST
NOORDHOEK
38 km (24 miles) southwest of Cape Town.

This popular beach community has stunning white sands that stretch all the way to Kommetjie along the aptly named Long Beach. The Noord-hoek Farm Village is a welcome rest stop with several great restaurants and a few galleries and boutiques showcasing the work of local artists and craftspeople. Long Beach is popular with surfers and runners, and

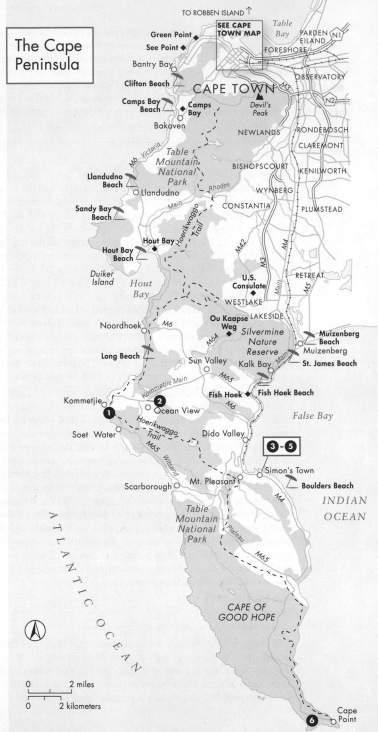

The Cape
Peninsula

TO ROBBEN ISLAND ↑

SEE CAPE
TOWN MAP

*Table
Bay*

PARDEN
EILAND

N1

Green Point ◆
See Point ◆

FORESHORE

OBSERVATORY

Bantry Bay

Clifton Beach

CAPE TOWN

M3

N2

**Camps Bay
Beach**
**Camps
Bay** ◆

*Devil's
Peak*

Bakoven

NEWLANDS

RONDEBOSCH

CLAREMONT

M6. *Victoria*

*Table
Mountain
National
Park*

BISHOPSCOURT

KENILWORTH

**Llandudno
Beach**

○ Llandudno

Rhodes

WYNBERG

Main

CONSTANTIA

PLUMSTEAD

**Sandy Bay
Beach**

Hoerikwaggo Trail

Hout Bay ◆

**Hout Bay
Beach**

*Duiker
Island*

*Hout
Bay*

**U.S.
Consulate**

RETREAT

WESTLAKE

Noordhoek

M6

**Ou Kaapse
Weg**

LAKESIDE

*Silvermine
Nature
Reserve*

M3

M4

Main

M5

**Muizenberg
Beach**

Muizenberg

Long Beach

Sun Valley ○

M64

Kalk Bay

St. James Beach

Kommetjie ○

2

Ocean View ○

M65

Fish Hoek ◆

Fish Hoek Beach

1

*Hoerikwaggo
Trail*

Kommetjie Main

M6

False Bay

Soet Water ○

M65

Dido Valley

Scarborough ○

Mt. Pleasant ●

Witsand

3 - 5

Simon's Town ○

Boulders Beach

M4

*INDIAN
OCEAN*

*Table
Mountain
National
Park*

Plateau

M65

A T L A N T I C   O C E A N

*CAPE OF
GOOD HOPE*

0   2 miles

0   2 kilometers

6

Cape
Point

you can walk all the way to Kommetjie. Just don't walk alone or when the beach is deserted, as attacks are not uncommon. Horseback riding along the beach and through the fynbos-covered dunes is a memorable and highly worthwhile excursion.

2

NEED A BREAK?

Café Roux. Nestled behind Chapman's Peak—and minutes away from Noordhoek Beach—Café Roux is an unpretentious outdoor café with great homemade food and fabulous South African wines at competitive prices. Kids (and parents) will love the adjacent play area. ✉ *Noordhoek Farm Village, Chapman's Peak Dr., Noordhoek* ☎ *021/789–2538* ⊕ *www.caferoux.co.za.*

The Food Barn Deli & Tapas Restaurant. Sister venue to the fabulous Food Barn Restaurant, this casual but excellent deli serves delicious and reasonably priced breakfasts, lunches, and snacks from a cozy book-lined space that invites lingering. From Tuesday through Saturday, a mouthwatering array of tapas is served in the evenings until 9 pm. ✉ *Noordhoek Farm Village, Chapman's Peak Dr., Noordhoek* ☎ *021/789–1966* ⊕ *www.thefoodbarn.co.za/deli.*

KOMMETJIE

3 km (1 mile) south of Noordhoek; 41 km (25 miles) southwest of Cape Town.

A pleasant, somewhat isolated, and almost entirely residential neighborhood, Kommetjie's main attraction is its beach. Take the scenic 45-minute walk down Long Beach to the wreck of the *Kakapo*, a steamship that ran aground on her maiden voyage in 1900. This area is also a surfer's paradise, with some really big waves, a few gentler breaks, and for swimmers, a dangerous undertow. Because of a few muggings on Long Beach a couple of years back, people generally walk here in groups or in couples in the early mornings and at sundown.

FAMILY

Imhoff Farm. This historic Cape farmstead offers a hodgepodge of shops and activities, including an excellent if small wineshop, a deli-style farm stall, several decent casual eateries and boutiques, and various animal-related attractions that kids will love. The latter include a petting farm, camel and horse rides, and a snake park. ✉ *Imhoff Farm, Kommetjie Rd.* ☎ *021/783-4545* ⊕ *www.imhofffarm.co.za.*

Slangkop Point Lighthouse. At 111 feet, this is the tallest cast-iron tower on South Africa's coast. Located almost exactly midway between Robben Island and Cape Point, the lighthouse has a 5-million-candlepower light and a range of 30 nautical miles. Since the lamp was officially lit in 1919 it has been capable of producing four flashes every 30 seconds. It's one of the few lighthouses in the world still to be manned by a keeper—known these days as a "lighthouse officer." Unfortunately famed lighthouse keeper Peter Dennett, who was known for his great tours—passed away in 2012. ✉ *Kommetjie* ☎ *021/449–2400.*

SCARBOROUGH

9 km (5½ miles) south of Kommetjie; 50 km (30½ miles) southwest of Cape Town.

This tiny seaside community has one of the best beaches on the peninsula, and is populated by a disproportionate number of conservation biologists. Look no further than the setting to explain that one.

From Kommetjie to Scarborough, the M65 hugs the shoreline, snaking between the mountains and the crashing surf. This part of the shore is considered unsafe for swimming, but experienced surfers, Boogie boarders, and windsurfers revel in the wind and waves, and the scenery is heart-stopping. The beach here has its own baboon troop.

FALSE BAY COAST
KALK BAY
30 km (19 miles) south of Cape Town.

This small but fascinating harbor shelters a weathered fishing fleet, and takes its name from the seashells that were once baked in large kilns to produce lime (*kalk* in Afrikaans). Charming cottages and Edwardian villas cling to the mountain above narrow, cobbled streets. Exploring the town's funky clothing shops, galleries, antiques shops, and cozy bistros can fill a whole day of rambling. Here gnarled fisherfolk rub shoulders with artists, surfers, yuppies, New Age trendies, and blue-haired ladies. During whale-watching season the gentle giants sometimes enter the harbor, and if you time your visit right, you can almost touch them. You can also walk up any of the steep stairways to Boyes Drive, and from there continue up the mountain on one of many hiking trails. If that's too strenuous, rather head down to the water and relax with a few beers at the Brass Bell, watching local surfers strutting their stuff on Kalk Bay reef. Other possibilities on your to-do list might include dropping your own line off the pier (fishing supplies are available from the small supermarket on the Main Road) or watching the harbor seals lolling around waiting for fishy discards when the boats come in. If you go to haggle for a fresh fish at the harbor, bear in mind that declining fish stocks mean this way of life may soon be a thing of the past.

NEED A BREAK?

Kalky's. Right on the harbor, this cash-only establishment is a first choice for a generous portion of fish-and-chips. The seagulls will fight for your leftovers, as will Robby, the resident seal. ✉ *Kalk Bay Harbour, Kalk Bay* ☎ *021/788–1726.*

Olympia Café. With a menu of Mediterranean-influenced specialities, this favorite local café is usually packed to capacity, especially on weekends. At the affiliated bakery just around the corner, you can buy takeaway cappuccinos, pastries, and legendary ciabatta bread. ✉ *134 Main Rd., Kalk Bay* ☎ *021/788–6396* ⊕ *www.olympiacafe.co.za.*

SIMON'S TOWN
10 km (6 miles) south of Kalk Bay; 45 km (28 miles) south of Cape Town.

Picturesque Simon's Town has many lovely old buildings and some of the peninsula's best swimming beaches at Seaforth and Boulders, the latter being a gem that is also home to a large colony of African penguins. The town has a long association with the Royal Navy. British troops landed here in 1795 before defeating the Dutch at the Battle of Muizenberg, and the town served as a base for the Royal Navy from 1814 to 1957, when it was handed over to the South African navy. Today you are bound to see plenty of men and women decked out in crisp white uniforms.

Jubilee Square, a dockside plaza that serves as the de facto town center, is just off the main road (St. George's Road). Next to the dock wall stands a statue of **Just Nuisance,** a Great Dane adopted as a mascot by the Royal Navy during World War II. Just Nuisance apparently liked his pint of beer and would accompany sailors on the train into Cape Town. He had the endearing habit of leading drunken sailors—and only sailors—that he found in the city back to the station in time to catch the last train. The navy went so far as to induct him into the service as an able seaman attached to the HMS *Afrikander.* He died at the age of seven in April 1944 and was given a military funeral. Just below Jubilee Square is the small but popular Simon's Town Waterfront. Fronted by shops and restaurants, this harbor is the point from which day cruises, deep-sea fishing trips, whale-watching excursions, and kayaking trips depart.

If you're looking to entertain children, the area has several options, including the SAS *Assegaai,* the South African Naval Museum's submarine, which is moored in the harbor with former submariners as guides, a toy museum, and the nearby Scratch Patch.

NEED A BREAK?

The Sweetest Thing Patisserie. The Sweetest Thing serves Simon's Town's best homemade cakes, pastries, and cookies, as well as breakfast until noon, and light lunch options like savory pies and quiches. It's a must-visit if you're hungry and in town during lunchtime. ✉ *82 St. George's St., Simon's Town* ☎ *021/786–4200.*

The Lighthouse Cafe. Arguably Simon's Town's best restaurant, regulars come here for good food and a charming host with a great story: A big-city Jo'burg boy met his girl and came to live by the sea. A friendly place to stop for breakfast (till 11), lunch, or dinner. ✉ *90 St. George's St., Simon's Town* ☎ *021/786–9000* ⊕ *www.thelighthousecafe.co.za* ⊗ *No dinner Sun.–Tues.*

FAMILY **Scratch Patch.** At Scratch Patch, a gemstone factory about 1 km (½ mile) north of Simon's Town, you can buy and fill a bag (you pay according to the size of the bag) with gemstones that you pick from a garden filled ankle-deep with semiprecious stones, such as tiger's eye, rose quartz, amethyst, jasper, agates, and crystals. Obviously this is a winner with children, and since 1970, when Scratch Patch opened, the owners claim it has been copied around the world. If you're lucky, you might find the rare Blue Lace Agate, which has a really interesting story linking it to mineral-rich Namibia and South Africa's little town of Springbok. Attached is Mineral World, a store that sells gemstone jewelry. Another branch of both is found at the V&A Waterfront in Cape Town. ✉ *Dido Valley Rd., Simon's Town* ☎ *021/786–2020* ⊕ *www.scratchpatch.co.za* ✎ *Free; bags of gemstones R17–R95.*

FAMILY **South African Naval Museum.** The naval museum is filled with model ships, old navigational equipment, old South African navy divers' equipment, a few real, life-size boats, and, oddly enough, a helicopter. You can also climb to the top of the building's clock tower. The newer "Transformation" section includes a display about the SS *Mendi* and information about how the navy has changed in democratic South Africa. It's staffed by naval personnel and volunteers. ✉ *Naval Dockyard, St. George's St., Simon's Town* ☎ *021/787–4686* ⊕ *www.simonstown.com/navalmuseum/index.htm* ✎ *Free (donations accepted).*

FAMILY **Warrior Toy Museum.** Dinky Toys, boats, trains, soldiers, airplanes, some 4,000 model cars, and 500 dolls—what's not to like about this toy museum that is equally enjoyable for both kids and adults? It's packed with hundreds of models of all things locomotive: from cars to trains and tanks, these miniature vehicles date from the 1920s to the present. Some are on sale at the attached collectibles shop. ⊠ *St. George's St., Simon's Town* ☏ *021/786–1395* ☏ *R10.*

CAPE OF GOOD HOPE
Cape Point is 60 km (37 miles) southwest of Cape Town.

Once a nature reserve on its own, this section of Table Mountain National Park covers more than 19,000 acres. Much of the park consists of rolling hills covered with fynbos and laced with miles of walking trails, for which maps are available at the park entrance. It also has beautiful deserted beaches (you can swim at some of these beaches, but note that there are no amenities or lifeguards). Eland, baboon, ostrich, and bontebok (a colorful antelope nearly hunted to extinction in the early 20th century) are among the animals that roam the park. A paved road runs 12½ km (8 miles) to the tip of the peninsula, and a turnoff leads to the Cape of Good Hope, a rocky cape that is the southwesternmost point of the continent. A plaque marks the spot—otherwise you would never know the site's significance.

The park has some excellent land-based whale-watching spots. About June to November, whales return to these waters to calve. You're most likely to see the Southern Right whale in False Bay, but the occasional humpback and Bryde's whale also show up. When the water is calm, you may even be lucky enough to see a school of dolphins looping past. The Rooikrans parking lot is good for whale-watching, but there are a number of lookout points. It's just a matter of driving around until you see the characteristic spray or a shiny black fluke.

FAMILY   **Cape Point Nature Reserve.** Cape Point is a dramatic knife's edge of rock
Fodor's Choice   that slices into the Atlantic. Looking out to sea from the viewing
★   platform, you feel you're at the tip of Africa, even though that honor officially belongs to another dramatic point at Cape Agulhas, about 160 km (100 miles) to the southeast. From Cape Point the views of False Bay and the Hottentots Holland Mountains are astonishing. The walk up to the viewing platform and the old lighthouse is very steep; a funicular makes the run every three or four minutes. Take a jacket or sweater—the wind can be fierce. It took six years, from 1913 to 1919, to build the old lighthouse, 816 feet above the high-water mark. On a clear day the old lighthouse was a great navigational mark, but when the mists rolled in it was useless, so a new and much lower lighthouse (286 feet) was built at Dias Lookout Point. The newer, revolving lighthouse, the most powerful on the South African coast, emits a group of three flashes every 30 seconds. It has prevented a number of ships from ending up on Bellows or Albatross Rock below. You can't go into the lighthouses, but the views from their bases are spectacular.

Stark reminders of the ships that didn't make it are dotted around the Cape. You'll see their rusty remains on some of the beaches. One of

2

the more famous wrecks is the *Thomas T. Tucker,* one of hundreds of Liberty Ships produced by the United States to enable the Allies to move vast amounts of supplies during World War II. It wasn't the German U-boats patrolling the coastline that did the ship in. Rather the fog closed in, and on her maiden voyage in 1942, she ended up on Olifantsbos Point. Fortunately, all on board were saved, but the wreck soon broke up in the rough seas that pound the coast.

The mast you see on the western slopes of Cape Point near the light-house belongs to the Global Atmosphere Watch Station (GAW). The South African Weather Bureau, together with the Fraunhofer Institute in Garmisch, Germany, maintains a research laboratory here to monitor long-term changes in the chemistry of the earth's atmosphere, which may impact climate. This is one of 20 GAWs throughout the world, chosen because the air at Cape Point is considered particularly pure most of the time.

The large sit-down Two Oceans Restaurant has spectacular views, and the food is also decent. Also found here are snack kiosks and three gift shops. During peak season (December–January), visit Cape Point as early in the day as possible to avoid being swamped by an armada of tour buses.

The best way to experience the park is to hike on one of the numerous walking trails (our favorites include the boardwalk trail to Diaz Beach and the shipwreck trail) and/or enjoy a picnic and dip at the Bordjiesrif or Buffels Bay tidal pools, or on Platboom or Oliphantsbos beaches. A fantastic alternative is to stay overnight in the comfortable basic accommodations, booked through South African National Parks.

⚠ **Do not feed the indigenous resident chacma baboons, which are increasingly under threat.** Despite the peninsula's population being estimated at only 450 individuals, baboons continue to be shot for raiding homes and stealing food; baboon-feeding tourists are largely responsible for this serious situation, and you should always be wary of them; they can be dangerous if provoked or if they think you have food. ⊠ *Off M65 (Plateau Rd.)* ✛ *60 km (37 miles) southwest of Cape Town* ☎ *021/780–9010* ⊕ *capepoint.co.za* ⊠ *R135 park entrance; funicular R50 (one way).*

BEACHES

With panoramic views of mountains tumbling to the ocean, the stunning white beaches of the Cape Peninsula are a major draw for Capetonians and visitors alike. Beautiful as the beaches may be, don't expect to spend hours splashing in the surf: the water around Cape Town is very, very cold (there's a slim chance you might get used to it). Beaches on the Atlantic are washed by the Benguela Current flowing up from the Antarctic, and in midsummer the water hovers around 10°C–15°C (50°F–60°F). The water on the False Bay side is usually 5°C (9°F) warmer, so if it's warmer waters you seek, head to False Bay beaches such as Muizenberg, Fish Hoek, and Boulders. Numerous **man-made "tidal pools"** are dotted around the peninsula, and although the water is not that much warmer, they make for lovely and protected places to swim. Some of our favorites on the False Bay side are St. James, Dalebrook (in Kalk Bay), and Miller's Point; and on the Atlantic side: Camps Bay, Maiden's Cove (also in Camps Bay), Soetwater (in Kommetjie), and Buffels Bay (in Cape Point nature reserve). The beaches in the Cape are renowned for their clean, snow-white, powdery sand. Beachcombers will find every kind of beach to suit them, from intimate boulder-strewn coves to sheltered bays and wild, wide beaches stretching forever. If you are looking for more tropical water temperatures, head for the warm Indian Ocean waters of KwaZulu-Natal, the Eastern Cape, or the Garden Route.

The major factor that affects any day at a Cape beach is wind. In summer howling southeasters, known as the Cape Doctor, are all too common and can ruin a trip to the beach; during these gales you're better off at Clifton or Llandudno, Atlantic beaches that remain protected by the mountain from even the worst southeast wind. On the False Bay side, the sheltered but very small St. James Beach and sometimes the southern corner of Fish Hoek Beach or one of the pools along Jager's Walk can still be pleasant. Boulders and Seaforth are also relatively sheltered from southeasters.

Every False Bay community has its own beach, but most are not reviewed here. In comparison with Atlantic beaches, most of them are rather small and often crowded, sandwiched between the sea and the commuter rail line, with Fish Hoek being a major exception. South of Simon's Town, the beaches tend to be wilder and less developed, except for the very popular Seaforth and Millers Point beaches.

TIMING AND PRECAUTIONS

The closest beaches to town are Clifton (which are numbered one to four) and Camps Bay, all of which are just minutes away during non-rush-hour traffic. But in summer, when you can't move for traffic, getting anywhere—and especially to the beaches—can take a frustratingly long time. If you want an adventure and are eager to avoid the holiday traffic, jump on the train that runs by the False Bay beaches of Muizenberg, Fish Hoek, and Boulders. From the center of town it will take you about 40 minutes to get to Fish Hoek, and the views from the train across the bay from Muizenberg onward are absolutely spectacular. Just be sure to get a seat in the first-class car, and do not carry obvious valuables.

At many beaches there may be powerful waves, a strong undertow, and dangerous riptides. The lifeguard situation is haphazard and varies according to funding and the availability of the lifeguards; the service combines voluntary and professional guards. Lifeguards work the main beaches, but only on weekends and during school breaks. Other beaches are unpatrolled. Although it's nice to stroll along a lonely beach, remember it's risky to wander off on your own in a deserted area. ■TIP➜ Toilet facilities at beaches are limited.

Sharks, including great whites, do share the Cape's waters, but thanks to the Shark Spotters (⊕ *sharkspotters.org.za*), your chances of an unexpected encounter are extremely low. Pay attention to the flags that will alert you to danger, and if you're worried, consider avoiding the water when it's murky.

Southeasters can also bring blue bottles—Portuguese men-of-war. As these jellyfishlike creatures can sting, you should avoid swimming at these times. (If you see them washed up on the shore, that's a good sign to stay out of the water.)

CAPE TOWN BEACHES

BLOUBERG

FAMILY

Fodor'sChoice

★

Blouberg Beach. A half-hour drive north of Cape Town, this is the beach from which all those iconic "sea with Table Mountain" postcards are shot. Blouberg is divided into two parts: Big Bay, which hosts surfing and windsurfing contests, and Little Bay, better suited to sunbathers, rock-pool explorers, and families. It can be windy here, which is great for kite flying and kite surfing. Kite surfing has become extremely popular along this side of Table Bay, and adrenaline junkies blow off work to come here and ride the waves. For safety, swim in front of the lifeguard club. **Amenities:** food and drink; lifeguards; parking; water sports. **Best for:** surfing; walking; windsurfing. ⊠ *Blouberg* ✛ *Take the N1 north to R27 to Milnerton and Bloubergstrand. Hug the road following the bay.*

CLIFTON

FAMILY

Fodor'sChoice

★

Clifton Beach. Almost always wind-free, these fantastic white-sand beaches are primarily enjoyed by locals, with certain sections known to attract certain crowds. Granite outcroppings divide the beach into four segments, unimaginatively known as First, Second, Third, and Fourth beaches. Fourth Beach is popular with families and teens, whereas the others support a strong social and singles' scene. Dogs are technically allowed only on First. Swimming is reasonably safe, although the undertow is strong and the water, again, freezing. Lifeguards are on duty on weekends and in peak season. Clifton is also a favorite for drinks and sunset picnics, but take care with containers, as alcohol is officially prohibited. Fairly steep staircases provide access to all four beaches, but once you arrive, you will find vendors with drinks, ice cream, and beach loungers for rent in summer. Some of the Cape's most desirable houses cling to the slopes above Clifton, and elegant yachts often anchor in the calm water beyond the breakers. **Amenities:** food and drink; lifeguards; parking; showers; toilets. **Best for:** partiers; sunset; surfing; walking. ■TIP➡ **Parking can be a nightmare in season; rather take an Uber or the MyCiti bus, which has convenient stops here.** ⊠ *Off Victoria Rd., Clifton.*

CAMPS BAY

Camps Bay Beach. The spectacular western edge of Table Mountain, known as the Twelve Apostles, provides the backdrop for this long, sandy beach that slopes gently to the very cold water from a grassy verge. Playing Frisbee or volleyball is very popular on this beach. The surf is powerful, but sunbathers can cool off in a tidal pool on the west end of the beach or under the outdoor showers. Camps Bay's ubertrendy, popular bar-and-restaurant strip lies yards away across Victoria Road. The wind can blow hard here—or not. The strip is alternately a refreshment break for groups of cyclists training for the annual Cape Argus; a watering hole for movie stars, models, and the wannabe rich and famous; and a tourist trap. As such, it tends toward the pretentious on weekends. **Amenities:** food and drink; parking; showers. **Best for:** partiers; surfing; walking. ⊠ *Victoria Rd., Camps Bay* Ⓜ *Hout Bay bus from OK Bazaars on Adderley St.*

BEACHES IN THE SOUTHERN SUBURBS

LLANDUDNO

Llandudno Beach. Die-hard fans return to this beach again and again, and who can blame them? Its setting, among giant boulders at the base of a mountain, is glorious, and sunsets here attract their own aficionados. The surf can be very powerful on the northern side of the beach (where you'll find all the surfers, of course), but the southern side is fine for a quick dip—and in this water that's all you'll want. Lifeguards are on duty on weekends and in season. If you come by bus, brace yourself for a long walk down (and back up) the mountain from the bus stop on the M6. Parking is a nightmare, but most hotels run shuttles in summer. There are no shops here, so take what snacks you need with you. **Amenities:** parking; showers; toilets. **Best for:** partiers; sunset; surfing; swimming; walking. ⊠ *Llandudno* ✛ *Take the Llandudno exit off M6.*

HOUT BAY

Hout Bay Beach. Cradled in a lovely bay of the same name and guarded by a 1,000-foot peak known as the Sentinel, Hout Bay is the center of Cape Town's crayfishing industry (legal and otherwise) and operates several fish-processing plants. It also has knockout views of the mountains, gentle surf, and easy access to the restaurants and bars of Mariner's Wharf. The fact that this is a working harbor, added to the raw sewage of the Inzamo Yethu informal settlement a short walk upstream, means this is unfortunately a polluted beach, however beautiful it looks. You are advised not to swim here. **Amenities:** food and drink; parking. **Best for:** solitude; walking. ⊠ *Off M6, Hout Bay.*

CAPE PENINSULA ATLANTIC BEACHES

KOMMETJIE

Long & Noordhoek Beaches. A vast expanse of white sand stretching 6½ km (4 miles) from the base of Chapman's Peak (Noordhoek Beach starts here) to Kommetjie (where you find Long Beach), this is one of the wildest and least populated stretches of uninterrupted beach, with fluffy white sand and dunes, behind which sit a lagoon and private nature reserve. Because of the wind and the space, these beaches attract horseback riders and walkers rather than sunbathers, and the surfing is excellent (especially off Long Beach). There are no lifeguards and there is no bus service, and, as at some other beaches, at the wrong times and more isolated spots there are real safety concerns (particularly the lonely stretch of sand right in the middle). Despite patrollers on horseback and the occasional all-terrain vehicle, crime is an issue here, and women in particular should be careful. Tourists always do best not to look like tourists. Hang out with other people, just in case, unless you're part of a group. **Amenities:** parking; toilets (Noordhoek). **Best for:** solitude; sunset; surfing; walking. ⊠ *Off M6, Noordhoek.*

CAPE PENINSULA FALSE BAY COAST BEACHES

FISH HOEK

FAMILY **Fish Hoek Beach.** With the southern corner protected from southeasters by Elsie's Peak, this sandy beach attracts retirees and families with young kids, who appreciate the calm, clear water—it may be the safest swimming beach in the Cape, although sharks are sighted fairly regularly in the bay between September and March (though that doesn't stop people from swimming, surfing, and Boogie boarding here); shark spotters are employed to keep an eye out. The middle and northern end of the beach are also popular with catamaran sailors and windsurfers, who often stage regattas offshore. The snorkeling is good, and it's a great beach for Boogie boarding. It's also one of the best places to see whales during calving season—approximately August to November—though there have been whale sightings as early as June and as late as January. **Amenities:** food and drink; lifeguards; parking (fee); showers; toilets; water sports. **Best for:** surfing; swimming; walking; windsurfing. ⊠ *Beach Rd., Fish Hoek* ✥ *Parking is at southern end of the beach.*

> **SPOTTING SHARKS**
>
> Shark spotters are employed at several of Cape Town's False Bay beaches—and on Boyes Drive looking down on the bay—to warn swimmers when great white sharks are out and about. Great whites are usually found close to the shore in the summer months (September–March), and spotters record around 170 sightings per year.

SIMON'S TOWN

FAMILY
Fodor's Choice
★
Boulders Beach. This series of small coves lies among giant granite boulders on the southern outskirts of Simon's Town. Part of Table Mountain National Park, the beach is best known for its resident colony of African penguins. You must stay out of the fenced-off breeding beach, but don't be surprised if a wandering bird comes waddling up to your beach blanket to take a look. Penguin-viewing platforms, accessible from either the Boulders Beach or Seaforth side, provide close-up looks at these comical birds. When you've had enough penguin peering, you can stroll back to Boulders Beach for some excellent swimming in the quiet sheltered coves. This beach is great for children because it is so protected, and the sea is warm(ish) and calm. It can get crowded in summer, though, so go early. Without traffic, it takes about 45 minutes to get here from town, less from the Southern Suburbs. **Amenities:** none. **Best for:** walking. ⊠ *Kleintuin Rd., Sea Forth, Simon's Town* ✥ *Follow signs from Bellvue Rd.* ☎ *021/786–2329* ⊕ *www.sanparks.org* ⊠ *R70 adults, R35 children 2–11.*

■ **QUICK BITES**

C'est La Vie. Just off the beach, this excellent French-style bakery and café is an unexpected gem in the otherwise fairly depressing food scene that is Fish Hoek. Serving some of Cape Town's best artisanal loaves, fresh juices, great coffee, and, of course, fantastic sweet treats, this café also serves yummy breakfast and lunch options. ⊠ *4 Recreation Rd., Fish Hoek* ☎ *083/676–7430.*

MUIZENBERG

FAMILY **Muizenberg Beach.** Once the fashionable resort of South African high society, this beach is now the place where locals—including plenty of kids from townships—learn to surf: a happy example of the evolving new South Africa. A long, sandy beach with a reliable break, this grand old lady of the city's warm-water beaches is known for the colorful bathing boxes of the type once popular at British resorts. Lifeguards are on duty, and the sea is shallow and reasonably safe. If you're keen on stretching your legs, you can walk along the beach or take the picturesque concrete promenade known as the Catwalk, which connects Muizenberg to St. James. **Amenities:** food and drink; lifeguards; parking; showers; toilets; water sports. **Best for:** sunrise; surfing; swimming; walking; windsurfing. ✉ *Off M4, Muizenberg.*

> ### ENDANGERED AFRICAN PENGUINS
>
> Populations of the African penguin (*Spheniscus demersus*) have plummeted because of declining anchovy and sardine stocks, as well as predation by a growing seal population. Up to 50,000 of the birds—who call Boulders Beach and Stony Point near Betty's Bay *(Chapter 3, Western Cape)* in the Overberg home—were lost in just two years, and the current population hovers around 2,700. Penguins mate for life and have been known to return to the same nesting site for up to 15 years.

WHERE TO EAT

Cape Town is the culinary capital of South Africa and quite possibly the continent. It certainly has the best restaurants in southern Africa. Nowhere else in the country is the populace so discerning about food, and nowhere else is there such a wide selection of high-quality restaurants. Western culinary history here dates back to the 17th century—Cape Town was founded specifically to grow food—and that heritage is reflected in the city's cuisine and the fact that a number of restaurants operate in historic town houses and 18th-century wine estates.

Cape Town dining today offers a global culinary experience, with Cape chefs showing the same enthusiasm for international food trends as their counterparts worldwide. French and Italian fare has long been available, but with Thai, Japanese, and Pan-Asian influences flooding in, accents of lemongrass, miso, and yuzu have become de rigueur in fine-dining kitchens. Middle Eastern cuisine is finally making some headway, and the Americas have also come to the fore, with plenty of burgers and ribs, and even chicken and waffles popping up on menus these days, not to mention a few South American and passable Mexican eateries. Ubiquitous pan-Asian fare is probably not as good as what you might be used to in major American cities; sushi is also easily found, though largely limited to tuna and salmon, and often prepared with lots of drizzled mayo and sauces. The locavore trend toward organic produce and healthful dishes is also gaining popularity, though attitudes toward vegetarianism in this meat-happy land remain somewhat backward.

WINE

Wine lists at many restaurants reflect the enormous expansion and resurgence of the Cape wine industry, with some establishments compiling exciting selections of lesser-known gems. More and more restaurants employ a sommelier to offer guidance on wine, but diners, even in modest establishments, can expect staff to be well versed about both wine lists and menus. Wines are expensive in restaurants (often three times what you'd pay in a wineshop), and connoisseurs may be irritated by corkage charges (around R40), but only a handful of restaurants will refuse to open a bottle you bring.

TIMING AND WHAT TO WEAR

During summer months restaurants in trendier areas are geared up for late-night dining but will accept dinner orders as early as 6. In winter locals tend to dine earlier and kitchens can often close by 9:30 if customers aren't waiting. That said, there are venues that stay open late year-round, particularly at the V&A Waterfront and the Camps Bay beachfront along the Atlantic seaboard. Other areas that are meccas for food lovers include Kloof Street and Bree Street in the City Bowl up through Gardens. Many restaurants are crowded in high season, so it's best to book in advance whenever possible; top-rated restaurants can be fully booked months in advance. With the exception of a very few high-end restaurants—where a jacket is suggested but never required—the dress code in Cape Town is very casual.

For more information on South Africa food, see Flavors of South Africa, in Chapter 1. Restaurant reviews have been shortened. For full information, visit Fodors.com.

WHAT IT COSTS IN SOUTH AFRICAN RAND			
	$	$$	$$$	$$$$
Restaurants	under R100	R100–R150	R151–R200	over R200

Restaurant prices are the average cost of a main course at dinner or, if dinner is not served, at lunch.

CAPE TOWN CENTRAL

Hardly a month goes by without a new café or restaurant opening in the city center. Many are housed in historic buildings, and most are open only for lunch and breakfast, as "town" tends to get quiet after hours. However, the areas of Heritage Square and Long and Bree streets are an exception, and you'll find some fantastic dinner choices listed here.

$$$$
INDIAN

✕ **Bombay Brasserie.** Turning the old Reserve Bank Building into a scene of fantastical opulence with ornate, handblown glass chandeliers, lots of dark wood, and luxurious fabrics, the Taj Hotel's Indian fine-dining restaurant does not disappoint when it comes to either ambience or flavor. Choose between the five-course chef's menu, or order à la carte from a menu that is filled with new takes on authentic Indian classics. **Known for:** luxurious ambience; fabulous renditions of classic Indian dishes. $ *Average main: R210* ⊠ *Taj Cape Town, Wale St., Cape Town Central* ☎ *021/819–2000* ⊕ *www.tajcapetown.co.za* ⊘ *No lunch.*

$

AMERICAN

✕**Clarke's bar & dining room.** A Bree Street institution beloved by the young and hip but very much welcoming to all, Clarke's is known for many things, among them its burgers (with their famously butter-fried brioche buns), drinks (from smoothies and fresh juices to excellent cocktails and everything else you'd expect from a place with the word "bar" in its name), and delicious breakfasts (the huevos rancheros are yummy if not strictly authentic). As day turns to night, this light and bright restaurant (seating options range from a few tables on the sidewalk, to a designer-diner interior, to a small plant-filled courtyard) morphs from a child-friendly brunch spot to a casual coffee and burger joint, to a vibey nighttime bar, where DJs and parties are not unusual. **Known for:** burgers and other Americana-style comfort food; hipster-skater hangout that remains friendly to all; fun drinks spot. $ *Average main: R75* ⊠ *133 Bree St., Cape Town Central* ☎ *021/424–7648* ⊕ *www. clarkesdining.co.za* ⊘ *No dinner Sat.–Mon.*

$$

CAFÉ

✕**Culture Club Cheese.** This homey shop behind the bright-yellow front on popular Bree Street trades in an exceptional variety of artisanal cheeses, as well as super-fresh and tasty meals, many of which incorporate (surprise) some kind of cheese or dairy product. Mostly from South African farms, but also including imports, the cheeses feature in the excellent platters, famous grilled-cheese sandwiches, and dishes like a Camembert mac 'n' cheese. **Known for:** friendly, knowledgeable cheese-maker owner gives great cheese recommendations; special events like fondue nights, or pairings with wine, olives, honey, or mushrooms; incredible freshness of ingredients and emphasis on local small-batch and fermented products. $ *Average main: R125* ⊠ *215 Bree St., Cape Town Central* ☎ *072/428–9572* ⊕ *www.cultureclubcheese.co.za.*

$$

PORTUGUESE

✕**Dias Tavern.** This Portuguese taverna in District Six is Cape Town's answer to a dive-bar-meets-diner. Serving classic South African Portuguese fare—think spicy *trinchado* (braised beef), *prego* rolls (rump steak fried in wine and garlic with a fried egg), spicy peri-peri chicken livers, and grilled sardines—for lunch and dinner, Dias Tavern is an institution. **Known for:** Portuguese South African fare—heavy on the garlic and spice; cheap, cheerful fun (don't be surprised if there's a 60th birthday and bachelor's party at the same time. $ *Average main: R110* ⊠ *15 Caledon St., District Six, Cape Town Central* ☎ *021/465–7547* ⊕ *www.diastavern.co.za* ⊘ *Closed Sun.*

$$

ECLECTIC

Fodor'sChoice

★

✕**Hemelhuijs.** Super-stylish Hemelhuijs is both a showcase for a range of exquisite and fanciful ceramicware, and a centrally located restaurant serving equally fanciful and exquisite food. Though a little pricey for lunch, the owner-chef's inventive seasonal dishes burst with freshness and flavor (think pear-and-celeriac salad with hazelnuts and trout, or a crispy panfried veal of sublime flavor and texture) are well worth it. **Known for:** super-creative and seasonal menu; constantly evolving designer interior; intimate friendly service. $ *Average main: R140* ⊠ *71 Waterkant St., Cape Town Central* ☎ *021/418–2042* ⊕ *hemelhuijs.co.za* ⊘ *Closed Sun. No dinner.*

$$$ BISTRO Fodor's Choice ★ 🍴 **La Tête.** Although the chef-owner at this small French-influenced bistro would rather people see his menu as "sensibly sustainable" versus "nose-to-tail," whatever you call it, the dishes served (all in tapas portions at lunch) make fantastic use of the freshest local ingredients, resulting in food that is both uniformly excellent and refreshingly simple. Naturally the menu changes regularly, but favorites include an octopus, cucumber, and mint salad and a mind-blowing pig-cheek, watercress, and radish dish. **Known for:** delightful, experimental food that, in addition to offering lovely fresh produce, employs less commonly favored animal parts; perfect freshly baked madeleines; minimalist ambience. [$] *Average main: R170* ✉ *17 Bree St., Foreshore* ☎ *021/418–1299* 🌐 *latete.co.za* 🕒 *Closed Sun. and Mon. No lunch Sat.*

$$$ EUROPEAN 🍴 **Mink & Trout.** This stylish and centrally located Bree Street bistro draws diners with exquisitely rendered food in an elegant heritage building where exposed brick and ancient yellowwood beams contrast with chartreuse velvet banquettes and sleek furnishings. The menu is small and changes regularly, but the inspiration is modern European served in three courses; expect dishes like risotto arancini, duck confit with braised cabbage, and crème brûlée. **Known for:** fine yet unpretentious food; great location in beautiful heritage building on buzzy Bree Street. [$] *Average main: R160* ✉ *127 Bree St., Cape Town Central* ☎ *021/426–2534* 🕒 *Closed Sun. No dinner Mon.*

$$$$ CONTEMPORARY Fodor's Choice ★ 🍴 **mulberry & prince.** Exceptionally delicious things are happening in this dinner-only designer space of exposed brick, funky lighting, and leather seats. Having adopted the sharing plates concept to great effect, the chef-owners are serving an inventive and changing selection of high-quality "small" dishes that leave a big impression: think buffalo stracciatella on a glaze of strawberry gazpacho with toasted puffed rice, or oysters with a shaved-ice kick of yuzu and grapefruit. **Known for:** kitchen stays open late; understated designer interior; extremely creative small "sharing" plates. [$] *Average main: R250* ✉ *12 Pepper St., Cape Town Central* ☎ *021/422–3301* 🌐 *www.mulberryandprince.co.za* 🕒 *Closed Sun. and Mon. No lunch.*

$$$$ BISTRO 🍴 **The Shortmarket Club.** This darkly gorgeous restaurant with its ambience of an opulent supper club from another era serves a small and well-considered à la carte menu of bistro classics made modern. The oyster and bubbly trolley upon your arrival sets the scene for the level of service and sense of fun that follows. **Known for:** star-chef Luke Dale Roberts co-owns with chefs previously at his other restaurants; breakfast treats like a Scotch egg with mango tahini or Parmesan-and-miso waffles; fanciful trolley service, delivering goodies from oysters to cheeses. [$] *Average main: R259* ✉ *88 Shortmarket St., Cape Town Central* ☎ *021/447–2874* 🌐 *www.theshortmarketclub.co.za* 🕒 *Closed Sun. No breakfast Mon.–Thurs.*

$$$ JAPANESE 🍴 **Tjing Tjing Torii.** Serving dinners and snacks comprised of crowd-pleasing Japanese bar food—think deep-fried sushi rice, excellent tempura, and karaage chicken—this beautifully moody evening venue is located between its vibey sister rooftop bar upstairs, and the excellent and more casual daytime brasserie, Dear Me, downstairs. All three venues share a chef, great design style, and a location in a centrally located

200-year-old heritage building. **Known for:** friendly and efficient service; fantastic cocktails; romantic atmosphere. [$] *Average main: R160* ✉ *165 Longmarket St., Cape Town Central* ☎ *021/422–4920* 🌐 *www.tjingtjing.co.za/torii* 🕒 *Closed Sun. and Mon.*

WOODSTOCK

$$$$ ECLECTIC Fodor's Choice ★

🍴 **The Pot Luck Club.** A meal at this playful and inventive tapas-style venture from Cape Town star-chef Luke Dale Roberts always promises fabulous fun. With great harbor and mountain views from its position on the sixth floor of a renovated silo, this hip eatery serves an eclectic but clearly Asian-influenced array of fine-dining nibbles. **Known for:** super-creative and umami-packed dishes with distinct Asian flair; simultaneously hip, elegant, and casual ambience; two seatings for dinner—don't expect to linger if you choose the early one. [$] *Average main: R250* ✉ *Old Biscuit Mill, 375 Albert Rd., Silo top fl., Woodstock* ☎ *021/447–0804* 🌐 *www.thepotluckclub.co.za* 🕒 *Brunch only on Sun.*

$$$$ ECLECTIC Fodor's Choice ★

🍴 **Reverie Social Table.** Enjoying a wonderful evening with a dozen or so strangers is almost as much of the pleasure of this unique fine-dining experience as is the exquisite five-course meal paired with boutique wines, all served at a single 18-seater wooden table in the gritty, industrial neighborhood of Observatory. The young and vibrant local chef-owner was raised in the nearby winelands, and her knowledge of terroir and experience in some of the region's best kitchens are both reflected in how brilliantly she creates and executes her menus with specific estates in mind. **Known for:** unusual and thoroughly enjoyable group dining experience with strangers; great informal lunches; wonderful pairings of the excellent cuisine with boutique wines. [$] *Average main: R700* ✉ *226A Lower Main Rd., Observatory* ☎ *021/447–3219* 🌐 *www.reverie.capetown* 🕒 *Closed Sun. No lunch Sat. No dinner Mon. and Tues.*

$$$$ ECLECTIC Fodor's Choice ★

🍴 **The Test Kitchen.** Consistently rated South Africa's top restaurant and on the top 50 restaurants in the world list, this industrial-elegant boutique eatery in Cape Town's trendy Woodstock neighborhood is a struggle to get a table at, but the fantastical sensory and culinary journey that awaits you is a worthy and potentially life-changing reward. Since opening in 2009, TTK, as it's known, has led fine-dining trends in foodie-mecca Cape Town. **Known for:** sensory-culinary food-theater experience; intense flavors from all over the globe presented in unexpected and thrilling ways; great cocktails (served from a delightful trolley), amazing wine pairings; bevy of excellent servers. [$] *Average main: R1600* ✉ *The Old Biscuit Mill, 375 Albert Rd., Shop 104A, Woodstock* ☎ *021/447–2337* 🌐 *www.thetestkitchen.co.za* 🕒 *Closed Sun. and Mon.*

GARDENS

$$$$ EUROPEAN

🍴 **Aubergine.** In this warm space of yellowwood tables, sash windows, and reed ceilings, chef-owner Harald Bresselschmidt has served classic European-with a-twist cuisine since 1996 at one of the city's oldest fine-dining establishments. Using the freshest South African produce prepared with classical European methods, the chef cooks with wine in mind, and Aubergine's cellar and pairings are unsurprisingly superb.

Known for: consistency of the classic European cuisine; warmly elegant and unpretentious dining room has great acoustics; old-school approach and feel. [$] *Average main: R233* ✉ *39 Barnet St., Gardens* ☎ *021/465–0000* 🌐 *www.aubergine.co.za* 🕒 *Closed Sun. and some Mon. No lunch Mon., Tues., and Sat.*

$$$ ECLECTIC 🍴 **Chefs.** The concept at this casual cafeteria-style bistro serving excellent lunch and early dinner fare encourages diners to wander in (no reservations) and enjoy a beautifully prepared meal without spending special-occasion amounts of time or money. The three options change daily, but whether meat, fish, or vegetarian, they all make great use of the wood-fired oven prominently on view in the exposed kitchen. **Known for:** high-quality, super-fresh ingredients are the base for beautifully executed homey meals; streamlined ordering system and limited (but entirely adequate) food and beverage options simplify your dining experience; convenient location just a block from Company's Garden and Iziko museums (parking can be difficult, however). [$] *Average main: R155* ✉ *81 St John's St., Gardens* ☎ *021/461–0368* 🌐 *www.chefscapetown.co.za* 🕒 *Closed weekends.*

$$$$ ECLECTIC 🍴 **Planet Restaurant.** Occupying one of Cape Town's most glamorous spaces at the iconic Mount Nelson Hotel, this restaurant with its whimsical design, smooth service, and exceedingly fresh and well-considered menu offers diners a beautifully understated fine-dining experience befitting its elegant location. With a galaxy of starry lights cascading from the high-domed ceiling and tall bay windows looking onto bucolic rose gardens, this gorgeous, all-white space rarely fills to capacity, but it's a great choice for an intimate and stylish night out. **Known for:** fantastical decor and amazing adjoining bar make great choice for intimate evening; chef's attention to sustainable ingredients and excellent vegetarian options; good value for this level of dining, often running winter or other specials. [$] *Average main: R223* ✉ *Mount Nelson Hotel, 76 Orange St., Gardens* ☎ *021/483–1948* 🌐 *www.belmond.com* 🕒 *Closed Mon. No lunch.*

$$ BISTRO 🍴 **Societi Bistro.** This much-loved neighborhood bistro offers a reliable and seasonal menu of French- and Italian-style classics. In a renovated 19th-century Georgian-style home just off Kloof Street, the dining room is all exposed brick and wooden floors, with roaring fires in the winter and a large, lovely garden in the summer. **Known for:** roasted chicken with crispy potatoes; excellent wine list; convivial atmosphere. [$] *Average main: R148* ✉ *50 Orange St., Gardens* ☎ *021/424–2100* 🌐 *www.societi.co.za* 🕒 *Closed Sun.*

TAMBOERSKLOOF

$$$ MEDITERRANEAN 🍴 **Kloof Street House.** Set in a fanciful garden under palm trees illuminated by strings of fairy lights, this magnificently dolled-up Victorian house on trendy Kloof Street serves a menu of Mediterranean-inspired fare with a distinctly South African twist. Expect starters like panfried halloumi cheese with dukkah spice and honey, or baked whole Camembert with caramelized onions and cranberry jelly. **Known for:** Moroccan-spiced lamb rump; festive atmosphere; excellent cocktails. [$] *Average main: R200* ✉ *30 Kloof St., Tamboerskloof* ☎ *021/423–4413* 🌐 *www.kloofstreethouse.co.za* 🕒 *No lunch Mon.*

$$$$ JAPANESE Fodor's Choice ★ 🍴 **Kyoto Sushi Garden.** Elegant and tranquil, this small oasis near the Kloof Street drag serves pricey but beautifully executed Japanese fare for dinner only. Sourcing as much as possible from Japan, the owner verges on obsessive in his effort to maintain a high standard of both ingredients and technique, evidenced in the lightness of the tempura and the freshness and variety of seafood. **Known for:** most authentic Japanese food in Cape Town; amazing Japanese whiskey and sake selections. [$] *Average main: R225* ✉ *11 Lower Kloofnek Rd., Tamboerskloof* ☎ *021/422–2001* 🌐 *www.kyotogardensushict.com* 🕑 *Closed Sun. No lunch.*

V&A WATERFRONT

Generally speaking, restaurants here tend to cater to tourists (i.e., they have no need to gain diners' loyalty). There are, however, some very good exceptions (though you'll pay for them), as well as plenty of cheap fast-food options.

$$$$ STEAKHOUSE 🍴 **Belthazar.** Boasting one of the largest selections of wines by the glass (more than 250) in the world, Belthazar is also recommended for its consistently good if pricey steak and seafood. Enjoy gorgeous Table Mountain and harbor views from the all-weather outdoor seating at lunch, or at dinner, the moodier interior, where a team of sommeliers can recommend the best wine match for your meal. **Known for:** In-house butchers cut and mature the locally sourced beef; award-winning wine list that exceeds 600 vintages, including a few rare treats; great steaks. [$] *Average main: R250* ✉ *Victoria Wharf, V&A Waterfront, Shop 153, Victoria and Alfred Waterfront* ☎ *021/421–3753, 021/421–3756* 🌐 *www.belthazar.co.za.*

$$$ BELGIAN 🍴 **Den Anker.** Take a break from your Waterfront wanderings at this Belgian-style eatery, where you can enjoy great views while also savoring an impressive range of Belgian beers and as good a pot of mussels with frites as you're likely to find anywhere in Cape Town. With its focus on meat and seafood, expect other dishes like fillet béarnaise, rabbit simmered in Belgian beer, or Norwegian salmon in a beurre blanc. **Known for:** wide range of imported Belgian beers, with six served on tap; attractive glassed-in space with harbor and mountain views; mussels, seafood, and Wagyu burger. [$] *Average main: R180* ✉ *Alfred Mall, Pierhead, Waterfront* ☎ *021/419–0249* 🌐 *www.denanker.co.za.*

$$$$ SEAFOOD 🍴 **Harbour House V&A.** Sister restaurant to the original Harbour House in Kalk Bay, the V&A location serves the same reliably fresh and tasty seafood menu from an enviable spot overlooking the harbor. As with the Kalk Bay location, the fresh fish of the day is always a good bet, and desserts are excellent. **Known for:** great location with beautiful harbor and mountain views; reliable fresh seafood; sushi bar upstairs is a great cocktail spot in summer. [$] *Average main: R202* ✉ *Quay 4, V&A Waterfront, Victoria and Alfred Waterfront* ☎ *021/418–4744* 🌐 *www.harbourhouse.co.za.*

$$$$ JAPANESE FUSION 🍴 **Nobu.** If you've always wanted to try Nobuyuki "Nobu" Matsuhisa's famous Japanese cuisine, but were put off by the potential bill in New York or London, Nobu Cape Town offers a chance to sample what may not constitute exactly the same level of cuisine, but will

nonetheless make for a highly enjoyable experience. A vast modern space in the Waterfront's One&Only resort provides a fitting backdrop for the splurge of the Omakase multicourse tasting menu, which will likely include dishes such as the signature Alaskan black cod with miso. **Known for:** branch of the famous Nobu chain; glitzy, bold atmosphere. [$] *Average main: R475* ✉ *One&Only Cape Town, Dock Rd., Victoria and Alfred Waterfront* ☎ *021/431–4511* 🌐 *www.oneandonlyresorts.com* 🕒 *No lunch.*

$$$ JAPANESE 🍴 **Willoughby & Co.** Though unfortunately inside the mall, this buzzing hive of activity consistently churns out what many say is the city's best sushi along with a surprisingly good array of other Japanese dishes as well as seafood favorites like English fish-and-chips and a prawn pasta. It is probably fair to say that South African sushi was defined by Willoughby & Co., with its fanciful and decadent signature rolls, such as the creamy rock-shrimp maki (a tuna-style roll graced with large chunks of tempura-fried crayfish in a spicy mayo-based sauce) and the rainbow nation roll (salmon, avocado, and tuna topped with caviar and a few squizzles of delicious sesame-oil and sweet chili sauces). **Known for:** excellent and decadent sushi rolls; long lines during dinner, alleviated by free wine samples. [$] *Average main: R200* ✉ *Victoria Wharf, Shop 6132, Victoria and Alfred Waterfront* ☎ *021/418–6115* 🌐 *www.willoughbyandco.co.za.*

GREEN POINT

$$ MEXICAN 🍴 **El Burro.** On the second floor of a heritage building in the heart of Greenpoint, this fun and funky Mexican joint serves great margaritas and very reasonable Mexican food that may fall short of "auténtico," but will certainly scratch the itch for most of us. The ceviche is a winner, as are the tacos, which come with the choice of corn or flour tortillas, and which you assemble yourself with a mass of nice fixings. **Known for:** great margaritas, and check out Cabrito Tequila bar downstairs for more; festive ambience, but unfortunate acoustics can make it hard to hear; a South African take on Mexican, but still delicious. [$] *Average main: R150* ✉ *1st Exhibition Bldg., 81 Main Rd., Green Point* ☎ *021/433–2364* 🌐 *www.elburro.co.za* 🕒 *Closed Sun.*

$ CAFÉ 🍴 **Giovanni's Deliworld.** With floor-to-ceiling shelves stacked with everything delicious from French Champagne to truffle oil, Giovanni's is a great place to stock up for a gourmet picnic or enjoy a bite to eat at the counter. Fridges have fresh pasta dishes and greens, but the deli section and espresso bar are where most customers congregate. **Known for:** excellent stock of Italian deli meats and cheeses; great vibe at the always-busy espresso counter; fantastic prepared meals for takeaway. [$] *Average main: R75* ✉ *103 Main Rd., Green Point* ☎ *021/434–6893.*

$$$$ AFRICAN FAMILY 🍴 **Gold Restaurant.** In a huge brick warehouse space decorated with Africana-like giant Malian puppets, beautiful beadwork, and wooden carvings, Gold instantly prepares you for the touristy but thoroughly enjoyable meal and show to come. Your 14-course pan-African "taste safari" may include dishes from Cape Malay curry to Moroccan tagine; the food is fine but not the sole reason you are here. **Known for:** great way to experience a variety of African cuisines; fantastic puppets and

Where to Eat in Cape Town

ATLANTIC OCEAN

WATERFRONT

Granger Bay

Victoria Basin

MOUILLE POINT

GREEN POINT

THREE ANCHOR BAY

Signal Hill

SEA POINT

FRESNAYE

BANTRY BAY

Lion's Head

0   500 yards

0   500 meters

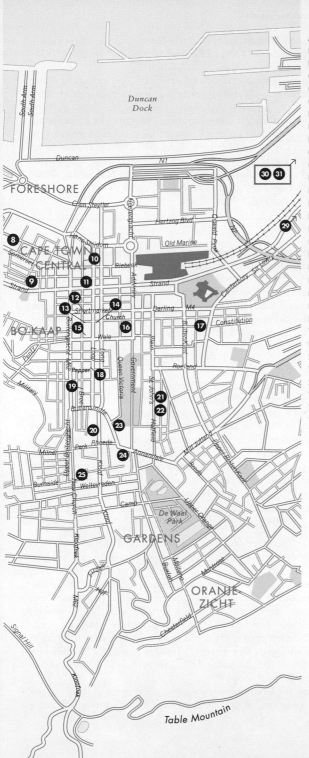

great dancing and drumming show; lively dinner entertainment experience. $ *Average main: R355* ✉ *15 Bennett St., Green Point* ☎ *021/421–4653* ⊕ *www.goldrestaurant.co.za* ⊘ *No lunch.*

$$$$
JAPANESE
FUSION

✕ **Shio Restaurant.** This intimate and sexy izakaya-style eatery in a charming part of the De Waterkant neighborhood serves super-creative if somewhat pricey Japanese and Asian fusion tapas plates. Brilliant flavor combinations are evidenced in dishes like the black rice risotto with a tom yum coconut cream. **Known for:** sister restaurant to the beloved Cheyne's in Hout Bay; great location in trendy DeWaterkant encourages making a night of it; creative Japanese-fusion tapas that are mostly fabulous. $ *Average main: R210* ✉ *49 Napier St., Green Point* ☎ *064/661–7474* ⊕ *www.thegreyhotel.co.za/shio* ⊘ *Closed Sun. No lunch Mon. and Tues.*

SEA POINT

$$
MEDITERRANEAN

✕ **La Boheme Wine Bar & Bistro.** Serving hearty unpretentious Mediterranean fare and tapas at reasonable prices, this unassuming wine bar and bistro on Sea Point's Main Road is often packed. The menu changes frequently, but focuses on Mediterranean-inspired dishes like ostrich meatballs and tagliatelle in a spicy Neapolitan sauce, sesame-crusted fish cakes with a chunky Greek salad, and a good selection of classically Spanish-style tapas. **Known for:** reasonably priced and hearty prix-fixe menus; great wine by the glass selection; tasty tapas. $ *Average main: R138* ✉ *341 Main Rd., Sea Point* ☎ *021/434–8797* ⊕ *www.labohemebistro.co.za* ⊘ *No lunch Sun.*

$$$$
FRENCH FUSION

✕ **La Mouette.** La Mouette serves an extremely reasonably priced tasting menu of modern French-fusion-style cuisine in a beautiful old Sea Point home that is all sash windows, working fireplaces, and bold color. With a choice of three or six courses, you'll be treated to inventive and delicious seasonal fare such as tuna tartare or duck breast with fermented red cabbage. **Known for:** reasonably priced tasting menu; great, friendly service; only fine-dining in Sea Point. $ *Average main: R375* ✉ *78 Regent Rd., Sea Point* ☎ *021/433–0856* ⊕ *www.lamouetterestaurant.co.za* ⊘ *Closed Mon. No lunch Tues.–Sat.*

CAMPS BAY

$$$$
ECLECTIC

✕ **Azure.** Although Azure's blue-and-white nautical-theme decor may feel a bit outdated to some, the restaurant's jaw-dropping sea and mountain views are reason enough to come experience the mostly inspired menu. Signature dishes like the crayfish-and-prawn cocktail, beef Stroganoff, and rice pudding have a classic old-school bent and are divinely comforting. **Known for:** founder Bea Tollman's classically delicious comfort food; amazing ocean views from nautically themed dining room; fantastic breakfast buffet that includes fresh oysters and sparkling wine. $ *Average main: R225* ✉ *Twelve Apostles Hotel & Spa, Victoria Rd., Camps Bay* ☎ *021/437–9029* ⊕ *www.12apostleshotel.com.*

$$$$
SEAFOOD

✕ **The Codfather.** The Codfather serves an excellent array of fresh seafood in a casual yet buzzing environment by way of a slightly unorthodox system. Rather than ordering from a menu, you instead head to a display of fresh seafood on ice, where, with the help of your waiter, you select everything from fish to shellfish in the quantities and style of your choice (you're charged by weight, as in Greece). **Known for:** excellent fresh seafood; unadorned cooking style (most seafood is grilled, no fancy sauces, etc.); order your seafood Greek-style, from a display. $ *Average main: R350* ✉ *37 The Drive, Camps Bay* ☎ *021/438–0782, 021/438–0783* ⊕ *www.codfather.co.za.*

$$
STEAKHOUSE
FAMILY

✕ **Hussar Grill.** This branch of one of the Cape's favorite steak houses offers an unpretentious and friendly place to enjoy excellent and reasonably priced steaks and ribs in an area where restaurants tend to focus more on views than food. A few minutes' drive away from Camps Bay's main beach drag, the interior here is more Boston than Miami—all leather booths and historic photographs, well suited to the carnivorous feast that awaits. **Known for:** excellent steaks and game meat; unpretentious old-school vibe; friendly, efficient service. $ *Average main: R135* ✉ *108 Camps Bay Dr., Shop 2, Camps Bay* ☎ *021/438–0151* ⊕ *www. hussargrill.co.za* ◯ *No lunch Mon.–Sat.*

$$
CAFÉ

✕ **Melissa's Mantra Cafe.** This welcome addition to Camps Bay delivers great and unfussy café food from a gorgeously casual space whose second-floor vantage provides sweeping views of the beach and sea while also lifting you above the street-level irritations of cars and hawkers. The scones and smoothies are fantastic at breakfast (it's quickly become a favorite local breakfast joint), while tapas, salads, pizzas, and heartier mains from mussels to burgers to pork ribs are available from 11:30 till closing. **Known for:** catering to locals in both price and quality, an anomaly in touristy Camps Bay; a full bar and cocktail menu makes this a great sundowner spot, occasionally with live music; nice small gift shop attached with some lovely local goods. $ *Average main: R145* ✉ *43 Victoria Rd., Camps Bay* ☎ *021/437–0206* ⊕ *www. mantracafe.co.za.*

TABLE MOUNTAIN NATIONAL PARK

$$$$
MODERN
EUROPEAN

✕ **The Roundhouse.** Known for its exceptional natural beauty, Cape Town is surprisingly short on restaurants with killer views; The Roundhouse, serving modern South African cuisine, is helping close that gap. Converted from its origins as an 18th-century Table Mountain–side hunting lodge, this unique fine-dining restaurant overlooking Camps Bay specializes in applying creative flavor combinations to local ingredients—think Karoo ostrich with a fennel seed glaze or hake with carrot and cashew puree. **Known for:** excellent and exceptionally suave team of waiters; gorgeous views over Camps Bay. $ *Average main: R665* ✉ *The Glen, Round House Rd., Table Mountain National Park* ☎ *021/438–4347* ⊕ *www.theroundhouserestaurant.com* ◯ *Closed Mon. No dinner Sun. No lunch May–Sept.*

HOUT BAY

$$$$ ASIAN FUSION

🍴 **Cheyne's & Lucky Bao.** Serving Pacific Rim cuisine from a funky and intimate location in Hout Bay, Cheyne's is the place to go for inventive, pan-Asian small plates. The menu changes entirely each season but is generally divided into the categories of sea, land, earth, poké bowls, and happy endings. **Known for:** fun and intensely flavored pan-Asian cuisine; vibey graffiti-mural interior. [$] *Average main: R240* ✉ *1 Pam Arlene Pl., Main Rd., Hout Bay* ☎ *021/790–3462* ✍ *cheynesrestaurant@gmail.com* ⏲ *Closed Sun. No lunch Mon.–Wed.*

$$ ITALIAN FAMILY

🍴 **Massimo's.** Having begun as a pizza joint, this casual Hout Bay eatery located in an old barn now serves a range of delightfully simple Italian fare from antipasti to pastas, as well as what is still arguably Cape Town's best pizza. The "spuntini" or antipasti include classics like Italian meatballs, Caprese salad, and panfried spinach with toasted pine nuts. **Known for:** excellent Italian-style pizza; friendly, warm service; frequent specials. [$] *Average main: R120* ✉ *Oakhurst Farm Park, Main Rd., Hout Bay* ☎ *021/790–5648, 073/390–1373* 🌐 *www.pizzaclub.co.za.*

SOUTHERN SUBURBS

CONSTANTIA

$$ ITALIAN

🍴 **Blanko.** Located in a historic manor house, this restaurant serves tasty and hearty Italian fare from multiple dining rooms whose white walls are adorned with an impressive collection of contemporary South African art. Classics like white anchovies in a shallot-and-olive-oil dressing, escalopes of veal, and fresh ravioli are all pleasing, filling, and reasonably priced, if not culinary events. **Known for:** edgy South African art collection; unpretentious and tasty Italian fare; location in historic manor house. [$] *Average main: R145* ✉ *Alphen Boutique Hotel, Alphen Dr., Constantia* ☎ *021/795–6300* 🌐 *www.blanko.co.za.*

$$$ EUROPEAN

🍴 **Buitenverwachting.** On a historic wine estate in Constantia, this fine-dining restaurant serves excellent fare from an original Cape Dutch building with charming views of the vineyards. The menu is divided into a "rustic" section, where you can find the likes of roasted pork belly and gnocchi or fish-and-chips, and an "indulge" section, where the chef gets more innovative with dishes like a grilled beef fillet served with a mouthwatering bone-marrow crust. **Known for:** beautiful views of one of the Cape's oldest wine estates; a menu that includes both "rustic" and "haute" cuisine; hushed, attentive service. [$] *Average main: R190* ✉ *Klein Constantia Rd., Constantia* ☎ *021/794–3522* 🌐 *www.buitenverwachting.com* ⏲ *Closed Sun.*

$$$$ ECLECTIC Fodor's Choice ★

🍴 **Chef's Warehouse at Beau Constantia.** Enjoy soaring views of the Constantia winelands from this coolly elegant space of carved wood and huge glass windows, where a fantastic and well-priced "tapas for two" menu reminds you why long lunches were invented. Eight dishes—all marked by freshness of ingredients and a globe-trotting host of inspiration—served in three courses are available for lunch and dinner, and change with the seasons or chef's inspiration. **Known for:** fantastic "tapas for two" menu that delightfully takes the decision making out of your hands; amazing views and beautiful interior space; sister restaurant

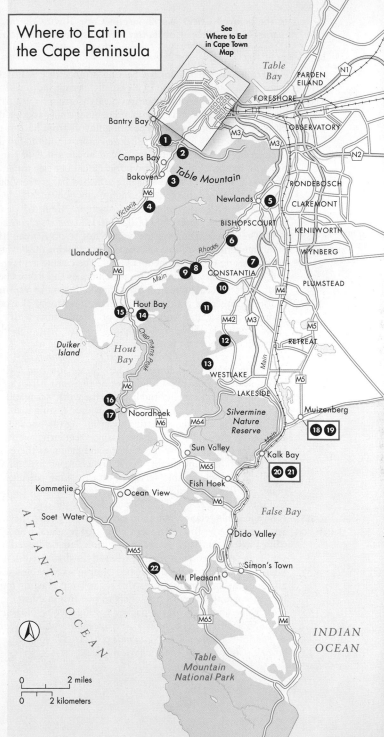

Where to Eat in the Cape Peninsula

See
Where to Eat
in Cape Town
Map

Table
Bay

PARDEN
EILAND

N1

FORESHORE

OBSERVATORY

Bantry Bay

❶

❷

Camps Bay

Bakoven

❸

Table Mountain

Newlands

❺

RONDEBOSCH

CLAREMONT

BISHOPSCOURT

KENILWORTH

M6

❹

Victoria

❻

Rhodes

WYNBERG

Llandudno

M6

Main

❾ ❽

❼

CONSTANTIA

PLUMSTEAD

M4

Hout Bay

❶❺ ❶❹

❶❶

❿

M42

M3

Duiker
Island

Chapman's Peak

Hout
Bay

❶❷

RETREAT

M5

❶❸

WESTLAKE

LAKESIDE

M6

Silvermine
Nature
Reserve

Muizenberg

M5

❶❻

❶❼

Noordhoek

M64

M6

❶❽ ❶❾

Kalk Bay

❷⓿ ❷❶

Sun Valley

M65

Kommetjie

Ocean View

Soet Water

Fish Hoek

M6

False Bay

Dido Valley

ATLANTIC OCEAN

M65

❷❷

Mt. Pleasant

Simon's Town

INDIAN
OCEAN

M65

M4

N

Table
Mountain
National Park

0   2 miles

0   2 kilometers

to the beloved Chef's Warehouse in Cape Town Central. [$] *Average main: R325* ✉ *Beau Constantia Wine Estate, Constantia Main Rd., Constantia* ☎ *021/794–8632* 🌐 *www.beauconstantia.com/eat* ⏲ *Closed Mon. No dinner Sun.*

$$$ ECLECTIC Fodor's Choice ★

🍴 **Foxcroft Restaurant & Bakery.** Serving a range of exquisitely prepared international fusion cuisine in a casually elegant-industrial setting, this restaurant and bakery in the heart of leafy Constantia is a true gem. The extremely seasonal menu changes often, but includes about a dozen mind-blowing tapas options—incorporating flavors from harissa to ponzu to smoked garlic—as well as a half dozen more traditional mains, such as chalmar beef with duck fat fries and café au lait sauce, or pan-seared line fish with mussel chowder. **Known for:** casual but elegant ambience that captures Capetonian style; amazing attached bakery serving breakfast; surprisingly affordable for such high-quality cuisine. [$] *Average main: R170* ✉ *High Constantia Centre, Constantia Main Rd. at Groot Constantia Rd., Constantia* ☎ *021/202–3304* 🌐 *www.foxcroft.co.za.*

$$$$ SOUTH AFRICAN

🍴 **The Greenhouse.** Discover the wonders of South African haute cuisine in this modern, glassed-in conservatory overlooking the beautiful gardens of the historic Cellars-Hohenort Hotel. The cuisine is playful but high-end, with a medley of multicultural techniques and flavors being used to great effect on local ingredients, resulting in dishes like a springbok (local venison) loin served with tempura shiitake mushrooms, karoo lamb with pumpkin mousse and fynbos honey, or Atlantic tuna with kimchee and apple. **Known for:** inventive and playful South African modern cuisine; stylish dining room with garden views. [$] *Average main: R1100* ✉ *Cellars-Hohenort Hotel, 93 Brommersvlei Rd., Constantia* ☎ *021/795–6226* 🌐 *www.greenhouserestaurant.co.za* ⏲ *Closed Sun. and Mon. No lunch.*

$$$$ ECLECTIC Fodor's Choice ★

🍴 **La Colombe.** Rightfully known as one of South Africa's most lauded fine-dining establishments and listed in the world's top 100 restaurants, La Colombe's sublime French-Asian inspired tasting menus are served in a delightful minimalist setting overlooking the bucolic green of the Constantia wine valley. The menu changes regularly, but the best option is to order the full eight-course gourmand menu, as there is not a false note to be found. **Known for:** stellar French-Asian fusion haute cuisine; excellent, knowledgeable service; fantastic wine pairings. [$] *Average main: R990* ✉ *Silvermist Mountain Lodge, Main Rd., Constantia Nek, Constantia* ☎ *021/795–0125* 🌐 *www.lacolombe.co.za.*

$$$$ ASIAN FUSION

🍴 **Myoga.** This relaxed but glam eatery in the posh Vineyard Hotel & Spa outside Cape Town attracts well-heeled regulars, who come for chef Mike Basset's consistently excellent fusion flair, evidenced in dishes like squid ink spaghetti with yuzu pearls and the divine truffle-teriyaki beef fillet topped with perfectly crisped tempura vegetables. Evenings are all about the amazingly good-value seven-course tasting menu. **Known for:** one of Cape Town's first chefs to put fusion cuisine on the map; great value and super flavor-packed tasting menus; pleasant ambience of the Vineyard Hotel & Spa. [$] *Average main: R220* ✉ *Vineyard Hotel & Spa, 60 Colinton Rd., Newlands* ☎ *021/657–4545* 🌐 *www.myoga.co.za* ⏲ *Closed Sun. No lunch Mon.*

TOKAI

$$$ ✕ **Bistro Sixteen82.** Named for the year the Steenberg wine estate on
ECLECTIC which it sits was established, this not-to-be-missed bistro serves dishes
Fodor'sChoice intended to be paired with the estate's vintages, but remains the opposite
★ of hoity-toity fine dining. Dishes like beef tataki with shimeji mush-
rooms or sustainable fish with kimchi and umami cream are the perfect
foil to a minimalist environment of bleached wood, metallic accents,
and high ceilings. **Known for:** fantastic but unpretentious fare from
breakfast to lunch to tapas; great location to while away an after-
noon on Steenberg wine estate; excellent estate wines for reasonable
prices. $ *Average main: R161* ✉ *Steenberg Estate, Steenberg Rd., Tokai*
☎ *021/713–2211* ⊕ *www.steenbergfarm.com/bistro1682* ☉ *No dinner.*

$$$ ✕ **Catharina's.** Serving good, unpretentious fare in an elegantly quirky
EUROPEAN space with lovely views across the historic Steenberg wine estate, this
is a decent fine-dining go-to no matter the time of day. An oak-shaded
terrace overlooking manicured lawns makes for a lovely, lazy lunch
spot, and the restaurant's interior with its origami swans hanging from
high ceilings and huge windows is a stylishly bright space. **Known
for:** standard European fine-dining style cuisine at reasonable prices;
beautiful setting; Sunday lunch extravaganza. $ *Average main: R195*
✉ *Steenberg Hotel, Steenberg Rd. at Tokai Rds., Tokai* ☎ *021/713–
7178* ⊕ *www.steenberghotel.com.*

CAPE PENINSULA

ATLANTIC COAST

NOORDHOEK

$$ ✕ **Café Roux.** Easy eating in a family-friendly atmosphere doesn't get much
CAFÉ better than this café, deservedly beloved by the outdoorsy crowd that
FAMILY populates the Cape Peninsula. Sit outside under the oak trees or in, where
reed-covered ceilings and a wood-burning stove create a cozy ambience,
and enjoy hearty and tasty breakfasts and lunches. **Known for:** reliable,
unfussy food with lots of choice; live music some afternoons and eve-
nings; super-relaxed and casual setting is great for families. $ *Average
main: R110* ✉ *Noordhoek Farm Village, Noordhoek Main Rd., Noord-
hoek* ☎ *021/789–2538* ⊕ *www.caferoux.co.za* ☉ *No dinner.*

$$$$ ✕ **The Foodbarn.** Probably the best restaurant on the Cape Peninsula,
FRENCH FUSION the aptly named Foodbarn serves delicious, unpretentious French-influ-
Fodor'sChoice enced cuisine in the relaxed setting of a renovated barn near Noord-
★ hoek Beach. The chef makes a point of only using sustainable seafood,
which he puts to great use in starters like fish tartar with miso cream
and a sublime whitefish soup with saffron. **Known for:** extremely well-
priced tasting menus for dinner and generous winter and lunch spe-
cials; the only fine-dining location on the peninsula. $ *Average main:
R203* ✉ *Noordhoek Farm Village, Noordhoek Main Rd., Noordhoek*
☎ *021/789–1390* ⊕ *www.thefoodbarn.co.za* ☉ *Closed Jan. 1. No din-
ner Sun. and Mon.*

FALSE BAY COAST

MUIZENBERG

$$ ITALIAN 🍴 **Casa Labia.** Sitting atop fynbos-covered hills overlooking the magnificent False Bay surf, this Italian-inspired restaurant serves tasty and well-priced meals in the opulent setting—think gold-coffered ceilings, Venetian wallpaper, and marble fireplaces—that once served as home to South Africa's first Italian ambassador, Count Natale Labia. The weekend breakfasts are lovely, with treats like a cheese soufflé omelet, and the lunch menu features hearty dishes like braised beef rib with bone marrow and popcorn-crusted chicken roulade. **Known for:** gorgeous museum-like setting, where children are surprisingly welcome; all-day (10–4) "tea time" menu with scones and cake; excellent pianist ups the ambience ante on weekend afternoons and Friday evenings when dinner is served. [$] *Average main: R145* ✉ *192 Main Rd., Muizenberg* ☎ *021/788–6062* 🌐 *www.casalabia.co.za* ⏲ *Closed Mon. No dfinner Sat.–Thurs.*

$$ CAFÉ 🍴 **Empire Cafe.** Overlooking Muizenberg's surfers' beach, Empire is a place to come barefoot with sand still between your toes for unexpectedly good food, though often with less-than-great service. The chalkboard menu changes regularly, but expect items from burgers and wraps to pastas and sticky pork ribs. **Known for:** tasty food in super-casual environment; service can be slow; delicious sweet treats. [$] *Average main: R120* ✉ *11 York Rd., Muizenberg* ☎ *021/788–1250* 🌐 *www.empirecafe.co.za* ⏲ *No dinner.*

KALK BAY

$$ CAFÉ FAMILY 🍴 **Foragers Deli & Wholefoods Deck Café.** Helping to fill the gaping lack of good eateries between Noordhoek and Cape Point, this café and deli serves great coffee, fresh baked goods (made on-site), sandwiches, and pizza from a child- and pet-friendly covered outside "deck" that is also popular with cyclists. The deli and bakery also sell plenty of takeaway treats for stocking a picnic (fresh fruit, high-quality deli meats and cheeses, freshly made dips and spreads, etc.). **Known for:** great coffee and fresh juices; child-friendly play area; fantastic selection of high-quality deli and some fresh items for picnics, etc. [$] *Average main: R120* ✉ *2 Watsonia St.* ☎ *071/342–5210* 🌐 *www.thevillagehub.co.za.*

$$$$ SEAFOOD 🍴 **Harbour House.** Built on the breakwater of a working harbor, this iconic seafood restaurant has an unbeatable location—waves are known to crash against the huge plate-glass windows at high tide and many tables literally feel perched over the sea. Large, light filled, and orchid adorned, this jaw-droppingly beautiful space of white wood and lots of decking makes the perfect place to enjoy fresh seafood. **Known for:** insane sea views from just about everywhere; freshness of the seafood. [$] *Average main: R202* ✉ *Kalk Bay Harbour, Main Rd., Kalk Bay* ☎ *021/788–4133* 🌐 *www.harbourhouse.co.za.*

$$ CAFÉ Fodor's Choice ★ 🍴 **Olympia Café.** This tiny Kalk Bay institution with its mismatched tables and open kitchen is much beloved by locals as a super-casual destination for consistently excellent food and a great cup of coffee. The quality of the mostly Mediterranean fare is high, and the servers sassy (some might call it something else). **Known for:** amazing treats from the café's bakery around the corner; fantastic fresh seafood and unpretentious Mediterranean fare; no reservations often mean waiting for a table. [$] *Average main: R145* ✉ *134 Main Rd., Kalk Bay* ☎ *021/788–6396* 🌐 *www.olympiacafe.co.za.*

WHERE TO STAY

Finding lodging in Cape Town can be a nightmare during peak travel season (December–January), as many of the more reasonable accommodations are booked up. It's worth traveling between April and August, if you can, to take advantage of the "secret season" discounts that are sometimes half the high-season rate. Other reduced rates can be scored by booking directly online, checking the "Best Available Rate" at large hotels, or simply asking if any specials or discounts are available. If you arrive in Cape Town without a reservation, head for any branch of the Tourism office, which has a helpful accommodations desk.

First-time, short-term, or business visitors will want to locate themselves centrally. The historic city center is a vibrant and pedestrian-friendly place by day, but at night can feel a bit deserted and edgy, depending on where you are. Night owls may prefer to stay amid the nonstop action of Long Street or Kloof Street, or at the V&A Waterfront, with its plethora of pedestrian-friendly shopping and dining options (though be aware that locals don't consider the Waterfront the "real" Cape Town). Boutique hotels and bed-and-breakfasts in the more residential Gardens, Tamboerskloof, and Higgovale areas are often within walking distance of attractions and dining but will be quieter and often enjoy lovely views. Options along the Atlantic Seaboard (from Mouille Point to Camps Bay) are also relatively close to action and (mostly) pedestrian-friendly, with the added advantage of sea and sunset views. Staying farther out on the Cape Peninsula, whether the False Bay or Atlantic side, provides the closest thing in Cape Town to a beach-vacation atmosphere despite the cold ocean waters. The Southern Suburbs, especially around Constantia or Tokai, can make a good base from which to explore the area's wine estates as well as the peninsula, but are truly suburban, meaning you'll need a car for everything, and should plan on 25 to 45 minutes to get into town.

Most international flights arrive in the late morning, and return flights depart in the evening. Because most hotels have an 11 am checkout and 2 pm check-in, you may find yourself with a lodging gap on travel days. All hotels will hold your luggage, and most will try to accommodate you (some of the larger hotels have lounges where you can spend the hours before your flight), but in peak season you may need to organize a backup plan. Also note that many small, luxury accommodations either do not permit children or have minimum-age restrictions. Always inquire in advance if traveling with kids. Cape Town also follows the global trend of not smoking in public places. All hotels will have no-smoking rooms, and most are entirely smoke-free. *Hotel reviews have been shortened. For full information, visit Fodors.com.*

LODGING ALTERNATIVES

When South Africans travel, they often stay in guesthouses or B&Bs, which are numerous in Cape Town and range from simple and "homey" lodgings to some of the most elegant and professionally run establishments available; the latter will offer everything a hotel does but on a smaller, more personal scale. If you prefer more anonymity or want to save money, consider renting a fully furnished apartment or even a room in a shared space, especially if you're staying two or more weeks. **Airbnb** has hundreds of listings in Cape Town, and several agencies can help you make bookings. *For agency recommendations, see Accommodations in Travel Smart.*

Cape Stay. Cape Stay offers a huge selection of accommodations to suit different needs, from very simple and affordable apartments to luxurious villas to special rates at well-known hotels, covering both Cape Town and popular Western Cape destinations. ⊠ *Cape Town* ⊕ *www.capestay.co.za.*

CAPSOL Property & Tourism Solutions. CAPSOL has more than 2,000 high-quality, furnished, fully stocked luxury villas and apartments along the Atlantic seaboard from Cape Town to Bakoven, including Clifton, Bantry Bay, and Camps Bay. Apartments range from R3,000 to R40,000 per night, most with a minimum three-night stay depending on season. ⊠ *The Penthouse, 13 Totnes Ave., Camps Bay* ☎ *021/438–9644* ⊕ *www.capsol.co.za.*

Village N Life. Village N Life manages **De Waterkant Village,** a collection of beautifully restored, self-catering (with cooking facilities) apartments and houses scattered around the charming, central, and gay-friendly De Waterkant area. Rentals include studios and one- to three-bedroom places, all of which enjoy daily housekeeping services and upmarket decor. A plethora of cafés, shopping, and restaurants are within walking distance. Rates for a studio start at R1,200. The collection also includes rooms in The Charles and De Waterkant House guesthouses. ⊠ *1 Loader St., Cape Town Central* ☎ *021/437–9700* ⊕ *www.villagenlife.com.*

WHAT IT COSTS IN SOUTH AFRICAN RAND			
$	**$$**	**$$$**	**$$$$**
Hotels under R1,500	R1,500–R2,500	R2,501–R3,500	over R3,500

Prices are the lowest price for a standard double room in high season.

CAPE TOWN CENTRAL

$$$
HOTEL
🛏 **Cape Heritage Hotel.** Built as a private home in 1771, this centrally located boutique hotel's spacious rooms are individually decorated, melding the best of South Africa's dynamic contemporary art scene with colonial elegance, and making the most of the building's teak-beamed ceilings, foot-wide yellowwood floorboards, and numerous other details that recall its gracious past. **Pros:** excellent eateries in adjoining Heritage Square and Bree Street; beautiful old building and quirky style; great location in Cape Town's historic district. **Cons:** bordered by one busy road; parking isn't free; lighting in some rooms is too dark. $ *Rooms from: R3135* ⊠ *90 Bree St., Cape Town Central* ☎ *021/424–4646* ⊕ *www.capeheritage.co.za* ⇆ *20 rooms* ⦿ *Breakfast.*

$
B&B/INN
🛏 **Daddy Long Legs Boutique Hotel.** Independent travelers with artistic streaks love this place, which was built to represent the creative community of Cape Town, and the location is great if you are looking for

nearby nightlife. **Pros:** lots of dash for the cash; central location for party animals; friendly, helpful service. **Cons:** small rooms; Long Street is noisy until late into the night; breakfast not included. $ *Rooms from: R1450* ⊠ *134 Long St., Cape Town Central* ☎ *021/422–3074* ⊕ *www. daddylonglegs.co.za* ↦ *13 rooms* ⦿ *No meals.*

$$
B&B/INN

Dutch Manor Antique Hotel. Steeped in old-world charm, this antique hotel in the charming and centrally located Bo-Kaap is chockablock with one of the Cape's finest collections of antiques. **Pros:** the decor makes you feel as if you're sleeping in a beautiful museum; great central location; generally helpful, friendly staff. **Cons:** parking is two minutes' walk from the entrance (though the guard will valet for you if needed); multiple changes in management mean sometimes inconsistent service; downstairs rooms a bit dark and overall aesthetic does not suit all tastes. $ *Rooms from: R1800* ⊠ *158 Buitengracht St., Cape Town Central* ☎ *021/422–4767* ⊕ *www.dutchmanor.co.za* ↦ *6 rooms* ⦿ *No meals.*

$$
B&B/INN

Long Street Boutique Hotel. The upper floors of a beautifully restored Victorian building on trendy Long Street house this incredibly good-value boutique hotel made up of 12 luxurious rooms. **Pros:** surprisingly opulent for the price; free unlimited Wi-Fi and air-conditioning; in the heart of Cape Town's nightlife. **Cons:** no elevator; not a tranquil neighborhood; must pay for parking (R100 per night). $ *Rooms from: R1800* ⊠ *230 Long St., Cape Town Central* ☎ *021/426–4309* ⊕ *www. longstreethotel.com* ↦ *12 rooms* ⦿ *No meals.*

$$
HOTEL

Rouge on Rose. This owner-managed boutique hotel in the colorful and very central Bo Kaap neighborhood offers spacious and comfortable suites with a surprising number of amenities—think espresso makers, slippers and robes, and super-fast Wi-Fi—for the price. **Pros:** great location in walking distance to city center attractions and restaurants; personalized, friendly service from owners; tasty hot breakfast choices. **Cons:** off-street parking is limited (but free); a few quiet blocks adjacent to Rose Street prevent complete confidence in walking at night; three-story building with no elevator. $ *Rooms from: R2300* ⊠ *25 Rose St., Bo-Kaap* ☎ *021/426–0298* ⊕ *www. capetownboutiquehotel.co.za* ↦ *9 rooms* ⦿ *Breakfast.*

$$$$
HOTEL
Fodor's Choice
★

Taj Cape Town. With an amazing location in the heart of historic Cape Town, the Taj sits in the grand former headquarters of the South African Reserve Bank and provides the professional and luxurious hospitality that one would expect from this brand. **Pros:** one of the few five-star hotels that attracts a truly multicultural clientele; excellent Indian fine-dining restaurant and gorgeous Twankey bar; fantastic spa. **Cons:** can have a bit of business feel; breakfast is not great; despite warm service, it lacks the intimacy of a smaller hotel. $ *Rooms from: R12625* ⊠ *Wale St., Cape Town Central* ☎ *021/819–2000* ⊕ *www.tajcapetown.co.za* ↦ *176 rooms* ⦿ *Breakfast.*

GARDENS

$$$$
HOTEL
FAMILY
Fodor's Choice
★

Belmond Mount Nelson Hotel. An icon of Cape Town since it opened its doors in 1899, this superbly located landmark sits on 9 beautifully landscaped acres and retains a charm and gentility unusual even in the world of luxury hotels. **Pros:** decor achieves the perfect balance between colonial elegance and contemporary style; great location in walking distance to Company's Garden and downtown, or Kloof Street attractions;

Where to Stay in Cape Town

ATLANTIC
OCEAN

*Victoria
Basin*

1

*Granger
Bay*

2   3
WATERFRONT
5   4
6

MOUILLE
POINT

Beach

9

Fritz Sonnenberg

GREEN
POINT

7

8

10

Western Blvd. Mtr.

Main Mtr.

High Level

Springbok

THREE
ANCHOR
BAY

Three Gallagardt

11

Signal Hill ▲

Rhine

12

Hall

London

Marais

High Level

13

SEA POINT

St. John's

High Level

Des Highlands
Fresnaye

FRESNAYE

Queens

BANTRY
BAY

0   500 yards
0   500 meters

14

Lion's Head ▲

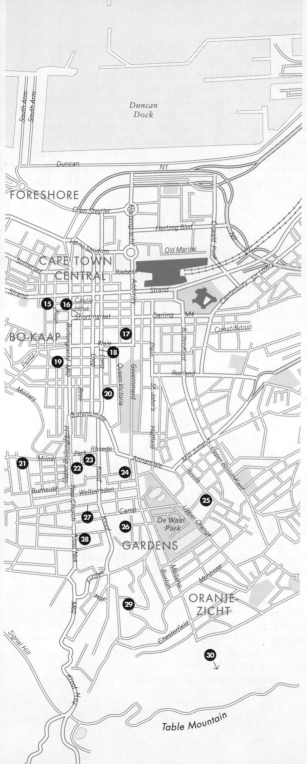

the "Nellie's" lavish high tea is an institution, and the glam Planet Bar an ideal place for a cocktail. **Cons:** breakfast restaurant Oasis lacks the charm of the rest of the hotel; may be booked out during high season as much as a year in advance; spread out across multiple buildings, each with its own style, so you must be sure to state your preferences. [$] *Rooms from: R13335* ✉ *76 Orange St., Gardens* ☎ *021/483–1000* 🌐 *www.belmond.com/mount-nelson-hotel-cape-town* 🛏 *198 rooms* 🍴 *Breakfast.*

$$$$ HOTEL FAMILY **Cape Cadogan Boutique Hotel & More Quarters.** The lovely and well-located Georgian and Victorian Cape Cadogan boutique hotel dates back to the beginning of the 19th century, and boasts a style that successfully blends contemporary and antique furnishings. **Pros:** free shuttle within 6-km (4-mile) radius; unique apartment-hotel concept at More Quarters gives best of both worlds; walking distance to great restaurants, bars, and shops. **Cons:** traffic noise from nearby intersection can be a problem; rooms can be quite uneven in size at Cadogan; not accessible. [$] *Rooms from: R4510* ✉ *5 Upper Union St., Gardens* ☎ *021/480–8080* 🌐 *www.capecadogan.co.za* 🛏 *33 rooms* 🍴 *Breakfast.*

$$$$ B&B/INN **Kensington Place.** A beautiful garden entrance leads you into this stylish oasis of a guesthouse where you can expect an atmosphere of luxurious privacy and attentive concierge service from on-site management. **Pros:** gorgeous peaceful location that is still walking distance to upper Kloof Street attractions; great breakfast and other meals available from on-site kitchen; fantastic staff and service. **Cons:** steep hill might dissuade walking back from town; no kids under 12; lots of stairs make it wheelchair-unfriendly. [$] *Rooms from: R4200* ✉ *38 Kensington Crescent, Higgovale, Gardens* ☎ *021/424–4744* 🌐 *www.kensingtonplace.co.za* 🛏 *9 rooms* 🍴 *Breakfast.*

$$ B&B/INN FAMILY Fodor's Choice ★ **La Grenadine Petit Hotel.** Built around a verdant courtyard shaded by pomegranate, guava, and avocado trees, the five gorgeous rooms at this well-located and good-value hotel are all Gallic charm meets South African vintage hipster: hand-embroidered bed linens, badminton paddles repurposed as mirrors, and art deco light fittings. **Pros:** great bustling location in walking distance to dozens of restaurants and attractions; excellent Continental breakfast filled with homemade treats; wonderful fusion of French and South African vintage style. **Cons:** no TVs in rooms and Wi-Fi can be slow; limited off-street parking; some rooms have bathrooms that are not fully closed off. [$] *Rooms from: R1860* ✉ *15 Park Rd., Gardens* ☎ *021/424–1358* 🌐 *www.lagrenadine.co.za* 🛏 *10 rooms* 🍴 *Breakfast.*

$$ HOTEL **Protea Fire & Ice! by Marriott** Initially built around somewhat kitschy themes—think interior elements like elevators kitted out as a shark cage underwater or a Table Mountain cable car mid-journey—this large hotel (one of the few in the area) will appeal to those who value a vibey social atmosphere and proximity to Cape Town's nightlife. **Pros:** proximity to restaurants and other activities on foot; brilliant views of Table Mountain from rooms above the fifth floor; friendly and helpful staff. **Cons:** zany decoration won't suit all tastes; rooms are small. [$] *Rooms from: R2200* ✉ *New Church St. at Victoria St., Gardens* ☎ *021/488–2555* 🌐 *www.marriott.com/hotels/travel/cptcf-protea-hotel-fire-and-ice-cape-town* 🛏 *201 rooms* 🍴 *No meals.*

$$$ B&B/INN FAMILY 🏨 **Welgelegen Boutique Hotel.** In Dutch, *welgelegen* means "well situated," and this charming boutique hotel in two beautifully restored Victorian mansions is just that: nestled under Table Mountain in a quiet street just minutes away from city attractions. **Pros:** great staff make guests feel like part of the family; walking distance to Kloof Street cafés; one of the few boutique hotels that welcomes children of all ages. **Cons:** it's an old building, so the occasional creaky floorboard is to be expected; Wi-Fi can be slow; breakfast dining room is a bit dark. [$] *Rooms from: R2880* ✉ *6 Stephen St., Gardens* ☎ *021/426–2373, 021/426–2374* 🌐 *www.welgelegen.co.za* 🛏 *13 rooms* 🍴 *Breakfast.*

TAMBOERSKLOOF

$$$ HOTEL 🏨 **Cape Milner Hotel.** The only midsize hotel in the lovely Tamboerskloof area, the clean and comfortable Milner makes a convenient location from which to explore trendy nearby Kloof Street and beyond. **Pros:** great location minutes from city; good dining options within walking distance; great views of Table Mountain from pool. **Cons:** one-way roads make it tricky to access; overlooks a road that's busy (and loud) at peak times; Table Mountain views from rooms that have them are partially obscured by strange window awnings. [$] *Rooms from: R3400* ✉ *2A Milner Rd., Tamboerskloof* ☎ *021/426–1101* 🌐 *www.capemilner.com* 🛏 *57 rooms* 🍴 *Breakfast.*

$$$ B&B/INN 🏨 **Derwent House.** The nine rooms comprising this beautiful Victorian house in a very central Tamboerskloof location make for a stylish and convenient base while exploring Cape Town. **Pros:** super-convenient location to Kloof Street eateries and attractions; well-stocked honesty bar and complimentary afternoon cake and treats; gracious management by owners with decades in the hospitality industry. **Cons:** some rooms a bit small; can hear creaks and noises on occasion; only two rooms have unobstructed mountain views. [$] *Rooms from: R2800* ✉ *14 Derwent Rd., Tamboerskloof* ☎ *021/422–2763* 🌐 *www.derwenthouse.co.za* 🛏 *9 rooms* 🍴 *Breakfast.*

ORANJEZICHT

$ B&B/INN 🏨 **Cactusberry Lodge.** This great-value guesthouse in an appealing shade of cinnamon terra cotta (aka cactusberry) is in a quiet neighborhood that is still within walking distance of many attractions and restaurants. **Pros:** personalized concierge service from the owner; homey, friendly place to meet other travelers; great breakfast. **Cons:** rooms on the small side; creaky floors if downstairs; no TV in rooms. [$] *Rooms from: R1400* ✉ *30 Breda St., Oranjezicht* ☎ *021/461–9787* 🌐 *www.cactusberrylodge.com* 🛏 *6 rooms* 🍴 *Breakfast.*

$$$$ HOTEL Fodor's Choice ★ 🏨 **Manna Bay.** On the slopes of Table Mountain with stupendous views overlooking the whole of Cape Town, this uber-luxurious boutique hotel is all tranquil privacy and bold designer style. **Pros:** amazing views and style; attentive service; great food. **Cons:** set back from the city, so you'll need a car to go anywhere; hard to get a booking; no kids under 12. [$] *Rooms from: R7000* ✉ *8 Bridle Rd., Oranjezicht* ☎ *021/461–1094* 🌐 *www.mannabay.com* 🛏 *9 rooms* 🍴 *Breakfast.*

V&A WATERFRONT

$$$$ HOTEL FAMILY 🏨 **Cape Grace.** Enjoying a stellar location in the working harbor section of the Waterfront—and rightfully renowned for its excellent service—the discreetly refined Cape Grace is popular with American celebrities, including the likes of Bill and Hillary Clinton. **Pros:** mountain or harbor views from all rooms; excellent, personalized service; extremely family-friendly for such a posh hotel. **Cons:** unconventional decor may not suit all tastes and some rooms a bit dark; Wi-Fi capped at 1GB per day; spa is great, but facilities like sauna and steam room are coed. [$] *Rooms from: R9261* ✉ *W. Quay Rd., Waterfront* ☎ *021/410–7100* 🌐 *www.capegrace.com* 🛏 *120 rooms* 🍴 *Breakfast.*

$$$$ HOTEL 🏨 **The Dock House Boutique Hotel.** Victorian splendor meets modern glam at this small and intimate boutique hotel perched over Cape Town's trendy and ever-popular V&A Waterfront. **Pros:** elegant, stylish oasis that feels amazingly private given location; great service; can walk to all the V&A Waterfront's restaurants, shops, and entertainment options. **Cons:** guests have to walk outside to reach the gym and spa; those wishing to socialize with other guests should look elsewhere; no kids under 12. [$] *Rooms from: R8600* ✉ *Portswood Close, Portswood Ridge, Victoria and Alfred Waterfront* ☎ *021/421–9334* 🌐 *www.dockhouse.co.za* 🛏 *6 rooms* 🍴 *Breakfast.*

$$$$ RESORT FAMILY 🏨 **One&Only Cape Town.** In the spirit of founding investor Sol Kerzner's "go big or go home" philosophy, the One&Only Cape Town is a splendid tribute to excess with its four-story glass window views onto Table Mountain from the aptly named Vista Bar and decadent island spa surrounded by a moat. **Pros:** conveniently located in the heart of the Waterfront; oceans of space and great views from all rooms; great kids' programs. **Cons:** Marina Rise guests must walk through the lounge in their swimsuit/robe to reach the pool or spa; lacks the intimacy of a smaller hotel; Reuben's restaurant not as good as it used to be. [$] *Rooms from: R12000* ✉ *Dock Rd., Victoria and Alfred Waterfront* ☎ *021/431–5888* 🌐 *www.oneandonlyresorts.com* 🛏 *131 rooms* 🍴 *Breakfast.*

$$$$ HOTEL 🏨 **The Silo Hotel.** Brilliantly melding industrial grit and sumptuous glamour, Cape Town's hottest new luxury hotel rises out of the old grain silo in the working harbor section of the Waterfront. **Pros:** surprisingly child-friendly; mind-blowing decor and artwork; incredible views from rooftop bar. **Cons:** policy towards nonresidents still being worked out, resulting in guests potentially being treated as strangers; starting category rooms are small; extremely pricey. [$] *Rooms from: R20300* ✉ *Silo Sq., Victoria and Alfred Waterfront* ☎ *021/670–0500* 🌐 *www.theroyalportfolio.com/the-silo/overview* 🛏 *28 rooms* 🍴 *Breakfast.*

$$$$ HOTEL 🏨 **Table Bay Hotel.** This glitzy hotel that is part of the Sun International group sits in a prime spot at the tip of the V&A Waterfront, enjoying fabulous views from all sides. **Pros:** wonderful high tea and public lounge spaces; all rooms have sea/harbor or mountain views; incredibly convenient location with direct access to the V&A Waterfront mall. **Cons:** service is friendly but sometimes a bit slow; breakfast quality doesn't quite meet expectations based on its grand presentation; lacks the intimacy and personality of a smaller hotel. [$] *Rooms from: R8500*

✉ *Quay 6, Victoria and Alfred Waterfront* ☎ *021/406–5000* 🌐 *www.suninternational.com* 🛏 *329 rooms* 🍴 *Breakfast.*

$$$$ HOTEL 🏨 **Victoria & Alfred Hotel.** Smack in the middle of the Waterfront and surrounded by shops, bars, and restaurants, 94 luxurious rooms occupy the three floors that once served as a warehouse for cargo from the ships visiting what was once a purely working harbor. **Pros:** best value at the Waterfront; excellent breakfasts with great views include healthy and diabetic options; great service from restaurant and hotel staff. **Cons:** economical loft rooms are very small; buskers in the piazza can be loud; pool and gym located at nearby sister property are an effort to find. [$] *Rooms from: R5105* ✉ *On the Waterfront Pierhead, Victoria and Alfred Waterfront* ☎ *021/419–6677* 🌐 *www.newmarkhotels.com* 🛏 *94 rooms* 🍴 *Breakfast.*

MOUILLE POINT

$$ B&B/INN 🏨 **Dolphin Inn.** An excellent value-for-money location on Mouille Point's sought-after strip, this simple inn's rooms are basic but neat and comfortable, a few even enjoying sea views. **Pros:** great location; good value for money; lovely, friendly service. **Cons:** basic amenities might leave you wanting more; sea-facing rooms are noisy, located by the entrance and over the road; restaurant serves breakfast only. [$] *Rooms from: R1750* ✉ *75 Beach Rd., Mouille Point* ☎ *021/434–3175* 🌐 *www.dolphin-inn.co.za* 🛏 *11 rooms* 🍴 *Breakfast.*

$$ HOTEL 🏨 **La Splendida Luxury Suites.** This good-value chic hotel enjoys a great location between the popular seafront promenade and Green Point park, and is also just a 15-minute walk from the V&A Waterfront. **Pros:** expansive views from sea-facing rooms; very reasonably priced for location and room size; friendly staff. **Cons:** noise from restaurant downstairs and the road from some rooms; limited off-street parking; horn from nearby lighthouse can ruin one's sleep on a foggy morning. [$] *Rooms from: R1930* ✉ *121 Beach Rd., Mouille Point* ☎ *021/439–5119* 🌐 *www.lasplendida.co.za* 🛏 *24 suites* 🍴 *Breakfast.*

GREEN POINT

$$$$ HOTEL 🏨 **Cape Royale Luxury Hotel & Spa.** Just a stone's throw from the Green Point stadium and the V&A Waterfront—and surrounded by restaurants and public transportation—the Cape Royale offers spacious apartment-style accommodations that make a great base for longer-term travelers. **Pros:** roomy, well-designed suites; great location surrounded by restaurants and cafés; lovely spa with reasonable prices. **Cons:** Skybar pool area is not child-friendly (smoking allowed, and not spacious); in-house restaurant dinner menu is fairly limited; lack of views from lower floors. [$] *Rooms from: R7600* ✉ *47 Main Rd., Green Point* ☎ *021/430–0500* 🌐 *www.caperoyale.co.za* 🛏 *55 rooms* 🍴 *No meals.*

$$ B&B/INN 🏨 **Dysart Boutique Hotel.** This small and stylish boutique hotel in Green Point is perfect for those who appreciate a minimalist-artsy decor, seeking a quiet stay in a convenient location. **Pros:** minimalist style with small contemporary art collection; nice views from pool and common

areas; quiet and peaceful. **Cons:** located between Green Point and Sea Point, it's a (little) bit of a walk to restaurants, etc.; light switches for bedside annoyingly located by doorway/entrance; no phone in room. $ *Rooms from: R2300* ✉ *17 Dysart Rd., Green Point* ☎ *021/439–2832* ⊕ *www.dysart.de* ⇆ *8 rooms* ⫙ *Breakfast.*

SEA POINT

$$$$
B&B/INN
Fodor's Choice
★

⛭ **Blackheath Lodge.** Conveniently located on a quiet street in upper Sea Point, this small good-value hotel in a beautiful Victorian-era home boasts concierge-level owner-rendered service and gorgeous quirky style in spades. **Pros:** excellent 24-hour service; complimentary treats throughout the day; gorgeous style. **Cons:** only three rooms have bathtubs; no gym; no kids under 10. $ *Rooms from: R3600* ✉ *Blackheath Rd., Sea Point* ☎ *021/439–2541* ⊕ *www.blackheathlodge.com* ⇆ *16 rooms* ⫙ *Breakfast.*

$$$$
HOTEL
Fodor's Choice
★

⛭ **Ellerman House.** Built in 1906 for shipping magnate Sir John Ellerman, what may be Cape Town's finest hotel sits high on a hill up from Sea Point in Bantry Bay, graced with stupendous views of the sea, and an art collection that puts the National Gallery to shame. **Pros:** amazing sense of intimacy and privacy to enjoy this spectacular environment; lovely treats like canapés and cocktails at sunset; fully stocked complimentary guest pantry available 24 hours. **Cons:** Kloof Road is busy (though noise not audible from hotel); often booked a year in advance. $ *Rooms from: R10000* ✉ *180 Kloof Rd., Bantry Bay, Sea Point* ☎ *021/430–3200* ⊕ *www.ellerman.co.za* ⇆ *15 rooms* ⫙ *Breakfast.*

$$$
HOTEL

⛭ **Glen Boutique Hotel.** This midsize boutique hotel on a quiet street in Sea Point is one part playful, Ibiza-inspired style—think orchids and a bright Greek Isle palette of white and turquoise—and one part elegant African colonial. **Pros:** great dual pool area with seaside vibey atmosphere; very close to Sea Point promenade; full-service restaurant with an elegant ambience. **Cons:** a bit clubby for some tastes; no kids under 16; decor in the two sections is very different—be sure to state preference. $ *Rooms from: R2980* ✉ *3 The Glen, Sea Point* ☎ *021/439–0086* ⊕ *www.glenhotel.co.za* ⇆ *24 rooms* ⫙ *Breakfast.*

$$$
HOTEL

⛭ **Winchester Mansions Hotel.** Built in the 1920s, this old-school hotel enjoys a wonderful position overlooking the beautiful Seapoint promenade, with an elegant sea-facing terrace that is deservedly popular for tea and afternoon drinks. **Pros:** great location with lots of dining options within walking distance; some rooms have nice sea views; friendly warm service. **Cons:** furnishings in some rooms need to be replaced; overall style is quite old-fashioned; otherwise nice hotel bar allows smoking inside. $ *Rooms from: R3080* ✉ *221 Beach Rd., Sea Point* ☎ *021/434–2351* ⊕ *www.winchester.co.za* ⇆ *76 rooms* ⫙ *Breakfast.*

2

CAMPS BAY

$$$$ HOTEL **The Bay Hotel.** The only large hotel in glitzy Camps Bay, this luxurious yet beachy property—vintage motorcycles and surfboards serve as decor—sits directly across the street from a famously beautiful stretch of white sand and is backed by the towering cliffs of the Twelve Apostles. **Pros:** very popular beach a few steps away; at the epicenter of high-season social life; intimate old-school hotel bar "Caamil's". **Cons:** road between hotel and beach is often busy and sometimes gridlocked; extra small charges like using the Nespresso pods in your room can be irritating; commercial feel with things like posters advertising classic car rentals in your room. [$] *Rooms from: R6400* ✉ *69 Victoria Rd., Camps Bay* ☎ *021/430–4444 host manager, 021/430–4013 bookings* 🌐 *www.thebayhotel.com* 🛏 *78 rooms* 🍴 *Breakfast.*

$$$ B&B/INN **Boutique @10.** Up against the mountainside right in the middle of Camps Bay, this small, intimate guesthouse enjoys stunning views over the popular seaside neighborhood below and across the ocean beyond. **Pros:** amazing views; owner-managed; nice touches like complimentary wine tastings. **Cons:** no fridges in rooms (except one); decor in some rooms tending toward a 1970s vibe, in need of small updates; lots of stairs. [$] *Rooms from: R3295* ✉ *10 Medburn Rd., Camps Bay* ☎ *021/438–1234* 🌐 *www.boutique10.co.za* 🛏 *4 rooms* 🍴 *Breakfast.*

$$$ B&B/INN FAMILY **Ocean View House.** Located in huge garden filled with indigenous succulents, ancient milkwood trees, and koi-filled water features, this good value family-owned and -managed B&B also enjoys gorgeous views of both the Atlantic Ocean and the majestic Twelve Apostles. **Pros:** amazing location with great views and just a few minutes' walk to Bakoven Beach; friendly, warm service; gorgeous indigenous garden and natural stream running through property. **Cons:** decor in some of the older rooms needs a bit of an update; not all rooms have full sea views; Wi-Fi can be a bit slow. [$] *Rooms from: R3200* ✉ *33 Victoria Rd., Camps Bay* ☎ *021/438–1982* 🌐 *www.oceanview-house.com* 🛏 *24 rooms* 🍴 *Breakfast.*

$$$$ HOTEL **Pod.** This compact designer boutique hotel that blends modern sleekness with accents of stone, rough wood, and slate to create a sexy Zen ambience enjoys a great location on a quiet corner just a block from Camps Bay's main drag. **Pros:** excellent breakfast; wellness room with shower for use by late check-outs; eco-friendly additions like door sensor to switch air-conditioning off and tree planting for guests of three nights or more. **Cons:** classic rooms are small, and open-plan bathrooms might be too much sharing; no on-site restaurant after breakfast; eyesore apartment block across the street from some rooms. [$] *Rooms from: R6400* ✉ *3 Argyle Rd., Camps Bay* ☎ *021/438–8550* 🌐 *www.pod.co.za* 🛏 *17 rooms* 🍴 *Breakfast.*

$$$$ HOTEL Fodor's Choice ★ **Twelve Apostles Hotel & Spa.** If you fancy taking a helicopter to the airport or lazing in a bubble bath while looking out floor-to-ceiling windows at breathtaking sea and mountain views, then this award-winning, luxurious hotel and spa that is the only such property within Table Mountain National Park may be for you. **Pros:** wonderfully attentive staff; stunning and unique location in Table Mountain National Park; great breakfast in Azure restaurant with insane sea views.

Cons: overlooks a road that gets busy; nearest off-site restaurant is at least 10 minutes by car; views and room size are extremely varied. $ *Rooms from: R7855* ✉ *Victoria Rd., Camps Bay* ☎ *021/437–9000* ⊕ *www.12apostleshotel.com* ⇱ *70 rooms* �101 *Breakfast.*

SOUTHERN SUBURBS

HOUT BAY

$$
B&B/INN

⊡ **Cube Guest House.** This stylish, modern guesthouse high on a hill in residential Hout Bay enjoys stunning bay and mountain views and makes the perfect pampered base from which to explore all the Cape's offerings. **Pros:** great service; no end-time for breakfast; free unlimited Wi-Fi. **Cons:** not kid-friendly; all rooms accessed by stairs; you'll need a car for most activities. $ *Rooms from: R2400* ✉ *20 Luisa Way, Hout Bay* ☎ *071/441–8161* ⊕ *www.cube-guesthouse.com* ⇱ *5 rooms* 101 *Breakfast.*

$$
B&B/INN

⊡ **Hout Bay Hideaway.** Tranquil and intimate with only four rooms, this owner-managed guesthouse tucked away in a lush neighborhood setting is perfect for those seeking peace and privacy. **Pros:** lovely private breakfast on your patio; wood-burning fires and underfloor heating; barbecue grills for guests. **Cons:** smokers aren't welcome; you'll want to have a car for most activities; no indoor public lounge space. $ *Rooms from: R2100* ✉ *37 Skaife St., Hout Bay* ☎ *021/790–8040* ⊕ *www.houtbay-hideaway.com* ⇱ *4 rooms* 101 *Breakfast.*

$$$$
RESORT
Fodor'sChoice
★

⊡ **Tintswalo Atlantic.** Visitors attracted to the Cape Peninsula for its natural grandeur will think they've died and gone to heaven when arriving at this discreetly luxurious boutique hotel. **Pros:** unique mind-blowing location; attentive service and setup creates a bit of a "safari by the sea" ambience; fantastic breakfast in one of the most beautiful spots imaginable. **Cons:** must drive to all activities and sights; building requirements in the national park mean exteriors of buildings have a prefab look; about a 35- to 40-minute drive from Cape Town Central. $ *Rooms from: R12250* ✉ *Chapman's Peak Dr., Km 2, Hout Bay* ☎ *021/201– 0025* ⊕ *www.tintswalo.com/atlantic* ⇱ *11 rooms* 101 *Breakfast.*

CONSTANTIA

$$$$
HOTEL

⊡ **Alphen Boutique Hotel.** Situated on 11 acres of gardens in leafy Constantia, this glamorous and avant-garde boutique hotel was originally an 18th-century Cape Dutch manor house and working farm. **Pros:** convenient beautiful location for exploring Constantia winelands; great pool area (although unheated); spacious rooms with bold voluptuous style. **Cons:** no gym; no elevator; need a car. $ *Rooms from: R5200* ✉ *Alphen Dr., Constantia* ☎ *021/795–6300* ⊕ *www.alphen.co.za* ⇱ *19 rooms* 101 *Breakfast.*

$$$$
HOTEL

⊡ **Cellars-Hohenort Hotel & Spa.** With acres of gardens and spectacular views across the Constantia Valley, this idyllic old-school getaway in two historic buildings makes the world beyond disappear. **Pros:** beautiful gardens; two pools (one for children); fantastic breakfast in lovely Conservatory Restaurant. **Cons:** need a car to get around; more modern rooms on Cellars side are starting to feel old-fashioned; a lot of stairs to access best rooms. $ *Rooms from: R5700* ✉ *93 Brommersvlei Rd.,*

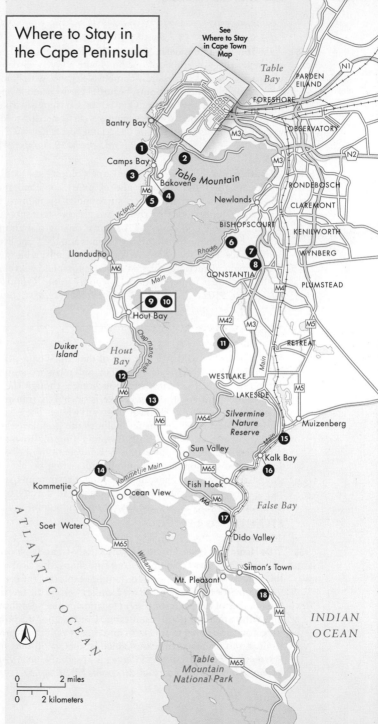

Where to Stay in the Cape Peninsula

Constantia ☎ *021/794–2137* 🌐 *www.collectionmcgrath.com/hotels/the-cellars-hohenort* 🛏 *53 rooms* 🍴 *Breakfast.*

$$$$ HOTEL 🏨 **The Last Word Constantia.** A great base for exploring the Constantia winelands, this peaceful boutique hotel with a lovely garden and incredibly spacious rooms successfully combines elegance with homey intimacy. **Pros:** incredibly spacious rooms; beautiful gardens and lovely pool; convenient location in the heart of Constantia. **Cons:** music from restaurant next door can be loud some evenings; a car is needed to do anything; no gym. [$] *Rooms from: R7600* ✉ *Spaanschemat River Rd., Constantia* ☎ *021/794–7657* 🌐 *www.thelastword.co.za* 🛏 *9 rooms* 🍴 *Breakfast.*

TOKAI

$$$$ HOTEL FAMILY 🏨 **Steenberg Hotel.** Located on the Cape's oldest—and still working—wine estate, this intimate and beautiful luxury hotel built mostly within renovated heritage structures is surrounded by manicured gardens, vineyards, a modern tasting room, two great restaurants, and a championship 18-hole golf course. **Pros:** great on-site restaurants; tranquil location between the Constantia winelands and the Cape Peninsula; free shuttle twice a day to the V&A Waterfront. **Cons:** a bit far from Cape Town's main attractions for first-time visitors; entry-level rooms a bit small; need a car to get around. [$] *Rooms from: R5800* ✉ *Steenberg Rd., Tokai* ☎ *021/713–2222* 🌐 *www.steenbergfarm.com* ⛳ *18-hole course* 🛏 *24 rooms* 🍴 *Breakfast.*

CAPE PENINSULA

The gorgeous but wild Atlantic side of the Cape Peninsula is primarily residential where there is development, and most accommodations are in the form of self-catering vacation homes, though there are a few lovely hotels and guesthouses. There is no public transport to speak of, and you'll need your own car to go anywhere. The eastern, or False Bay side of the Cape Peninsula includes the popular seaside villages of Muizenberg, St. James, Kalk Bay, and Simon's Town. It's a lovely base for those seeking more of a beach-vacation vibe, with some of the Cape's most popular swimming and surfing beaches found here, along with clusters of charming shops and restaurants, and plenty of hiking opportunities. The train connects you to the city, but for full-on exploration, a car remains the easiest option by far.

ATLANTIC COAST

NOORHOEK

$$ HOTEL FAMILY 🏨 **De Noordhoek Hotel.** Situated in the family-friendly Noordhoek Farm Village with its great restaurants and cute shops, this clean and comfortable hotel is a practical option for families exploring the peninsula. **Pros:** connecting rooms are suitable for families; one of the few hotels on the Atlantic side of the peninsula; great location in the Noordhoek Farm Village, with numerous good restaurants. **Cons:** a good 35-minute drive to Cape Town; no views to speak of, and nearby pub can be noisy at night; service from management can be inconsistent. [$] *Rooms from: R2500* ✉ *Noordhoek Farm Village, Village La., Noordhoek* ☎ *021/789–2760* 🌐 *www.denoordhoek.co.za* 🛏 *20 rooms* 🍴 *Breakfast.*

KOMMETJIE

$$$$

HOTEL

Fodor's Choice

★

⊞ **The Last Word Long Beach.** All the spacious rooms at this elegant beach-themed boutique hotel—decor is clean and minimalist in shades of white, sand, and pale blue—have balconies with superb sea views making the most of the fact that you are literally on the beach. **Pros:** fabulous location right on Kommetjie's Long Beach; the only stellar hotel on this side of the peninsula; friendly staff make you feel like they are there to serve only you. **Cons:** a good 45-minute drive to Cape Town; very limited dinner options in immediate vicinity; Wi-Fi can be slow. $ *Rooms from: R7600* ⊠ *1 Kirsten Ave., Kommetjie* ☎ *021/794–6561* ⊕ *www.thelastword.co.za* ⇥ *6 rooms* ⦿ *Breakfast.*

FALSE BAY COAST

KALK BAY

$

B&B/INN

FAMILY

Fodor's Choice

★

⊞ **Chartfield Guesthouse.** This surprisingly stylish and great-value guesthouse is within walking distance of all the bohemian pleasures in the charming fishing village of Kalk Bay. Located in a grand old house above the harbor, bright and airy rooms are decorated in a contemporary beach-chic style, and most have sea views. **Pros:** great value for the location; within walking distance of numerous restaurants and the train; funky and charming decor. **Cons:** no parking; lots of stairs (some very steep); Wi-Fi is not free. $ *Rooms from: R950* ⊠ *30 Gatesville Rd., Kalk Bay, Kalk Bay* ☎ *021/788–3793* ⊕ *www.chartfield.co.za* ⇥ *17 rooms* ⦿ *Breakfast.*

ST JAMES

$$$$

HOTEL

FAMILY

Fodor's Choice

★

⊞ **St. James Seaforth & Manor.** For a luxurious and private seaside retreat, a room in this casually elegant seaside retreat—or even better, the whole house—is just the ticket. **Pros:** lots of perks like inclusive beverages; intimacy and privacy; great views and ambience of old-world luxury. **Cons:** noise from the road out front can be irritating; not all rooms are equally stunning; some of the fixtures in the Manor feel in need of an update. $ *Rooms from: R4255* ⊠ *Main Rd., Peninsula False Bay, St. James* ☎ *021/788–4543* ⊕ *www.stjamesguesthouses.com* ⇥ *3 rooms* ⦿ *Breakfast.*

SIMON'S TOWN

$

B&B/INN

Fodor's Choice

★

⊞ **Residence William French.** The French-born owner of this gem of a guesthouse just past Boulders Beach takes his vocation seriously, providing a level of engagement and service that truly make you feel like a guest in this gorgeous retreat where edgy, rustic, and super-elegant design features combine to great effect, all bolstered by fantastic views of False Bay. With only five rooms—each styled differently, but all mixing polished concrete surfaces in neutral tones with a few carefully selected ornate pieces of furniture—it's all intimate, quiet relaxation. **Pros:** lovely, personalized service from owner; wonderful breakfasts and dinners (the latter by request); gorgeous views of False Bay from quiet location just past Boulders Beach. **Cons:** no children under 14; lacks facilities of a larger hotel (gym, concierge service, etc.); location is residential and you'll want a car to get around. $ *Rooms from: R1350* ⊠ *44 Dorries Dr.* ☎ *021/786–1068* ⊕ *williamfrench.co.za* ⇥ *5 rooms* ⦿ *Breakfast.*

$$
B&B/INN   ⊡ **Simon's Town Guest House.** This clean and contemporary African-themed guesthouse in a residential area about 3 km (2 miles) outside of Simon's Town offers spacious rooms with magnificent views over False Bay. All five spacious rooms have their own sitting areas with unobstructed views of the ocean and the surrounding mountain. **Pros:** delicious full English and Continental breakfast; amazing views; friendly staff. **Cons:** not actually in Simon's Town; breakfast ends at 9:30; very steep hill. Ⓢ *Rooms from: R1600* ⊠ *20 Bennett Close, Simon's Town* ☎ *021/786-5552* ⊕ *www.simonstownguesthouse.co.za* ⇨ *5 rooms* ◎ *Breakfast.*

NIGHTLIFE AND PERFORMING ARTS

NIGHTLIFE

There's plenty to do in Cape Town after dark. The city's nightlife is concentrated in a number of areas, so you can explore a different one each night or move from one hub to another. Unfortunately walking isn't always advisable, as some parts of the city are completely deserted and unsafe. Anyone who isn't very street savvy should avoid walking alone or even in pairs (sorry ladies, this especially affects you) at night.

NIGHTLIFE AREAS

One of the safest places after dark is the V&A Waterfront, where you can choose from movies, restaurants, bars, and pubs and walk between them quite happily, as there are plenty of security guards and other people walking around. The top end of Long Street is probably the city's best-known young nightlife area. Here you'll find several blocks of bars, restaurants, and backpacker lodges that are open till the wee hours. The area bounded by Loop, Long, Wale, and Orange streets is the best place to get a feeling for Cape Town's always-changing nightclub scene, but the district known as the Fringe—around Roeland, Harrington, and de Villiers streets—is increasingly where the club set hang out. De Waterkant in Green Point is also very busy at night and is home to many of Cape Town's gay venues; if you're in the area, you can take in the Green Point strip, where restaurants and bars open out onto the streets. On weekends these bars are packed, and you'll get a good idea of how Capetonians let down their hair. Heritage Square, in Cape Town Central, hosts an ever-changing mix of bars and restaurants generally catering to a more discerning (think wine bars and microbrewery) crowd. Mouille Point's Platinum Mile and Granger Bay are also good for evening cocktails; with breathtaking views over the Atlantic and onto Robben Island, this is where a more moneyed set hangs out after a hard day at the beach or gym. Be prepared to line up to get in to places, especially on a Friday night.

PUBLICATIONS

The weekly entertainment roundup for Cape Town is called *48 Hours* and is available all over town. Websites like ⊕ *www.capetownmagazine. com* and ⊕ *www.insideguide.co.za* are great resources, as are the "Top of the Times" in Friday's *Cape Times*, along with the *Argus* newspaper's "Tonight" section.

Cape Town is a very gay-friendly city. Geared toward gay (and to a far lesser extent lesbian) travelers, the site ⊕ *www.gaycapetown4u.com* provides information on events and venues in Cape Town.

CAPE TOWN CENTRAL

BARS AND PUBS

Beerhouse. Cape Town has jumped on the craft-beer bandwagon, and with 25 taps and 99 of the best local and international beers available, this is the place to come see what the fuss is all about. ⊠ *223 Long St., Cape Town Central* ☎ *021/424–3370* ⊕ *www.beerhouse.co.za.*

Orphanage Cocktail Emporium. This upmarket contemporary cocktail bar on Bree Street is a great spot for a well-composed drink. ⊠ *227 Bree St., Cape Town Central* ☎ *021/244–1995* ⊕ *www.theorphanage.co.za.*

The Perseverance. South Africa's oldest pub is traditional and recommendable, with decent food and pizza, craft beers, and even an inviting outdoor area. Plus, you'll find plenty of TV screens to watch football. ⊠ *83 Buitenkant St., Cape Town Central* ☎ *021/461–2440* ⊕ *www. perseverancetavern.co.za.*

Publik Wine Bar. Perhaps the best place in Cape Town to acquaint yourself with lesser known, boutique, and very special vintages, this well-located bar off Heritage Square shares a space with Ash Restaurant, meaning you can also get something to eat. ⊠ *81 Church St., Cape Town Central* ⊕ *www.publik.co.za.*

CAFÉS

Truth Coffee. This great spot captures the happening atmosphere in Cape Town's creative Fringe, in District Six. With steam-punk design, a coffee shop, bar, and live music or other performances on many nights, the fun usually spills out onto the pavement. It's open from 7 am to 6 pm weekdays (till late on Fridays), and from 8 am to late on Saturdays. It's also a great Sunday brunch spot (open 8–2). ⊠ *36 Buitenkant St., Cape Town Central* ☎ *021/200–0440* ⊕ *www.truthcoffee.com.*

LIVE MUSIC

blah blah blah bar. Located in an old Victorian house on Kloof Street, this bar and live music venue hosts musicians of all stripes, as well as DJs. They promise you won't hear anything "faintly commercial." ⊠ *84 Kloof St., Gardens* ☎ *082/349–8849* ⊕ *www.blahblahblahbar.co.za.*

District. District is the live music component of a three-part nighttime venue in the space formerly known as The Assembly. Catering to live-music and electronica, this space features everything from South African indie-rock to Afro-Brazilian electronica. The crowd is typically pretty young, with plenty of guests in their late teens, and smoking is allowed. Adjacent sister venues Harringtons Cocktail Lounge and SurfaRosa are an upscale drinks and punk-styled outdoor patio bar, respectively. ⊠ *61 Harrington St., District 6, Cape Town Central* ☎ *076/070–4474* ⊕ *www.theassembly.co.za.*

Mama Africa. Among the clubs with live African music, a good spot is Mama Africa. It has a live marimba band Monday through Saturday, as well as authentic African food, music, and pulse. ⊠ *178 Long St., Cape Town Central* ☎ *021/426–1017* ⊕ *www.mamaafricarestaurant.co.za.*

V&A WATERFRONT

BARS AND PUBS

Bascule Whisky Bar and Wine Cellar. Built right on the water's edge adjacent to the yacht marina, Bascule Whisky Bar and Wine Cellar is a fancy watering hole for well-heeled, cigar-puffing locals. Its 400 whiskies are reputed to be the biggest selection in the Southern Hemisphere. ⊠ *Cape Grace Hotel, West Quay Rd., Victoria and Alfred Waterfront* ☎ *021/410–7238* ⊕ *www.capegrace.com/culinary-delights/bascule-bar.*

PERFORMING ARTS

Tickets for almost every cultural and sporting event in the country (including movies) can be purchased through Computicket.

Contacts Computicket. ☎ *0861/915–8000* ⊕ *www.computicket.co.za.*

FILM

The Waterfront and Cavendish Mall both have movie houses: respectively, the NuMetro, which plays mainstream fare, and the Cinema Nouveau theater, which concentrates on foreign and art films. Check newspaper listings for what's playing.

The Galileo Open Air Cinema. Screening films of all types from classics to rom-coms to documentaries in great outdoor venues across the city, this is one of summer's treats (October–April). Our favorite venue was the original: Kirstenbosch Botanical Gardens, where movies play on Wednesdays an hour after sunset. Delicious food and drinks are for sale at every screening, and you can also rent backrests and blankets. ☎ *021/447–1641 office hrs, 071/471–8728 available till 8 pm on show days* ⊕ *www.thegalileo.co.za* ⊠ *From R89.*

Labia. The Labia is a local gem—an independent art house and Cape Town institution that screens good-quality mainstream and alternative films. There are four screens, and a small coffee bar serves snacks and wine. ⊠ *68 Orange St., Gardens* ☎ *021/424–5927* ⊕ *www.labia.co.za.*

THEATER AND PERFORMING ARTS

Alexander Upstairs. Upstairs from the classy Alexander Bar on Strand Street is the eponymous theater, an intimate performance space that features drama, comedy, cabaret, and even readings, much of which has proven itself in recent festivals in SA and beyond. ⊠ *76 Strand St., Cape Town Central* ☎ *021/300–1088* ⊕ *alexanderbar.co.za/shows-upstairs.*

Artscape Theatre Centre. Cape Town's premier performing arts venue is where you come for opera, dance, and bigger theater productions. Opened in 1971, it includes an opera house that seats more than 1,400, a theater auditorium seating more than 500, and a second smaller theater space seating more than 100. ⊠ *D.F. Malan St., Foreshore* ☎ *021/410–9800* ⊕ *www.artscape.co.za.*

Baxter Theatre Complex. The Baxter Theatre Complex, part of the University of Cape Town, hosts a range of productions from serious drama to satirical comedies, as well as some rather experimental stuff. The complex includes a 666-seat theater, a concert hall, a smaller studio, and a restaurant and bar. ⊠ *Main Rd., Rondebosch* ☎ *021/685–7880* ⊕ *www.baxter.co.za.*

Fugard Theater. This theater is named after legendary and internationally renowned playwright Athol Fugard, who was at the heart of the protest theater movement in 1980s apartheid South Africa. Anything cutting edge and politically relevant arrives at the Fugard. The 320-seat theater itself sits on the edge of the historical and oh-so politically relevant District Six area. ⊠ *Caledon St., Cape Town Central* ☎ *021/461–4554* ⊕ *www.thefugard.com.*

Maynardville Open-Air Theatre. Cape Town's own version of New York City's Shakespeare in the Park happens every summer at the excellent Maynardville Open-Air Theatre. Theatergoers often bring a picnic supper to enjoy before the show. ⊠ *Maynardville Park, Wolfe St. at Church St., Wynberg* ☎ *021/421–7695* ⊕ *www.maynardville.co.za.*

Theatre on the Bay. This 256-seat theater in lovely Camps Bay is a great place to enjoy a night of theater. ⊠ *1A Link St., Camps Bay* ☎ *021/438–3301* ⊕ *www.theatreonthebay.co.za.*

VISUAL ARTS

Already known as South Africa's creative and design hot spot, Cape Town's growing portfolio of contemporary art galleries—mostly clustered downtown and in Woodstock—and the 2017 opening of the Zeitz MOCAA are positioning the Mother City to assume the title of continental art hub. *See Cape Town Central and Woodstock Exploring sections for more information on the respective galleries, and V&A Exploring for Zeitz MOCAA.*

Fodor's Choice ★ **First Thursdays Cape Town.** On the first Thursday of every month, art galleries in Cape Town's center stay open until 9 pm or later. With them, some retail shops (mostly design-oriented) extend their hours, and often other cultural events and openings are held in the area's hotels (The Taj) and restaurants. The main axes are Bree and Church streets. It is one of the few times the city feels truly pedestrian-friendly after dark, and you can expect a crowd. In summer, food trucks gather in parking lots to add to the festivity. ■**TIP→ Don't even think about driving—parking will be impossible and you will want to save your strolling for the gallery-crawl.** ⊠ *Cape Town Central* ⊕ *www.first-thursdays.co.za* 🖾 *Free.*

SPORTS AND THE OUTDOORS

Cape Town is the adventure capital of the universe. Whatever you want to do—dive, paddle, fly, jump, run, slide, fin, walk, or clamber—this is the city to do it, and there is always somebody to help make it happen.

For spectator sports, it's easy to get tickets for ordinary club matches and interprovincial games. Getting tickets to an international test match is more of a challenge, though of course for a price, you will almost always win.

BIKING

Bike & Saddle. Offering trips from the "sip and cycle" tour through the winelands to a day around the Cape Peninsula or even a cycle safari, this "eco-active" outfit has all your cycling needs covered. They also organize multiday journeys that combine cycling, hiking, and paddling (or whatever combination thereof appeals). ⊠ *32 Jamieson St., Gardens* ☎ *021/813–6433, 076/540–4249 mobile, 202/643–3689 text messages in U.S.* ⊕ *www.bikeandsaddle.com.*

Up Cycles. Cape Town's first drop-and-go bike rental company has a network of stations around the city, making two wheels the most fun and easy way to get around town on a gorgeous day. Their main location in town also has a lovely café where you can enjoy a coffee or juice and free Wi-Fi while you rent or return a bike, or even get your own wheels serviced. Helmets and locks are inclusive, and child seats can be rented. ⊠ *Waterkant St., Cape Town Central* ☎ *076/135–2223, 074/100–9161* ⊕ *www.upcycles.co.za* ⊠ *From R60 per hr.*

BIRD-WATCHING

Birding Africa Tours. One of the top five bird tour companies in the world according to Birding Africa, these are the go-to guides in Cape Town. They organize customized birding trips of any length, and can also take you far beyond the Mother City. ■TIP➜ **All of their guides are great, but consider asking for Callan Cohen.** ⊠ *Hilltop St.* ☎ *021/531–4592* ⊕ *www.birdingafrica.com.*

CLIMBING

Cape Town has hundreds of bolted sport routes around the city and peninsula, ranging from an easy 10 to a hectic 30. To give you some idea of difficulty, a route graded a 10 in South Africa would be equivalent to a 5.5 climb in the United States. A grade 20 climb would register around 5.10c, and the hardest you'll find in South Africa is probably a 35, which American climbers would know as a 5.14c. The toughest climb up Table Mountain rates about 32, which is a 5.14a. Both Table Mountain sandstone and Cape granite are excellent hard rocks.

There's a wide range of traditional as well as sport climbing and bouldering areas scattered throughout the peninsula: a few favorite climbing areas include Table Mountain (from various angles), Lion's Head, Silvermine, and Muizenberg Peak. There are trad and sport climbing route guides that cover all the major climbing areas, plus a number of friendly climbing schools in Cape Town. The climbing forum is a great source (⊕ *www.climbing.co.za*), as are books by Tony Lournes. *For more information, see Hiking and Canyoning, below.*

High Adventure. High Adventure specializes in climbing in the Cape Town area but also organizes trips farther afield that can be anything from short two- to four-hour hikes, to half-day outings or full-day trips. A minimum group is two clients; there's a singles supplement of 80% for a solo traveler. ⊠ *11 Belmont Rd., Claremont* ☎ *021/689–1234* ⊕ *www.highadventure.co.za* ⊠ *From R550.*

FISHING

Hooked on Africa. Based in Hout Bay harbor, this operation is in one of the richest fishing grounds left in the world today. If you're keen to take to the open ocean for some deep-sea fishing, you'll have plenty of choices, as South Africa has excellent game fish, such as dorado, yellowfin tuna, and broadbill swordfish. The company offers private, full-boat charters of a 32-foot catamaran for a full day of deep-sea fishing. Call to inquire about current rates and to see if there are any organized trips you could join in lieu of a full-boat charter. ☎ *021/790–5332* ⊕ *www. hookedonafrica.co.za* ✉ *From R10,000.*

Inkwazi Fly-Fishing Safaris. In the mountains, just an hour or so away from Cape Town, you'll encounter wild and wily fish in wild and wonderful rivers. The season runs September–May and Inkwazi Fly-Fishing Safaris offers escorted tours, all the equipment you'll need, and plenty of good advice. Regulations allow them to guide no more than two anglers, and trips are frequently just one person. ☎ *083/626–0467* ⊕ *www.inkwaziflyfishing.co.za.*

HIKING AND CANYONING

Cape Town and the surrounding areas offer some of the finest hiking in the world. Kloofing, known as canyoning in the United States, is the practice of following a mountain stream through its gorge, canyon, or kloof by swimming, rock hopping, and jumping over waterfalls or cliffs into deep pools, so it's definitely more hard-core than simple hiking. There are some exceptional kloofing venues in the Cape. *For more information on the Hoerikwaggo Trail, see Table Mountain Exploring section, above.*

Hike Table Mountain. This fully South African, owner-operated mountain guiding service specializes in hikes and climbs (mountaineering) on Table Mountain and the Cape Peninsula. Guides, many of whom seem to practically live on the mountain, are passionate and knowledgeable. ☎ *021/422–0560, 083/683–1876 mobile* ⊕ *www.hiketablemountain. co.za* ✉ *From R750.*

Mother City Hikers. Originally from Chicago, Lauren Medcalf came to Cape Town on an extended vacation in 2006 and has never left. With Table Mountain standing tall over the city and surrounded by the southern oceans, it has become her home away from home. Mother City Hikers uses qualified and accredited mountain guides, who have fulfilled the requirements for Adventure Guiding/Mountaineering and are also qualified to offer mountain walking and overnight trips. All guides are also certified in first aid and CPR with the National First Aid Academy in South Africa. Prices include pickup at your hotel and transportation to the hiking site. ☎ *072/530–3464* ⊕ *mothercityhikers. co.za* ✉ *From R850.*

RidgwayRamblers. Binny Ridgway is one of the most experienced Table Mountain guides. If you want to get the most out of this iconic rock, it's best to learn a little about the area and its flora and fauna while getting some exercise and not having to think too hard for yourself. Hikes may go from Skeleton Gorge to Maclears Beacon (on the mountain) or to the Twelve Apostles (above Camps Bay). Binny also runs overnight hikes on Table Mountain, and other hikes around the Western Cape. ☎ *082/522–6056* ⊕ *www.ridgwayramblers.co.za* ◳ *From R850.*

HORSEBACK RIDING

Cantering down one of the Cape's long white-sand beaches or riding through the fynbos-covered dunes at sunset is a unique and tranquil pleasure, and Noordhoek is the place to do it, whatever your level.

Sleepy Hollow Horse Riding. Sleepy Hollows Horse Riding is the oldest operating horse riding business in Noordhoek, and has three guided rides a day. The two-hour beach ride goes mostly at a walking pace, but the company also has some specialized offerings and has experience with riders with disabilities. Pony rides for children are also available. ✉ *Sleepy Holly La., Noordhoek* ☎ *021/789–2341* ⊕ *www.sleepyhollowhorseriding.co.za* ◳ *From R530 for beach ride; R150 for pony rides.*

KAYAKING

kaskazi kayaks & adventures. You don't have to be a pro to discover Cape Town by kayak. Kaskazi has regular sunset and sunrise paddles off Sea Point, no experience necessary. The delightful two-hour paddles are reasonably priced and popular for good reason. ✉ *179 Beach Rd., Mouille Point* ☎ *021/439–1134* ⊕ *www.kayak.co.za* ◳ *From R350.*

Kayak Cape Town. Join this friendly operator based in Simon's Town for a paddle to see the penguins on Boulders Beach—there is nothing else quite like it. They also run full-moon-rising evening trips. ✉ *Cape Town* ☎ *082/501–8930* ⊕ *www.kayakcapetown.co.za* ◳ *From R300.*

PARAGLIDING AND SKYDIVING

Icarus Tandem Paragliding. The friendly and highly experienced folks at Icarus take their time with you, which is important when you're about to jump off a mountain with someone. Literally a breathtaking experience. ✉ *Signal Hill Rd.* ☎ *072/209–0119* ⊕ *www.icarusparagliding.co.za.*

Skydive Cape Town. You can do a tandem sky dive (no experience necessary) and have a video taken of you hurtling earthward with Table Mountain in the background with Skydive Cape Town—in business since 2002. On a tandem jump, you are strapped to an instructor with a special harness that's attached to a specially designed parachute large enough to support both of you. After only 15 minutes of ground briefing you will enjoy a spectacular 20-minute aircraft ride, with views of the West Coast, Cape Town, Robben Island, and Table Mountain before making the jump. Then it's a 25- to 30-second free fall from 9000 feet, followed by 3–4 minutes of peaceful parachuting back to earth. If you're hooked, you can do a full course with the same team. ✉ *Cape Town* ☎ *082/800–6290* ⊕ *www.skydivecapetown.co.za* ◳ *From R2,300.*

RAPPELLING

Abseil Africa. Abseil Africa offers a 350-foot abseil (rappel) off the top of Table Mountain. Another excursion—the "Kamikaze Kanyon"—takes you abseiling over a waterfall in the Helderberg Mountains (about an hour away), along with a whole lot of hiking and kloofing (canyoning). Tours include both transportation and lunch. This is a good operation that's been around a long time. ⊠ *297 Long St., Cape Town Central* ☎ *021/424–4760* ⊕ *www.abseilafrica.co.za* ⊠ *From R895.*

SCUBA DIVING

The diving around the Cape is excellent, with kelp forests, cold-water corals, very brightly colored reef life, and numerous wrecks. An unusual experience is a dive in the Two Oceans Aquarium. CMSA, NAUI, and PADI dive courses are offered by local operators; open-water certification courses begin at about R2,800 (all-inclusive).

Adrenalised Diving. Adrenalised can introduce you to some of Cape Town's amazing dive options, from diving with Seven Gill Cow sharks in Simon's Town to scuba diving with Cape Fur Seals in Cape Town, or just exploring wrecks and kelp forests. They also run PADI certification courses, free-diving courses and trips, and snorkeling trips. ⊠ *V&A Waterfront, Shop 8, Quay 5, Waterfront* ☎ *021/418–2870* ⊕ *www. adrenaliseddiving.co.za* ⊠ *From R990 (single dive with equipment).*

Scuba Shack. The friendly Scuba Shack is based out of Kommetjie and can organize dives around the peninsula—both the Atlantic and the warmer False Bay, with Simon's Town as the meeting point. Options include diving with cow sharks, traveling through kelp forests, and snorkeling with seals. It's a refreshing experience—and not just the water temperature—but so very different from the more typical vacation diving world of subtropical corals. ⊠ *Mountain Rd.* ☎ *072/603–8630* ⊕ *www.scubashack.co.za* ⊠ *From R1,300.*

SHARK DIVING

Seeing great white sharks hunting seals around False Bay's Seal Island is one of the most exhilarating natural displays you're likely to witness. And if witnessing it all from a boat is not thrill enough, you can get in the water (in a cage).

Apex Predators. Run by marine biologists, Apex Predators operates small-group trips from Simon's Town during season (February–September). If the great whites aren't around, try the Ocean Predator Trip, in which you cage dive with makos and blues. Co-founder Chris Fallows is a local legend in the shark photography and observation world, and the go-to guy for many international broadcasters. ⊠ *Quayside Bldg., Main Rd., Shop 3, Simon's Town* ☎ *079/051–8558, 021/786–5717* ⊕ *www. apexpredators.com.*

SURFING

Cape Town has some great but cold surf, and conditions can be complicated by the winds. Though it's no J-Bay (Jeffreys Bay), Cape Town still has some killer spots, Bloubergstrand (beach) being host to regular international events.

FAMILY **Gary's Surf School.** Gary's was the first surf school in South Africa, and is still going strong, offering surfing lessons to youngsters and the young at heart in the relatively warm and gentle waters at Muizenberg. You can also rent boards and wet suits. A basic two-hour lesson includes an hour of instruction and an hour of practice. All lessons are conducted at low tide to make things as safe and simple as possible. ⊠ *Balmoral Bldg., 34 Beach Rd., Muizenberg* ☎ *021/788–9839* ⊕ *www.garysurf. com* ✉ *From R450.*

SHOPPING AND SPAS

When it comes to shopping, Cape Town has something for everyone—from sophisticated malls to trendy markets and street vendors. Although African art and curios are obvious choices (and you will find some gems), South Africans have woken up to their own sense of style and creativity; the results are fantastic, and Cape Town is the epicenter of the South African design explosion. In a single morning you could bag some sophisticated tableware from Mervyn Gers, a funky wire-art object from a street vendor, and a beautifully designed handbag made by HIV-positive women working as part of a community development program.

Cape Town also has great malls selling well-known international brands. The V&A Waterfront is an excellent place to start by virtue of its location at the harbor and its mix of international labels with the fantastic Watershed Market, where you can also find unique local goods. But it's beyond the malls that you're most likely to have a shopping experience that can give you greater insight into the soul of the city and its people.

Shopping malls usually have extended shopping hours beyond the normal 9–5 on weekdays and 9–1 on Saturday. Most shops outside of malls (except for small grocery stores) are closed on Sunday.

CAPE TOWN CENTRAL

ARTS AND CRAFTS

A number of stores in Cape Town sell African art and crafts, much of which come from Zululand or neighboring countries. Street vendors, particularly on St. George's Mall and Greenmarket Square, often sell the same curios for half the price of a shop. Pick up the excellent Arts & Crafts Map at Cape Town Tourism for listings of excellent and cutting-edge galleries, boutiques, and designers.

African Image. Look here for contemporary and funky African art and township crafts, colorful cloth from Nigeria and Ghana, plus West African masks, Malian blankets, and beaded designs from

2

southern African tribes. Local and international collectors, as well as local institutions such as the South African National Gallery and the Standard Bank Collection of African Art, buy goods here. It's a top-notch place offering fair-trade pricing. They also have a branch at the Watershed Market in the V&A Waterfront. ⊠ *Burg St. at Church St., Cape Town Central* ☎ *021/423–8385* ⊕ *www.african-image.co.za* ⊗ *Closed Sun.*

Pan-African Market. You'll see some glorious cultural contradictions here. The lobby boasts lovely if dusty Victorian tiling, while the first and second floors are a beehive of traders in new and old folk art, with representatives from most locales in West, sub-Saharan, and southern Africa. Order a custom-tailored garment, choose a mask from among the many thousands, and don't be afraid to bargain. ⊠ *76 Long St., Cape Town Central* ☎ *021/426–4478, 082/747–2308* ⊕ *www.panafricanmarket.co.za.*

Streetwires. You'll see streetwire art everywhere in Cape Town, but this shop is a trove of the form, which uses a combination of wire, beads, and other recycled materials to create bowls, lights, mobiles, and expressive sculptures. ⊠ *Maxton Center, 1st fl., 354 Albert Rd., Woodstock* ☎ *021/426–2475* ⊕ *www.streetwires.co.za* ⊗ *Closed Sun.*

BOOKS AND MUSIC

The Book Lounge. Cape Town's best independent bookstore has a fantastic selection of titles, with many classics and contemporary must-haves on all things African. It also frequently hosts readings and book launches and has a nice café downstairs where you can enjoy a cappuccino while browsing. ⊠ *71 Roeland St., Cape Town Central* ☎ *021/462–2425* ⊕ *www.booklounge.co.za.*

MARKETS

Greenmarket Square. Visit this historic square to find a plethora of African jewelry, art, crafts, and fabrics, as well as good buys on clothing (especially T-shirts), and locally made leather shoes and sandals. It's one of the best places in town to purchase souvenirs and gifts, but it's lively and fun whether or not you buy anything. More than half the stalls are owned by people from other parts of Africa, and if you stop to chat, you'll find political and economic refugees from Ethiopia, Eritrea, Zimbabwe, and the Democratic Republic of Congo trying to eke out a living. Bargain, but do so with a conscience. ⊠ *Longmarket, Burg, and Shortmarket Sts., Cape Town Central.*

GARDENS

Vino Pronto. You can't go wrong at this small but carefully curated boutique wineshop. Ask for recommendations—the people here can be trusted to assemble a bespoke selection at all price points. They also host tastings, can ship wine overseas, supply carrying cases for international travel, and are open on Sundays. ⊠ *42 Orange St., Gardens* ⚙ *Dedicated parking spots at the gas station* ☎ *021/424–5587* ⊕ *www. vinopronto.co.za.*

Wine Concepts. Another great boutique wineshop in Gardens' Lifestyle Center mall, this one hosts tastings daily from 4 pm. ⊠ *Lifestyle on Kloof, 50 Kloof St., Gardens* ☎ *021/426-4401* ⊕ *www.wineconcepts. co.za* ☉ *Closed Sun.*

SEA POINT

FAMILY **Mojo Market.** This fantastic seven-day-a-week food-and-lifestyle market in Sea Point boasts 45 designer retail stalls selling everything from fashion to home decor to funky local souvenirs, as well as 25 food vendors representing some of Cape Town's favorite city restaurants and craft wine and beer makers. Large tables enjoying views of the Sea Point promenade and free weekend events like live music encourage hanging out as much as shopping. ⊠ *30 Regent Rd., Sea Point* ⊕ *www. mojomarket.co.za.*

WOODSTOCK

MARKETS
The Neighbourgoods Market. Known as the Biscuit Mill, this market is partially responsible for putting ever-gentrifying Woodstock on the map with Cape Town's hip, organic types who scoot in on their Vespas looking for artisan breads, pesto, home-cured olives, and fancy cheeses. It gets frantically busy by 10 am, which indicates just how popular it is, but if you want to rub shoulders with trendy design types and eat fabulous artisanal everything, this is the place to be. The prepared foods are wonderful, and many of Cape Town's most beloved eateries got their start here (most maintain a presence). When you're done browsing the food market, check out the crafts section with its lovely handmade leather goods, designer clothing, and jewelry, or carry on to the great stores in the same complex. Get there before 9:30 (or after 1:30) or be crushed by the crowds. Music events are not uncommon, and craft beer and boutique wines are also for sale. ⊠ *373–375 Albert Rd. (Lower Main Rd.), Woodstock* ⊕ *www. neighbourgoodsmarket.co.za.*

V&A WATERFRONT

BOOKS AND MUSIC
Exclusive Books Waterfront. The biggest bookstore chain in the country, this well-stocked branch carries a wide selection of local and international periodicals and coffee-table books on Africa, all the best sellers making literary waves around the world, an extensive magazine selection, and also has a nice coffee shop. You'll find branches at all the big malls and the airports. ⊠ *V&A Waterfront, Victoria Wharf, Shop 6160* ☎ *021/419–0905* ⊕ *www.exclusivebooks.co.za.*

MARKETS

FAMILY **Oranjezicht City Farm Market Day.** Held every Saturday from 9 till 2 at the Granger Bay part of the V&A Waterfront, the OZCF Market Day is a community farmers'-style market for independent local farmers and artisanal food producers where you can buy everything from fresh organic veggies to unique artisanal products (meats, cheeses, chocolates, etc.). The prepared foods are also fabulous (everything from shakshuka to eggs Benedict on a rosti to homemade muesli) and can be enjoyed at the big tables set up with sea views. Some lovely crafts and fashion vendors also trade here. Great for the whole family. ⊠ *Granger Bay, Beach Rd., Victoria and Alfred Waterfront* ✛ *Parking available adjacent to market* ⊕ *www.ozcf.co.za/market-day.*

Watershed. This market brings together the best of local arts and crafts with 150 vendors selling more than 365 brands of jewelry, fashion and accessories, pottery and home decor, and artwork, all of which is made in South Africa and the majority of which is of extremely high quality. ⊠ *Dock Rd., next to the aquarium, Victoria and Alfred Waterfront* ⊕ *www.waterfront.co.za/shop/markets.*

CAPE QUARTER

ARTS AND CRAFTS

Africa Nova. If you aren't crazy about traditional African artifacts à la Greenmarket Square, you might want to visit this store, which stocks contemporary and elegant African art and jewelry. ⊠ *Cape Quarter, 72 Waterkant St., Cape Town Central* ☎ *021/425–5123* ⊕ *www.africanova.co.za* ⊗ *Closed Sun.*

HOUT BAY

MARKETS

FAMILY **Bay Harbour Market.** This funky market in Hout Bay's working harbor offers more than 100 stalls selling everything from great food and drinks to clothing, crafts, and some truly worthwhile "made in South Africa" memorabilia. With good-quality live music performances, a wide and affordable selection of tasty treats, and a kids' play area, this all-weekend shopping spot is a great place for the whole family to shop, eat, or just hang out—by day or night—in the Hout Bay Harbour area. ⊠ *31 Harbour Rd., Hout Bay* ☎ *083/275–5586* ⊕ *www.bayharbour.co.za* ⊗ *Closed Mon.–Thurs.*

OBSERVATORY

ARTS AND CRAFTS

Mnandi Textiles. Here you'll find a range of African fabrics, including South African *shweshwe*, traditional West African prints, and Dutch wax prints. The store sells ready-made African clothing for adults and children, and you can also have garments made to order. ⊠ *90 Station Rd., Observatory* ☎ *021/447–6814* ⊗ *Closed Sun.*

SPAS

V&A WATERFRONT

Mai Thai Wellness Spa. This excellent, reasonably priced, and owner-managed boutique spa is one of the few not associated with a hotel. The highly trained therapists offer an extensive range of Thai-inspired massage therapy, as well as facials, luxury hand and feet treatments, and waxing and tinting services for men and women. Located in a charming building in De Waterkant, the spa also has a bamboo court-yard relaxation room where you can enjoy post-treatment teas and a cool breeze. ✉ *18 Dixon St., Green Point* ☎ *021/418–0713* ⊕ *www. maithaiwellness.com* ⊘ *Closed Sun.*

THE WESTERN CAPE

Including the Cape Winelands

Updated by
Mary Holland

Anchored by Cape Town in the southwest, the Western Cape is an alluring province, a sweep of endless mountain ranges, empty beaches, and European history dating back more than three centuries. The cultures of the indigenous Khoekhoen and San people—the first inhabitants of this enormous area—also contribute to the region's richness. You can reach most of the province's highlights in less than two hours from Cape Town, making the city an ideal base from which to explore.

The historic Winelands, in the city's backyard, produce fine wine amid the exquisite beauty of rocky mountains, serried vines, and elegant Cape Dutch estates. Here farms have been handed down from one generation to another for centuries, and old-name families like the Cloetes and Myburghs have become part of the fabric of the region.

Wildflowers are an extraordinary element of this natural setting. The Western Cape is famous for its fynbos (pronounced *fane*-boss), the hardy, thin-leaf vegetation that gives much of the province its distinctive look. Fynbos composes a major part of the Cape floral kingdom, the smallest and richest of the world's six floral kingdoms. More than 8,500 plant species are found in the province, of which 5,000 grow nowhere else on Earth. The region is dotted with nature reserves where you can hike through this profusion of flora, admiring the majesty of the king protea or the shimmering leaves of the silver tree. When the wind blows and mist trails across the mountainsides, the fynbos-covered landscape takes on the look of a Scottish heath.

Not surprisingly, people have taken full advantage of the Cape's natural bonanza. In the Overberg and along the West Coast, rolling wheat fields extend to the horizon, while farther inland jagged mountain ranges hide fertile valleys of apple orchards, orange groves, and vineyards. At sea, hardy fisherfolk battle icy swells to harvest succulent crayfish (similar to lobster), delicate *perlemoen* (abalone), and line fish, such as the delicious *kabeljou*. Each June–November hundreds of whales return to the Cape shores to calve, and the stretch of coastline that includes Hermanus, now referred to as the Whale Coast, becomes one of the best places for land-based whale-watching in the world.

For untold centuries this fertile region supported the Khoekhoen (Khoikhoi) and San (Bushmen), indigenous peoples who lived off the land as pastoralists and hunter-gatherers. With the arrival of European settlers, however, they were chased off, killed, or enslaved. In the remote recesses of the Cederberg Mountains and along the West Coast you can still see the fading rock paintings left by the San, whose few remaining clans have long since retreated into the Kalahari Desert. The population of the Western Cape today is of mixed race and descendants of imported slaves, the San, the Khoekhoen, and European settlers.

TOP REASONS TO GO

Land of Divine Wine: Few places in the world can match the drama of the Cape Winelands, where mountains rise above vine-covered valleys and 300-year-old homesteads. Against this stunning backdrop you can visit scores of wineries, tour their cellars, relax under old oaks with a picnic basket, and dine at the many excellent restaurants in the area. You'll be hard-pressed to decide which wines to take home with you.

Whale of a Time: Come spring, when the winter rains are no longer lashing the Cape, the icy seas teem with Southern Right whales, which come here to calve. Towns like Hermanus offer some of the best land-based whale-watching in the world, and you can also take a boat trip out to see these gentle giants. If it's adrenaline you're after, head to Gansbaai, where you can go diving amid great white sharks.

Flower Power: In summer, when the temperatures soar and the land is dusty, parched, and brown, it's hard to imagine the transformation that takes place each spring when millions of flowers carpet the West Coast hills. It's a photographer's dream, with the blue ocean in the background and swaths of yellow, white, and orange daisies.

Fabulous Food: South African food has come into its own. Boring *boerekos* (directly translated as "farmer's food"), characterized by meat and overcooked vegetables, has given way to an explosion of great cuisine. A new generation of chefs is making the most of the area's fabulous fresh produce, and restaurants in Franschhoek and Stellenbosch regularly get voted among the world's best.

The Great Outdoors: The Western Cape's real charm lies outdoors. Erinvale and the Arabella Western Cape Hotel & Spa, near Kleinmond, have some of the most spectacular golf courses in the world. In the Cederberg you can hike for days and explore ancient rock formations while learning about the leopard-conservation programs. You can also ride horses through the vineyards of the Cape Winelands or go boating in the Klein River lagoon near Hermanus.

3

ORIENTATION AND PLANNING

GETTING ORIENTED

The Cape Winelands, 45 minutes east of Cape Town, is the Napa Valley of southern Africa. The region boasts some of South Africa's best restaurants and hotels, not to mention incredible wine. Running in a broad band from northeast to southeast is the beautiful Breede River valley, home to farms, vineyards, and orchards.

East of the Cape Winelands and bordering the Atlantic Ocean, the Overberg is home to the small towns and villages of Gordon's Bay, Betty's Bay, Kleinmond, Hermanus, Stanford, and Gansbaai. Inland, Overberg villages of Elgin, Greyton, Swellendam, and Elim embody a bygone age.

Heading north out of Cape Town is the drier, more windswept West Coast. Small fishing villages hunker down next to the sea and offer visitors plenty of space to roam.

The Cape Winelands. This area fans out around three historic towns and their valleys. Founded in 1685, Stellenbosch's oak-lined streets, historic architecture, good restaurants, interesting galleries and shops, and vibrant university community make it an ideal base for wine travel. Franschhoek, enclosed by towering mountains, is the original home of the Cape's French Huguenots, whose descendants have made a conscious effort to reassert their French heritage. Paarl lies beneath huge granite domes, its main street running 11 km (7 miles) along the Berg River past some of the country's most elegant historical monuments.

Breede River Valley. Farms, vineyards, and orchards make up most of the Breede River valley. (So it should come as no surprise that one of the towns in the area is called Ceres, after the Roman goddess of agriculture.) Small-town hospitality, striking mountains, and wide-open spaces are hallmarks of this area. In summer the heat can be overwhelming, and in winter the mountain peaks are often covered with snow.

The Overberg. The genteel atmosphere of the southwestern Cape fades quickly the farther from Cape Town you go. The Overberg, separated from the city by the Hottentots Holland Mountains, presides over the rocky headland of Cape Agulhas, where the Indian and Atlantic oceans meet (officially) at the southernmost tip of the continent. Unspoiled beaches, coastal mountains, and small towns are the lure of this remote area.

West Coast. North of Cape Town on the West Coast, civilization drops away altogether, save for a few lonely fishing villages and mining towns. Each spring, though, the entire region explodes in a spectacular wildflower display that slowly spreads inland to the desiccated Namaqualand and the Cederberg mountains. For nature lovers, the West Coast provides some unique opportunities, including birding at West Coast National Park at the Langebaan Lagoon and hiking or rock climbing in the remote wilderness areas of the Cederberg.

PLANNING

Many people come to the Western Cape after getting a big-game fix in Kruger. Although it's possible to explore Cape Town and the Cape Winelands in three or four days—the area is compact enough to allow it—you need six or seven to do it justice. You can get a good sense of either the Overberg or the West Coast on a three- or four-day jaunt, but set aside a week if you plan to tackle more than one or two of the regions in this chapter.

WHEN TO GO

Summer (late November–January) is high season in the Western Cape, and during that time you will seldom visit major places of interest without encountering busloads of fellow visitors. The weather is warm and dry, and although strong southeasterly winds can be a nuisance, they do keep the temperature bearable. ■ **TIP→** The UV index in the Western

Cape is exceptionally high in summer, so if you do plan to visit then, make sure you take precautions to avoid severe sunburn. If soaking up the sun is not of primary importance and you prefer to tour during quieter times, spring (September and October) and autumn–early winter (late March through May) are ideal. The weather is milder, and the lines are shorter. Spring also brings Southern Right whales close to the shores of the Western Cape to calve, and late August–October are the months to see the wildflowers explode across the West Coast. If the Cape Winelands are high on your list of must-dos, remember that the busiest time in the vineyards and cellars is January–April, when they begin harvesting and wine making.

GETTING HERE AND AROUND

The best way to explore the Western Cape is to rent a car and take to the roads. You need to be flexible to enjoy all this region has to offer, and public transportation is too limited. Navigating your way around is not difficult. There are three main routes out of the city: the N1, N2, and N7. The N1 and N2 take you to the Cape Winelands of Stellenbosch, Franschhoek, and Paarl, and the N7 heads up the West Coast. To reach the Overberg, take the N2 out of town and head up over Sir Lowry's Pass. ■TIP➜ Getting lost after taking a wrong turn can take you into unsafe areas, so plan your route before setting out and use GPS.

PLANNING YOUR TIME

3 Days: You could devote a couple of days to touring the wineries, spending perhaps one day visiting Stellenbosch-area wineries such as Simonsig and Villiera, and another day around Franschhoek or Paarl. Consider breaking up your wine touring with horseback riding at one of the vineyards and a night in Franschhoek. A third day could be devoted to a long, scenic route back to Cape Town after lunch at one of Franschhoek's many good restaurants. Another option is to spend the first day wine tasting, and then drive over Sir Lowry's Pass through Elgin and on to Greyton, where you can wander around the village and visit the Moravian Mission complex in Genadendal. The last morning of your stay could be spent in Greyton before you head back to Cape Town via coastal Clarence Drive, which passes Kleinmond, Betty's Bay, Pringle Bay, and Gordon's Bay.

5 Days: With five days, you can work in time to see the Cape Winelands as well as Clanwilliam, at the edge of the Cederberg. (The drive to the Clanwilliam area will take you through the Swartland and the beginning of the wildflower route, which is best in spring.) If nature beckons, head into the Cederberg, where you can easily spend two nights in some of the country's most spectacular scenery. You can hike, swim in crystal-clear rock pools, and admire ancient San rock art. You could also combine a trip to the Cape Winelands or Cederberg with a visit to the coast's Langebaan and West Coast National Park, where the birding is exceptional.

HEALTH AND SAFETY

If you plan to go hiking in the mountains, come prepared with the right clothing and the correct attitude—each year tourists get lost in the mountains. Cape weather is notoriously changeable, so you need something warm and preferably waterproof. Take at least 2 liters of water per person and something to eat. If possible, hike with somebody who knows the area well, but if you're walking alone, be sure to take a cell phone and program in some emergency numbers (but be aware that cell phones won't work in all areas). Let somebody know of your route and when you expect to return, and don't stray from the paths if the mist closes in.

HOTELS

The Cape Winelands are sufficiently compact that you can make one hotel your touring base. Stellenbosch and Paarl, situated close to dozens of wineries and restaurants as well as the major highways to Cape Town, offer the most flexibility. Here bed-and-breakfasts and self-catering (with cooking facilities) options are often less expensive than hotels and provide a better taste of life in the country. Franschhoek is comparatively isolated, which many visitors consider a blessing. The West Coast, the Cederberg, and the Overberg are much more spread out, so you'll want to stay in one place for a day or two and then move on. During the peak season of December–January, book well in advance and be prepared for mandatory two-night stays on weekends. Although the winter months of June–September are usually a lot quieter and bring negotiable rates, seaside towns get really busy (and booked up) when the whales arrive to calve. The same is true up the West Coast during flower season. *Hotel reviews have been shortened. For full information, visit Fodors.com.*

RESTAURANTS

The dining scene ranges from fine South African cuisine complete with silver service to local, laid-back, country-style cooking. Franschhoek restaurants attract some of the country's most innovative chefs, who aren't afraid to experiment with unusual ingredients or food-and-wine combinations, and offer up a very sophisticated dining experience in a gorgeous setting. West Coast fare is not as urban as what you find in the Cape Winelands, and coastal towns usually concentrate on seafood, often served in open-air restaurants. Farther inland the cuisine tends to be less trendy and the portions more generous. Be sure to try some Cape Malay cuisine, characterized by mild, slightly sweet curries and aromatic spices. The only places you're likely to be disappointed in the food are in smaller agricultural towns in the Overberg, where overcooked veggies and an uninspiring and indistinguishable roast are still the norm. But this is changing from month to month as weary city slickers head out of town to open lovely restaurants serving high-quality food.

Country restaurants tend to serve lunch from noon and dinner from 6, and do not cater to late diners except on weekends. Because these areas rely heavily on tourists and local day-trippers, most restaurants in the Cape Winelands and seaside towns are open on weekends, especially for leisurely Sunday lunches, but may catch their breath on Sunday evenings or quieter Mondays. Dress codes vary as much as the dining experiences. Casual wear is acceptable during the day and at most restaurants in the evening. On the coast people pull shorts and T-shirts

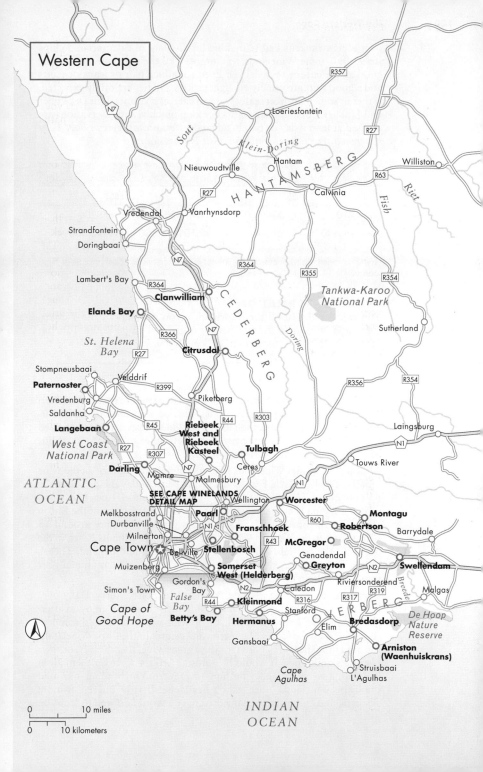

Western Cape

R357

R27

Loeriesfontein

Klein-Doring

HANTAMSBERG

Hantam

Williston

Sout

Nieuwoudtville

R63

Calvinia

R27

Fish

Riet

Vredendal

Vanrhynsdorp

Strandfontein

Doringbaai

N7

R364

R355

R354

Tankwa-Karoo
National Park

Lambert's Bay

R364

Clanwilliam

C
E
D
E
R
B
E
R
G

Sutherland

Elands Bay

St. Helena
Bay

R366

R27

N7

Citrusdal

Doring

Stompneusbaai

Velddrif

R399

Piketberg

R356

R354

Paternoster

Vredenburg

Saldanha

Langebaan

West Coast
National Park

R45

R27

R307

Riebeek
West and
Riebeek
Kasteel

R44

R303

Laingsburg

N1

Darling

Mamre

N7

Tulbagh

Ceres

Touws River

Malmesbury

N1

SEE CAPE WINELANDS
DETAIL MAP

Melkbosstrand

Durbanville

Milnerton

Wellington

Worcester

Montagu

Paarl

R60

Robertson

Barrydale

Cape Town

Bellville

Franschhoek

McGregor

N1

R43

Stellenbosch

Genadendal

Swellendam

Muizenberg

Somerset
West (Helderberg)

Greyton

N2

Riviersonderend

Breede

Malgas

Simon's Town

Gordon's
Bay

N2

Caledon

R316

R317

R319

Cape of
Good Hope

False
Bay

R44

Kleinmond

Stanford

Elim

Bredasdorp

De Hoop
Nature
Reserve

Betty's Bay

Hermanus

Gansbaai

Arniston
(Waenhuiskrans)

ATLANTIC
OCEAN

Struisbaai

Cape
Agulhas

L'Agulhas

INDIAN
OCEAN

0   10 miles

0   10 kilometers

over their swimsuits before tucking into a plate of calamari and chips (fries), but some Winelands restaurants like their patrons to look as good as the cuisine they deliver. Even so, a nice pair of jeans or pants and a good shirt are usually enough; jackets and ties are rarely expected. If there's someplace you really want to eat, reserve ahead. In December and January, popular restaurants book up quickly, and reservations are advised at least a day or two in advance. *Restaurant reviews have been shortened. For full information, visit Fodors.com.*

WHAT IT COSTS IN SOUTH AFRICAN RAND			
$	$$	$$$	$$$$
Restaurants	under R100	R100–R150	R151–R200	over R200
Hotels	under R1,500	R1,500–R2,500	R2,501–R3,500	over R3,500

Restaurant prices are the average cost of a main course at dinner or, if dinner is not served, at lunch. Hotel prices are the lowest cost of a standard double room in high season.

VISITOR INFORMATION

You can get almost all the information you need about the Western Cape and Winelands from the very organized Cape Town Tourism offices. *See Visitor Information in Cape Town.*

THE CAPE WINELANDS

Frank Prial, wine critic for the *New York Times,* wrote that he harbored "a nagging suspicion that great wines must be made in spectacular surroundings." If that's true, then the Cape Winelands are perfectly poised to produce fantastic wines, because the setting of dramatic mountains and lush valleys is absolutely stunning.

Although the Cape Winelands region is largely thought of as the wine centers of Stellenbosch, Franschhoek, and Paarl, today these areas make up only about 33% of all the land in the Cape under vine. This wine-growing region is now so vast, you can trek to the fringes of the Karoo Desert, in the northeast, and still find a grape. There are around 18 wine routes in the Western Cape, ranging from the Olifants River, in the north, to the coastal mountains of the Overberg and beyond. There's also a well-established Winelands brandy route, and an annual port festival is held in Calitzdorp, in the Little Karoo.

The secret to touring the Cape Winelands is not to hurry. Dally over lunch on a vine-shaded veranda at a 300-year-old estate, enjoy an afternoon nap under a spreading oak, or sip wine while savoring the impossible views. Of the scores of wineries and estates in the Cape Winelands, the ones listed here are chosen for their great wine, their beauty, or their historic significance. It would be a mistake to try to cover them all in less than a week. You have nothing to gain from hightailing it around the Cape Winelands other than a headache. If your interest is more aesthetic and cultural than wine driven, you would do well to focus on the historic estates of Stellenbosch and Franschhoek. Most Paarl wineries stand out more for the quality of their wine than for their beauty.

GETTING HERE AND AROUND

Driving yourself is undoubtedly the best way to appreciate the area. Each wine route is clearly marked with attractive road signs, and there are complimentary maps available at the tourism bureaus and at most wine farms. Roads in the area are good, and even the dirt roads leading up to a couple of the farms are nothing to worry about.

The best way to get to the Cape Winelands is to take the N2 out of Cape Town and then the R310 to Stellenbosch. Outside of rush hour, this will take you around 45 minutes. Expect some delays during the harvest months (generally late January–late March), when tractors ferry grapes from farms to cellars on the narrower secondary roads. On your way back to Cape Town, stick to the R310 and the N2. Avoid taking the M12, as it gets very confusing, and you'll end up in suburbs that aren't on tourist maps.

The major car-rental agencies have offices in the smaller towns, but it's best to deal with the Cape Town offices. Besides, you'll probably want to pick up a car at the airport. Since driving yourself around limits the amount of wine you can taste, unless you have a designated driver, it's best to join a tour, take a taxi, or Uber.

Paarl Radio Taxis will transport up to three people at about R10 per kilometer (half mile). Waiting time is around R60 per hour. Larger groups can arrange transportation by minibus. Go!Shuttle, a shuttle service based in Stellenbosch, works on a trip rate rather than a per-kilometer basis. A trip to a local restaurant costs around R200 regardless of the number of people. Go!Shuttle also provides shuttle service to the airport.

There's no regular bus service to the Cape Winelands suitable for tourists. If you are based in Stellenbosch, however, and don't want to drive to the wineries, you can make use of the Vine Hopper, a hop-on, hop-off minibus service that follows three different routes through the wine country. Tickets cost around R300 for a one-day ticket and R540 for a two-day ticket, and you'll be given a timetable so that you can get on and off as you please.

We do not recommend Cape Metro trains to Stellenbosch and Paarl because of an increase in violent muggings.

Contacts Go!Shuttle ☎ *072/368–3455* ⊕ *www.goshuttle.co.za.* **Paarl Radio Taxis.** ☎ *021/872–5671.* **Paarl Taxis & Tours.** ✉ *111 Loop St., Paarl* ☎ *021/872–5671.* **Vine Hopper.** ✉ *Black Horse Centre, Dorp St. at Mark Rd., Stellenbosch* ☎ *021/882–8112* ⊕ *www.vinehopper.co.za.* **Way 2 Go.** ☎ *021/638–0300* ⊕ *www.way2gotours.co.za.*

SAFETY AND PRECAUTIONS

If you spend a day out in the Cape Winelands and return at dusk or after dark, be on the lookout for pedestrians, especially on weekends, when people are likely to have been drinking. There is, unfortunately, a high incidence of pedestrian-related accidents on these roads. Also, be sure to designate a driver to avoid the risks associated with drinking

and driving. ■TIP➜ Under no circumstances do you want to spend even a night in a South African jail. If you are stopped by traffic police, they may well try to solicit a bribe. Do not offer a bribe.

TOURS

Most tours of the Cape Winelands are operated by companies based in Cape Town; most have half- or full-day tours, but they vary by company and might include a cheese tasting or cellar tour in addition to wine tasting. Expect to pay around R700 for a half day and R1,000 for a full day. Though you stop for lunch, it is not included in the cost.

African Eagle Day Tours. Great half- and full-day Winelands tours are offered by African Eagle. On the full-day tour (about R990), you"ll be whisked through Stellenbosch, Paarl, and Franschhoek. In Stellenbosch there's a walking tour of the town, followed by a cellar tour and cheese and wine tasting at a local wine estate. In Paarl you'll take a drive around before visiting a wine estate, then it's on to Franschhoek, where you can visit the Huguenot memorial and do some (more) wine tasting before journeying over the Helshoogte Pass. On the way back to town, you'll also see Nelson Mandela's former prison (Victor Verster Prison). The half-day tour—you can choose morning or afternoon—is all about Stellenbosch: you'll see the sights, take a cellar tour, do some cheese and wine tasting, and even experience a biltong and wine pairing. This tour costs R730. ✉ 4 Malta Rd., Salt River ☎ 021/464–4266 ⊕ www. daytours.co.za ⌧ From R730.

Amber Wine Tours. Lesley Cox from Amber Wine Tours is wildly enthusiastic about Cape wines and knows many of the Cape winemakers and wine-farm owners. Lesley prefers visiting boutique farms not on the tourist map, but she'll tailor tours to your tastes. So if you want to sample only Sauvignon Blancs, for instance, she'll know just where to take you. If you're not crazy about wine but want to tour the Winelands, Lesley can tell you about Cape Dutch architecture and the history of the area. ✉ 44 Hastings St., Tamboerskloof ☎ 083/448–7016 ⊕ www.ambertours.co.za ⌧ From R1,900.

Cape Fusion Tours. Foodie Pam McOnie from Cape Fusion Tours is a breath of fresh air and has an eye for the quirky. Pam and her team focus on small to medium wine farms and will really tailor your trip to incorporate the things you love. They can make plenty of suggestions, too, and have the inside scoop on what's new in Cape Town and the Winelands' food-and-wine world. ✉ Cape Town ☎ 021/461–2437, 083/235–9777 ⊕ www.capefusiontours.com.

Easy Rider Wine Tours. This outfitter has a great all-day tour that's very reasonably priced—around R650, including all fees and even lunch. You get picked up around Stellenbosch about 10:30 for a visit to four estates in the three regions, including Fairview, Simonsig, and Boschendal. The day starts with a cellar tour at Simonsig Wine Farm, and then it's on to Fairview for some cheese tasting. Next you'll stop for lunch in Franschhoek—vegetarians are catered for, too—where you can expect a variety of tasty dishes, from salads and burgers to pasta. After lunch you'll visit Dieu Donne and Boschendal for some more wine tasting.

✉ *12 Market St., Stellenbosch* ☎ *021/886–4651* ⊕ *www.winetour.co.za* 🖃 *From R650.*

Gourmet Wine Tours. This is an excellent choice for individuals or small groups wanting a tour of the greater Winelands area, including Constantia, Durbanville, Elgin, Franschhoek, Paarl, Somerset West, Stellenbosch, and Hermanus. The mountain and coastal views are reason enough to take a tour, and each of these towns has unique wines to offer. Tour operator Stephen is well informed and great at selecting the right wine…and restaurant. He's happy to tailor the itinerary to suit your personal tastes. Expect to pay around R2,650 for the first person and R1,350 per additional person per day for a personalized tour. ✉ *213 Fernbridge, Alnwick Rd., Diep River, Cape Town* ☎ *021/710–5454, 083/299–3581* ⊕ *www.gourmetwinetours.co.za* 🖃 *From R1,800.*

Hylton Ross Tours. A full-day Winelands tour with Hylton Ross starts with a cellar tour and cheese and wine tasting before moving on to Franschhoek via the Groot Drakentein Prison, where Nelson Mandela was incarcerated. In Franschhoek you'll have a second wine tasting of the day and lunch (not included) before heading to Stellenbosch. A full-day tour costs around R990 per person; a half-day tour is R720 per person. ✉ *94 Voortrekker Rd., Salt River* ☎ *021/506–2575* ⊕ *www. hyltonross.co.za* 🖃 *From R720.*

iKapa Tours & Travel. The itinerary for a full-day Winelands tour includes wine tasting and cellar tours in Paarl, Stellenbosch, and Franschhoek. The day starts with a vist to the stunning Paarl Valley before a quick photo op at the prison where Nelson Mandela was incarcerated at the time of his release in 1990. Then it's on to Franschhoek for lunch and wine tasting, followed by a drive over the majestic Helshoogte Pass. If there's time, you'll end the day with a final wine tasting before heading back to Cape Town. ✉ *94 Voortrekker Rd., Salt River* ☎ *021/506–3700* ⊕ *www.ikapa.co.za* 🖃 *From R995.*

Springbok Atlas Tours & Safaris. This tour outfitter offers full-day tours of the Winelands that include Paarl, Franschhoek, and Stellenbosch and cost around R995 per person, excluding lunch. A three-hour afternoon tour includes wine tasting at one or two estates in Stellenbosch and costs R740 per person. ✉ *Chiappini Sq., 17 Chiappini St., Cape Town Central* ☎ *021/460–4700* ⊕ *www.springbokatlas.com* 🖃 *From R740.*

Vineyard Ventures. For those serious about wine, Vineyard Ventures is the best of the Winelands tour companies. Glen Christie and her team are knowledgeable and passionate about wine and will tailor tours to your interests. The cost ranges from around R4,000 for one to four people and includes transport and refreshments. The rates come down as the number of people increases, so it's good to team up with another couple for a great day out. ✉ *Punta Del Mar, Milton Rd., Sea Point* ☎ *021/434–8888, 082/920–2825* ⊕ *www.vineyardventures.co.za* 🖃 *From R4,000.*

Wellington Wine Walk. A great way to combine wine tasting with exercise, this three- or four-day walking tour leads you from one upscale guesthouse to the next through vineyards and indigenous fynbos in the picturesque Wellington Valley. Your guides and hosts know all there is to know about the history and culture of the area, as well as the wines. They're also passionate about good food, and each day you'll have a light lunch and a dinner paired with the appropriate wines. The walking isn't tough, but you cover around 12 km (8 miles) each day. Your luggage is transferred for you from place to place, so all you have to carry is a light day pack. The best times to go are in autumn (April–May) and then again in spring (September–November) before the temperatures soar. ⊠ *Wellington* ☎ *083/313–8383* ⊕ *www.winewalk.co.za* ✉ *From R7,400.*

Windward Coach Charters. Take a tour of the premier wine-producing regions of Paarl, Franschhoek, and Stellenbosch with Windward Charters. The full-day tour includes cheese and wine tasting, a stop at the historical Taal Monument, a tour of the town of Stellenbosch, and a visit to some of the local shops and markets. The half-day version is a trip to Stellenbosch, either in the morning or afternoon, with a tour of the town, wine tasting, and a cellar tour. ⊠ *277 Koeberg Rd., Cape Town* ☎ *021/510–0961* ⊕ *www.windward.co.za* ✉ *From R650.*

EMERGENCY SERVICES
Police. ☎ *10111.*

SOMERSET WEST (HELDERBERG)

45 km (28 miles) southeast of Cape Town on the N2.

Somerset West, nestled at the foot of the Helderberg Mountains, is just 30 minutes from the center of Cape Town and close to Gordon's Bay and the Strand beaches. Once an important farming town, its former dairy fields are now covered with dreary town houses and faux Tuscan villas. But a few historic estates still remain and are worth visiting.

Just before you reach the center of town you'll see the turnoff to Lourensford Road, which runs 3 km (2 miles) to Vergelegen and Morgenster. If you're keen to stretch your legs, the Helderberg Nature Reserve overlooks the beautiful False Bay and is home to plenty of fauna and flora.

GETTING HERE AND AROUND
Somerset West is 30 minutes southeast of Cape Town on the N2 and 20 minutes from the airport. Public transport in these outlying towns leaves a lot to be desired. Your best bet is to rent a car and invest in a good map or GPS. Don't be tempted to catch trains out to the Cape Winelands after dark—you run the risk of being mugged.

VISITOR INFORMATION
Contacts Cape Town Tourism–Helderberg Branch. ⊠ *186 Main Rd., Somerset West* ☎ *021/840–1400* ⊕ *www.capetown.travel.*

EXPLORING
Morgenster. A leading producer of excellent extra-virgin olive oils and wines is the historic estate Morgenster (Morning Star), which was part of Cape Governor Willem Adriaan van der Stel's original 17th-century farm. In the mid-1990s the estate was restored to its original splendor, and thousands of olive trees were imported from Italy and planted. It

South African Wine

The South African wine industry is booming. Buried by sanctions during apartheid, South African wines were largely unknown internationally. But today there's enormous interest in South African reds *and* whites. Although South Africa has a reputation for delivering good quality at the bottom end of the market, more and more ultrapremium wines are emerging. Good-quality wines at varied prices are readily available—even in supermarkets.

Currently white wine production outstrips red, but the quality continually improves for both, and they regularly win international awards. Particularly notable is Pinotage, South Africa's own grape variety, a cross between Pinot Noir and Cinsaut (formerly Hermitage). Chenin Blanc is the country's most widely planted variety and is used in everything from blends to bubbly (known in South Africa as Méthode Cap Classique).

The industry is transforming itself slowly. The illegal *dop* (drink) or tot system, in which farmers pay some of laborers' wages in wine, is finally on its way out, and there's a concerted effort among producers to uplift their laborers' quality of life. Many international companies refuse to import wine from farms that don't secure their workers' rights, and many farms are working at black empowerment. Tukulu, Riebeek Cellars, Thandi Wines, Ses'Fikile (which translated means "we have arrived"), M'hudi, and Freedom Road are just some of the pioneers. Three farms that deserve a special mention when it comes to transformation are Bosman Family Vineyard (Wellington), Solms-Delta wine estate (Franschhoek), and Van Loveren Family Cellar (Robertson). Tragically, South Africa has one of the highest incidences of fetal alcohol syndrome, a legacy left over from the dop system.

If you're serious about wine, arm yourself with *John Platter's Wine Guide* or visit ⊕ *www.winemag. co.za* (the new digital form of *Wine* magazine), featuring local wineries. For an in-depth read and fantastic photos, pick up *Wines and Vineyards of South Africa* by Wendy Torein or *New World of Wine from the Cape of Good Hope: The Definitive Guide to the South African Wine Industry* by Phyllis Hands, David Hughes, and Keith Phillips. *Wines of the New South Africa: Tradition and Revolution* by Tim James is also recommended reading.

is now producing some of the best oils in the country and internationally. Seventeen different olive cultivars on the farm have been carefully selected from all the regions in Italy; these are pressed and stored individually before they're blended. For R40 you can taste the olives, the oil, balsamic vinegar, and the delicious olive paste. It's also worth lingering in the beautiful wine-tasting room, which was designed by acclaimed South African architect Revel Fox. To avoid disappointment, phone a day ahead if you're traveling in a group bigger than six. ⊠ *Vergelegen Ave., off Lourensford Rd., Somerset West* ☎ *021/852–1738* ⊕ *www. morgenster.co.za* ✉ *Olive tasting R40, wine tasting R35–R65.*

Rust en Vrede. Nestled against the base of Helderberg Mountain and shaded by giant oaks, the peaceful Rust en Vrede winery looks over steep slopes of vines and roses. This comparatively small estate specializes entirely in red wine and produces some of the very best in South Africa. In fact, Nelson Mandela chose this wine to be served at his Nobel Peace Prize dinner when he was president. Rust en Vrede Estate is the flagship wine, a blend of predominantly Cabernet Sauvignon, Syrah, and around 10% Merlot grapes. The 2014 vintage is the current hot seller; its lush flavors are testimony to the hot Stellenbosch summers that give the fruit their flavor. Enjoy it now, but you can also put it away to mature in the bottle for another 10 years or more. Another weighty wine is the 1694 Classification (named after the year the farm was established). Look out for raspberry, cedar, and pencil shavings on your palate and nose. ⊠ *Annandale Rd., off R44, between Somerset West and Stellenbosch, Somerset West* ☎ *021/881–3881* ⊕ *www.rustenvrede. com* 🍷 *Tastings R50–R100.*

Fodor'sChoice
★

Vergelegen. Established in 1700 by Willem Adriaan van der Stel, who succeeded his father as governor of the Cape, this traditional Cape Dutch homestead with thatch roof and gables looks like something out of a fairy tale. An octagonal walled garden aflame with flowers surrounds it, and huge camphor trees, planted more than 300 years ago, stand as gnarled sentinels. These trees were declared a National Monument in 1942, and you can picnic in the adjacent camphor forest (which are descendents from the historic trees) during the summer months. The homestead is now a museum and is furnished in period style. Other historic buildings include a magnificent library and the old stables, which is now the Stables Restaurant, where you can have breakfast and lunch while looking onto the magnificent Hottentots Holland Mountains. Behind the house is the farm's signature restaurant, Camphors at Vergelegen.

Vergelegen wines rake in the accolades year after year, and there's no award that they haven't won—usually more than once. Vergelegen's flagship wines include the Vergelegen V (a full-bodied Cabernet Sauvignon), and the Vergelegen GVB Red, a Bordeaux blend of Cabernet Sauvignon, Merlot, and Cabernet Franc. If you prefer white wine for summer drinking, the Vergelegen GVB White is a Sauvignon-Semillon blend. Reservations are recommended for the wine tours, but no children are allowed. There are also 70 steep stairs up and down into the state-of-the-art cellar, so you need to be able to manage these. Cellar tours last an hour. Apart from their award-winning wine, there are 18 themed gardens, including the newly relaid rose garden, agapanthus garden (at its best during January), and International Camellia Garden of Excellence—an amazing collection of more than 1,000 plants and 550 different species which flower during the winter months (June–August). There's a lovely children's play area that will keep children happy for hours. ⊠ *Lourensford Rd., Somerset West* ☎ *021/847–2122* ⊕ *www.vergelegen.co.za* 🍷 *Entrance fee R10, tastings R30.*

OFF THE
BEATEN
PATH

Mooiberge Farm Stall. You can't drive down the R44 between Somerset West and Stellenbosch without noticing the remarkable scarecrows at Mooiberge Farm Stall. They're riding bicycles, driving tractors, and working in the strawberry fields, where you can spend a morning picking the luscious red fruit. The strawberry season varies from one year

CLOSE UP

Cape Dutch Architecture

As you travel around the region, the most visible emblems of settler culture you'll encounter are the Cape Dutch–style houses. Here 18th- and 19th-century manor houses share certain characteristics: thick, whitewashed walls, thatch roofs curving around elegant gables, and small-pane windows framed by wooden shutters. It's a classic look—a uniquely Cape look—ideally suited to a land that is hot in summer and cold in winter. The Cape Dutch style developed in the 18th century from traditional long houses: simple rectangular sheds capped by thatch. As farmers became more prosperous, they added the ornate gables and other features. Several estates, most notably Vergelegen (near Somerset West) and Boschendal (on the Franschhoek wine route), have opened their manor houses as museums. The Oude Drostdy Museum just outside of Tulbagh is another fine example of classic Cape Dutch architecture.

to the next but usually begins in October and runs to January. You pay for what you pick, and you can also buy jams, dried fruit, and other refreshments at the farm stall. Look for the interesting display of old farm implements at the side of the building. ✉ *R44, between Somerset West and Stellenbosch, Somerset West* ☎ *021/881–3222* 🎫 *Free.*

WHERE TO EAT

$$$$ INTERNATIONAL

🍴 **Camphors at Vergelegen.** In summer, you'll need to reserve a table weeks in advance at this idyllic restaurant on the Vergelegen Estate (ask for a table on the terrace). With a big emphasis on fresh, free-range, and ethically farmed produce, the innovative menu from chef Micahel Cooke, is ever-changing with seasonal items like seafood potjie with seaweed and herbs or tea-smoked duck with farm berries and hibiscus. **Known for:** extravagant tasting menu; local ingredients; gorgeous setting. [$] *Average main: R395* ✉ *Vergelegen Estate, Lourensford Rd., Somerset West* ☎ *021/847–2131* 🌐 *www.vergelegen.co.za* 🕒 *Closed Mon. and Tues. No lunch Wed.–Sun. No dinner Fri. and Sat. during summer* 👔 *Jacket required.*

$$ INTERNATIONAL

🍴 **96 Winery Road.** This relaxed venue is always buzzing with folk from the wine industry, regulars, and up-country visitors. The menu changes regularly but tempts with favorites such as the classic Gatriles Duck and Cherry Pie, the "Hollandse" Pepper Fille, and the decadent crème brûlée. **Known for:** cozy setting; impressive wine list; local favorite. [$] *Average main: R125* ✉ *Zandberg Farm, Winery Rd., between Somerset West and Stellenbosch, Somerset West* ☎ *021/842–2020* 🌐 *www.96wineryroad.co.za* 🕒 *No dinner Sun.*

$$$$ FRENCH FUSION Fodor's Choice ★

🍴 **The Restaurant at Waterkloof.** Having quickly become one of South Africa's most notable dining destinations, this modern cliffside restaurant can't be missed. The dishes on the menu change according to availability and seasonality, but the poached freshwater lobster served with tomato concassé and hollandaise sauce remains a crowd-pleaser. **Known for:** stunning setting; superb wines; tasting menu. [$] *Average* *main: R420 ⊠ Sir Lowry's Pass Rd.* ☎ *021/858–1292* ⊕ *www.waterk-loofwines.co.za* ☉ *Closed Sun. evenings.*

STELLENBOSCH

15 km (9½ miles) north of Somerset West.

You could easily while away a week in this small, sophisticated, beautiful, and absolutely delightful town. South Africa's second-oldest municipality, after Cape Town, Stellenbosch actually *feels* old, unlike so many other historic towns. Wandering the oak-shaded streets, which still have open irrigation furrows (known as the *lei water*, pronounced lay *vaa*-ter), you'll see some of the finest examples of Cape Dutch, Georgian, Victorian, and Regency architecture in the country. The town was founded in 1679 by Simon van der Stel, first governor of the Cape, who recognized the agricultural potential of this fertile valley. Wheat was the major crop grown by the early settlers, but vineyards now blanket the surrounding hills. Stellenbosch is considered the center of the Cape Winelands, and many of the older and more established wineries are nearby. Wine routes fan out like spokes of a wheel, making excellent day trips if you're staying in town. The town is also home to the University of Stellenbosch, the country's first and most prestigious Afrikaner university.

GETTING HERE AND AROUND

The best way to get to this area is by renting a car. Expect to pay around R340 for an entry-level car per day and up to R900 for a Mercedes C Class. Once you're there, walking around is an excellent way to explore. Parking is hard to find, so once you've found a spot, leave your rented car while you explore on foot. There is usually a fee, so be sure to find out before venturing off. Avoid public transportation.

TOURS

The historic area of Stellenbosch is so pretty and compact that it's a pity just to drive through. Pull on your walking shoes and stride out with Stellenbosch on Foot for their 1½-hour walking tour.

Stellenbosch on Foot. Take a walking tour with one of the knowledgeable guides from Stellenbosch on Foot. Tours last around 1½ hours and take in all the well-known sights. Expect to pay around R120 per person if there are two of you, or around R170 if you're alone. Twilight tours cost R195 per person and include a wine tasting at one of the wine bars in Stellenbosch. ⊠ *36 Market St.* ☎ *021/887–9150, 083/497–7262* 🖭 *From R100.*

VISITOR INFORMATION

Contacts Stellenbosch Tourism and Information Bureau. ⊠ *36 Market St.* ☎ *021/883–3584* ⊕ *www.stellenbosch.travel.*

EXPLORING

Start your tour of the town at the corner of Dorp Street and the R44, where you first enter Stellenbosch. Look for street names written in yellow on curbs; they're easy to miss, so remember to look down and not up.

Sip and Spoeg Like an Expert

South Africa currently has more growing areas than ever that yield a huge selection of very different wines. One of the best ways to find your way around the enormous selection is to visit ⊕ *www.winemag.co.za* (formally *Wine* magazine), devoted to the subject. Wine prices ex-cellar are significantly cheaper than most retail outlets, so if you're looking for a bargain, buy directly from the farm.

AH, BUT YOUR LAND IS BEAUTIFUL

When it comes to South African terroir, think sun, sea, and soil. Whereas Northern Hemisphere farmers work hard to get as much sunlight onto their grapes as possible, local viticulturists have to deal with soaring summer temperatures (this is why the cooling influence of the two oceans is so welcome). South Africa also has some of the world's oldest soil, and there's a mineral element to its wines, a quality that's most prominent in the top-end Sauvignon Blancs like those produced by Cape Point Vineyards, Steenberg, Thelema, Diemersdal, Groote Post, Cederberg, and Springfield.

YOU CAN'T LEAVE WITHOUT TRYING PINOTAGE

In the 1920s, a professor at Stellenbosch University decided to create a truly South African varietal. He crossed Pinot Noir (a tricky grape to grow) with Cinsaut (a vigorous and very hardy grape)—he liked the idea of combining a drama queen with a pragmatic, no-nonsense type—and came up with Pinotage. Though it's had its ups and downs, including being accused by everyone from critics to connoisseurs of being bitter and rubbery, strides are being made

to express the grape's character. One example is the coffee Pinotage. It's been on the market for just a few years and is hugely popular because it's a ballsy, bold wine. There's a distinct mocha flavor to it that's a combination of the soil and the winemaking technique. A good example of this is the Diemersfontein Carpe Diem Pinotage. Other Pinotages to keep an eye out for: Stellenzicht Golden Triangle Pinotage, Spier Private Collection Pinotage, and Kanonkop Pinotage. Former Kanonkop cellar master Beyers Truter is known as the Pinotage King in South Africa; be sure to try Beyerskloof Pinotage.

HUNDREDS AND THOUSANDS TO CHOOSE FROM

Wines that have helped put South Africa on the map include Chenin Blanc, Sauvignon Blanc, and Bordeaux-style red blends of Cabernet Sauvignon, Merlot, and Cabernet Franc. South African red blends have done well at international competitions, and the quality rivals some of the world's best producers. Until recently, Chenin Blanc was something of a Cinderella varietal. It accounts for the bulk of South African white wine plantings but, because of its versatility, was largely overlooked. Luckily, this has shifted, and there are now more than 100 Chenin Blancs out there demanding attention and commanding top prices.

■ Good Sauvignon Blancs: Alexanderfontein Sauvignon Blanc, Springfield Estate Life from Stone Sauvignon Blanc, and Cape Point Vineyards Sauvignon Blanc.

■ Great red blends: Stellenrust Timeless, Rustenberg John X Merriman, and Kanonkop Paul Sauer.

■ Great Chenin Blancs: Kleine Zalze Chenin Blanc, Rudera Robusto Chenin Blanc, and Ken Forrester FMC Chenin Blanc.

A ROSÉ BY ANY OTHER NAME
Though it legally can't be called Champagne, Méthode Cap Classique, South Africa's version of the bubbly, is made in exactly the same way. You'd be unwise to pass on an offer of Graham Beck Cuvée Clive or Villiera Brut Tradition.

NAME-DROPPING
There are some iconic South African wines you really should try before you leave the country. Of course, the list of such wines varies depending on whom you talk to, but keep an eye out for these:

■ Boekenhoutskloof Cabernet Sauvignon

■ Boplaas Vintage Reserve Port

■ Cape Point Isliedh

■ De Toren Fusion V

■ Hamilton Russell Chardonnay and Pinot Noir

■ Jordan Chardonnay

■ Kanonkop Pinotage or Paul Sauer

■ Klein Constantia Vin de Constance

■ Meerlust Rubicon

■ Springfield Méthode Ancienne Cabernet Sauvignon

■ Steenberg Sauvignon Blanc Reserve

■ Vergelegen V

Potential future icons include Columella and Palladius, both made by Eben Sadie, and Raats Family Vineyard Cabernet Franc.

TO SHIP OR NOT TO SHIP
You're bound to want to take some great South African wine home with you, but it's not as easy as cramming your hand luggage with your favorite tipple. Travelers to the United States can take only two bottles on board. Any more than that and it will need to be shipped to you by an agent. Each person is allowed two cases (or 24 bottles), but some states won't allow you to import a single bottle without an importer's license. Expect to pay between R1,800 and R3,400 per case (East Coast destinations are usually cheaper than those on the West Coast) and that it will take anywhere from 6 to 18 days to reach you. Alternately, when you're wine tasting, ask the estate if they distribute in the United States, as you might find a local agent closer to home. The Vineyard Connection (⊕ *www.vineyardconnection.co.za*) is just one of the agents who can help you get your favorite bottle delivered to your destination.

Architecture buffs will be happy to know that there are still examples of 19th-century Stellenbosch design around. To check them out, turn left off Market Street onto Herte Street. (Market is Mark in Afrikaans; some maps use the names interchangeably, which can be confusing.) The whitewashed cottages along this street were built by and for freed slaves after the Emancipation Act of 1834. Although they are no longer thatch, the houses on the left-hand side of the road are still evocative of this era.

TOP ATTRACTIONS

Dorp Street. Stellenbosch's most historic avenue is oak-lined Dorp Street. Almost the entire street is a national monument, flanked by lovely restored homes from every period of the town's history. ⊠ *Dorp St. at Papegaai Rd.*

Oom Samie Se Winkel. Redolent of tobacco, dried fish, and spices, this 19th-century-style general store is one of Stellenbosch's most popular landmarks. In addition to the usual Cape kitsch, Oom Samie sells some genuine South African produce, including *witblitz* and *mampoer,* both Afrikaner versions of moonshine. The shop has a restaurant, too. ⊠ *84 Dorp St.* ☎ *021/887–0797.*

WORTH NOTING

Die Braak. Some of Stellenbosch's most historic buildings face the Braak, the grassy town square, which is a national monument. **St. Mary's Church** stands at the far end of the Braak. Built in 1852 as an Anglican church, it reflects the growing influence of the English in Stellenbosch. Across Bloem Street from St. Mary's is the **Burgher House,** built in 1797. Today it houses the offices of Historical Homes in South Africa. At the southern end of the Braak is the **Rhenish Mission Church,** erected by the Missionary Society of Stellenbosch in 1823 as a training school for slaves and blacks. ⊠ *Bordered by Bloem, Alexander, and Bird Sts.*

La Gratitude. This early 18th-century Dorp Street home was built in traditional Cape Dutch town-house style. The all-seeing eye of God molded on its gable was designed as a talisman to watch over the owner's property and keep him and his family safe from harm. ⊠ *95 Dorp St.*

Oude Werf. Possibly the country's oldest boardinghouse and now a welcoming guesthouse, Oude Werf (formally d'Ouwe Werf) first took in paying guests in 1802. To get here from Dorp Street, turn onto Andringa Street and then right onto Church (aka Kerk) Street; Oude Werf will be on your left. ⊠ *30 Church St.* ☎ *021/887–4608* ⊕ *www. oudewerfhotel.co.za.*

Rhenish Complex. One of the most impressive restoration projects ever undertaken in South Africa and a good example of what early Stellenbosch must have been like, this complex consists of an art center, which melds elements of English and Cape architecture; and a two-story building that is typically English. The complex is just east of the Tourism and Information Bureau on Market Street, on your left, facing a large lawn. The **Toy and Miniature Museum** (🖾 *R20,* ☎ *079/981–7067)* houses a collection of scale dollhouses and antique toys, as well as a miniature model of the famous Blue Train. ⊠ *Bordered by Herte, Market, Bloem, and Dorp Sts.*

Stellenbosch Museum. This museum comprises four dwellings scattered within a two-block radius. Dating from different periods in Stellenbosch's history, the houses have been furnished to reflect changing lifestyles and tastes. The oldest is the very basic Schreuderhuis, built in 1709. The others date from 1789, 1803, and 1850. ⊠ *18 Ryneveld St., at Church St.* ☎ *021/887–2948* ⊕ *www.stelmus.co.za* ✍ *R35.*

V.O.C. Arsenal. Next to the Burgher House, just across from the Braak on a traffic island in Market Street, stands the V.O.C. Arsenal, often called the **V.O.C. Kruithuis** (*kruithuis* means "powder house"). It took 91 years for the political council to decide that Stellenbosch needed its own magazine, and just six months in 1777 to complete the structure. Today the arsenal contains a wide selection of guns, gunpowder holders, and cannons. If the arsenal is closed, call or pop into the Toy and Miniature Museum and someone will open it up for you. ⊠ *Market St.* ☎ *021/886–4153* ✍ *By donation.*

Voorgelegen. This 19th-century home and the houses on either side of it form one of the best-preserved Georgian buildings in town. ⊠ *116 Dorp St.*

WINERIES

Many wine estates are wheelchair friendly, and you'll be able to access the tasting rooms without a problem. But some don't have restroom facilities for those using wheelchairs. You might want to phone ahead so you know what to expect.

TOP ATTRACTIONS

Fodor'sChoice ★ **Kanonkop.** In the days when ships of the Dutch East India Company used Cape Town as a refreshment station on their way to the East, a ship would fire a cannon as it entered the harbor to let farmers know provisions were needed, and a set of relay cannons, all set on hilltops, would carry the message far inland. One such cannon was on this farm, which was then called Kanonkop, Afrikaans for Cannon Hill. The beauty of Kanonkop today is not in its history or its buildings but in its wine. Winemaker Abrie Beeslaar has taken over from the legendary Beyers Truter (a very hard act to follow), but Kanonkop continues to reel in numerous awards and accolades. Paul Sauer, a blend of about 70% Cabernet Sauvignon and 15% each Merlot and Cabernet Franc, rakes in awards both in South Africa and internationally year after year. Bow before the Kanonkop Black Label Pinotage. It's an iconic wine that is produced only in small quantities (fewer than 5,000 bottles a year) and is sold only from the farm. It recently scored 97 points out of 100 at an international tasting. There are no guided cellar tours, but during harvest you can do a walkabout in the cellar to see all the action. An added attraction to this farm is the art gallery that features art from around 50 leading South African artists. It's a wonderful selection of the really modern to totally traditional and gives good insight into the artist soul of the nation. ⊠ *R44, between Paarl and Stellenbosch* ☎ *021/884–4656* ⊕ *www.kanonkop.co.za* ✍ *Tastings R30.*

Meerlust. A visit to Meerlust, probably South Africa's most celebrated estate, provides an introduction to Cape history. In the same family for generations, the wine farm was bought by Johannes Albertus Myburgh

Stellenbosch Wine Route

ALONG R310

West of Stellenbosch, the R310 (also known locally as Baden Powell Drive) forks to the left, but go straight on the M12 (also known as Polkadraai Road); Asara is first up on your right, followed by **Neethlingshof**. Turn right on Stellenbosch Kloof Road, where **Overgaauw** is a Merlot mainstay. Follow the winding road through pretty vineyards; at the end is **Jordan,** known for its excellent Chardonnay. Double back to Stellenbosch, and at the set of traffic lights, take the R310 to your right to the touristy but fun **Spier**. Next up this road is **Meerlust**, with its submerged windmill.

If you drive east on the R310 from Stellenbosch, detour up the Idasvallei Road and follow a narrow lane through cattle pastures and oak groves to **Rustenberg,** which focuses on reds. Then it's up and over the scenic Helshoogte Pass to **Thelema Mountain Vineyards,** which has knockout reds and whites. Its neighbor, **Tokara,** is a great lunch spot, and **Delaire Graff Estate,** over the road, has breathtaking views and an upmarket wine-tasting lounge.

ALONG R44

Some important wineries are on the R44 north of Stellenbosch. At **Morgenhof** you can sip Chardonnay and Pinotage and linger for lunch. About 3 km (2 miles) farther along on the R44, turn right on Knorhoek Road to reach low-frills **Muratie,** with some good reds. Back on the R44, travel a short way and then turn left on Kromme Rhee Road to visit **Simonsig,** home to wonderful bubbly. On the R44 once more, continue to **Kanonkop,** which has won numerous awards, and **Warwick,** with great red blends and lots of place to picnic. Carry on to Klapmuts and take the Simondium Road to the right to get to Babylonstoren, not to be missed for its gardens and interesting restaurant.

ALONG R304

This road shoots northwest from Stellenbosch past several wine farms. Stop at **Mulderbosch** for its excellent white wines (and great pizzas). Cross over Kromme Rhee Road and on to **Villiera,** known for sparkling wine and lush Sauvignon Blanc.

in 1757. When Nicolaas Myburgh, eighth-generation Myburgh and father of Hannes (the current owner), took over the reins in 1959, he began restoring the farm's Cape Dutch buildings. The entire complex was declared a national monument in 1987. But Nico Myburgh did more than just renovate. He took a fresh look at red wines and broke with tradition by deciding to make a red blend. In the '70s, conventional wisdom had it that Cabernet Sauvignon was king, but Nico went against the grain and opted for a Bordeaux-style blend, planting both Merlot and Cabernet Franc. The first wine, made in 1980 and released in 1983, was named Rubicon (an allusion to Julius Caesar) to symbolize the crossing of a significant barrier. Rubicon garners awards year after year and is rated as an international best seller. The estate makes only one white, a delicious, full-bodied Chardonnay. If a vintage of any of their grapes isn't good enough to bottle, they don't bother, so you can be assured of outstanding quality. Scoop up a bottle of the Rubicon 2009. Meerlust's other wines—Chardonnay 2016, Cabernet Sauvignon 2013, Pinot Noir 2016, and Merlot 2014—are also notably good. ⌂ *Off R310* ☎ *021/843–3587* ⊕ *www.meerlust.co.za* ✇ *Tastings R30.*

Thelema Mountain Vineyards. On the slopes of the Simonsberg, just off the Helshoogte Pass, this is an excellent example of the exciting developments in the Cape Winelands since the early 1980s, when farmers began to eye land that hadn't traditionally been earmarked for wine farming. When Gyles and Barbara Webb started the farm in 1983, there was nothing here but very good soil and old fruit trees. It's a testament to their efforts that the winery has regularly won prizes for both its reds and whites ever since. To cap it all off, the view of the Groot Drakenstein Mountains from the tasting room is unforgettable. Ever the pioneers, the Webbs have also bought Sutherland, an old fruit farm (not open to the public) in the Elgin area, an exciting new wine-growing region at the top of Sir Lowry's Pass. The Sutherland vineyard sits in the middle of the Kogelberg Biosphere, where many rare and endangered species of protea can be found. The Sutherland wines, which can be tasted at Thelema, are wonderfully fragrant; look out for the Pinot Noir and Chardonnay. The Mint Cabernet Sauvignon is a firm favorite, exhibiting light mint and herbal flavors. The locals' favorite, however, is Ed's Reserve, a single-vineyard Chardonnay named after the farm's matriarch, the late, legendary Edna McLean, Barbara's mother; she originally bought the Thelema farm, was a stalwart in the tasting room, and received all the farm's visitors. ⌂ *Off R310, between Stellenbosch and Franschhoek* ☎ *021/885–1924* ⊕ *www.thelema.co.za* ✇ *Tastings R50.*

FAMILY
Fodor'sChoice
★
Tokara. Perched on the crest of the Helshoogte Pass between Stellenbosch and Franschhoek, Tokara is the brainchild of banker G. T. Ferreira. For a city slicker with lots of money, he's done everything right by employing an excellent winemaker in the super-sexy Miles Mossop and paying careful attention to the quality of his vines. From the start, Tokara has scooped up awards; its Chardonnay was voted one of the top 10 wines from around the world at the Chardonnay-du-Monde Awards. The flagship red, a blend of Cabernet Sauvignon, Merlot, Petit Verdot, and Malbec, is well worth taking home. Be on the lookout for the farm's limited-release Pinotage 2012. A fire destroyed a chunk of the farm's vineyards a few years ago, and only 1,400 bottles of Pinotage were produced, so this is bound to be a hot collector's item. Tokara also has farms in the cooler Elgin and Hemel-en-Aarde regions, which means it can produce a stunning white wine blend (Sauvignon Blanc and Semillon) with plenty of complexity. The farm also produces its own premium olive oil, which you can buy from the Olive Shed. The restaurant is a foodie's delight, and the Delicatessen is a perfect venue for a breakfast or light lunch. Kids love the free-form jungle gym—as good-looking as any contemporary sculpture—and the weaver's nest they can climb into that hangs in a huge oak; the nest is the creation of visionary South African artist Porky Hefer. ⌂ *Off R310, between Stellenbosch and Franschhoek* ☎ *021/808–5900, 021/808–5959 restaurant* ⊕ *www.tokara.com* ✇ *Tastings free.*

WORTH NOTING

Delaire Graff Estate. This has to be one of the most spectacular settings of any winery in the country. Sit on the terrace of the tasting room or restaurant and look past a screen of pin oaks to the valley below and the majestic crags of the Groot Drakenstein and Simonsberg Mountains. It's an ideal place to stop for lunch, and you'll need at least three hours to do your meal and the wines justice. The wine lounge has an upmarket, clubby feel, and the staff are slick and on top of their game. So are the crew in the vineyard and cellar. Within just three years the estate has gone from so-so to stellar, and now it's regarded as one of the country's top 10 wine producers. Although the Botmaskop Red Blend is the farm's flagship wine, do try the Cabernet Franc Rose. It's a new release and a lovely take on a varietal that usually gets added to the Bordeaux Blend. The Coastal Cuvée Sauvignon Blanc is exceptional and is reeling in the awards. The Chardonnay is very elegant with fresh lime and creamy butterscotch flavors. ✉ *Helshoogte Pass Rd., between Stellenbosch and Franschhoek* ☏ *021/885–8160* ⊕ *www.delaire.co.za* ▣ *Tastings R70 for 5 wines.*

Jordan. At the end of Stellenbosch Kloof Road, this meticulous winery, flanked by the Bottelary hills, overlooks rolling vineyards and jagged mountains. Husband-and-wife team Gary and Kathy Jordan studied at the University of California at Davis and worked at California's Iron Horse Winery. The family made its fortune producing practical shoes, and although it produced its first vintage only in 1992, it has already established a formidable reputation. The Sauvignon Blanc, with refreshing hints of asparagus, makes for good summer drinking; the multi-award-winning, dense but fruity Chardonnay is extremely popular and has regulars stocking up on cases at a time. The 2013 Chardonnay won the Decanter wine of the year award. The Sauvignon Blanc and Chardonnay are combined in the versatile, flavorful, and well-priced Chameleon dry white. Another wine to try is the Cobblers Hill Bordeaux blend. The wine estate has an excellent restaurant on-site, as well as a bakery where you can have breakfast or a light lunch. Cellar tours are available by appointment; book at least a day ahead. ✉ *Stellenbosch Kloof Rd.* ☏ *021/881–3441 cellar, 021/881–3612 restaurant, 021/881–3004 bakery* ⊕ *www.jordanwines.com* ▣ *Tastings R35.*

Morgenhof Wine Estate. This beautiful Cape Dutch estate, with a history stretching back 300 years, lies in the lee of a steep hill covered with vines and pine trees. In 1993 Morgenhof was acquired by Anne Cointreau of Cognac, France, who spared no expense in making this a showpiece estate with a lovely rose garden on top of the working underground cellar. The estate has a talented winemaker, Andries de Klerk, and some distinguished wines. The Morgenhof Estate Blend 2006 is a complex wine made from a blend of Cabernet Sauvignon, Merlot, Malbec, Petit Verdot, and Cabernet Franc. Look out for black cherries, prunes, hints of chocolate, and spice on your palate. On a hot summer's day (and the temperatures can soar in Stellenbosch) try the 2015 Chardonnay with fresh pear, passion fruit, and pineapple flavors. Morgenhof is an excellent place to stop for lunch while you watch the peacocks roaming around. There's also a coffee shop if you want a snack before heading off to the next farm. Tour reservations are advisable in summer. ⊠ *R44, between Paarl and Stellenbosch* ☎ *021/889–2000* ⊕ *www.morgenhof. com* 🖃 *Tastings R35.*

FAMILY **Mulderbosch Vineyards.** Nobody likes change, and the wine industry—steeped in tradition—was twitchy when Mulderbosch was sold in 2011 to an overseas investor and the extremely talented winemaker Mike Dobrovic moved on. However, Mulderbosch fans have not been let down. The team continues to revise the wines and is still producing some stunners. Do try the Single Vineyard Chenin Blanc series (current 2015 vintage); these wines capture all that's good about the underrated Chenin varietal. Look for mango, pineapple, and citrus flavors with crisp acidity, perfect for summer drinking. A huge portion of the farm has been left to indigenous vegetation and wildlife, and they're attempting to restore endangered renosterveld and fynbos. The tasting room is relaxed and family-friendly and serves a selection of wood-fired pizzas to complement the wines. ⊠ *M12, Polkadraai Rd.* ☎ *021/881–8140* ⊕ *www.mulderbosch.co.za* 🖃 *R50* ⊗ *Closed Mon. and July.*

Muratie. Ancient oaks and a cellar that truly seems to be more concerned with the business of producing wine than with decor make this a refreshing change from the "prettier" wineries. It's a small estate, specializing in rich, earthy reds and full-bodied dessert wines. Muratie's port is an old favorite in the Cape, and the well-balanced amber is a fortified dessert wine of note, with pleasing citrus overtones to counter the sweetness. The cellar produces some fine red wines. Worth looking out for are the Pinot Noirs, from some of the oldest vines of this cultivar in the Cape. The farm's flagship wine is the Ansela van der Caab, a red blend of Cabernet Sauvignon, Cabernet Franc, and Merlot, named after the freed slave who married the first owner of the farm, Laurens Campher, and helped set up the vineyards in the early 1700s. The Ronnie Melck Shiraz and Muratie Martin Melck Family Reserve Cabernet Sauvignon also come highly recommended. Cellar tours by appointment only. ⊠ *Knorhoek Rd., off the R44, between Stellenbosch and Paarl* ☎ *021/865–2330* ⊕ *www.muratie.co.za* 🖃 *Tastings R35 for 5 wines.*

FAMILY **Neethlingshof.** A long avenue of pines leads to this lovely estate, which traces its origins to 1692. The magnificent 1814 Cape Dutch manor house looks out across formal rose gardens to the Stellenbosch Valley and the Hottentots Holland Mountains. There's even a large play area, complete with jungle gyms, for kids. The Gewürztraminer is an off-dry, very elegant wine with rose-petal and spice aromas, and the Maria Noble Late Harvest (named after the feisty woman who built the manor house, now the restaurant) is one of the best of its kind, having scooped up almost every local award since 1990. The farm's Owl Post Pinotage is a single-vineyard wine matured in Hungarian oak, which makes it a funkier take on an old South African favorite. Look out for mocha, chocolate, and licorice flavors. Try the food-and-wine parings, which include five bite-size tastes of food paired with the estate wines. On Wednesday evenings in summer enjoy live music, food, and wine as the sun sets. ⊠ *Neethlingshof Estate, 7599 Polkadraai Rd. (M12)* ☎ *021/883–8988* ⊕ *www.neethlingshof.co.za* 🖃 *Tastings R45, food-and-wine pairings R100, cellar tours R65.*

Overgaauw. Among the established estates on Stellenbosch Kloof Road, Overgaauw definitely deserves a visit. You can admire the pretty Victorian tasting room while exploring the range of big red wines. David van Velden took over as winemaker in 2007; he's the fourth-generation winemaker on the farm. Tradition hasn't stood in the way of innovation, however. In 1982 Overgaauw was the first South African estate to make a Merlot, but it also experiments with other varietals, and you should, too. Try the Cape Vintage Port made with Portuguese varietals such as *touriga*, *tintas*, *souzao*, and *cornifesto*. Confused? Don't be. The result is a wonderful richly balanced blend. The Tria Corda sells out faster than it can be released. The spicy, fruity Sylvaner is named for a grape of the same name. To date, Overgaauw is the only Cape estate to grow this varietal, which comes from the Alsace region of France, so it's definitely worth exploring. ✉ *Stellenbosch Kloof Rd., Vlottenburg* 🕿 *021/881–3815* ⊕ *www.overgaauw.co.za* 🍷 *Tastings R30 by appointment only.*

Rustenberg. This estate may date back to 1682, but it's been brought thoroughly up to date with a state-of-the art winery and underground vaulted maturation rooms. It is known for red wine, particularly its 100% Cabernet Peter Barlow (named after the present owner's father), which is made from grapes from one lovely, well-tended vineyard. The Five Soldiers Chardonnay is delicious and also made from a single vineyard, which gives it its unique character; it's named for the five tall pine trees that stand guard on top of the hill above the Chardonnay grapes. The farm uses screw caps on about half of its wines for quality and environmental reasons. Make time to explore the estate's beautiful gardens and labyrinth. These are open year-round but are best in summer. The lovely manor house gardens are open to the public only once a year over the last weekend of October, alas. ✉ *Rustenberg Rd., off Leslie St./R310, Ida's Valley* 🕿 *021/809–1200* ⊕ *www.rustenberg. co.za* 🍷 *Tastings R25.*

FAMILY **Simonsig.** Sitting in a sea of vines is this estate with tremendous views back toward Stellenbosch and the mountains. Simonsig has more than a dozen white and red wines of impressive range, both in terms of taste and price. But quantity certainly doesn't mean that it has compromised on quality. This family-run farm produces exciting and consistent wines. Kaapse Vonkel was South Africa's first Méthode Cap Classique, and since 1971 this classic blend of Chardonnay, Pinot Noir, and a touch of Pinot Meunier has been among the best. The 2010 Tiara is a great Bordeaux blend. The Pinotage demonstrates how well this varietal fares with no wood aging, but the Red Hill Pinotage, from old bush vines, shows just how much good oaking can improve it. This is a good place for kids, with a small playground, a labyrinth that takes about 10 minutes to walk through, and a small vineyard of all the grape varietals; here you can see which grape is used for the different wines and taste grapes directly from the vine. Cuvee restaurant offers seasonal, locally inspired dishes in a relaxed environment. Cellar tours are free at 11 from Monday to Saturday for less than five people. ✉ *Kromme Rhee Rd., Koelenhof* 🕿 *021/888–4900* ⊕ *www.simonsig.co.za* 🍷 *Tastings range R50–R75, R100 including sabrage; cellar tour R50.*

FAMILY **Spier.** Spier has undergone some serious restructuring and ditched some of its touristy trappings, which is probably a good thing; you can spend a very happy day here. This is one of the oldest farms in the area, established in 1692 on the banks of the Eerste River. The farm produces excellent wines, which go from strength to strength. The latest flagship wine is the Frans K. Smit 2012, named after its winemaker. Also try the 21 Gables Chenin Blanc—the 2015 looks set to be a winner. The 2014 Pinotage in the 21 Gables range is also excellent. The farm's owners value biodiversity and arts and culture: their enormous art collection is displayed across the farm's public spaces, and their farm-grown produce is used in the restaurant, Eight, and the deli. You can also order a picnic and enjoy it on the banks of the river. Visit Eagle Encounters, an on-site rehabilitation center for raptors—your kids will never want to leave. ⊠ *R310 (Lynedoch Rd.)* ☎ *021/809–1100* ⊕ *www.spier.co.za* 🍷 *Tastings R40–R90.*

Villiera. Since it started wine making in 1984, the Grier family has notched numerous successes. As John Platter, one of South Africa's foremost wine writers, says, "Other winemakers might jog or work out in the gym; Jeff Grier gets all the exercise he needs stepping up to the podium for wine industry awards." The farm is famous for its range of Méthode Cap Classique sparkling wines. Try the Brut Natural, which is 100% Chardonnay and made using wild yeast. It has no added sulfur and no added sugar, making it the perfect bubbly—delicious and good for you. The creamy Monro Brut made of Chardonnay and Pinot Noir is a multiple award winner. The barrel-fermented Chenin Blanc is also very popular. Registered as a biodiversity farm, the winery produces chemical-free wines as much as possible; they use ducks to help control the snails and work to attract raptors to scare off the smaller birds that feast on the ripening grapes. You can combine a wine tasting with a drive through the 545-acre wildlife sanctuary (2 hours, R220), where you'll see eland, gemsbok, giraffe, bush pig, and other wild animals. Booking is essential. ⊠ *R101 and R304 (Old Paarl and Stellenbosch Rds.), Koelenhof* ☎ *021/865–2002, 021/865–2003* ⊕ *www.villiera.com* 🍷 *Tastings R30.*

Warwick. This Ratcliffe-family-run farm is all business. Norma Ratcliffe, the grande dame of the estate, spent a couple of vintages in France perfecting traditional techniques, which have influenced Warwick's reds. The first female winemaker in South Africa, Norma pioneered the way for a new breed of young women who are now making their mark in the industry. Trilogy is a stylish and complex red made predominantly from 54% Cabernet Sauvignon 2013, with about 14% Merlot and 32% Cabernet Franc. The 2004 Trilogy was voted one of the top five wines in the world by *Wine Spectator*—no mean feat! The 2010 vintage was also voted best wine on show and was awarded five stars, the highest rating any wine can receive. Another great red, the Three Cape Ladies, was named after the indomitable Ratcliffe women. It's been described as a "feminine" blend of Cabernet Sauvignon, Shiraz, and Pinotage. Their Cabernet Franc is undoubtedly one of the best wines made from this varietal in the Winelands. Cellar tours on request. ■ **TIP→ On the hour-long Big 5 Vineyard tour (R85), the grape**

varietals are compared to South Africa's famous Big Five wild animals; afterward you can relax with a farm picnic (prices change) on the lawn or in one of the picnic pods. ✉ *R44, between Stellenbosch and Klapmuts, Elsenburg* ☎ *021/884–4410* 🌐 *www.warwickwine.com* 🎟 *Standard tastings R50, exclusive tastings R100.*

TASTING TIP

One of the funny things about small, family-owned farms is that they won't charge you for a tasting if they don't feel like it. But it's at the owners' discretion, and it all depends on whether they wake up in a good or a bad mood. If they like you, you could end up with a tasting, tour, and lunch at their home. So be at your best and most charming. But don't tell them we told you.

WHERE TO EAT

$$$ ECLECTIC

🍴 **Bodega.** On the huge veranda of a historic barn, a languid air of well-fed ease wafts around Bodega. An enormous blackboard announces the tapas of the day: crispy squid tubes, figs wrapped in Serrano ham, and chicken croquettes are just some of the options. **Known for:** casual vibe; family-friendly; fantastic desserts. [$] *Average main: R165* ✉ *Blaauwklippen Rd.* ☎ *021/880–0557* 🌐 *www.dornier.co.za* 🕒 *No lunch Mon. and Tues. No dinner.*

$$$$ ECLECTIC

🍴 **Overture.** At the end of Annandale Road, Hidden Valley Estate perches on a mountain ridge, flanked by the splendor of fynbos-covered hills and a silvery grove of olive trees. It has a constantly changing menu of seasonal ingredients that manifests a pure love of food with distinctly South African dishes like Chip & Dip Before a Braai (a refined version of the "chip and dip"), Mom's Cabbage Bake (a modern take on his mother's cabbage recipe), and black bream with cauliflower. **Known for:** friendly service; excellent tasting menu; great value. [$] *Average main: R480* ✉ *Hidden Valley Wines, Annandale Rd.* ☎ *021/880–2721* 🌐 *www.dineatoverture.co.za* 🕒 *No dinner Sun.–Wed.*

$$$$ ECLECTIC Fodor's Choice ★

🍴 **Rust en Vrede.** When you arrive at this gorgeous old Dutch farmhouse, a staff member greets you outside the door, suggesting a predinner drink on the rose-trellised terrace: the perfect introduction to your evening at one of South Africa's top-ranked restaurants. A four- (R220) or six-course (R850) tasting menu keeps things deceptively simple with complex flavors like the sublime *ajo blanco* (white gazpacho) soup with white peach, Champagne jelly, and fresh honeycomb as well as the roasted baby chicken with curried mango and coriander. **Known for:** over-the-top tasting menu; exquisite service; reasonably priced wines. [$] *Average main: R720* ✉ *Annandale Rd.* ☎ *021/881–3757* 🌐 *www.rustenvrede.com* 🕒 *No lunch. No dinner Sun. and Mon.* 👔 *Jacket required.*

$$ SOUTH AFRICAN Fodor's Choice ★

🍴 **Spek & Bone.** Hidden in the center of town, Spek and Bone is a cozy restaurant with a lush courtyard with tables and chairs set under a canopy of vines. The menu is filled with bold, comforting dishes: sautéed potato gnocchi with mushroom, spring onion and Parmesan sauce, and Tannie Hetta's Apple Pie with homemade vanilla ice cream. **Known for:** chef Bertus Basson; hearty dishes; local wines. [$] *Average main: R100* ✉ *84 Dorp St.* ☎ *082/569–8958* 🌐 *www.bertusbasson.com* 🕒 *Closed Sun.*

$$$$ ECLECTIC FAMILY Fodor's Choice ★ 🍴 **Terroir.** The setting on a golf estate and wine farm is pretty, but it's the excellent food and service that really stand out here. The menu changes regularly to make use of the fresh produce, with options that might include smoked duck breast with chestnut purée, orange, and sesame. **Known for:** chef Michael Broughton; local ingredients; prawn risotto. [$] *Average main: R265* ✉ *Kleine Zalze Residential Golf Estate, Strand Rd. (R44), between Somerset West and Stellenbosch* ☎ *021/880–8167* 🌐 *www.kleinezalze.co.za* 🕒 *No dinner Sun.*

$$$$ ECLECTIC Fodor's Choice ★ 🍴 **Tokara.** At the top of the Helshoogte Pass with absolutely amazing views of the valley and mountains, Tokara is a Winelands must-visit, known for innovation and playful twists. The adventurous menu changes seasonally but could include dishes like beef tartare with Parmesan custard, cured egg, and anchovy and pepper vinaigrette or tempura line fish with sushi rice, avocado, sesame, and wasabi mayonnaise. **Known for:** chef Richard Carstens; surprising flavors; child-friendly fine dining. [$] *Average main: R205* ✉ *Helshoogte Pass Rd. (R310)* ☎ *021/885–2550* 🌐 *www.tokara.co.za* 🕒 *Closed Mon. No dinner Sun.*

3

WHERE TO STAY

$$ HOTEL 🏨 **Asara Wine Estate & Hotel.** This hotel on the outskirts of Stellenbosch might not have the most breathtaking setting that the Winelands has to offer, but what it lacks in location it more than makes up for in luxury and attention to detail. **Pros:** easy access to both Cape Town and the Winelands; highly rated wines produced on the estate. **Cons:** not far from the Stellenbosch municipal garbage dump; lacks the gracious charm of some historic wine farms; you'll need a deep pocket. [$] *Rooms from: R2000* ✉ *Polkadraai Rd. (M12), Vlottenburg* ☎ *021/888–8000* 🌐 *www.asara.co.za* 🛏 *41 rooms* 🍽 *Breakfast.*

$$$$ HOTEL Fodor's Choice ★ 🏨 **Delaire Graff Estate Lodges.** At the top of the Helshoogte mountain pass and looking onto two surrounding mountain ranges, the luxurious Delaire Graff enjoys one of the wine country's most dramatic locations. **Pros:** stunning natural setting; lodge guests enjoy free tastings and shuttles into Stellenbsoch; staff accounts for personal preferences from pillows to newspapers. **Cons:** this level of luxury doesn't come cheap. [$] *Rooms from: R14550* ✉ *Helshoogte Pass Rd., between Stellenbosch and Franschhoek* ☎ *021/885–8160* 🌐 *www.delaire.co.za* 🛏 *10 lodges* 🍽 *Breakfast.*

$$$ HOTEL 🏨 **Majeka House.** This complex of creeper-encrusted buildings nestled in gardens overflowing with roses, lavender, frangipani, and jasmine in an upmarket residential corner of Stellenbosch is a perfect oasis and a great base for exploration. **Pros:** fantastic and convenient location; outstanding restaurant; three of the four pools are heated. **Cons:** you will need a car to explore the area. [$] *Rooms from: R3000* ✉ *26–32 Houtkapper St., Paradyskloof* ☎ *021/880–1549* 🌐 *www.majekahouse.co.za* 🛏 *23 rooms* 🍽 *Breakfast.*

$$ B&B/INN 🏨 **Oude Werf Hotel.** A national monument, this attractive 1802 inn is thought to be the oldest continuously running inn in South Africa. **Pros:** perfect location in the heart of Stellenbosch; landmark in-house restaurant; two family-size, self-catering houses available; heated outdoor swimming pool. **Cons:** can get a bit noisy in the center of town; some rooms are dark. [$] *Rooms from: R2500* ✉ *30 Church*

St. ☎ 021/887–4608 ⊕ www.oudewerfhotel.co.za ⇆ 58 rooms
|◎| Breakfast.

$$
HOTEL
FAMILY

⊞ **Spier Hotel.** The design of these two-story buildings grouped around six courtyards, each with its own pool and leisure area, makes this complex feel like a Mediterranean village, albeit a very luxurious one. **Pros:** plenty of entertainment on hand; perfect for the whole family; very accessible and close to the N2. **Cons:** can get busy in peak season; you'll have to share the wine farm with day visitors. $ Rooms from: R2100 ⊠ Spier Estate, Lynedoch Rd. ☎ 021/809–1100 ⊕ www.spier. co.za ⇆ 158 rooms |◎| Breakfast.

NIGHTLIFE AND PERFORMING ARTS
NIGHTLIFE
Wijnhuis. Take a stroll into the Church Street part of town, where shops stay open late and bars and cafés spill onto the streets. A good place to start, the Wijnhuis quickly fills up with trendy locals wanting to unwind. ⊠ Church St. at Andringa St. ☎ 021/887–5844 ⊕ www.wijn-huis.co.za.

PERFORMING ARTS
For tickets to most events in South Africa, contact **Computicket** (☎ 083/915–8000 ⊕ www.computicket.co.za).

Oude Libertas Amphitheatre. Each summer, performances ranging from African jazz to opera to ballet are staged at the Oude Libertas Amphitheatre, a delightful open-air venue across from and run and owned by Distell, a South African liquor company. Book tickets online through Computicket. ⊠ Adam Tas St. at Oude Libertas Rd. ☎ 021/809–7473 ⊕ www.oudelibertas.co.za.

EN ROUTE

From Thelema the **R310** runs down into the fruit orchards and vines that mark the beginning of the Franschhoek Valley. The R310 dead-ends at the R45. To the left is Paarl, to the right Franschhoek. When you head up the R310 from Franschhoek back to Stellenbosch, keep a look out for the "angel" etched onto the mountain in among the vines. Well-known land artist Strijdom van der Merwe was asked to help create the Bartinney Wine Estate's winged figure of Élevage in the landscape. Élevage is a French wine-making term that describes the art of liberating grapes to reveal their true characteristics. The image was created by planting endemic fynbos among the new Chardonnay vines.

FRANSCHHOEK

22 km (14 miles) northeast of Stellenbosch.

Franschhoek (French Corner) takes its name from its first white settlers, French Huguenots who fled to the Cape to escape Catholic persecution in France in the late 1600s. By the early 18th century about 200 Huguenots had settled in the Cape; today their descendants—with names like de Villiers, Malan, and Joubert—number in the tens of thousands. With their experience in French vineyards, the early Huguenots were instrumental in nurturing a wine-making culture in South Africa.

Franschhoek is the most spectacular of the three wine centers: a long valley encircled by towering mountain ranges and fed by a single road that runs through town. As spectacular as the valley is today, it must have been even more so in the 17th century, when it teemed with game. In calving season herds of elephants would migrate to the valley via the precipitous Franschhoek Mountains. The last wild elephant in the valley died in the 1930s. Some leopards still survive high in the mountains, but you won't see them.

What you will see today is an increasingly upscale village with beautifully renovated cottages and gorgeous gardens. Although it can get very busy during the summer season, you will always be able to find a quiet spot with a view of the mountains, roses, and swaths of lavender, which do well here. Franschhoek has developed into a culinary mecca, with some of the country's best restaurants and cafés lining the pretty main street. In May the fabulous Franschhoek Literary Festival (⊕ *www.flf. co.za*) features local and international writers. Bastille Day (⊕ *www. franschhoekbastille.co.za*) is a huge draw, when the town is decked out in red, white, and blue, and events commemorate the town's French history. The town is more touristy than agrarian, although you will see the occasional wine farmer steaming into town with his dogs on the back of his *bakkie* (pickup truck), looking for tractor tires or other essentials. It's a great place for lunch or for a couple of days, as there are excellent small hotels and guesthouses to choose from.

GETTING HERE AND AROUND
The best way to explore this area is by renting a car and braving the Cape's highways and byways. Be aware that drunken walking is a real hazard in wine-growing areas, and you need to keep a sharp eye out for staggering pedestrians, especially over the weekends.

VISITOR INFORMATION
Contacts Franschhoek Vallée Tourisme. ⊠ *62 Huguenot Rd.* ☎ *021/876–2861* ⊕ *www.franschhoek.org.za.*

EXPLORING
Huguenot Memorial Museum. To trace the history of the Huguenot community here, visit the Huguenot Memorial Museum. Its main building is modeled after the Saasveld house, built in 1791 by renowned Cape architect Louis Thibault in Cape Town. Wall displays profile some of the early Huguenot families. Exhibits also focus on other aspects of the region's history, such as the development of Cape Dutch architecture and the relationship of the Huguenots with the Dutch East India Company. Displays in the annex cover the culture and life of the Khoekhoen, or Khoikhoi, once derogatorily known as Hottentots, as well as the role of slaves and local laborers in the development of the Franschhoek Valley. Bring a picnic basket and take advantage of the lovely garden. Be sure to visit the adjacent Huguenot Museum gardens and the graveyard next to the monument. The graves date back 300 years; note that most are marked with simple, rectangular headstones or the obelisk, pointing toward heaven, rather than the symbol associated with the church the Huguenots were so desperate to escape. ⊠ *Lambrecht St.* ☎ *021/876–2532* ⊗ *R10.*

Huguenot Monument. At the end of the main road through Franschhoek is the Huguenot Monument, built in 1948 to commemorate the

Franschhoek Wine Route

ALONG R310

The drive out of Stellenbosch up the Helshoogte Pass is spectacular. In winter you'll more than likely find snow on the mountain peaks; in summer, once you top the pass you enter a verdant valley of fruit trees and ordered vineyards.

Then head to **Boschendal,** one of the oldest and most established estates in the country.

ALONG R45

There are well more than 40 estates to choose from here, and there's something for everyone—from enormous farms covering hundreds of acres to smaller, boutique vineyards producing just a few hundred bottles each year. If you turn right on R45 from the R310, **L'Ormarins** is one of the first wine farms you'll come to (off the R45 through a tunnel of trees). It's a well-established estate that's undergone some massive changes since the founder, Anthonij Rupert, died in 2001. Just outside town, **La Motte** is a sister farm to L'Ormarins. Closer to town the estates come thick and fast. Amid this flurry—Môreson (up the aptly named Happy Valley Road), Rickety Bridge, Agusta, Chamonix, and Dieu Donne—is **Mont Rochelle,** a relatively small producer of lovely wine and home to a boutique hotel. Outside town and up the Franschhoek Pass toward Villiersdorp, the fabulous **Cabrière,** at Haute Cabrière, is built into the mountain. **La Petite Ferme** is worth phoning ahead for (you can't just pop in).

If you turn left on the R45 from the R310, you'll find more outstanding wine farms, including **Plaisir de Merle,** which makes a distinctive Cabernet and Sauvignon Blanc.

contribution of the Huguenots to South Africa's development. The three arches symbolize the Holy Trinity, the sun and cross reference the Huguenots' emblem, and the female figure in front represents Freedom of Conscience. ⊠ *Lambrecht St. at Huguenot St.*

WINERIES

It should come as no surprise that the Franschhoek Valley produces excellent wines. After all, the original French settlers brought with them an extensive and intimate understanding of viticulture. Some of the country's oldest estates nestle at the base of the spectacular Groot Drakenstein Mountains, and the wine farmers here are constantly trying to top themselves.

TOP ATTRACTIONS

Boschendal. With a history that dates back three centuries, this lovely estate is one of the Cape's major attractions. You can easily spend half a day here, and recent renovations have added polish to an already premier estate. Cradled between the Simonsberg and Groot Drakenstein Mountains at the base of Helshoogte Pass, the farm—formerly called Bossendaal—was originally granted to Jean le Long, one of the first French Huguenot settlers in the late 17th century. Boschendal runs one of the most pleasant wine tastings in the region: you can sit inside at the Taphuis, a Cape Dutch *langhuis* (longhouse), or outside at wrought-iron tables under a spreading oak. In 1981 Boschendal was the first to pioneer a Blanc de Noir, a pink wine made in a white-wine style from black grapes. The Boschendal Blanc de Noir remains one of the best-selling wines of this style. From the Taphuis it's a two-minute drive through vines and fruit trees to the main estate complex. The recently renovated Werf Restaurant serves excellent country-style cuisine, and picnic baskets are available from Werf and Rhone that can be enjoyed on the lawns; reservations are essential for both. Hour-long vineyard tours and cellar tours are available; be sure to book ahead. ✉ *R310 between Franschhoek and Stellenbosch, Groot Drakenstein* ☎ *021/870–4200, 021/870–4211 winery, 021/870–4272 restaurants* ⊕ *www.boschendal.co.za* 🍷 *Tastings R35–R65.*

L'Ormarins. Dating from 1811, the archetypal Cape Dutch manor house is festooned with flowers and framed by majestic peaks, but instead of remaining in the past, this winery has embraced the future and pumped serious money into a major revamp. L'Ormarins is the main estate and part of the Rupert empire, but there are five labels produced by their various farms dotted around the Western Cape. The wines include the premium Anthonij Rupert range, the L'Ormarins label, Terra Del Capo, Cape of Good Hope, and Protea range. The farm has three state-of-the-art cellars and two tasting rooms. At the Anthonij Rupert Tasting Room, in the manor house, you can try the Cape of Good Hope and Anthonij Rupert wine ranges. High tea is served here in the afternoon (by reservation only). You can try the other ranges at the Terra Del Capo Tasting Room. There's an antipasto bar below the tasting room, where you can enjoy tasty tapas. Chat with the winemakers, and they'll tell you that the farm has introduced revolutionary farming practices, from transporting the grapes to the cellar in cool trucks to optical sorting and hand-stemming. The results are impressive, and you're likely to find something to suit your taste and pocket. The AR Merlot is exceptional: look out for mulberries, blackberries, and hints of fynbos along with fruitcake and cloves. The TDC Sangiovese is a brilliant, light drinking wine, and the Pinot Grigio is always a pleasure. ■ **TIP➔ Visit the estate's Franschhoek Motor Museum, home to more than 80 cars of varying ages in mint condition (R80 per person).** ✉ *R45 (Franschhoek Rd.), Groot Drakenstein* ☎ *021/874–9000* ⊕ *www.rupertwines.com* 🍷 *Tastings R25–R90 (per flight of 3–4 wines), Motor Museum R80* ☉ *Anthonij Rupert Tasting Room closed Sun.; Terra del Capo Tasting Room and antipasto bar closed Mon.*

WORTH NOTING

FAMILY **Allée Bleue.** Set against the dramatic Drakenstein Mountains, surrounded by vineyards and orchards, Allée Bleue is one of the oldest wine farms in the Cape. This picturesque estate is well known for its fresh and fruity white wines and well-matured, spicy reds. You can taste their award-winning wines on the tree-shaded terrace overlooking the vineyards, or by an open fire in the tasting room. Bistro Allée Bleue offers breakfast and light lunches, or seasonal set picnic baskets, which have a selection of salads, homemade ciabatta sandwiches, quiches, cheeses, and desserts. There's even a kids' picnic menu, and a jungle gym, trampoline, sand pit, and jumping castle to keep the little ones occupied. The farm also produces a range of fruit including pears, plums, and nectarines).

✉ *Intersection of R45 and R310, Groot Drakenstein* ☎ *021/874–1021* ⊕ *www.alleebleue.co.za* ☜ *Tastings R45.*

Haute Cabrière. Built in 1994 on the lower slopes of the Franschhoek Mountains, Haute Cabrière is the brainchild of Achim von Arnim, one of the Cape's most colorful winemakers. To avoid scarring the mountain, the complex, which includes the fine Haute Cabrière restaurant and terrace, hunkers into the hillside. There are three Cap Classique sparkling wines under the Pierre Jordan label, and four Haute Cabrière wines. The fruity, mouth-filling unwooded Pinot Noir is consistently one of the best. Also delicious is the Chardonnay–Pinot Noir blend, an ideal, extremely quaffable wine to enjoy at lunchtime. Take a Saturday-morning cellar tour with von Arnim or his son, Takuan, and watch him perform his trademark display of *sabrage*—the dramatic decapitation of a bottle of bubbly with a saber. ✉ *R45 (Franschhoek Pass Rd.)* ☎ *021/876–8500* ⊕ *www.cabriere.co.za* ☜ *Tastings R45–R70, cellar tours at 11 daily R75, Sat. cellarmaster's tour R90.*

La Motte Estate. This estate is owned by a branch of the same Rupert family that owns L'Ormarins, and is a partner in Rupert & Rothschild, a vineyard closer to Paarl. There's a lot happening at this farm: try the Pierneef Experience (a guided tour of the estate's museum followed by a wine-and-cheese tasting) or take a hike along one of the farm's stunning trails. And then there's great wine tasting, food-and-wine pairings, and high tea; the Pierneef à La Motte restaurant on the estate is regularly voted one of the country's top 20. The farm also has a wonderful collection of Jacob Hendrik Pierneef's art; view his iconic landscapes in the gallery. But don't get too sidetracked—the wine is excellent as well. The Pierneef Collection is the farm's premium range, and the Shiraz Viognier blend is being snapped up for its whiffs of dark chocolate, smoked beef, black cherry, and blackberry. The estate's Sauvignon Blanc is also outstanding. ✉ *R45 (Main Rd.)* ☎ *021/876–8000* ⊕ *www.la-motte.com* ☜ *Tastings R50, cellar tour and tasting R70* ☉ *Restaurant, museum, and farm shop closed Mon.*

La Petite Ferme. You'll have to phone ahead to arrange a tasting here, but it's worth it, because then you'll know what to have with your lunch if you decide to dine here. True to its name, this is a small estate producing just enough wine for the restaurant and to keep its faithful customers happy. Try the full-bodied, barrel-fermented Chardonnay or the Merlot, which scoops up awards year after year. The Verdict, a Cape-style blend, is also a crowd-pleaser. ✉ *R45 (Franschhoek Pass Rd.)* ☎ *021/876–3016 Ext. 8* ⊕ *www.lapetiteferme.co.za.*

Mont Rochelle. This picture-pretty estate has one of the best views in the valley. Mont Rochelle, owned by Sir Richard Branson, boasts more than 90 acres of vineyard, and the wines produced here are excellent. If the sun is shining, consider a picnic at the vineyards. You can order wine to accompany your picnic, or visit the tasting center and sample a variety of Mont Rochelle wines—try the Mont Rochelle Syrah and the signature Miko Chardonnay. If you have the time, take a tour of the 150-year-old cellar, which was originally a fruit-packing shed. For relaxed and formal dining, the hotel has two restaurants: the Country

Kitchen, which is the perfect place for a light lunch or relaxed dinner, and Miko, a contemporary gourmet restaurant, where you can enjoy a cocktail at sunset or an intimate meal. ✉ *Dassenberg Rd.* ☎ *011/325–4405* 🌐 *www.montrochelle.co.za* 🎫 *Tastings R35, cellar tours free.*

Plaisir de Merle. The name means "Pleasure of the Blackbird" and has its origins with the original French owners of the farm. This huge estate is the showpiece of Distell, a big wine and spirit producer. With its innovative architecture and conservation area, it truly feels different from the ubiquitous oak-and-gable wineries that you see all over the Cape. But forget all the frills—it really is about the wine. Don't miss the full-bodied barrel-fermented Chardonnay, which spends nine months in the barrel developing its lovely rich and layered flavor. The farm's flagship wine is the Grand Plaisir, a complex red blend; the 2010 vintage is currently available. When tasting, look out for flavors of sweet ripe plums, oak with hints of tobacco, vanilla, and cedar. ✉ *R45, Simondium* ☎ *021/874–1071, 021/874–1072* 🌐 *www.plaisirdemerle.co.za* 🎫 *Tasting and food pairing R90, cellar tour with tastings R120* 🕒 *Closed Good Friday, Christmas Day, and New Year's Day.*

Solms-Delta. In 2002 neuroscience professor Mark Solms took charge of Delta wine estate and set about altering wine-making traditions in the region; the grapes grown at Solms-Delta are French, but the technique used is from ancient Greece. This process is called desiccation: grapes are clamped on the vine, cutting off the flow of nutrients, leading to dehydrated fruit with intense flavor. The estate produces three ranges: the Lifestyle, Heritage, and Terroir collections. On the farm you can also visit the Museum van de Caab, where you'll learn the story of the farm and the fascinating history of the Cape. Produce from the estate's 5-acre garden of *veldkos* (indigenous edible plants) is used in Fyndraai Restaurant, which serves traditional Cape cuisine with strong European and Cape Malay influences. If you'd prefer an informal lunch, you can opt to picnic on the grounds. ✉ *Delta Rd., off R45* ☎ *021/874–3937* 🌐 *www.solms-delta.co.za* 🎫 *Tastings Lifestyle Collection R25, Heritage collection R50, Terroir collection R100.*

WHERE TO EAT

$$$$ ECLECTIC FAMILY

🍴 **Bread & Wine Vineyard Restaurant.** This rustic restaurant on Môreson Farm has won numerous accolades for its food and is a great place to stop for lunch on the Wine Tram route. The menu changes often, and on a whim, but you can expect dishes like butter roasted kingklop with chicken wing confit and twice-cooked Boschendal Chuck with mushroom, garlic, and potato. **Known for:** local and seasonal produce; charcuterie; comfort food. [$] *Average main: R360* ✉ *Môreson Farm, Happy Valley Rd.* ☎ *021/876–3692* 🌐 *www.moreson.co.za* 🕒 *No dinner.*

$$$$ ECLECTIC Fodor's Choice ★

🍴 **Haute Cabrière.** Try to reserve a window table for views across the vine-clad valley at this restaurant atop a working winery built into the mountainside. The menu is distinctly South African but rooted in French techniques, with dishes like a Pinot Noir barrel-smoked trout with Huguenot cheese sauce or grilled line fish with Bombay potatoes and sweet curry sauce. **Known for:** tasting menu; local ingredients; wine pairings. [$] *Average main: R265* ✉ *Franschhoek Pass Rd. (R45)*

☎ *021/876–3688* 🌐 *www.cabriere.co.za* ⏲ *Closed Mon. and for a period during winter. No dinner Sun.*

$$ INDIAN 🍴 **Marigold.** Located in the Heritage Square along Franschhoek's bustling main street, Marigold offers classic Indian cuisine in the center of town. The menu features a range of fragrant dishes from all-time favorites like butter chicken to lesser-known (but no less delicious) dishes like *tamatar machli* (marinated fish cooked in a tomato gravy and Indian spices). **Known for:** chef Vanie Padayachee (formerly of Le Quartier Francais); polished interior; lovely courtyard. [$] *Average main: R140* ✉ *Heritage Sq., 9 Hueguenot St.* ☎ *021/876–8970* 🌐 *www.marigoldfranschhoek.com.*

$$$ INTERNATIONAL 🍴 **Miko.** Miko is a contemporary fine-dining restaurant with seating indoors and out, offering spectacular views of the Franschhoek valley and mountains. The menu consists of dishes like gluwhein marinated trout with beetroot puree or beef fillet encrusted with basil and marrow, and everything is made with local, seasonal produce. **Known for:** quirky decor; global South African fare; inventive desserts. [$] *Average main: R195* ✉ *Dassenberg Rd.* ☎ *011/325–4405* 🌐 *www.montrochelle.co.za* ⏲ *No dinner Sun.*

$ BAKERY 🍴 **Ou Meul Farmstall.** This rustic bakery has become well known for its savory pies, fresh baked goods, Bootleggers coffee, and an assortment of goods such as rusks (South African biscuits), sun hats, and soaps. You can also get excellent food from the café, including salads and sandwiches, which can be eaten on the front porch. **Known for:** coffee; breakfast. [$] *Average main: R55* ✉ *Portion 8 of farm Tonis Fontyn, R45 (Franschhoek Rd.), Groot Drakenstein Handelshuis, Simondium.*

$$$$ ECLECTIC 🍴 **The Restaurant at Grande Provence.** The chic and industrial decor of The Restaurant at Grande Provence is a bold contrast to the old-world charm of whitewashed Huguenot architecture: high-back white leather chairs, blue-gray walls, steel doors that open onto a sculpture garden, and skylights make for a striking setting at this restaurant. Starters include a wild porcini and salt-cured foie gras mousse and risotto of seared scallop with barbecue langoustine. **Known for:** exceptional service; formal dining; elaborately creative meals. [$] *Average main: R725* ✉ *Grande Provence, off R45* ☎ *021/876–8600* 🌐 *www.grandeprovence.co.za.*

$$$ ECLECTIC 🍴 **Reuben's.** Reuben cooks food he would like to eat, and so, it seems, would everyone else. For starters, consider the chili-salted squid with grapefruit, mint, and pineapple, or peppered springbok steak with honey parsnip, beets and smoked mushroom crème. **Known for:** chef Reuben Riffel; local favorite; globally inspired fare. [$] *Average main: R179* ✉ *2 Daniel Hugo St.* ☎ *021/876–3772* 🌐 *www.reubens.co.za.*

$$$ SOUTH AFRICAN Fodor's Choice ★ 🍴 **The Werf Restaurant.** Set in the manor house of one of the oldest wine farms in the country, The Werf does an excellent job at serving refined farm-to-table meals. The restaurant has an old Cape Dutch feel with a cozy interior and an old wooden table at the entrance, reminiscent of a traditional Afrikaans farmhouse. **Known for:** chef Christiaan Campbell; farm-sourced ingredients; rustic setting; friendly service. [$] *Average main: R160* ✉ *R310 (Pniel Rd.), Groot Drakenstein* ☎ *021/870–4207* 🌐 *www.boschendal.com* ⏲ *Closed Sun. and Mon.*

WHERE TO STAY

$$$$ ⛶ **Akademie Boutique Hotel.** With eight individually designed suites hid-
B&B/INN   den on a leafy street in the town of Franschhoek, this peaceful and mod-
Fodor's Choice   ern 19th-century Cape Dutch house is one of the area's best-kept secrets.
★   **Pros:** rooms are unique and beautifully designed; lovely courtyard.
Cons: must book far in advance. $ *Rooms from: R6000* ✉ *5 Akademie St.* ☎ *082/517–0405* ⊕ *www.aka.co.za* ⤳ *8 rooms* ⎟⊙⎟ *Breakfast.*

$ ⛶ **Le Ballon Rouge.** If you fancy being in the heart of the village, Le
B&B/INN   Ballon Rouge makes a good base: here you're just a five-minute walk
from galleries, restaurants, and the general buzz. **Pros:** central location;
personal and attentive service; airport shuttle can be arranged. **Cons:**
few rooms available; children under 12 not allowed. $ *Rooms from:
R1100* ✉ *7 Reservoir St.* ☎ *021/876–2651* ⊕ *www.ballonrouge.co.za*
⤳ *10 rooms* ⎟⊙⎟ *Breakfast.*

$$$$ ⛶ **Leeu Estates.** The stunning flagship property of the Leeu Collection
B&B/INN   (which also includes Leeu House), this luxurious and sprawling retreat
has stunning views of the mountains and vineyards of the Franschhoek
Valley. **Pros:** stunning views; incredible spa; wine tasting on-site.
Cons: outside of the town. $ *Rooms from: R9900* ✉ *Dassenberg Rd.*
☎ *021/492–2222* ⊕ *www.leeucollection.com/leeu-estates* ⤳ *17 rooms*
⎟⊙⎟ *Breakfast.*

$$$$ ⛶ **Leeu House.** Although this contemporary and luxurious guesthouse
B&B/INN   is located on the main street in the middle of town, it's so tranquil,
you'd think it was in the countryside. **Pros:** intimate setting; rooms
are beautifully designed; stunning pool area. **Cons:** spa and gym are
located a short drive away. $ *Rooms from: R6700* ✉ *12 Huguenot Rd.*
☎ *021/492–2221* ⊕ *www.leeucollection.com/leeu-house* ⤳ *12 rooms*
⎟⊙⎟ *Breakfast.*

$$$$ ⛶ **The Owner's Cottage.** You know you're in good company at the under-
B&B/INN   stated and elegant Owner's Cottage on Grande Provence wine estate
when the visitors' book includes Jude Law and British royals Sophie
and Prince Edward. **Pros:** you'll be made to feel right at home; close
to Franschhoek action but far enough to escape; lovely pool. **Cons:**
some people don't like the smell of thatch; unless you rent the whole
house, you'll have to share it with other guests. $ *Rooms from: R6000*
✉ *Grand Provence, off R45* ☎ *021/876–8600* ⊕ *www.grandeprovence.
co.za* ⤳ *5 rooms* ⎟⊙⎟ *Breakfast.*

PAARL

21 km (13 miles) northwest of Franschhoek.

Paarl takes its name from the granite domes of Paarl Mountain, which
looms above the town—*paarl* is Dutch for "pearl." The first farmers
settled here in 1687, two years after the founding of Stellenbosch. The
town has its fair share of historic homes and estates, but it lacks the
charm of its distinguished neighbor simply because it's so spread out.
Main Street, the town's oak-lined thoroughfare, extends some 11 km (7
miles) along the western bank of the Berg River. You can gain a good
sense of the town's history on a drive along this lovely street.

GETTING HERE AND AROUND
As in the rest of the area, driving yourself is your best option in and around Paarl. Estates are spread so there is distance between them, and to really get the best out of the area you do need your own wheels.

VISITOR INFORMATION
Contacts Paarl Visitor Information Center. ⊠ *216 Main St.* ☎ *021/872–4842* ⊕ *www.paarlonline.com.*

EXPLORING
Most visitors to Paarl drive down the town's main street, take in the historic buildings, and then head off to the Cape Winelands, golf estates, and restaurants. If you have the time, check out the Afrikaanse Taalmonument (Afrikaans Language Monument) and Jan Phillips Mountain Drive. For some excellent examples of Cape Dutch, Georgian, and Victorian homes, head to Zeederberg Square, a grassy park on Main Street just past the Paarl Tourism Bureau.

Afrikaanse Taalmonument (*Afrikaans Language Monument*). The towering Afrikaanse Taalmonument, set high on a hill overlooking Paarl, is a fascinating step back into the past. It was designed by architect Jan van Wijk and built with Paarl granite and cement. The rising curve of the main pillar represents the growth and potential of Afrikaans. When it was unveiled in 1975, the monument was as much a gesture of political victory as it was a paean to the Afrikaans language. Ironically, the monument—although built during apartheid—gives recognition to all the diverse origins of Afrikaans (from Africa, Europe, and Asia) and has even become a symbol for reconciliation. In the new South Africa, Afrikaans is one of 11 official languages and although it is gradually coming under threat, attempts are being made to ensure that the rich culture isn't lost. The view from the top of the hill is incredible, taking in Table Mountain, False Bay, Paarl Valley, and the various mountain ranges of the Winelands. ■TIP→ **You can buy a picnic basket at the monument's restaurant (or bring your own) and find a pretty spot to enjoy the wonderful view; baskets are crammed with cold meats, salad, cheese, breads, fresh fruit, and something sweet.** A short, paved walking trail leads around the hillside past impressive fynbos specimens, particularly proteas. After the N1 bridge, a sign on your right points the way to the monument. ⊠ *Afrikaanse Taalmonument Rd.* ☎ *021/863–0543* ⊠ *R30.*

Afrikaanse Taalmuseum (*Afrikaans Language Museum*). It was from the Gideon Malherbe House, now the Afrikaanse Taalmuseum, that the Society of True Afrikaners launched its campaign in 1875 to gain widespread acceptance for Afrikaans, hitherto considered a sort of inferior kitchen Dutch. To get here from the Paarl Museum, walk about 200 yards along Pastorie Street. ⊠ *11 Pastorie Ave.* ☎ *021/872–3441* ⊕ *www.taalmuseum.co.za* ⊠ *R20.*

Bain's Kloof Pass Road. The Bain's Kloof Pass Road, built by engineer Andrew Geddes Bain and opened in 1853, links Wellington to Ceres and Worcester. The road (an extension of the R303 from Paarl through Wellington) winds north from Wellington, through the Hawekwa Mountains, revealing breathtaking views across the valley below. On a clear day you can see as far as the coast. The road has a good tar surface, but

Paarl Wine Route

Wineries here are spread far apart, so you might want to select only a couple or take a whole day to taste at leisure. Start in Paarl, home to the impressive **KWV**, with cellars covering 55 acres and a wide selection of wines.

Along R301/303. On its way to Franschhoek, the R301/303 runs past **Avondale Wine**, a relatively new farm with a state-of-the-art cellar, a gorgeous rose garden, and excellent wines.

Between R44 and R45. On your way from Franschhoek to Paarl, take a quick detour down the Simondium Road to **Backsberg** and, a bit farther, **Glen Carlou**. Backsberg has more going on than Glen Carlou, but they both have wines that are worth tasting and buying. Be sure to make time to visit Babylonstoren, just

beyond Glen Carlou, where you could easily spend a day. Continue on, and turn right on the R44. At a four-way stop, turn right onto the R101 and cross over the N1. Follow the goat signs to Suid-Agter-Paarl Road and Fairview.

Along Suid-Agter-Paarl and Noord-Agter-Paarl roads. Fairview is as famous for its goats and cheese as it is for its wines. Leave yourself plenty of time here. From Fairview, turn right onto the Suid-Agter-Paarl Road and make your way to **Landskroon**, known for full-bodied reds. Turn right on the R44 and, after about 10 km (6 miles), right onto the WR8 (Noord-Agter-Paarl Road), and then right again to **Rhebokskloof Private Cellar**. If you continue on the R44 toward Wellington, you'll pass Nelson Wine Estate (aka Nelson's Creek) on your left.

unlike many Western Cape passes, Bain's Kloof has not been widened much since it was built, so take your time and enjoy the views. There are places where you can park and walk down to lovely, refreshing mountain pools—great on a hot summer's day. ⊠ *Paarl.*

Jan Phillips Mountain Drive. Halfway down the hill from the Afrikaans Language Monument is a turnoff onto a dirt road and a sign for the Paarl Mountain Nature Reserve. The dirt road is Jan Phillips Mountain Drive, which runs 11 km (7 miles) along the mountainside, offering tremendous views over the valley. Along the way it passes the **Mill Water Wildflower Garden** and the starting points for several trails, including hikes up to the great granite domes of Paarl Mountain. The dirt road rejoins Main Street at the far end of Paarl. ⊠ *Paarl.*

Paarl Museum. Main Street North doglegs to the right at Lady Grey Street before continuing as Main Street South. On your left, the Paarl Museum, formerly the Oude Pastorie, occupies a gorgeous Cape Dutch home built as a parsonage in 1787. In fact, the building itself is of more interest than the collection, which includes odds and ends such as silver, glass, and kitchen utensils, donated by local families. ⊠ *303 Main St.* ☏ *021/872–2651* ⊠ *R10.*

WINERIES
TOP ATTRACTIONS

Avondale Wine. Although the farm was established as early as 1693, current owners Johnny and Ginny Grieve have done some serious reorganizing in the vineyards and built a state-of-the-art cellar, which is dug into a dry riverbed. Avondale started producing wines only in 1999, making it one of the newer kids on the block. No matter. The winery hit the ground running, and its wines win one award after another. The reds are especially good, and the intense Paarl summers result in full-bodied grapes that deliver knockout flavors. Be sure to try the Armilla Blanc de Blanc 2009, a rich wine with a balance of hazelnut bread, fresh quince, and gardenia flavors. The Grieves are also farming as biodynamically as possible, and Avondale is now registered as biodiversity-compliant by South African authorities. Great care is taken to maintain top-quality soil, and no pesticides or herbicides are used. If you're interested in the wine-making process, book an Eco Wine Safari (R250) and visit Avondale's state-of-the-art gravity-flow cellar, constructed three stories underground. Many farms have absent owners, but the Grieve family takes a hands-on approach here. The casually dressed guy behind the wine-tasting counter is, in all likelihood, the owner. ✉ *Lustigan Rd., off R301* ☎ *021/863–1976* ⊕ *www.avondalewine.co.za* 🍷 *Tastings R50.*

FAMILY **Fairview.** This is one of the few wineries that are good for families. Children get a kick out of seeing peacocks roaming the grounds and goats clambering up a spiral staircase into a goat tower. In fact, Fairview produces a superb line of goat cheeses and olive oil, all of which you can taste. But don't let Fairview's sideshows color your judgment about the wines. Charles Back is one of the most successful and innovative winemakers in the Cape, and the estate's wines are top-drawer and often surprising. Back doesn't stick to the tried-and-true Cape varietals. The Fairview Eenzaamheid 2014 is excellent, as is the 2015 La Beryl Blanc. The winery also makes creative use of the farm's many Rhône varieties. Perhaps it's just because the pun was irresistible, but (as claimed by the label) goats are sent into the vineyard to personally select grapes for the Goats-do-Roam, which is indeed like a young Côtes du Rhône (infuriating French winemakers). The cheese at Fairview is not to be missed. Visit the Vineyard Cheesery, the first carbon-neutral cheesery on the African continent, and taste the Roydon Camembert. If you care to linger, you can have a light meal and freshly baked bread at the Goatshed restaurant for around R100. ✉ *WR3, off R101 (Suid-Agter-Paarl Rd.)* ☎ *021/863–2450* ⊕ *www.fairview.co.za* 🍷 *Wine-and-cheese tastings R40, cheese tastings R20, Beryl Back Master Tasting R80.*

Spice Route Winery. Charles Back, the owner of Fairview, has bought the neighboring farm in Paarl. The Spice Route produces deep-flavored wines, using mostly bush vines (untrellised vines). This practice, which is uncommon outside of South Africa, leads to fruit with great flavor intensity but lower volumes. Try the Spice Route Chakalaka 2014, a signature Swartland blend, which has clove and savory notes. The farm's flagship wine, Malabar, is produced in a separate cellar where the fruit is sorted by hand to ensure top quality. There is good reason to spend an entire day on the estate: artisan shops include Barley & Biltong

Emporium; DV Café, where they roast their own small batches of coffee; and the Cape Brewing Company, which offers craft beer tasting. At the Grapperia, you can taste grappa and schnapps made on-site with pizzas and charcuterie. Bertus Basson at Spice Route is a great place to enjoy the estate wines with a gourmet lunch under the trees. ⊠ *Suider-Agter-Paarl Rd., off R44* ☏ *021/863–5200* ⊕ *www.spiceroutewines.co.za* ⊠ *Tastings R50 for Spice Route wines, R30 for CBC beers.*

WORTH NOTING

FAMILY **Backsberg.** Framed by the mountains of the Simonsberg, this lovely estate is run by the Back family, well known for producing great wines of good value. Backsberg has a comprehensive range of red and white wines and a very fine brandy made from Chenin Blanc. Among the wines to look out for are Backsberg Family Reserve White 2016 and the Backsberg Family Reserve Red 2015. It also produces five kosher wines that are palatable: an unwooded Chardonnay, a Merlot, a Kiddush, a sparking MCC Brut, and a Pinotage. The restaurant does a lamb spit every Sunday, so you can taste some excellent wines before digging in to a typical South African meal, or enjoy a picnic under the trees. The estate has guided cellar tours. Concerned about climate change and the environment, the Back family has put measures in place to reduce the farm's carbon footprint. They've done a good job, and Backsberg is the first carbon-neutral wine estate in South Africa. Here's hoping others will soon follow suit. ⊠ *WR1 (Simondium Rd.), between R44 and R45* ☏ *021/875–5141* ⊕ *www.backsberg.co.za* ⊠ *Tastings R20, cellar tours by appointment* ⊙ *Restaurant closed Mon. and Tues.*

Glen Carlou. What comes out of Glen Carlou is rather special. The Quartz Stone Chardonnay 2015 is exceptional, "The Welder" dessert wine is excellent, and the Gravel Quarry Cabernet 2012 is also remarkable. A unique feature of the estate is the Zen Fynbos Garden, a great place to relax after you've stocked up on some seriously good wines. You can always enjoy a meal at the restaurant; expect to pay around R300 for two courses. The menu changes seasonally, but you can expect dishes like goat cheese and Gorgonzola soufflé and roast pork belly with crisp crackling, celeriac, and apple puree. ⊠ *WR1 (Simondium Rd.), between R44 and R45, Klapmuts* ☏ *021/875–5528* ⊕ *www.glencarlou.co.za* ⊠ *Tastings R50.*

KWV. Short for Ko-operatieve Wijnbouwers Vereniging (Cooperative Winegrowers' Association), KWV regulated and controlled the Cape wine industry for decades. This is no longer the case, and KWV is seeking to redefine itself as a top wine and spirit producer. KWV has won numerous awards, including Best Producer at Veritas from 2011 to 2015. They also make some of the finest spirits, with the KWV 15-year-old winning the Best Brandy in the World at the 2016 International Spirits Challenge (ISC). KWV produces an enormous selection of excellent wines, and its cellars are some of the largest in the world, covering around 55 acres. Cellar tours here are very popular; among the highlights is the famous Cathedral Cellar, with a barrel-vaulted ceiling and giant vats carved with scenes from the history of Cape wine making. The tour ends with a tasting of two white wines, two red wines, a fortified wine, and a brandy. The new facility, House of Fire, is an old distillery, where you can learn all about KWV brandy (R170 per person). ⊠ *André du Toit Bldg., Kohler St.* ☏ *021/807–3007* ⊕ *www. kwv.co.za* ⌧ *Tastings, pairings, and cellar tours R40–R70.*

Landskroon. With a name meaning "crown of the land" in Afrikaans, this venerable estate, run by the ninth generation of the de Villiers family, produces a lovely Cabernet Sauvignon—with hints of spice and oak—that's up there with the best. Look out for the Paul de Villiers Wine Range. In particular, the 2014 Paul de Villiers Shiraz is deliciously fruity. For a little something to sip after a long, leisurely dinner, try the Cape Vintage (Port) 2012 —a dark, fortified wine with aromas of black prunes and tobacco. ⊠ *Suid-Agter-Paarl Rd., off R44, Suider Paarl* ☏ *021/863–1039* ⊕ *www.landskroonwines.com* ⌧ *Tastings free.*

Nabygelegen. Before you head up the spectacular Bain's Kloof Pass, do a quick detour to a quieter corner of the busy Winelands. Situated in the heart of the Bovlei upper valley outside Wellington, Nabygelegen is known for its handcrafted wines. Their motto is "good wine takes time," and they are dedicated to producing top-quality wine with concentrated flavors. Try the Seventeen Twelve 2014, with richness of black currant and plum overlaid with smoky tannins. Nabygelegen's Chenin Blanc 2008 and Snow Mountain Pinot Noir 2009 were served at Queen Elizabeth II's 60th jubilee lunch, earning the winery international acclaim. The tasting room, in the old forge—remember this would have been the old wagon route out of Cape Town—offers wine tastings. ⊠ *Bovlei Division Rd., Wellington* ☏ *021/873–7534* ⊕ *www. nabygelegen.co.za* ⌧ *Tastings R10; cellar tours by appointment only.*

Rhebokskloof Private Cellar. This winery sits at the head of a shallow valley, backed by hillsides covered with vines and fynbos. It's a lovely place for lunch on a sunny day, and you can also take horseback rides through the vineyards. The Victorian Restaurant serves à la carte meals and teas on an oak-shaded terrace overlooking the gardens and mountains. You can also order a picnic basket for two, brimming with fresh baguettes, cold meats, and delicious cheeses for around R185 per person excluding beverages (must be booked in advance). The Estate makes an excellent Shiraz, thanks to its unique terroir, which is composed of old decomposed granite soils. Other wines to look out for are the Pinotage, Chardonnay, and Chenin blanc. ⊠ *WR8* ☏ *021/869–8386* ⊕ *www.rhebokskloof.co.za* ⌧ *Tastings R20.*

Wellington Wines. Driving down Bain's Kloof Road, as you approach the initial slopes of Bain's Kloof, look out for the BOVLEI, the tasting room of Wellington Wines, on the right. Constructed in 1907 in traditional style, the building itself is not noteworthy, but it has a vast picture window offering a stupendous view of the undulating vineyards beyond. This winery celebrated its centennial in 2007, and its wines just keep getting better. Be sure to try the Centennial range Shiraz-Mourvèdre blend, which promises great things. With plenty of well-priced, good-quality wines to choose from, you likely won't go away empty-handed. ⊠ *Bain's Kloof Rd., Wellington* ☏ *021/873–1567* ⊕ *www.wellington-wines.com* ⌧ *Tastings vary in price.*

WHERE TO EAT

$$$$ ✕**Babel.** Set on the grounds of one of the Cape's oldest Dutch farms,
ECLECTIC Babel and the Babylonstoren boutique hotel are a vision in white sur-
Fodor'sChoice rounded by lush fruit and vegetable gardens with a gorgeous backdrop
★ of mountain views. Everything about this farm is stylish: the restaurant
is in a converted cow shed, and the menu includes inventive dishes
influenced by what is bountiful in the garden. **Known for:** bold flavors
and unusual combinations; spectacular farm setting. $ *Average main:
R225* ⊠ *Klapmuts Rd.* ☎ *021/863–3852* ⊕ *www.babylonstoren.com*
⊗ *No lunch Mon. and Tues. No dinner Sun.–Thurs.*

$$$ ✕**Bertus Basson at Spice Route.** Set on the Spice Route wine estate, Bertus
SOUTH AFRICAN Basson at Spice Route is one of the most acclaimed restaurants in the
FAMILY Paarl area. The menu at this casual eatery changes every two months
at the casual eatery, but you can always expect to find Tannie Hetta's
Apple Pie (his mom's recipe) and traditional dishes like lamb bobotie
with braised lamb, sambals, and yellow rice. **Known for:** South African
cuisine; summertime picnics; homemade apple pie. $ *Average main:
R160* ⊠ *Suid Agter Paarl Rd., Suid Agter* ☎ *021/863–5200.*

$$$$ ✕**Bosman's.** Set amid the heady opulence of the Grande Roche hotel,
ECLECTIC this elegant restaurant ranks as one of the country's finest. The food is
Fodor'sChoice classic international cuisine with an innovative spin, with dishes like
★ sweet-and-sour pickled Mozambican prawn with cauliflower mousse
and passion fruit coulis or oven-roasted sirloin with slow braised cele-
riac roots and pommes dauphines. **Known for:** Michelin-trained execu-
tive chef Roland Gorgosilich; decadent tasting menu; extraordinary
service; award-winning wine list. $ *Average main: R525* ⊠ *Grande
Roche, Plantasie St.* ☎ *021/863–5100* ⊕ *www.granderoche.com.*

$$$$ ✕**The Table at De Meye.** Set on De Meye wine farm, between Stellenbosch
SOUTH AFRICAN and Paarl, The Table is run by a husband-and-wife team tirelessly churn-
Fodor'sChoice ing out hearty, family-style dishes which are devised according to what's
★ seasonal or available from local producers that day. Meals are served
family-style: slow-cooked grass-fed beef flat rib, baked quince and gar-
den kale salad, and wood-fired sourdough loaf. **Known for:** outdoor
dining in summer; friendly service; hard-to-get reservation. $ *Average
main: R325* ⊠ *Muldersvlei, Old Paarl Rd., Stellenbosch* ☎ *072/696–
0530* ⊕ *www.thetablerestaurant.co.za* ⊗ *Closed Mon.–Thurs.*

$$$ ✕**Terra Mare.** Owner-run Terra Mare has become a favorite with locals
ECLECTIC and tourists alike, offering not just great freshly prepared meals and
affordable wine but a wonderful dining experience in a friendly and
laid-back setting. The owners produce opulent food with French, Italian, Afrikaans, and German influences; kudu fillet and chef Thabo salad
are favorites, as is the three-mushroom risotto. **Known for:** cozy atmosphere; tiramisu; friendly owners. $ *Average main: R170* ⊠ *90A Main
St.* ☎ *021/863–4805* ⊗ *Closed Sun.*

WHERE TO STAY

$$$$ 🏨**Babylonstoren.** Set on a 500-acre working farm that is one of the
HOTEL Cape's oldest, Babylonstoren is a bucolic farmhouse-chic lodging with
Fodor'sChoice a dozen lovingly renovated thatched roof cottages. **Pros:** option to har-
★ vest your own produce and enlist the help of a chef to prepare; five
additional rooms in the 17th-century manor house available on special

request; 8 acres of organic landscaped gardens to wander. **Cons:** in-cottage book selection dominated by Afrikaans titles. [$] *Rooms from: R4900* ✉ *45 Klapmuts Rd., Klapmuts* ☎ *021/863–3852* 🌐 *www.babylonstoren.com* 🛏 *22 rooms* 🍴 *Breakfast.*

$$$$ B&B/INN Fodor's Choice ★ 🏨 **Bartholomeus Klip Farmhouse.** This Victorian guesthouse on a nature reserve and working farm offers luxurious accommodations and excellent food in the middle of 17,000 acres of rare renosterveld scrubland, home to the endangered geometric tortoise. **Pros:** separate house available for self-catering families; very tranquil setting close to wine farms and small towns; gobs of wildlife. **Cons:** may be a bit intimate for some, as all the rooms are in the manor house; this part of the Western Cape can get unbearably hot in summer. [$] *Rooms from: R8750* ✉ *Off the R44, near Bo-Hermon* ☎ *082/829–4131, 021/300–1113* 🌐 *www.bartholomeusklip.co.za* ⏲ *Closed July* 🛏 *5 rooms, 1 self-catering house (sleeps 8)* 🍴 *Some meals.*

$ B&B/INN 🏨 **De Leeuwenhof Estate.** Situated on 30 acres of farmland in the Klein Drakenstein area, De Leeuwenhof Estate promises a tranquil and intimate stay. **Pros:** exceptional service with a personal touch; air-conditioning in all rooms. **Cons:** TV reception is poor in some rooms; children over the age of two are charged as adults. [$] *Rooms from: R1450* ✉ *Sonstraal Rd.* ☎ *021/862–1384* 🌐 *www.deleeuwenhof.co.za* 🛏 *16 rooms* 🍴 *Breakfast.*

$ B&B/INN 🏨 **Diemersfontein Wine & Country Estate.** Built in the 19th century, this historic farmstead is set in a lush garden with rolling lawns and abundant roses and azalea bushes. **Pros:** lots to do, including fishing, horseback riding, wine tasting; lovely gardens; airport shuttle can be arranged. **Cons:** frequently used as wedding and conference venue so can get quite busy. [$] *Rooms from: R1399* ✉ *Jan van Riebeek Dr. (R301), Wellington* ☎ *021/861–5060 lodging, 021/864–5060 restaurant, 021/864–5050 winery* 🌐 *www.diemersfontein.co.za* 🛏 *30 rooms* 🍴 *Breakfast.*

$$$$ HOTEL Fodor's Choice ★ 🏨 **Grande Roche.** Part of the Small Luxury Hotels of the World Collection, this establishment can stake a claim to being one of the best hotels in South Africa. **Pros:** estate declared a national monument in 1993; award-winning cuisine. **Cons:** not within easy walking distance of town; rarefied atmosphere doesn't suit everybody. [$] *Rooms from: R5130* ✉ *Plantasie Str.* ☎ *021/863–5100* 🌐 *www.granderoche.com* 🛏 *28 suites* 🍴 *Breakfast.*

$ B&B/INN 🏨 **Lemoenkloof Guest House.** This classic guesthouse on the Paarl Wine Route is run by owners Dion and Hanlie Naude, who are prepared to go the extra mile to make your stay a happy one. **Pros:** walk-in guests are welcome until 11 pm; very reasonable rates and weekend specials; 10-minute drive from Pearl Valley and Boschenmeer golf courses. **Cons:** no room service. [$] *Rooms from: R800* ✉ *396A Main St.* ☎ *021/872–7520, 021/872–3782* 🌐 *www.lemoenkloof.co.za* 🛏 *31 rooms* 🍴 *Breakfast.*

SPORTS AND THE OUTDOORS

BALLOONING

Wineland Ballooning. This company makes one-hour flights over the Winelands every morning from about end of November through April, weather permitting. The balloon holds a maximum of six passengers, and the trip costs about R3,900 per person. After the flight there's a Champagne breakfast at the Grand Roche. ☎ *021/863–3192, 083/983–4687* ⊕ *www.kapinfo.com.*

GOLF

Boschenmeer Golf Club. This picturesque 18-hole golf course has stunning mountain views. The course is covered with trees and dotted with water hazards. There's a pro shop, driving range, and terrace that looks out over the course. ✉ *848 Wemmershoek Rd.* ☎ *021/863–1140, 021/863–2828 pro shop* ⊕ *www.boschenmeergolf.co.za* ✉ *R520* ⅃ *18 holes, 6368 yards, par 72* ☞ *Facilities: driving range, putting green, pitching area, golf carts, caddies, rental clubs, golf academy/lessons, restaurant, bar.*

Pearl Valley Signature Golf Estate & Spa. In a breathtaking setting in the valley, the course, designed by Jack Nicklaus, has golfers in rapture. Anyone can play a round of golf, but the clubhouse, pool, and spa are for members only. ✉ *R301* ☎ *021/867–8000* ⊕ *pearlvalley.co.za* ✉ *R795* ⅃ *18 holes, 6654 yards, par 72* ☞ *Facilities: driving range, putting green, golf carts, rental clubs, golf academy/lessons, restaurant, bar.*

HORSEBACK RIDING

Wine Valley Horse Trails. Michelle Mazurkiewicz guides scenic rides around the Rhebokskloof vineyards or up into the surrounding Paarl Mountain Nature Reserve. If horses aren't your thing, you can have fun on an all-terrain vehicle. It costs R450 for one hour on a horse or all-terrain vehicle. A two-hour ride will cost you R800, and half-day wine tasting on horseback costs R1300. ✉ *Rhebokskloof wine farm, WR8, off the R44* ☎ *083/226–8735, 021/869–8687* ⊕ *www.horsetrails-sa.co.za.*

BREEDE RIVER VALLEY

The upper and central part of the catchment of the Breede River extends over a large area. It's a beautiful part of the country, with a combination of fantastic mountain scenery, fabulous fynbos, pretty, bucolic farmlands, and small towns. A short drive over any one of the scenic mountain passes is sure to bring you into a secluded valley resplendent with the greens of spring, the grape-laden vines of summer, the myriad colors of autumn, or the snowcapped peaks and crisp misty mornings of winter.

A natural climatic combination of comparatively mild but wet winters followed by long, warm summers makes this area perfectly suited for the cultivation of deciduous fruit, especially viticulture. In the summer the intense sunshine allows the wine and table grapes to develop rich ruby colors. Virtually deprived of rain in summer, the vines nurture their precious crop, irrigated from the meandering Breede River and the huge Brandvlei dam, near Worcester.

GETTING HERE AND AROUND

Driving is definitely the way to go when exploring the Breede River valley, as it will give you the flexibility you need to discover interesting back roads or to linger at a lovely lunch spot. The roads in the Western

Cape are generally good. Although you might have to navigate some dirt roads, they tend to be graded regularly and are in fine condition.

The major car-rental agencies have offices in some of the smaller towns, but it's best to deal with the Cape Town offices. An alternative is to pick up a car in Stellenbosch. *For car-rental agencies, see Travel Smart.*

The best way to get to this area is to take the N1 from Cape Town past Paarl. You can either go through the Huguenot toll tunnel (around R29 per vehicle) or over the spectacular Bain's Kloof mountain pass to Worcester. From there take the R60 to Robertson and Montagu.

Greyhound, Intercape Mainliner, and Translux provide daily bus service throughout most of the Western Cape, stopping at bigger towns such as Worcester and Robertson on their way upcountry. Although each company's timetable varies, most have approximately four trips a day from Cape Town. From Cape Town it takes about 1½ hours to Worcester and about 2 hours to Robertson. A one-way trip to Worcester costs around R325, and the drop-off spot is a service station on the side of the N1. It is a little way out of town, but shuttle buses will take you into town for a small fee. *For detailed information about traveling by bus, see Bus Travel in Travel Smart.*

TOURS

Instead of big tour companies, there are a couple of individual guides operating in Breede River towns. Because the guides are usually from the area, they provide rare insights about the towns. Your best bet is to ask at local tourism offices for names and numbers. If you wish to hike in the Montagu Mountain Reserve, where trails are not well marked, go with someone familiar with the area; ask at the local tourism office for names of people to hike with. There's a strenuous hike of just over 15 km (9 miles) and an easier one of just over 11 km (7 miles). Best times to go are in spring or autumn, as it can get very hot in summer.

TULBAGH

60 km (37 miles) north of Paarl.

Founded in 1743, the town of Tulbagh is nestled in a secluded valley bound by the Witzenberg and Groot Winterhoek mountains. A devastating earthquake in September 1969 shook the city and destroyed many of the original facades of the historic town. After this disaster, well-known South African architect Gawie Fagan—together with his wife, Gwen—helped rebuild the buildings in the style of an 1860s hamlet, and the result is a photographer's paradise. The 32 buildings that make up Church Street were all declared national monuments and constitute the largest concentration of national monuments in one street in South Africa. It's not all white gables and brass doorknobs, however. The workaday side of town is quite dreary, and unemployment is rife.

GETTING HERE AND AROUND

You won't be able to experience the beauty of this area unless you can explore on your own terms, so be sure to rent a car. If you want to travel on the back routes, do some asking around first—you might need a 4x4 in winter after heavy rains, when the gravel roads become very slippery.

VISITOR INFORMATION

Contacts Tulbagh Tourism. ⊠ *4 Church St.* ☎ *023/230–1375* ⊕ *www.tulbagh-tourism.co.za.*

EXPLORING

Church Street. Much of the town is unlovely, having simply been rebuilt, often prefab style, on old foundations, but the real attraction of Tulbagh is Church Street, parallel to the main Van der Stel Street, where each of the 32 buildings was restored to its original form and subsequently declared a national monument. ⊠ *Tulbagh.*

De Oude Drostdy Museum. Around 4 km (2½ miles) out of town, set on high ground commensurate with its status, is the majestic De Oude Drostdy Museum. Built by architect Louis Thibault in 1804, the structure was badly damaged by fire in 1934 and later by the 1969 quake, but it has been carefully restored and is a fine example of neoclassical architecture. The building now houses an impressive collection of antique furniture and artifacts. Look for the gramophone collection and the Dutch grandfather clock that has a picture of Amsterdam harbor painted on its face. As the original magistrate's house, the Drostdy had a cellar that served as the local jail; it's now used by Drostdy-Hof as their wine-tasting area. Linger and taste some of their flavorful and fruity wines. ⊠ *Winterhoek Rd.* ☎ *023/230–0203* ⊠ *Museum R10, museum and wine tasting R25.*

Oude Kerk (*Old Church*). The Oude Kerk museum stands at the entrance to Church Street and is the logical departure point for a self-guided tour of the area, which is well marked. The church has been extensively restored and has an interesting collection of artifacts from the area, including carvings made by Boer prisoners of war. A ticket includes admission to another two buildings on Church Street, which operate as annexes of the main museum. These show a practical history of events before, during, and after the quake. The buildings have been painstakingly reconstructed. ⊠ *21 Church St.* ☎ *023/230–1041* ⊠ *R15.*

Twee Jonge Gezellen. If you stand in front of the church on Van der Stel Street, you will see a wine barrel indicating the road to Twee Jonge Gezellen estate, which is about 8 km (5 miles) from town. The House of Krone at Twee Jonge Gezellen specializes in the production of MCC sparkling wine. One of the finest and oldest wineries in the area, it's best known for its fantastic Cap Classique—Krone Borealis Vintage Cuvée Brut. But many Capetonians are also familiar with the tried and trusted still wine, Krone Chardonnay Pinot Noir (72% Chardonnay, 26% Pinot Noir), a crisp and elegant wine that is light pink in color. After the farm underwent a renovation, they released the Phoenix Prestige Cuvée, a stunning, complex MCC produced in a snazzy bottle imported from France. ⊠ *Twee Jonge Gezellen Rd.* ☎ *023/230–0680* ⊕ *www.tweejongegezellen.co.za* ⊠ *Tastings free.*

OFF THE BEATEN PATH

Waverley Hills Estate. If you're looking for a day trip, Waverley Hills Estate is a 20-minute drive from Tulbagh. This 320-acre estate is known for its organic wines with robust fynbos characteristics. ⊠ *Off R46, between Tulbagh and Ceres, Wolseley* ☎ *023/231–0002* ⊕ *www.waverleyhills.co.za* ⊘ *Closed Mon. No dinner Sat.–Tues. and Thurs.*

WHERE TO EAT

$$ SOUTH AFRICAN

🍴 **Olive Terrace Bistro & Lounge Bar.** At the Tulbagh Hotel, the Olive Terrace Bistro serves local wines and tasty food on a pretty terrace, shaded by a white karee tree for warm summer days, and in a cozy indoor dining area with a view of the snow-covered mountains. The à la carte menu features South African dishes made with locally sourced fresh produce and homemade breads, jams, and chutneys, and all eggs are free-range. **Known for:** decadent breakfasts; hearty sandwiches; cozy atmosphere. [$] *Average main: R100* ✉ *Tulbagh Hotel, 22 Van der Stel St.* ☎ *023/230–0071* 🌐 *tulbaghhotel.co.za/dining.*

$$ ECLECTIC

🍴 **Readers.** The historic residence makes a cozy setting for this restaurant with consistently high-quality food and service. The innovative fare offers sophisticated contrasts with simple presentation and a small seasonal menu that changes daily. **Known for:** local flavors, like wildebeest; homemade ice cream; well-priced wine list. [$] *Average main: R115* ✉ *12 Church St.* ☎ *023/230–0087, 082/894–0932* 🌐 *www.readersrestaurant.co.za* ⏲ *Closed Tues. and Aug.*

WHERE TO STAY

$$ B&B/INN

🏨 **Rijk's Country House.** This country house is on the outskirts of the village, on a ridge overlooking a dam where you can enjoy sweeping views of the surrounding mountains. **Pros:** tranquil and remote location; fine dining on your doorstep. **Cons:** quite far from bigger towns; pool, dam, and river not fenced, so kids need to be under adult supervision at all times. [$] *Rooms from: R1780* ✉ *Van Der Stel Extension, Winterhoek Rd.* ☎ *023/230–1006* 🌐 *www.rijkscountryhouse.co.za* 🛏 *12 rooms* 🍽 *Breakfast.*

$ B&B/INN

🏨 **Tulbagh Country Guest House & Cape Dutch Quarters.** This 200-year-old manor house, on historic Church Street, offers authentic Cape Dutch living with modern amenities. **Pros:** in the heart of Tulbagh; stunning manor house; swimming pool. **Cons:** the guesthouse is small, so you will be aware of other guests. [$] *Rooms from: R900* ✉ *24 Church St.* ☎ *023/230–1171* 🌐 *www.cdq.co.za* 🛏 *10 rooms* 🍽 *Breakfast.*

WORCESTER

45 km (28 miles) southeast of Tulbagh; 50 km (31 miles) east of Paarl.

You're unlikely to linger in Worcester, by far the largest town in the Breede River valley. It's often termed the region's capital by locals, and with good cause. Much of the town's burgeoning commerce and industry is connected to agriculture—viticulture, in particular. But the town itself is unexciting and serves as a pit stop for prettier inland destinations. Pause to visit the Karoo Desert National Botanical Garden or pop in at the Worcester Museum.

GETTING HERE AND AROUND

Worcester is east of Paarl on the N1, on the other side of the du Toits Kloof Pass or tunnel, an 80-minute drive from Cape Town. Renting a car is the only way to get around.

Contacts **Worcester Tourism Association.** ✉ *60 Fairburn St.* ☎ *023/342–6244* ⊕ *www.worcestertourism.com.*

EXPLORING

Karoo Desert National Botanical Garden. With several hundred species of indigenous flora, including succulents, bulbs, aloes, and trees, the Karoo Desert National Botanical Garden has been billed as one of the most important such collections in the world. The Braille Garden is geared toward the visually impaired. If you phone ahead, you can arrange to be taken on a guided tour through the gardens and the collection houses for around R120 per person (inclusive of entrance fee). Unfortunately, they won't do the tour unless there are at least seven people. The garden lies on the opposite side of the N1 highway from the town of Worcester but is easy to find if you follow the signs eastward from the last set of traffic lights on High Street. Follow the road from the entrance to the garden to the main parking area, the starting point of three clearly marked walks. ✉ *Roux Rd.* ☎ *023/347–0785* 🗓 *June.–Oct. R20, Nov.–May R10.*

FAMILY **Worcester Museum.** A welcome change from dusty artifacts in glass cases, this fascinating museum is actually a collection of original buildings from the area that have been re-erected around a working farmyard. After a narrated slide show, venture into the farmyard and watch the museum staff, intent on keeping traditional skills alive, as they bake bread, twist tobacco, make horseshoes in a smithy, and distill *witblits* (directly translated it means "white lightning" because of the astonishing effect it has on you). The museum also has a shop where you can buy produce from the farmyard. They run bread-baking demonstrations, and you can do some coffee and witblits tastings as well. Considering that some witblits has an alcohol content of almost 80%, you might want to do that tasting first and then sober up with the coffee afterward. ✉ *Kleinplasie Agricultural Showgrounds, Robertson Rd.* ☎ *023/342–2226* ⊕ *www.worcestermuseum.org.za* 🗓 *R15.*

SPORTS AND THE OUTDOORS
RAFTING AND CANOEING
The Breede River has tiny rapids near Worcester, where it twists and turns between clumps of *palmiet* (river reeds) and overgrown banks.

River Rafters. Using two-person inflatables, River Rafters offers a one-day trip for R765 (R640 for children under 18). This is inclusive of two meals (breakfast and lunch) and transport can be arranged on request. ✉ *R43* ☎ *021/975–9727* ⊕ *www.riverrafters.co.za.*

Wildthing Adventures. Now part of the well-established Felix Unite river-rafting company, Wildthing Adventures runs river trips down the Breede. Enjoy a two-night stay at River Camp Round The Bend on the banks of the Breede River and head out each day to negotiate some rapids or drift lazily along, depending on the water levels. An all-inclusive two-day trip will cost around R1,900 (R1,100 for children under 12). Check their website, as prices change regularly. ✉ *Swellendam* ☎ *087/354–0578* ⊕ *www.wildthing.co.za.*

3

ROBERTSON

48 km (30 miles) southeast of Worcester.

Robertson was founded primarily to service the surrounding farms, and it retains its agricultural and industrial character. The town largely lives up to its mantra of "small town, big heart"—the townsfolk are welcoming and friendly, which makes up for the lack of action. Some effort has been made to beautify the town with tree-lined roads, and the town comes alive each year during two festivals: the Wacky Wine Weekend (⊕ *www.wackywineweekend.com*) in June and the Robertson Slow festival (⊕ *www.robertsonslow.com*) in August, which will also give you an insight into farming life. If, however, you're on your way to McGregor or Montagu, don't be in too much of a rush. There are some excellent—and underrated—wine farms in the area.

GETTING HERE AND AROUND

Robertson is less than a 30-minute drive from Worcester. Renting a car is the only way to get around in a reasonable amount of time.

VISITOR INFORMATION

Contacts Robertson Tourism Bureau. ⊠ *2 Reitz St.* ☎ *023/626–4437* ⊕ *www.robertsonr62.com.*

EXPLORING

Graham Beck Wines. Who needs French Champagne when you have top-class South African MCC at very affordable prices? The Robertson cellar of Graham Beck Wines, on the road between Worcester and Robertson, produces some very sophisticated wines. Winemaker Pieter Ferreira is known as Mr. Bubbles for his wonderful sparkling wines, which are so popular that the farm no longer produces any still wines (only MCCs). The iconic Cap Classique flagship, Cuvée Clive, is produced with Chardonnay grapes from the Robertson estate and with Pinot Noir fruit from the Graham Beck Stellenbosch estate. It is the undisputed favorite in the Cap Classique range. The other wine farm in the Graham Beck stable is the super-stylish Steenberg estate in Constantia, Cape Town. ⊠ *R60, about 10 km (6 miles) northwest of Robertson* ☎ *023/626–1214* ⊕ *www.grahambeckwines.com* ⊠ *Classic tastings free, MCC tasting R75, Delux MCC tasting R125.*

Rooiberg Winery. Capetonians in the know have long considered Rooiberg Winery, between Worcester and Robertson, one of the best value-for-the-money wineries in the area. The Pinotage was ranked in the top 10 Pinotages in SA 2016, and the Rooiberg, Shiraz, and Merlot are all award winners for good reason. ■TIP→ **The Bodega de Vinho restaurant serves light lunches and delectable pastries, making this a good place to stop for something to eat.** ⊠ *R60, about 10 km (6 miles) northwest of Robertson* ☎ *023/626–1663* ⊕ *www.rooiberg.co.za* ⊠ *Tastings free.*

Springfield Estate. Abrie Bruwer, winemaker and viticulturist at Springfield Estate, has a fan club, and for good reason. Quality is assured, and if the wine doesn't meet Bruwer's stringent standards, it isn't released. Although the Cabernet has its loyal following, this innovative estate is best known for its unusual approach to white wines, especially

Chardonnay. The Méthode Ancienne Chardonnay 2012 is made in the original Burgundy style, a technique that uses wild yeast and no fining/filtration. It has tropical fruit flavors, layered with lime and cream. The creamy Wild Yeast Chardonnay 2016, with its all-natural fermentation, is an unwooded version of the above and comes highly recommended. Another great white is the 2016 Special Cuvée. It originates from the estate's prime Sauvignon Blanc vineyard and has notes of passion fruit and nettle. Their latest release, Miss Lucy, an unusual white blend of Sauvignon Blanc, Semillon, and Pinot Gris, was created as an ode to the ocean. ✉ *R317, to Bonnievale* ☎ *023/626–3661* 🌐 *www.springfieldestate.com* 🎫 *Tastings free.*

3

FAMILY **Van Loveren Winery.** This winery between Robertson and Bonnievale produces around 60 wines, as well as whisky, brandy, and craft beers, so there's something to suit everybody's palate. In addition to sampling the extensive wines, be sure to visit the unusual grounds of this family-owned and family-run farm. An established garden of indigenous and exotic plants and trees surrounds a water fountain that supplies the entire farm. Weather permitting, instead of visiting the usual tasting room, sit out under the trees and have the various wines brought to you. It's very relaxed and friendly, and you may feel like part of the family before you know it. The tasting room offers 10 different tastings, including cheese and wine, chocolate and wine, and charcuterie and wine. There are even nonalcoholic tastings and a pairing for kids. As a broad-based black economic empowerment (BBBEE) deal, De Goree farm, which is 52% worker owned, signed a long-term grape-supply contract with Van Loveren Private Cellar. The farm has been profitable ever since, and Van Loveren Winery takes great pride in their involvement in this project. ✉ *Off R317* ✥ *15 km (9 miles) southeast of Robertson* ☎ *023/615–1505* 🌐 *www.vanloveren.co.za* 🎫 *Tastings R20–R55.*

WHERE TO EAT

$$$ SOUTH AFRICAN FAMILY 🍴 **Bosjes Kombuis.** The Bosjes farm, which has stunning views of the Slanghoek Mountains, has a small guesthouse and a restaurant, Bosjes Kombuis. The menu is small and simple, featuring rustic dishes that are big on flavor, like panfried sea bass with mussel and herb risotto and slow-braised lamb shank with garden vegetables. **Known for:** modern church on-site; beautiful farm setting. [$] *Average main: R165* ✉ *R43* ☎ *023/004–0496.*

EN ROUTE

On the R60 out of Robertson you can either take the clearly marked turnoff to McGregor, which snakes between vineyards and farms—a picture of bucolic charm—or continue on toward Montagu on the R62. Before reaching the latter, you'll pass through the unlovely agricultural town of Ashton. Keep left (don't turn off to Swellendam), and enter the short but spectacular **Cogman's Kloof Pass.** On either side of the pass, which runs in a river gorge, you can see the magnificent fold mountains, which are ultimately the source for Montagu's hot springs.

MCGREGOR

20 km (12 miles) south of Robertson.

Saved from development as a result of a planned mountain pass that never materialized, McGregor is the epitome of the sleepy country hollow, tucked away between the mountains, and is one of the best-preserved examples of a 19th-century Cape village. As you approach McGregor from Robertson, farmsteads give way to small cottages with distinctive red-painted doors and window frames. McGregor Wines, on the left, heralds your entry into the town with its thatch cottages in vernacular architecture.

McGregor has become popular with artists who have settled here permanently and with busy executives from Cape Town intent on getting away from it all. Frankly, this is an ideal place to do absolutely nothing, but you can take a leisurely stroll through the fynbos, watch birds from one of several blinds on the Heron Walk, or follow one of the hiking or mountain-bike trails if you are feeling more energetic. There is a great hiking trail across the Riviersonderend Mountains to Greyton.

GETTING HERE AND AROUND

McGregor is a 10- to 15-minute drive from Robertson.

EXPLORING

FAMILY **Esletjiesrus Donkey Sanctuary.** About 15 km (9½ miles) outside Robertson on the road to the village of McGregor, Esletjiesrus Donkey Sanctuary provides a place of safety for neglected and abused donkeys and is a great place to visit with kids. They can meet the residents while you relax at the restaurant, which serves teas and light lunches. ✉ *On main road to McGregor* ☎ *023/625–1593* 🌐 *www.donkeysanctuary.co.za.*

McGregor Wines. An unpretentious and popular attraction, McGregor Wines makes surprisingly inexpensive wines, considering their quality. Try the 2014 unwooded Chardonnay; previous vintages won Veritas Gold awards. Their fortified wines are perfect for sipping near a log fire in winter. The white Muscadel and the Cape ruby port are very different, but both are delicious. The off-dry Colombar gets rave reviews year after year. ✉ *On main road to McGregor* ☎ *023/625–1741* 🌐 *www.mcgregorwinery.co.za* 🎫 *Tastings free.*

WHERE TO STAY

$ B&B/INN 🏨 **Green Gables Country Inn.** In the manor house that used to serve the mill, Green Gables is a good place to escape. **Pros:** amazing setting; good food; you'll soon feel part of the village; pool. **Cons:** limited accommodations; not the place if you're wanting anonymity. [$] *Rooms from: R850* ✉ *Smith St. at Mill St.* ☎ *023/625–1626* 🌐 *www.greengablescountryinn.co.za* 💳 *No credit cards* 🛏 *8 rooms* 🍴 *Breakfast.*

SPORTS AND THE OUTDOORS

HIKING

Vrolijkheid Nature Reserve. The 19-km (12-mile) Rooikat Trail through the Vrolijkheid Nature Reserve takes about eight hours to complete. It's a strenuous, circular route winding up into the Eldandsberg Mountains, and an early start is recommended. There are five self-catering cottages available for overnight visitors. They each accommodate a maximum of four people and are fully equipped. The cottages start from R1,000 per night in low season and around R1,600 during high season. Day visitors need to get a permit (around R40 per adult and R20 per child under 12 years) at the entrance of the reserve; overnight visitors can add it to the booking fees. It's based on the honor system, and you put your money in a box on entry. If you don't want to hike, there are two bird blinds and a mountain-bike trail. ✉ *5 km (3 miles) outside McGregor* ☎ *023/625–1621* ✍ *reservation.alert@capenature.co.za.*

MONTAGU

29 km (18 miles) northeast of Robertson.

Montagu bills itself as "the Gateway to the Little Karoo," and its picturesque streets lined with Cape Victorian architecture lend this some credence. Today the town's main attraction is its natural hot springs, and many of the Victorian houses have been transformed into B&Bs and guesthouses. You know you're in a special place when farmers drop off their produce at the Honesty Shop (an unmanned shop that operates on the honor system) and buyers leave money for what they owe. There are a number of resorts where you can stay and "partake of the waters."

GETTING HERE AND AROUND
Montagu is a 20-minute drive from Robertson.

VISITOR INFORMATION
Contacts Montagu/Ashton Tourism Bureau. ✉ *24 Bath St.* ☎ *023/614–2471* ⊕ *www.montagu-ashton.info.*

EXPLORING
FAMILY **Avalon Springs.** Popular Avalon Springs, the only resort open to day visitors, is not the most stylish, and the architecture leaves a lot to be desired. But if you look beyond this and the numerous signs carrying stern warnings and instructions, you'll get good insight into South African life and culture, as people float and splash around in the various pools. If you're not staying at the resort, you can rent bikes from the village and cycle to the springs, where you can spend a few hours before heading home again. ✉ *Uitvlucht St., 3 km (2 miles) outside Montagu* ☎ *023/614–1150* ⊕ *www.avalonsprings.co.za* 💲 *Weekdays R55, weekends R100.*

FAMILY **Langeberg Tractor Ride.** The popular three-hour Langeberg Tractor Ride takes you to the summit of the Langeberg (Long Mountain) and back. The tractor winds up some tortuously twisted paths, revealing magnificent views of the area's peaks and valleys. After a short stop at the summit, a similarly harrowing descent follows, but you won't be disappointed by the views or the driver's chirpy banter. If you're here in spring or summer when the flowers are in bloom, you might even get to pick some gorgeous proteas on the way down. Following your trip, you can enjoy a delicious lunch of *potjiekos* (traditional stew cooked over a fire in a single cast-iron pot). Reservations are essential. ✉ *Protea Farm, R318* ☎ *023/614–3012* 💲 *R260 for tractor ride and lunch.*

WHERE TO STAY

$$ HOTEL [icon] **Montagu Country Hotel.** This salmon-color hotel was built in Victorian times but was extensively remodeled in the early 1930s; the present owner, Gert Lubbe, highlights its many art-deco features and collects furniture and artifacts from this era to complement the interior. **Pros:** on-site spa and restaurant; centrally located; spacious luxury rooms. **Cons:** Sundays very quiet generally; avoid if you're not a fan of art deco. [$] *Rooms from: R1600* ✉ *27 Bath St.* ☎ *023/614–3125, 082/899–3670* 🌐 *www.montagucountryhotel.co.za* 🛏 *32 rooms* 🍴 *Breakfast.*

$ B&B/INN [icon] **7 Church Street.** In the heart of the village sits this guesthouse in a lovingly restored Victorian home; each room is individually and stylishly decorated with hand-embroidered cotton percale linens. **Pros:** peaceful and secluded location; within easy walking distance of the hot springs. **Cons:** young adults "by appointment only"; may be too quiet for some. [$] *Rooms from: R1200* ✉ *7 Church St.* ☎ *023/614–1186, 084/507–8941* 🌐 *www.7churchstreet.co.za* 🛏 *5 suites* 🍴 *Breakfast.*

THE OVERBERG

Overberg, Afrikaans for "over the mountains," is an apt name for this remote but beautiful region at the bottom of the continent, separated from the rest of the Cape by mountains. Before 19th-century engineers blasted a route over the Hottentots Holland mountain range, the Overberg developed in comparative isolation. To this day it possesses a wild emptiness far removed from the settled valleys of the Cape Winelands.

It's a land of immense contrasts, and if you're planning a trip along the Garden Route, you would be well advised to add the Overberg to your itinerary. The coastal drive from Gordon's Bay to Hermanus unfolds a panorama of deserted beaches, pounding surf, and fractured granite mountains. Once you pass Hermanus and head out onto the windswept plains leading to Cape Agulhas, you have to search harder for the Overberg's riches. Towns are few and far between, and the countryside is an expanse of wheat fields, sheep pastures, and creaking windmills. The occasional reward of the drive is a coastline of sublime beauty. Dunes and unspoiled beaches extend for miles. Currently no roads run parallel to the ocean along this stretch, and you must repeatedly divert inland before heading to another part of the coast.

Unfortunately, the ocean's bounty has been the undoing of communities along this coastline. Perlemoen (abalone) poaching is an enormous problem. These sea mollusks are being illegally poached faster than they can reproduce and are then shipped to the East, where they are considered a powerful aphrodisiac. Violent Western Cape gangs are involved in perlemoen trafficking, and children as young as 11 are used as runners in exchange for drugs.

Naturally, the coast also has plenty of good things on tap. Hermanus is one of the best places in South Africa for land-based whale-watching during the annual migration of Southern Right whales between June and November. Spring is also the best time to see the Overberg's wildflowers, although the region's profusion of coastal and montane fynbos is beautiful year-round. The raw, rugged beauty of Africa's southernmost coastline can be found at De Hoop Nature Reserve. The Whale Trail, a five-day hike mapped out through De Hoop, might just oust the Garden Route's Otter Trail as South Africa's most popular. In fact, walking is one of the Overberg's major attractions, and almost every town and nature reserve offers a host of trails.

The upper part of the Overberg, north of the N2 highway, is more like the Cape Winelands, with 18th- and 19th-century towns sheltered in the lee of rocky mountains. Here the draws are apple orchards, inns, and hiking trails that wind through the mountains. The historic towns of Swellendam and Greyton are good places to spend a night before moving on to your next destination. Stanford, a tiny hamlet just outside of Hermanus, is also a lovely place to stay if you want to avoid the crowds that clog the streets of Hermanus on holidays.

3

Touring the whole area would take three to four days, but you could easily spend a week in the Overberg. For a shorter trip, focus on the splendors of the coastal route from Gordon's Bay to Hermanus, and then head north toward Greyton and Swellendam.

GETTING HERE AND AROUND

Driving yourself is undoubtedly the best way to appreciate this lovely and diverse area. The roads here are generally good. They are sign-posted, and major routes are paved. For the most part, you'll come across gravel roads only around Elim and Napier and from Swellendam to Malgas, and they may be a bit rutted and bumpy. A two-wheel-drive vehicle is fine, but take it easy if it's been raining, as gravel roads can get slippery. You'll need a 4x4 only if you're planning to tackle some of the more remote back roads or want to do a 4x4 route.

The major car-rental agencies have offices in the bigger towns, such as Hermanus and Swellendam. However, it's best to deal with the Cape Town offices; you'll probably want to pick up a car at the airport anyway. *For car-rental agencies, see Travel Smart.*

The Overberg stretches over an enormous area, so you need to decide where you're heading before planning your route. If you want to enjoy the beauty of the coast, then take the N2 from Cape Town, but, instead of heading up Sir Lowry's Pass, turn off to Gordon's Bay and follow the R44, also known as Clarence Drive, along the scenic route. Just after Kleinmond the road becomes the R41 and turns inland to bypass the Bot River lagoon. It becomes the R43 as it makes its way toward Hermanus. If you want to explore inland, however, take the N2 over Sir Lowry's Pass and past Caledon and Swellendam. To get to the pretty hamlet of Greyton, take the R406 to your left just before Caledon.

Intercape Mainliner, Greyhound, and Translux have daily bus service throughout most of the Western Cape, especially to the bigger towns on the N2. Swellendam is a major hub and a good transit point, but to enjoy smaller towns such as Greyton or those along the coast, you'll need your own transportation. *For more information about traveling by bus, see Bus Travel in Travel Smart.*

SAFETY AND PRECAUTIONS

Keep in mind that on Sunday afternoons and in early evenings traffic returning to the city via Sir Lowry's Pass can be very congested. Expect delays as you enter Somerset West, and be very careful if it is misty (which it often is on the pass), as this stretch of road sees numerous accidents each year. Leaving Cape Town on a Friday afternoon can also take time, so try to leave by lunchtime to avoid traffic jams.

TOURS

A number of individuals and small companies offer customized tours. A day trip, which should cost R1,850 per person per day (excluding transport, accommodations, and meals), could involve an excursion to De Hoop Nature Reserve, with plenty of time to admire the birds, fynbos, and whales; a ride on the ferry at Malgas; and time at Bontebok National Park. Or, you could start in Swellendam and then head over picturesque Tradouw Pass through the spectacular Cape Fold Mountains to Barrydale, where you could do some wine tasting before heading on to Robertson. Other tours concentrate on the historic fishing village of Arniston (Waenhuiskrans), Bredasdorp, and Elim.

Cape Adventure Zone. Adventure guide Brenhan Van Niekerk focuses on anything and everything adventure related (day and overnight hikes, canyoneering) in the Overberg region, specifically the Hottentots Holland. He also specializes in fynbos and has a strong interest in nature and wildlife—he is involved in setting up camera traps for the Cape Mountain Leopard Trust in the Hottentots Holland region. ☎ 071/354–1222 ✉ brenhan@capeadventurezone.com.

Stephen Smuts. A distant relative of the famous South African prime minister General Jan Smuts, Stephen Smuts is passionate about fynbos and will be able to give you an insiders' guide to the amazing flora of the area. He owns a private nature reserve and the Sunbird Lodge (⊕ www. thesunbirdlodge.co.za), and you can organize a day walk with him as well. ☎ 028/423–3049, 076/972–0450.

Thoza Tours. Run by Thomazile Stuurman (AKA "Mr. T"), Thoza Tours offers tailor-made tours for individuals or groups. Stuurman specializes in the whole Western Cape area, but has become known for his township tour, a cultural and historic tour which takes place in the Zwelihle (which means "place of beauty" in Xhosa) township (R700 for two people). He also offers full-day tours of the Overberg and the Cape Peninsula (where you can see the Indian Ocean meet the Atlantic Ocean), but Mr T. is very flexible and will cater to your interests. A full-day tour costs approximately R2,400 for two people. ☎ 072/203–7806 ⊕ www.thozatours.co.za.

VISITOR INFORMATION

Contacts Overberg Tourism. ⊠ 22 Plein St., Caledon ☎ 028/214–3370 ⊕ www.overberg.co.za.

EN ROUTE Gordon's Bay, 70 km (43½ miles) southeast of Cape Town, is built on the steep mountain slopes of the Hottentots Holland Mountains overlooking the vast expanse of False Bay. You can often see whales and their calves in the bay in October and November. This is a good

3

point to start on the fantastic coastal route known as **Clarence Drive** (R44), one of the country's most scenic drives, particularly if you take the time to follow some of the dirt roads leading down to the sea from the highway. There are numerous paths down to the seashore from the road between Gordon's Bay and Rooiels. It's worth walking down to watch the waves pounding the rocky coast, but take care. If there are no other people around and the waves are quite big, stay a few yards back from the water, as this section of coast is notorious for rogue waves in certain swell and wind conditions. Note the many crosses on the side of the road—each one denotes somebody who has been swept off the rocks and drowned at sea. The road passes the tiny settlement of **Rooiels** (pronounced *roy*-else), then cuts inland for a couple of miles. A turnoff leads to **Pringle Bay,** a collection of vacation homes sprinkled across the fynbos. The village has little to offer other than a beautiful wide beach (check out the sign warning of quicksand). If you continue through Pringle Bay, the tar road soon gives way to a gravel road, now closed by shifting sand dunes, that used to lead to Betty's Bay (you now have to backtrack and take the inland route to get to Betty's Bay).

BETTY'S BAY

30 km (19 miles) southeast of Gordon's Bay.

Betty's Bay, or Betty's, as the hamlet is fondly known, is worth visiting for its penguins and botanical garden. The village is made up of retirees and weekenders wanting to escape the city hustle. The scenery is wild and untamed and the settlement unfussy, but don't go unless you're happy to hunker down inside when the summer wind is howling or when the winter rains set in.

If you're in the area, the colony of African penguins at Stony Point is definitely worth exploring. They are one of only two mainland colonies in southern Africa (the other is at Boulders Beach on the Cape Peninsula, where it is much easier to see them). The Stony Point colony lies about 600 yards from the parking area along a rocky coastal path. Along the way you pass the concrete remains of tank stands, reminders of the days when Betty's Bay was a big whaling station. The African penguin is endangered, so the colony has been fenced off for protection, but this still doesn't stop leopards from making forays into the colony.

To get to the penguins from Pringle Bay, return to Clarence Drive (the R44) and continue 2 km (1¾ miles) to the turnoff to Stony Point, on the edge of Betty's Bay. Follow Porter Drive for 2¼ km (1¾ miles) until you reach a sign marked "mooi hawens" and a smaller sign depicting a penguin.

GETTING HERE AND AROUND
Head out of Cape Town on the N2 toward Somerset West. Once you've made your way through the town (the traffic can be torturous on a Friday afternoon), take the R44 turnoff to Gordon's Bay. From there the road hugs the coast. It takes 45 minutes from Cape Town to Gordon's Bay if there are no traffic jams and then about 30 minutes to Betty's Bay, but this will vary depending on the traffic and weather—and how often you stop to admire the view.

VISITOR INFORMATION

The Hangklip-Kleinmond Tourism Bureau has information on Betty's Bay.

Contacts Hangklip–Kleinmond Tourism Bureau. ✉ *Protea Centre, Main Rd., Shop 1, Kleinmond* ☎ *028/271–5657* 🌐 *www.kleinmondtourism.co.za.*

EXPLORING

Harold Porter National Botanical Garden. This 440-acre nature reserve is in the heart of the coastal fynbos, where the Cape floral kingdom is at its richest. The profusion of plants supports 96 species of birds and a wide range of small mammals, including troops of chacma baboons. You couldn't ask for a more fantastic setting, cradled between the Atlantic and the towering peaks of the 3,000-foot Kogelberg Range. Walking trails wind through the reserve and into the mountains via Disa and Leopard's kloofs, which echo with the sound of waterfalls. Back at the main buildings, a pleasant restaurant serves light meals and teas. Book at least two weeks in advance for a guided tour to take you around the gardens. To get to the garden from the penguin colony, return to Porter Drive and turn right to rejoin the R44. Drive another 2 km (1 mile) to get here. ✉ *Clarence Dr. at Broadwith Ave.* ☎ *028/272–9311* 🌐 *www.sanbi.org/gardens/harold-porter* 🎟 *Around R22.*

WHERE TO EAT

$$ SEAFOOD 🍴 **Hook, Line and Sinker.** At this small restaurant, expect fish—which is fresher than you'll find just about anywhere else—prepared simply, usually with salsa verde or a bourbon-and-mustard sauce. The dishes, all cooked on a wood fire, come only with fries. **Known for:** fresh fish; simple meals. [$] *Average main: R125* ✉ *382 Crescent Rd., Pringle Bay* ☎ *028/273–8688.*

WHERE TO STAY

$$ B&B/INN 🏨 **Moonstruck on Pringle Bay.** About 60 km (37 miles) from Hermanus, Pringle Bay is a great place to be if you want to escape the Hermanus holiday crush, and situated within 1,600 feet of sandy beach, this modern, four-star guesthouse has spectacular sea and mountain views and is an excellent location for whale-watching. **Pros:** stunning views; close to restaurants; near the beach. **Cons:** the guesthouse is small, so you may be aware of other guests. [$] *Rooms from: R2200* ✉ *264 Hangklip Rd., Pringle Bay* ☎ *028/273–8162* 🌐 *www.moonstruck.co.za* 🛏 *4 rooms* 🍽 *Breakfast.*

KLEINMOND

25 km (15½ miles) southeast of Gordon's Bay.

The sleepy coastal town of Kleinmond (Small Mouth) presides over a magnificent stretch of shoreline, backed by the mountains of the Palmietberg. It's a favorite among retirees, but more and more city-weary folks are moving here preretirement as well. A harbor development near the old slipway is bustling with restaurants and shops.

GETTING HERE AND AROUND

Kleinmond is about 45 minutes from Gordon's Bay, depending on the weather and traffic on the R44.

VISITOR INFORMATION

Contacts Hangklip–Kleinmond Tourism Bureau. ⊠ *Protea Centre, Main Rd., Shop 1* ☎ *028/271–5657* ⊕ *www.kleinmondtourism.co.za.*

EXPLORING

Beaumont Family Wines. The R44 becomes the R41 and cuts inland around the Bot River lagoon. About 10 km (6 miles) past Kleinmond is the junction with the R43. Hermanus is to the right, but take a quick detour to the left through the sleepy town of Bot River to the big, old white gates of Beaumont Wines. This is a fabulous family-run winery. It's just sufficiently scruffy to create an ambience of age and country charm without actually being untidy. But, charm aside, it's the wine you come here for, and it really is worth the detour. Beaumont produces a range of dependable, notable wines, like their flagship Hope Marguerite, a wooded Chenin Blanc. ⊠ *Compagnes Drift Farm, R43, Bot River* ☎ *028/284–9194* ⊕ *www.beaumont.co.za* 🍷 *Tastings R40.*

OFF THE
BEATEN
PATH

Forage at Wildekrans. A 20-minute drive from Kleinmond, Forage at Wildekrans lies on the sprawling Wildekrans wine estate. Here, the chefs forage for ingredients to create an "Indigenous Dining" experience with seasonal ingredients like forest mushroom bubbles, edible soil, truffle moss, and ground weeds, or hay-baked quail breast with barley, knotweed jelly, and root vegetables. **Known for:** foraged foods; stunning interior; tasting menu. ⊠ *R43, Bot River* ☎ *028/284–9488* ⊕ *www.wildekrans.com.*

Gabriëlskloof. As you're heading out of the confines of the city and inland to explore the Overberg or Garden Route, be sure to stop at the impressive Gabriëlskloof, 10 km (6 miles) outside Bot River on the right as you're driving up the N2. Try the Decanter award–winning Gabriëlskloof Shiraz 2010 and Five Archers 2009. You can taste the estate wines in front of a log fire in the tasting room or in the garden. You can also sample the estate's extra-virgin olive oil, and olive products can be purchased from the deli. The Gabriëlskloof restaurant (R110) is a great place to stop for lunch if you're in the area. The menu changes regularly, but the food is always no-fuss home-cooked fare made with fresh local Overberg farm produce. If you visit Gabriëlskloof in December, aim for the weekend they host an evening market with 30 local produce and crafts stalls. ⊠ *Bot River* ☎ *028/284–9865* ⊕ *www.gabrielskloof.co.za* 🍷 *Tastings R30, cellar tours by appointment only.*

Kogelberg Nature Reserve. Close to town, on the Cape Town side and clearly marked with signs from the main street, is the Kogelberg Nature Reserve, a 66,000-acre area of fynbos that extends from the mountains almost to the sea and includes most of the course of the Palmiet River. Declared a UNESCO World Heritage Site in the 1990s, it has fauna and flora found nowhere else in the world. Take one of the well-marked nature walks through the reserve and you are sure to see some of the area's magnificent flora and birdlife. ■**TIP➜ One of the best-kept secrets of this nature reserve are the five Oudebosch eco-cabins, which sleep four people each.** ⊠ *Kleinmond* ☎ *021/483–0190* ⊕ *www. capenature.co.za* 🍷 *R40.*

NEED A BREAK

The Milkwood. Overlooking the lagoon in Onrus, the Milkwood is a great place for a languid lunch. You can sit on the deck after a quick dip and eat some fresh fish (what kind of fish depends on the day's catch), grilled and served with a lemon or garlic-butter sauce. ✉ ***95 Atlantic Dr., Onrus*** ☎ ***028/316–1516.***

Onrus. Head back toward Kleinmond, continuing on the R43 toward Hermanus and across the Bot River. The R43 swings eastward around the mountains, past the not particularly attractive fishing village of Hawston, one of the Overstrand communities hardest hit by abalone poaching and drug peddling, and the small artists' colony of Onrus. The Onrus lagoon is a great swimming spot for children; the water is always a couple of degrees warmer than the sea and is safe for the newly waterborne. ✉ *Onrus.*

Sandown Bay. About 10 km (6 miles) of sandy beach fringes the impressive Sandown Bay, at the eastern edge of town. Much of the beach is nothing more than a sandbar, separating the Atlantic from the huge lagoon formed by the Bot River. Swift currents make swimming risky, although there is a sheltered corner near the rocks close to the old Beach House hotel, which burned down in 2006. Keep an eye out for the famous Bot River horses that live on *vlei* (pronounced flay), or marsh. There are lots of theories about just how the horses got here. One has it that they were turned loose during the Boer War to save them from being killed and ended up on the vlei for safety. DNA tests show that these horses are descendants of the Kaapse Waperd (Cape wagon horse), a sturdy breed used to help settle the wild regions of the Overberg. **Amenities:** food and drink; parking (fee); showers; toilets; water sports. **Best for:** solitude; swimming; walking. ✉ *Beach Rd.*

WHERE TO STAY

$$$ HOTEL FAMILY Fodor's Choice ★

🏨 **The Arabella Hotel & Spa.** Gone are the days when heading out into the country meant staying in pokey hotels with dodgy beds: the Arabella Hotel & Spa is luxurious lodging in the most amazing setting—on the edge of the Bot River lagoon. **Pros:** plenty of activities to keep both adults and children entertained; world-rated golf course. **Cons:** windy during summer months. [$] *Rooms from: R2660* ✉ *Arabella Country Estate, R44* ☎ *028/284–0000* 🌐 *www.arabellacountryestate.co.za* 🛏 *145 rooms* 🍴 *Breakfast.*

SPORTS AND THE OUTDOORS

GOLF

Arabella Golf Club. The setting of the Arabella Golf Club is so beautiful that you'd do well to take time to admire the views at the 8th hole, with the lagoon, the mountains, and the sea in the distance. This is Ernie Els's favorite spot and the most photographed hole on the course. Don't lose your head to the views—the course is fairly challenging. It's also expensive. ✉ *R43* ☎ *028/284–0000* 🌐 *www.arabellacountryestate.co.za/arabella-golf-course* 🎫 *R1,425 includes halfway house meal* 🏌 *18 holes, 6651 yards, par 72* ☞ *Facilities: driving range, putting green, golf carts, rental clubs, restaurant, bar.*

RAFTING

The Palmiet River is a low-volume, technical white-water river of about Grade III.

Gravity Adventures. The Palmiet River, which runs through the Kogelberg Nature Reserve, is perfect for white-water adventures. In high water in winter, Gravity Adventures offers rafting trips in two- or four-seater inflatable rafts. During summer in low water, it does the same trip but on specially designed one-person inflatable crafts called "geckos." A full-day rafting trip (including a snack) costs R695. Tubing costs R595 for a full day; you can order lunch for an extra R95 or bring your own. Remember to take along plenty of sun protection. ✉ *21 Selous Rd., Claremont* ☎ *021/683–3698, 082/574–9901* ⊕ *www.gravity.co.za.*

SA Forest Adventures. Tubing and river rafting trips down the Palmiet River are offered by SA Forest Adventures in Kleinmond. Expect to pay around R550 for a half day of fun and heart-stopping action. If this isn't enough, ask about their sand-boarding trips, where you get to ski down sand dunes that overlook Betty's Bay and the Atlantic Ocean. ✉ *Harbour Rd., Unit B1* ☎ *083/517–3635* ⊕ *saforestadventures.co.za.*

HERMANUS

34 km (21 miles) southeast of Kleinmond.

Pristine beaches extend as far as the eye can see, and the Kleinriviersberg provides a breathtaking backdrop to this popular resort, the Overberg's major coastal town. Restaurants and shops line the streets, and Grotto Beach was awarded Blue Flag status (an international symbol of high environmental standards as well as good sanitary and safety facilities) in 2003 and is still going strong. Though the town has lost much of its original charm—thanks to the crowds and fast-food joints—it is still most definitely worth a visit. If you're in Hermanus for the weekend, visit the Saturday morning organic farmers' market to get a real feel for the area.

GETTING HERE AND AROUND

Hermanus is about a 40-minute drive from Kleinmond on the R41 and the R43. In summer expect delays, as the traffic into town is often gridlocked.

VISITOR INFORMATION

Contacts Hermanus Tourism Bureau. ✉ *Lord Robert St. at Mitchell St.* ☎ *028/312–2629* ⊕ *www.hermanustourism.info.*

EXPLORING

Hermanus sits atop a long line of cliffs, which makes it one of the best places in South Africa for land-based whale-watching. The town is packed during the Whale Festival in late September as well as over Christmas vacation. The 11-km (7-mile) Cliff Walk allows watchers to follow the whales, which often come within 100 feet of the cliffs as they move along the coastline. Keep an ear and an eye out for the whale crier, who makes his rounds during the season. Using horns made from dried kelp, he produces a long note to indicate where you can find him on the harbor wall. Once you've located him, he will tell you where to catch the best sighting of these mighty giants of the deep.

Bouchard Finlayson. West of town off the R43, the R320 (Hemel-en-Aarde Valley Road) leads through the vineyards and orchards of the scenic Hemel-en-Aarde Valley and over Shaw's Pass to Caledon. A bit past Hamilton Russell Vineyards and with only 44 acres under vine, Bouchard Finlayson nevertheless thrills critics and wine lovers year after year. Winemaker Peter Finlayson makes good use of the cool sea breeze and unique terroir of the estate to create some fantastic deep-south wines. Finlayson, who has a great voice, maintains that Pinot Noir "is like opera. When it's great, it is pure seduction, almost hedonistic. There is no middle road." You might wish to lay down a few bottles of the much-lauded Tête de Cuvée Galpin Peak Pinot Noir, a velvety and fruity wine. ⊠ *Off Hemel-en-Aarde Valley Rd. (R320)* ☎ *028/312–3515* ⊕ *www.bouchardfinlayson.co.za* ⊠ *Tastings R20 for 3 wines, R40 for 6 wines.*

> ## WONDER OF WHALES
>
> Whale sightings off South African shores weren't always so frequent, but each year it seems whales are arriving earlier and leaving later. In the 1960s, whale populations, especially Southern Right whales, showed an increase around the coast. The population was probably around 1,000 in the '80s, and in 1984 the Dolphin Action and Protection Group, an organization campaigning to stop whaling, finally won year-round protection for the creatures. Today, around 4,000 Southern Right whales call SA waters home.

Hamilton Russell Vineyards. A short way down the R320 (Hemel-en-Aarde Valley Road) in a thatch building overlooking a small dam, Hamilton Russell Vineyards produces only two varietals: the temperamental Pinot Noir and Chardonnay. Their wines are regarded as some of the best in the world. The Chardonnay, with lovely pear aromas and flavors, won the Chardonnay category at the 2014 South African Wine Index Awards. The Pinot Noir, great for pairing with veal, pork, and gamey meats, was also a winner at the 2014 SAWi Awards. The farm doesn't do official picnics, but they don't mind you bringing your own nibbles and enjoying the remarkable setting; there's a lawn outside the tasting room where you can spread your blanket. ⊠ *Off Hemel-en-Aarde Valley Rd. (R320), Walker Bay* ☎ *028/312–3595* ⊕ *www.hamiltonrussellvineyards.co.za* ⊠ *Tastings R50.*

FAMILY **Old Harbour Museum.** Originally, Hermanus was a simple fishing village. Its Old Harbour, the oldest original harbor in South Africa that is still intact, has been declared a national monument. The Old Harbour Museum bears testimony to the town's maritime past. A small building at the old stone fishing basin displays a couple of the horrific harpoons used to lance whales and sharks, as well as some interesting whale bones. There are also exhibits on fishing techniques, local marine life, and angling records. The white building next to the harbor parking lot on Market Square is **De Wetshuis Photo Museum,** which houses the Old Harbour Museum Photographic Exhibition. Here are photos of old Hermanus and of many of the town's fishermen proudly displaying their catches of fish, sharks, and dolphins—yes, dolphins.

The museum's third component is the **Whale House**, with an interactive display. Although the exhibit is still only 75% complete, the touch screens, submarine, and skeleton of a whale make it a great place for kids. A whale movie runs twice a day, at 10 am and 3 pm. A crafts market every Sunday and first Friday of the summer months (behind De Wetshuis Photo Museum) is fun for browsing. ✉ *Old Harbour, Marine Dr.* ☎ *028/312–1475* 🌐 *www.old-harbour-museum.co.za* 🎟 *R20.*

Rotary Way. On the outskirts of town a pair of white gateposts set well back from the R43 signal the start of Rotary Way. This scenic drive climbs along the spine of the mountains above Hermanus, with incredible views of the town, Walker Bay, and the Hemel-en-Aarde (Heaven and Earth) Valley, as well as some of the area's beautiful fynbos. It's a highlight of a trip to Hermanus and shouldn't be missed. The entire mountainside is laced with wonderful walking trails, and many of the scenic lookouts have benches. ✉ *Hermanus.*

WHERE TO EAT

$$ SEAFOOD FAMILY

🍴 **Fishermans Cottage.** It's hard to believe this unassuming stone cottage serves some of the best food in town. The menu focuses on seafood, but don't let that put you off the non-seafood options like smoked pork belly and seafood curry with freshly made roti. **Known for:** hake and chips; fresh, seasonal ingredients; local wines. [$] *Average main: R135* ✉ *Main St. at Harbour Rd* ☎ *028/312–3642* 🌐 *www.fishermanscottage.co.za.*

$$$ ECLECTIC Fodor's Choice ★

🍴 **Marianas.** Mariana and Peter Esterhuizen started out selling organic vegetables at the Hermanus farmers' market before converting a house in the little village of Stanford, just 25 minutes away, into a restaurant. Produce from the garden dictates the menu, and ingredients are sourced from local producers, with dishes that lean toward a Mediterranean style with a strong element of Cape cooking present. **Known for:** Gruyère soufflé; Overberg lamb; decadent lunch. [$] *Average main: R160* ✉ *12 du Toit St., Stanford* ☎ *028/341–0272* 💳 *No credit cards* 🕒 *Closed Mon.–Wed. No dinner.*

$$ ECLECTIC

🍴 **Mogg's Country Cookhouse.** Don't be put off by the bumpy dirt road heading up the Hemel-en-Aarde Valley—this restaurant on a fruit farm at the top of the valley is worth any amount of dust and corrugations. The seasonal menu is scribbled on a chalkboard, with dishes like caramelized pear, Gorgonzola, avocado, and walnut salad, or smoked trout and sautéed prawns in a phyllo pastry basket with lime-wasabi vinaigrette. **Known for:** BYOB; Moroccan-style lamb; homemade desserts. [$] *Average main: R100* ✉ *Nuwe Pos Farm, off the Hemel-en-Aarde Valley Rd. (R320)* ☎ *076/314–0671* 🌐 *www.moggscookhouse.com* 🕒 *Closed Mon. and Tues. No dinner.*

$$$ SOUTH AFRICAN

🍴 **The Restaurant at Newton Johnson.** If you're keen to escape the crowds in Hermanus, head to the Restaurant at Newton Johnson in the picturesque Hemel-en-Aarde Valley Road, where vines and fynbos cover the slopes. Here, the menu changes depending on available produce and what's been foraged on the farm, featuring bold, flavorful dishes with a country flair: gnocchi with cauliflower, crispy potato skins, and home-cured mustard or lamb shoulder with pumpkin and porcini soil. **Known for:** chef Rickey Broekhoven; tasting room on-site; stunning setting.

$ *Average main: R190* ✉ *R320, Hemel-en-Aarde Valley* ☎ *021/200–2148* 🌐 *www.newtonjohnson.com.*

WHERE TO STAY

If you want to avoid the crowds of Hermanus, consider lodging in the nearby tiny hamlet of Stanford.

$ B&B/INN 🏨 **Auberge Burgundy Guesthouse.** If you want to be in the center of the village, this stylish guesthouse is an excellent choice; you're a stone's throw from the famous whale-watching cliffs and the market, and three minutes from the Old Harbour Museum. **Pros:** close proximity to everything Hermanus has to offer; very friendly staff; less than 200 feet from the sea. **Cons:** some suites facing the street are noisy; no children under 12 (exceptions made during winter months). $ *Rooms from: R1440* ✉ *16 Harbour Rd.* ☎ *028/313–1201* 🌐 *www.auberge.co.za* 🛏 *18 rooms* 🍴 *Breakfast.*

$ SOUTH AFRICAN 🍴 **Betty Blue Bistro.** This bistro located on the main road is a welcome addition to the Hermanus dining scene, with a bright and playful interior featuring hand-painted Moroccan tiles and colorful planters. The menu is simple but packs a full punch with fresh, flavorful daytime dishes, with everything from freshly squeezed juices to the burgers, salads, and sandwiches. **Known for:** decadent pancakes; sweet and savory breakfast; no dinner. $ *Average main: R90* ✉ *126 Main Rd.* ☎ *028/125–0037* 🌐 *www.bettybluebistrohermanus.com.*

$$$$ B&B/INN 🏨 **Birkenhead House.** If whale-watching is on your agenda, then consider this stunning hotel mandatory; it's unlikely you'll come across a better ocean-facing position than the one of Birkenhead House. **Pros:** stunning views; excellent service; homey feel. **Cons:** far from town. $ *Rooms from: R7550* ✉ *11th St. at 7th Ave., Voelklip* ☎ *028/314–8051* 🌐 *www.theroyalportfolio.com/birkenhead-house* 🛏 *11 rooms* 🍴 *All-inclusive.*

$$ B&B/INN 🏨 **Blue Gum Country Estate.** Husband-and-wife team Anton and Tarryn de Kock run a top-notch establishment on the banks of the Klein River just 10 minutes from Stanford and 30 minutes from Hermanus. **Pros:** brilliant base from which to explore the area; feels like home away from home with added luxury. **Cons:** you'll need to drive a distance to get to the busier areas; pitiful nightlife in Stanford. $ *Rooms from: R2400* ✉ *Off R326, Stanford* ☎ *028/341–0116* 🌐 *www.bluegum.co.za* 🛏 *13 rooms* 🍴 *Breakfast.*

$$$$ RESORT FAMILY Fodor's Choice ★ 🏨 **Grootbos Private Nature Reserve.** Only a 30-minute drive from Hermanus and two hours from Cape Town, this private nature reserve is on 2,500 acres of Western Cape landscape overlooking Walker Bay. Here you can observe protea, fynbos, and milk-wood forests, as well as aquatic life: penguins, dolphins, great white sharks, seals, and Southern Right whales in early spring. **Pros:** certified green property; secluded natural surroundings; whale-watching. **Cons:** confining for longer stays; expensive. $ *Rooms from: R9100* ✉ *Gansbaai* ☎ *028/384–8000, 028/384–8053* 🌐 *www.grootbos.com* 🛏 *27 suites* 🍴 *All meals.*

$$$$ HOTEL FAMILY Fodor's Choice ★ 🏨 **The Marine.** The Marine is one of the Southern Hemisphere's most spectacular seaside properties, with an incomparable cliff-top setting and sumptuously decorated rooms. **Pros:** wonderful views of the ocean; old-world service excellence and attention to detail. **Cons:** you'll need a tony wardrobe to blend in; not a super-relaxed environment. $ *Rooms*

from: R4450 ✉ *Marine Dr.* ☎ *021/794–5535* ⊕ *www.collectionmc-grath.com/marine* ⇌ *40 rooms* ❍ *Breakfast.*

$$
B&B/INN ⊡ **The Vishuis.** Located in the center of town (within walking distance of a host of shops and restaurants), this renovated fisherman's cottage and heritage building is now a stylish urban retreat. **Pros:** convenient location; beautifully decorated. **Cons:** no views; rooms have to share communal area. $ *Rooms from: R1500* ✉ *7 Hope St.* ☎ *082/576–1355* ⊕ *www.thevishuis.co.za* ⇌ *4 rooms* ❍ *Some meals.*

SPORTS AND THE OUTDOORS

East of Hermanus the R43 hugs the strip of land between the mountains and the Klein River lagoon. The lagoon is popular with water-skiers, boaters, and anglers.

KAYAKING

Walker Bay Adventures. For a really fun outing, join a gentle paddling excursion from the Old Harbour operated by Walker Bay Adventures. You paddle in safe, stable double sea kayaks accompanied by a guide, and will pay between R400 and R450 for a two-hour trip (depending on the season). Children 10 and older are welcome to join. From July to December, Walker Bay is a whale sanctuary, and this is the only company with a permit to operate here. ✉ *Old Harbour, off Marine Dr.* ☎ *082/739–0159* ⊕ *www.walkerbayadventures.co.za.*

WHALE-WATCHING AND SHARK DIVING

Although Hermanus is great for land-based whale-watching, you get a different perspective on a boat trip into Walker Bay. Boats leave on 2½-hour whale-watching trips (around R900) from both Hermanus and Gansbaai.

Dyer Island Cruises. This company, which strives to create awareness about conservation, is a good bet for whale-watching, and the guides are full of information. You're likely to see some of the Marine Big Five—whales, dolphins, penguins, seals, and sharks—on the guided boat trip. Expect to pay R1100 per adult. A free visit to the African Penguin and Seabird Sanctuary is also included. Transfers to and from Cape Town can be arranged. ✉ *5 Geelbek St., Kleinmond* ☎ *082/801–8014* ⊕ *www.dyer-island-cruises.co.za.*

White Shark Diving Company. Shark diving is extremely popular (even Brad Pitt took the plunge), and Gansbaai has a number of operators working from the small harbor, including White Shark Diving Company. A roughly 4½-hour trip (with plenty of adrenaline) costs around R1,750, including breakfast, snacks on the boat, and a light lunch after the trip. If you don't want to take the plunge—which you do in a cage, to keep you safe from the sharks—you can just stay in the boat and watch the sharks from the deck for a slightly reduced rate. A volunteer program is also available, offering those passionate about the ocean a chance to contribute to great white shark research and marine conservation. ✉ *Kleinbaai Harbour, 9 Kus Dr., Gansbaai* ☎ *082/559–6858* ⊕ *www.sharkcagediving.co.za.*

SHOPPING

Wine Village. This shop carries a good selection of South African wines, including wines from neighboring vineyards Hamilton Russell and Bouchard Finlayson as well as Southern Right. ⊠ *Hemel-en-Aarde Rd., Hemel-en-Aarde Village* ☎ *028/316–3988* ⊕ *www.winevillage.co.za.*

BREDASDORP

89 km (55 miles) east of Hermanus; 60 km (37 miles) east of Stanford.

This sleepy agricultural town has a certain charm, as long as you don't catch it on a Sunday afternoon, when everything's closed and an air of ennui pervades the brassy, windswept streets. Each spring, however, the usual lethargic atmosphere is abandoned, and a radical sense of purpose takes its place when Bredasdorp hosts the Foot of Africa Marathon. Don't be lulled by the small-town country setting into thinking that this race is a breeze; word has it that the undulating landscape has the fittest athletes doubting their perseverance.

GETTING HERE AND AROUND

Travel time from Hermanus is around 45 minutes and from Stanford 30 minutes. From Hermanus you travel on the R43 to Stanford; then you take the R326 and then the R316. The route is well signposted.

VISITOR INFORMATION

The Cape Agulhas Tourism Bureau has two offices with information for Bredasdorp.

Contacts Cape Agulhas Tourism Bureau. ⊠ *19 Long St.* ☎ *028/424–2584* ⊕ *www.discovercapeagulhas.co.za.*

EXPLORING

Bredasdorp Shipwreck Museum. Housed in a converted church and rectory, the Bredasdorp Shipwreck Museum has an extensive collection of objects salvaged from the hundreds of ships that have gone down in the stormy waters off the Cape. In addition to the usual cannons and figureheads, the museum displays a surprising array of undamaged household articles rescued from the sea, including entire dining-room sets, sideboards, china, and phonographs. Be sure to visit the buildings out back, which contain old wagons and the first fire engines used in South Africa. ⊠ *6 Independent St.* ☎ *028/424–1240* ⊕ *www.western-cape.gov.za/facility/shipwreck-museum* ☎ *R50.*

De Hoop Nature Reserve. This huge conservation area covering 88,900 acres of isolated coastal terrain as well as a marine reserve extending 5 km (3 miles) out to sea is a World Heritage Site and well deserving of this status. Massive white-sand dunes, mountains, and rare lowland fynbos are home to eland, bontebok, and Cape mountain zebra, as well as more than 250 bird species. Though the reserve is only three hours from Cape Town, it feels a lifetime away. Access is via the dirt road between Bredasdorp and Malgas. This is a fantastic place to watch whales from the shore—not quite as easy as in Hermanus but much less crowded. You can also hike the enormously popular **Whale Trail,** which runs through this reserve. A shuttle service takes your bags to each new stop, so all you have to carry is a small day pack and some water between overnight stops. You need to book up to a year in advance to enjoy the Whale Trail, or you might get lucky and snag a last-minute cancellation. In fact, this hike is now so popular that it's beginning to appear in online auctions. Self-catering cottages sleep up to four people and range from basic to fully equipped. The trail costs R1,695 per person (off peak) and R2,195 (peak season), but there's a minimum of six people each time, so you'll have to drum up other happy hikers. You can still enjoy De Hoop without doing the Whale Trail; they have lovely accommodations ranging from camping to luxurious rooms in the old manor house. ⊠ *Bredasdorp* ☏ *028/542–1253* ⊕ *www.capenature.co.za.*

3

OFF THE
BEATEN
PATH

Elim. Little has changed in the last hundred years in the Moravian mission village Elim, founded in 1824. Simple whitewashed cottages line the few streets, and the settlement's coloured residents all belong to the Moravian Church. At the Sunday 10 am church service, which you're welcome to attend, just about the whole town turns out in their Sunday best, and voices soar in the white church at the top of the main street. The whole village has been declared a national monument, and it's the only town in the country that has a monument dedicated to the freeing of the slaves in 1838. It's also home to the country's oldest working clock and biggest wooden waterwheel. Elim is 36 km (22 miles) west of Bredasdorp, the easiest access is via the R317, off the R319 between Cape Agulhas and Bredasdorp.

Malgas. Past De Hoop Nature Reserve on the dirt road from Bredasdorp is the small hamlet of Malgas, a major port in the 19th century before the mouth of the Breede River silted up. In addition to a tiny village, you will find the last hand-drawn car ferry in the country (R42 round-trip). It's fascinating to watch the technique, as the ferry operators "walk" the ferry across the river on a huge cable, leaning into their harnesses.

OFF THE
BEATEN
PATH

Cape Agulhas. From Bredasdorp it's just 39 km (24 miles) through rolling farmland to the tip of the African continent. Although this cape is not nearly as spectacular as Cape Point, it's a wild and lonely place—rather fitting for the end of a wild and wonderful continent. For R24, you can climb the Cape Agulhas lighthouse tower from 9 to 5 daily. ⊠ *Lighthouse St., Cape Agulhas.*

ARNISTON (WAENHUISKRANS)

25 km (15½ miles) southeast of Bredasdorp.

Although its official name is Waenhuiskrans, and that's what you'll see on maps, this lovely, isolated vacation village is almost always called Arniston—after a British ship of that name that was wrecked on the nearby reef in 1815. Beautiful beaches, water that assumes Caribbean shades of blue, and mile after mile of towering white dunes attract anglers and vacationers alike. Only the frequent southeasters that blow off the sea and the chilly water are likely to put a damper on your enjoyment.

For 200 years a community of local fisherfolk has eked out a living here, setting sail each day in small fishing boats. Today their village, **Kassiesbaai** (translation: "suitcase bay," supposedly for all the suitcases that washed ashore from the frequent shipwrecks), is a national monument. It's fascinating wandering around the thatch cottages of this still-vibrant community, although declining fish stocks have left many families vulnerable. Perlemoen poaching is also a problem here. The adjacent village of Arniston has expanded enormously in the last two decades, thanks to the construction of vacation homes. Unfortunately, not all of the new architecture blends well with the whitewashed simplicity of the original cottages.

Waenhuiskrans is Afrikaans for "wagon-house cliff," a name derived from the vast cave 2 km (1 mile) south of town that is theoretically large enough to house several wagons and their spans of oxen. Signs point the way over the dunes to the cave, which is accessible only at low tide. You need shoes to protect your feet from the sharp rocks, and you should wear something you don't mind getting wet. It's definitely worth the trouble, however, to stand in the enormous cave looking out to sea.

GETTING HERE AND AROUND

It'll take drivers about 20–30 minutes to get here from Bredasdorp. Don't bother with public transport. Rent a car and you'll have the freedom to explore this vast area.

VISITOR INFORMATION

The Cape Agulhas Tourism Bureau has information for Arniston.

WHERE TO STAY

$$ HOTEL FAMILY **Arniston Spa Hotel.** You could easily spend a week here and still need to be dragged away: the setting, a crescent of white dunes, has a lot to do with Arniston's appeal, but the hotel also strikes a fine balance between elegance and beach-vacation comfort. **Pros:** great views of the beach; located on a beach safe for children. **Cons:** windy in summer; a bit noisy during high season. [$] *Rooms from: R1880* ✉ *Beach Rd., Arniston* ☎ *028/445–9000* 🌐 *www.arnistonhotel.com* 🛏 *67 rooms* 🍴 *Breakfast.*

SWELLENDAM

72 km (45 miles) north of Arniston (Waenhuiskrans).

Beautiful Swellendam lies in the shadow of the imposing Langeberg Range. Established in 1745, it is the third-oldest town in South Africa, and many of its historic buildings have been elegantly restored. Even on a casual drive along the main street you'll see a number of lovely Cape Dutch homes, with their traditional whitewashed walls, gables, and thatch roofs.

GETTING HERE AND AROUND

Swellendam is about an hour's drive from Arniston. Rent a car to get around.

VISITOR INFORMATION

Contacts Swellendam Tourism Bureau. ✉ *22 Swellengrebel St.* ☎ *028/514–2770* 🌐 *www.swellendamtourism.co.za.*

3

EXPLORING

Bontebok National Park. Covering just 6,880 acres of coastal fynbos, Bontebok National Park is one of the smallest of South Africa's national parks. Don't expect to see big game here—the park contains no elephants, lions, or rhinos. What you will see are bontebok, graceful white-face antelope nearly exterminated by hunters in the early 20th century, as well as red hartebeest, Cape grysbok, steenbok, duiker, and the endangered Cape mountain zebra. There are simple, self-catering accommodations in the reserve, a three-star facility, and camping facilities. ✉ *Off N2, 2 km (1.2 miles) from Swellendam* ☎ *028/514–2735* 🌐 *www.sanparks.org* 🎟 *R80.*

Drostdy Museum. The centerpiece of the town's historical past is the Drostdy Museum, a collection of buildings dating from the town's earliest days. The Drostdy was built in 1747 by the Dutch East India Company to serve as the residence of the *landdrost,* the magistrate who presided over the district. The building is furnished in a style that dates back to the late 1700s and early 1800s. A path leads through the Drostdy herb gardens to Mayville, an 1855 middle-class home that blends elements of Cape Dutch and Cape Georgian architecture. Across Swellengrebel Street stand the old jail and the Ambagswerf, an outdoor exhibit of tools used by the town's blacksmiths, wainwrights, coopers, and tanners. ✉ *18 Swellengrebel St.* ☎ *028/514–1138* 🌐 *www.drostdy.com* 🎟 *R25.*

Dutch Reformed Church. Swellendam's Dutch Reformed Church is an imposing white edifice built in 1911 in an eclectic style. The gables are baroque, the windows Gothic, the cupola vaguely Eastern, and the steeple extravagant. Surprisingly, all the elements work together wonderfully. Inside is an interesting tiered amphitheater with banks of curving wood pews facing the pulpit and organ. ✉ *7 Voortrek St.* ☎ *028/514–1225* 🎟 *R10; services free* 🕒 *Closed Sat.*

Marloth Nature Reserve. If you'd like to stretch your legs, take a hike in the Marloth Nature Reserve in the Langeberg above town. Five easy walks, ranging from one to four hours, explore some of the mountain gorges. An office at the entrance to the reserve has trail maps and hiking information. If you're doing a day walk, park outside the entrance boom. Although you can stay in the reserve until sunset, the gates close at the time advertised. ✉ *Swellendam* ✥ *1½ km (1 mile) from Voortrek St. on Andrew White St. to golf course, and follow signs* ☎ *028/514–1410* 🌐 *www.capenature.co.za* 🎟 *R40.*

WHERE TO STAY

$ RENTAL FAMILY 🏨 **A Hilltop Country Retreat.** Set in the foothills of the Langeberg Mountains, A Hilltop Retreat offers spacious and luxurious self-catering accommodations. **Pros:** beautiful setting; children of all ages are welcome. **Cons:** no oven in the kitchenette; rooms are close together. [$] *Rooms from: R1000* ✉ *7 Bergsig Ave.* ☎ *028/514–2294* 🌐 *www.ahilltop.co.za* 🛏 *10 rooms* 🍴 *No meals.*

$ B&B/INN 🏨 **Augusta de Mist.** This elegant Cape Dutch homestead, established in 1802, now serves as a comfortable retreat on 3½ acres of fynbos; the house still has original reed and mud ceilings, yellowwood shutters, and authentic metalwork. **Pros:** quiet, peaceful setting; highly acclaimed restaurant. **Cons:** no children under 14. [$] *Rooms from: R1000* ✉ *3 Human St.* ☎ *028/514–2425* 🌐 *www.augustademist.com* 🛏 *6 suites* 🍴 *Breakfast.*

$$ HOTEL 🏨 **De Kloof Luxury Estate.** Situated in manicured gardens with breathtaking scenery, De Kloof Luxury Estate is a chic, upmarket boutique hotel that offers five-star accommodations in one of the oldest Cape Dutch manors in Swellendam. **Pros:** set in manicured gardens; swimming pool; family suite available. **Cons:** prior approval is needed for children under 8. [$] *Rooms from: R2100* ✉ *8 Weltevrede St.* ☎ *028/514–1303* 🌐 *www.dekloof.co.za* 🛏 *8 suites* 🍴 *Breakfast.*

$$$ HOTEL 🏨 **Schoone Oordt.** The ultimate luxury getaway, this renovated Victorian manor house, with original ceilings, wooden floors, and antique furnishings, boasts five-star accommodations. **Pros:** lush gardens with a swimming pool; the staff are happy to cater to special dietary requirements. **Cons:** not all rooms are in the beautiful main house. [$] *Rooms from: R3150* ✉ *1 Swellengrebel St.* ☎ *028/514–1248* 🌐 *www.schooneoordt.co.za* 🛏 *11 rooms* 🍴 *Breakfast.*

SPORTS AND THE OUTDOORS

HORSEBACK RIDING

Two Feathers Horse Trails. You can take just a little trot or a longer excursion through the Marloth Nature Reserve on horseback with Two Feathers Horse Trails. Expect to pay around R400 for a 1½-hour excursion. Full-day rides can be arranged on request and include a picnic lunch. ✉ *5 Liechtenstein St.* ☎ *082/494–8279* 🌐 *www.twofeathers.co.za.*

EN ROUTE From Swellendam return to the N2 and turn right toward Cape Town. The road sweeps through rich, rolling cropland that extends to the base of the Langeberg. In the town of Riviersonderend (pronounced riff- *ear*-son-der-ent), stop at the excellent Ou Meul Bakkery (Old Mill Bakery) to stock up on succulent pies, rusks (dry biscuits), and home produce. A few kilometers on, turn right onto the R406, a good gravel road that leads to the village of Greyton, in the lee of the Riviersonderend Mountains.

GREYTON

94 km (58 miles) west of Swellendam.

The charming village of Greyton, filled with white thatch cottages and quiet lanes, is a popular weekend retreat for Capetonians as well as a permanent home for many retirees. The village offers almost nothing in the way of traditional sights, but it's a relaxing place to stop for a meal or a night, and a great base for walks into the surrounding mountains. There are plenty of small B&Bs and guesthouses to stay in, but no large hotels.

GETTING HERE AND AROUND

If you're driving from Swellendam, take the N2 west. Expect the trip to take an hour to an hour and a half.

VISITOR INFORMATION

Contacts Greyton Tourism Bureau. ✉ *29 Main Rd.* ☎ *028/254–9564, 028/254–9414* 🌐 *www.greytontourism.com.*

EXPLORING

Genadendal (*Valley of Grace*). The neighboring village to Greyton is Genadendal, a Moravian mission station founded in 1737 to educate the Khoi-Khoi and convert them to Christianity. When the first missionary George Schmidt arrived in South Africa, the Khoi-Khoi were at the verge of extinction. His focus was to develop them into a self-sustainable community. The first school in the interior opened its doors in 1738. By 1806, Genadendal was the second-largest settlement in the colony (after Cape Town) and in 1838, the first Teachers Training College in South Africa opened its doors. Seeing this impoverished hamlet today, it's difficult to comprehend the major role the mission played in the early history of South Africa. Some of the first written works in Afrikaans were printed here, and the coloured community greatly influenced the development of Afrikaans as it is heard today. None of this went down well with the white government of the time. By 1909 new legislation prohibited coloured ownership of land, and in 1926 the Department of Public Education closed the settlement's teachers' training college, arguing that coloureds were better employed on neighboring farms. In 1980 all the buildings on Church Square were declared national monuments (it's considered the country's most authentic church square), but despite a number of community-based projects, Genadendal has endured a long slide into obscurity and remains impoverished. In 1995, then president Nelson Mandela renamed his official residence Genadendal. You can walk the streets and tour the historic buildings facing Church Square. Ask at the Genadendal Mission Museum for somebody to show you around or phone ahead for a guided tour. With luck you'll meet up with Samuel Baatjes, a fourth-generation Genadendal resident. Tours last as long as you would like them to and depend on your level of interest. ⊠ *Genadendal* ☎ *028/251–8582* ⊕ *www.overberg.co.za/content/view/21/27.*

Genadendal Mission Museum. Of particular note in Genadendal is the Genadendal Mission Museum, spread through 15 rooms in three buildings. The museum collection, the only one in South Africa to be named a National Cultural Treasure, includes unique household implements, books, tools, and musical instruments, among them the country's oldest pipe organ, which arrived in the village in 1832. Wall displays examine mission life in the Cape in the 18th and 19th centuries, focusing on the early missionaries' work with the Khoekhoen. ⊠ *Church Sq., Genadendal* ☎ *028/251–8582* ⊕ *www.museumsonline.co.za* ⊡ *Adults R10, children R5* ☉ *Closed Sun.*

SPORTS AND THE OUTDOORS

HIKING

Boesmanskloof Trail. In addition to day hikes and short walks, you can take the 14-km (8½-mile) Boesmanskloof Trail through the Riviersonderend Mountains between the exquisite hamlets of Greyton and McGregor. In the good old days, youngsters used to walk from Greyton to McGregor for an energetic game of tennis before walking home again the same evening. Hikers often book the following night's accommodations at a local B&B and have a good meal and a good night's sleep before heading home. In McGregor the trailhead is about 14 km (8½ miles) away from the town, but most guesthouses will have someone pick you up and drop you off. Note that cell-phone coverage is sporadic on the trail. You do need a permit from CapeNature to do the hike; buy one from the Greyton or McGregor Tourism Bureau. Take water and adequate protective clothing, as the weather can change quickly. A great place to stay if you're walking from Greyton to McGregor is the Eagle's Nest guesthouse (⊕ *www.boesmanskloofmcgregor.com*) and Onverwacht Cottages (at the end of the trail, R300 per person). Both have have spectacular views. Simpler accommodations, in hiking huts on a private farm (R150 per person with bedding), can be booked through **Japie and Sandra Oosthuizen** (☎ *072/514–4209 or* ☎ *023/625–1667*), who will also buy groceries and leave them at the hut before you arrive. He can also arrange for your permit for the full hiking route, for R80.

EN ROUTE

To head back toward Cape Town, follow the R406 to the N2. After the town of Bot River, the road leaves the wheat fields and climbs into the mountains. It's lovely country, full of rock and pine forest interspersed with orchards. **Sir Lowry's Pass** serves as the gateway to Cape Town and the Cape Winelands, a magnificent breach in the mountains that opens to reveal the curving expanse of False Bay, the long ridge of the peninsula, and, in the distance, Table Mountain.

WEST COAST

The West Coast is an acquired taste. It's dry and bleak, and other than the ubiquitous exotic gum trees, nothing grows higher than your knees. But it's a wild and wonderful place. An icy sea pounds long, deserted beaches or rocky headlands, and the sky stretches for miles.

Historically, this area has been populated by hardy fisherfolk and tough, grizzled farmers. Over the years they have worked out a balance with the extreme elements—responding with a stoic minimalism that is obvious in the building styles, the cuisine, and the language.

Unfortunately, minimalism became fashionable, and urban refugees started settling on the West Coast. The first lot wasn't bad—they bought tattered old houses and renovated them just enough to make them livable. Then came those who insisted on building replicas of their suburban homes at the coast. And then—worst of all—came the developers. They bought up huge tracts of land and cut them into tiny little plots, popping horrid little houses onto them. Or perhaps they'd turn a whole bay into a pseudo-Greek village. As a result, the austere aesthetic that makes the West Coast so special is fast disappearing. But it's not gone—at least not yet.

Just inland from the West Coast is the Swartland (Black Ground, a reference to the fertile soil that supports a flourishing wheat and wine industry). Rolling wheat fields extend as far as the eye can see to mountains on either side. In summer the heat is relentless, and there's a sea of golden-brown grain, but in winter the landscape is a shimmery green, and when there's snow on the mountains, it's as pretty as can be. The Swartland includes Piketberg, Malmesbury, Yzerfontein, Darling (also considered part of the West Coast), and the twin towns of Riebeek West and Riebeek Kasteel.

To the north, the Cederberg is an absolutely beautiful and rugged range of mountains, most of which is a designated wilderness area. In South Africa that means you may hike there with a permit, but there are no laid-out trails and no accommodations or facilities of any kind. Fantastic rock formations, myriad flowering plants, delicate rock art, and crystal-clear streams with tinkling waterfalls and deep pools make this a veritable hiker's paradise.

3

A loop around the West Coast, Swartland, and the Cederberg, starting from Cape Town, will take a minimum of three days, but the distances are long, so plan to spend more time here if you can.

GETTING HERE AND AROUND

The roads up the West Coast are generally good, but some dirt roads are rutted and bumpy. If you plan to head into the Cederberg Mountains rather than just sticking to the small towns, consider renting a 4x4, especially in winter, when roads become muddy and you run a small risk of being snowed in.

The major car-rental agencies have offices in the smaller towns, but it's best to deal with the Cape Town offices; you'll probably want to pick up a car at the airport anyway. *For car-rental agencies, see Travel Smart.*

To get up the West Coast and to the Cederberg, take the N1 out of Cape Town. Just before Century City shopping center, take Exit 10, which is marked "Goodwood, Malmesbury, Century City Drive and Sable Road" and leads to the N7, the region's major access road. Though the highway is well marked, get yourself a good GPS or map from a bookstore or tourism office and explore some of the smaller roads, which offer surprising vistas or a glimpse into the rural heart of the Western Cape. The Versveld Pass, between Piketberg and the hamlet of Piket-Bo-Berg, at the top of the mountains, has views that stretch for miles.

Intercape Mainliner heads from Cape Town daily up the N7, which is the main route up to the Cederberg. The bus stops at Citrusdal and Clanwilliam, but not coastal towns such as Langebaan and Elands Bay. Expect to pay around R324 to Citrusdal and R333 to Clanwilliam. The journey to Clanwilliam from Cape Town takes about four hours. *For detailed information about travel by bus, see Bus Travel in Travel Smart.*

Although there's public train service to major West Coast towns, it's not recommended, as there have been regular on-board muggings.

TOURS

To see the exceptional rock art in the Cederberg, it's recommended that you take a tour to fully appreciate and understand this ancient art form, about which experts still have questions.

Clanwilliam Living Landscape Project. The community-driven Clanwilliam Living Landscape Project has trained locals to act as guides. Expect to pay around R120 for a one-hour tour that includes a visit to two sites, and R220 for a full tour, which takes about three hours. If you don't have your own vehicle, the guide can pick you up, but you'll be charged a little extra for gas. To see some majestic scenery, take a three-day hike from the Living Landscape Project headquarters through the dramatic Cederberg mountain range. Donkey carts are used to transport your luggage from cottage to cottage in the Moravian Mission villages of Heuningvlei, Brugkraal, and Wupperthal. Expect to pay R2,175–R3,250 per person. ✉ *18 Park St., Clanwilliam* ☎ *027/482–1911* ⊕ *www.cllp.uct.ac.za.*

Donkey Cart Adventures. For something completely out of the ordinary, try a Donkey Cart Adventure, which starts at the top of the Pakhuis Pass and ends a couple of hours later in the tiny hamlet of Heuningvlei in the heart of the Cederberg Wilderness Area. The donkey-cart route is windy and takes you through some spectacular scenery and flora. It's best to plan this trip for spring, when the fynbos is at its best, or in autumn. In summer, temperatures soar in the Cederberg. ✉ *Pakhuis Pass, Clanwilliam* ✛ *17 km (10½ miles) outside Clanwilliam* ☎ *027/492–3070 Heuningvlei Tourism* ⊕ *www.cedheroute.co.za.*

Elandsberg Eco Tourism. Rooibos tea is a big part of this region's economy, and a rooibos tour with Elandsberg Eco-Tourism should fill you in on all you need to know. The shorter tour (which focuses on rooibos), around 1½ hours, costs R150 per person, and the 2½- to 3-hour tour (which focuses on rooibos and fynbos) costs around R260 per person. They will still do a tour if there are fewer people, but they will charge a little extra to cover their costs. Because the tour is out on a farm, they will arrange to pick you up in town. Booking is essential. ✉ *Off R364, 22 km (14 miles) outside Clanwilliam, Graafwater* ☎ *027/482–2022* ⊕ *www.elandsberg.co.za.*

VISITOR INFORMATION

There are tourist offices in most small towns along the West Coast, but the West Coast Regional Tourism Organization has information on the entire area. Visit its website to get a good overview of the area.

The Flowerline is a central hotline that provides details about where the flowers are best seen each day. You can call 24 hours a day July–September.

Contacts Flowerline. ☎ *072/938–8186.* **West Coast Regional Tourism Organization.** ✉ *65 Long St., Moorreesburg* ☎ *022/433–8505* ⊕ *www.capewestcoast.org.*

DARLING

82 km (51 miles) north of Cape Town.

Darling is best known for three draws: its beautiful wildflowers; its sensational performer, Pieter-Dirk Uys, otherwise known as Evita Bezuidenhout; and the hugely popular rock music festival Rocking the Daisies, held each October on Cloof Wine Estate. Evita is at her best all year-round *(see Nightlife and Performing Arts, below)*. The wildflowers are usually at their best August–October, and an annual Wildflower and Orchid Show is held in September. Also in September, the whole town comes alive during the Voorkamerfest (directly translated as "Front Room Festival"), when different homes host a variety of performers for the weekend and you can enjoy pop-up food stalls and wine tasting. When driving into Darling, ignore the rather unattractive new houses on the Cape Town side of the village and head straight through to the Victorian section of town, where pretty period houses line up amid lush gardens.

GETTING HERE AND AROUND
Darling is an easy hour's drive from Cape Town along the N7 north and then west on the R315. Alternately, you could go north on the R27 out of town, then east on the R315.

VISITOR INFORMATION
Contacts Darling Tourism Bureau. ⊠ *Darling Museum, Pastorie St. at Hill St.* ☎ *022/492–3361* ⊕ *www.darlingtourism.co.za.*

EXPLORING
Darling Brew. Started in 2010 (the brewery only opened in 2015), Darling Brew has quickly become one of the Western Cape's most-loved craft beer brands. The beers can be found at many local restaurants and bars, but the microbrewery is located in the town of Darling. Visitors can taste the selection of craft beers in the tasting room, which also serves typically South African snacks and meals. While heavyweights have their pick of seven core and nine speciality beers, lightweights can opt for the "beginner's beer tasting." Some of the favorite brews include the Slow Beer, a refreshing, golden lager and the Bone Crusher, a white beer. ⊠ *48 Caledon St.* ☎ *021/286–1099* ⊕ *www.darlingbrew. co.za* ۩ *Closed Mon.*

Darling Cellars. This large producer makes wines under a number of labels. Look out for the Premium range as well as the award-winning Darling Cellars Blanc de Blanc MCC 2015. Other suggestions include the Reserve Bush Vine Sauvignon Blanc 2017 with notes of peas, passion fruit, green figs, traces of guava on the nose, and a zingy aftertaste. Don't miss out on the Sweet Darling range, a selection of white, red, and rosé wines cultivated from local grapes. It's all good, drinkable stuff at very affordable prices. ⊠ *R315* ☎ *022/492–2276* ⊕ *www.darlingcellars. co.za* ۩ *Tastings R20.*

Groote Post Vineyard. Former dairy farmer Peter Pentz had enough of getting up at 4 am to milk his cows, so together with his son, Nick, he turned instead to wine farming at Groote Post Vineyard. Groote Post fans couldn't be happier. The large, environmentally sensitive winery got off to a fantastic start when its maiden 1999 Sauvignon Blanc was judged one of the best in the Cape, and Groote Post has been garnering awards ever since. Try the Groote Post Kapokberg Sauvignon Blanc, packed with flavors of granadilla, green fig, and green pepper, or taste the Groote Post Kapokberg Pinot Noir, with hints of plum and raspberry. There are no cellar tours. The restaurant, Hilda's Kitchen, is a really excellent choice for lunch and a scrumptious picnic basket, teeming with local cheeses and cured meats, quiche, and chocolate brownies can be ordered in advance at around R350 per couple. A large portion of the farm has been left uncultivated and is covered with endangered *renosterveld* (literally, "rhino vegetation" in Afrikaans), which is found only in this area. These scrubby bushes might not look like much, but in the past they supported large herds of game. Because the vegetation grows in fertile soil, a lot of renosterveld has been lost to agriculture. Game drives (R170 per person) through this unique vegetation for groups of 4 to 10 people take place during the summer; advanced bookings are essential. ✉ *Off R307* ☎ *022/492–2825* 🌐 *www.grootepost.com* 🎫 *Tastings R25.*

!Kwa ttu If you love nature and history, you'll love !Khwa ttu, a culture and education destination, located on a former wheat farm. Vistors can take part in numerous outdoor activities including hiking and cycling. There are also guided tours, which provide insight into the culture and heritage of the San people. Simple accommodations are available as well as a laid-back restaurant that serves local food and wine. ✉ *R27 West Coast Rd.* 🌐 *www.khwattu.org.*

Tienie Versfeld Wildflower Reserve. During the flower season, usually August–October, the Tienie Versfeld Wildflower Reserve is just fantastic: a wonderful, unpretentious, uncommercialized little gem, boasting a range of uniquely South African veld types. This variation has produced some amazing flowers. Look out for the Geophytes (bulbous plants), which are striking in their diverse sizes and colors. ✉ *R315, 12 km (7½ miles) west of Darling* 🌐 *www.sa-venues.com/game-reserves/wc_tienie-versveld.htm* 🎫 *Free.*

WHERE TO STAY

$ B&B/INN 🏨 **Darling Lodge.** You'll soon be made to feel at home at this pretty Victorian B&B with a lovely garden in the heart of the village. **Pros:** centrally located in Darling; perfect accommodations for families; only 15 minutes from the coast. **Cons:** limited number of rooms. [$] *Rooms from: R980* ✉ *22 Pastorie St.* ☎ *022/492–3062* 🌐 *www.darlinglodge.co.za* 🛏 *6 rooms* 🍴 *Breakfast.*

NIGHTLIFE AND PERFORMING ARTS

Fodor's Choice ★ **Evita se Perron.** One of Darling's main attractions is Evita se Perron, the theater and restaurant started by satirist and social activist Pieter-Dirk Uys. The caberet venue is on the platform of the Darling station (*perron* is the Afrikaans word for "railway platform"). Pieter-Dirk Uys has made his alter ego, Evita Bezuidenhout, a household name in South Africa. Performances cost R150 and take place Saturday afternoon and evening and Sunday afternoon. Come early to enjoy a buffet meal in the restaurant (around R100 per person). In the same complex, **Evita's A en C** (get the pun on the name of the ruling party, the ANC?) is the gallery of an arts-and-crafts collective and skills-development center. Here you can see and buy works from West Coast artists; it's open Tuesday–Sunday 10–4. ✉ *Darling Station, 8 Arcadia St.* ☎ *022/492–2851, 022/492–2831* 🌐 *www.evita.co.za.*

LANGEBAAN

50 km (31 miles) northwest of Darling.

Probably the most popular destination on the coast, Langebaan is a great base from which to explore the region, and the sheltered lagoon makes for fantastic water sports, especially windsurfing, kite surfing,

CLOSE UP

Pieter-Dirk Uys: Everyone's Darling

It's fitting that Pieter-Dirk Uys (⊕ *www. pdu.co.za*) and his alter ego, Evita Bezuidenhout (⊕ *www.evita.co.za*), live in a village called Darling. He's the darling of South African satire, and his speech is peppered with dramatic and warmhearted "dahlings." *Tannie* (Auntie) Evita is as much a South African icon as braais and biltong.

Evita Bezuidenhout debuted in a newspaper column written by playwright Pieter-Dirk Uys in the 1970s. He dished the dirt as though he were an insider at the Nationalist Party. His mysterious source's voice grew so strong that she was soon nicknamed the "Evita of Pretoria." She hit the stage in the early 1980s, when apartheid was in full swing and the ruling Nationalist Party was short on humor.

Uys's first production, *Adapt or Dye,* was performed at a small venue in Johannesburg at 11 pm, a time when he hoped the censors would be in bed. The titles of his shows and some characters (all of which he plays himself) are intricately wound up with South African politics and life. *Adapt or Dye,* for instance, was based on a speech by former prime minister P. W. Botha, who said, "South Africans have to adapt to a changing world or die." Thirty-five years later his latest show is *Adapt or Fly,* a title out of the mouth of an ANC politician.

Every performance shows an intricate understanding of the country and her people. Over the years, Uys's richest material has come from the government. Most politicians were happy to be lampooned; in an inhumane society, laughing at themselves made them seem more human. If there's any criticism leveled at Uys, it's that for all his biting remarks, he played court jester to the apartheid government and held back too much. He would argue that too many punches don't put people in seats; too many tickles can be vacuous.

Uys is not just about comedy and satire, however. He's deeply committed to transforming society. Before the first democratic elections in 1994, he embarked on self-funded voter-education tours. He's now channeling his considerable energy into tackling HIV/AIDS. He speaks at schools, where he uses humor and intelligence and pulls no punches. During his presentation he demonstrates how to put a condom on a banana. This he swiftly replaces with a rubber phallus, "because," he explains with a twinkle, "men and boys don't have bananas between their legs. A condom on a banana on the bedside table is not going to protect you!" Of course, the kids shriek with laughter. As always, humor is his weapon of mass distraction.

In 2002, Uys was awarded the Truth and Reconciliation Award, as well as nominated a national living treasure by the South African Human Sciences Research Council. Tannie Evita also has more than a few fans. She received the Living Legacy 2000 Award in San Diego by the Women's International Center for "her contribution to the place of women in the last century." Pieter-Dirk Uys's autobiographies, *Between the Devil and the Deep—A Memoir of Acting and Reacting* and *Elections & Erections,* make for good reading. In 2017 Uys is 72 and Evita is 82. Here's to both of you, dahlings!

—Karena du Plessis

and sea kayaking. The town has a truly laid-back, beachy feel. To quote a local: "There is nowhere in Langebaan you can't go barefoot." Lots of Capetonians have weekend houses and head here on Friday afternoon with boats, bikes, and boards in tow. If you're not into water sports and serious tanning, however, Langebaan doesn't have that much to offer. The town grew up around a slipway, yacht club, and cluster of brick-faced beach houses, and the main drag is unexciting. Though the town comes alive in summer as youngsters crowd the beach and flex their muscles, during the off-season Langebaan quickly reverts to a quiet settlement where people retire to fish and mess about on boats.

GETTING HERE AND AROUND
It's about 30 minutes by car from Darling to Langebaan.

VISITOR INFORMATION
Contacts Langebaan Tourism Bureau. ✉ *Municipal Bldg., Bree St.*
☎ *022/772–1515* ⊕ *www.westerncape.gov.za/facility/langebaan-tourism-bureau.*

EXPLORING

FAMILY **West Coast Fossil Park.** About 20 minutes from Langebaan on the R45 on the way to Paternoster is the West Coast Fossil Park, one of the richest fossil sites in the world. It was discovered by chance while the area was being mined for phosphates in the 1950s. Since then, more than 200 kinds of fossilized animals have been collected, including the Africa bear, which used to roam this area. The park has been declared a national monument, and the curators have done much to make the park and information about the fossils as accessible as possible. There are interactive guided tours, cycling trails through the areas, and interesting archaeological workshops for all ages. There's also a children's play park and a simple coffee shop where you can have a toasted sandwich. ■TIP➜ **Kids will love the tour.** ✉ *R27* ☎ *022/766–1606* ⊕ *www.fossilpark.org.za* ✉ *R20, tours R55.*

West Coast National Park. Even if you don't stop in West Coast National Park, consider driving the scenic road that runs through it rather than the R27 to Langebaan. The park is a fabulous mix of lagoon wetlands, pounding surf, and coastal fynbos. On a sunny day the lagoon assumes a magical color, made all the more impressive by blinding white beaches and the sheer emptiness of the place. Birders can have a field day identifying waterbirds, and the sandveld flowers are among the best along the West Coast. Postberg, the little mountain at the tip of the reserve where ships would drop off their mail on their trip around the Cape, is open only in flower season, which changes from year to year but usually falls between August and October. It's easy to run out of superlatives when describing West Coast flowers, but imagine acres of land carpeted in multicolored blooms—as far as the eye can see. If you're lucky, you may catch glimpses of zebra, wildebeest, or bat-eared fox. Accommodations in the park are rarer than hen's teeth, and families book cottages at the little village of Churchhaven here for years at a time (make sure you book well in advance). ✉ *Off the R27, 11 km (7 miles) north of the R315* ☎ *022/772–2144* ⊕ *www.sanparks.org* ✉ *R120 in flower season, R60 out of season.*

WHERE TO EAT

$$$$ SEAFOOD 🍴 **Die Strandloper Seafood Restaurant.** For a no-frills lunch on the beach, book a table at Die Strandloper. Bring your own drinks and games, and expect to linger for the afternoon. **Known for:** BYOB; kid-friendly; seafood. [$] *Average main: R295* ✉ *Langebaan* ☎ *022/772–2490, 083/227–7195* 🌐 *www.strandloper.com* 💳 *No credit cards* 🕑 *Days and times are seasonal.*

$$ SOUTH AFRICAN FAMILY 🍴 **Geelbek Restaurant.** Passionate about food and history, Elmarie Leonard created this restaurant to preserve the area's fast-disappearing old recipes like fragrant Malay chicken curry and traditional bobotie. Every month the menu is planned around the ingredients, herbs, and fresh produce of the area. **Known for:** historical setting; denningsvleis, a Cape Malay lamb stew; afternoon tea. [$] *Average main: R120* ✉ *West Coast National Park* ☎ *022/772–2134* 🕑 *No dinner.*

WHERE TO STAY

$$ HOTEL 🏨 **The Farmhouse Hotel.** Centered on a restored farmstead built in the 1860s, this hotel has thick white walls, tile floors, and timber beams. **Pros:** great views over the lagoon; relaxed atmosphere. **Cons:** avoid rooms above the kitchen area, as they can be noisy; only two rooms have air-conditioning; area is very windy—expect a few bad hair days. [$] *Rooms from: R1900* ✉ *5 Egret St.* ☎ *022/772–2062* 🌐 *www.thefarmhousehotel.com* 🛏 *18 rooms* 🍽 *Breakfast.*

$ HOTEL FAMILY 🏨 **Friday Island.** If you like water sports or cycling or are generally active, then this guesthouse is a great choice: it's bright, airy, and right on the beach. **Pros:** perfect for family vacations; fall out of bed onto the beach. **Cons:** young, hip, and happening crowd might not suit those wanting a quiet escape; sports center next door can get noisy during the flower season in spring and the summer holidays over Christmas and New Year. [$] *Rooms from: R480* ✉ *92 Main St.* ☎ *022/772–2506* 🌐 *www.fridayisland.co.za* 🛏 *12 rooms* 🍽 *No meals.*

SPORTS AND THE OUTDOORS

The sheltered Langebaan Lagoon is a haven for water-sports enthusiasts, but you don't have to be energetic all the time. There are expansive stretches of beach that are good for walking, sunbathing, and kite flying. Be warned, however: the water might look calm and idyllic, but it's still cold, and the wind can blow unmercifully for days at a stretch. It's fantastic for wind- or kite surfing, but not so great if you want to spend a peaceful day under your umbrella with a book.

Cape Sports Centre. You'll find everything you need here to kite surf, windsurf, kayak, SUP, or canoe or even learn how. You can rent gear or take lessons from qualified instructors. Cape Sports Centre also has a café and bar. ✉ *98 Main St.* ☎ *022/772–1114* 🌐 *www.capesport.co.za.*

PATERNOSTER

47 km (29 miles) northwest of Langebaan.

Paternoster is a mostly unspoiled village of whitewashed thatch cottages perched on a deserted stretch of coastline. The population here consists mainly of fisherfolk, who for generations have eked out a living harvesting crayfish and other seafood. Despite the overt poverty, the village has a character and sense of identity often lacking in larger towns. It helps if you turn a blind eye to the rather opulent houses on the northern side of the village.

GETTING HERE AND AROUND

Paternoster is about a half-hour drive from Langebaan. Take Langebaanweg out of town until you reach the junction with the R45. Turn left and head northwest toward Paternoster. At Vredenburg the road name changes to the R399.

EXPLORING

Columbine Nature Reserve. Along the coast just south of Paternoster, the Columbine Nature Reserve is a great spot for spring wildflowers, coastal fynbos, and succulents. Cormorants and sacred ibis are common here, and the population of the endangered African black oystercatcher is growing each year. You can walk anywhere you like in the 692-acre park (map provided); a round-trip through the reserve is 7 km (4 miles). It's very exposed, however, so don't plan to walk in the middle of the day, or you'll end up with some serious sunburn. Die-hard anglers and their families camp here during the Christmas holidays and revel in the abundant fish. The dusty road has no name, but head south out of town and ask directions of anybody along the way—it's impossible to get lost. There aren't that many roads to choose from. ⊠ *8 km (5 miles) south of Paternoster* ☎ *022/752–2718* 🎫 *R15.50.*

WHERE TO EAT

$$
SOUTH AFRICAN
✕**Oep ve Koep.** Don't be fooled by the appearance of this tiny rustic bistro with a retro garden area. The sensational menu is narrated and inspired by owner Kobus van der Merwe, who creates innovative, smart, and scrumptious dishes from traditional recipes. **Known for:** foraged ingredients; limited menu; fresh baked goods. Ⓢ *Average main: R140* ⊠ *St. Augustine Rd.* ☎ *022/752–2105* ⊗ *No dinner.*

$$
SEAFOOD
✕**Voorstrand.** A little West Coast gem, this old corrugated-iron shack on the beach stood empty for years, then suddenly metamorphosed into a truly innovative seafood restaurant. Voorstrand serves all the expected seafood and fish, but the fish curries and fresh local crayfish are favorites. **Known for:** setting on the beach; fresh seafood; Malay-inspired dishes. Ⓢ *Average main: R100* ⊠ *Strandloper St.* ☎ *022/752–2038* ⊕ *www.voorstrand.com.*

$$$$
SEAFOOD
Fodor's Choice
★
✕**Wolfgat.** The set tasting menu is fierce and precise with small offerings of seafood, seaweeds, veldkos, and pickings from the garden, like breadsticks with bokkom-infused butter, or baked oyster with veld findings. Overlooking the glistening ocean and beach below, Wolfgat has one of the best locations on the West Coast. **Known for:** chef Kobus van de Merwe; experimental and innovative dishes; foraged ingredients; hard-to-get reservation. Ⓢ *Average main: R650* ⊠ *10 Sampson St.* ⊕ *www.wolfgat.co.za* ⊗ *Closed Mon. and Tues. No dinner Wed., Thurs., and Sun.*

WHERE TO STAY

$$$$
HOTEL
⌂ **Abalone House and Spa.** This luxurious boutique hotel set in indigenous gardens has eclectic decor—a mix of restored antiques and modern furniture, with bold paintings adorning the walls. **Pros:** great restaurant with a vibey wine and cocktail bar; swimming pool; spa. **Cons:** no children under 12. ⓢ *Rooms from: R6350* ⊠ *3 Kriedoring St.* ☎ *087/820–5974* ⊕ *www.southofafrica.co.za* ⇄ *10 suites* ⑩ *Breakfast.*

$
B&B/INN
⌂ **Paternoster Lodge & Restaurant.** This lodge makes the most of the sweeping views of the Atlantic Ocean; the rooms are simply decorated, but who needs artwork when at every turn you catch glimpses of the azure sea and pretty bay? At any rate, the rooms are comfortable, with good linens and firm beds, and—a big plus—they all open onto verandas. **Pros:** easy stroll to the beach; kids under five stay free. **Cons:** hold your hat during summer as the wind can blow; rooms are close together. ⓢ *Rooms from: R1300* ⊠ *64 St. Augustine Rd.* ☎ *022/752–2023* ⊕ *www.paternosterlodge.co.za* ⇄ *7 rooms* ⑩ *Breakfast.*

ELANDS BAY

75 km (46½ miles) north of Paternoster.

Mention eBay auctions here, and most people will stare at you blankly. But mention the E'bay left-hand break, and you'll get nods of approval and instant admission into the inner circle of experienced surfers, who make the pilgrimage to Elands Bay to experience some of the Western Cape's best surfing.

This lovely destination is at the mouth of the beautiful Verlorenvlei Lagoon. Verlorenvlei (Afrikaans for "lost wetland," a testimony to its remoteness) is a birder's delight; you're likely to see around 240 species, including white pelican, purple gallinule, African spoonbill, African fish eagle, and the goliath and purple herons. Nearby are some fantastic walks to interesting caves with well-preserved rock art that dates back to the Pleistocene era, 10,000 years ago.

GETTING HERE AND AROUND
Elands Bay is a two-hour drive from Paternoster. To get here, double back on the R399 to Vredenburg, then take the R399 north to Velddrif. You'll join the R27 at a junction just outside Velddrif. Follow the signs to Elands Bay through town and continue on to what looks like a secondary road. It may not seem to have a number, but it's still the R27.

WHERE TO EAT

$$$$
SOUTH AFRICAN
✕ **Muisbosskerm.** For the true flavor of West Coast life, come to the original open-air seafood restaurant, on the beach south of Lambert's Bay. You'll watch food cook over blazing fires, where snoek is smoked in an old drum covered with burlap, bread bakes in a clay oven, and everywhere fish sizzles on grills and in giant pots. **Known for:** local specialties; rustic beachy setting; tourists. ⓢ *Average main: R280* ⊠ *Elands Bay Rd., 5 km (3 miles) south of Lambert's Bay* ☎ *027/432–1017* ⊕ *www.muisbosskerm.co.za.*

3

CLANWILLIAM

46 km (28½ miles) northeast of Elands Bay.

Although the town itself is uninspiring, it's no surprise that half the streets are named after trees or plants. Clanwilliam is at the edge of one of the natural jewels of the Western Cape—the Cederberg Wilderness Area, which takes its name from the cedar trees that used to cover the mountains. In spring the town is inundated with flower-watchers. Clanwilliam is also the center of the rooibos-tea industry.

Clanwilliam was home to Dr. Christiaan Louis Leipoldt, poet and Renaissance man. He is buried in a lovely spot in the mountains a little way out of town; you can visit his grave, which is on the way to the Pakhuis Pass (R364; there's a small signpost). You could also pop into the Clanwilliam Museum, which houses a room devoted to Leipoldt.

GETTING HERE AND AROUND

Driving to Clanwilliam takes close to three hours from Cape Town without stopping, but half the fun is checking out what local farm stands have to offer and stopping to admire the scenery. In spring this trip will take much longer, as you'll likely want to stop to photograph the flowers that carpet the countryside.

VISITOR INFORMATION

Contacts Clanwilliam Tourism Bureau. ⌧ *Main Rd.* ☎ *027/482–2024* ⊕ *www.clanwilliam.info.*

EXPLORING

Cape Leopard Trust. Sheep farming in the Cederberg is a precarious business. Not only are the winters harsh, but valuable sheep may be killed by the leopards that live in the mountains. Farmers have resorted to using gin traps to keep their flocks safe, but with devastating consequences for any animals caught in them. Two researchers, Quinton and Nicole Martins, in conjunction with the farmers in the area, were keen to find a solution to this problem. They established the Cape Leopard Trust. The trust aims to track the movement of the predators to see exactly how many cats remain in the Cederberg and to pinpoint which farmers are most at risk. The trust is also working to introduce Anatolian shepherds—dogs that are bred to bond with sheep and act as their protectors against leopards. Several farmers have already had great success with these dogs. Their flocks are safe, and the leopards aren't at risk of dying an agonizing death in a trap. Cederberg Conservancy has subsequently been formed as a successful PPP initiative between landowners and conservation bodies in the area to improve leopard management. The Cape Leopard Trust does a lot of outreach and educational work with local schools and offers outdoor holiday programs for kids—and adults. ☎ *027/004–1208, 076/552–1201* ⊕ *www.capeleopard.org.za.*

Fodor's Choice ★ **Cederberg.** Clanwilliam is close to the northern edge of the Cederberg, a mountain range known for its San paintings, its bizarre rock formations, and, once upon a time, its cedars. Most of the ancient cedars have been cut down, but a few specimens still survive in the more remote regions. The Cederberg is a hiking paradise—a wild, largely unspoiled

San Rock Art

The Cederberg has astonishing examples of San rock art, and there is a concerted effort to find ways of managing these sites. On your explorations you'll come across paintings of elephants, eland, bees, people, and otherworldly beings that seem to be half human and half beast. Some examples are in pristine condition, whereas others are battered and scarred from a time when hikers saw nothing wrong with scribbling their names across the art, or lighting fires in the caves and overhangs where the paintings occurred. For centuries, people believed the rock art was simply a record of what happened during the daily lives of the San. But since about 1970, there has been a belief that the art is much richer and carries enormous spiritual meaning that tells us about the inner lives of the San. The art is riddled with metaphors, and it's unpacking the rich symbolism that poses a real challenge. Drawings of an eland, for instance, are not simply depictions of animals the San have seen or hope to hunt. Rather the eland serves as an intermediary between the physical and spiritual worlds.

area where you can disappear from civilization for days at a time. About 172,900 acres of this mountain range constitute what has been declared the Cederberg Wilderness Area. Try to visit in spring when the flowers are out and the area is carpeted in orange, yellow, and white flowers. You can get hiking permits from Cape Nature or the local tourism offices in Clanwilliam or Citrusdal. Be sure to tell somebody if you are planning to hike in the area.

A scenic dirt road that heads south out of town, past the tourism bureau and museum, winds for about 30 km (18 miles) into the Cederberg to Algeria, a Cape Nature campsite with self-catering cottages and tent sites set in an idyllic valley. Algeria is the starting point for several excellent hikes into the Cederberg. The short, one-hour hike to a waterfall is great, but it's worth going into the mountains for a day or two, for which you will need to book and obtain a permit through **CapeNature** or from one of the local farms, many of which have simple, self-catering cottages on their land. ⊠ *Clanwilliam* ⊕ *www.capenature.co.za.*

Cederberg Private Cellar. The Cederberg mountain range might be the last place you'd expect to find a vineyard, but that's what makes Cederberg Private Cellar so unusual. It's been in the Nieuwoudt family for five generations. When old man Nieuwoudt, known to everyone as "Oom Pollie," planted the first vines in 1973, all his sheep-farming neighbors thought he had gone mad. Today, however, winemaker David Nieuwoudt and his small team are laughing all the way to the awards ceremonies. At an altitude of around 3,300 feet, this is the highest vineyard in the Western Cape, and consequently is almost completely disease-free. They don't have to spray for the mildew and mealybugs that are the bane of wine farmers in the Winelands of the Western Cape. All the wines are excellent; in fact, you'll struggle to see the labels for all the wine accolades pasted on the bottles. Wine sales staff laugh when you ask them to identify their favorite wines and remark that it's like somebody asking you which child you like most. The farm has self-catering accommodations at Sanddrif. The Cederberg Observatory also operates on this farm on Saturday (but not during full moon and cloudy evenings). It's an open-air wonder run by passionate stargazers, who give a slide presentation when the weather permits and then help you spot faraway galaxies on their super-powerful telescopes. The little farm shop usually stocks delicious koeksisters served with strong coffee, which cuts through the sweetness. ⊠ *Dwarsrivier Farm, Algeria turnoff from the N7* ☎ *027/482–2827* ⊕ *www.cederbergwine.com* ✍ *Tastings R40.*

Clanwilliam Museum (*Ou Tronk Museum*). The display is old-fashioned and not particularly well curated at the Clanwilliam Museum but still gives a sense of remarkable native son Dr. Christiaan Louis Leipoldt and early settler life in the mountains. The wagons, carts, and rudimentary household equipment speak of much harder times, when pioneers headed into the high country wanting to farm or escape colonial control in the cities. ⊠ *Main Rd.* ☎ *027/482–1090* ⊕ *clanwilliammuseum.webs. com* ✍ *R10.*

Pakhuis Pass. East of Clanwilliam the R364 becomes a spectacularly scenic road called Pakhuis Pass. Fantastic rock formations glow in the early morning or late afternoon. There's even a mountain range called the Tra-Tra Mountains, derived from an old Khoi-San word. A steep, narrow road to the right leads to the mission town of **Wupperthal,** with its characteristic white-thatch houses and sleepy air. This used to be a thriving Moravian mission station, and remnants of the old industries remain—a baker still turns out soft, yeasty loaves that are snapped up as fast as they come out of the oven, and you can see shoes being made in the local shoe factory. You can drive this road in an ordinary rental car, but be very careful in wet weather. Donkey Cart Adventures leave from the top of the pass and go down to the tiny remote village of Heuningvlei (which is not on the pass), a former Moravian mission station. Currently only 20 families live here, making a modest living as subsistence farmers.

Ramskop Wildflower Garden. At its best in August—when the Clanwilliam Flower Show takes place at the old Dutch Reformed church, and almost every available space in town is filled with flowers—the Ramskop Wildflower Garden is a wonderful opportunity to see many of the region's flowers all growing in one place. The best time to go is between 11 am and 3 pm, when the sun is at its apex and the flowers are open. You pay to enter the flower garden at the entrance of the Clanwilliam Dam, on the road out of town past the garden. They won't charge you if the weather isn't great and the flowers aren't at their best—that's small-town hospitality for you. There is a simple coffee shop in the garden. Expect opening times to vary for no particular reason. ⊠ *Ou Kaapseweg* ☎ *027/482–8012* ✍ *R20–R30.*

CLOSE UP

Rooibos Tea

Chances are you will either love or hate *rooibos* (red bush) tea, which South Africans drink in vast quantities. It has an unusual, earthy taste, and is naturally sweet. People drink it hot with lemon and honey or with milk or as a refreshing iced tea with slices of lemon and a sprig of mint. It's rich in minerals, such as copper, iron, potassium, calcium, fluoride, zinc, manganese, and magnesium; contains antioxidants; and is low in tannin. Best of all, it has no caffeine. Trendy chefs are incorporating it into their cooking, and you might see rooibos-infused sauces or marinades mentioned on menus. Good coffee shops also serve red cappuccinos and lattes—a delicious and healthful alternative to their coffee counterparts. Rooibos leaves are coarser than regular tea and look like finely chopped sticks. When they're harvested, they're green; then they're chopped, bruised, and left to ferment in mounds before being spread out to dry in the baking summer sun. The fermentation process turns the leaves red—hence the name.

3

WHERE TO STAY

$$$$ HOTEL Fodor's Choice ★ **Bushmans Kloof Wilderness Reserve & Wellness Retreat.** It's no surprise that Bushmans Kloof garners awards each year—the lodge is in an area of rich cultural significance and a South African National Heritage site, and if you spend some time here, you're unlikely to want to leave. **Pros:** you can fly in to the reserve from Cape Town, which takes about an hour; many outdoor activities on offer; stunning rock art on the property; Western Cape is malaria-free, unlike other parts of the country with wildlife lodges. **Cons:** no kids under 12; very expensive. [$] *Rooms from: R8000* ✉ *Off Pakhuis Pass* ☎ *027/482–8200* 🌐 *www.bushmanskloof.co.za* 🛏 *16 rooms* 🍴 *All meals.*

$ RESORT **Traveller's Rest.** If you're on a tight budget, this farm is the place to stay; there are no frills at these basic but comfortable cottages, but the surrounding mountain scenery is spectacular. **Pros:** nearby rock-art route; cottages have self-catering facilities; very reasonable rates; the owner is a real character. **Cons:** amenities are basic; service at the restaurant can be annoyingly slow. [$] *Rooms from: R500* ✉ *Off Pakhuis Pass* ☎ *027/482–1824* 🌐 *www.travellersrest.co.za* 🛏 *25 cottages* 🍴 *Some meals.*

SHOPPING

Strassberger Shoe Factory. *Veldskoen,* or *Vellies,* as they're fondly known, are something of a South African institution. All you have to do is think of the singer David Kramer and his signature red shoes to understand the place they hold in most South Africans' hearts. Vellies used to be the preserve of hardy farmers, who would wear these sturdy shoes with socks and shorts in winter, and without socks and shorts in summer. Thankfully, the styles have changed somewhat, and now you can get the softest shoes made to order from the Strassberger Shoe Factory. The shoemakers you see working here come from generations of craftspeople dating back to when the Moravian missionaries first started shoemaking in Wupperthal. ✉ *12 Ou Kaapseweg* ☎ *027/482–1439* ⊕ *www.strassbergers.co.za.*

CITRUSDAL

53 km (33 miles) south of Clanwilliam.

As you might guess from the name, Citrusdal is a fruit-growing town. It sits by the Olifants River valley, surrounded by the peaks of the Cederberg, and is known as the gateway to the Cederberg. For the most part it's a sleepy farming town, but in spring the smell of fruit blossoms as you come over the Piekenaarskloof Pass (also known as the Piekenierskloof Pass) is incredible.

GETTING HERE AND AROUND

It's usually 45 minutes on the N7 from Clanwilliam to Citrusdal, but factor in delays because of roadwork.

VISITOR INFORMATION

Contacts Citrusdal Tourism Bureau. ✉ *Kerk St. at Miller St.* ☎ *022/921–3210* ⊕ *www.citrusdal.info.*

EXPLORING

Baths. After a grueling hike in the Cederberg, there's no better way to relax than at the Baths, where hot mineral water gushes from a natural spring. The waters' curative powers have been talked about for centuries, and although the formal baths were established in 1739, there's little doubt that indigenous San and Bushmen spent time here as well. On-site are a restaurant and self-catering facilities, which were upgraded following renovations in 2015. You can also go as a day visitor, but you must book at least a day in advance. ✉ *16 km (10 miles) outside Citrusdal; follow signs* ☎ *022/921–8026* ⊕ *www.thebaths.co.za* ▣ *R100 for adults, R50 for children.*

RIEBEEK WEST AND RIEBEEK KASTEEL

104 km (65 miles) south of Citrusdal.

Drive through the small agricultural town of Malmesbury and over the Bothman's Kloof Pass to these twin towns named after Jan van Riebeeck, the 17th-century Dutch explorer of the Cape. The towns developed only a few miles apart because of a disagreement about where to build a church. In the end, two separate places of worship were built, and two distinct towns grew up around them.

Riebeek West is the birthplace of Jan Christiaan Smuts, one of the country's great politicians and leader of the United Party in the 1940s. D. F. Malan, prime minister of the Nationalist Party in 1948, was born on the farm Allesverloren, just outside Riebeek Kasteel. This wine estate produces some great red wines, an exceptional port, and world-class olives and olive oil. The *kasteel*, or castle, in question is the Kasteelberg (Castle Mountain), which stands sentinel behind the towns.

Disenchanted city dwellers have been buying up cottages here to use as weekend getaways, and others are moving out to the small towns and commuting into the city. It's not hard to understand why. Children play in the street and people keep sheep in their huge gardens—a far cry from Cape Town life. There are numerous restaurants, some galleries, and plenty of olive products to buy, including excellent olive oils and bottled olives. Huge groves in the area do well in the Mediterranean climate.

You'll hear the distinctive, rolling accent of the Swartland here. Known as the "Malmesbury *brei,*" it's characterized by long "ghrrrr" sounds that seem to run together at the back of the throat. In Afrikaans, *brei* means "to knit" or "temper," both of which make sense when listening to somebody from the Swartland.

GETTING HERE AND AROUND
The Riebeek Valley is an hour and a half from Citrusdal via the N7 and R311 without traffic. Roadwork will slow you down.

VISITOR INFORMATION
Contacts Riebeek Valley Tourism. ⊠ *7 Plein St., Riebeek Kasteel* ☎ *022/448–1545* ⊕ *www.riebeekvalley.info.*

EXPLORING

Allesverloren. Translated from Afrikaans, Allesverloren means "all is lost." The bleak name derives from a story from the early 1700s, when the widow Cloete owned this farm. Legend has it that she left the farm for a few weeks to attend a church gathering in town, and in her absence the resentful indigenous tribespeople set her homestead alight. When she came back to a smoldering ruin, she declared, "Allesverloren," and the name stuck. Today the farm's prospects are a lot brighter. It has been in the Malan family for generations. The infamous D. F. Malan, regarded as one of the architects of apartheid, gave up the farm for politics. Happily, his descendants are doing a better job at wine making than he did at shaping a country's destiny, and their reds are big, bold, and delicious. Packed with black-currant and tobacco flavors, and with a lingering fruitcake finish, the port (called the Allesverloren Fine Old Vintage) is perfect for cool winter evenings. A family-friendly restaurant and pub on the premises means you can dine in a beautiful setting. ⊠ *R311, between Riebeek Kasteel and Riebeek West* ☎ *022/461–2320* ⊕ *www.allesverloren.co.za* ⊠ *R30.*

Kloovenburg Wine Estate. You have to move fast if you want to snap up any wines from the Kloovenburg Wine Estate. This family-run farm has many awards under its belt and is probably best known for its excellent Shiraz. Wines to take home are the Shiraz 2015, a ruby red wine with smoky flavors and a chocolaty aftertaste, and the Merlot 2015, with sweet berry and oak flavors and excellent aging potential. The 2016 Eight Feet is a fun but very drinkable testimony to the generations of du Toits who have worked the land: it alludes to the eight grape-stomping feet of the owners' four sons. Don't miss out on Annalene du Toit's olive products. Kloovenburg olives and olive oils are exceptional, and they manufacture olive oil beauty products, too. ⊠ *R46, just outside Riebeek Kasteel as you come down the pass into Riebeek Valley* ☎ *022/448–1635* ⊕ *www.kloovenburg.com* ⊠ *Wine tastings R30, olive tastings R30.*

OFF THE BEATEN PATH

Swartland Winery. Because of its location in the less fashionable part of the Winelands, this large cellar a few miles outside Malmesbury has had to work hard for its place in the sun. Previously a well-kept secret among local cost- and quality-conscious wine experts, it's garnering an international reputation. In 2013 and 2014 alone, the winery won four bronze and two silver Decanter World Wine Awards. It is particularly proud of its Bushvine range, and the Bushvine Shiraz and Bushvine Pinotage were ranked among the top 100 SA wines in 2012. ✉ *R45, Dooringkuil, Malmesbury* ☎ *022/482–1134* 🌐 *www.swwines.co.za* 🎫 *Tastings free.*

WHERE TO EAT

$$ ITALIAN

🍴 **Mama Cucina.** The restaurant is dotted with tables dressed in red-and-white-checkered tablecloths, and the outside area is shaded by an awning and trees—the perfect place to sit on a balmy evening. The pasta is all made in-house, but other highlights on the menu include the vitello tonnato, lamb shank, prawn and pea risotto, and the wood-fired pizzas. **Known for:** outdoor dining; traditional Italian cuisine. [$] *Average main: R100* ✉ *Sarel Cilliers St.* ☎ *022/448–1676* 🌐 *www.mamacucina.co.za.*

WHERE TO STAY

$ HOTEL

🏨 **Riebeek Valley Hotel.** At the top of town, with a great view over vineyards and mountains, this small luxury hotel in a converted farmhouse is an oasis from the sweltering Swartland summer heat as well as a winter getaway. **Pros:** in-house spa treatments available; indoor heated pool. **Cons:** avoid Room 8, as it's near the kitchen and can get noisy. [$] *Rooms from: R750* ✉ *4 Dennehof St., Riebeek West* ☎ *022/461–2672* 🌐 *www.riebeekvalleyhotel.co.za* 🛏 *33 rooms* 🍽 *Breakfast.*

THE NORTHERN CAPE

Updated by
Christopher
Clark

South Africa's largest province, the Northern Cape, is also its least populated. Covering almost a third of the country, its deserts and semi-deserts—the Karoo, Kalahari, Namaqualand, and Richtersveld—stretch from the Orange River in the north to the Western Cape border in the south. From the small towns of Springbok and Port Nolloth in the west across 1,000 km (630 miles) to Pofadder and Hotazhel to the diamond capital, Kimberley, in the east, this is a place of large and rugged beauty—a far cry from the verdant Mpumalanga.

The Northern Cape's appeal is in its sense of loneliness, its sparse but remarkable vegetation, and its occasional lunar landscapes. All told, it covers an area of 363,389 square km (225,665 square miles), roughly a third bigger than the entire United Kingdom, but it has a population of just over a million people (only about two per square km), and most are concentrated in a handful of towns.

The province boasts the country's second-largest national park, Kgalagadi Transfrontier Park, the first transfrontier (i.e., crossing a national border) park in Africa. Together with an adjoining national park in Botswana, this park forms one of the largest conservation areas in the world. Ecotourism also draws an annual pilgrimage to see the spectacular Namaqualand flowers far southwest of the park.

The Northern Cape is a harsh province that begs to be driven—flying is an expensive luxury—but therein lies its beauty. There's plenty to see if you're the type who's not afraid to ask questions and to go where your nose leads you. You have to look hard if you're after luxurious accommodations and fine cuisine, but when you find them, it'll be worth it. Such is the joy of discovery in one of South Africa's less-traveled provinces. What you can expect, given a little time and patience, are sleepy villages and charming locals who appreciate visitors tremendously, albeit in very broken, accented English. This is a place of natural wonders, the ancestral land of the Khoi San first people and known for unusual, unique crafts. It's an off-the-beaten-path getaway that could well turn out to be the highlight of your trip to South Africa.

ORIENTATION AND PLANNING

GETTING ORIENTED

The Northern Cape's vastness makes it a difficult place to travel, and on a first trip you'll probably see only a small part of it, such as Namaqualand in flower season, the Kalahari, or Kimberley. Namaqualand is most easily visited from Cape Town and the Western Cape, whereas

Kimberley and the Kalahari are far more accessible from Johannesburg. If you are planning to drive from Johannesburg to Cape Town or vice versa, Kimberley makes an ideal stopover. The Kimberley route (along the N12) is less than 100 km (63 miles) longer than the sterile N1 route with its huge gas stations, toll plazas, and fast-food places. It's also more scenic and not as busy. Although Upington and the Kgalagadi Transfrontier Park are about the same distance from Cape Town as they are from Johannesburg, the roads from Johannesburg are far better.

PLANNING

WHEN TO GO

By South African standards the Northern Cape's climate is exceptionally hot in summer (late November–February), often rising to above 35°C (95°F). It's hottest in Kimberley and just about intolerable in Upington and the Kalahari. Conversely, the region can get seriously cold in winter (mid-May–early August), sometimes dropping below 0°C (32°F) at night. In fact, the province has the dubious honor of being home to the hottest town in South Africa in summer (Upington) and the coldest in winter (Sutherland, in the Karoo), so come prepared to sweat or shiver (mostly by night). The best time to see the flowers in Namaqualand is usually between the middle of August and the end of September, depending on when and how much rain has fallen. Other dates to be aware of: the four-day Gariep Annual Festival (*Gariep* means "orange" in Tsetswana, the language of the Tswana people) in September. Sporting events also bring crowds to Kimberley, but dates change annually.

PLANNING YOUR TIME

To get the most out of this province, plan to visit between mid-August and late September, which would allow for a visit to Kgalagadi Transfrontier Park, a couple of days following the Orange River between Upington and Augrabies National Park, and taking in the culture and flowers of Namaqualand. Ten days would let you see the highlights. Most people have less time and choose to do one of these in two or three days.

3 Days: If you have three days, spend them soaking up the history and culture of Kimberley. On your first day, tour the town and its landmarks, perhaps starting your morning with one of the reasonably priced registered guides. Day 2 can be spent taking an underground tour of a working diamond mine, followed by an afternoon of diamond-rush history at a mine museum. To rest your weary feet, ride on a historic restored tram. On your third day take a side trip, either northwest of town toward Barkly West, where you can see alluvial diggings with a guide or view ancient rock engravings, or south of Kimberley to the evocative Anglo-Boer War battlefield Magersfontein. Take a picnic and have it under one of the ubiquitous thorn trees scattered across the battlefield.

5 Days: If it's spring (August–September), it's worth sharing five days between the florally quite phenomenal Nieuwoudtville, Springbok, and Port Nolloth to get the best of Namaqualand.

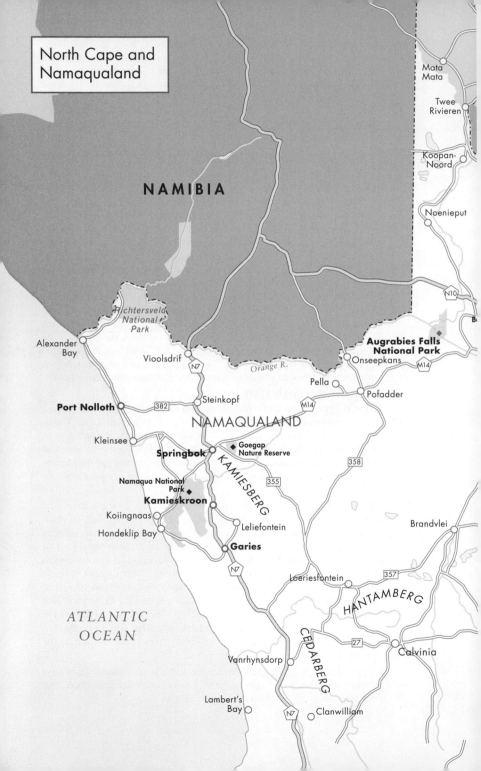

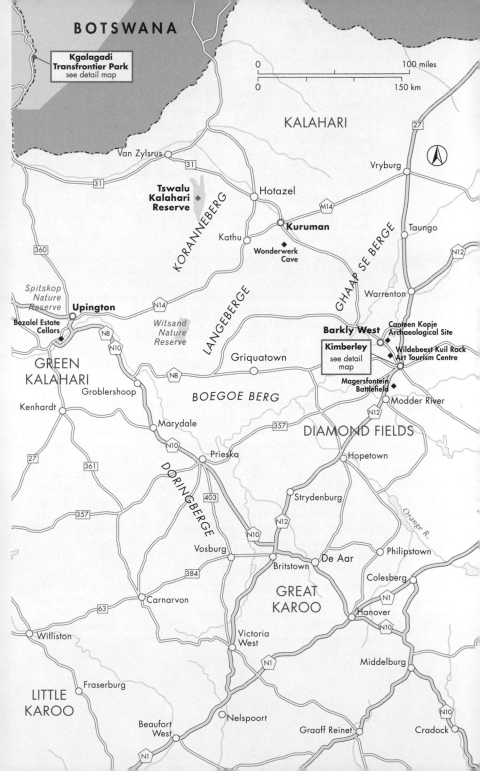

TOP REASONS TO GO

Getting Off the Beaten Path: This is South Africa's emerging, undiscovered province, where less is indisputably more.

Scenery: Mixed in with inevitable boring stuff, there are some awesome landscapes of rugged beauty.

Spring Flower Season: The magnificent wildflowers in Namaqualand must be seen to be believed,
and they are easily reachable from Cape Town.

Starry Skies: The Southern Hemisphere's largest telescope is in off-the-beaten-track Sutherland for good reason.

Desert Game: Excellent game reserves mean an experience very different from Kruger; you'll see more cheetahs and rhinos and fewer elephants.

If you visit between mid-May and late July (winter in South Africa), head for the huge spaces of the Kgalagadi, then spend a night along the Orange River between Upington and Augrabies Falls National Park. Some excellent accommodations and wining (this is serious grape country) and dining establishments have set up in the region in recent years, and these are viable alternatives to the better-known Cape Winelands. Take note that the Northern Cape is a renewable energy hub, and that Upington has a large solar energy project under way. Next try a few days of roughing it in the ruggedly beautiful Kgalagadi Transfrontier Park, cooking your own meals and driving your own vehicle in search of the black-maned Kalahari lions and the beautifully symmetrical gemsbok. Then head for the decadent luxury of two nights at Tswalu Kalahari Reserve, where you'll appreciate the game drives, bush walks, and attention to detail all the more for having roughed it for the past few days. A worthwhile, more affordable, and geographically logical luxury option is Tutwa Desert Lodge, outside Augrabies Falls.

If you visit between October and mid-May, Port Nolloth makes an excellent entry point for the Richtersveld, South Africa's last true wilderness. The Port Nolloth region is an undiscovered country of shipwrecks, diamonds, and crayfish, and is well worth at least two nights and a day in itself. Crayfish season begins in October, so during this time you may want to find a crayfish braai (barbecue) on the beach somewhere. This is off-the-beaten-track stuff. But note: there is no fresh fish in the winter months.

In summer Upington is a good base for day trips to Pella and Klein Pella (visually arresting date-palm plantations), Witsand (wildlife and white sand dunes), the occasional wine estate on the banks of the Orange River, and Augrabies Falls, but be sure to make your visits in early morning or late afternoon, leaving time for a rest or a swim in the midday heat.

GETTING HERE AND AROUND
AIR TRAVEL
The small Kimberley Airport, 12 km (7½ miles) southwest of town, is served by South African Express, which connects to Johannesburg and Cape Town daily (except Saturday), SA Airlink, and South African Airways. CEMAIR flies between Johannesburg and Sishen Kathu—an important mining hub, but these flights aren't really for tourists.

A five-minute drive from the city center, Upington International Airport has the longest runway in the Southern Hemisphere—5 km (3 miles)—and has been the scene of a few global land-speed records. Upington is the gateway to the Kalahari region of South Africa. South African Airways operates a daily service between Upington and both Johannesburg and Cape Town.

BUS TRAVEL
For those travelers with plenty of time, daily bus service between Kimberley and both Cape Town (about 11 hours, R420–R595) and Johannesburg (about 6 hours, R400) is offered by Greyhound and Translux. The local company Tickets for Africa provides schedules, prices, and other information and sells tickets for all buses in and out of Kimberley.

Intercape Mainliner runs daily and night coach services three times a week between Upington and Johannesburg/Pretoria (approximately 10½ hours, R850–R980) and Sunday–Friday service from Upington to Cape Town (about 12 hours, R600–R750) and to Windhoek (approximately 12½ hours, R570–R680).

Intercape Mainliner operates bus service up the West Coast from Cape Town to Springbok (9 hours) on Sunday, Tuesday, Thursday, and Friday evenings, stopping en route at Piketburg and Vanrhynsdorp in the Western Cape and Garies in the Northern Cape. Return service to Cape Town runs Sunday, Monday, Wednesday, and Friday late at night.

CAR TRAVEL
From Johannesburg it is an easy 4½-hour drive (480 km/298 miles) to Kimberley on the N12 and N14; however, the trip from Cape Town is considerably longer, at 954 km (600 miles), and takes approximately 10 hours. The trip from Kimberley to Upington can take another 4 hours. And it's another 2½ hours from Upington to Kgalagadi Transfrontier Park. The drive from Upington to Augrabies Falls is almost 2 hours, and this leg of the N14 is excellent.

Namaqualand, however, is considerably closer to Cape Town than it is to Johannesburg. The drive from Johannesburg to Springbok, the "capital" of Namaqualand, is 1,344 km (835 miles) and takes a little over 12 hours driving straight through with refreshment stops; from Cape Town, it's only 7 hours driving (562 km/349 miles).

TRAIN TRAVEL
Trains between Kimberley and Johannesburg (8 hours) run daily, with extra trains on Wednesday, Friday, and Sunday. There are daily trains to Cape Town (7 hours), with an additional one on Thursday. Sleepers are available only in first and second classes, but you'll want to travel first or second class for safety reasons anyway, and preferably with a companion. Make sure you book tickets together so that they are issued

4

for the same compartment. First- and second-class passengers must reserve in advance. The one-way fare between Kimberley and Johannesburg is R240, R470 between Kimberley and Cape Town, but prices increase for the December to January school vacation. Information on these routes can be obtained from Shosholoza Meyl, the long-distance passenger division of Spoornet. A private security company (Spoornet Security), train assistants, and a manager are on every train. *See Train Travel in Travel Smart.*

HOTELS

The newest tourism kid on the South African provincial block, the Northern Cape is fast developing some outstanding products. Although homey cooking and accommodations remains the norm for this rural province, high-quality guesthouses and even luxury lodgings have emerged around the major business centers and tourist attractions. Guesthouses can be found in just about every little town; the bigger centers like Kimberley and Upington are brimming with them—from basic self-catering units with cooking facilities to luxurious bed-and-breakfasts. There are also comfortable farm accommodations, which offer overnight stays that can be a saving grace late at night on the province's long and lonely roads. In and near the parks and nature reserves, accommodations are in public rest camps, lodges, bungalows, and cottages, which often sleep up to six people, and the odd luxury lodge. Though the price categories given for all lodgings reflect the cost for two people, many places (especially chalets in the national parks) can hold more than two and are, therefore, often a better value if you're traveling as a family or larger party.

Remember that most safari lodges are all-inclusive experiences, with all meals, alcoholic beverages, and activities (like game-viewing) accounted for in the price, but that may not be the case in this region. *Hotel reviews have been shortened. For full information, visit Fodors.com.*

RESTAURANTS

The Northern Cape has never been gastronomically exciting, but some standout additions to the province's tourism map offer food as good as anything you'll find in Cape Town. In the larger towns of Kimberley, Upington, and Springbok—where local residents generally traditionally like a lot of red meat and regard chicken as salad—it may be hard to find what you're looking for. Your most memorable meal might be the legendary delicacy Karoo lamb—often roasted on a *braai*. It can be savored not only on the farms of the Karoo but also in restaurants in Kimberley, Upington, and the Kalahari. Vegetarians will find their needs very difficult to meet in large towns and almost unheard of in small villages. However, fresh fruits, especially grapes, are delicious and abundant in the summer months in the Orange River valley, from Upington to Kakamas. In winter look out for homemade preserves like peach chutney and apricot jam. Other than the more sophisticated hotels and such national steak-house chains as Spurs and Saddles, many restaurants are closed on Sunday evening. Unless you are a large group, reservations are not essential or even expected. Dining in the Northern Cape, even in Kimberley, is a casual affair in all but the few elegant and chic establishments. *Restaurant reviews have been shortened. For full information, visit Fodors.com.*

WHAT IT COSTS IN SOUTH AFRICAN RAND			
	$	$$	$$$	$$$$
Restaurants	under R100	R100–R150	R151–R200	over R200
Hotels	under R1,500	R1,500–R2,500	R2,501–R3,500	over R3,500

Restaurant prices are the average cost of a main course at dinner or, if dinner is not served, at lunch. Hotel prices are the lowest cost of a standard double room in high season.

TOURS

The African Chapter Tours. This operator based near Johannesburg is forging a different path. Specializing in unusual experiences and vast landscapes—for those with both specific and general interests—owner Megan Alves impresses in that she's seen and tested everything she recommends. From the bed to the dinner to the itineraries, she never includes a feature without having had a firsthand look. She and her team will ensure that your tastes, styles, and wishes are satisfied. She offers a range of carefully crafted itineraries into the Northern Cape, and you can be assured that environmental, socioeconomic, and conservation ethics are carefully considered in every compelling journey. ⊠ *Pretoria* ☎ *012/941–2033* ⊕ *www.africanchapter.co.za.*

VISITOR INFORMATION

Northern Cape Tourism Authority. ⊠ *15 Villiers St., Kimberley* ☎ *053/832–2657, 053/833–1434* ⊕ *www.experiencenortherncape.com.*

KIMBERLEY

480 km (298 miles) west of Johannesburg; 954 km (600 miles) northwest of Cape Town.

Kimberley was born in the dust, dreams, and disappointments of a rudimentary mining camp that grew into a city of grace and sophistication in some quarters, still evident in many of its early buildings. Today Kimberley is a city of about 200,000 people spread out around its diamond mines—giant holes in the earth, like inverted *koppies* (hills). Kimberley has a host of comfortable guesthouses and many historical attractions, making it a wonderful place to spend a few days. It's an easy trip of about 4 to 4½ hours from Johannesburg on a good highway, but is almost 11 hours from Cape Town.

GETTING HERE AND AROUND

If you arrive in Kimberley by air, you'll find only two local taxi companies. Although Rikkis Taxis try to meet most flights on arrival, their presence isn't guaranteed, so it's best to reserve a taxi in advance.

If you don't drive to Kimberley, renting a car there is a good idea (Avis, Budget, and Europcar can all be found at Kimberley Airport), as it gives you more freedom, but it's not mandatory if you're staying only a day or two and you hire a good tour guide. Strategically placed monuments and good signage make this an easy town to find your way around in. Just remember to drive within the speed limits, as there are plenty of hidden cameras. Parking is no problem, and gas stations are visible and plentiful. Roads out of town are very straight and generally do not have shoulders.

A restored 1914 tram travels through Kimberley between the other side of the Big Hole and City Hall. The cost is R10 round-trip. Trams leave from the Big Hole when at least four people are ready to go. (Kimberley was the first South African city to have tram service.)

Airport Contacts Kimberley Airport. ✉ *N12, Kimberley* ☎ *053/830-7101.*

Airport Transfers Rikkis Taxis. ☎ *053/842-1764, 083/342-2533* ⊕ *www. rikkistaxis.co.za.*

TOURS

Consider a tour by chartered township taxi (minibus), which will pick you up from wherever you wish. These tours focus on the history and culture of Galeshewe, Kimberley's largest township, named after an important Tswana chief. Places visited include the homes of legendary human-rights activists Sol Plaatje and Robert Sobukwe, as well as the Northern Cape legislature. The tours also take in a traditional *shebeen* (drinking place) and a restaurant serving traditional South African meals. Those wanting a longer township visit can stay at one of several guest-houses catering to tourists there. Galeshewe tours are offered by a variety of local operators; in most cases you'll need to take a taxi to Galeshewe to meet your tour operator, so ask at your hotel to make arrangements.

The Kimberley Ghost Route is another popular tour, starting at night with sherry inside the Honoured Dead Memorial and then proceeding to several of Kimberley's (purportedly) haunted places, such as the Kimberley Club and Rhodes's boardroom. The tour ends with a visit to the historic Gladstone Cemetery, where a certain Mr. Frankenstein and his wife are buried. Prices vary according to the size of the group. Book this one at least two days in advance, and make sure you specify that you want to go inside the haunted buildings, or the tour can be disappointing. The best guides for the ghost tour should be booked through Jaco (*Yako*) Powell or Steve Lunderstedt.

Guide fees are not regulated, and guides therefore charge different rates. A half-day tour should not cost more than R600 per person, a full day not more than R1,200. This excludes transportation, entrance fees, and refreshments.

BOOKING AGENT
Contacts Steve Lunderstedt. ☎ *083/732-3189.* **Jaco Powell.** ☎ *082/572-0065.*

VISITOR INFORMATION
The Northern Cape Tourism Authority, in Kimberley, has information on the entire province. The Kimberley Visitors' Centre has maps and brochures on the Northern Cape and the Kimberley region in particular, and can make referrals. Local guides can also provide good information *(see Tours).*

Contacts Kimberley Visitors' Centre. ✉ *121 Bultfontein Rd., Kimberley* ☎ *053/830-6271* ⊕ *www.solplaatje.org.za.*

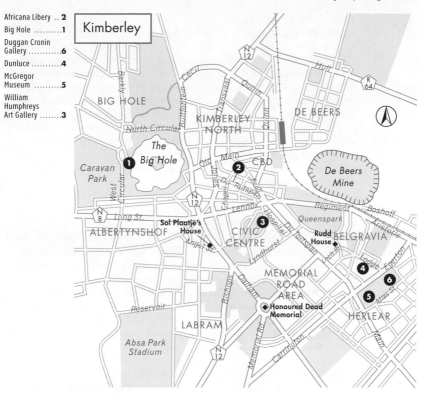

EXPLORING

The hub of business activity, in the CBD (Central Business District), is defined by Jones Street, George Street, and Du Toitspan Road, with its small manufacturing concerns. Victorian-style architecture abounds in Belgravia, Kimberley's first residential suburb, which, beginning in the late 1880s, was associated with the town's mines. De Beers, another suburb that grew up around the De Beers mine, originally constituted part of Johannes Nicholas De Beer's farm. (Both the Kimberley and De Beers mines are now closed, leaving three remaining working mines.) Also on land originally owned by De Beers and of even greater historical interest, the residential area around the Civic Centre is similar to Cape Town's District Six in sociopolitical terms. Called Malay Camp, it was where freed Asian slaves (largely Muslim and erroneously lumped together under the name Cape Malays) settled. Given to the municipality as an open area in 1939, today it is a well-maintained, treed garden area stretching out from the base of the municipal building.

One of the two oldest townships in South Africa, Greenpoint, is located south of town. Despite its age, no standing buildings predate the 1930s. Galeshewe is the settlement to the west of town.

TOP ATTRACTIONS

Africana Library. Housed in the old Kimberley Public Library, which was built in 1887, this is one of the country's premier reference libraries. Books are shelved from floor to ceiling, and an ornate wrought-iron staircase connects the floors. Included among the 20,000 books in the collection are such rarities as the Setswana Bible, the first-ever Bible in an African language, printed by Robert Moffat in the 1850s. The library also has four books dating from the 1400s and a good selection of locally published, limited-edition books for sale. If there's enough interest on tours or when requested by researchers, books are removed from the safe, and visitors can—under surveillance—have hands-on contact with some literary jewels. The library is said to be haunted by the ghost of Bertram Dyer, the first qualified librarian in the country. After he was caught defrauding the library of money, he committed suicide. He now purportedly stacks files on the floor and rattles teacups in the kitchen. ✉ *63–65 Du Toitspan Rd., Kimberley* ☎ *053/830–6247* ⊕ *www.africanalibrary.co.za* ✉ *Donations accepted* ⊘ *Closed weekends.*

FAMILY
Fodor's Choice
★

Big Hole. If you do one thing in Kimberley, visit the Big Hole, at 2,690 feet deep, the largest hand-dug hole in the world. Although water now fills most of its depth, it's still an impressive sight, particularly from the observation post. On the lip is the extensive open-air Kimberley Mine Museum, comprising a host of authentic 19th-century buildings, many of which were moved here from the city center instead of being torn down. They include the first house erected in Kimberley (1877), which was brought piece by piece from Britain to the diamond fields by ship and ox wagon; Barney Barnato's boxing academy; and a bar reminiscent of a Wild West saloon. Replicas of the world's most famous diamonds, including the Eureka, a 21-carat yellow diamond that was South Africa's first recorded diamond discovery in 1866, are also on view. Kids can dig through gravel for a real diamond, and learn about 19th-century attire at the museum. Allow a few hours here, and wear comfortable shoes. ✉ *Tucker St., Kimberley* ☎ *053/839–4600* ⊕ *www.thebighole.co.za* ✉ *R100* ⊘ *Closed Christmas Day.*

McGregor Museum. This graceful Kimberley landmark, built at Rhodes's instigation, was first used as a sanatorium, then an upscale hotel, and later as a girls' convent school. Rhodes himself stayed here during the siege, and you can see rooms he once occupied. Today the building houses a museum that focuses on Northern Cape history (prehistoric to early 20th century) within a global context. It contains quite a good display on the Anglo-Boer War and the even more impressive Hall of Ancestors—an extensive exhibition on the history of humanity that includes prehistoric human skulls dating back some 3 million years. The natural history of the area can be seen in the EnviroZone, and a chapel once stood on what is today the Hall of Religion. ✉ *Atlas St., Belgravia, Kimberley* ☎ *053/839–2700* ⊕ *www.museumsnc.co.za* ✉ *R25* ⊘ *Closed Sun.*

William Humphreys Art Gallery. This renowned art museum in Kimberley's Civic Centre is at once sedate and lively. It's an air-conditioned haven of tranquility on a hot summer day and an active site for community projects, such as the Whag Ubuntu Project, which teaches unemployed black women crafting skills. The gallery's impressive collection features South African works as well as Dutch, Flemish, British, and French masters. One area is devoted to local work, and a very popular exhibit is a permanent display on rock art of the Northern Cape. Free guided tours (preferably booked in advance) cater to specific interests on request. Light meals are available in the gallery's downstairs tearoom, the Palette. ✉ *Cullinan Cresent, Civic Centre, Kimberley* ☎ *053/831–1724, 053/831–1725* 🌐 *www.whag.co.za* 🎟 *R5.*

WORTH NOTING

Duggan Cronin Gallery. This gallery houses early photographs of southern Africa and its inhabitants taken by A. M. Duggan Cronin, an Irishman who arrived in 1897 to work as a night watchman for De Beers. A keen photographer, he traveled widely through southern Africa, capturing his impressions—mostly of African peoples—on film. There are also occasional temporary photographic exhibitions. ✉ *4 Edgerton, adjacent to the McGregor Museum, Belgravia, Kimberley* ☎ *053/839–2743* 🌐 *www.museumsnc.co.za* 🎟 *Donations accepted* 🕒 *Closed weekends.*

Dunluce. A well-known Kimberley landmark, the family home of merchant John Orr has a colonial wraparound veranda painted a distinctive green and white. To see the house you need to take a personalized tour (run by the McGregor Museum), on which you'll hear about such details as the swimming pool (the first in Kimberley) and the red dining room, which took a shell through its ceiling during the siege. ✉ *10 Lodge Rd., Belgravia, Kimberley* ☎ *053/839–2700* 🌐 *www.museumsnc.co.za* 🎟 *R25.*

WHERE TO STAY

$ B&B/INN Fodor's Choice ★ 🏨 **Belgravia Bed and Breakfast.** In a 100-year-old house on leafy Elsemere Road, in the heart of historic Belgravia, this charming guesthouse is within easy walking distance of many of Kimberley's historic attractions, including the McGregor Museum, Dunluce, and the Rudd House. **Pros:** within easy walking distance of many historic attractions; beautiful period-piece architecture; comfortable, small, and intimate. **Cons:** must be booked well in advance; breakfast is a bit basic; rooms are a little small. [$] *Rooms from: R700* ✉ *10 Elsemere Rd., Belgravia, Kimberley* ☎ *053/832–8368, 082/224–3605* 🌐 *www.belgraviabb.co.za* 🛏 *3 rooms* 🍴 *Breakfast.*

$ B&B/INN 🏨 **Milner House.** In a tranquil part of the already sedate Belgravia, this big old, beautiful B&B offers all the comforts of home, with modern and comfortable rooms. **Pros:** refreshing swimming pool; the garden attracts 20 bird species; good breakfast. **Cons:** rooms don't maintain the Victorian period decor of the main house; some furnishings are a little gaudy; no air-conditioning. [$] *Rooms from: R800* ✉ *31 Milner St., Belgravia, Kimberley* ☎ *053/831–6405* 🌐 *www.milnerhouse.co.za* 🛏 *10 rooms* 🍴 *Breakfast.*

$ B&B/INN Fodor's Choice ★ 🏨 **Oleander Guest House.** Close to a number of attractions in the historic suburb of Belgravia, Oleander is a beautifully-renovated Victorian property with luxurious accommodations and an excellent fine-dining restaurant. **Pros:** probably the best dining in Kimberley; smooth service; lovely architecture. **Cons:** some rooms are a little small; French windows opening onto the pool area don't afford maximum privacy;

the extensive security features can feel a bit disconcerting. $ *Rooms from: R900* ⊠ *28 Carrington St., Kimberley* ☎ *053/832–7088* ⊕ *www. oleander.co.za* ⇗ *10 rooms* ⦿ *Breakfast.*

NIGHTLIFE

Halfway House. Cecil John Rhodes used to stop for a drink at Halfway House, halfway between the Kimberley and Bultfontein mines. Because he was short and it was difficult for him to mount and dismount, he was served on his horse. Thanks to the building of a 6-foot wall to prevent people from drinking in public, this novel tradition still lives on at this Kimberley institution. You can drive into the parking lot at "the Half," honk your horn, and a waiter will appear. Today, though, most of the action is inside, where the under-30 crowd can get rowdy at night, making the most of the wide drinks selection. If you go on a drinking spree, you can even spend the night at the attached hotel, at which point no amount of noise will wake you. ⊠ *229 Du Toitspan Rd., Belgravia, Kimberley* ☎ *053/831–6324.*

SHOPPING

Annette's Gift Shop. The gift shop at Big Hole has Kimberley's best assortment of postcards, slides, books, videos, and knickknacks as well as a wide range of ethnic souvenirs such as T-shirts and pillow covers. (Postcards mailed in the pre-1902 Victorian mailbox outside the shop will receive a Kimberley Mine Museum postmark.) You can also buy diamonds and diamond jewelry here, but it may be useful to compare pieces and prices with the Jewel Box, down the road. ⊠ *Big Hole, W. Circular Rd., Kimberley* ☎ *053/831–2681* ⊙ *Closed Christmas Day and Good Friday.*

Jewel Box & Big Hole Diamond Cutting Factory. The Jewel Box & Big Hole Diamond Cutting Factory specializes in diamond jewelry and can custom-make a piece if you will be in town for a day or two. Although the Jewel Box doesn't boast about its prices, they are among the country's most reasonable, and they draw customers from as far as Johannesburg. On weekdays you can watch goldsmiths at work in the on-premises factory. ⊠ *18 W. Circular Rd., Big Hole, Kimberley* ☎ *053/832–1731* ⊙ *Closed Sun.*

SIDE TRIPS FROM KIMBERLEY

BARKLY WEST

32 km (20 miles) north of Kimberley on the R31.

The town of Barkly West, on the Vaal River, was the site of some of the earliest alluvial diamond diggings in South Africa.

EXPLORING

Canteen Kopje Archaeological Site. Today you can visit the open-air Canteen Kopje Archaeological Site to view both archaeological and geological treasures, ranging from Stone Age artifacts more than a million years old to rock axes, found in a recent excavation, that date from the late 1800s. Walk the 1-km (½-mile) trail to take in the exhibits. Students of history—and South Africa in particular—will really appreciate this off-the-beaten-path stuff. ⊠ *Barkly West* ✛ *10 km (6 miles) southeast of Barkly West, toward Kimberley* ☏ *082/222–4777* ☙ *Free.*

NEED A BREAK

Pump House Bar. Finish off your tour of Barkly West with a drink or light snack at the Pump House Bar, on the important Vaal River and within a stone's throw of the town's small, neglected but still-interesting museum, which can be opened up for visitors on request by staff at the Pump House. The pub itself is a great place to meet locals, enjoy a good steak or other pub fare, and contemplate the waters of the Vaal River. ⊠ *Barkly West* ✛ *On Vaal River just south of Barkly West* ☏ *053/531–0867.*

Fodor's Choice ★

Wildebeest Kuil Rock Art Tourism Centre. At the Wildebeest Kuil Rock Art Tourism Centre, the 1-km-long (½-mile-long) San Rock Art Trail takes you on a short walk back through time. Billed as "helping to protect the future of the past," this memorable community-based rock art experience includes engravings made by ancestors of the Khoisan, dating between 1,000 and 2,000 years ago. (Ancestors of the Khoisan are believed to be some of the earliest humans to walk the face of the Earth.) Listening to an audio player, you take a boardwalk to the best of more than 400 images—eland, elephant, rhino, wildebeest, hartebeest, ostrich, and dancing human figures—on a low ridge of ancient andesite rock. The center also offers a 20-minute introductory film and display on the subject and a crafts shop run by the !Xun and Khwe San (refugees from the Angolan and Namibian wars), whose land surrounds the site. ⊠ *Between Barkly West and Kimberley* ✛ *15 km (9 miles) northwest of Kimberley on the R31, en route to Barkly West* ☏ *053/833–7069* ⊕ *www.museumsnc.co.za/wildebeestkuil.htm* ☙ *R35.*

WHERE TO STAY

$$ RESORT

▣ Mattanu Private Game Reserve. Most accommodations at this small, family-operated game reserve are in luxury tents under the shade of the indigenous camel-thorn trees, with each intimate and secluded tent including a viewing deck overlooking a water hole. **Pros:** small and intimate atmosphere; eco-friendly environment; family-run by caring owners. **Cons:** popular local wedding venue, so it can be booked up; not a Big Five reserve; in winter the early morning game drives can be an icy affair. $ *Rooms from: R1800* ⊠ *Barkly West* ✛ *17 km (10½ miles) north of Barkly West* ☏ *060/988–5555* ⊕ *www.mattanu.com* ⤢ *7 rooms* ☉ *Some meals.*

THE KALAHARI

With Namibia to its west and Botswana to its north, the Kalahari is an area of arid dunelands that rightfully conjures up images of desolation. Much of the area is vast, semi-desert terrain with minimum rainfall, and it's largely uninhabited—by humans, that is. It is home to the oryx, springbok, and black-maned lion.

Paradoxically, the southern Kalahari—stretching west along the R64 from Upington to Kakamas and beyond—turns that stereotype on its head. This is the so-called Green Kalahari, the basin of the Orange River, South Africa's largest. It is where the hunter-gatherer San (Bushmen) marked the dry Kalahari as their home, and the fertile land around the Orange was originally occupied by the pastoral Khoi people. Here irrigation has created a literal oasis that today includes thousands of acres of vineyards and the largest date farm in the Southern Hemisphere. Along the roads, irrigation canals are punctuated with waterwheels, an old-fashioned irrigation technique that elevates water so it can be directed into the vineyards, particularly in Kakamas and Keimoes.

In winter the fields and vineyards are brown and bare, but in spring they turn from the neon green of new growth into a deep, lush summer green that makes the area look more like the Winelands of Paarl and Stellenbosch. Grapes are one of the province's major industries: 80% of South African sultanas are grown in the Northern Cape, and table grapes are a rapidly growing export.

Acting as a gateway to both these Kalaharis is the river town of Upington, known countrywide for its intense heat.

GETTING HERE AND AROUND

Because of its isolation, most people with limited time fly into the region via Upington, and many lodgings provide shuttle service from Upington Airport. You can also rent a car or 4x4 (Avis, Budget, and Europcar serve Upington Airport), but if you plan to do so, reserve it far in advance, because their numbers are limited.

If you are driving, Upington and the Kalahari are usually approached from Kimberley along the scenic and winding R64, a distance of 411 km (257 miles). The N14, on the northern side of the Orange River, is a slightly longer alternative—450 km (313 miles)—but it's faster because it is straighter. Upington is 375 km (233 miles) from Springbok along an excellent paved road. There are several 4x4 trails within the Kgalagadi at Bitterpan and Gharagab, but it is not necessary to have one to get there or for getting around inside the park.

Most towns, game parks, and even remote areas have gas, but use common sense and anticipate long distances by refueling when passing a gas station. Roadside car wrecks bear testimony to what locals say is the biggest danger on these roads: falling asleep at the wheel.

Airport Contacts Upington International Airport. ✉ *Diedricks St., Upington* ☎ *054/337–7900.*

TOURS

Day trips from Upington to Augrabies Falls start at R630 per person. Kalahari Desert tours start at R2,500 per person for a few days. The latter are usually fully inclusive of entrance fees, food, and beverages.

Kalahari Safaris. Catering to all levels of the market, from budget to luxury, this popular company is widely praised and booked months in advance. The owner, Pieter Hanekom, was trained in bush lore by the San Bushmen and often says, "People say if the sand of the Kalahari gets in your shoes, you always come back." He calls the Kalahari one of the last true wilderness areas, and he brings his expertise to small groups of travelers. ⊠ *6 Morant St., Upington* ☎ *087/233–5067, 082/435–0007* ⊕ *www.kalaharisafaris.co.za.*

Kalahari Tours and Travel. Dantes Liebenberg of Kalahari Tours and Travel customizes trips to Kgalagadi Transfrontier Park from an afternoon to two weeks. Other specialties are the Witsand Nature Reserve, Augrabies Falls, the Kalahari, Namaqua flower tours (in season), and farther afield to Namibia and Botswana. The all-inclusive three-day desert experience, which includes interacting with the San community, is a must. Tours range from the four-star variety to backpacker style. Even better, the company is committed to responsible tourism and supports local communities and projects whenever possible. ⊠ *12 Mazurkadraai, Upington* ☎ *054/338–0375, 082/493–5041* ⊕ *www.kalahari-tours.co.za.*

VISITOR INFORMATION

Local guides are often more reliable, knowledgeable, and helpful in disseminating information than the local government tourist office.

UPINGTON

411 km (257 miles) northwest of Kimberley.

Home to about 74,000 residents, Upington is a thriving agricultural center on the north bank of the Orange River. In the 1870s a Koranna (a group within the Na'ama culture) captain named Klaas Lucas invited missionary Christiaan Schroder to come to Olyvenhoudtsdrift (Ford at the Olive-wood Trees), as Upington was first known. Construction on the first mission buildings, now part of the Upington museum complex, was started in 1873. The town was renamed after Sir Thomas Upington, a Cape attorney general who was responsible for ridding the area of its notorious bandits in the 1880s. Although convention has it that the first person to irrigate crops from the Orange was Schroder himself, recent historical research has revealed that this honor should go to Abraham September, a freed coloured slave, who first led water from the Orange in about 1882.

EXPLORING

Bezalel Estate Cellars. If you are a fan of cognac and liqueurs, then a stop here is a must. From his pot still, Tinus Bezuidenhout produces and sells really good brandies, and especially high-quality liqueurs. His (or his son Martiens's) generous hand with the tastings will be appreciated by all except the designated driver. It's a family-operated business, and Tinus also knows everyone in the area, so think of him as a tourism resource, too. ✉ *N14, between Upington and Keimos* ☎ *054/491–1141* 💻 *Free.*

Orange River Wine Cellars. In Upington's industrial area is Orange River Wine Cellars, the second-largest wine cooperative in the world (the largest is also in South Africa). Tastings of a variety of white wines—from the sweet and rich dessert wine Hanepoort to the lighter Steens and Chenin Blancs—as well as grape juice are offered. Between January and March you can also take a tour of the cellars. ✉ *32 Industrial Rd.* ☎ *054/337–8800* ⊕ *orangeriverwines.com* 💻 *Tastings R25 for 5 wines; R35 for 7* ⊙ *Closed Sun.*

Sakkie se Aartjie (*Sakkie's Ark*). If you're missing the sea, a sedate sunset cruise on the Orange River may be just the thing. Sakkie se Aartjie offers a 90-minute trip on a double-decker raft complete with cash bar. After dark you may see monkeys, fish, eagles, and other birds, as well as catfish. ✉ *Park St., below O Hagans Restaurant* ☎ *082/564–5447* ⊕ *www.arkie.co.za* 💻 *R120* ⊙ *Closed weekdays, and only available for group bookings during winter months.*

WHERE TO EAT

$$
SOUTH AFRICAN

✗ **Dros.** You can drop in for a meal or just a drink at the bar in this large, rowdy, and rustic franchise steak house and wine cellar. Wine bottles are packed into the walls from floor to ceiling, and numerous archways give the place a Mediterranean feel. **Known for:** quality meat cuts; festive atmosphere; very reasonable prices. 💲 *Average main: R100* ✉ *Pick 'n Pay Centre, Hill St.* ☎ *054/331–3331* ⊕ *www.dros.co.za.*

WHERE TO STAY

$
B&B/INN
Fodor's Choice
★

⌨ **African Vineyard Guesthouse.** Just outside Upington on Kanon-Eiland, an island in the Orange River (South Africa's largest), this luxurious and peaceful guesthouse sits among expansive vineyards and beautiful labyrinthine gardens. **Pros:** brilliant mix of accommodation styles; superb cuisine; convivial hosts. **Cons:** bit of a distance from Upington; rooms can be a little cold in winter; a popular wedding venue, so can be booked out. 💲 *Rooms from: R1300* ✉ *Kanon-Eiland, Plot 79* ☎ *083/461–1724, 071/607–4582* ⊕ *www.africanvineyard.co.za* ⇄ *12 rooms* ⊙ *Breakfast.*

$
B&B/INN

⌨ **A Riviera Garden B&B.** In the middle of a row of guesthouses, the Riviera is an oasis of personal attention, charm, and tasteful interiors. **Pros:** beautiful garden on the river; very good breakfast; secure parking. **Cons:** you have to prepay to confirm booking; only two units; some furnishings are a little tacky. 💲 *Rooms from: R1100* ✉ *16 Budler St.* ☎ *054/332–6554* ⊕ *upington.co.za/ariviera* ⊟ *No credit cards* ⇄ *2 rooms* ⊙ *Breakfast.*

$
B&B/INN

⌨ **Kalahari Guest House.** A perfect overnight stop on the way to or from the Kgalagadi National Park, this typical South African homestead, 50 km (31 miles) north of Upington, caters to all budgets. **Pros:** countryside atmosphere with a lot of local flavor; proximity to Kgalagadi Transfrontier Park; very reasonable prices. **Cons:** accommodations are a little basic; far from other amenities; no meals included in the rates. 💲 *Rooms from: R600* ✉ *R360* ☎ *073/194–2864* ⊕ *www.kalahariguesthouse.co.za* ⊟ *No credit cards* ⇄ *4 rooms* ⊙ *No meals.*

$ RESORT [hotel] **Witsand Kalahari Nature Reserve Lodge.** It's worth staying a few nights in one of the chalets or bungalows at this beautiful site in the southern Kalahari, especially if you can't get all the way to Kgalagadi. **Pros:** roaring sand dunes; good game; desert bush sounds at their best. **Cons:** off the well-worn track; self-catering only; chalets could do with a face-lift. [$] *Rooms from: R630* ✢ *220 km (137 miles) east of Upington on the road to Griquatown and then another 45 km (28 miles) down a sometimes rocky road to Witsand* ☎ *083/234–7573* 🌐 *www.witsandkalahari.co.za* 🛏 *17 rooms* 🍴 *No meals.*

AUGRABIES FALLS NATIONAL PARK

4

120 km (75 miles) west of Upington; 40 km (25 miles) northwest of Kakamas.

The Khoi, early pastoralists who lived in this area for thousands of years before the arrival of Europeans, called these falls Aukoerabis (Place of Great Noise), and though Augrabies is a relatively small national park (696,850 acres), its falls are truly impressive. Reports of sightings of a river monster in the gorge have been made frequently but are probably fanciful accounts of shoals of giant barbels, which reach about 7 feet in length.

Augrabies Falls National Park. South Africa's largest falls in volume of water, Augrabies plunges 653 feet over terraces and into a gorge 18 km (11 miles) long, which was carved into smooth granite over millions of years. It is strangely otherworldly. Legend has it that an unplumbed hole beneath the main falls is filled with diamonds washed downriver over millennia and trapped there.

Depending on what you're looking for, you can hike in the park for an hour or several days. You don't need a guide. You can also drive around the park to its beautiful and well-appointed lookout points, which offer spectacular views of the gorge below the falls. Unfenced Ararat provides the best views. Oranjekom, which is fenced with a shaded hut, is particularly welcome in the blistering summer heat, and the Swartrante lookout offers a view over the rugged, barren areas of the park. All are easily accessible and well marked. For the energetic, the Gariep 3-in-1 Adventure is a day trip that consists of canoeing down the Orange for 4 km (2½ mile), hiking another 4 km (2½ miles), and taking a 12-km (7½-mile) mountain-bike ride. During peak times, the park also offers worthwhile night drives. Recently renovated, reception is at the main gate, and the visitor center, with an information office, shop, and restaurant, is a few miles down the road. All accommodations here were renovated in mid-2014. ✉ *Augrabies* ☎ *054/452–9200* 🌐 *www.sanparks.org/parks/augrabies* 🎟 *R176 per person per day.*

WHERE TO STAY

$ RESORT [hotel] **Augrabies Rest Camp.** South African National Parks (SANParks) offers a variety of modern, clean units near both the main visitor center and the falls that were renovated in mid-2014. **Pros:** beautiful, peaceful environment; great hikes and walks; chalets recently renovated (some with better views). **Cons:** can get crowded; SANParks food is not the best (better to bring your own); the rest camp's shop can be a little under-stocked. $ *Rooms from: R1000* ✉ *Augrabies* ☎ *012/428–9111 parks board, 054/452–9200 park* ⊕ *www.sanparks.org* ↻ *59 rooms* ❏ *No meals.*

$
B&B/INN
❏ **Damas Guesthouse.** In a real story of community uplift, a Nama teacher (originally from Namibia) and her family in the Augrabies Falls village have uniquely decorated rooms in their old house near the hot springs on the Riemvasmaak community trust land. **Pros:** a real community project; beautiful environment; solitude and peace. **Cons:** not the easiest place to get to; few mod cons; no catering for breakfast. $ *Rooms from: R400* ✉ *Riemvasmaak Community, Augrabies* ☎ *071/966–5200* ▭ *No credit cards* ↻ *3 rooms* ❏ *No meals.*

$
HOTEL
❏ **Dundi Lodge.** Situated just 3 km (2 miles) from the falls, this stylish luxury lodge, which oozes hospitality, is a recent addition to this desert oasis. **Pros:** excellent dinner menu; beautiful rooms; dirt runway outside for that 4-km (2½-mile) morning run. **Cons:** bit of a drive to the falls; bathrooms are a little small; the restaurant also takes outside guests, so can get busy. $ *Rooms from: R1390* ✉ *4 Airport Blvd., Rooipad, Augrabies* ☎ *054/451–9201* ⊕ *www.dundilodge.co.za* ↻ *11 rooms* ❏ *Breakfast.*

$$$$
HOTEL
Fodor's Choice
★
❏ **Tutwa Desert Lodge.** Only a few lodges in South Africa are blessed with truly phenomenal locations, and Tutwa is one of them, but it's not for the seekers of the Big Five. **Pros:** a standout South African location; acceptable isolation and solitude; attention to details. **Cons:** animals can be few and far between; fairly isolated; prices may be prohibitive to some. $ *Rooms from: R8780* ✉ *Southern Cross Game Reserve, Schuitdrift, Augrabies* ☎ *054/451–9200* ⊕ *www.tutwalodge.co.za* ↻ *9 rooms* ❏ *All-inclusive.*

$
HOTEL
❏ **Vergelegen Guesthouse.** This well-placed guesthouse for travelers on the road from Upington to Riemvasmaak Hot Springs also has a good restaurant, curio shop, and cocktail lounge (and even swings for kids in the garden). **Pros:** excellent amenities; good restaurant; accepts pets. **Cons:** a little isolated; not the most intimate option in the area; rooms might be too modern for those seeking something more rustic. $ *Rooms from: R1000* ✉ *Kakamas* ⊹ *Just off the N14, a few km from Kakamas* ☎ *054/431–0976* ⊕ *www.augrabiesfalls.co.za* ↻ *25 rooms* ❏ *Breakfast.*

KGALAGADI TRANSFRONTIER PARK

260 km (162 miles) north of Upington on the R360.

If you're looking for true wilderness, remoteness, and stark, almost surreal landscapes and you're not averse to foregoing luxury and getting sand in your hair, then this uniquely beautiful park within the Kalahari Desert is for you.

The Kgalagadi Transfrontier Park is less commercialized and developed than Kruger. The roads aren't paved, and you'll come across far fewer people and cars. There's less game on the whole than in Kruger, but because there's also less vegetation, the animals are much more visible. Also, because the game and large carnivores are concentrated in two riverbeds (the route that two roads follow), the park offers unsurpassed game-viewing and photographic opportunities. Perhaps the key to really appreciating this barren place is in understanding how its creatures have adapted to their harsh surroundings to survive—like the gemsbok, which has a sophisticated cooling system allowing it to tolerate extreme changes in body temperature. There are also insects in the park that inhale only every half hour or so to preserve the moisture that breathing expends.

The landscape—endless dunes punctuated with blond grass and the odd thorn tree—is dominated by two *wadis* (dry riverbeds): the Nossob (which forms the border between South Africa and Botswana) and its tributary, the Auob. The Nossob flows only a few times a century, and the Auob flows only once every couple of decades or so.

The park is famous for its gemsbok, the desert-adapted springbok, and its legendary, huge, black-maned Kalahari lions. It also has leopard, cheetah, eland, blue wildebeest, jackal, and giraffe, as well as meerkat and mongoose. Rarer desert species such as the elusive aardvark, and the pretty Cape fox, also make their home here. Among birders, the park is known as one of Africa's raptor meccas; it's filled with bateleurs, lappet-faced vultures, pygmy falcons, and the cooperatively hunting red-necked falcons and gabar goshawks.

The park's legendary night drives depart most evenings around 5:30 in summer, earlier in winter (check when you get to your camp), from Twee Rivieren Camp and Nossob. The drives set out just as the park gate closes to everyone else. You'll have a chance to see rare nocturnal animals like the brown hyena and the bat-eared fox by spotlight. The guided morning walks—during which you see the sun rise over the Kalahari and could bump into a lion—are also a must. Reservations are essential and can be made when you book your accommodations.

WHEN TO GO

The park can be superhot in summer and freezing at night in winter (literally below zero, with frost on the ground). Autumn—from late February to mid-April—is perhaps the best time to visit. It's cool after the rains, and many of the migratory birds are still around. The winter months of June and July are also a good time. It's best to make reservations as far in advance as possible, even up to 11 months if you want to visit at Easter or in June or July, when there are school vacations.

GETTING HERE AND AROUND

Upington International Airport is 260 km (162 miles) south of Kgalagadi Transfrontier Park; many lodgings provide shuttle service, or you can rent a car at the airport. If you reserve a car through an agency in Upington, you can pick it up from the Twee Rivieren Camp. If you drive from Johannesburg, you have a choice of two routes: either via Upington (with the last stretch a 60-km [37-mile] gravel road) or via Kuruman, Hotazel, and Vanzylrus (with about 340 km [211 miles] of gravel road). The gravel sections on both routes are badly corrugated, so don't speed.

VISITOR INFORMATION

There's a daily conservation fee for all visitors, which can be paid at the Twee Rivieren reception desk. Reservations for most accommodations, bush drives, wilderness trails, and other park activities must be made through South African National Parks, and it's recommended to book all of the above well in advance.

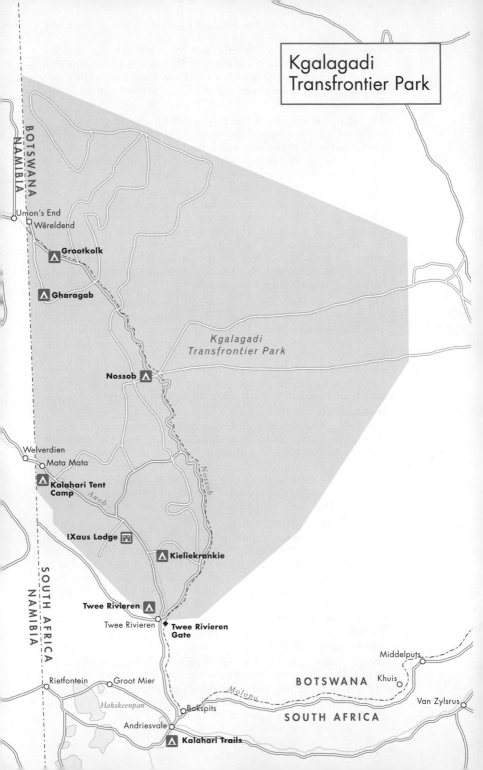

EXPLORING

Kgalagadi Transfrontier Park. Originally called Kalahari Gemsbok National Park when it was first incorporated in 1931, Kgalagadi was combined with Botswana's Gemsbok National Park to create this internationally protected area of nearly 9 million acres. Unlike Kruger, South Africa's other mammoth national park, this is a desert park, with sparse vegetation and even sand dunes. The game seen here is mostly concentrated around two roads, which follow the park's two (mostly) dry riverbeds. Black-maned Kalahari lions, springbok, oryx, pygmy falcons, and martial eagles are among the star animal attractions. You will not find the broad range of big mammals that you see in Kruger, but because of the sparse vegetation and limited grazing areas, they are more visible here. Among the noteworthy plant species are plenty of beautiful camel-thorn acacia trees. The park has several lodges and more rustic rest camps for accommodations, but its isolation means that it's never as crowded as Kruger. ⊠ *Twee Rivieren Rest Camp* ☎ *054/561–2000* ⊕ *www.sanparks.co.za* ⊠ *R304 per adult per day.*

WHERE TO STAY

Accommodations within the park are in three traditional rest camps and several highly sought-after wilderness camps (try to reserve these if possible) that are spread around the park. All of the traditional rest camps have shops selling food, curios, and some basic equipment, but Twee Rivieren has the best variety of fresh fruit, vegetables, milk, and meat, and is the only camp with a restaurant. Twee Rivieren is also the only camp with telephone and cell-phone reception (although cell-phone reception quickly disappears as you head into the dunes) and 24-hour electricity; the other camps have gas and electricity, but the electricity runs only part of the day, at different times in each camp.

For all national park accommodations, contact South African National Parks (✉ *reservation@sanparks.org*), or you can reserve directly through the park if you happen to be there and would like to stay a night or add another night onto your stay.

For a private luxury lodge, !Xaus, owned by the Khomani San community, is deep in the west of the park. Because it's roughly 50 km (32 miles) in from the gate, guests are met by a vehicle at the Kumqwa rest area, where they park their car. From there it is exactly 91 dunes to the lodge in a 4x4—and well worth it.

BOOKING

South African National Parks. It's usually safest and quickest to book through the central booking office in Pretoria, although oftentimes when that office says "full," the camp itself has vacancies. ☎ *012/428–9111 Pretoria* ⊕ *www.sanparks.org.*

LODGES

$$$$
RESORT
Fodor's Choice
★

🏨 **!Xaus Lodge** If you want to experience one of South Africa's most beautiful and isolated parks without hassle, then this luxury lodge owned by the Khomani San and Mier communities and jointly managed with Transfrontier Parks Destinations is the place for you. **Pros:** unique wilderness setting; only private lodge in area; opportunities to interact with the local indigenous people. **Cons:** it doesn't get much

San Culture and Language

The Northern Cape has a long and rich human history. Also called the !Xam, the hunter-gatherer San (most of whom prefer to be called Bushmen, as it describes their skill) have a culture that dates back more than 20,000 years, and their genetic origins are more than 1 million years old, contemporary humans' oldest. Fast-forward a few years—about 2,000 years ago, to be inexact—when Korana or Khoi (Khoe) herders migrated south, bringing their livestock and settling along the Orange (Gariep/Garieb), Vaal, and Riet rivers. During the 18th and 19th centuries the Griquas—thought to be part Khoi and part African and Malay slaves—moved into the Northern Cape with their cattle and sheep.

At one time 20–30 languages pertaining to various San/Bushmen clans flourished, but colonialism brought with it devastating results for most of these languages, which lost out to Tswana and Afrikaans. In the nick of time in the 1870s, British doctor Wilhelm Bleek (who spoke !Xam) and Lucy Lloyd recorded the last activities of !Xam culture and tradition. (Some of these records can be found at the McGregor Museum in Kimberley.)

Still, thousands of Northern Cape residents today acknowledge an ancestral connection to the largest San or !Xam group of the 18th and 19th centuries. The two biggest remaining groups are the !Xu and the Khwe, who live at Schmidtsdrift, 80 km (50 miles) from Kimberley. Among the best-known groups in South Africa today is the Khomani San, some of whom still speak the ancient Nu. For a good overview on the languages, culture, and peoples who migrated to the Northern Cape, check out the McGregor Museum.

---

more remote than this; not a Big Five destination; chalets in need of a spruce-up. $ *Rooms from: R4390* ⊠ *Dune 92 Kgalagadi* ☎ *021/701–7860* ⊕ *www.xauslodge.co.za* ⇌ *12 rooms* ⦿ *All-inclusive.*

REST CAMPS

$

B&B/INN

⛺ **Kalahari Trails.** Offering clean, comfortable self-catering accommodations just a short drive away from the Twee Rivieren gate to the Kgalagadi Transfrontier Park, this is the kind of unique place that's worth seeking out. **Pros:** individual and unique; Anna is engaging and a font of information; very reasonably priced. **Cons:** accommodations are a bit basic; it's a bit of a way from many of the Kgalagadi's wildlife hot spots; due to her age, Anna doesn't lead the walks any more, which is a loss. $ *Rooms from: R600* ⊠ *Andriesvale* ☎ *054/511–0900* ⊕ *www.kalaharitrails.co.za* ⇌ *8 rooms* ⦿ *No meals.*

$

RESORT

⛺ **Mata Mata.** This camp, 120 km (74 miles) from Twee Rivieren on the Namibian border, has good game-viewing due to the proximity of the water holes, and is particularly well known for regular giraffe sightings. **Pros:** you're allowed to drive into Namibia without visas for a certain distance; great water holes; giraffes galore. **Cons:** dry and dusty year-round; can get crowded; a long drive from the park's entrance on the South African side. $ *Rooms from: R945* ⊠ *Kgalagadi Transfrontier*

Park ☎ 012/428–9111 reservations 🌐 www.sanparks.org 🛏 12 rooms 🍴 Some meals.

$ RESORT 🏨 **Nossob Rest Camp.** In the central section of the park, this camp is on the Botswana border, 166 km (103 miles) from Twee Rivieren. **Pros:** riverbed location in a desert landscape makes it a great place to see predators, particularly lions; there's a predator information center; it's right in the thick of the action. **Cons:** barren, unattractive camp; no phone reception; perpetually in need of a spruce-up. [$] *Rooms from: R995 ✉ Kgalagadi Transfrontier Park ☎ 012/428–9111 reservations 🌐 www.sanparks.org 🛏 18 rooms 🍴 No meals.*

$ RESORT FAMILY 🏨 **Twee Rivieren Rest Camp.** On the Kgalagadi's southern boundary, this camp is home to the park's headquarters. **Pros:** modern, well-equipped chalets; on-site grocery store selling basics; not-to-be-missed guided morning and night drives. **Cons:** the biggest and noisiest camp in the park; not particularly attractive; a fair drive from the park's best wildlife hot spots. [$] *Rooms from: R1110 ✉ Kgalagadi Transfrontier Park ☎ 012/428–9111 reservations 🌐 www.sanparks.org 🛏 31 rooms 🍴 No meals.*

WILDERNESS CAMPS

Kgalagadi is the first national park to provide accommodations deep in the wilderness, where several unfenced wilderness camps with their own water holes for game-viewing put you deep in the heart of the Kalahari. These enchanting camps are very popular, so make your reservations well in advance—up to 11 months ahead, if possible. Each camp is slightly different, but all have the same facilities and are similarly priced. All have an equipped kitchen with a gas-powered refrigerator, solar-powered lights, gas for hot water, and a deck with braai facilities. You do need to supply your own water and firewood.

Because all of these camps are unfenced (which is part of their desirability and charm), it's probably best not to walk away from your accommodations at night. There's a very real chance of face-to-face encounters with nocturnal hunters like lions, leopards, and hyenas.

$ RENTAL 🏨 **Bitterpan.** This elevated camp overlooks an enormous expanse of sand and a water hole, where you can watch game come and go from your deck or from the communal areas. **Pros:** spectacular game-viewing from your accommodations; beautiful desert scenery; only four cabins. **Cons:** 4x4s only; no children under 12; it's a long drive to get here from any starting point. [$] *Rooms from: R1495 ✉ Kgalagadi Transfrontier Park ☎ 012/428–9111 reservations 🌐 www.sanparks.org 🛏 4 rooms 🍴 No meals.*

$ RENTAL 🏨 **Gharagab.** Although you'll need a 4x4 to negotiate the two-track road to Gharagab, it's worth every dusty mile for the chance to feel like you're the only person on Earth. **Pros:** you've probably never experienced solitary wilderness such as this; great views from your private deck; only four units means guaranteed intimacy. **Cons:** 4x4s only; not much in the way of big game; guests must bring their own drinking water and firewood. [$] *Rooms from: R1495 ✉ Kgalagadi Transfrontier Park ☎ 012/428–9111 reservations 🌐 www.sanparks.co.za 🛏 4 rooms 🍴 No meals.*

$$ RENTAL 🏨 **Grootkolk.** Surrounded by camel-thorn trees and close to the Nossob River bed, this lovely camp has good game-viewing, with lions, cheetahs, hyenas, and lots of antelope, including oryx and springbok, and it

4

can book up months in advance. **Pros:** spotlighted water hole; sublime wilderness; ceiling fans in the cabins. **Cons:** a long drive from other camps; no children under 12; the cabins are not the prettiest. [$] *Rooms from: R1630* ✉ *Kgalagadi Transfrontier Park* ☎ *012/428–9111 reservations* 🌐 *www.sanparks.org* 🛏 *4 rooms* 🍴 *No meals.*

$$ RENTAL FAMILY 🏠 **Kalahari Tent Camp.** Many visitors say that this good game-viewing camp overlooking the Auob River bed and water hole is one of the most beautiful places in the park, so try to stay for more than one night. **Pros:** near Mata Mata, which has a shop and gas; excellent game; family-friendly. **Cons:** guests must bring their own drinking water and firewood; not as intimate as some of the other wilderness camps; camp kitchen not the best equipped. [$] *Rooms from: R1600* ✉ *Kgalagadi Transfrontier Park* ☎ *012/428–9111 reservations* 🌐 *www.sanparks.org* 🛏 *15 rooms* 🍴 *No meals.*

$$ RENTAL 🏠 **Kieliekrankie.** Perched high on a big sand dune only 8 km (5 miles) from the game-rich Auob River road, this small camp overlooks seemingly infinite red Kalahari sands, creating an amazing sense of space and isolation. **Pros:** easily accessible with a sedan; you can start your game drives before residents of the other camps reach the area so you have the game to yourself for a while; the red Kalahari sands are unforgettable. **Cons:** no children under 12; guests must bring their own drinking water and firewood; no double beds. [$] *Rooms from: R1630* ✉ *Kgalagadi Transfrontier Park* ☎ *012/428–9111 reservations* 🌐 *www.sanparks.org* 🛏 *4 rooms* 🍴 *No meals.*

$$ RENTAL 🏠 **Urikaruus.** Four cabins with kitchens, bedrooms, and bathrooms are built on stilts among camel-thorn trees with beautiful vistas overlooking the Auob River. **Pros:** accessible with a sedan; stunning location; game to yourself on early-morning and late-afternoon drives. **Cons:** no children under 12; guests must bring their own drinking water and firewood; only single beds available. [$] *Rooms from: R1630* ✉ *Kgalagadi Transfrontier Park* ☎ *012/428–9111 reservations* 🌐 *www.sanparks.org* 🛏 *4 rooms* 🍴 *No meals.*

TSWALU KALAHARI RESERVE

250 km (155 miles) southeast of Kgalagadi Transfrontier Park; 262 km (163 miles) northeast of Upington; 145 km (90 miles) northwest of Kuruman.

Near the Kgalagadi Transfrontier Park is the malaria-free Tswalu Kalahari Reserve, at 1,000 square km (386 square miles) the largest privately owned game reserve in Africa; it's the perfect place to photograph a gemsbok against a red dune and big blue sky. Initially founded as a conservation project by the late millionaire Stephen Boler (how he made his money is a story in itself), primarily to protect and breed the endangered desert rhino, he left it to the Oppenheimer (of De Beers diamonds fame) family in his will. Today it spreads over endless Kalahari dunes covered with tufts of golden veld and over much of the Northern Cape's Korannaberg mountain range. Its initial population of 7,000 animals has grown, and it's now home to lions, cheetahs, buffalos, giraffes, and a range of antelope species—including rare species such as roan and sable antelope, black wildebeest, and mountain zebra. For (sadly) financial reasons a fence keeps the lion and the sable antelope separate in this massive reserve. There's not as much game as in some of Mpumalanga's private reserves because the land has a lower carrying capacity (the annual rainfall is only about 9¾ inches). But when you do see the animals, the lack of vegetation makes sightings spectacular.

GETTING HERE AND AROUND
The lodge operates a direct flight between its Johannesburg airport hangar and Tswalu (this has to be booked directly through the reserve). It's also easy (and cheaper) to fly to Kimberley or Upington and be picked up from there by the lodge. Daily charter flights are available from Johannesburg, Durban, and Cape Town with Airlink. Road transfers from Kimberley or Upington can be arranged, or you can book a charter flight from Johannesburg.

EXPLORING

FAMILY **Tswalu Kalahari Reserve.** This reserve northeast of Upington is one of the most child-friendly game reserves in southern Africa. Children are welcomed and well catered to, with lots of freedom and special activities. No other game reserve offers such flexibility, and the dedication of the field guides and butlers here allows you to plan your days as you please: you might prefer a Champagne breakfast in your stunning accommodations to going out on a game drive, or you may want to sleep under the stars on the "Malori" open deck. The reserve plays a particularly important conservation role: backed by funds from the De Beers family, its desert black rhino population represents one-third of South Africa's entire remaining animals. In addition to rhino sightings, the interactive experience with the meerkats is a highlight when staying at Tswalu, as are visits to 380,000-year-old rock engravings from the earliest residents of these phenomenal landscapes. ☎ 053/781–9331 ⊕ www.tswalu.com.

WHERE TO STAY

$$$$ ▦ **The Motse.** Tswalu's main lodge is made up of freestanding thatch-
RESORT and-stone suites clustered around a large main building with a heated
FAMILY natural-color pool and a floodlighted water hole. **Pros:** special children's room and babysitting services and nannies available; unique desert landscape; wonderful library with rare books. **Cons:** no elephants; sable antelopes kept separate from the lions, making the experience feel a little manufactured; if being waited on hand and foot isn't your thing, this may not be the place for you. $ *Rooms from: R17000* ⊠ *Tswalu Kalahari Reserve* ⊕ *www.tswalu.com* 🛏 *8 rooms* ¶❍¶ *All meals.*

$$$$ ▦ **Tswalu Tarkuni Lodge.** In a private section of Tswalu, Tarkuni is an
RENTAL exclusive, self-contained house decorated similarly to The Motse and
FAMILY offering a comparable level of luxury. **Pros:** this is excellent value for money if you're a group who can fill the house; a children's paradise; black-maned Kalahari lions, occasional wild dogs, cheetahs, and one-third of South Africa's endangered desert black rhino population. **Cons:** no elephants; not for couples or small groups; no chance to mingle with guests outside your group. $ *Rooms from: R18000* ⊠ *Tswalu Kalahari Reserve* ⊕ *www.tswalu.com* 🛏 *5 rooms* ¶❍¶ *All meals.*

4

KURUMAN

250 km (156 miles) northeast of Upington.

If you have a car while in the Kalahari region, it's worth stopping in Kuruman, the hub of a dairy, cattle, and game-farming area. With flat, wide streets, the town is a rush of green in the middle of the Kalahari. Camel-thorn and stinkwood trees are everywhere, but cleanliness is not high on this municipality's priority list, so arrive without expectations. Follow signs to "The Eye" or "Die Oog," an amazing natural spring that bubbles out 5 million gallons of water daily. This is the source of the Kuruman River and of massive significance to the arid Northern Cape, though the river's polluted appearance can be a bit disappointing.

EXPLORING

Kuruman Moffat Mission. Established in 1816, the Kuruman Moffat Mission is the most famous mission station in Africa. It was headed by Robert Moffat from 1820 until his retirement in 1870. The site, with stone-and-thatch buildings dating from the 1820s and 1830s and surrounded by huge trees, represents an interface between precolonial history and the present. A complete Setswana Bible was printed here in 1857—the first time the Bible was printed in its entirety in a previously unwritten African language. The mission served as a springboard for many early adventures into the interior, including David Livingstone's expeditions. It's a lovely and gentle place full of memories, though it's in need of some TLC. It still functions as a mission and community center, and has a small curio shop. ⊠ *Moffat La., Kuruman* ✚ *5 km (3 miles) north of Kuruman on Hotazel Rd.* ☎ *053/712–1352* 💰 *R10.*

OFF THE BEATEN PATH

Wonderwerk Cave. This fascinating heritage site contains a spectacular 460-foot-long cave that shows evidence of 800,000 years of Stone Age occupation and early fire use. Some 10,000-year-old engravings were found in the deposit, and the cave has unusual rock paintings on its walls. A good museum adjacent to the cave provides detailed interpretation, and a resident guide will show you around. The cave is administered by Kimberley's McGregor Museum, which can provide additional information, and advance reservations are advised. ⊠ *Off the R31, 50 km (31 miles) south of Kuruman* ☎ *053/839–2700, 082/222–4777 direct line for Professor David Morris* ⊕ *www.museumsnc.co.za* 💰 *R30* ⊗ *Closed weekends except by special arrangement.*

NAMAQUALAND

This huge, semi-desert region extending north from the West Coast to Namibia, hundreds of miles north of Cape Town and west of Kimberley, is a highlight of South Africa. It's a remote, unpopulated area, with few facilities and comforts. In spring, however, it puts on a spectacle that must be the greatest flower show on Earth. Vast fields that seemed barren only a month before blush with blossoms—and in two months they're gone again. *Vygies* (a type of succulent fynbos) and Namaqualand daisies brightly splash the hillsides and valleys with color. Known as the Succulent Karoo, the area is dependent on the right weather conditions—staggered and regular rainfall and particular temperature and light—to show off its full beauty. As with many South African village businesses, the flowers tend to open at 10 and close at 4. Unless it's flower season, think twice about trekking to Namaqualand. As in parts of the American West, distances are vast, and the landscape looks harsh, mostly hills dotted with giant boulders and swollen-trunked *kokerbooms* (quiver trees, so named because Bushmen cut arrow quivers from them).

Khoisan populations have lived in Namaqualand for thousands of years. The first Europeans to venture into the area were Dutch settlers from the Cape, who came in search of the copper they knew existed here because the Khoi had used it in trade. Though Simon van der Stel, a governor of the Cape Colony, sank test shafts in 1685 and realized there were rich quantities of copper in the hills around Okiep and Carolusberg, it wasn't until the 1840s, when the Okiep Copper Mining Company came to Namaqualand, that copper was mined on a large scale. Today the region's commercial activity is clustered in the *dorps* (small towns) of Okiep, Concordia, and Nababeep, and in the region's most prominent town, Springbok—all of whose roots lie in copper. The area is littered with heritage sites harking back to the early copper days, from the smokestack in Okiep to the Messelpad Pass, south of Springbok.

GETTING HERE AND AROUND

If traveling from Johannesburg, you can fly to Upington and rent a car from the airport. It's a lovely four hour drive from Upington to Springbok.*For more information, see Air Travel in Travel Smart.*

Intercape Mainliner provides bus transportation to Springbok from both Cape Town and Johannesburg. *For more information, see Bus Travel in Travel Smart.*

Namaqualand is more than 320 km (200 miles) north of Cape Town and 900 km (563 miles) west of Kimberley. With the great distances involved and the absence of any real public transportation, the only way to get around is by car. Roads are generally well paved, but signage to tourist attractions is not always good. From Springbok to Hondeklipbaai there is an 80-km (50-mile) stretch of sandy gravel road. Traffic to Springbok picks up on Friday and Saturday, when people from neighboring communities converge on the town.

If you arrive by bus, you can rent from Titis or Namaqualand 4x4 Hire, which also rents camping equipment. Make your reservations early. If you're going to the Richtersveld, rent a bakkie (pickup truck) or 4x4, as sedans are not permitted.

Car-Rental Contacts Namaqualand 4x4 Hire. ⊠ *15 Jurie Kotze St., Springbok* ☎ *027/712–1905.* **Titus Car Rental.** ⊠ *7 van den Heever, Springbok* ☎ *027/718–2544.*

TOURS

Local trips around Springbok lasting several hours start from around R350 per person. Three-day Richtersveld trips cost around R5,000 per person, all-inclusive, with a minimum of two people.

Contacts Aukwatowa Tours. ⊠ *47 Flosse St., Port Nolloth* ☎ *027/851–7047* ⊕ *www.aukwatowatours.co.za.*

VISITOR INFORMATION

The Namakwa Tourism office is across from the Agenbag gas station in Springbok. Springbok Lodge's tourist-friendly, welcoming approach often makes it the first place visitors stop for information and free maps.

Tourist Offices Namakwa Tourism. ✉ *Voortrekker Rd., Springbok* ☎ *027/718–2985* 🌐 *www.namakwa-dm.gov.za.* **Springbok Lodge/Tourist Information.** ✉ *37 Voortrekker St., Springbok* ☎ *027/712–1321* 🌐 *www.springboklodge.com.*

GARIES

58 km (36 miles) northeast of Vanrhynsdorp.

Garies is a one-horse town cradled amid sunbaked, granite-dominated hills, and one of the best flower routes runs just north of it for 100 km (60 miles) to Hondeklipbaai, on the coast. The road winds through rocky hills before descending onto the flat coastal sandveld. Flowers in this region usually bloom at the end of July and early August. If you're lucky, fields along this route will be carpeted with purple vygies, but also look for Namaqualand daisies, aloes, and orchids. Quiver trees are common along this route, too.

WHERE TO STAY

$$ RESORT 🏨 **Agama Tented Camp.** This camp is open in and out of Namaqualand's world-renowned wildflower season. **Pros:** phenomenal scenery, especially in the (spring) flower season; very intimate experience; good meals. **Cons:** isolation could be an issue for some out of flower season; no cell reception; no children under 12. [$] *Rooms from: R2300* ✉ *Klipfontein* ✣ *20 km (12 miles) north of Garies* ☎ *072/0400–614* 🌐 *www.agamacamp.co.za* 🛏 *5 rooms* 🍴 *Some meals.*

KAMIESKROON

49 km (30 miles) north of Garies; 72 km (45 miles) south of Springbok on the N7.

Another base for exploring Namaqualand in spring, Kamieskroon is the only place to stay close to Namaqua National Park—unless you're in the park itself. The Kamieskroon Hotel, although no great shakes for accommodations, is a good source of information on wildflowers in Namaqualand. The SANParks information center at the gate to the park should also help.

EXPLORING

Namaqua National Park. During its flower season (August through early October), Namaqua National Park can usually be counted on for superb wildflower displays, even when there are no flowers anywhere else. Covering an area of almost 200,000 acres, 21 km (11 miles) west of Kamieskroon, the park is the world's only arid biodiversity hot spot. Recent upgrades include more routes and new rest camps; game (tsetsebe, oryx, springbok, and eland) has been reintroduced. Visitors look for Namaqua daisies in oranges and yellows as well as succulents, such as the many-colored vygies in hues of purple, magenta, and orange. Roads are good throughout the park. Driving from Soebatsfontein toward Springbok yields spectacular views over the coast from the top of the Wildeperdehoek Pass. Two short hiking trails take a few hours each. A visitor center is at the Skilpad entrance, and an on-site restaurant across the road caters to those in need. ✉ *Skilpad Rd.* ☎ *027/672–1948* ⊕ *www.sanparks.co.za* 💳 *R74.*

**OFF THE
BEATEN
PATH**

Leliefontein. A 29-km (18-mile) detour from Kamieskroon brings you to this old Methodist mission station at the top of the Kamiesberg, which has spectacular views across the desert to the sea. The church, a national monument, was finished in 1855, but the adjacent parsonage is much older. The wildflowers in Leliefontein bloom much later than those on the coast, often lasting as late as the end of October. Even if there are no flowers, it's a beautiful drive back down the Kamiesberg to Garies, 72 km (45 miles) away. ✉ *Liliefontein.*

4

WHERE TO STAY

**$$$
RESORT**

🏨 **Namaqua Flower Skilpad Camp.** During flower season, this rustic camp puts you in the middle of things, as you are surrounded by low-lying mountains and, of course, fields of orange, yellow, and white flowers with superb views all around. **Pros:** gorgeous setting, with low-lying mountains on the surrounding horizon; the Namaqua National Park never fails to deliver a natural flower spectacular; real off-grid experience. **Cons:** pricey for what you get; unsatisfactory meals for the price; there's no self-catering option. 💲 *Rooms from: R3300* ✉ *Skilpad Nature Reserve* ☎ *084/299–577* ⊕ *www.flowercamps.co.za* 🕐 *Closed Oct.– July* 🛏 *20 rooms* 🍽 *All meals.*

SPRINGBOK

117 km (73 miles) north of Kamieskroon; 375 km (233 miles) south-west of Upington.

The capital of Namaqualand is set in a bowl of rocky hills that form part of the Klipkoppe, a rocky escarpment that stretches from Steinkopf, in the north, to Bitterfontein, in the south. Quiver trees proliferate in the area, and flower season brings the town alive with multicolored carpets. Though the town owes its existence to the discovery of copper, its architecture is mostly modern, with very few buildings dating from the 1800s. Compared with most of the dorps in the Northern Cape, Springbok is a buzzing little town, with a fair number of things to see in the area if you need to take a break from flower gazing.

EXPLORING

Goegap Nature Reserve. Each spring this reserve transforms into a wild-flower mosaic, which you can discover on either of two short—4- and 6-km (2½- and 4-mile)—walking trails. Goegap is also home to the Hester Malan Wildflower Garden, which displays an interesting collection of succulents, including the bizarre *halfmens,* or "half person" (*Pachypodium namaquanum*), consisting of a long, slender trunk topped by a passel of leaves that makes it resemble an armless person—hence the name. During flower season, there's a small kiosk open on-site where you can get a bite to eat. ✉ *R355* ✛ *16 km (10 miles) southeast of town via airport road* ☎ *027/718–9906* 💳 *R30.*

Namaqualand Museum. Displays at the Namaqualand Museum tell the history of Namaqualand, the town of Springbok, and the people who lived here. Articles range from some 17th-century pieces to an old fridge and washing machine made from *kokerboom* wood (from the distinctive "half-man" tree). The museum is housed in an old synagogue, and pays tribute to the era when Jews lived in Springbok (180 Jews lived here until 1972, but there are none left today). The earliest Jewish traders had a significant impact on the growth of business not only in the area, but in the country as a whole. The massive and nationwide Lewis chain of stores had its origins here in the little town of Springbok. ✉ *Monument St.* ☎ *053/132–2645* 🎟 *Donations accepted* 🕒 *Closed weekends.*

WHERE TO EAT

$$ SOUTH AFRICAN FAMILY
🍴 **Herb Garden Restaurant & Coffee Shop.** This tucked-away, family-friendly eatery is an unusual and very welcome little gem in Springbok's otherwise limited dining scene. Expansive breakfast, lunch, and dinner menus are available. **Known for:** slow-cooked lamb dishes; very reasonable prices. [$] *Average main: R100* ✉ *4 Kruis St.* ☎ *027/712–1247* 🌐 *www.herb-garden.co.za.*

WHERE TO STAY

$ B&B/INN
🏨 **Apollis Cottage.** Remote in location, 30 minutes from Springbok, this is the real deal if you want comfort and solitude with big skies in a desertlike location. **Pros:** remote location provides solitude; modern accommodations; good value for money. **Cons:** bedroom color combinations are not attractive; parts of the road are rough when it rains; while the area is beautiful, the buildings are a little bland. [$] *Rooms from: R800* ✉ *Homeb 6* ✈ *20 km (12 miles) off the N2* ☎ *079/429–3022* 🌐 *www.theapolliscottage.com* 💳 *No credit cards* 🛏 *3 rooms* 🍽 *Breakfast.*

$$$ HOTEL
🏨 **Naries Namakwa Retreat.** This picturesque and upscale Cape Dutch–style guesthouse west of Springbok looks out over the mountains of the Spektakelberg. **Pros:** beautiful location in the mountains; excellent cuisine; the mountain suites are a truly special offering. **Cons:** location is pretty isolated; the dining room can feel a bit sparse and uninviting; no Wi-Fi and patchy cell reception in the mountain suites. [$] *Rooms from: R2620* ✉ *Kleinzee Rd.* ✈ *27 km (17 miles) west of Springbok on the R355* ☎ *027/712–2462* 🌐 *www.naries.co.za* 🛏 *12 rooms* 🍽 *Some meals.*

$ HOTEL
🏨 **Okiep Country Hotel.** About 8 km (5 miles) from Springbok, this hotel is one of the nicest places to stay in Namaqualand, not only for the above-average accommodations and dining ($–$$), but also because owner Malcolm Mostert has created a homey atmosphere and goes out of his way to be helpful and friendly. **Pros:** hands-on, longtime owner/manager; hearty meals; good value. **Cons:** style is a subjective matter; some rooms are in need of a spruce-up; not the most intimate option in the area. [$] *Rooms from: R950* ✉ *Main St., Okiep* ☎ *082/569–7158, 082/744–1000* 🌐 *www.okiep.co.za* 🛏 *37 rooms* 🍽 *No meals.*

EN ROUTE For an excellent **flower drive,** take a 320-km (200-mile) rectangular route that heads north on the N7 from Springbok to Steinkopf and then west on the paved R382 to Port Nolloth. From there a dirt road leads south through the Sandveld to Grootmis, then east along the Buffels River before climbing the Spektakel Pass back to Springbok. If the rains have been good, the route offers some of the best flower viewing in the region. Note that this depends entirely on the time of the season and the rains—there might be little in obvious evidence. Try to time your return to Springbok to coincide with the sunset, when the entire Spektakel Mountain glows a deep orange red.

PORT NOLLOTH

4

110 km (69 miles) northwest of Springbok.

Port Nolloth—a lovely drive from Springbok, particularly during flower time—started life as a copper port, but it's better known today as a fishing and diamond center. With only one (decent) road leading into it, the flat, desertlike coastal dorp is a ghost town at night, as the little life that exists by day dies completely after dark. If the few establishments in town are full, MacDougall Bay a mile down the coast has accommodations.

Port Nolloth is also the springboard to the Richtersveld, the vast region of mountains and desert to the north, which is well known for its exquisite succulents and other flora but should be visited only on an organized tour or once you have armed yourself with a considerable amount of information. It's extremely remote, and you'll definitely need a 4x4 or *bakkie* to avoid breakdowns. If you're a newbie to deserts, a guide will help you get the most out of your visit to the Richtersveld. In fact this arid country comes alive when interpreted, whether that means learning about its flowers or the Richtersveld Mountains (look out for Conrad Mouton of Aukwatoa Tours).

Port Nolloth's bay is safe for swimming, although the water is freezing cold almost any time of the year. Head over to the harbor to check out the diamond-vacuuming boats, with their distinctive hoses trailing astern. Divers use the hoses to vacuum under boulders on the seabed in search of any diamonds that have washed into the sea from the Orange River over many millennia. It's a highly lucrative endeavor but not without its dangers; at least one diver has been sucked up the vacuum hose to his death.

George Mouyses, at the local museum, has done it all (except for the diamond-vacuum). He can keep you enthralled for hours and asks only for a small donation for his time, which may feel invaluable as you depart.

WHERE TO STAY

$ **Bedrock Lodge.** The interiors of this guesthouse (made up of some of the very first houses in town) are delightful, decorated with an eclectic collection of Africana and antiques; each room has its own bathroom, although not always in the room. **Pros:** beautiful period-piece accommodations; convenient location, with the town's museum on-site; very

RENTAL

reasonable prices. **Cons:** some accommodations are a little dated; the main road in front can be noisy; more nostalgia than luxury. [$] *Rooms from: R850* ✉ *2 Beach Rd.* ☎ *027/851–8865* ⊕ *www.bedrocklodge. co.za* ⮫ *19 rooms* ⦿ *Breakfast.*

$ ⛺ **Port Indigo Guest House.** A range of spotless, fully equipped, self-cater-
RENTAL   ing units across the road from the beach can accommodate individuals and groups. **Pros:** friendly hosts; the rooms have everything a traveler needs; across the road from the beach. **Cons:** ugly facade; some accommodations lack soul; only one bed-and-breakfast option. [$] *Rooms from: R650* ✉ *1245 Kamp St., McDougalls Bay* ☎ *027/851–8012, 2782/892–6344* ⊕ *www.portindigo.co.za* ⮫ *12 rooms* ⦿ *No meals.*

THE GARDEN ROUTE AND THE LITTLE KAROO

Updated by
Kate Turkington

This region is a study in contrasts. The forested mountain ranges of the Outeniqua and Tsitsikamma that shadow the coastline trap moist ocean breezes that then fall as rain on the verdant area known as the Garden Route. Meanwhile, these same mountains rob the interior of water, creating the arid semi-deserts of the Little and Great Karoo. Even within these areas, however, there is significant variety.

The Garden Route, which generally refers to the 208-km (130-mile) stretch of coastline from Mossel Bay to Storms River, encompasses some of South Africa's most spectacular and diverse scenery, with long beaches, gentle lakes and rivers, tangled forests, impressive mountains, and steep, rugged cliffs that plunge into a wild and stormy sea. It's this mix that has earned the Garden Route its reputation for being one of the most scenic routes in South Africa. Though the ocean may not be as warm as it is in KwaZulu-Natal the accommodations are equally superb.

The Garden Route also offers great variety for all ages. The backpacking crowd loves it for its great beaches, adventure activities, and accessibility, whereas more sophisticated visitors revel in the excellent seafood, scenery, golf courses, and superior guesthouses and hotels—many with attached spas—where pampering is the name of the game. A Garden Route trip also makes a fabulous family vacation destination, where little ones can frolic on a beach, visit an animal sanctuary, or go for a magical forest walk. Few would wish to pass up the opportunity to see whales and dolphins. With numerous guided, catered, and portered multiday hikes and loads of pretty day walks, the Garden Route is ideal for avid ramblers.

A trip into the Little Karoo in the interior, on the other hand, offers a glimpse of what much of South Africa's vast hinterland looks like. This narrow strip of land, wedged between the Swartberg and Outeniqua ranges, stretches from Barrydale in the west to Willowmore in the east. It's a sere world of rock and scrub, famous for its ostrich farms and the subterranean splendors of the Cango Caves. Unlike more classic safari destinations, the Little Karoo's treasures are not handed to you on a plate. Scour the apparently dry ground to spot tiny and beautiful plants. Hike into the hills to admire the fascinating geological formations of the Cape Fold Mountains and to look for rock art. Or simply pause and drink in the space and the silence.

■TIP➜ The Garden Route National Park encompasses the national parks of Wilderness, Knysna, and Tsitsikamma. Each area offers a distinct experience from lakeside to forest to dramatic shoreline.

ORIENTATION AND PLANNING

GETTING ORIENTED

Although it *is* possible to get from place to place by bus, the best way to explore this region is by car. There are two practical routes from Cape Town to Port Elizabeth. You can follow the N2 along the Garden Route, or you can take Route 62, which goes through the Little Karoo. These two roads are separated by the Outeniqua Mountains, which are traversed by a number of scenic passes. So it is possible—even desirable, if you have the time—to hop back and forth over the mountains, alternating between the lush Garden Route and the harsher Little Karoo. The inland border of the Little Karoo is formed by the Swartberg Mountains; the Great Karoo is on the other side, beyond the mountains.

Garden Route. This beautiful 208-km (130-mile) stretch of coast takes its name from a year-round riot of vegetation. Here you'll find some of the country's most inspiring scenery: forest-cloaked mountains, rivers and streams, and golden beaches. The area draws a diverse crowd, from backpackers and adventure travelers to family vacationers and golfers. The main towns along the route are (from west to east) Mossel Bay, George, Wilderness, Knysna, Plettenberg Bay, the Crags, Tsitsikamma, and Storms River.

Little Karoo. Presenting a striking contrast to the Garden Route is the semiarid region known as the Little Karoo (also known as the Klein Karoo). In addition to a stark beauty that comes with its deep gorges and rugged plains, the Little Karoo offers the chance to visit ostrich farms, to stay at the Sanbona Wildlife Reserve, to explore the impressive Cango Caves, and to relax at vineyards.

PLANNING

WHEN TO GO

There's no best time to visit the Garden Route, although the water and weather are warmest November through March. The high season is from mid-December to mid-January, when South African schools break for the summer holidays and families flock to the coast. Between May and September the weather cools down with some rain (though there is no single rainy season here). The winter months are the low season, and some establishments choose this time of year to take a break. Yet, even in these colder months it's rarely cold for more than two or three days at a stretch, after which you'll get a few days of glorious sunshine. Wildflowers bloom along the Garden Route from July to October, the same time as the annual Southern Right whale migration along the coast.

The Little Karoo can be scorchingly hot in summer. In winter, days are generally warm and sunny, though it can get bitterly cold at night.

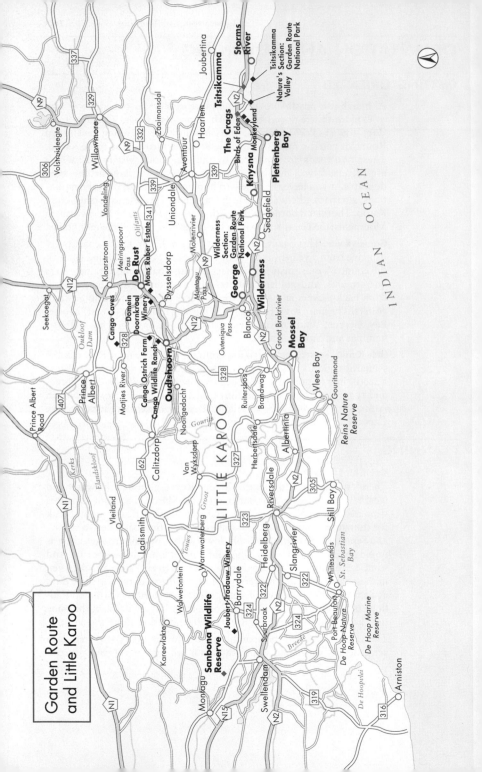

Garden Route and Little Karoo

TOP REASONS TO GO

Whale-Watching: Some of the best boat-based whale- and dolphin-watching in the world can be found at Plettenberg Bay on the Garden Route. And although Plett is the best, there are also good trips to be had at Mossel Bay and Knysna. You can often watch these friendly cetaceans frolicking from the shore, as well. If you really want to feel part of the ocean, your best bet is a kayaking trip in Plett.

Animal Encounters: The Crags area, just outside Plettenberg Bay, is the place to go if you want to spend a day with the animals. Visit with rescued primates at Monkeyland Primate Sanctuary or amble through the world's largest free-flight aviary next door at Birds of Eden. Other spots for animal-watching include the ostrich farms and Cango Wildlife Ranch at Oudtshoorn and—for free-roaming big game like elephants and lions—the Sanbona Wildlife Reserve close to Barrydale.

Adventure Sports: If you're itching for a taste of freefall, you've come to the right place. The highest commercial bungee jump in the world (at 700 feet) can be found at Bloukrans Bridge. If you really have an appetite for heights, you can leap out of a plane with Skydive Plett. For something a little bit closer to the ground, nothing beats the canopy tour at Tsitsikamma, where you fly through the trees (via cables and a harness) with the greatest of ease.

Scenic Hiking: Enjoy the best of nature in comfort on an escorted, guided, portered, and catered hike, locally called "slackpacking." The Dolphin Trail, in the Tsitsikamma section of the Garden Route National Park, offers the chance to walk along remote and rugged coastal terrain but with indulgent accommodations. The Oystercatcher Trail in Mossel Bay lets you explore a wide range of coastal scenery, from cliff-top paths to long beaches, and the food emphasizes traditionally cooked local seafood. The Garden Route Trail combines long and short day hikes with some paddling through the wonderful wetlands of the Wilderness section of the Garden Route National Park.

GETTING HERE AND AROUND
AIR TRAVEL

The only major airport serving the Garden Route and the Little Karoo is George Airport, 10 km (6 miles) southwest of town. George is well served by Airlink, SA Express, Mango, and Kulula airlines with daily flights from South Africa's three major cities (Cape Town, Durban, and Johannesburg). Flying times are 2 hours from Johannesburg, 1½ hours from Durban, and 1 hour from Cape Town. There are only a handful of flights from Johannesburg or Cape Town to the little airfield in Plett, 6 km (4 miles) west of town, but from here African Ramble runs charters to anywhere you may wish to go that has a landing strip (most commonly to the Eastern Cape game reserves). These scenic trips fly over the Robberg Peninsula and out over the bay (where you may see whales or dolphins) and then hug the coast up to Nature's Valley before heading inland. *For additional airline contact information, see Air Travel in Travel Smart.*

Airlines African Ramble Air Charter. ✉ *Plettenberg Bay Airport* ☎ *083/375–6514* ⊕ *www.africanramble.co.za.*

Airport George Airport *(GRJ).* ✉ *George Airport, George* ☎ *044/876–9310* ⊕ *www.airports.co.za.*

BUS TRAVEL

Intercape Mainliner and Greyhound offer regular service between Cape Town and Port Elizabeth, stopping at all major Garden Route destinations on the N2, although they often don't go into town but drop passengers off at gas stations along the highway. Another excellent service is the Baz Bus, which offers a handy door-to-door, hop-on, hop-off service to backpacking hostels along the Garden Route and beyond (all the way up to the Wild Coast in the Eastern Cape).

CAR TRAVEL

Most of the towns in this chapter can be found along the N2 highway. The road is in good condition and well signposted. A cautionary note, however: there is a wide shoulder along most of the route, but pull onto it to let faster cars overtake you *only* when you can see a good few hundred yards ahead. Also, stick to the speed limit, as speed traps are common.

■TIP➜ An alternative to the N2 is the less traveled—some say more interesting—inland route, dubbed Route 62, even though some of it is on the R60. From Worcester, in the Breede River valley *(see Chapter 3)*, you can travel the R60 and R62 to Oudtshoorn.

PLANNING YOUR TIME

3 Days: Choose a home base in the Garden Route: Wilderness, Knysna, and Plettenberg Bay (Plett) are all excellent options. You'll encounter wonderful crafts shops and studios in all these towns, so keep your credit card handy. On your first day, take a half-day walk through Plett's Robberg Nature Reserve, visit the Woodville Big Tree in Wilderness, or explore Knysna's Garden of Eden. Devote the afternoon to a boat or kayak trip; you may see dolphins, seals, and/or whales, particularly around Plett. Dedicate the second day to whatever activity suits your fancy—lounging on the beach, paddling, horseback riding, or abseiling (rappelling). If you're staying in Plett, you could drive out to Storms River on the third day to do the treetop canopy tour. If you're staying farther west, head over one of the scenic passes to Oudtshoorn, visit the Cango Caves, and take a different scenic drive back.

5 Days: Start with the three-day itinerary *above.* Then spend the next two days at the Little Karoo's Sanbona Wildlife Reserve, where you can see the Big Five and take in lovely flora. Alternatively, you could spend some extra time at any of the Garden Route destinations from the first itinerary; you may want to linger, for example, in Storms River, which will put you right near the spectacular Tsitsikamma section of the Garden Route National Park.

HEALTH AND SAFETY

The whole area is malaria-free, the climate is mild, and the water is safe to drink. Avoid sunburn by wearing a hat and slathering on sunscreen, and take care when swimming, as some beaches have dangerous currents. Never feed wild animals, especially vervet monkeys, who can become a nuisance.

HOTELS

The region would not have such allure if it weren't for its exclusive seaside getaways and colonial manor houses, as well as its more rustic inland farms and national-park log cabins. Many of the better establishments are set on little islands of well-tended gardens within wild forests. Breakfast is included in most lodgings' rates, and if your guest-house serves dinner, eating the evening meal in situ often has a welcome intimacy after a day of exploring. On the flip side, some cottages are self-catering (with cooking facilities), giving you the chance to pick up some local delicacies and make yourself a feast.

Note that the prices listed are for high season, generally October–April. In some cases these prices are significantly higher than during low season, and they may go up higher still for the busiest period—mid-December to mid-January. (If you're traveling during South Africa's winter, be sure to inquire about seasonal specials.) *Hotel reviews have been shortened. For full information, visit Fodors.com.*

RESTAURANTS

Most medium-size towns along the Garden Route offer a decent selection of restaurants, and the smaller towns of the Little Karoo usually have one or two good restaurants and a handful of lesser eateries. On the Garden Route the emphasis is often on seafood in general and oysters in particular. (Knysna has an oyster festival in July.) Restaurants in the Little Karoo feature fresh ostrich meat and organic mutton or lamb, which is delicious accompanied by a good South African red wine. Look out for farm shops between towns. These make excellent comfort stops where you can buy traditional home-baked fare, dried fruit, and other snacks for the road. *Restaurant reviews have been shortened. For full information, visit Fodors.com.*

WHAT IT COSTS IN SOUTH AFRICAN RAND			
$	**$$**	**$$$**	**$$$$**
Restaurants	under R100	R100–R150	R151–R200	over R200
Hotels	under R1,500	R1,500–R2,500	R2,501–R3,500	over R3,500

Restaurant prices are the average cost of a main course at dinner or, if dinner is not served, at lunch. Prices are the lowest price for a standard double room in high season.

VISITOR INFORMATION

Most local tourism bureaus are very helpful. Typical hours are week-days 8:30 to 5, Saturday 8 to 1. In peak season (generally October to April), you may find them open longer; in very quiet periods the staff may close up shop early.

MOSSEL BAY

384 km (238 miles) east of Cape Town.

Mossel Bay's main attractions are an excellent museum complex; several beautiful historic stone buildings (some of which are exceptionally well preserved); some of the best oysters along the coast; excellent golf; and good beaches with safe, secluded swimming. The area has some of the few north-facing (read: sunniest) beaches in South Africa, which means it's very popular with local families and is always packed in December. Dolphins—sometimes hundreds at a time—frequently move through the bay in search of food, and whales swim past during their annual migration (July–October). You could take a cruise out to Seal Island, home to a breeding colony of more than 2,000 Cape fur seals or, if you're feeling brave, a cage dive to view the numerous white sharks (blue pointers) that hang around the seal colony.

GETTING HERE AND AROUND

Mossel Bay, at the western end of the Garden Route, lies 384 km (238 miles) east of Cape Town along the N2 highway. It usually takes about four hours to drive from Cape Town to Mossel Bay—unless you stop to take in a view, have lunch, or browse in a roadside produce or crafts store.

VISITOR INFORMATION

Contacts Mossel Bay Tourism. ⊠ *Mossel Bay Tourism Office, Church St. at Market St.* ☎ *044/691–2202* ⊕ *www.visitmosselbay.co.za.*

EXPLORING

Bartolomeu Dias Museum Complex. Named for the 15th-century Portuguese navigator, the Bartolomeu Dias Museum Complex concentrates on the early history of Mossel Bay, when it was a regular stopover for Portuguese mariners en route to India from Europe. The most popular exhibit is the full-size (340-foot-long) replica of Dias's ship (a caravel), which was sailed to Mossel Bay from Lisbon as part of the quincentenary celebrations in 1988. If you pay the extra fee to board it, you'll find it all pretty authentic, except for the modern galley and heads. Also here is the Post Office Tree. In 1501 Pedro de Alteide left a letter here, which was picked up and delivered by another Portuguese navigator on his way to India and thus South Africa's first post office was born. De Alteide was so grateful that he built a small chapel here, reputed to be the first place of Christian worship in South Africa. Pop a postcard into the shoe-shaped mailbox and your mail will arrive with a special postmark. ⊠ *Church St. at Market St.* ☎ *044/691–1067* ⊕ *www.dias-museum.co.za* 🖾 *R20; caravel additional R40.*

WHERE TO EAT

$$ ✕ **Café Gannet.** This is Mossel Bay's premium seafood house serving
SEAFOOD fresh oysters and seafood alongside inventive dishes like ostrich fil-
let with caramelized onions and port-soaked apricots. In summer, it's
virtually mandatory to sip a cocktail on the deck of the Blue Oyster
bar with its great sea view. **Known for:** seafood casserole; coastal oys-
ters; black mussels. $ *Average main: R150* ✉ *Church St. at Market St.*
☎ *044/691–1885* ⊕ *www.cafegannet.co.za.*

$ ✕ **Carola Ann's.** Carola Ann is passionate about food and brings her
EASTERN international experience to whipping up tasty, innovative dishes from
EUROPEAN locally sourced meat, fish, and veggies in a historic little house close
Fodor's Choice to the Dias Museum. Superb coffee, delicious smoothies, scrumptious
★ lunches, and to-die-for breakfasts have made this one of the town's
not-to-be-missed eateries. **Known for:** healthy breakfasts; excellent
coffee; Mediterranean food. $ *Average main: R75* ✉ *Carola Ann's,*
12 Church St. ☎ *044/690–3477* ⊕ *www.carolaann.com* ⊘ *Closed*
weekend afternoons.

$$ ✕ **Delfino's Espresso Bar and Pizzeria.** Good coffee, yummy pizzas and
ITALIAN pastas, tables on the lawn right next to the beach, and a fantastic view
FAMILY of the bay and the Cape St. Blaize lighthouse make this a great place to
spend a sunny afternoon. **Known for:** Italian food; great views. $ *Average*
main: R100 ✉ *2 Point Village* ☎ *044/690–5247* ⊕ *www.delfinos.co.za.*

WHERE TO STAY

$$ ⛉ **Protea Hotel Mossel Bay.** Just yards away from the museum com-
HOTEL plex, this stylish hotel is close to most of what's happening in Mossel
Bay. You can take in the great view of the harbor, beach, and sea
while relaxing at the Blue Oyster Pool Lounge. **Pros:** location very
central for museum, restaurants, and the beach; stylish and modern
rooms; great views. **Cons:** swimming pool is small and overlooked
by the terrace; street-facing rooms can be noisy; crowded in season;
view is slightly obstructed by building below. $ *Rooms from: R1540*
✉ *Church St. at Market St.* ☎ *044/691–3738* ⊕ *www.proteahotels.*
com ⇦ *31 rooms* ⦿ *Breakfast.*

$ ⛉ **Santos Express Train Lodge.** And now for something completely differ-
B&B/INN ent: In an old train parked on the beach, this lodging uses real train com-
partments for accommodations. **Pros:** all the cabins face the sea; town
center is a 10-minute walk away; funky, fun accommodations. **Cons:**
compartments are very cramped; you need to supply your own towel
and soap; no air-conditioning; only suites have private bathrooms.
$ *Rooms from: R350* ✉ *Munro Rd., Santos Beach* ☎ *083/900–7797*
⊕ *www.santosexpress.co.za* ⇦ *33 rooms* ⦿ *Breakfast.*

SPORTS AND THE OUTDOORS

BOATING

Romonza Boat Trips. For a closer look at the Cape fur seals lounging
around on Seal Island or to check out whales and dolphins, take a trip
with Romonza Boat Trips on a 54-foot sailing yacht. One-hour Seal

Island trips (all year) cost R160 and whale-watching trips cost R700 (from July to October). ✉ *Church St.* ☎ *044/690–3101* ⊕ *romonzaboat-trips.co.za.*

HIKING

Fodor's Choice **Oystercatcher Trail.** The guided, catered Oystercatcher Trail offers the ★ best of both worlds, providing a multiday hiking experience along the beach and over rocky shorelines while you carry only a day pack. The trail starts in Mossel Bay, with the first day spent on the lovely clifftop Cape St. Blaize Trail, and continues to the mouth of the Gouritz River. Nights are spent in a guesthouse or a thatched cottage, where delicious traditional food is prepared for you on open fires. Knowledgeable guides point out birds and plants and discuss local history and customs along the way. Walking on the beach can be hard if the tide is in, but most people of average fitness should manage. A typical trip is four days and five nights but shorter hikes of one or two days can be arranged. ✉ *Sandpiper Safaris, Boggoms Bay* ☎ *044/699–1204* ⊕ *www. oystercatchertrail.co.za* ✐ *R6,850 per person.*

EN ROUTE The small town of Albertinia, about 40 km (25 miles) west of Mossel Bay, is an interesting place to break your journey into the Garden Route from Cape Town or the Winelands. It's the center of the aloe ferox industry. The gel of this indigenous aloe has even greater therapeutic benefits than the better-known aloe vera. Two factories in Albertinia make cosmetics and health-care products from this interesting plant and sell them on-site.

GEORGE

45 km (28 miles) northeast of Mossel Bay; 50 km (31 miles) southeast of Oudtshoorn.

About 11 km (7 miles) from the sea, George is the largest town and the de facto capital of the Garden Route. Although the surrounding countryside is attractive and there is a thriving farming and crafts community on its outskirts, George itself is not particularly appealing unless you are a golfer or a steam train enthusiast eager to visit its excellent transportation museum.

GETTING HERE AND AROUND

The only true airport serving the Garden Route and the Little Karoo is George Airport, 10 km (6 miles) southwest of town. Most people who arrive by plane rent a car to continue their journey on the Garden Route. Avis, Budget, Europcar, and Hertz all have car-rental offices at George Airport.

It takes about half an hour to get to Mossel Bay and Oudtshoorn from George, and the roads are good. ■**TIP**→ **The area between George and Wilderness is notorious for speed traps, especially in the Kaaimans River Pass, just west of Wilderness.**

VISITOR INFORMATION

Contacts George Tourism Information. ✉ *124 York St.* ☎ *044/801–9299* ⊕ *www.georgetourism.co.za.*

EXPLORING

Outeniqua Transport Museum. This museum in a huge hangarlike building is a steam train enthusiast's delight, with 13 beautifully kept steam locomotives and other examples of vintage vehicles. One of the museum's highlights is the original "White Coach" in which Queen Elizabeth and her sister Margaret slept during their 1947 visit to South Africa. ✉ 2 *Mission Rd.* ☎ *044/801–8289* ⊕ *www.outeniquachootjoe.co.za* 🎫 *R20.*

WHERE TO EAT

$

CONTEMPORARY

✗ **Meade Café.** This light and airy bistro-style restaurant in an 18th-century town house with a lovely outdoor seating area serves breakfast and lunch favorites like eggs Benedict and fish-and-chips. They also have an excellent selection of salads and sandwiches with interesting ingredients such as hickory-smoked pork loin, roasted vegetables, or marinated chickpeas and apricots. **Known for:** creative sandwiches; chicken curry; excellent salads. $ *Average main: R95* ✉ *91 Meade St.* ☎ *044/873–6755* ⊕ *meadecafe.co.za* ⊘ *Closed Sun. No dinner.*

WHERE TO STAY

$$$$

RESORT

🏨 **Fancourt Hotel and Country Club Estate.** If you're one of those people who believe we were created with opposable thumbs for the sole purpose of gripping a golf club, you'll *love* Fancourt, a luxury resort in the shadow of the Outeniqua Mountains that resembles a country club with numerous leisure and business facilities. **Pros:** on-site spa; kids' program; spectacular golf. **Cons:** non-golfers might feel out of place; little nightlife in George; cocooned away from real world. $ *Rooms from: R4500* ✉ *Montagu St., Blanco* ☎ *044/804–0000* ⊕ *www.fancourt.com* 🛏 *133 rooms* ⊙I *Breakfast.*

WILDERNESS

12 km (7 miles) southeast of George.

Wilderness is a popular vacation resort for good reason. Backed by thickly forested hills and cliffs, the tiny town presides over a magical stretch of beach between the Kaaimans and Touw rivers, as well as a spectacular system of waterways, lakes, and lagoons strung out along the coast, separated from the sea by towering vegetated dunes. Many of the Garden Route's other attractions are within an hour or two's drive, making Wilderness a good base for exploring.

GETTING HERE AND AROUND

Many hotels offer a transfer from George Airport, but your best bet is to rent a car there and drive yourself, as the roads are good and you'll be able to see a lot more of the country.

EXPLORING

Wilderness Section of the Garden Route National Park. This 299,000-acre reserve stretches east along the coast for 31 km (19 miles). A wetlands paradise, the park draws birders from all over the country to its two blinds. Several walking trails wind through the park alongside lakes, rivers, and the sea. A relatively gentle option is the 45-minute Woodville Big Tree Walk, which takes you past an 800-year-old yellowwood tree and into the indigenous forest. ✉ *Wilderness* ☎ *044/877–0046* 🌐 *www.sanparks.org* 🎟 *R120.*

WHERE TO EAT

$$$$ SOUTH AFRICAN Fodor's Choice ★

🍴 **Serendipity.** Start your evening at this award-winning restaurant with predinner drinks on the patio overlooking the river, then move inside to a candlelit table for a fabulous five-course menu that takes classic South African ingredients and gives them an original, modern twist. Dishes could include Cape salmon served with sautéed niçoise vegetables and hollandaise sauce or desserts with a South African touch, such as Amarula crème brûlée or saffron-infused milk tart. **Known for:** creative flavors; excellent service; attention to detail. [$] *Average main: R445* ✉ *Freesia Ave.* ☎ *044/877–0433* 🌐 *www.serendipitywilderness.com* 🕒 *Closed Sun. No lunch.*

$$ SOUTH AFRICAN FAMILY Fodor's Choice ★

🍴 **Zucchini.** Zucchini is all about free-range, organic, locally sourced, and seasonal ingredients, and chances are the garnishes on your plate will have been freshly picked from the organic herb garden outside. The menu changes regularly and features homemade pastas, soups, sandwiches, and a range of salads served either roasted or raw. **Known for:** vegetarian-friendly dishes; homemade pasta; craft beer on tap; rustic setting. [$] *Average main: R140* ✉ *Timberlake Farm Stall, off the N2* ☎ *044/882–1240* 🌐 *www.zucchini.co.za.*

WHERE TO STAY

$ RESORT

🏨 **Ebb and Flow Restcamp, Wilderness Section of the Garden Route National Park.** This rest camp, along a lovely, meandering stretch of river, is divided into two sections (north and south) and includes a variety of accommodations options, ranging from cottages and cabins to huts and campsites. **Pros:** activities like hiking and canoeing available; tranquil; good base. **Cons:** accommodations utilitarian, in style of national parks; crowded in season; river is prone to flooding. [$] *Rooms from: R760* ✉ *Wilderness section of Garden Route National Park* ☎ *044/877–1197* 🌐 *www.sanparks.org* 🛏 *181 rooms* 🍽 *No meals.*

$$$$ HOTEL Fodor's Choice ★

🏨 **Views Boutique Hotel & Spa.** This boutique hotel offers stupendous views of the seemingly endless Wilderness beach from rooms that have floor-to-ceiling windows and private verandas looking straight onto the ocean. **Pros:** superb ocean views; a pillow menu for picky guests; service is attentive and friendly. **Cons:** about 3 km (2 miles) from village center and safe swimming area; limited dining options on-site; the three DeLuxe suites do not have sea views. [$] *Rooms from: R3560* ✉ *South St.* ☎ *044/877–8000* 🌐 *www.viewshotel.co.za* 🛏 *27 rooms* 🍽 *Breakfast* ☞ *No children under 14.*

$$ ⊡ **Xanadu.** Deep-pile carpets, double-volume spaces, spectacular floral
B&B/INN   arrangements, and voluminous drapes framing the sea-view windows
Fodor's Choice   add to the sense of opulence at this beachfront establishment. **Pros:** just
★   a short walk to the beach; bathrooms are modern and large; free Wi-Fi.
Cons: too far to walk into town; breakfast is eaten communally; only
one restaurant in immediate vicinity. $ *Rooms from: R2500* ⊠ *Xanadu,
43 Die Duin* ☎ *083/357–8000* ⊕ *www.xanadu-wilderness.co.za* ⇄ *6
rooms* ⭢⭠ *Breakfast.*

SPORTS AND THE OUTDOORS

The Wilderness section of the Garden Route National Park and its
environs provide opportunities for lovely walks, paddling, and birding.

ADVENTURE TOURS

Eden Adventures. Based close to the Wilderness section of the Garden
Route National Park, Eden Adventures offers canyoneering in Kaaimans
Gorge (R600), which includes a leisurely walk through indigenous for-
est to the confluence of the Kaaiman and Silver rivers. You then have
to jump into deep pools and swim through canyons on your way back.
Wet suits are provided. Other adventures in their bag of tricks include
abseiling (rappelling) and canoeing. Custom tours can also be arranged.
⊠ *Fairy Knowe Hotel* ☎ *044/877–0179* ⊕ *www.eden.co.za.*

HIKING

Fodor's Choice   **Garden Route Trail.** Mark Dixon is the highly qualified nature guide
★   behind this operation. Excursions include guided day walks and multi-
day hikes in the forest and around the lakes and beaches of this beautiful
part of the world. His signature offering is the five-day guided Garden
Route Trail, starting at the Ebb and Flow Restcamp at Wilderness.
The trip takes you east along the coast, with long beach walks and
coastal forest included, before ending at Brenton on Sea near Knysna.
The emphasis is on the natural environment rather than covering great
distances, with Mark's expert guiding along the way. The trip is catered
and portered, and you do some canoeing in addition to hiking. Another
popular offering is the Moonlight Meander on the beach at full moon.
⊠ *Wilderness* ☎ *044/883–1015, 082/213–5931* ⊕ *www.gardenroutet-
rail.co.za.*

PARAGLIDING

Cloudbase Paragliding. Wilderness is one of the best paragliding spots in
the country. You can ridge-soar for miles along the dune front, watching
whales and dolphins in the sea. If you've never done it before, don't
worry: you can go tandem (R650) with an experienced instructor from
Cloudbase Paragliding. Their season is from mid-September to mid-
April as weather conditions in winter are not suitable for paragliding.
They also use launch sites at Sedgefield and Brenton-on-Sea depending
on weather conditions. ⊠ *Wilderness* ☎ *082/777–8474, 044/877–1414*
⊕ *www.cloudbase.co.za.*

5

KNYSNA

40 km (25 miles) east of Wilderness.

Knysna (pronounced *nize*-nuh) is one of the most popular destinations on the Garden Route. The focus of the town is the beautiful Knysna Lagoon, ringed by forested hills dotted with vacation homes. Several walking and mountain-bike trails wind through Knysna's forests, many offering tremendous views back over the ocean. With luck you may spot the Knysna turaco, a brilliantly plumed forest bird also known as the Knysna loerie, or the brightly colored but even more elusive Narina trogon.

Towering buttresses of rock, known as the Heads, guard the entrance to the lagoon, funneling the ocean through a narrow channel. The sea approach is often hazardous, which is why Knysna never became a major port, and may explain why it developed instead into the modern resort town it is today, with the attendant hype, commercialism, and crowds, especially in summer. About the only aspect of the town that hasn't been modernized is the single-lane main road (the N2 goes straight through the middle of town), so traffic can be a nightmare. Walking is the best way to get around the town center, which is filled with shops, galleries, restaurants, and coffeehouses. Knysna's main claims to fame are edible and drinkable. The former are cultivated oysters, and the latter is locally brewed Mitchell's beer, on tap at most bars and pubs.

GETTING HERE AND AROUND

The main N2 highway travels straight through the center of Knysna, so the road can get rather busy (and noisy) in the high season.

VISITOR INFORMATION

Contacts **Knysna Tourism.** ⊠ *40 Main St.* ☎ *044/382–5510* ⊕ *www.visitknysna.com.*

EXPLORING

Featherbed Nature Reserve. Unlike its eastern counterpart, the western side of the Heads (part of the Featherbed Nature Reserve) is relatively unspoiled. In addition to a bizarre rock arch and great scenery, the reserve is home to various small mammals, more than 100 species of birds, and 1,000 plant species. There is a morning standard trip here, plus more in high season (generally October–April). The morning trip costs R635, leaves at 10, and lasts four hours. It consists of a ferry ride across the Lagoon to the Western Head, a 4x4 tractor ride onto the reserve, and a guided 2.2-km (1.3-mile) downhill walk through the Reserve and along the coastline. After this there's a buffet lunch under the trees. ⊠ *Cruise Cafe Bldg., Waterfront Dr.* ☎ *044/382–1693* ⊕ *www.knysnafeatherbed.com.*

Heads. You can't come to Knysna without making a trip out to the Heads, at the mouth of the lagoon. The rock sentinels provide great views of both the sea and the lagoon. Only the developed, eastern side is accessible by car, via George Rex Drive off the N2. You have two options: to park at the base of the Head and follow the walking trails that snake around the rocky cliffs, just feet above the crashing surf, or drive to the summit, with its panoramic views and easy parking. ⊠ *Knysna.*

BEACHES

Although Knysna is very much a seaside destination, there are no beaches actually in the town—unlike in Plett or Mossel Bay—but there are some fabulous ones nearby.

Brenton on Sea. The beach at Brenton on Sea, past Belvidere, is a beautiful, long, white-sand beach popular for its 6-km (4-mile) walk to neighboring Buffalo Bay. It's about a 10-minute drive from the exit off the N2 highway, about 12 km (7½ miles) west of Knysna. Although spectacular, this beach is not particularly good for swimming because of a strong undertow (hence the warning signs in German!). Lifeguards are present in season, but swimmers are cautioned to swim only between the flags where indicated. **Amenities:** food and drink; lifeguards; parking; toilets. **Best for:** sunrise; sunset; walking. ⊠ *Brenton-on-Sea.*

Buffalo Bay Beach. About 20 km (12 miles) from Knysna, Buffalo Bay beach offers safe swimming and excellent surfing and body-boarding conditions. It's around a half-moon bay with a sandy beach next to a grassy peninsula. The little village has been spared overdevelopment because of its proximity to the nearby Goukamma Nature Reserve. There is a popular beach walk in the direction of Brenton-on-Sea, and there are accommodations in the nature reserve (booked through Cape Nature). **Amenities:** food and drink; lifeguards; parking; showers; toilets; water sports. **Best for:** surfing; swimming; walking. ⊠ *Buffalo Bay.*

Leisure Isle. In the middle of the Knysna lagoon, Leisure Isle has a few tiny strands of beach but is essentially a low-lying island populated with vacation and residential homes. The surrounding mudflats of the lagoon provide bait for the local fisherfolk. For those lucky enough to stay here, the best views are out toward The Heads of Knysna, but the only swimming to be had is knee-height paddling. **Amenities:** parking. **Best for:** solitude; swimming; windsurfing. ⊠ *Knysna.*

WHERE TO EAT

$$ ✕ **Ile de Pain.** Almost every South African you meet on the Garden Route
ECLECTIC will tell you to visit Ile de Pain and its stellar reputation is well deserved;
Fodor's Choice owners Liezie Mulder and Markus Farbinger have an uncompromis-
★ ing attitude toward quality that shows in their wonderful bread and pastries, as well as on the short, perfectly executed menu. Local and organic suppliers are used wherever possible, the menu changes seasonally, and everything is made on the premises. **Known for:** fresh-baked pastries; indulgent breakfasts; duck confit. $ *Average main: R100* ⊠ *The Boatshed, Thesen Island* ☎ *044/302–5707* ⊕ *www.iledepain. co.za* ⊙ *Closed Mon. No dinner Sun.*

$$
SEAFOOD

✕ **34° South.** Right on the water's edge in what appears to be a dolled-up warehouse, 34° South manages to combine elements of a fishmonger, a bar, a bistro, a deli, a coffee shop, and a seafood restaurant. Choose from the huge array of fresh fish, including sushi; opt for a rustic pizza; or just fill a basket with tasty breads, pickles, cheeses, meats, and other delights. **Known for:** oysters and fresh seafood; good wine selection; outdoor dining with a view. ⑨ *Average main: R100* ✉ *Knysna Quays* ☎ *044/382–7331* ⊕ *www.34south.biz.*

$$$$
MODERN
EUROPEAN

✕ **Zachary's.** Knysna is a bit of a gourmet destination, and Zachary's at the Pezula Resort Hotel and Spa, about a 10- to 15-minute drive from Knysna, has helped to cement that reputation. The restaurant specializes in high-quality organic and seasonal dishes that might include shiitake mushroom broth, butter-poached crayfish, venison, line fish, scallops, and Karoo lamb. **Known for:** elegant dining in a stylish setting; six-course tasting menu; excellent wine list. ⑨ *Average main: R250* ✉ *Pezula Resort Hotel and Spa, Lagoon View Dr.* ☎ *044/302–3333* ⊕ *www.zacharys.co.za.*

WHERE TO STAY

There are more bed-and-breakfasts than you can possibly imagine, as well as some fantastic guesthouses, self-catering resorts, and hotels, so you will not be short of choices.

$$
B&B/INN

▦ **Belvidere Manor.** There are lovely views across the lagoon to Knysna, some 6½ km (4 miles) away, at this attractive establishment where accommodation is offered in airy cottages that face each other across a lawn sloping down to a jetty. **Pros:** British-style pub on-site; great views; well-equipped cottage accommodations. **Cons:** out of town, so dining options are limited; no air-conditioning; in the center of a retirement village. ⑨ *Rooms from: R2100* ✉ *169 Duthie Dr.* ☎ *044/387–1055* ⊕ *www.belvidere.co.za* ⇄ *28 rooms* ⑩ *Breakfast.*

$$$$
HOTEL
Fodor's Choice
★

▦ **Phantom Forest Eco Reserve.** On a private 450-acre nature reserve, this stunning lodge, set in the tree canopy of the indigenous Knysna forest, offers guests the opportunity to sleep in luxury tree houses built from sustainable woods. **Pros:** spacious and luxurious bathrooms, with under-floor heating; lodge has a secluded feel although it's in the center of Knysna; food and service are excellent. **Cons:** lodge is up a steep hill so you need to be ferried up the hill by a lodge vehicle; the N2 highway is some distance away, but the road noise does filter through; views of the Knysna lagoon only from the Eyrie lounge area. ⑨ *Rooms from: R5418* ✉ *Phantom Pass* ☎ *044/386–0046* ⊕ *www.phantomforest.com* ⇄ *14 rooms* ⑩ *Breakfast.*

$
B&B/INN

▦ **St. James of Knysna.** This elegant lodging right on the edge of Knysna Lagoon offers individually decorated rooms with uninterrupted views of the water, a landscaped formal garden with tranquil koi ponds, and a private pier with free use of canoes or fishing equipment. **Pros:** some rooms are enormous, and all are decorated individually; views of the lagoon are stunning; rooms have air-conditioning. **Cons:** old-fashioned decor; swimming pool is on the small side; a bit out of town. ⑨ *Rooms* *from: R1180* ✉ *Eastford, The Point* ☎ *044/382–6750* 🌐 *www.stjames.co.za* 🛏 *15 rooms* 🍴 *Breakfast.*

$$$ HOTEL Fodor's Choice ★ 🏨 **Turbine Hotel & Spa.** A former timber mill, this unique eco-friendly boutique hotel has incorporated some of the unmovable heavy machinery and restored it to blend in seamlessly with the warm bright colors and funky furniture in state-of-the-art bedrooms and suites, each themed to reflect Knysna's rich historical and cultural diversity. **Pros:** excellent Armani Spa; location, location, location; unique boiler room chic; superb food at Turbine's Tapas Bar. **Cons:** far from the real world; no beaches; crowded in school vacation times during July and December. [$] *Rooms from: R3462* ✉ *TH 36 Sawtooth La.* ☎ *044/302–5746* 🌐 *www.turbinehotel.co.za* 🛏 *25 rooms* 🍴 *Breakfast.*

SPORTS AND THE OUTDOORS

BOATING

Featherbed Company. In addition to running the ferry to the nature reserve, the Featherbed Company operates sightseeing boats on the lagoon (trips start at R130 per person), as well as a Mississippi-style paddle steamer that does lunch and dinner cruises. ✉ *Off Waterfront Dr.* ☎ *044/382–1693* 🌐 *www.knysnafeatherbed.com.*

Springtide Charters. This charter company operates a luxury 50-foot mono-hull yacht, *Outeniqua*, that takes visitors out on scenic cruises on the lagoon and through The Heads (weather permitting). The boat takes a maximum of 12 passengers, and can also be rented out for private parties. Their most popular outing is the sunset cruise (R860 per person) which includes Mediterranean-style snacks and a couple of glasses of bubbly. Springtide Charters also operates the *Ocean Odyssey*, Knysna's only accredited close-encounter whale-watching vessel, which takes visitors through The Heads to the open ocean (R850 per person). ✉ *Knysna Quays* ☎ *044/382–0321* 🌐 *www.springtide.co.za.*

HIKING

Diepwalle Elephant Walk. This lovely trail takes you deep into the indigenous forest. The full trail is about 20 km (12 miles) long and should take around six to seven hours. For those who don't have a whole day to spare, there are three color-coded shorter routes of 9 km (5½ miles), 7 km (4½ miles), and 6½ km (4 miles). These should take between two and four hours. Day hikes cost R68. ✉ *Off N2, Uniondale Rd., Diepwalle Forest Estate* ✣ *24 km (15 miles) east of Knysna* ☎ *044/382–9762/3.*

Garden of Eden. If you'd like to sample the Harkerville Forest but don't want to commit to a strenuous, two-day hike, try the easy stroll in the Garden of Eden. The short trail goes into the forest on a wheelchair-friendly wooden boardwalk. You'll see some ancient giant trees, plus tables where you can picnic. The kiosk at the Garden of Eden is open daily 8–5 and on weekends 8–6, and entry is R12 per person. ✉ *Off N2 between Plett and Knysna* ☎ *044/532–7793* 🌐 *www.sanparks.org.*

Harkerville Trail. The two-day, 26-km (16-mile) Harkerville Trail passes through the indigenous forests, pine plantations, and "islands" of

5

fynbos, as well as fairly taxing sections on the coast. (This is not a beginner's trail.) Homesick Californians can hug a familiar tree in a small stand of huge redwoods (*Sequoia sempervirens*), planted as part of a forestry experiment years ago. Overnight accommodation is in a hut with beds and mattresses, water, and firewood, but you'll need to bring your own bedding and food provisions. There's also no electricity. The trail costs R300 per person including conservation fee. ⊠ *Off N2 ⚹ 15 km (9 miles) east of Knysna* ☎ *044/382–2095* ⊕ *www.sanparks.org.*

Knysna Forest Tours. If you don't fancy heading off into the forest on your own, take a guided walk or even a trail run through the area with Knysna Forest Tours. Prices start at R410 for a trail run, while a full-day outing, including lunch, will cost R1,010. The parent company, Tony Cook Adventures, also offers surfing, kiteboarding, stand-up paddleboarding, and sea and river kayaking trips. ⊠ *Thesen Island* ☎ *082/783–8392* ⊕ *www.knysnaforesttours.co.za.*

MOUNTAIN BIKING

The Garden Route is ideal for mountain biking, and Harkerville, 20 km (12 miles) east of Knysna, is where mountain bikers usually head first. Here you'll find four color-coded circular trails of varying length and difficulty, starting and ending at the Garden of Eden. The most challenging of these is the Red route, which is a 22-km (13½-mile) ride through forest with some coastal scenery along the way. The others are Blue (11 km/7 miles), Yellow (13 km/8 miles), and Green (14 km/9 miles). There's a fifth 22-km (13½-mile) trail, Petrus se Brand, that is not circular but can be ridden in either direction between Diepwalle and Garden of Eden. It's tight and twisty, and you'll zip downhill (if you start at Diepwalle) over the springy forest floor, dodging enormous trees. It costs R165 to cycle any of these trails.

Outeniqua Biking Hire. You can rent mountain bikes from Outeniqua Bike Hire, which is conveniently located right on the forest edge and close to the trails. Only adult bikes are available and booking is essential. The SANParks entrance fee is R165. ⊠ *Off N2, Harkerville ⚹ 20 km (12.4 miles) east of Knysna* ☎ *044/532–7644, 083/252–7997.*

PLETTENBERG BAY

32 km (20 miles) east of Knysna.

Plettenberg Bay is South Africa's premier beach resort, as the empty houses on Beachy Head Road (known as Millionaires' Mile) during the 11 months when it's not high season will attest. But in December inland visitors with all their teenage offspring arrive en masse. Even then you can find yourself a stretch of lonely beach if you're prepared to walk to the end of Keurboomstrand or drive to Nature's Valley. Plett, as it is commonly known, is one of the best places in the world to watch whales and dolphins. Boat-based trips are run from Central Beach, as are sea-kayaking trips.

GETTING HERE AND AROUND

There is an airport in Plett, but it's not currently in operation. There's no public transportation to and around Plett, so your best bet is renting a car and driving yourself.

VISITOR INFORMATION

Contacts Plettenberg Bay Tourism Association. ✉ *Shop 35, Melville's Corner, Marine Dr. at Main Rd.* ☎ *044/533–4065* ⊕ *www.pletttourism.co.za.*

BEACHES

Plett presides over a stretch of coastline that has inspired rave reviews since the Portuguese first set eyes on it in 1497 and dubbed it *bahia formosa* (the beautiful bay). Three rivers flow into the sea here, the most spectacular of which—the Keurbooms—backs up to form a large lagoon. For swimming, surfing, sailing, hiking, and fishing you can't do much better than Plett, although the water is still colder than it is around Durban and in northern KwaZulu-Natal.

■**TIP→ Keep in mind that the beach facilities (i.e., lifeguards, food concession, and so on) are available only during the summer months (November–April).**

Central Beach. All the dolphin-watching boats and kayak trips leave from Central Beach. A constant stream of tenders going out to the fishing boats moored in the bay makes this area quite busy, but it's still a great spot. Just keep away from the boat-launching area and swim in the southern section. **Amenities:** food and drink; lifeguards; parking; toilets. **Best for:** surfing; swimming; walking. ✉ *Plettenberg Bay.*

Keurboomstrand. This beach is about 10 km (6 miles) from Plett—right on the eastern edge of the bay. If you're fit, you can walk all the way from here to Nature's Valley, but you need to watch both the tides and the steep, rocky sections. It's best to ask locals before tackling this. Even if you're not fit, you can walk about a mile down the beach, relax for a while, and then walk back. **Amenities:** food and drink; lifeguards; parking; showers; toilets. **Best for:** walking. ✉ *Plettenberg Bay.*

Lookout Beach. Traditionally one of Plettenberg Bay's most popular beaches, Blue Flag–status Lookout Beach is a favorite spot for swimmers and surfers, and families and toddlers enjoy paddling on the lagoon side of what is essentially a large sandy spit. **Amenities:** food and drink; lifeguards (in season); parking; toilets; water sports. **Best for:** surfing; swimming; walking. ✉ *Plettenberg Bay.*

Robberg Beach. Just on the other side of the Beacon Isle hotel, the unmissable building at the end of the tombolo (a sand spit linking the island to the mainland), is Robberg Beach, a great swimming beach that continues in a graceful curve all the way to Robberg Peninsula. You can get pretty good sightings of dolphins and whales just behind the back break. **Amenities:** food and drink; lifeguards; parking; showers; toilets. **Best for:** swimming; sunbathing. ✉ *Beachy Head Dr.*

WHERE TO STAY

Plett has plenty of fabulous places to eat and overnight, although dining options are generally better in Knysna, so guests in Plettenberg Bay usually eat in their hotel.

$$
B&B/INN
Fodor's Choice
★

⊡ **Bitou River Lodge.** About 3 km (2 miles) upstream from the Keurboom Lagoon, this lovely, quiet, restful B&B has a wonderful location on the bank of the Bitou River, with rooms overlooking a pretty garden and a quiet bird-rich and lily-filled pond. **Pros:** beautiful river running past the property; friendly and helpful staff; private verandas. **Cons:** no air-conditioning in the rooms; 10-minute drive to restaurants; self-catering facilities limited. $ *Rooms from: R1700* ⊠ *Off the N2* ✛ *About 3 km (2 miles) on the R340 to Wittedrif* ☎ *044/535–9577, 082/978–6164* ⊕ *www.bitou.co.za* ⊲ *5 rooms* ⦿ *Breakfast.*

$$$
B&B/INN
Fodor's Choice
★

⊡ **Emily Moon River Lodge.** Only 10 minutes away from the hubbub of Plettenberg Bay but a world away in time and ambience, this delightfully quirky lodge set on the banks of the Bitou River combines an enchanting eclectic mix of African, Asian, and Polynesian decor. **Pros:** lovely views; stunningly original decor and design; car wash, bicycles, and river canoes all included. **Cons:** restaurant crowded at weekends; no air-conditioning; some suites have lots of steps so check in advance. $ *Rooms from: R3440* ⊠ *Rietvlei Rd.* ☎ *044/501–2500* ⊕ *www.emilymoon.co.za* ⊲ *10 rooms* ⦿ *Breakfast.*

$$
B&B/INN

⊡ **The Grand Café and Rooms.** Although the entrance is on the town's main street, walking into the Grand is like walking into a different world. **Pros:** central location; unique, quirky decor; well-behaved dogs welcome. **Cons:** rooms can be a bit dark; on main road; no children under 12. $ *Rooms from: R2230* ⊠ *27 Main Rd.* ☎ *044/533–3301* ⊕ *www.grandafrica.com* ⊲ *8 rooms* ⦿ *Breakfast.*

$$$$
HOTEL

⊡ **The Plettenberg.** High on a rocky point in Plettenberg Bay, this luxury hotel has unbelievable views of the bay, the Tsitsikamma Mountains, and Keurbooms Lagoon; miles of magnificent beach; and, in season, whales frolicking just beyond the waves. **Pros:** watch dolphins frolicking from your room; walk down to the beach in minutes; the view from the breakfast terrace is incredible. **Cons:** standard rooms are small; some rooms look out onto the car park; pricey. $ *Rooms from: R5540* ⊠ *Lookout Rocks* ☎ *044/533–2030* ⊕ *www.collectionmcgrath.com* ⊲ *37 rooms* ⦿ *Breakfast.*

$$$$
HOTEL

⊡ **Plettenberg Park.** The setting of this stylish, minimalist lodge—in splendid isolation on a cliff top in a private nature reserve on the western (wild) side of Robberg Peninsula—is one of the best anywhere, and the view of the open ocean across fynbos-clad hills is spectacular. **Pros:** spacious rooms; on-site spa; private beach. **Cons:** no cell phone reception; no air-conditioning; out of town. $ *Rooms from: R8700* ⊠ *Off Robberg Rd.* ☎ *044/533–9067* ⊕ *www.plettenbergpark.co.za* ⊲ *10 rooms* ⦿ *Some meals.*

$$$$
HOTEL
Fodor's Choice
★

⊡ **Tsala Treetop Lodge.** At this lodge, glass, stone, metal, and wood chalets are built on stilts overlooking a steep forested gorge and, in some cases, extending into the forest canopy. **Pros:** beautiful infinity plunge pools; vegetarians are well looked after; Wi-Fi throughout. **Cons:** suites don't have valley views as trees are in the way; pools not heated. $ *Rooms* *from: R10160 ⊠ Hunter's Estate, off N2 ✛ 10 km (6.2 miles) west of Plettenberg Bay ☎ 044/501–1111 ⊕ www.hunterhotels.com ⟋ 16 rooms ⵑ⃝⃒ Breakfast.*

SPORTS AND THE OUTDOORS

KAYAKING

Dolphin Adventures. This company offers regular trips in sleek but stable tandem kayaks (all gear provided). From May to the end of August their trips depart at 10 and 2; the rest of the year the times are 6, 9, noon, and 3. They also offer surf rentals. ⊠ *Central Beach* ☎ *083/590–3405* ⊕ *www.dolphinadventures.co.za.*

Ocean Blue Adventures. Ocean Blue runs regular paddling trips on which you may see whales and dolphins. They go out at 9, noon, and 3; fees are R500 per person. ⊠ *Hopwood St., Central Beach* ☎ *044/533–5083* ⊕ *www.oceanadventures.co.za.*

Plettenberg Bay. Kayaking on Plettenberg Bay is a great way to see the sights and possibly enjoy a visit from a whale or dolphin. Though you aren't likely to see as many animals as the people on the big boats will, it's a far more intimate and exciting experience if you do. You also get to paddle past the Cape fur seal colony on Robberg.

WHALE-WATCHING

Fodor's Choice
★
Plettenberg Bay is one of the very best locations worldwide for boat-based whale- and dolphin-watching. Most days, visitors see at least two cetacean species and Cape fur seals, as well as a variety of seabirds, including Cape gannets and African penguins. On some days people have seen up to six cetacean species in the course of a few hours.

Two similar operators, Ocean Blue Adventures and Ocean Safaris, have you step directly onto a boat at the beach. Boats are fast, safe, and dry, even though the beaching after a trip can be a bit adventurous, as it's a bumpy ride. Both operators offer similar trips, and boats are licensed to come as close as 164 feet to the whales.

Ocean Blue Adventures. Ocean Blue has a 1½- to 2-hour whale-watching trip that costs from R750 and a dolphin-watching trip that costs from R500. Sightings are not guaranteed, but the adventure of going out to sea in a launch and beaching again is worth the trip alone. En route, they take you past Robberg, which is home to a colony of Cape fur seals. ⊠ *Hopwood St., Central Beach* ☎ *044/533–5083* ⊕ *www.ocean-adventures.co.za.*

Ocean Safaris. This group runs regular whale-watching trips from the beach area. These last 1½ to 2 hours and cost R750. Trips to see dolphins cost R500. ⊠ *Hopwood St., Central Beach* ☎ *082/784–5729* ⊕ *www.oceansafaris.co.za.*

THE CRAGS

16 km (10 miles) northeast of Plettenberg Bay.

Although technically part of Plett, the Crags is very different. It's rural and forested and is home to a primate refuge as well as a free-flight aviary. Although there's no beach, the Crags region is close to the lagoon and beautiful beach at Nature's Valley—although swimming here can be dangerous because of the currents. There are loads of accommodation options and exciting activities, most of which are part of a great little marketing initiative called Cruise the Crags.

GETTING HERE AND AROUND

The Crags falls within the greater Plett area, so the same travel information applies. There's no public transportation to and around Plett, so renting a car and driving yourself is your best option.

VISITOR INFORMATION

Contacts Cruise the Crags. ⊕ *www.cruisethecrags.co.za.*

EXPLORING

FAMILY   **Birds of Eden.** Built over a natural valley in the indigenous forest, Birds of Eden is a giant free-flight aviary spanning five dome-enclosed acres. A stream, waterfalls, ponds, paths, benches, and rest areas make it a great place to spend the day. About 200 species of birds, some of which are quite tame, stay here, among them many African species. ⊹ *16 km (10 miles) east of Plettenberg Bay along the N2, just before Nature's Valley turnoff* ☏ *044/534–8906* ⊕ *www.birdsofeden.co.za* ✉ *R230; combined ticket with visit to Monkeyland R360; plus Jukani cat sanctuary R450.*

FAMILY   **Monkeyland.** This refuge houses abused and abandoned primates, most of which were once pets or laboratory animals. They now roam in a huge enclosed area of natural forest and are free to play, socialize, and do whatever it is that keeps primates happy. There are lemurs, gibbons, spider monkeys, indigenous vervet monkeys, howler monkeys, and many more. Guided walks are offered throughout the day, and the tamer "inmates" often play with guests. You can also just visit the coffee shop without paying an entrance fee. ✉ *The Crags* ⊹ *16 km (10 miles) east of Plettenberg Bay along the N2* ☏ *044/534–8906* ⊕ *www.monkeyland.co.za* ✉ *R160, combined ticket with Birds of Eden R360, and R450 including Jukani (big-cat sanctuary).*

WHERE TO STAY

$$$$ ☷ **Hog Hollow Country Lodge.** This lovely lodge, set on the edge of a forested gorge with the Tsitsikamma Mountains beyond, is well located for many of the Garden Route's most popular attractions, although you will be hard-pressed to find a reason to leave your room with its private veranda, sumptuous views, and cozy in-room fire place. **Pros:** excellent service; lavish breakfasts; privacy and space. **Cons:** dining is communal (although you can opt to have a separate table); Wi-Fi only available in the main lounge area; vervet monkeys (while cute) might pester you while

B&B/INN
Fodor'sChoice
★

you're sitting out on your veranda. $ *Rooms from: R3975* ⊠ *Askop Rd.* ☎ *044/534–8879* ⊕ *www.hog-hollow.com* ⇨ *19 rooms* ⦿ *Breakfast.*

$$$$
HOTEL
Fodor's Choice
★

⊞ **Kurland.** On the road to Tsitsikamma, this magnificent 1,500-acre estate offers spacious guest suites that make you feel like you're staying in your own country home. **Pros:** excellent Wi-Fi; rooms are individually decorated and supremely comfortable; suites have loft rooms for children. **Cons:** about a 15-minute drive out of Plettenberg Bay; no other dining options nearby; far from beach. $ *Rooms from: R5590* ⊠ *The Crags* ☎ *044/534–8082* ⊕ *www.kurland.co.za* ⇨ *13 rooms* ⦿ *Breakfast.*

TSITSIKAMMA

31 km (19 miles) east of Nature's Valley; 42 km (26 miles) east of Plettenberg Bay.

Administered as its own park, the Tsitsikamma section of the Garden Route National Park is a narrow belt of coastline extending for 80 km (50 miles) from Oubosstrand to Nature's Valley, encompassing some of the most spectacular coastal scenery in the country, including deep gorges, evergreen forests, tidal pools, and beautiful empty beaches.

GETTING HERE AND AROUND
Pickup can be arranged with most lodges. There's no public transportation in this area, so your best bet is renting a car and driving yourself. The roads are in good condition.

EXPLORING

Tsitsikamma Section of the Garden Route National Park. If you want to see some of the most fantastic scenery along the Garden Route by foot, then this area that hugs the coast between Nature's Valley and Plettenberg Bay should be your top choice. One of the best ways to see this section of the park is on the five-day Otter Trail, one of South Africa's most popular hikes—but this is usually booked out a year ahead. The somewhat easier and more comfortable portered Dolphin Trail is another option. A less strenuous highlight is to visit the suspension bridge at Storms River Mouth, where the river enters the sea through a narrow channel carved between sheer cliffs. Storms River was aptly named: when gale winds blow, as they often do, the sea flies into a pounding fury, hurling spray onto the rocks and whipping spume high up the cliffs. From the Tsitsikamma section's visitor center, a trail descends through the forest (different tree species are all labeled) and over a narrow suspension bridge strung across the river mouth. It's a spectacular walk, a highlight of any trip to the Garden Route. On the other side of the bridge a steep trail climbs to the top of a bluff overlooking the river and the sea—the turning point of the Storms River MTB (mountain bike) Trail, which starts and finishes in Storms River village. Other trails, ranging from 1 to 3 km (½ to 2 miles), lead either to a cave once inhabited by hunter-gatherers or through the coastal forest. The Cattle Baron restaurant (part of a steak-house chain) has great views of the river and ocean. It serves breakfast, lunch, and dinner to park visitors. ☎ *042/281–1607* ⊕ *www.sanparks.org* ⊠ *R196.*

WHERE TO STAY

$ **Storms River Mouth Rest Camp.** The lodgings here are clean and com-
HOTEL fortable (as are most lodgings in South Africa's national parks), and the
setting, almost within soaking distance of the pounding surf, is spectacular, making this spot a must-visit for international visitors. **Pros:** you
couldn't get closer to the sea; restaurant and shop on-site; everything is
well cared for and clean. **Cons:** there's a daily conservation fee on top
of accommodation rates; the Otter Trail is generally booked out a year
ahead; inclement weather means activities like kayaking and snorkeling
are not always available. $ *Rooms from: R1485* ✉ *Storms River Mouth*
☎ *042/281–1607* ⊕ *www.sanparks.org* ↩ *85 rooms* ⏀ *No meals.*

SPORTS AND THE OUTDOORS

BOATING

Spirit of Tsitsikamma. For a really good look at the gorge, take a boat
trip (R108) on the *Spirit of Tsitsikamma.* The boat departs every 45
minutes between 9:30 and 2:45 from the jetty below the suspension
bridge. ☎ *042/281–1607* ⊕ *www.sanparks.org.*

HIKING

Fodor'sChoice **Dolphin Trail.** This trail is the perfect marriage of exercise and relaxation,
★ rugged scenery and comfort. Starting at Storms River Mouth, the trail
continues east along the coast, with scenery similar to the Otter Trail
but with infinitely more comfortable lodging. The trail covers 17 km
(10½ miles) over two days, and the best part is that you carry only a day
pack (your luggage is transported by vehicle to the next spot). Accommodations on the first night are in very comfortable cabins with private
baths at Storms River Mouth. The next two nights are spent in lovely
guesthouses with awesome views and great food. The price includes
a guide, all meals from dinner on arrival to breakfast on the last day,
transportation, and three nights' accommodations. ☎ *042/280–3588*
⊕ *www.dolphintrail.co.za* ✉ *R5,900 per person.*

STORMS RIVER

*4 km (2½ miles) east of Tsitsikamma section of the Garden Route
National Park.*

Although it's a small, isolated village, Storms River absolutely buzzes
with activity. A hotel, a couple of guesthouses, and a few backpackers'
lodges all cater to the numerous adrenaline junkies and nature lovers
who frequent this hot spot for adventure and ecotourism activities.
Bear in mind that Storms River Mouth, the SANParks camp in the
Tsitsikamma section of the Garden Route National Park, and Storms
River village are not the same place.

GETTING HERE AND AROUND

Storms River Mouth is 18 km (11 miles) south of the Storms River
Bridge. There's no public transportation around the area, so you will
need your own transport, though the Baz Bus will drop you off at various hostels around town.

WHERE TO STAY

$$ **At the Woods Guest House.** Built with care and attention to detail, this lovely owner-managed guesthouse is a winner. **Pros:** rooms are spacious; comfortable guest lounge; knowledgeable hosts. **Cons:** swimming pool is small; limited dining options in the area; no air-conditioning (ceiling fans only); some rooms don't have mountain views. [$] *Rooms from: R2000* ✉ *Formosa St.* ☎ *082/328–2371* 🌐 *www.atthewoods.co.za* 🛏 *8 rooms* 🍴 *Breakfast.*
B&B/INN

$$ **Tsitsikamma Village Inn.** The guest rooms here are in pretty, colorful buildings that are neatly arranged around a village green, and the public rooms are in an old hunting lodge built in 1888. **Pros:** three restaurants on-site; pretty, spacious gardens; adventure center close by. **Cons:** on the main road (although it is a very quiet, little town); very busy in season. [$] *Rooms from: R1590* ✉ *Darnell St.* ☎ *042/281–1711* 🌐 *www.tsitsikammahotel.co.za* 🛏 *49 rooms* 🍴 *Breakfast.*
HOTEL

SPORTS AND THE OUTDOORS

CANOPY AND FOREST TOUR

Fodor's Choice ★ **Storms River Adventures.** Want a turaco's-eye view of the treetops? Storms River Adventures will take you deep into the forest, where you don a harness, climb up to a platform, clip in, and "fly" on long cables from platform to platform. You can even control your speed. The cost is R595 (including a light lunch), and a double DVD with video and downloadable photos costs an extra R160. Storms River Adventures also offers the Woodcutter's Journey, a gentle, open-vehicle tour of the forest and the old Storms River Pass. Knowledgeable guides expound on the flora and fauna, as well as the interesting history of the region. You end it all with lunch or tea at a beautiful picnic site next to the Storms River, where wagons would stop more than a century ago. The tea trip costs R300, and the lunch trip R400. ✉ *Main Rd.* ☎ *042/281–1836* 🌐 *www.stormsriver.com.*

MOUNTAIN BIKING

Storms River Mountain Bike Trail. This trail, in the Plaatbos area of the Garden Route National Park, is a scenic, circular 22-km (14-mile) trail that navigates the old Storms River Pass (fitness is a prerequisite here). The 5-km (3-mile) descent through the forest to the bottom of the pass offers beautiful gorge views and a refreshing dip in the river. The starting point is near the police station at Storms River; be sure to pick up a self-issue permit at the start of the trail. ✉ *Main Rd.* ☎ *042/281–1557* 🌐 *www.sanparks.org.*

Tsitsikamma Segway Tours. Part of the Tsitsikamma Backpackers hostel, Tsitsikamma Segway Tours rents mountain bikes and offers Segway tours. A two-hour Segway tour into the forest costs from R550 per person (including a short safety lesson in advance). ✉ *54 Formosa St.* ☎ *081/320–3977* 🌐 *www.segwayfun.co.za.*

5

LITTLE KAROO

The landscape of the Little Karoo—austere, minimal, and dry—stands in stark contrast to the Garden Route. In summer it resembles a blast furnace, and winter nights are bitterly cold. In its own way, however, it is absolutely beautiful. The Little Karoo, also called the Klein Karoo (*klein* is Afrikaans for "small"; *karoo* derives from the San [Bushman] word for "thirst"), should not be confused with the Great Karoo, a vast semi-desert scrubland on the interior side of the Swartberg Mountains. Everything here is a little surreal—giant birds of prey soar overhead, huge caves stretch for miles underground, and bright-green vineyards contrast with intricately eroded, deep-red hills.

EXPLORING

Ronnie's Sex Shop. No, your eyes are not playing tricks on you. That sign definitely says Ronnie's Sex Shop. And no, it's not a country brothel or a sex shop. It's actually a Route 62 icon that started out as a joke. Ronnie Price (a real person) planned to open a shop here near the road, but his friends painted the word "sex" in big red letters next to the sign to read "Ronnie's Sex Shop." It stayed like that for years—a local landmark—until Ronnie thought he would cash in on the unintentional marketing, and opened a pub instead. It's a far cry from a sophisticated venue, but it's a great place to meet the locals, some of whom spend a large proportion of the day here. It's also a mandatory stop on most motorcycle rallies. It's open from 10 in the morning until the last person leaves at night, which is usually pretty late. You can't miss it—it's right on Route 62, just on the Ladysmith side of Barrydale. ⊠ *Off R62, Barrydale* ☎ *028/572–1153* ⊕ *www.ronniessexshop.co.za.*

EN ROUTE

Joubert-Tradauw. Set between Montagu and Barrydale on the R62, the Op-de-Tradouw region, named after a pass through the mountains, is best known for its excellent wines. Joubert-Tradauw is a great place to stop for a wine tasting or for lunch or tea. Owner Meyer Joubert makes wine in the age-old French tradition—unfiltered and unrefined. His Chardonnay is sublime, and he has publicly stated that it is his ambition to make the best Syrah in the world. (Try it; he's definitely on the right track.) While he works his magic in the winery, his wife Beate waves her star-spangled wand over the small deli–coffee shop, where you can sit under the pergola and spend ages over a superb cheese platter or Gruyère salad, or just have a quick coffee and cheesecake. It's tapas alfresco with a traditional Afrikaner touch. ⊠ *R62, Barrydale* ✛ *12 km (7½ miles) west of Barrydale* ☎ *028/125–0086* ⊕ *www.joubert-tradauw.co.za* 🖼 *Free* ⊗ *Closed Sun.*

SANBONA WILDLIFE RESERVE

27 km (17 miles) west of Barrydale.

Roughly the size of Singapore, this enormous private wildlife reserve supports a free-roaming population of wild animals that were indigenous to the Western Cape before European settlers arrived. Here you'll find the Big Five (lion, rhino, elephant, buffalo, and leopard) and many smaller desert creatures. One of the more unique experiences is to spend time on foot with the wild cheetahs that have grown accustomed to being approached by the rangers. But don't expect to be able to touch them. Remote, tranquil, and beautiful, Sanbona has the added benefits of offering luxurious accommodations options and being malaria-free.

GETTING HERE AND AROUND

There's no public transportation in the area, so you will need a car to get around. The drive from Cape Town is about three hours along the N1, R60, and then R62.

EXPLORING

Fodor's Choice
★
Sanbona Wildlife Reserve. Arguably the Western Cape's most authentic Big Five reserve, Sanbona Wildlife Reserve is within relatively easy reach of Cape Town (270 km/168 miles). Animals like elephants, lions, and cheetahs roam free in the reserve's some 135,000 acres, and guides make use of tracking devices to locate them. The scenery is spectacular, too. Rugged gorges alternate with gently rolling plains featuring unique plant life that comes into its own in spring. Crystal-clear night skies promise exceptional stargazing. Three luxury lodges cater to a variety of tastes and life stages: historic Tilney Manor has an old-world farmhouse feel, Gondwana Lodge is geared toward families, and Dwyka Tented Camp, magnificently situated beneath soaring cliffs, is styled as a bush safari camp. ⊠ *Off R62, Montagu* ✛ *43 km (27 miles) from Montagu, en route to Oudtshoorn* ⊕ *www.sanbona.com.*

WHERE TO STAY

$$$$
HOTEL
Dwyka Tented Camp. This luxury tented camp, on a horseshoe bend of a dry riverbed at the foot of soaring cliffs, is a great place to reconnect with yourself, your partner, and nature. **Pros:** luxuriously appointed tents; spa treatments available; spectacular setting. **Cons:** paths to tents are unpaved and a bit rough; wilderness environment might not be to everyone's taste; no kids under 16. $ *Rooms from: R16500* ⊠ *Sanbona Wildlife Reserve, Montagu* ☎ *021/010–0028* ⊕ *www.sanbona.com* ⇥ *9 rooms* ‖○‖ *All meals.*

$$$$
HOTEL
FAMILY
Gondwana Lodge. Within easy striking distance of the best game-viewing areas and overlooking the Bellair Dam, Gondwana Lodge marries contemporary design with traditional thatched, Karoo-style architecture and is unashamedly family-friendly. **Pros:** staff are attentive and accommodating; lots of options for kids; on-site spa. **Cons:** stairs to the upper level are steep; not ideal for couples because very family-orientated; not ideal for a secluded stay. $ *Rooms from: R15616* ⊠ *Sanbona Wildlife Reserve, Montagu* ☎ *021/010–0028* ⊕ *www.sanbona.com* ⇥ *12 rooms* ‖○‖ *All meals.*

$$$$
ALL-INCLUSIVE
Fodor's Choice
★
Tilney Manor. A warm welcome awaits when you arrive at the historic manor house at Tilney Lodge, where staff wait outside to greet new arrivals with hot face towels to freshen up after the hour-long drive from the reserve entrance. **Pros:** hands-on staff will attend to every need; indoor and outdoor dining; on-site spa. **Cons:** Wi-Fi connectivity does not reach all rooms; communal dinner tables may not suit everyone's tastes; formal atmosphere in lodge. $ *Rooms from: R15616* ⊠ *Sanbona Wildlife Reserve, Montagu* ☎ *021/010–0028* ⊕ *www.sanbona.com* ⇥ *6 rooms* ‖○‖ *All meals.*

5

OUDTSHOORN

85 km (53 miles) north of Mossel Bay.

Oudtshoorn has been famous for its ostriches since around 1870, when farmers began raising them to satisfy the European demand for feathers to adorn women's hats and dresses. In the years leading up to World War I, ostrich feathers were almost worth their weight in gold thanks to the continuing demands of fashion, and Oudtshoorn experienced an incredible boom. Many of the beautiful sandstone buildings in town date from that period, as do the "feather palaces," huge homes built by prosperous feather merchants and buyers. Although feathers are no longer a major fashion item, these huge birds are now bred for their tough and distinctive leather and almost completely fat- and cholesterol-free red meat, although a few feathers make their way to Las Vegas for the showgirls. Almost as much of a moneymaker, though, is the tourist potential of these weird and wonderful birds. In addition to visiting an ostrich farm, you can buy ostrich products ranging from the sublime—feather boas—to the ridiculous—taxidermic baby ostriches emerging from cracked eggs. Several farms compete for the tourist buck, offering almost identical tours and a chance to eat an ostrich-based meal. Be warned—these can be real tourist traps: glitzy, superficial, and crowded.

Note that most of the restaurants, guesthouses, and attractions listed here are on Baron van Reede Street. This street becomes the R328, which heads north from Oudtshoorn to the Cango Caves, the Swartberg Pass, and Prince Albert.

GETTING HERE AND AROUND
The most convenient and efficient way of getting around is driving yourself. The roads are good, and parts are very scenic. Intercape buses now travel to Oudtshoorn.

VISITOR INFORMATION
Contacts Oudtshoorn Tourism Bureau. ⊠ *12 Baron van Reede St.* ☎ *044/279–2532* ⊕ *www.oudtshoorn.com.*

EXPLORING
Cango Caves. Between Oudtshoorn and Prince Albert, the huge and stunningly beautiful Cango Caves, filled with weird and wonderful stalactite and stalagmite formations, are deservedly one of the most popular attractions in the area. Only a small fraction of the caves, which extend for several miles through the mountains, is open. Unfortunately, due to shortsighted tourism schemes in the 1960s and vandalism, there's some damage, especially to the first chamber, but they are still very impressive and get more magnificent the more the tour progresses. One of the highlights is "Cleopatra's Needle," which is 29 feet high and at least 150,000 years old. You can choose between two tours: the hour-long standard tour and the aptly named adventure tour, which lasts 1½ hours. Think long and hard before opting for the latter if you're overweight, very tall, claustrophobic, or have knee or heart problems. It's exhilarating, but the temperature and humidity are high, there's not much oxygen, and you'll be shimmying up narrow chimneys on your belly, wriggling your way through tiny tunnels, and sliding on your

bottom. Wear old clothes and shoes with a good tread. Standard tours leave on the hour, adventure tours on the half hour. ✉ *Off R328* ✥ *29 km (18 miles) north of Oudtshoorn* ☎ *044/272–7410* 🌐 *www.cango-caves.co.za* 🎫 *Standard tour R80, adventure tour R100.*

FAMILY **Cango Ostrich Farm.** Cango Ostrich Farm is one of the least commercialized ostrich show farms. Guides explain the bird's extraordinary social and physical characteristics, and there are lots of interactive opportunities, including feeding and petting the ostriches and posing with one for a photograph. The farm is conveniently located en route to the Cango Caves from town. From September to February, you may see babies hatching. ✉ *R328* ✥ *14 km (9 miles) north of Oudtshoorn* ☎ *044/272–4623* 🌐 *www.cangoostrich.co.za* 🎫 *R100.*

NEED A BREAK? **Wilgewandel.** At the turnoff to the Cango Caves, Wilgewandel serves well-cooked simple food such as hamburgers, toasted sandwiches, ostrich steaks, and sweet treats. Shady outdoor tables overlook a big lawn and duck-filled pond. **Known for:** tasty simple meals. ✉ *R328* ✥ *2 km (1 mile) from the caves* ☎ *044/272–0878* 🌐 *www.wilgewandel.co.za.*

WHERE TO EAT

$$ ECLECTIC 🍴 **Jemima's Restaurant.** Named after the mythical guardian angel of love, good taste, and good cooking, this restaurant would not disappoint its muse. All the ingredients are sourced locally from farmers in the district, and the menu focuses on such local delicacies as olives, Karoo mutton, and, of course, ostrich. **Known for:** Karoo lamb, beef, ostrich, and venison; butternut cheesecake; local wines. [$] *Average main: R150* ✉ *94 Baron van Reede St.* ☎ *044/272–0808* 🌐 *www.jemimas.com.*

WHERE TO STAY

$$ B&B/INN 🏨 **Hlangana Lodge.** Conveniently situated on the edge of town on the road out to the caves, this great option is warm and friendly and has a lovely garden surrounding a swimming pool. **Pros:** superior rooms have huge bathrooms; staff is friendly and helpful; lovely garden and pool. **Cons:** rooms not very private; lodge is on the main road; they don't serve dinner. [$] *Rooms from: R1600* ✉ *Baron van Reede St. at North St.* ☎ *044/272–2299* 🌐 *www.hlangana.co.za* 🛏 *19 rooms* 🍽 *Breakfast.*

$ B&B/INN 🏨 **Kleinplaas.** Comfortable, well-appointed chalets with fully equipped cooking facilities are neatly arranged in a huge, shady lawn area at Kleinplaas, which means "small farm"—although it isn't really a farm despite the ostriches and ducks on the premises. **Pros:** chalets serviced daily; a private patio area for each chalet; conveniently located at edge of town. **Cons:** only the open-plan chalets have air-conditioning; Wi-Fi available only in the office; not particularly scenic. [$] *Rooms from: R897* ✉ *171 Baron van Reede St.* ☎ *044/272–5811* 🌐 *www.kleinplaas.co.za* 🛏 *54 rooms* 🍽 *No meals.*

$$ B&B/INN Fodor's Choice ★ 🏨 **La Plume Guest House.** This stylish guesthouse is set on a working ostrich farm on the Calitzdorp side of Oudtshoorn. **Pros:** beautiful views of the valley from the patio; spacious bedrooms and en suite bathrooms; terrific attention to detail (candles in bathrooms, sprigs of lavender on the pillow, etc.). **Cons:** a 10-minute drive out of town; no room phones; not for trendy types. [$] *Rooms from: R1720* ✉ *Volmoed*

⊕ *14 km (9 miles) west of Oudtshoorn* ☎ *044/272–7516, 082/820–4373* 🌐 *www.laplume.co.za* 🛏 *20 rooms* 🍴 *Breakfast.*

$ B&B/INN 🏨 **Le Petit Karoo.** Perched high on a hill just off the R328, three en-suite bush tents, with spa-baths on the veranda, have fabulous mountain views where you can feel like you're in your own little private paradise. **Pros:** breakfasts (not included) are great; the Jacuzzis in the tents are wonderful; the French owner/hosts are charming. **Cons:** it's rustic; tents can get hot in summer; dinners only by arrangement. [$] *Rooms from: R850* ✉ *Off R328* ⊕ *14 km (9 miles) north of Oudtshoorn* ☎ *044/272–7428* 🌐 *www.lepetitkaroo.za.net* 🛏 *8 rooms* 🍴 *No meals.*

$$ B&B/INN FAMILY Fodor's Choice ★ 🏨 **Rietfontein Ostrich Palace.** The world's oldest established working ostrich farm since 1897, this former feather palace surrounded by spectacular red mountains has authentically furnished accommodations. **Pros:** swimming pool with panoramic views; wheelchair- and child-friendly; authentic and historic. **Cons:** very hot in summer, very cold in winter; no single rooms; Emma unit has only shower, not bath. [$] *Rooms from: R1800* ✉ *Oudtshoorn* ⊕ *18 km (11 miles) from Calitzdorp on Route 62 towards Oudtshoorn, well-signposted* ☎ *044/213–3784* 🌐 *www.rop.co.za* 🛏 *6 rooms* 🍴 *Breakfast.*

$$$$ B&B/INN 🏨 **Rosenhof.** For luxury and indulgence in the heart of Oudtshoorn, look no further than Rosenhof, where you'll be greeted with fresh cut flowers in garden cottages boasting under-floor heating, baths and showers, and patios facing a pretty stone fountain. **Pros:** excellent restaurant; lovely gardens, with many places to sit and relax; on-site art gallery. **Cons:** outside areas of rooms are not private; small pool area; close to main road. [$] *Rooms from: R3800* ✉ *264 Baron van Reede St.* ☎ *044/272–2232* 🌐 *www.rosenhof.co.za* 🛏 *14 rooms* 🍴 *Breakfast.*

SPORTS AND THE OUTDOORS

BALLOONING

Oudtshoorn Ballooning. Oudtshoorn Ballooning offers a scenic balloon flight over the town and neighboring farms at dawn. Flights are R2,500 per person and include tea and coffee on arrival and sparkling wine on landing. In the high season, book well in advance. ✉ *Oudtshoorn* ☎ *082/784–8539* 🌐 *www.oudtshoornballooning.co.za.*

MOUNTAIN BIKING

Joyrides. Joyrides, based at Backpackers Paradise, runs a fabulous mountain-biking trip. You get transported to the top of the Swartberg Pass, where you (and your fellow cyclists) are left with a mountain bike, helmet, and water. It's pretty much downhill all the way back to town, and the route passes Cango Caves (it's a bit of a steep uphill detour to get there), Wilgewandel coffee shop, Cango Ostrich Farm, Cango Wildlife Ranch, and Le Petit Karoo and then back to Backpackers Paradise. So you've got all day to visit the main tourist attractions. The tour costs R450 and an extra R100 if you want to be picked up somewhere on route. ✉ *148 Baron van Reede St.* ☎ *044/272–3436* 🌐 *www.backpackersparadise.net.*

SHOPPING

Oudtshoorn has loads of stores selling ostrich products, but it pays to shop around, as prices vary significantly. The smartest shops strung out along Baron van Reede Street have a great variety but are a tad pricey.

Klein Karoo Boutique. The Klein Karoo Co-op, that coordinates the marketing of ostrich products, has a boutique on its premises near the airport, on the western side of town. (This is really just an airfield, but it's called the airport.) Here you can purchase bags, feather boas, shoes, and other smaller items. It can be a little tricky to find, so it's best to phone for directions or ask for help at your hotel. ⊠ *Kooperasie St.* ☎ *044/203–5242* ⊕ *www.kleinkarooboutique.co.za.*

Lugro Ostrich. This small factory in town manufactures ostrich handbags and wallets, as well as belts and smaller items such as key rings. These can be bought in the shop on the premises. ⊠ *133 Langenhoven Rd.* ☎ *044/272–7012* ⊕ *www.lugro-ostrich.co.za.*

DE RUST

40 km (25 miles) northeast of Oudtshoorn.

De Rust is a sleepy Little Karoo village. The main road is lined with crafts stores, coffee shops, restaurants, and wineshops.

GETTING HERE AND AROUND

There's no public transportation here. You will need your own vehicle to travel around, but the roads are good, and the scenery is very beautiful.

VISITOR INFORMATION

Contacts De Rust Tourism Bureau. ⊠ *29 Schoeman St.* ☎ *044/279–2532* ⊕ *www.derust.org.za.*

EXPLORING

Domein Doornkraal. This one-stop farm shop features wines from 25 cellars and has an excellent selection of pot-still brandies, dessert wines, dry wines, and blends. They also make their own superb range of fortified wines and an inexpensive white blend (Chenin Blanc, Sauvignon Blanc, and Colombard). The shop also stocks local olive oil products from 10 local suppliers, preserves, honey, sweets, and cookies, all sourced from local farms and bakers. In season, they operate a small outdoor restaurant focusing on old-fashioned home cooking. ⊠ *R62, 10 km (6 miles) southwest of De Rust* ☎ *044/251–6715* ⊕ *www. doornkraal.co.za* ⌺ *Free.*

Mons Ruber Estate. This estate is named after the red hills that dominate the landscape and whose soil creates the perfect environment for growing grapes with a high sugar content. So it's not surprising that this winery specializes in dessert wines as well as a fine brandy. There is a lovely restored 19th-century kitchen, and an easy hiking trail stretches 1½ hours into the fascinating red hills. ⊠ *N12, 15 km (9 miles) southwest of De Rust* ☎ *044/251–6550* ⌺ *Free.*

5

WHERE TO STAY

$$$

B&B/INN

Fodor's Choice

★

⊞ **Madi-Madi Karoo Safari Lodge.** Tucked away in a hidden valley between the mighty Outeniqua peaks and the Swartberg Mountains, this lovely lodge with six traditional riverfront cottages is one of South Africa's most tranquil places to stay. **Pros:** true isolation and peace; delicious traditional country food; lovely pool. **Cons:** very isolated; very hot in summer, very cold in winter; limited activities. ⑤ *Rooms from: R3000* ⊠ *Oudtshoorn* ✚ *9.3 km (5.8 miles) northeast of Dysseldorp on Main Rd.* ☎ *044/696–6055* ⊕ *www.madi-madi.co.za* ⇌ *6 rooms* �◎⎮*Breakfast.*

THE EASTERN CAPE

Updated by
Christopher
Clark

The Eastern Cape is South Africa's most diverse province and has some of its best vacation destinations, but it is often glossed over by overseas visitors. Starting where the Garden Route ends, it includes much of the Great Karoo—a large, semidesert region of ocher plains, purple mountains, dramatic skies, and unusual, hardy vegetation—and abuts KwaZulu-Natal in the northeast and Lesotho's mountain lands in the north. But a glance at a map will reveal the region's main attraction: its coastline, still largely undeveloped and running for some 640 km (400 miles) from temperate to subtropical waters.

The climate is mild across the region and throughout the year, with temperatures at the coast ranging between winter lows of 5°C (41°F) and summer highs of 32°C (90°F). It has many of the country's finest and least crowded beaches, Afro-montane forests (one of South Africa's eco-regions) and heathlands, an ever-increasing number of fantastic malaria-free game reserves, and some of the most interesting cultural attractions in South Africa.

ORIENTATION AND PLANNING

GETTING ORIENTED

The Eastern Cape is a big space with many tiny gems. The towns, and even the cities, of the province are relatively small and often quaint, and the distances between them are often fairly large. Since the only airports are in Port Elizabeth, East London, and Mthatha (previously Umtata), the best way to experience the region is on a self-driving tour, leaving yourself plenty of time to explore (but be prepared for some poorly maintained roads in some regions of the Transkei).

Frontier Country and the Sunshine Coast. Formerly known as Settler Country, the Frontier Country stretches from the outskirts of Port Elizabeth to Port Alfred in the east, Grahamstown in the northeast, and the Zuurberg Mountains in the north. The area also encompasses Addo Elephant National Park and game reserves including Shamwari and Kwandwe. The Sunshine Coast overlaps part of this area, running roughly from Cape St Francis for 500 km (310 miles) as far as East London via Port Elizabeth.

Amatole. This undulating region stretches along the coast from just beyond Port Alfred almost up to Port St Johns, overlapping with the Wild Coast from East London onward. But the larger part of this region

TOP REASONS TO GO

Take a Walk on the Wild Side: The Wild Coast is a fabulous "slackpacking" destination. You can walk all day on long, lovely beaches, past turquoise lagoons and through unspoiled villages. Wonderful day-hiking opportunities include the 37-km (23-mile) walk between Bulungula and Coffee Bay—which takes you along beaches, cliff tops, and rolling hills—plus guided hikes run by many of the lodges.

Take a Look at the Wildlife: With its rich and varied topography and flora, the Eastern Cape supports a wide range of game, much of which was once hunted to near extinction by farmers and settlers. Initiatives to reclaim this area for some of its original inhabitants include Addo Elephant National Park, Shamwari Game Reserve, and Kwandwe Private Game Reserve. Most of the terrain here is hilly with thick bush, so you won't see vast herds of animals wandering across open plains, and some areas bear visible scars from farming. But the game is here: elephants, antelope, rhinos, buffalo, and much more. And best of all—it's malaria-free.

Take a Dive on the Wild Side: If you've cage-dived with great whites, plumbed the depths of dark and narrow caves, and dived under ice, you probably think you've done it all. Wrong. Diving with a "baitball"—fish herded together by dolphins for dining purposes—in the sardine run off the Wild Coast is the ultimate adrenaline dive. Sharks, Cape gannets, Bryde's whales, and even humpbacks have all been known to join in the feast.

Take in the Culture and History: From rustic Xhosa villages—where women paint their faces with ocher clay and boys undergo circumcision rites of passage—to colonial mansions, the range and depth of the Eastern Cape's cultural heritage is amazing. Since the early 19th century, the Eastern Cape has been a frontier and a focus of black resistance. In almost every town you'll find fascinating museums and art galleries and a good tour operator who can expose you to the history and culture of this heterogeneous society. A particular cultural highlight of the Eastern Cape is the annual National Arts Festival, which runs for 10 action-packed days every late June and/or July in Grahamstown.

See the Other Side: The Transkei is a truly unadulterated vision of rural South Africa. Taking a tour will allow you to interact with locals while traversing the spectacular Wild Coast on foot, horse, bicycle, or ATV. If you're more interested in culture than adventure, a visit to Bulungula will let you meet locals and generally interact on a far more personal level.

stretches far into the hinterland, almost to Queenstown, with the picturesque mountain village of Hogsback found more or less at its heart.

Wild Coast. Lovely, long beaches stretch as far as the eye can see, often with nothing but a few cows breaking the isolation. Strictly speaking, the Wild Coast originally reached from the Kei River mouth to Port Edward (which were the borders of the then nominally independent Transkei), but today it has spread almost to the outskirts of East London.

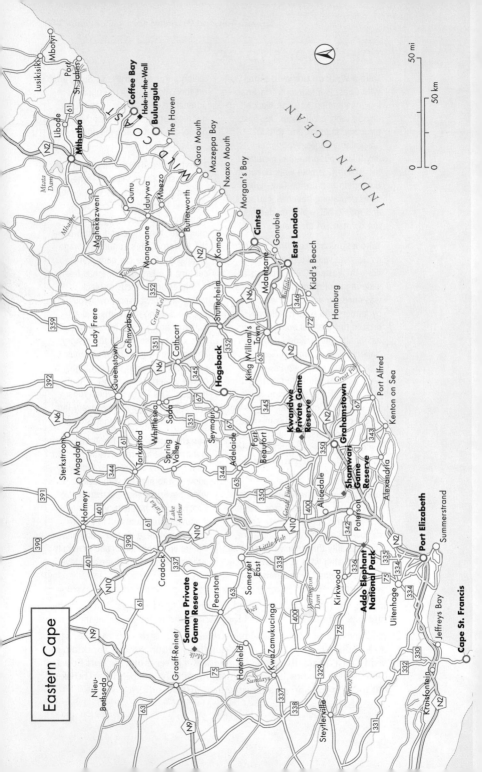

PLANNING

WHEN TO GO

Although winters are pretty mild, especially farther north along the Wild Coast, summer—from September to April—is the most popular time to visit, especially for sun worshippers. (The beaches are best avoided at Christmas and New Year's, when they become severely overcrowded with reveling locals.) But even winter has its attractions. The sardine run, usually in June or early July (see "The Food Chain Up Close" box, in Wild Coast), is becoming a major draw, and July's (sometimes late June's) National Arts Festival draws thousands of cultural pilgrims to the delightful university town of Grahamstown.

PLANNING YOUR TIME

3 Days: Fly in to Port Elizabeth in the morning and head straight out to Grahamstown. Do a historical tour in the afternoon followed by dinner at your guesthouse or one of the restaurants in town. The next morning, drive out to Shamwari, Kwandwe, or Addo; plan to spend two days in one of these reserves (staying at one of the private luxury lodges or, at Addo, at an inexpensive SANParks camp) and then drive back to Port Elizabeth to fly out. Or if you choose to visit Kwandwe, you can cut the game-viewing down to one day, keep heading north from Grahamstown, and spend the third day exploring the pretty village of Hogsback and taking a brisk hike into the Amatola Mountains. Alternatively, you could spend two days in Port Elizabeth or its beautiful coastal environs—soaking up the sun, playing a round of golf, taking a cultural tour, and just relaxing—and a third day on a day trip to Addo for an animal fix.

5 Days: With five days you could fly in and out of East London to join the Wild Coast Meander tour with Wild Coast Holiday Reservations (see East London)—your days filled with walking this wonderful coastline, and each night spent at a different beach hotel. For a glimpse of South Africa not on the usual tourist route, fly to Mthatha from Johannesburg; spend two days and three nights at Bulungula, immersing yourself in the local culture, and then drive from Mthatha to Addo, Shamwari, or Kwandwe for a good game fix. If you spend these last couple of nights at one of the private lodges, you can revel in the indulgence of absolute luxury after a few days of roughing it. Or if game parks aren't your thing, head to Hogsback and hike through the mountains and forests for a day or two before returning to Port Elizabeth to fly out. A third option is to start in Grahamstown, as with the three-day itinerary; two days in Grahamstown will give you the opportunity to appreciate the history and culture of this lovely city. Then spend two days at the game destination of your choice—Addo, Shamwari, or Kwandwe—and one more day on the Sunshine Coast soaking up some culture, lounging on the beach, or playing golf.

GETTING HERE AND AROUND

AIR TRAVEL

Port Elizabeth (PLZ) airport, small and easy to navigate, is the primary air entry point for the Eastern Cape and has a number of daily services with South African Airways, and the affiliated SA Airlink and SA Express, as well as British Airways (operated by Comair). Mango, a local no-frills budget airline, also offers a good service but usually

6

has only a couple of flights a day. You can fly here from Cape Town (1 hour), Johannesburg (1½ hours), and most other major cities; there are no direct international flights.

The small and easy-to-navigate East London (ELS) airport is the best entry for the Amatole region and is served daily by South African Airways, SA Express, SA Airlink, and Kulula.

SA Airlink also flies between the tiny airport at Mthatha (UTT)—for travel to the Wild Coast—and Johannesburg. There are three flights a day, which take about an hour and 40 minutes. *For information on airlines, see Air Travel in Travel Smart.*

Contacts East London Airport (*ELS*). ☎ *043/706–0306* ⊕ *www.acsa.co.za.* **Mthatha Airport** (*UTT*). ☎ *047/536–0023.* **Port Elizabeth Airport** (*PLZ*). ☎ *041/507–7319* ⊕ *www.acsa.co.za.*

BUS TRAVEL

Greyhound and Intercape Mainliner have pretty reliable and reasonably priced bus services, but the distances are long. In Port Elizabeth, both services depart and arrive at Greenacres shopping complex, in the Newton Park suburb 3 km (2 miles) from the city center. This area is perfectly safe during the day, but you do need to arrange to be picked up in advance. If you are concerned about your budget, consider saving money by staying at a backpackers' lodge and spending a bit more on the Baz Bus (which travels door-to-door); an added benefit is that you won't have to wander around town with your luggage. *For information on buses, see Bus Travel in Travel Smart.*

CAR TRAVEL

Traveling by car is the easiest and best way to tour the Eastern Cape. The major rental agencies have offices at the various airports in the region and in downtown Port Elizabeth. One-way rentals are available. Roads are generally in fairly good shape. *For information on car-rental agencies, see Car Travel in Travel Smart.*

SAFETY AND PRECAUTIONS

One thing to keep in mind is that although most of the Central area of Port Elizabeth is safe, a few parts of it can be dicey. The lower section along Govan Mbeki is lively and vibrant, and the upper section is quiet and peaceful, but the parts in between have seen some crime. The area is slowly improving, but it's still best to get advice from your hotel or the tourism office before wandering around. The same goes for most of the bigger cities in the Eastern Cape; smaller towns and villages tend to be less affected by crime.

The Eastern Cape is malaria-free, and the climate is generally good. The tap water in the deep rural areas may be a bit unpredictable, but it's fine in the cities and towns. Avoid driving east of Grahamstown at night: the roads are unfenced and animals wander onto—or even sleep on—the warm tarmac, which is a serious hazard. Be sure to bring protection against sunburn, and be careful swimming in the sea—the Wild Coast beaches don't have lifeguards.

In case of an emergency, call the general emergencies number (☎ *10111*). For vehicle breakdown, call your car-rental company.

HOTELS

Most hotels along the coast get booked up over summer vacation (December and January), and the Wild Coast hotels are even busy over the winter school vacation, usually around June. Most establishments run winter specials, but there are exceptions. Grahamstown is packed in late June and/or early July for the National Arts Festival; every guesthouse is full, the campsite bulges, and even school and university dorms rent out rooms. Hotels on the Wild Coast often offer packages for the sardine run, usually in June or early July, but it's always a bit of a gamble, as the sardines are just not as reliable as the artists of the Grahamstown festival.

The best way to secure a reservation is by phone or via the lodging's website. Another thing to keep in mind is that some of the more remote or rural lodgings on the Eastern Cape (particularly on the Wild Coast) still have limited Internet services provided for guest use, though almost all lodgings in the urban areas have good, fast Wi-Fi service these days. ■TIP➜ **If the ability to connect to the Web is important to you, it's always worth clarifying the type of service available when you make your reservation.**

Hotel reviews have been shortened. For full information, visit Fodors.com.

RESTAURANTS

Generally speaking, the restaurants of the Eastern Cape are good but rarely great. Of course there are always a few exceptions to every rule, and in the Eastern Cape the number of these exceptions is steadily increasing. But for really good food, choose a great hotel or guesthouse, some of which are noted for their cuisine. Not surprisingly, most restaurants are reasonably casual, and there are none where men would be expected to wear a dinner jacket or a tie. *Restaurant reviews have been shortened. For full information, visit Fodors.com.*

WHAT IT COSTS IN SOUTH AFRICAN RAND				
	$	$$	$$$	$$$$
Restaurants	under R100	R100–R150	R151–R200	over R200
Hotels	under R1,500	R1,500–R2,500	R2,501–R3,500	over R3,500

Restaurant prices are the average cost of a main course at dinner or, if dinner is not served, at lunch. Hotel prices are the lowest cost of a standard double room in high season.

TOURS

African Dive Adventures. This well-established and family-run tour company offers Sardine Run Packages along the Wild Coast from its base at the lovely Ocean View Hotel in tranquil Coffee Bay. The best time to see this remarkable natural phenomenon, which draws an array of shark species as well as pods of dolphins, whales, and even gannets plunging into the sea from the skies above, is usually between late June and late July. You'll often be joined by co-owner Roland, who can spin a good yarn or two from his many thousands of dives in this area, as can the company's highly experienced dive masters and instructors, who'll make you feel right at home both in and out of the water. ⊠ *Ocean View*

Hotel, Coffee Bay ☎ *039/317–1483, 082/456–7885 mobile* ⊕ *www. afridive.com* ✉ *R27,500, 5 nights and 4 days diving and food.*

Calabash Tours. The tour company offers some of the best cultural, township, and shebeen tours in Port Elizabeth. In recognition of its commitment to community development, this operator has been accredited by Fair Trade Tourism in South Africa. A tour of the local townships costs R550. An evening shebeen tour (R650) includes visits to a couple of township taverns, dinner, and, almost certainly, some good music. For a more intimate and personal experience, a new storytelling route has recently been added to the list, incorporating a traditional lunch with one of the local storytellers (R695). Calabash also has multiday tours to Addo Elephant National Park, as well as three- to five-day African heritage tours. ✉ *Summerstrand Hotel, Central* ☎ *041/585–6162* ⊕ *www.calabashtours.co.za.*

Mosaic Tourism. From a short and informative city or township tour with knowledgeable local guides to an all-day game-viewing excursion, the award-winning Mosaic Travel offers a variety of immersing tailor-made tours in and around Port Elizabeth and right across the Eastern Cape. ☎ *083/656–8329 mobile* ⊕ *www.mosaictourism.co.za.*

VISITOR INFORMATION

Contacts Nelson Mandela Bay Tourism. ✉ *39 and 41 Donkin St., Central* ☎ *041/582–2575* ⊕ *www.nmbt.co.za.*

FRONTIER COUNTRY AND THE SUNSHINE COAST

Frontier Country and the Sunshine Coast offer the perfect mix of well-maintained sunny coastal towns, beaches and resorts, historic and cultural sites, and a plethora of great game reserves all within a relatively concentrated (and malaria-free) area. Combined with good roads and infrastructure and a fine climate almost throughout, it's not hard to see why this part of the Eastern Cape is a particularly popular playground for South African tourists. It's richer and more developed here than in many other parts of the Eastern Cape, and although towns like Jeffreys Bay can become a little overrun during the holidays, there's a lot to see and do, with most of the highlights within very short and easy driving distances of each other. Sometimes unkindly referred to as the Detroit of South Africa, Port Elizabeth is the Sunshine Coast's (as well as the whole of the Eastern Cape's) main urban hub and has great transport links to and from the rest of the region and beyond. Both the city and the surrounding region also boast many of the province's best accommodations options and restaurants.

PORT ELIZABETH

770 km (477 miles) east of Cape Town.

Port Elizabeth, or PE, may not have the range of attractions found in Cape Town or on the Garden Route, but it's a pleasant town that's worthy of a couple of days' exploration. There are some beautiful beaches (although you'll need to visit them early in the day in summer, as the wind tends to pick up by midday) and some wonderfully preserved historic buildings in the older part of the city, called Central. A large part of the town's charm lies in its small size and laid-back environment, but PE is not a total sleepy hollow. If you feel the need for a bit of nightlife, head to the Boardwalk complex near the beach for its restaurants, cafés, theater, and casino, or to the pedestrianized Parliament Street in Central, which has a vibrant restaurant and nightlife scene.

GETTING HERE AND AROUND

PE is a good base for exploring some other fantastic destinations, both wild and cultural, including Addo Elephant National Park. If you are traveling to any of the game reserves east of Port Elizabeth (such as Shamwari or Kwandwe), it may be a good idea to spend the night before in PE, as many places advise you to check in before lunch and it could be a scramble to get there if you're driving or flying in that morning.

Port Elizabeth's suburbs can be a little confusing. Humewood and Summerstrand are PE's two main coastal suburbs, with Humewood closer to the city center. The Humewood Golf Course, one of South Africa's best, is in Summerstrand, not Humewood, however (just to keep you on your toes).

There's a minibus shuttle at the Port Elizabeth airport that will drop you off at your hotel (about R90 one way, much less than a metered taxi), but you'll need to book in advance.

Contacts Blunden Minibus Shuttle. ☎ *041/451–4803* ⊕ *www.blunden.co.za.*

VISITOR INFORMATION

Port Elizabeth's Nelson Mandela Bay Tourism is open weekdays 8–4:30.

EXPLORING

Art Route 67. Consisting of 67 public artworks by the Eastern Cape's local artists, the route symbolizes the 67 years that the late Nelson Mandela dedicated to the South African fight for freedom. The route runs from the city center to Donkin Reserve and the old lighthouse above that overlook the harbor and the ocean beyond. Here there's a large pyramid built by the city's former governor Rufane Shaw Donkin in honor of his deceased wife, Elizabeth, from whom Port Elizabeth gets its name. Stretching from the pyramid toward a towering South African flag is a long and colorful mosaic that references various important parts of Port Elizabeth's and the Eastern Cape's history and cultural heritage. Beneath the huge flag is a life-size metal cutout of Mandela (he was taller than you might think) with his fist raised in triumph, and snaking down the steps behind him is a line of South Africans (also life-size) of all ages, colors, and creeds lining up to vote in the 1994 elections. Sixty-seven colored steps lead from this point back to the city below, and along the way you'll find a number of inspiring quotes from Mandela on sheets of metal made to look like pages ripped from a book. Combined with all the other colorful wall paintings, sculptures, and texts, the route has both revitalized and contextualized some of the previously more run-down areas of central Port Elizabeth, and tells important stories about where South Africa came from and where it is headed. ⊠ *Donkin Reserve.*

BEACHES

The beaches listed here are lined with restaurants, shops, and coffee bars, and there are flea markets on weekends. Beyond Hobie Beach the seafront is still built up with houses and apartments, but the frenetic commercialism is missing.

Hobie Beach. The pier marks the beginning of Hobie Beach, where sailing catamarans and Jet Skis launch, and where a number of annual events and festivals are held. There are a number of restaurants along the other side of the promenade, including Ginger at the Beach Hotel. The Hobie Beach Guesthouse is also close by. The section of beach closest to the pier is great for swimming and sunbathing, and there are also a number of rock pools to explore. Hobie Beach can get very busy on a hot summer's day. **Amenities:** food and drink; lifeguards; parking (fee); showers; toilets. **Best for:** snorkeling; swimming; walking. ✉ *Marine Dr.*

FAMILY **Humewood Beach.** Humewood Beach runs from King's Beach to Shark Rock Pier. This beach has fine white sand and is a great place for families, with shaded areas supplied by an overhead promenade. A convenient parking lot is behind the beach (behind John Dory's restaurant), and there are excellent facilities, including picnic tables, plus lifeguards on duty during peak times. Some grassy areas lead into Happy Valley, but it's not recommended that you walk into the valley, as it's often completely deserted and you may be in danger of being mugged. The beach slipway has a little reef, and the water beside it is great for snorkeling. Humewood Beach is close to the bustling Boardwalk Hotel and all its facilities (including a casino and mall) and the Beach Hotel. **Amenities:** lifeguards; parking (free); showers; toilets. **Best for:** snorkeling; swimming. ✉ *Marine Dr.*

King's Beach. Within the bay and starting closest to the city center and harbor (which is best avoided), the first beach you come to is King's Beach, so named because King George VI slept in the Royal Train here during a visit to the city before World War II. You may want to avoid the far end of King's Beach, as it can get pretty crowded. The beach is one of three Blue Flag beaches in PE (along with Hobie Beach and Humewood Beach), meaning that it has met international standards of cleanliness, safety, and facilities. It's another very family-friendly beach, too. The Macarthurs Baths pool complex is along the promenade. The Garden Court King's Beach Hotel offers rooms with views across King's Beach. **Amenities:** lifeguard; parking (free); showers; toilets. **Best for:** swimming; walking. ✉ *Kings Rd.*

FAMILY **McArthur Baths.** The section of beach near McArthur Baths is great for swimming and very popular. If you'd rather swim in flat water, head for the bath complex. Open from September through April, for a small fee you can use a range of pools, two of which are heated to a few degrees above sea temperature. There's no natural grass here, however, so you will need to rent a lounge chair to be comfortable. **Amenities:** lifeguard; showers; toilets. **Best for:** swimming. ✉ *McArthur Baths, Beach Rd., Humewood* ☎ *041/582–2285.*

Pollock Beach. Adjacent to the suburb of Summerstrand, Pollock Beach is one of the better swimming beaches, with a lovely small natural tidal pool. It also offers great surfing. (Generally the surfing in PE is not too challenging, unlike at Jeffreys Bay, just over an hour's drive to the west, which has some pretty exciting waves.) The far end of Pollock Beach is best avoided, as it can get crowded with somewhat boisterous, picnicking, partying crowds. **Amenities:** food and drink; lifeguard; parking (free); toilets. **Best for:** partiers; surfing. ⊠ *10th Ave., off Marine Dr.*

Sardinia Bay. For a truly fantastic Port Elizabeth beach experience, very little can beat Sardinia Bay Beach, outside the bay and about a 20-minute drive from the main beaches. Here, miles and miles of deserted, snow-white sand are great for long walks. It's best to come on weekends, however, as during the week it can be isolated and there have been a few incidents of muggings. On weekends there are plenty of people, and you will be perfectly safe. It's also a popular beach for scuba-diving and this part of the coast has been declared a marine reserve, so no fishing is allowed. There are also fire pits so come prepared for a braai. **Amenities:** food and drink; lifeguard; parking (free); toilets. **Best for:** snorkeling; swimming; walking. ⊠ *Sardinia Bay Dr.*

WHERE TO EAT

The beachfront is lined with reasonably priced hotels and restaurants, as well as a few higher-quality ones.

$$$
SOUTH AFRICAN
Fodor's Choice
★

✕**Ginger.** This is Port Elizabeth's most well-established fine-dining option, a stylish stalwart in the expanding beachfront dining scene. Located in the Beach Hotel opposite the pier and boasting sea views, Ginger serves up an expansive array of contemporary cuisine with local flair. **Known for:** sumptuous seafood; prime beachfront location; faithful clientele. Ⓢ *Average main: R160* ⊠ *The Beach Hotel, Marine Dr., Summerstrand* ☎ *041/583–1229* ⊕ *www.ginger-restaurant.co.za.*

$$
SOUTH AFRICAN

✕**The Stage Door.** Accessed by the back entrance of Port Elizabeth's oldest hotel, the Stage Door is one of the city's best-kept secrets and has long been a favorite with locals in the know for its cheap and cheerful menu, good range of beers, and an eccentric and old-fashioned pub feel. Although it can get very busy here, the service remains excellent, as do the steaks. **Known for:** friendly, welcoming staff; fun and festive atmosphere; a long history. Ⓢ *Average main: R120* ⊠ *5 Chapel St.* ☎ *041/586–3553* ⊕ *www.phoenixhotel.co.za.*

WHERE TO STAY

$
B&B/INN

🛏 **Forest Hall Guesthouse.** Located in the leafy and affluent suburb of Walmer, just a 5- to 10-minute drive from the airport, this friendly and family-run guesthouse is a great place to stop and recuperate for a night or two before traveling on from PE. **Pros:** owners are approachable and helpful; prices are very reasonable; private airport shuttle service. **Cons:** it's popular with business and conference groups so can get noisy at night; it's a bit of a trek to any of PE's best restaurants or attractions; no meals aside from breakfast except on special request. Ⓢ *Rooms from: R750* ⊠ *84 River Rd., Walmer* ☎ *041/581–3356* ⊕ *www.foresthall. co.za* ➷ *14 rooms* ◎| *Breakfast.*

6

$$$
B&B/INN
Fodor's Choice
★

Hacklewood Hill Country House. For superbly comfortable and gracious lodgings, try this inn set in English-style gardens in the leafy suburb of Walmer. **Pros:** it has a great air of tranquility; service and food are both excellent; prices are reasonable. **Cons:** decor is a bit old-fashioned; it's not in walking distance of the beachfront; not particularly well suited to the business traveler. $ *Rooms from: R2890* ✉ *152 Prospect Rd., Walmer* ☎ *041/581–1300* ⊕ *www.hacklewood.co.za* ↩ *8 rooms* |◎| *Breakfast.*

$
B&B/INN

Jikeleza Lodge. In a quiet part of the Central neighborhood, this friendly hostel tends to attract mature backpackers who are more interested in culture and adventure activities than partying. **Pros:** within walking distance of restaurants and bars in less touristy area than the beachfront; tables in the garden make dining (either brought in or cooked in the communal kitchen) a pleasure; free Wi-Fi. **Cons:** you will need to take a taxi to the beachfront; service is a little sloppy; bookings and deposits have been known to go awry on occasion. $ *Rooms from: R380* ✉ *44 Cuyler St., Central* ☎ *041/586–3721* ⊕ *www.jikelezalodge. co.za* ↩ *6 rooms* |◎| *No meals.*

$
HOTEL

Summerstrand Hotel. Two major attractions of this hotel are its good prices and its location—close to the beach on the quieter side of the bay and virtually on top of the excellent Humewood Golf Course. **Pros:** excellent on-site help with arranging tours and onward travel; friendly staff; good restaurant. **Cons:** exterior and bathrooms could use an update; it's a popular conference venue so can get a bit noisy; due to the size of the place, it can feel impersonal. $ *Rooms from: R1080* ✉ *Marine Dr., Summerstrand* ☎ *041/583–3131* ⊕ *www.summerstrand-hotel.co.za* ↩ *127 rooms* |◎| *Breakfast.*

CAPE ST FRANCIS

111 km (69 miles) southwest of Port Elizabeth; 693 km (430 miles) east of Cape Town.

Weaving its way between beautiful nature reserves, indigenous fynbos, wetlands, plush marinas, and rolling sand dunes, Cape St Francis is a pretty beachfront eco-village at the heart of the St Francis Peninsula, which also includes the equally pristine St Francis Bay and Oyster Bay. Though it's increasingly popular with South African tourists during the summer holiday season, it retains an air of calm and tranquility throughout the year, and there's plenty of sunshine even in the depths of winter, when the area's mostly empty. There's a historic lighthouse (the highest masonry building in southern Africa), a challenging links golf course, a handful of good restaurants and watering holes, and any number of fine accommodations options among the pretty whitewashed, thatch-roofed Cape Dutch–style beach cottages and villas that dominate the area's architecture. It's also a great destination for surfers and water-sports enthusiasts.

GETTING HERE AND AROUND

The best way to get here is to rent a car from Port Elizabeth and drive yourself; it's an easy and pleasant 1½-hour drive on the N2 and then the R330, and the roads are pretty good. There's no direct public transport between Cape St Francis and Port Elizabeth. There are local minibus taxis around, but they run fairly infrequently, as evinced by the many hitchhikers you'll see on the side of the road. If you're riding the Baz Bus from Cape Town, Cape St Francis is your first stop within the Eastern Cape. You can also book a private shuttle from Port Elizabeth's airport with J-Bay Cabs. St Francis Bay is roughly 10 km (6 miles) north of Cape St Francis, and Oyster Bay is 14 km (9 miles) west of St Francis Bay on a dirt road. *For information on car rentals, see Car Travel in Travel Smart.*

WHERE TO STAY

$$
RESORT
FAMILY

Cape St Francis Resort. This big, bright beachfront resort offers a wide range of different accommodations, from luxury self-catering villas with direct beach access over the dunes to simple backpacker rooms with shared bathrooms. **Pros:** great location; a wide range of activities can be organized at reception; very family-friendly. **Cons:** it can get overcrowded during holidays; because of the size, it can feel a little impersonal; it's not the quietest place with so many children about. [$] *Rooms from: R2462* ✉ *Da Gama Way, Cape St Francis* ☎ *042/298–0054* 🌐 *www.capestfrancis.co.za* 🛏 *92 rooms* 🍴 *Some meals.*

$$
B&B/INN
Fodor's Choice ★

Oyster Bay Lodge. Set on a secluded coastal reserve that incorporates magnificent dunes, woods, river deltas, lagoons, a 3½-km (2-mile) expanse of beach, free-roaming horses, and a plethora of birdlife, Oyster Bay Lodge truly is a hidden gem. **Pros:** location and activities are superb; service is smooth; room rates are very reasonable. **Cons:** not the easiest place to get to; Wi-Fi can be temperamental; some of the standard rooms don't get a lot of daylight. [$] *Rooms from: R2500* ✉ *Humansdorp* ✣ *Take the 632 Palmietvlei exit off the N2 highway and follow signs to Oyster Bay Lodge for 24 km (15 miles)* ☎ *042/297–0150* 🌐 *www.oysterbaylodge.com* 🛏 *14 rooms* 🍴 *Some meals.*

6

ADDO ELEPHANT NATIONAL PARK

72 km (45 miles) north of Port Elizabeth.

GETTING HERE AND AROUND

The closest airport to Addo Elephant Park is Port Elizabeth (PLZ) airport. Flights arrive daily from all of South Africa's main cities via South African Airways, SA Express, SA Airlink, British Airways, and the budget airline Mango. Flights from Cape Town take roughly 1 hour and from Johannesburg 1½ hours.

Traveling by car is the easiest and best way to tour this area, as public transport is limited. Some roads are unpaved but in decent condition. Most lodges will organize airport transfers for their guests. *For information on airlines, see Air Travel in Travel Smart.*

EXPLORING

Addo Elephant National Park. Smack in the middle of a citrus-growing and horse-breeding area, Addo Elephant National Park is home to a staggering 700 elephants not to mention plenty of buffalo, black rhino, leopards, spotted hyena, hundreds of kudu and other antelopes, and lions. At present the park has about 400,000 acres, but it's expanding all the time and is intended to reach a total of about 600,000 acres, including a fully incorporated marine section. The most accessible parts of the park are the original, main section and the Colchester, Kabouga, Woody Cape, and Zuurberg sections. The original section of Addo still holds most of the game and is served by Addo Main Camp. The Colchester section, in the south, which has one SANParks camp, is contiguous with the main area. The scenic Nyati section is separated from the main section by a road and railway line. Just north of Nyati is the mountainous Zuurberg section, which doesn't have a large variety of game but is particularly scenic, with fabulous hiking trails and horse trails. You can explore the park in your own vehicle, in which case you need to heed the road signs that claim "dung beetles have right of way." Addo is home to the almost-endemic and extremely rare flightless dung beetle, which can often be seen rolling its unusual incubator across the roads. Watch out for them (they're only about 2 inches long), and watch them: they're fascinating. Instead of driving you could take a night or day game drive with a park ranger in an open vehicle from the main camp. A more adventurous option is to ride a horse among the elephants. Warning: no citrus fruit may be brought into the park, as elephants find it irresistible and can smell it for miles. ✉ *Addo Elephant National Park* ☎ *042/233–8600* 🌐 *www.addoelephantpark.com* 🎫 *R248.*

Schotia Safaris. If you're short on time or budget, Schotia offers a good value, family-run, no-frills safari experience taking place in a privately owned wildlife reserve bordering the eastern side of Addo. Due to its small size (4,200 acres) and the fact that it's very densely stocked (more than 2,000 animals and 40 species) you're almost guaranteed to see a wide variety of wildlife—lion, giraffes, hippos, white rhinos, crocodiles, zebras, and all kinds of buck. The popular Tooth and Claw safari starts at 2:30 pm and includes a game drive and a tasty, generous buffet dinner served in an attractive open-air area with roaring fires. After dinner you're taken on a short night drive back to the reception area—keep your eyes peeled for some unusual nocturnal animals. There's also the option of going on a morning game drive into Addo, with lunch, and then the Tooth and Claw safari. Other packages include one or two nights' accommodations on the reserve. Tours are very good value and well run, and the guides are excellent. The Tooth and Claw half-day safari can be done easily as a day trip from Port Elizabeth, as it's only a 45-minute drive away. ✉ *Orlando Farm, Paterson* ☎ *042/235–1436* 🌐 *www.schotia.com.*

WHERE TO STAY

$ RESORT FAMILY 🏨 **Addo Elephant National Park Main Camp.** One of the best SANParks rest camps, this location has a range of self-catering accommodations, such as safari tents, forest cabins, rondavels, cottages, and chalets, and a shop that sells basic supplies as well as souvenirs. **Pros:** great value; you get to enter the game area before the main gates open and go on night drives; good amenities. **Cons:** the shop has only basic supplies; the rondavels have shared cooking facilities; can feel crowded. [$] *Rooms from: R1300* ✉ *Addo Elephant National Park* ☎ *012/428–9111* 🌐 *www.addoelephant.com* 🛏 *65 rooms* 🍴 *No meals.*

$$$$ RESORT 🏨 **Gorah Elephant Camp.** On a private concession within the main section of Addo, this picturesque colonial-themed camp has accommodations in spacious, luxurious safari tents with thick thatch canopies and furnished in fine antiques from the colonial era. **Pros:** the food and service are

top-notch; guests are not required to sit together at meals; the location and colonial style recall a bygone era. Cons: rooms don't have bathtubs; rooms can get cold at night in winter; you often have to leave the private concession area to find the best game. $ *Rooms from: R11000* ⊠ *Addo Elephant National Park* ☎ *044/501–1111* ⊕ *www.gorahelephantcamp. com* ⟿ *11 rooms* ¶○¶ *All-inclusive.*

$$$
B&B/INN
Fodor's Choice
★
⛫ **Hitgeheim Country Lodge.** This lovely lodge is set on a steep cliff overlooking the Sundays River and the town of Addo. Pros: attentive personal touches; friendly and helpful owners; excellent facilities. Cons: not for independent travelers, as the owners like to arrange your activities for you; the restaurant is not open to nonguests; a bit of a drive from the main gate into the national park. $ *Rooms from: R3325* ⊠ *Addo Elephant National Park* ⚓ *18 km (11 miles) from Addo Main Gate on R335, then follow R336 to Kirkwood* ☎ *042/234–0778* ⊕ *www. hitgeheim.com* ⟿ *16 rooms* ¶○¶ *Breakfast.*

$$$$
B&B/INN
FAMILY
⛫ **River Bend Lodge.** Situated on a 34,594-acre private concession within the Nyati section of Addo, River Bend perfectly balances the feel of a sophisticated, comfortable country house with all the facilities of a game lodge. Pros: kids are welcome, and there's an enclosed playground; the food is excellent, especially the seven-course dinner menu; all food and drinks are included in the rack rates. Cons: decor is more English colonial than African; only the honeymoon suite has a plunge pool; it's not the most exciting section of the park in terms of game. $ *Rooms from: R12000* ⊠ *Zuurberg* ☎ *042/233–8000* ⊕ *www.riverbendlodge. co.za* ⟿ *8 rooms* ¶○¶ *All-inclusive.*

SHAMWARI GAME RESERVE

72 km (45 miles) from Port Elizabeth.

GETTING HERE AND AROUND

The closest airport to Shamwari Game Reserve is the one in Port Elizabeth (PLZ), about 72 km (45 miles) away. Small and easy to navigate, the airport is served daily by South African Airways, SA Airlink, SA Express, British Airways, and Mango. Flights arrive from Cape Town (1 hour) and Johannesburg (1½ hours). From here it's best to rent your own car, as there isn't any reliable public transport. If you are flying into Port Elizabeth and visiting only Shamwari, it may be easier to arrange an airport transfer with the reserve. As with all of the luxury game reserves, it's advised that you arrive by midday so you can check in and have lunch before the afternoon game drive. *For information on airlines, see Air Travel in Travel Smart. For information on car rentals, see Car Travel in Travel Smart.*

EXPLORING

FAMILY
Born Free Centres. Part of the reserve has been set aside as the Born Free Centres (there's one in the northern part and one in the southern part of the reserve). Here African leopards and lions rescued from zoos, circuses, and even nightclubs around the world are allowed to roam in large enclosures for the rest of their lives, as they cannot safely be returned to the wild. Although these are interesting tourist attractions, the main purpose is educational, and about 500 local schoolchildren tour the centers every month. ⊠ *Shamwari Game Reserve* ⊕ *www.bornfree.org.uk.*

6

Fodor's Choice ★ **Shamwari Game Reserve.** In the Eastern Cape, an easy 1½-hour drive from Port Elizabeth, Shamwari Game Reserve is, in every sense of the word, a conservation triumph. Unprofitable farmland has been turned into a successful tourist attraction, wild animals have been reintroduced, and alien vegetation has been eradicated. The reserve, which officially opened in 1992, is constantly being expanded and now stands at about 62,000 acres. Its mandate is to conserve not only the big impressive animals (which are abundant), but everything else: indigenous plants, buildings, history, and the culture of the area. The reserve's six lodges are all top notch and each offers its own unique flavor. During the summer months (October to April), you can also enjoy a unique walking safari experience at Shamwari's Explorer Camp. ✉ *Shamwari Game Reserve* ☎ *041/509–3000* 🌐 *www.shamwari.com.*

WHERE TO STAY

$$$$ RESORT 🏨 **Bayethe Tented Lodge.** Huge air-conditioned safari tents under thatch roofs create comfortable accommodations, and private decks with plunge pools overlook the Buffalo River. **Pros:** each tent has an amazing outside shower and deck; tents have fabulous bathrooms; the king-size beds have comfortable 400-thread-count sheets. **Cons:** for those seeking privacy, the communal meals might be a nuisance; Wi-Fi is not available in the suites; the rustic style is not to everyone's liking. [$] *Rooms from: R8440* ✉ *Shamwari Game Reserve* ☎ *042/203–1111* 🌐 *www.shamwari.com* 🛏 *12 rooms* 🍴 *All-inclusive.*

$$$$ RESORT Fodor's Choice ★ 🏨 **Eagles Crag.** Very different from the other Shamwari options, this sleek, modern lodge makes use of light wood, pale sandstone, and stainless-steel finishes. **Pros:** a carefully selected choice of top local wines and spirits is included; the rooms are enormous; the food and service are excellent. **Cons:** the reception areas are very large and can feel impersonal; drinks are not included in the rates; the decor in the dining area doesn't live up to the rest of the lodge. [$] *Rooms from: R9000* ✉ *Shamwari Game Reserve* ☎ *042/203–1111* 🌐 *www.shamwari.com* 🛏 *9 rooms* 🍴 *All-inclusive.*

$$$$ RESORT 🏨 **Long Lee Manor.** Originally built in 1910 as the manor house of one of the private farms that would later be incorporated into Shamwari, this colorful and richly furnished Edwardian property continues to evoke the colonial era and all the opulence that went with it. **Pros:** the food and service are spectacular; the dining area is the best of any of Shamwari's lodges; there are spa facilities and a gym with great views. **Cons:** it's one of the bigger lodges at Shamwari, so not the most intimate; it's not as deep into the heart of the reserve as other lodges; it's certainly not for those looking for something more "African". [$] *Rooms from: R7642* ✉ *Shamwari Game Reserve* ☎ *042/203–1111* 🌐 *www.shamwari.com* 🛏 *15 rooms* 🍴 *All-inclusive.*

$$$$ RESORT FAMILY 🏨 **Riverdene Lodge.** Riverdene combines the great food and service of Shamwari's other lodges with a much more child-friendly atmosphere and facilities. **Pros:** there are special "Kids on Safari" programs for kids of all ages; seven of the nine suites are connectable; it's probably Shamwari's friendliest lodge. **Cons:** all those children means it can get noisy; not the place for privacy; has less character than the likes of Long Lee or Bayethe. [$] *Rooms from: R8062* ✉ *Shamwari Game Reserve* ☎ *042/203–1111* 🌐 *www.shamwari.com* 🛏 *9 rooms* 🍴 *All-inclusive.*

GRAHAMSTOWN

134 km (83 miles) northeast of Port Elizabeth.

Although billed as a city, much of Grahamstown looks more like an English village than anything else—if you discount that alter ego of most South African towns, the contiguous shanty townships. These are a big part of Grahamstown, and they contribute to the city's wealth of cultural history. Established as a garrison town to enforce the arbitrarily assigned border of the British Cape Colony, Grahamstown was the center of several battles during the last couple of centuries.

It's worth spending a day or two to explore the sights and to perhaps take a tour—just to reinforce the fact that history, no matter how accurately portrayed, is always subjective.

GETTING HERE AND AROUND

It's easiest and best to tour this area by car. Roads are generally in relatively good shape, though there is a slight difference in road conditions east and west of Grahamstown. To the west (that is, on the PE side) roads are wide, often dual lane, and well maintained. East of Grahamstown the N2 is a single-lane road and there are some sections with no shoulders, but for the most part it's good.

From PE, the drive is approximately 1½ hours. Bus services (Greyhound, Intercape) stop in the center of town. There's also Mini-Lux, a minibus shuttle that runs from PE Airport to Grahamstown on Tuesday, Thursday, and Friday and then on to East London.

Grahamstown is small enough that you can easily walk around on foot, although you should take a taxi late at night. *For information on car rentals, see Car Travel in Travel Smart. For information on buses, see Bus Travel in Travel Smart.*

TOURS

Ottours "Spirit of Life". One of South Africa's most seminal historical incidents was the 1819 Battle of Grahamstown, when the Xhosa prophet Makana tried to rid his area of British colonizers. Makana was arrested and sent to Robben Island, where he died trying to escape. You can relive this battle and other interesting parts of Grahamstown's history with Ottours "Spirit of Life" tours. Your guide, Otto Nteshebe, will inform you about the traditional way of life of the Xhosa people, and can also organize local township and shebeen tours, as well as give you a greater insight into the beautiful historic architecture of Grahamstown. ✉ *63 High St.* ☎ *082/214–4242.*

VISITOR INFORMATION

In Grahamstown, Makana Tourism is open weekdays 8:30–5 and Saturday 9–noon.

Contacts Makana Tourism. ✉ *63 High St.* ☎ *046/622–3241* ⊕ *www.grahamstown.co.za.*

EXPLORING

Home to Rhodes University and some of the country's top schools, Grahamstown is considered by many to be the seat of culture and learning in South Africa.

National Arts Festival. The 10-day National Arts Festival, which takes place in late June and/or early July and is purported to be second in size only to the Edinburgh Festival in Scotland, is the country's premier cultural event. ✉ *Grahamstown* ☎ *046/603–1103* 🌐 *www.nationalartsfestival.co.za.*

TOP ATTRACTIONS

FAMILY **Observatory Museum.** An intriguing study of Victorian-era cutting-edge science, the building was constructed by a watchmaker and amateur astronomer H. C. Gulpin, who built a cupola above his shop to house his instruments. The museum contains a two-story pendulum and the only genuine Victorian camera obscura in the Southern Hemisphere. You can stand in the tower and watch what's happening in the town below—pretty useful if you've lost your companions. ✉ *10 Bathurst St.* ☎ *046/622–2312* 🎟 *R20* 🕑 *Closed weekends and public holidays.*

WORTH NOTING

International Library of African Music. A teaching and research center for indigenous music, the library has a collection of more than 200 traditional African musical instruments, including *djembes* (drums), *mbiras* (thumb pianos), and marimbas (xylophones). ✉ *Rhodes University, Prince Alfred St.* ☎ *046/603–8557* 🎟 *Free* 🕑 *Closed weekends and public holidays.*

National English Literary Museum. The National English Literary Museum houses a comprehensive collection of books, articles, and press clippings on South African writers in the English language, including some unpublished works. There is also a bookshop. ✉ *87 Beaufort St.* ☎ *046/622–7042* 🌐 *www.dac.gov.za/national_english_literary_museum* 🎟 *Free* 🕑 *Closed weekends and public holidays.*

WHERE TO EAT

You won't find the greatest choice of dining establishments here, particularly when it comes to fine dining, as Grahamstown is largely a student town. However, there are a number of cafés on High Street that are adequate.

$$ CAFÉ 🍴 **Browns Restaurant.** Conveniently located inside a historic guesthouse in the heart of Grahamstown, this chic and recently renovated coffee shop and restaurant represents the town's diversity with a range of different culinary influences and themed menus. The whole place has managed to keep plenty of old-world charm while adding some overdue contemporary flourishes, and there's outside seating in a pretty, sunny courtyard. **Known for:** excellent location; beautiful old courtyard; historic building. [$] *Average main: R150* ✉ *137 High St.* ☎ *046/622–3242* 🌐 *www.grahamstownaccom.co.za* 🕑 *Restaurant closed mid-Dec.–mid-Jan.*

$$ SOUTH AFRICAN 🍴 **Haricot's.** Centrally located with a pretty outside courtyard area, Haricot's simple, bright, and clean decor and its good array of reasonably priced fresh fare has helped it become a local stalwart. More café and deli by day, it's popular with Rhodes University students and professors thanks to its great coffee, homemade cakes and baked goods, and a good lunch menu. **Known for:** friendly atmosphere; good central location; young clientele. [$] *Average main: R120* ✉ *32 New St.* ☎ *046/622–2150* 🌐 *www.haricots.co.za* 🕑 *Closed Sun.*

Grahamstown's Arts Festival

The National Arts Festival (⊕ *www.nationalartsfestival.co.za*) began in 1974 with some 60-odd performances, and now offers a staggering variety of entertainment. Besides theaters, every conceivable kind of venue is used, including churches, school halls, museums, and pubs. There is a formal program, an official fringe festival, and even a fringe of the fringe that gets seriously alternative. Some offbeat productions have included families of giant puppets and stilt walkers roaming the streets and a theater ensemble who create hair installations on its audience. You can also see local and international music, theater, ballet, comedy, and modern dance performances. There's a Children's Festival and a large outdoor market with vendors selling everything from hand-painted T-shirts to local crafts.

The large festival events and the film festival are staged at the **1820 Settlers National Monument,** a concrete edifice on Gunfire Hill, next to the old garrison, Fort Selwyn. Sundowner concerts at 5 pm in the monument's foyer give previews of the various shows.

TICKETS

Tickets are available via the official festival website (⊕ *www.nationalartsfestival.co.za*) up to two months before the festival.

GETTING TO AND AROUND THE FESTIVAL

If you are flying into Port Elizabeth, you can rent a car to make the 1½-hour-long journey to Grahamstown, or you can take the festival minibus that meets passengers at the airport. Check out the festival website for booking information.

In Grahamstown, the Festival Hopper Bus travels between the monument and various venues throughout the day. Timetables and booking information for all festival-related events are on the comprehensive website.

WHERE TO STAY

A wide variety of accommodations are available, ranging from rooms in university halls to private-home stays. It's advisable to plan your trip three months in advance or more, but it's still possible to find something at the last minute. Many overseas visitors stay in surrounding towns or on game farms in the area (which often have special packages) and make day trips into the town.

BE PREPARED

The festival takes place in midwinter, and it can get very cold at night. Days can be hot and sunny, but it's always advisable to have extra layers, and to bring a coat and scarf.

6

WHERE TO STAY

If you need help finding accommodations, the Grahamstown Accommodations Bureau should be able to give you a hand.

$ ⬚ **The Cock House.** Over the years, this charming building, a National
B&B/INN Monument built in 1826, has been the home of distinguished citizens, most notably academic and novelist André Brink, so it's fitting that the individually decorated rooms are named after previous owners. **Pros:** a small, lovely garden in the back; good restaurant; plenty of character. **Cons:** rooms are on the small side; no Wi-Fi in the rooms; in need of renovation.

$ Rooms from: R1180 ⊠ 10 Market St., at George St. ☎ 046/636–1295 ⊕ www.thecockhouse.co.za ⌑ 13 rooms ⑩ Breakfast.

$
B&B/INN

⊞ **High Corner Guesthouse.** This popular, quaint, and centrally located guesthouse is in the oldest cottage in Grahamstown (built in 1814) and is just a few paces from the main entrance to Rhodes University and most of Grahamstown's shops, cafés, restaurants, and bars. **Pros:** free Wi-Fi throughout the property;

THE ELASTIC CITY

Most of the year Grahamstown is pretty small, but around festival time (late June/early July) this elastic city expands to accommodate the tens of thousands of festivalgoers. Come December, it shrinks to a mere ghost of itself as the students and scholars go home.

prices are reasonable; great breakfast. **Cons:** it's popular with visiting professors and businessmen, so it can be hard to get a room; the rooms are not the biggest around; no meals apart from breakfast available. $ Rooms from: R1240 ⊠ 122 High St. ☎ 046/622–8284 ⊕ www.highcorner.co.za ⌑ 7 rooms ⑩ Breakfast.

KWANDWE PRIVATE GAME RESERVE

38 km (24 miles) northeast of Grahamstown.

GETTING HERE AND AROUND

Kwandwe is a 30-minute drive from Grahamstown, and air and road shuttles are available from Port Elizabeth, which is a 1½-hour drive.

EXPLORING

Kwandwe Private Game Reserve. Kwandwe Private Game Reserve is tucked away in the Eastern Cape, near the quaint, historic cathedral city of Grahamstown. Little more than a decade ago, the area was ravaged farmland and goat-ridden semidesert. Today it is a conservation triumph—more than 55,000 acres of various vegetation types and scenic diversity, including rocky outcrops, great plains, thorn thickets, forests, desert scrub, and the Great Fish River—that's home to more than 7,000 mammals, including the Big Five. Your chances of seeing the elusive black rhino are very good, and it's likely you'll see fauna you don't always see elsewhere, such as black wildebeest and the endangered blue crane (*Kwandwe* means "place of the blue crane" in Xhosa). If you come in winter, you'll see one of nature's finest floral displays, when thousands of scarlet, orange, and fiery-red aloes are in bloom, attended by colorful sunbirds. The reserve also has a strong focus on community development, as evinced by the Community Centre and village within the reserve, both of which are worth a visit. ⊠ Grahamstown ☎ 046/603–3400 ⊕ www.kwandwe.com ⊗ Closed June.

WHERE TO STAY

There are four great places to stay within the reserve; guests can choose between classic colonial or modern chic. You'll be cosseted, pampered, well fed, and taken on some memorable wildlife adventures. Kwandwe is a member of the prestigious Relais & Châteaux group. All the lodges listed here have cable TV in a communal area as well as a safari shop, and massages are available upon request. The child-friendly lodges have movies and games. In the single-use lodges, these are hidden away in a cupboard, so you can keep their existence a secret from your brood unless a rainy day makes them essential.

$$$$
RESORT

🔲 **Ecca Lodge.** This classy lodge combines understated modern elegance with vibrant African colors. **Pros:** superb food; an extensive self-service bar; magnificent open outdoor and indoor showers. **Cons:** some guides are young and slightly inexperienced; service can be a little disorganized; the lounge can feel big and impersonal. $ *Rooms from: R11850 ⊠ Kwandwe Private Game Reserve* ☎ *046/603–3400* ⊕ *www. kwandwe.com* ⊘ *Closed June* ⌁ *6 rooms* �‖ *All meals.*

$$$$
RESORT
Fodor's Choice
★

🔲 **Great Fish River Lodge.** If you have an artistic eye, you'll immediately notice how the curving thatch roof of the main buildings echoes the mountain skyline opposite. **Pros:** spectacular river views; unusual habitats (it's not often you find lions clambering up and down rocky outcrops); ultra-friendly staff. **Cons:** avoid if you're a bit unsteady as there are lots of tricky steps; also avoid if you don't like unfenced camps and predators potentially wandering around the lodge at night; not the most family-friendly lodge. $ *Rooms from: R11850 ⊠ Kwandwe Private Game Reserve* ☎ *046/603–3400* ⊕ *www.kwandwe.com* ⊘ *Closed June* ⌁ *9 rooms* �‖ *All meals.*

$$$$
RESORT

🔲 **Melton Manor.** Slightly bigger than Uplands Homestead, the Manor accommodates up to eight guests and offers the same superb service and exclusivity. **Pros:** exclusivity deluxe; great food; great service. **Cons:** as you're in your own group you miss out on the opportunity to meet other lodge guests; unlike other Kwandwe lodges, there are no private plunge pools and decks; you can only book for a minimum of four people. $ *Rooms from: R10000 ⊠ Kwandwe Private Game Reserve* ☎ *046/603–3400* ⊕ *www.kwandwe.com* ⊘ *Closed June* ⌁ *4 rooms* �‖ *All meals.*

$$$$
RESORT

🔲 **Uplands Homestead.** If you're a small family or a bunch of friends and want to have a genuine, very exclusive, out-of-Africa experience, then stay at this restored 1905 colonial farmhouse. **Pros:** perfect for that special family occasion or friends' reunion; great food and service; steeped in history. **Cons:** can only be booked for families or parties of up to six; the colonial nostalgia might be a little overwhelming for some; not a good option if you want to meet other guests. $ *Rooms from: R10000 ⊠ Kwandwe Private Game Reserve* ⊕ *www.kwandwe.com* ⊘ *Closed June* ⌁ *3 rooms* �‖ *All meals.*

SAMARA PRIVATE GAME RESERVE

55 km (34 miles) southeast of Graaff-Reinet; 258 km (160 miles) northeast of Port Elizabeth.

GETTING HERE AND AROUND

There are daily flights from Johannesburg, Durban, and Cape Town to Port Elizabeth. Air charters from Port Elizabeth to Samara (gravel airstrip) can be arranged on request; it's a 45-minute drive from the airstrip to the reserve. Transfers to and from the airport or airstrip can be arranged through the reserve.

The drive from Port Elizabeth should take about three hours. Take the R75 toward Graaff-Reinet for 258 km (160 miles). Turn right onto the R63 toward Pearston/Somerset East for 7 km (4 miles). Turn left onto the Petersburg gravel road and drive 23 km (14 miles) to reach Karoo Lodge.

EXPLORING

Samara Private Game Reserve. Nestled among 70,000 acres of achingly beautiful wilderness, Samara Private Game Reserve is located in a hidden valley deep in the Karoo Mountains of South Africa's Eastern Cape. Owners Sarah and Mark Tompkins opened the reserve in 2005 with a promise to return former farmland to its natural state. The malaria-free reserve now encompasses 11 former farms and is home to a variety of protected species that have been reintroduced, including cheetah, Cape mountain zebra, white rhino, giraffe, black wildebeest, and a variety of antelope; there are even meerkats and aardvarks. Because there aren't any big predators to pose a threat, rangers stop the trucks often and guests get a completely different safari experience on foot. The lack of predators also makes this a great place for families with children. ✉ *Samara Private Game Reserve, Graaff-Reinet* ☎ *031/262–0324* 🌐 *www.samara.co.za.*

WHERE TO STAY

$$$$ RESORT 🏨 **Karoo Lodge.** From the moment you reach this lovingly restored, 19th-century, green-roofed farmhouse set among purple mountains, 800-year-old trees, and rolling plains where cheetahs, rhinos, and giraffes roam, you'll forget another more stressful world even existed. **Pros:** unique beauty; exclusivity; great for families. **Cons:** lack of accessibility; Samara is not Big Five country, so some might find the game drives lacking; colonial decadence can be a bit over the top. [$] *Rooms from: R6340* ✉ *Samara Private Game Reserve, Graaff-Reinet* ☎ *031/262–0324* 🌐 *www.samara.co.za* 🛏 *9 rooms* 🍴 *All-inclusive.*

$$$$ RESORT 🏨 **The Manor House.** If you're looking for the perfect place to share a safari with a group of people, then look no further. **Pros:** complete run of the house for your group; attentive personal staff; lunch in the bush is an experience you'll not soon forget. **Cons:** not close to major airports; climate can get very hot and dry; if you're after the Big Five, this is not for you. [$] *Rooms from: R6250* ✉ *Samara Private Game Reserve, Graaff-Reinet* ☎ *031/262–0324* 🌐 *www.samara.co.za* 🛏 *4 rooms* 🍴 *All-inclusive* ☞ *4-guest minimum.*

AMATOLE

The Amatole region takes its name from the spectacular Amatola mountain range, which is home to a number of ancient indigenous forests, waterfalls, and rare flora and fauna, all presided over by impressive peaks that reach up to 5,905 feet above sea level. All of this sets the backdrop for the six-day Amatola hiking trail, one of the country's best trails. There are also game parks, beautiful beaches, and a number of cultural pursuits to discover in Amatole, in addition to plenty of history. Aside from the region's important role in South Africa's antiapartheid struggle, towns like Cathcart and Adelaide began their life as 19th-century British military outposts intended to defend the border of the Cape Colony and the white farmers in the area from the Xhosa nation to the east. One of the frequent border wars between these two sides was dubbed the Amatola War. There's still something distinctly reminiscent of rural England about parts of the region, and farming remains a central facet of life. As with the Wild Coast, there's certainly little risk of overdevelopment here.

East London, the largest city in the region, has excellent transport links with the rest of the country and is a good starting point for heading into the hinterland as well as joining the Wild Coast.

EAST LONDON

150 km (93 miles) east of Grahamstown.

The gateway to both the Wild Coast and Amatole, East London was built around the mouth of the Buffalo River, which forms South Africa's only river port. Although fairly urban, East London is still close to the rural heartland, so it retains a pleasantly small-town air. There's a great museum here, and you can take a half-day city tour, an escorted visit to a local township, or a full-day tour of a rural village. Although the beaches on the outskirts of the city are wonderful, those within the central business district are crowded and not very pleasant.

GETTING HERE AND AROUND

The East London airport has all the expected facilities. There's also an airport shuttle service called the Little Red Bus, which will drop you off at your hotel, but you'll need to book it in advance.

Greyhound and Intercape Mainliner have pretty reliable and reasonably priced bus services from the country's major cities, including Johannesburg and Cape Town, but the distances are long. The Mini-Lux minibus service also travels from Port Elizabeth to East London via Grahamstown. All the buses stop and depart from the coach terminal in town. A more convenient option is the Baz Bus, which travels to East London, Cintsa, and Coffee Bay and will drop you off at your lodgings. *For information on buses, see Bus Travel in Travel Smart.*

It's easiest and best to tour this region by car. The major rental agencies have offices at East London's airport and in the city's downtown. One-way rentals are available. Roads are wide, often dual lane, and well maintained. Northeast of East London there are long sections of road that are relatively broad and well maintained, but they are all unfenced—meaning livestock can wander onto the road—and some stretches have potholes. *For information on car rentals, see Car Travel in Travel Smart.*

TOURS

Imonti Tours. Based in East London, Imonti Tours runs a three- to four-hour tour through the local township, including a visit to a sangoma (traditional healer) and a local shebeen where you can enjoy a braai (barbecue) lunch and drinks with the locals, and listen to some awesome jazz. On Sunday, the tour includes a church visit. A tour of a rural Xhosa village takes the whole day. Imonti's full-day Nelson Mandela Freedom Trail takes in Mandela's childhood home in Qunu and the Nelson Mandela Museum in Mthatha, as well as some beautiful Transkei scenery. This tour includes lunch. The Pride of Amatole Heritage Tour is another full-day tour that takes you to a number of sites related to the iconic Steve Biko, as well as to the historical town of Alice, where most of South Africa's greatest black political figures received their education. ✉ *9 Chamberlain Rd.* ☎ *083/487–8975* ⊕ *www.imontitours.co.za.*

Fodor's Choice
★

Wild Coast Holiday Reservations. The Wild Coast has been a favorite hiking destination for years, but the overnight huts have practically disintegrated. Perhaps they will be repaired, but until then you can take advantage of some good options—perhaps better than the original— offered by the East London–based Wild Coast Holiday Reservations. The Wild Coast Meander and the Wild Coast Amble are five- or six-day guided hikes during which you walk between hotels and/or resorts on the southern section of the coast. Farther north, the Hole-in-the-Wall and Wild Coast Pondo walks traverse more remote and less densely populated terrain. The Pondo Walk is a series of treks to and from a comfortable base camp over far more spectacular, but also much steeper, terrain than what you'll find on the other hikes. The trips are all catered, and you can arrange to have your luggage driven or portered. Shorter walks can be organized by request. This really is the best of both worlds. You walk on deserted beaches during the day and stay in comfy hotels with all the modern conveniences at night. ⊠ *44 Drake Rd.* ☎ *043/743–6181* ⊕ *www.wildcoastholidays.co.za.*

VISITOR INFORMATION
Tourism Buffalo City, in East London, is open weekdays 8–4:30.

Contacts Tourism Buffalo City. ⊠ *Fire Station, Fleet St., 2nd fl.* ☎ *043/736–3019* ⊕ *www.bctourism.co.za.*

EXPLORING
East London Museum. There's definitely something fishy going on at the East London Museum. In addition to a whole section on the discovery of the coelacanth, the museum has a large display of preserved fish, including an enormous manta ray. For a different kind of fishy, check out what is claimed to be the world's only surviving dodo egg. *Jurassic Park,* here we come! Probably the most worthwhile exhibit, though, is the extensive beadwork collection; it's culturally interesting and just plain beautiful. ⊠ *319 Oxford St.* ☎ *043/743–0686* 🔖 *R15* ⊘ *Closed weekends and public holidays.*

Steve Biko Heritage Centre. The state-of-the-art heritage center, which opened in 2012, is in King William's Town's Ginsberg township, where Steve Biko grew up. It's actually about a 40-minute drive out of East London, but it's well worth a visit for anyone interested in South Africa's "struggle" history, as well as the development of its young democracy. There's a museum, an archive, a library resource center, a commemorative garden honoring human rights activists, performance and production spaces, training rooms, and a community media center. The center is also the focal point for a heritage trail that consists of various sites that pay tribute to Steve Biko, the South African activist and leading Black Consciousness Movement proponent who died in police custody in 1977 at the age of 31. Biko has often been held up as one of the greatest martyrs of the antiapartheid movement. You can organize a tour from East London with Imonti Tours, which will also incorporate lunch in the township. ⊠ *2429 Mbeka St., Ginsberg, King William's Town* ☎ *043/605–6700* ⊕ *www.sbf.org.za* 🔖 *Free* ⊘ *Closed Sun. and public holidays.*

BEACHES

East London is just far enough north of PE that the water and the weather are a bit warmer, but the inner-city beaches are not that great and would appeal more to surfers than to general loungers.

FAMILY **Gonubie Beach.** Gonubie Beach is at the mouth of the Gonubie River, about half an hour northeast of the city. The riverbank is covered in dense forest, with giant *strelitzias* (wild banana trees) growing right to the water's edge. A lovely white sandy beach, tidal pools, and a 500-yard-long wooden walkway make this a fantastically user-friendly beach. It's also a good place to watch whales and dolphins, and compared to some of the more central beaches it's pretty quiet. There are picnic tables, fire pits, and a playground. **Amenities:** food and drink; lifeguard; parking (free); showers; toilets. **Best for:** sunset; swimming; walking. ✉ *Riverside Rd., Gonubie.*

Nahoon Beach. Nahoon Beach, at the mouth of the Nahoon River, is about a 10-minute drive from the city. There's some fantastic surf—but only for people who know what they're doing. It's also just a beautiful beach for sunbathing, watching surfers, and evening walks, and the lagoon is good for swimming and snorkeling. From the end of the beach nearest the lagoon you can look straight across to the Blue Lagoon Hotel on the other side of the water. The walk from the parking lot to the beach takes you through a beautiful forest, which helps make the beach feel secluded despite its proximity to the city. There are picnic tables, fire pits, and a playground, making a perfect spot for a braai. **Amenities:** food and drink; lifeguards; parking (free); toilets. **Best for:** sunsets; surfing; walking. ✉ *Beach Rd., Nahoon.*

WHERE TO EAT

$$ SOUTH AFRICAN FAMILY 🍴 **Buccaneers.** An East London institution, Buccaneers has been open since 1992, and not a lot has changed here in the last 20 years or so. There's hearty, unpretentious pub fare and atmosphere, lots of seafood, sports, draft beer aplenty, live music, raucous student nights, and spectacular sea views from the big sun-soaked wooden deck. **Known for:** festive weekend atmosphere; beachfront location; fresh seafood. [$] *Average main: R100* ✉ *1 Tranrack Rd., Beachfront* ☎ *043/743–5171* 🌐 *www.buccaneers.co.za.*

$$ BURGER Fodor's Choice ★ 🍴 **Sanook Cafe.** This youthful, trendy, and relative newcomer to the East London dining scene is constantly busy and bustling thanks to its simple formula of good, well-presented gourmet burgers and thin-crust pizzas topped with only the freshest ingredients, combined with sharp but always friendly service. The decor and layout of the place are equally simple and effective, with heavy wooden tables and exposed brick walls and pillars, and lots of air and light. **Known for:** excellent burgers; lively atmosphere; central location. [$] *Average main: R100* ✉ *11 Chamberlain Rd.* ☎ *043/721–3215* 🌐 *www.sanook.co.za* ⏲ *Closed Sun.*

WHERE TO STAY

$$ HOTEL FAMILY 🏨 **Blue Lagoon Hotel.** Overlooking the mouth of the beautiful Nahoon River and within easy reach of Nahoon Beach, this is a great place for a low-key family beach break. **Pros:** staff are friendly and warm; there's an airport shuttle; location is hard to beat. **Cons:** it's a conference venue so

can get noisy; only the suites have river or sea views; service can be a little disorganized. [$] *Rooms from: R1700* ✉ *17–19 Blue Bend Pl.* ☎ *043/748–4821* 🌐 *www.bluelagoonhotel.co.za* 🛏 *103 rooms* 🍴 *Breakfast.*

$$ B&B/INN 🏨 **Meander Inn.** In the leafy suburb of Selborne, Meander Inn is close to the East London Museum, restaurants, and shops. **Pros:** pool and gardens are lovely; good business facilities are available; there's an airport shuttle. **Cons:** groups about to embark on the Wild Coast Meander stay here the night before, so it can be quite noisy; rooms don't have air-conditioning or phones; regular business groups mean it's often booked up. [$] *Rooms from: R1850* ✉ *8 Clarendon Rd., Selborne* ☎ *043/726–2310* 🛏 *11 rooms* 🍴 *Breakfast.*

$ B&B/INN 🏨 **Stratfords Guest House.** It's worth staying at this friendly, stylish guesthouse just to see the building, a masterpiece of design that makes excellent use of space and utilizes unusual materials like corrugated iron, bare concrete, wood, and glass in incredibly innovative ways to create a comfortable, stimulating environment. **Pros:** the building is unusual and was designed by the owner; the garden is sheltered from the elements; the business facilities are superb. **Cons:** as it's a conferencing venue it can get noisy; there are no meals available apart from breakfast; bathrooms are a little basic. [$] *Rooms from: R1200* ✉ *31 Frere Rd., Vincent* ☎ *043/726–9765* 🌐 *www.stratfordsguesthouse.co.za* 🛏 *14 rooms* 🍴 *Breakfast.*

CINTSA

40 km (25 miles) northeast of East London.

This lovely, quiet little seaside town a half-hour drive from East London is a winner. A nice long beach, pretty rock pools, and a beautiful lagoon on which to paddle make this a coastal paradise. Not much happens here, which is its main attraction. The town—if it can be called a town—is divided by the river mouth into an eastern and a western side. It's a drive of about 10 km (6 miles) between them, although you can walk across the river at low tide (most of the time). The town has a couple of restaurants and small shops, plus a good choice of accommodations.

GETTING HERE AND AROUND

It's best to tour this area by car, and the road from East London to Cintsa is paved and in good condition. The Baz Bus drops passengers off in Cintsa. Intercape and Greyhound buses go as far as East London on the coast and then carry on slightly inland to Mthatha before rejoining the coast at Durban. Neither go via Cintsa.

TOURS

African Heartland Journeys. African Heartland Journeys arranges excellent tours into the Transkei and Wild Coast. Tours generally focus on the people and culture but all include an element of adventure and are tailor-made to suit the needs, interests, and fitness levels of participants. You can choose to travel by vehicle, ATV, horse, canoe, mountain bike, on foot, or a combination thereof. Overnight accommodations may be in a village or at hotels—again, usually a combination of the two. The company also offers working holidays and volunteering programs focusing on education, conservation, and social betterment. ✉ *854 Cintsa Dr., Chintsa East* ☎ *043/738–5523* 🌐 *www.ahj.co.za.*

WHERE TO STAY

$$$$ RESORT Fodor's Choice ★ 🏨 **Prana Lodge.** With eight luxury suites tucked away inside a thick, lush indigenous dune forest, the exclusive Prana Lodge is Cintsa's first and best luxury offering, and you won't find a much better spot in which to unwind anywhere in the Eastern Cape. **Pros:** fantastic relaxation and wellness location; you can organize a combined luxury "Bush Beach" experience in conjunction with Kwandwe Private Game Reserve; great for romantic getaways. **Cons:** service can be a little overzealous at times; it's a bit of a walk from the main reception area to some of the suites; vervet monkeys can be a nuisance. [$] *Rooms from: R4200* ✉ *Chintsa Dr., Chintsa East* ☎ *043/704–5100* 🌐 *www.pranalodge.co.za* 🛏 *8 rooms* 🍴 *Some meals.*

HOGSBACK

139 km (87 miles) northwest of East London; 170 km (105 miles) northwest of Cintsa.

This peaceful and picturesque village is the perfect place from which to embark on some of South Africa's best hiking trails and experience a number of its finest waterfalls and oldest Afro-montane forests. Hogsback allegedly takes its name from the shape of the three striking peaks that overlook the village, referred to as the Three Hogs. One of the village's earliest inhabitants was a gardener from Oxford by the name of Thomas Summerton, who set about trying to re-create the English countryside in his new homeland; he's responsible for many of the pretty gardens, apple orchards, and tree-lined avenues that give the village its distinctly rural English feel. Today, Hogsback has become a mecca for artists and artisans, as well as a few other endangered species. The village has long been associated with J. R. R. Tolkien's *Lord of the Rings,* though there is nothing to actually prove this connection. But spend some time in this magical place and it's not hard to see why the rumors might have gained so much credence.

GETTING HERE AND AROUND

As is the case throughout most of Amatole, it's best to tour this area by car, and the roads to and from East London (2 hours) and Cintsa (2½ hours) are pretty good for the most part, aside from the occasional pothole. The Baz Bus also runs services to Hogsback from East London. Once you're in the village itself, most of the points of interest are within walking distance of the accommodations.

WHERE TO STAY

$ B&B/INN Fodor's Choice ★ 🏨 **The Edge Mountain Retreat.** This property boasts some of the best views in Hogsback, as well as 15 acres of gardens, a range of self-catering cottages that are perfect for families or groups—some are perched right on the cliff's edge—and 10 simple but comfortable en-suite rooms with whitewashed walls. **Pros:** breathtaking views; there's a lot of space; great for families. **Cons:** food can be a little disappointing; it's not the easiest place to get to; service can be a bit disorganized. [$] *Rooms from: R600* ✉ *Redcoat La.* ☎ *045/962–1159* 🌐 *www.theedge-hogsback.co.za* 🛏 *30 units* 🍴 *Breakfast.*

6

$ B&B/INN Fodor's Choice ★ 🏨 **Nutwoods Park.** This lovely old guesthouse is nestled amid 7 acres of beautifully well-kept gardens with expansive views across the treetops to the dramatic mountain peaks, and with easy access to all of Hogsback's outdoor pursuits. **Pros:** great location with lots of space and privacy; family-friendly options; prices are very reasonable. **Cons:** all meals must be arranged at least a day in advance; some of the room furnishings are a little gaudy; it's often fully booked. [$] *Rooms from: R760* ✉ *Nutwoods Dr. at Orchard La.* ☎ *045/962–1043* 🌐 *www.nutwoodspark.co.za* 🛏 *4 rooms* 🍴 *Breakfast.*

WILD COAST

As the name suggests, the Wild Coast is a haven of unspoiled wilderness. Whereas other areas of the country have become tourist playgrounds, the coast's lack of infrastructure has resulted in the large and mostly undeveloped swath of country east of Cintsa. The coastline consists of more than 280 km (174 miles) of desolate white-sand beaches, ragged cliffs, and secluded bays. Inland it's green and forested, with abundant birdlife. With mild year-round weather, this is a great destination for the adventure traveler.

To many, though, this part of the Eastern Cape is a glimpse of a very different South Africa. The mostly Xhosa population farm the land communally, domestic animals roam free, and traditional thatched *rondavel* huts dot the landscape. This is also one of South Africa's poorest regions, but the introduction of responsible tourism is helping to raise employment levels while simultaneously giving visitors unique insights into the traditional Xhosa culture.

BULUNGULA

295 km (183 miles) northeast of East London.

Bulungula is a tiny community near the mouth of the Bulungula River, about a 25-km (16-mile) walk from Coffee Bay's Hole-in-the-Wall. There are no shops, no banks, and no post office. There isn't even a decent road. The one lodge is run in partnership with the local community, making it a completely different destination for adventure travelers. Bulungula is a great place to just chill out on the beach, but there are also loads of great activities—all owned and run by members of the community in conjunction with the lodge. You can choose from a horseback ride, a canoe or fishing trip, an educational walk through the bush with an herbalist, a visit to a local restaurant, or a day spent with the women of the village, learning how they live. You might learn to carry water and firewood on your head, harvest wild foods and cook them for your lunch, make mud bricks, work in the fields, or weave baskets.

This is a really worthwhile destination, although it's not for everyone. But because Bulungula is such a small, isolated community, crime is practically nonexistent and it is very safe.

CLOSE UP

The Food Chain Up Close

Hailed by locals as "the greatest shoal on Earth," the sardine run is, in terms of biomass, the world's largest animal migration. Cold water traveling up the coast moves closer to shore and brings with it untold millions of sardines (actually pilchards). These tiny fish are, of course, highly edible, so they have quite a following. Cape gannets, Cape fur seals, common and bottlenose dolphins, sharks, and Bryde's whales all follow this movable feast. The run coincides with the northern migration of the humpback whales, so the sea is teeming with life. Local fishing folk revel in the huge catches to be had simply by wading into the shallows with makeshift nets, and sightseers can watch for the bubbling water and attendant cloud of seabirds that signal shoals moving past.

There are boat trips aplenty to take you out for a closer look, but the real thrill is in diving the run. It's awesome just being amid all those fish, but you often are also among a thousand common dolphins. What everyone is really hoping for is a "baitball"—when dolphins herd a big school of sardines into a circle, keep them there by swimming around them, and pick them off at will. Sharks almost always join in, and an acrobatic seal or two might take advantage of the free lunch. Bryde's and even humpback whales have been known to take a (rather large) passing bite out of the ball, and the sight of Cape gannets from underwater as they dive-bomb the fish is memorable. African Dive Adventures (🌐 *www.afridive.com*) offers Sardine Run Packages along the Wild Coast from a base at Coffee Bay. The best time to see the run is usually between late June and late July.

6

GETTING HERE AND AROUND

You'll need to travel on unpaved roads to get to Bulungula. The driving time from East London is 4½ hours. The lodge will provide you with a detailed map if you're driving yourself. Your best bet is to leave your car in the secure parking provided by the lodge at a small grocery store about 1½ km (1 mile) away, from which you can walk to the lodge (downhill for 45 minutes) or be picked up. If you arrive after 5 pm, leave your vehicle at the larger grocery store 15 km (9 miles) away and arrange for a pickup, as it's not advisable to drive the dirt road in the dark. In both instances, the owners of the stores will look after your vehicles for R15 per night. The lodge also runs a shuttle service to and from the bus stop at Mthatha.

WHERE TO STAY

$ HOTEL Fodor's Choice ★ 🏨 **Bulungula Lodge.** Bulungula's one lodge is, in spirit, just an extension of the village. **Pros:** interaction with local Xhosa people means you learn a lot about their culture; eco-friendly credentials; warm and friendly staff. **Cons:** accommodations are simple and low on creature comforts; not much privacy or solitude; tricky to get to. [$] *Rooms from: R450* ✉ *Bulungula River Mouth, Nqileni Village, Mthatha* ☎ *047/577–8900, 083/391–5525* 🌐 *www.bulungula.com* 🛏 *10 rooms* 🍴 *No meals.*

COFFEE BAY

295 km (183 miles) northeast of East London.

The village of Coffee Bay is a bit run-down, but the beaches and the scenery are great. (The surf is fantastic, but don't head out alone if you don't know what you're doing.)

You can do a fabulous 37-km (23-mile) hike from Coffee Bay to Bulungula (or vice versa) via Hole-in-the-Wall, across the cliff tops, and along the beach. It's best to take a guide, who can cut about two or three hours from the journey by taking a shortcut through rolling hills dotted with thatched huts. Arrange for a guide through Bulungula Lodge *(above)*, where you should plan to overnight at the end of your hike; the lodge can transport your luggage while you walk.

GETTING HERE AND AROUND

Coffee Bay is about 1½ hours from Mthatha. Greyhound buses and the Baz Bus stop at the Shell Ultra City just outside the town. The Coffee Shack *(below)* will also pick guests up from here. Otherwise, local minibus taxis run from Mthatha to Coffee Bay. They leave from the taxi stand in the center of town and change at Mqanduli, a small town on the way. They are a cheap and convenient way of getting around but are not always the safest option.

If you are driving, take the N2 to Viedgesville (about 20 km [12 miles] south of Mthatha) and then follow signs for Coffee Bay road. The coastal road is paved, but there are lots of potholes, and you're advised to travel only during daylight. The drive takes about 3½ hours from East London.

Coffee Bay itself is small, so you can walk to most places or take local minibus taxis to get around.

EXPLORING

Hole-in-the-Wall. What makes Coffee Bay stand out from all the other lovely destinations is its proximity—only 9 km (5½ miles)—to the spectacular Hole-in-the-Wall, a natural sea arch through a solid rock island. You can go here on a rather adventurous road from Coffee Bay, and it's included on almost any tour of the Wild Coast. The Xhosa name, Esikaleni, means "place of the water people," and it is believed to be a gateway to the world of the ancestors. If you try swimming through it in rough seas, it certainly will be, but some intrepid souls have made it on calm (very calm) days. ⊠ *Coffee Bay* ✛ *About 9 km (5½ miles) south of Coffee Bay along a coastal path.*

WHERE TO STAY

$

B&B/INN

⌖ **Coffee Shack on the Beach.** The main (but certainly not the only) attraction of this vibey beachside backpackers' lodge are the surfing lessons. **Pros:** surf lessons are great value; stay for four nights and get the fifth free throughout the year; dinner is free on Sunday night. **Cons:** can have a noisy, party atmosphere; you need to book ahead; no meals are included in your room rates. ⓢ *Rooms from: R400* ⊠ *Bomvu Beach, Mqanduli* ☎ *047/575–2048* ⊕ *www.coffeeshack. co.za* ⌖ *9 rooms* ⎁ *No meals.*

$$ ⊞ **Ocean View Hotel.** This old Wild Coast hotel is light and bright, with
HOTEL   white walls and blue fabrics with marine motifs. **Pros:** child-friendly;
FAMILY   there are tons of adventure activities to participate in; the hotel is close
to the beach. **Cons:** rooms are a bit basic; it's a family resort, so there
may be children around; service is not always the friendliest. $ *Rooms*
from: R2500 ✉ *Main Beach* ☎ *047/575–2005, 047/575–2006* ⊕ *www.*
oceanview.co.za ↪ *30 rooms* ⏐⊙⏐ *All meals.*

MTHATHA

295 km (183 miles) northeast of East London; 100 km (62 miles)
northwest of Coffee Bay.

Mthatha is largely poor and overcrowded, and a little dilapidated,
though it's certainly not boring. Most people don't stay here beyond
making a travel connection elsewhere; strangely, accommodations here
are generally very expensive, too. If you want some good, cheap local
food, try one of the numerous large storage containers around the cen-
ter of Mthatha that serve as makeshift (and very popular) restaurants.

GETTING HERE AND AROUND

Because Mthatha is a really small airport, it doesn't have all the expected
facilities. Greyhound and Baz Bus drop passengers off at the Shell Ultra
City just outside Mthatha. You can rent a car from either Avis or Bud-
get. *For information on buses, see Bus Travel in Travel Smart. For*
information on car-rental agencies, see Car Travel in Travel Smart.

EXPLORING

Nelson Mandela Museum. The Nelson Mandela Museum stands as evi-
dence of the love and respect that this awesome statesman inspired
in people all over the world, from rural schoolchildren to royalty.
The many gifts Mandela received through his life say more about the
givers than the receiver, and the exhibitions display the political and
personal journey of this beloved politician. In addition to the recently
renovated building in Mthatha, there are three other sites. Qunu, the
area where Mandela spent part of his childhood, was also the site
of his family residence in the years prior to his death; the house can
be seen from the N2, 32 km (20 miles) south of Mthatha, as can his
grave on the hill inside the property behind the house. On another
hill on the opposite side of the road is the Nelson Mandela Youth
and Heritage Centre, a beautifully designed building that combines
natural stone and unfinished wattle branches to create an interesting
pattern of light and shade that complements the black-and-white pho-
tographs documenting Mandela's early life and his period of activism
and incarceration. There's also a reconstruction of his prison cell
on Robben Island. Huge glass windows overlook the fields where
Madiba (an affectionate sobriquet for Mandela) herded cattle as a
boy, and you can also take a short walk to a smooth rock face that he
and his young friends used to use as a slide, and maybe even have a
go at it yourself. **Mvezo** was the birthplace of Mandela. Although the
foundations of the house in which Mandela was born are visible and
there is a small open-air museum, Mvezo is more a place of pilgrim-
age than a museum (since there isn't very much to see here). It's best

6

to visit Mvezo as part of a tour—both because it's hard to find and because you'll get much more out of it with a knowledgeable guide—which you can arrange through the museum, or with Imonti Tours. But you can get directions from the museum in Mthatha if you want to go on your own. You'll need to travel down a 19-km (12-mile) gravel road, but a 4x4 is not required. You can take a similar gravel road north of the N2 to **Mqhekezweni**, which is where Mandela went to live with his cousin under the guardianship of Jongintaba Dalindyebo, regent of the Tembu people, and where he began his education. The rondavel he and his cousin shared remains exactly as it would have been then, as does the great tree where Mandela used to sneak up and secretly listen to the elders during their meetings. ■**TIP→ It's possible to visit the Nelson Mandela Museum on Saturday and Sunday afternoon if you make an arrangement in advance.** ⊠ *Bhunga Bldg., Owen St. at Nelson Mandela Dr. (N2)* ☎ *047/501–9500* ⊕ *www. nelsonmandelamuseum.org.za* ✉ *Free.*

DURBAN AND KWAZULU-NATAL

Updated
by Ishay
Govender-
Ypma

Durban is a burgeoning arts and culture destination, but its main draw is the 320 days of sunshine a year that entices visitors and locals alike to the vast stretches of beautiful beach. The proximity to the beach has given the province's largest city a laid-back vibe that makes it a perfect vacation destination and the ideal springboard from which to visit the diverse beauty of the rest of the province of KwaZulu-Natal.

As one of the few natural harbors on Africa's east coast, Durban developed as a port city after the first European settlers landed in 1824 with the intention of establishing a trading post. It's the busiest port in South Africa, as it exports large volumes of sugar and is home to the country's largest import/export facility for the motor industry. The port also has a passenger terminal for cruise liners that operate mostly between November and May.

The city's Esplanade, known as the Golden Mile (an area much larger than the name implies) consists of high-rise hotels flanked by a popular promenade and beaches, with the Moses Mabhida Stadium in the background. The colonial-inspired suburbs of Berea and Morningside overlook the city and offer boutique hotels and packed restaurants.

Residential and upscale commercial development has seen coastal spots like Umhlanga to the north earn cult status with tourists, and collections of small villages along both the north and south coasts have access to pristine beaches. Add to the mix two World Heritage Sites (uKhahlamba-Drakensberg Park and iSimangaliso Wetland Park), and KwaZulu-Natal itself embodies South Africa's mantra: the world in one country. More important, it's truly representative of the country's diversity.

Durban's booming lifestyle scene can be enjoyed the moment you step onto the ocean-flanked Golden Mile, filled with cyclists (you can even hire a tandem bicycle), skateboarders, runners, and coffee aficionados enjoying the broad boardwalk. On weekends, locals and visitors head to the markets around the Moses Mabhida Stadium and the trendy boutiques near Station Road Precinct. The Rivertown Precinct, dubbed Durban's "cultural revival hot spot," hosts start-ups, unique retail pods, festivals, and music events.

KwaZulu-Natal—commonly referred to as KZN—is a premier vacation area for South Africans, and, despite being a comparatively small province, has the country's second-largest province population, at more than 10 million people. It's all but impossible to resist the subtropical climate and the warm waters of the Indian Ocean. In fact, the entire 480-km (300-mile) coastline, from the Wild Coast in the south to the Mozambique border in the north, is essentially one long beach, attracting hordes of swimmers, surfers, and anglers.

ORIENTATION AND PLANNING

GETTING ORIENTED

Hugging the country's east coast, Durban's amount of sunshine has earned the city the nickname "South Africa's playground." Here you'll find the colonial-inspired suburbs of Berea and Morningside, the coastal village of Umhlanga, and the warm waters and vacation towns that populate the areas known as the Dolphin Coast and South Coast. Spend some time exploring Durban's inner-city precincts that are currently undergoing rapid development—you'll find inexpensive local food, traditional fabrics and blankets, craft beer, and local music. There are numerous tours you can go on if you're a little shy to explore by yourself. Head inland to the KwaZulu-Natal Midlands and the dramatic Drakensberg Mountains for the antithesis of coastal beauty. Farther north you'll find the Battlefields and Zululand that portray the province's bloody history, as well as the Big Five (lion, elephant, Cape buffalo, leopard, rhinoceros) roaming in various game reserves.

Durban. South Africa's third-largest city, Durban is southern Africa's busiest port (chiefly cargo). The city's chief appeal to tourists is its long strip of high-rise hotels and its popular promenade—known as the Esplanade or Golden Mile (though it's actually several miles long)—fronting its beaches.

Side Trips from Durban. To find beaches unmarred by commercial development, you need to travel north to the Dolphin Coast or south to the aptly named South Coast. Moving inland takes you to the KwaZulu-Natal Midlands, just off the N3 between Durban and Johannesburg. Here racehorse and dairy farms stud rolling green hills and lush pastures that are reminiscent of England. The Midlands Meander (an ever-growing series of routes set up by the local tourism board) is a great way to experience the area's farms and crafts shops.

Zululand and the Battlefields. Zululand, the region north of the Tugela River and south of Swaziland and Mozambique, is the traditional home of the Zulu people. Prominent towns (though these are all relatively small) in this region are the industrial towns of Empangeni and Richards Bay, Eshowe, Pongola, and Ulundi. The farther north you go, the less populated and more rural the area becomes, with traditional Zulu huts known as rondavels and herds of long-horn brown-and-white and black-and-white Nguni cattle, tended by boys or young men, scattered over the hills.

The Battlefields (Anglo-Zulu and Anglo-Boer) are inland, to the north of the Midlands and northeast of the Drakensberg. The towns dotted among the Zululand battlefields tend to be a little dusty and forlorn during the dry winter months, but this is an area to visit more for its historic than its scenic value.

7

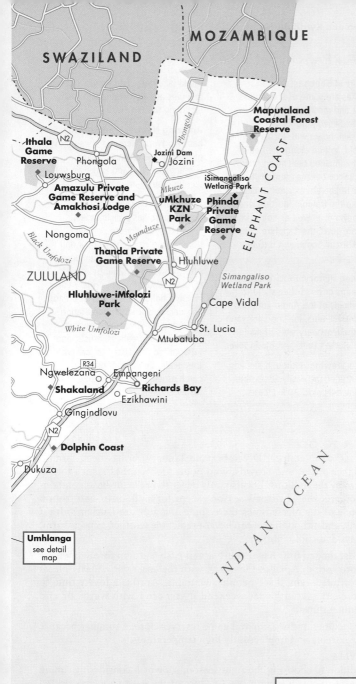

MOZAMBIQUE

SWAZILAND

Maputaland
Coastal Forest
Reserve

Ithala
Game
Reserve

N2

Phongola

Jozini Dam
Jozini

Louwsburg

iSimangaliso
Wetland Park

Amazulu Private
Game Reserve and
Amakhosi Lodge

Mkuze

uMkhuze
KZN
Park

Phinda
Private
Game
Reserve

Black Umfolozi

Nongoma

Msunduze

Thanda Private
Game Reserve

Hluhluwe

ZULULAND

N2

Simangaliso
Wetland Park

Hluhluwe-iMfolozi
Park

Cape Vidal

White Umfolozi

St. Lucia
Mtubatuba

R34

Ngwelezana

Empangeni

Shakaland

Richards Bay

Ezikhawini

Gingindlovu

N2

Dolphin Coast

Dukuza

ELEPHANT COAST

INDIAN OCEAN

Umhlanga
see detail
map

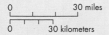

0   30 miles

0   30 kilometers

KwaZulu–Natal

TOP REASONS TO GO

Beautiful Beaches: Durban's beaches are some of the world's safest and most beautiful. Hire a bicycle, Segway, go-kart, or hop on your skateboard with locals (young and old) to ride along the beautifully maintained beachfront. The long, sandy beaches and inviting water temperatures extend all the way up the Dolphin (north) Coast and beyond, as well as south from Durban, down the Sapphire Coast, the Hibiscus Coast, and into the Eastern Cape.

Reliving History: Explore city's museums or go farther afield to the battlefields of the Anglo-Zulu and Anglo-Boer wars, making sure you visit the legendary sites of Isandlwana, Rorke's Drift, and Blood River.

Game-Viewing: Although smaller than Kruger, the easily accessible Hluhluwe-iMfolozi Park, Mkuze,

Ithala (aka Itala), and Pongola game reserves are all teeming with game, including the Big Five.

Amazing Natural Wonders: KZN has two World Heritage Sites—the uKhahlamba-Drakensberg and iSimangaliso Wetland Park—as well as numerous game reserves.

A Vibrant City: Durban, Africa's busiest port, has a distinct feel, flavored by its diverse populations. In the city center, you'll find mosques, temples, and churches. After browsing for Zulu beadwork, try a local "bunny chow" (fiery curry inside a hollowed-out loaf of bread). The design district around Station Road and the Rivertown Precinct are a hub for creatives, artists, and intrepid foodies. Listen to jazz with the locals, sip on craft beer, or catch a new band during one of the festivals.

PLANNING

WHEN TO GO

The height of summer (December and January) brings heat, humidity, higher prices, and crowds, who pour into "Durbs," as it's fondly known, by the millions. Locals know never to brave the beach on holidays or over the Christmas season except for an hour or two from 6 am—one of the nicest times there. June and July are Durban's driest months, and although you can never predict the weather, expect warm, dry days and cool nights.

The best time to tour KwaZulu-Natal is early autumn through winter and into spring (April to October), with the coast particularly pleasant in winter—you'll see people swimming. April is a lovely time to visit the city (avoid Easter weekend if you can), with warm air and sea temperatures.

Some facilities in the Zululand game reserves close in summer because of the extreme and unpleasantly high temperatures.

FESTIVALS

In addition to choosing the right season, it's worth considering timing your visit to coincide with one or more of the exciting events hosted within this region.

Ballito PRO. Around the end of June and the beginning of July, top surfers and surfing fans head to Ballito for one of the longest-running professional surfing events in the world, established in 1969. ✉ *Ballito* ☎ *031/310–8000* ⊕ *www.theballitopro.com.*

> **WARNING**
>
> It is essential that visitors to the northern parts of the province, including Zululand, take antimalarial drugs, particularly during the wet summer months.

Comrades Marathon. This is the world's oldest and largest ultra-marathon—approximately 90 km (56 miles) between Pietermaritzburg and Durban, the race route changes annually. It's a South African institution, creating an unparalleled camaraderie between runners. Many runners have earned their "life" permanent race number after competing in the gruelling marathon 10 times. ✉ *Durban* ☎ *033/897–8650* ⊕ *www.comrades.com.*

Durban International Film Festival. The Durban International Film Festival (DIFF), running for almost four decades, is a highlight on the KwaZulu-Natal and South African arts calendars. The largest film festival in southern Africa, it's a celebration of local, African, and international film, offering paid and free screenings. Many filmmakers and actors have cut their teeth here and gone on to international acclaim. ☎ *031/260–2506* ⊕ *www.durbanfilmfest.co.za.*

FNB Dusi Canoe Marathon. Paddlers compete in this 120-km (76-mile) kayak race between Pietermaritzburg and Durban along the Msindusi (Dusi) River. It's regarded as one of the toughest canoe events in the world and takes place over three days. The race is run by Natal Canoe Club. ✉ *Durban* ☎ *033/394–9994, 033/342–1528, 033/3421–1525* ⊕ *www.dusi.co.za.*

Sardine Run. Dubbed "The Greatest Shoal on Earth," the Sardine Run is regarded as one of nature's most amazing migrations. Starting along the South Coast and moving up to Durban, sardine shoals of 20–30 km (12–18 miles) are followed by some 23,000 dolphins, 500 whales, 1,000 sharks and countless birds. The spectacle can be viewed from the beach or at various dive spots. You can even grab a bucket and catch your own dinner. Ancillary events take place on land. ✉ *Durban* ☎ *039/682–7944 South Coast Tourism* ⊕ *www.tourismsouthcoast.co.za.*

Splashy Fen. South Africa's longest-running and most renowned annual music festival showcases the country's top bands, famous performers, and up-and-coming musicians. The outdoor event takes place every Easter long weekend on a Midlands farm in the Underberg. It's great fun and has an eclectic selection of the best local bands and a great Woodstock-esque vibe. ✉ *Bushman's Nek Rd., Underberg* ☎ *084/253–3164* ⊕ *www.splashyfen.co.za.*

Vodacom Durban July. South Africa's most prestigious horse race sees tens of thousands of spectators descend on Greyville Racecourse to partake in one of the year's biggest social events and to watch the ponies run. Fashionistas have a day in the sun, often in over-the-top designs as they compete for "best-dressed" prizes. ✉ *Greyville Racecourse, 150 Avondale Rd., Durban* ☎ *031/314–1651* ⊕ *www.vodacomdurbanjuly.co.za.*

7

PLANNING YOUR TIME

2 Days: If you have just two days, spend them in Durban. Start with an early morning walk or cycle along the Golden Mile to watch the surfers before grabbing brunch or take-away chili chicken burger from Afro's bright yellow container stand in South Beach, popular with locals.
■ TIP➜ Leave large items of jewelry and valuables in your hotel safe.
Safety has improved dramatically but exercise caution as the sun sets—don't walk alone on poorly lit sections of the promenade.

Spend three or four hours on a guided walking tour of the Indian District or downtown Durban. Tours (reservations are a must—you can call to book) leave from the Tourist Junction (Old Station Building). Wilson's Wharf, which overlooks the Durban harbor, and Morningside's trendy Florida Road offer great options for lunch or dinner. If you dine on Florida Road, make sure you stop by the African Arts Centre, which supports unemployed artists and youth, for beautiful Zulu beadwork, baskets, prints, textiles, and curios. You can also spend the afternoon strolling around Mitchell Park, which is known for its colorful flower beds at the top of Florida Road (also be sure to visit the small zoo here). On your second day, visit the aquarium at uShaka Marine World, one of the largest and best in the world, perhaps lunching on seafood at Cargo Hold, adjacent to the shark tank or at easygoing Surf Riders nearby. In the afternoon, visit the Natal Sharks Board for a show and fascinating shark dissection—yes, they actually do a dissection (Tuesday–Thursday only). You could also visit the Umgeni River Bird Park, whose live bird shows are a must-see (11 and 2 daily, except Monday).

5 Days: Spend at least one day in Durban*(see above)*before or after you explore KwaZulu-Natal following the Zululand and the more northern section option, which takes in the coastal strip and some of the northern game parks and private lodges. Start out with a tour of the battlefield sites of Isandlwana, Rorke's Drift, and the Talana Museum at Dundee. Afterward, travel north and take the R103 to pick up the Midlands Meander, which stretches north all the way to Mooi River, through the tranquil KZN Midlands.

If you decide to head up the north coast, spend a night at Shakaland or Simunye Zulu Lodge to get the total Zulu cultural experience. Then schedule at least two days in Hluhluwe-iMfolozi Park or Phinda Private Game Reserve to see the wildlife for which these reserves are known. A trip to iSimangaliso Wetland Park to see hippos and crocodiles in the wild is another great experience.

GETTING HERE AND AROUND
AIR TRAVEL

Durban's King Shaka International Airport, at La Mercy, on the north coast, became operational in 2010 and is three times the size of the old airport. About 17 km (11 miles) from Umhlanga and about 32 km (20 miles) north of Durban, it operates under the management of the Airports Company South Africa.

South African Airways (SAA) flies to Durban via Johannesburg. Domestic airlines serving Durban are SAA, BA/Comair, Kulula, SA Express, SA Airlink, and Mango. Perhaps the easiest way to book a ticket to or from

Durban is online. Kulula and Mango are the budget-priced airlines, so expect to buy your own snacks and drinks on board. SAA is usually the more expensive option, unless you're looking for a ticket at short notice (next day or two), when it may turn out to offer the lowest price.

The most inexpensive ground transfer into Durban and back is the Airport Shuttle Service, which costs R80 and departs every 30 to 45 minutes after incoming flights arrive and leaves the city center every hour. Its drop-off points are flexible within the city and include all hotels on the North Beach and South Beach, the Central Business District, the International Convention Centre, and the Moses Mabhida Stadium. On request, the driver is likely to drop you anywhere en route. Call ahead and the bus will pick you up at any hotel in the city; there's no need to reserve for the trip into Durban. A taxi ride into Durban will cost around R320. If you plan to go farther afield, call Magic Transfers or catch a cab or an Uber that will conveniently pick you up from a demarcated area just outside the terminal building. *For airline contact information see Air Travel in Travel Smart South Africa.*

Airports **Airports Company South Africa.** ☎ *032/436–6000* ⊕ *www.airports. co.za.* **King Shaka International Airport.** ☎ *032/436–6000* ⊕ *kingshakainternational.co.za.*

BUS TRAVEL

Greyhound and Translux Transfers offer long-distance bus service to cities all over South Africa from Durban. All intercity buses leave from the Durban Station on Masabalala Yengwa Avenue (N.M.R. Avenue), between Archie Gumede Road (Old Fort Road) and Sandile Thusi Road (Argyle Road). Bear in mind that you can often fly for much the same prices as traveling by bus, especially if you book well in advance or find a discount.

Three primary bus services are available in and around the city: Durban Transport, Mynah, and People Mover buses, operated by eThekwini Transport Authority. All of the fleet's buses are air-conditioned and equipped with electronic ramps for wheelchair access and strollers. All bus stops are staffed by security people. Small Mynah buses are ideal for short trips within the inner city, costing a couple of rand per ride; you pay as you board and exact change isn't required. Larger, more comfortable People Mover buses make longer city trips, including to the Golden Mile, the Central Business District (aka CBD), and out to the beachfront and back; fares are R9 per ride or R87 for 10 rides, and buses arrive every 15 minutes between 6:30 am and 10 pm. Durban Transport services city-to-suburb routes. If you plan to make frequent use of public transportation, it would be worth investing in a Muvo Card. This is a single secure smartcard that can be used interchangeably across the three bus lines. Call Muvo at ☎ *080/000–6886*.

The main bus depot is on Monty Naicker Road (Pine Street) between Samora Machel (Aliwal) and Dorothy Nyembe (Gardiner) streets. Route information is also available at an information office at the corner of Samora Machel Street and Monty Naicker Road.

Contacts **eThekwini Transport Authority** (*Durban City Transport*). ☎ *031/311–1111* ⊕ *www.durban.gov.za.*

CAR TRAVEL

Durban is relatively easy to navigate because the sea is a constant reference point. Downtown Durban is dominated by two parallel one-way streets, Dr. Pixley kaSeme Street (West Street) going toward the sea and Anton Lembede Street (Smith Street) going away from the sea, toward Berea and Pietermaritzburg; together they get you in and out of the city center easily. Parking downtown is a nightmare; head for an underground garage whenever you can. As with the rest of South Africa, wherever you go, self-appointed car guards will ask if they can watch your car. The going rate for a tip—if you want to give one—is R10, depending on how long you're away. The guards between North and South beaches are said to be very trustworthy. ∎**TIP**➔ **Don't leave any belongings visible in the car or your keys with anyone.**

The M4 (Ruth First Highway), which stretches north up to the Dolphin Coast—from Umhlanga to Ballito, about 40 km (25 miles) and beyond—is a particularly pretty coastal road, offering many views of the sea through lush natural vegetation and sugarcane fields. It's much nicer than the sterile N2 highway, which takes a parallel path slightly inland and offers no views.

Avis, Budget, Europcar, and Tempest have rental offices at the airport. Rates start at around R400 per day, including insurance and 200 km (125 miles), plus R2.10 per additional kilometer (half mile), or about R500 for the weekend. Avis offers unlimited mileage to international visitors, as long as you can produce your return ticket, international driver's license, and passport as proof.

RICKSHAW TRAVEL

Colorfully decorated rickshaws are unique to Durban—you won't find them in any other South African city. Though their origins lie in India, these two-seat carriages with large wheels are pulled exclusively by Zulu men dressed in feathered headgear and traditional garb. Limited to the beachfront, the rickshaw runners ply their trade all day, every day, mostly along the Golden Mile section. The going rate is R100 per person for about 15 minutes, and R15 for a photo (don't assume you can take a picture without paying for the privilege). With numerous other modes of transport for hire here, like bicycles and go-karts, the rickshaws are at the end of their life cycle, since many consider the practice cruel.

TAXI TRAVEL

Taxis are metered and start at R10, with an additional R12 per kilometer (half mile); after-hours and time-based charges apply. Fares are calculated per vehicle for up to four passengers. Expect to pay about R50 from City Hall to North Beach and R400 to Durban International Airport. The most convenient taxi stands are around City Hall, in front of the beach hotels, and outside Spiga d'Oro on Florida Road in Morningside. Some taxis display a "for-hire" light, whereas others you simply hail when you can see they're empty. Major taxi companies include Eagle Taxi, Mozzies, Umhlanga Cabs, and Zippy Cabs.

There's no need to contact a taxi yourself. They will either be easy to find or your hotel or restaurant can call one for you. Uber and app-based taxi services have made hailing one from anywhere in the city a breeze.

Contacts Mozzie Cabs. ☎ *031/303–5787* ⊕ *www.mozzie.co.za.*

HOTEL AND RESTAURANT PRICES

Restaurant and hotel reviews have been shortened. For full information, visit Fodors.com.

WHAT IT COSTS IN SOUTH AFRICAN RAND			
$	$$	$$$	$$$$
Restaurants	under R100	R100–R150	R151–R200	over R200
Hotels	under R1,500	R1,500–R2,500	R2,501–R3,500	over R3,500

Restaurant prices are the average cost of a main course at dinner or, if dinner is not served, at lunch. Hotel prices are the lowest cost of a standard double room in high season.

VISITOR INFORMATION

The Tourist Junction, in the restored Old Station Building, houses the Tourism KwaZulu-Natal offices, where you can find information about almost everything that's happening in the province of KwaZulu-Natal. It's open weekdays 8–4:30 and weekends 9–2. There's also a satellite office, conveniently located along the Golden Mile, one of the city's premier destinations. Sugar Coast Tourism (covering the Umhlanga and nearby Umdloti areas), is open weekdays 8:30–4:45 and Saturday 9–1, and Sapphire Coast Tourism (covering Amanzimtoti to Umkomaas) is open weekdays 8–4 and Saturday 9–2.

Contacts Durban Tourism Beach Office. ⊠ *1 K.E. Masinga Rd., Beachfront* ☎ *031/322–4203* ⊕ *www.durbanexperience.co.za.* **Durban Tourism Office.** ⊠ *90 Florida Rd., Durban* ☎ *031/322–4164* ⊕ *www.durbanexperience.co.za.* **Sapphire Coast Tourism.** ⊠ *95 Beach Rd., Amanzimtoti* ☎ *031/322–4173* ⊕ *www.sapphirecoasttourism.co.za.* **Sugar Coast Tourism.** ⊠ *Chartwell Centre, 15 Chartwell Dr., Shop 1A, Umhlanga* ☎ *031/561–4257* ⊕ *www.umhlanga-tourism.co.za.* **Tourism KwaZulu-Natal.** ☎ *031/366–7500* ⊕ *www.zulu.org. za.* **Tourist Junction.** ⊠ *160 Monty Naicker Rd. (Pine St.), at Soldiers Way, City Centre* ☎ *031/322–4164* ⊕ *www.zulu.org.za.* **Umhlanga Tourism Info Center.** ⊠ *Shop 1A, Chartwell Centre, 15 Chartwell Dr., Umhlanga* ☎ *031/561–4257* ⊕ *www.zulu.org.za.*

DURBAN

Durban has the pulse, the look, and the complex face of Africa. Then there's the summer heat, a clinging sauna that soaks you with sweat in minutes. If you wander into the Indian Quarter or drive through the Warwick Triangle—an area away from the sea around Julius Nyerere (Warwick) Avenue—the pulsating city rises up to meet you. Traditional healers closely guard animal organs for *muti* or medicine, vegetable and spice vendors crowd the sidewalks, and minibus taxis hoot incessantly as they trawl for business. It is by turns colorful, stimulating, and hypnotic.

It's also a place steeped in history and culture. Gandhi lived and practiced law here, and Winston Churchill visited as a young man. It's home to the largest number of Indians outside India; the massive Indian townships of Phoenix and Chatsworth stand as testimony to the harsh treatment Indians received during apartheid, though now thousands of Indians are professionals and businesspeople in Durban.

■TIP➔ Street names have all been updated, but the old ones remain in brackets, as some maps and locals still refer to streets by the old names.

SAFETY AND PRECAUTIONS

Durban has not escaped the crime evident in every South African city. Though far less prevalent nowadays, in the city center but also elsewhere, smash-and-grab thieves occasionally roam the streets, looking for bags or valuables in your car, even while you're driving, so lock any valuables in the trunk and keep your car doors locked and windows up at all times. Although there's no need to be fearful, be observant wherever you go. Hire a guide to take you around Durban, don't wander around the city center aimlessly or linger outside your hotel alone at night, and keep expensive cameras and other possessions concealed. The Durban Beachfront (with recently upgraded security features), Umhlanga, and the outlying areas are safe to explore on your own, though you'll need a taxi or car to get between them. If you plan to take a dip while you're at the beach, ask a neighboring beachgoer or lifeguard to keep an eye on your belongings, or put them in a locker—available in the vicinity of North and South beaches and on Umhlanga Main Beach.

TOURS

Durban Tourism. Three-hour walking tours depart from the Tourist Junction on weekdays at 9:30 and 1:30: the Oriental Walkabout explores the Indian District, including Victoria Market and several mosques, and the Historical Walkabout covers major monuments and museums. Reservations are essential; a two-person minimum applies. Durban Tourism can also provide details of various guided township tours by local tour operators such as SBRM Tours, Jikeleza Tours & Travel, and Kude Travel & Tours, which offer an insight into the social history and modern-day challenges of the townships. ☎ *031/322–4173* ⊕ *www. durbanexperience.co.za* ✉ *R100.*

Isle of Capri. This company offers sightseeing cruises around Durban Bay or out to sea, plus whale- and dolphin-watching tours and party cruises for the young at heart. Boats depart from Wilson's Wharf on Margaret Mncadi Avenue. ✉ *14–18 Boatman's Rd., Canal Rd., Victoria Embankment* ☎ *031/305–3099, 082/851–4787* ⊕ *www.isleofcapri.co.za.*

Ricksha Bus Tours. An inexpensive way to see the main attractions Durban has to offer is to join one of the bus tours, operated by Durban Tourism. They depart daily at 9 am and 1 pm from the North Beach Tourism Office and take 2½–3 hours to complete the circuit. The route includes the Beachfront, uShaka Marine World, Emmanuel Cathedral, Victoria Market, Florida Road, City Hall, KwaMuhle Museum, Mitchell Park, Moses Mabhida Stadium, Suncoast Casino, and more, and a tour guide provides commentary en route. ✉ *Durban* ☎ *031/322–4209* ✉ *R100.*

Sarie Marais Pleasure Cruises. Trips around the bay or out to sea are offered by this company. Half-hour harbor cruises run on the hour 9–4 and hour-long sea cruises run noon–3 daily. Deep-sea fishing and educational excursions are possible, or hire a boat and captain your own harbor cruise. Charters for up to 57 people are also available. ⊠ *Wilson's Wharf, 14–18 Boatman's Rd., Victoria Embankment* ☎ *031/305–4022* ⊕ *www.sariemaraiscruises.co.za* ⊠ *Harbor cruise R80; sea cruise R120; private charter R2,500.*

FAMILY
Fodor's Choice
★

Street Scene Tours. Offering responsible tours led by locals and benefiting local communities, Street Scene delves into the heart of Durban with well-curated guided walking tours. Book the city walking tour, heritage tour, or a township experience to connect with Durbanites in a way that a bus tour just can't achieve. ☎ *031/321–5079* ⊕ *www.streetscene.co.za.*

EXPLORING

By no means should you plan an entire vacation around Durban, because there is so much more to see beyond the city. Nevertheless, it's definitely worth a stopover. To get the most from your visit, get ready to explore the Central Business District (CBD), which includes the Indian Quarter; the Beachfront; and Berea and Morningside. If you're concerned about safety within the CBD, book tours through Tourist Junction.

CITY CENTER

The center of the city is indicative of South Africa's developing world status and first-world leanings. Large office buildings dominate streets filled with crowded taxis and buses, but every so often you'll stumble across a building that speaks of an imperial past. It can get horribly humid from December through February, so if you visit then, avoid walking too much during the midday heat. Browse the air-conditioned museums when it's hot, and save walking outside for later in the afternoon, making sure you get to the museums and galleries before they close, around 4:30.

TOP ATTRACTIONS

Durban Art Gallery. A vibrant, contemporary mix of local, southern African, and international work is presented here, though the main focus is on work from KwaZulu-Natal. Exhibits have included the cultural diversity of art and craft from KwaZulu-Natal and the rest of South Africa. Look out, too, for the traditional, patterned *hlabisa* baskets, regularly displayed at the gallery. Exhibits change every few months. ⊠ *City Hall, Anton Lembede [Smith] St. entrance, 2nd fl., City Centre* ☎ *031/311–2264* ⊕ *www.durban.gov.za/city_services/parksrecreation/ durban_art_gallery/pages/default.aspx* ⊠ *Free.*

KwaMuhle Museum. Pronounced kwa- *moosh*-le (with a light *e*, as in *hen*), this small museum, housed in what used to be the notorious Department of Native Affairs, tells of Durban's apartheid history. During apartheid the department was responsible for administering the movement of black people in and out of the city, dealing with the dreaded passes that blacks had to carry at all times, and generally overseeing the oppressive laws that plagued the black population. Ironically, the name means "place of the good one," Kwa meaning "place of" and "Muhle" meaning "good one" (after J. S. Marwick, the benevolent manager of the municipal native affairs department from 1916 to 1920). Exhibits provide the often heartbreaking background on this period through old photographs and documents, replicas of passbooks, and lifelike

7

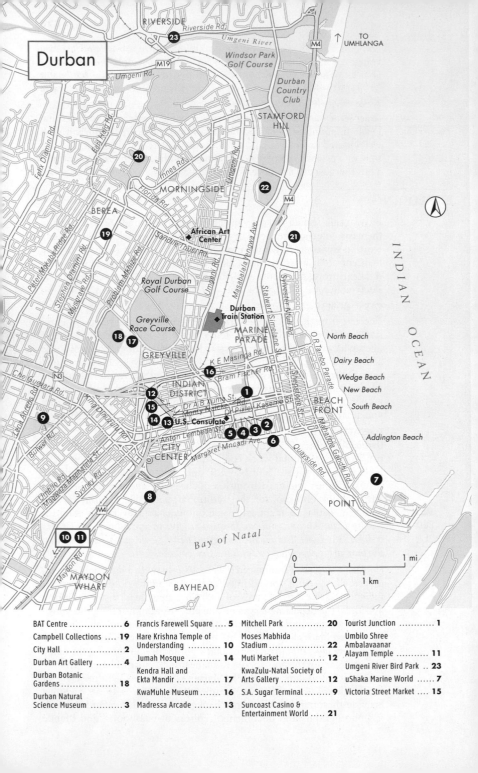

Durban

models of people involved in the pass system, including *shebeen* (informal bar) queens, who had to apply for permits to sell alcohol at a time of prohibition. ⊠ *130 Bram Fischer [Ordnance] Rd., City Centre* ☎ *031/311–2223* ✉ *Free* ⊘ *Closed Good Friday and Christmas Day.*

FAMILY
Fodor's Choice
★

Moses Mabhida Stadium. This handsome structure, an architectural jewel in Durban's skyline, was built for the 2010 Word Cup soccer tournament and seats just under 63,000. Named after General Moses Mabhida, the secretary general of the South African Communist party, it's a busy, multiuse stadium that is busy year-round with activities for tourists. You can take a two-minute ride to the viewing platform on the SkyCar (R60 for adults) for a panoramic view of the city, or glide around the stadium with a guide on a Segway. Daredevils can get their thrill on with the Big Rush Big Swing (R695 for adults, no children under 10), which has you strapped in and swinging across the stadium—named the tallest swing of its kind by Guinness Book of Records in 2011. Or, get a workout climbing 500 grueling steps on the adventure walk to the top of the arch, 106 meters above the ground. The People's Park is free and open to the public with rolling green lawns, a café with free Wi-Fi, and plenty of parking. ■TIP→ The vibrant I Heart Market is held here every Saturday, a premier food and lifestyle market loved by local families and visitors. ⊠ *44 Isaiah Ntshangase Rd. [Walter Gilbert]* ⊕ *www.mmstadium.com.*

WORTH NOTING

City Hall. Built in 1910 in Edwardian neo-baroque style, the hall looks as if it has been shipped straight from the United Kingdom column by column—hardly surprising, since it's an exact copy of Belfast City Hall. The main pediment carries sculptures representing Britannia, Unity, and Patriotism, and allegorical sculptures of the arts, music, and literature adorn the exterior. City Hall houses not only the mayor's parlor and other government offices, but also the Durban Art Gallery, the Natural Science Museum, and the City Library. Ask the guard to let you in to see the huge theater's ornate molding and grand parterre boxes, or join an official tour run by City of Durban. ⊠ *Anton Lembede [Smith] St., City Centre* ☎ *031/311–1111* ⊕ *www.durban.gov.za* ✉ *Free* ⊘ *Closed Good Friday and Christmas Day.*

NEED A
BREAK?

Royal Coffee Shoppe. This is a popular, if old-school meeting place for daytime breaks and for pre- and post-theater crowds. Crystal chandeliers, etched glass, formally dressed staff, and live piano music in the nearby lounge at lunchtime create a rich atmosphere of old-time colonial Durban. ⊠ *Royal Hotel, 267 Anton Lembede [Smith] St., City Centre* ☎ *031/333–6000* ⊕ *www.theroyal.co.za.*

FAMILY

Durban Natural Science Museum. Despite its small size, this museum provides an excellent introduction to Africa's numerous wild mammals (the displays include a stuffed elephant and leopard, as well as smaller mammals like wild dogs and vervet monkeys), plants, birds, reptiles, and insects. It's a great place to bring the kids or to familiarize yourself with the local wildlife before heading up to the game parks in northern KwaZulu-Natal. At one popular gallery, the KwaNunu Insect Arcade, giant insect replicas adorn the wall; another, the bird gallery, showcases a variety of stuffed birds, including flamingos, ostriches, eagles, and penguins. There are exciting, temporary art exhibitions next

7

door. ✉ *City Hall, 234 Anton Lembede [Smith] St., 1st fl., City Centre* ☎ *031/311–2256* 🖱 *Free* ⊘ *Closed Good Friday and Christmas Day.*

Francis Farewell Square. In the heart of Durban, the square (also known as Luthuli Square) is a lovely shady plaza bordered by some of the city's most historic buildings, including City Hall, the Central Post Office, and the Royal Hotel. Walkways lined with stately palms and flower beds crisscross the square and lead to monuments honoring some of Natal's important historic figures. The square stands on the site of the first European encampment in Natal, established by Francis Farewell and Henry Fynn in 1824 as a trading station to purchase ivory from the Zulus. A statue representing Peace honors the Durban volunteers who died during the Second South African War (1899–1902), also known as the Boer War or Anglo-Boer War. The Cenotaph, a large stone obelisk, commemorates the South African dead from the two world wars. In the same block is the Old Court House Museum, one of the city's oldest buildings. Apart from the historic attractions, it's an energetic, bustling part of the city center, with street stands selling inexpensive flowers, clothes, and food for the locals. You'll really feel the vibe of the city here. ⚠ **Pay attention to your valuables while walking in the square.** ✉ *Bounded by Anton Lembede [Smith], Dr. Pixley Kaseme [West], and Dorothy Nyembe [Gardiner] Sts. and the Church St. pedestrian mall, City Centre* ⊕ *www.heritagekzn.co.za.*

Tourist Junction. The city's principal tourist information outlet occupies Durban's old train station, an attractive brick building constructed in 1894 in Flemish Revival style. The "NGR" above the main entrance stands for Natal Government Railways. KwaZulu-Natal tourism authority also has a large office here, so it's a good place to pick up pamphlets and information about the city and province. ✉ *160 Monty Naicker Rd. [Pine St.], at Soldiers Way, City Centre* ☎ *031/322–4164* ⊕ *www.zulu.org.za.*

MORNINGSIDE

Dating back to Durban's colonial past, Morningside is an upscale suburb featuring prestigious residential properties such as the Dr. John L. Dube House, where the state president resides when in Durban. Below Jameson Park and Mitchell Park a slew of fashionable restaurants, boutique hotels, pubs, and clubs welcome patrons to trendy Florida Road.

WORTH NOTING

FAMILY **Mitchell Park.** The magnificent rose garden, colorful floral displays, and leafy lawns here are a real treat on a hot summer day. Attached to the park is a small zoo, named after Sir Charles Mitchell, an early governor of Natal. It was opened at the turn of the 19th century, and the Aldabra tortoises that were donated to the park in the early 1900s—now massive—are still in residence. There are also small mammals, reptiles, tropical fish, and birds in large aviaries. The park has a popular playground, and the leafy terrace of the park's Blue Zoo Restaurant is a great place for breakfast or a light lunch. ✉ *Bordered by Innes, Nimmo, and Ferndale Rds., and Havelock Crescent, Morningside* ☎ *031/303–2275* 🖱 *Gardens free; zoo R10 adults, R7 children.*

CLOSE UP

The Florida Road Strip

Florida Road leads a double life. By day, shoppers and tourists stroll up and down the tree-lined avenue, browsing art galleries and boutiques and indulging in lazy lunches; by night it transforms into a neon-lighted nightclub, where hordes of young and not-so-young revelers overflow from restaurants, lounges, and bars.

The thing that sets Florida Road apart is its historic character, with fine Edwardian architecture, well-preserved historic buildings, and half a dozen churches creating a timeless atmosphere that attracts the city's trendy set to meet and eat.

Since the strip is only about 0.8 km (less than ½ mile) long, you can enjoy it on foot in fine weather, but Mynah buses pass regularly, so there's transportation if you need it, and taxis are another option. The city has erected detailed and well-marked boards for walkers to navigate the city's most popular areas, including Florida Road and surrounds.

For a daytime visit, start in the morning at the top of the road where it meets Innes, opposite Mitchell Park, and work your way downhill, rather than battling an incline from the other end, where it intersects with Sandile Thusi (Argyle) Road.

Along the way, a bevy of coffee shops beckon for a light bite and good coffee, and clothing boutique Gorgeous adds a bit of glamour.

Chic home design outlet Ceclie & Boyd's showcases opulent style in a repurposed original home. After stopping there, head across the road to see the hundreds of locks that adorn the fence at Mandela Legacy Park.

Smokers will want to seek out the road's high-quality tobacconists selling imported cigars and cigarettes, of which Mojo Cairo Tobacconist, a coffee and cigar lounge, is the best.

There's an Apple Store, looking a little incongruous among the restaurants (though offering superb coffee at @ Coffee, inside), and Botica's leather bags and shoes woo passersby, but it's worth pressing on to the African Art Centre, which supports local artists and artisans and offers a good choice of unique and high-quality gifts and mementos. For more art, the Elizabeth Gordon Gallery showcases established South African artists in mixed media, and a small display of African artwork and wooden masks makes a stop at Art on Florida worthwhile.

Most of the numerous restaurants remain open all day, so there's no shortage of lunch venues. Spiga d'Oro, Cappello, or Butcher Boys are good choices.

As the sun goes down and Florida Road puts on its party face, restaurants begin filling up, and pubs and lounges—Dropkick Murphy's, Absolute, Velvet Lounge, Sinderella, The Keys on Florida, and Ice Bar & Grill—do a brisk trade. Find Italian fare at Mama's, Spiga d'Oro, Piatto, and Cappello; Afro-Portuguese at Mo-Zam-Bik; hot and spicy food at House of Curries; Mexican-inspired cuisine at Taco Zulu; and succulent steaks at Butcher Boys.

Should you choose to stay overnight on Florida Road, Quarters on Florida or the Benjamin are two classy boutique hotels at the lower end of the road, offering some respite from the hustle and bustle.

7

NEED A
BREAK

Love Coffee. On Lilian Ngoyi Road in Windemere, which some say is the "new" Florida Road, Love Coffee is your best bet for noncommercial, top-notch coffee in a veritable hole-in-the-wall, of the contemporary, well-designed kind. The bran muffins, rooibos cappuccino, fresh juice, packed salads, and brief breakfast menu come highly recommended. ⊠ *484 Lilian Ngoyi Rd., Morningside* ☎ *084/493–2802* ⊕ *www.lovecoffee.durban.*

BEACHFRONT

Of any place in Durban, the Beachfront most defines the city. Either you'll hate it for its commercial glitz, or love it for its endless activity. It extends for about 7 km (4½ miles) from uShaka Marine World, at the base of Durban Point, all the way past North Beach and the Suncoast Casino to Blue Lagoon, on the southern bank of the Umgeni River. The area received a R500-million upgrade that included creating a 65-foot-wide uninterrupted promenade and an additional pedestrian walkway linking the Beachfront to the Kings Park Sports Precinct and the Moses Mabhida Stadium. There are refreshment stands and places to relax every 980 feet. The section of Beachfront between South Beach and the Suncoast Casino is particularly safe, as police patrol often. It's lovely to take a stroll along here early or late in the day when it's less busy. Walk out onto one of the many piers and watch surfers tackling Durban's famous waves.

Depending on the weather, parts of the Beachfront can be quite busy, especially on weekends. There's always something to see, even in the early mornings, when people come to surf or jog before going to work.

TOP ATTRACTIONS

FAMILY

Fodor's Choice

★

uShaka Marine World. This aquatic complex combines the uShaka Sea World aquarium and the uShaka Wet 'n Wild water park. The largest aquarium in the Southern Hemisphere, it has a capacity of nearly 6 million gallons of water, more than four times the size of Cape Town's aquarium. Enter through the side of a giant ship and walk down several stories to enter a "labyrinth of shipwrecks"—a jumble of five different fake but highly realistic wrecks, from an early-20th-century passenger cruiser to a steamship. Within this labyrinth are massive tanks, housing more than 350 species of fish and other sea life and the biggest variety of sharks in the world, including ragged-tooth and Zambezi (bull sharks). Try to catch the divers hand-feeding fish and rays in the morning. The complex includes dolphin, penguin, and seal shows, and a variety of reptiles and amphibians populate the Dangerous Creatures exhibit.

The extensive water park comprises slides, pools, and about 10 different water rides. The intensity ranges from toddler-friendly to adrenaline junkie. Durban's moderate winter temperatures make it an attraction pretty much year-round, though it's especially popular in summer. ■TIP➔ Avoid on public holidays, and call ahead during winter when hours may change. ⊠ *1 King Shaka Ave., Beachfront* ☎ *031/328–8000* ⊕ *www.ushakamarineworld.co.za* 🎫 *Sea World R186; Wet 'n Wild R178; combo ticket R209. Dangerous Creatures Exhibit R55.*

WORTH NOTING

Suncoast Casino & Entertainment World. Part of the rejuvenation of Durban's Golden Mile, this casino is done in the art-deco style for which Durban is famous. Colorful lights make it a nighttime landmark, but it's established itself as a daytime hot spot as well. There are deck chairs beneath umbrellas on a grassy sundeck and a pretty beach. A paved walkway dotted with benches is a pleasant place to sit and watch cyclists, inline skaters, and joggers. Fairly regularly there's a band playing directly in front of the complex on weekends, with amphitheater-like stairs where you can sit and enjoy the show. ⊠ *20 Suncoast Blvd., Beachfront* ☎ *031/328–3000* ⊕ *www.suncoastcasino.co.za* ⊠ *Free.*

NEED A BREAK?

Milky Lane. Take respite from the summer sun and enjoy a cool treat at this ice-cream parlor, one of 20 or so restaurants, fast-food outlets, and coffee shops in the Suncoast Casino complex. Even in winter, the creamy ice-cream waffles and creative shakes are a welcome indulgence. ⊠ *Sun Coast Mall, Marine Parade, Shop L11* ☎ *031/332–1849* ⊕ *www.milkylane.co.za.*

BEREA

Durban's colonial past is very much evident in this suburb overlooking the city. Built on a ridge above the sea, it's characterized by old homes with wraparound balconies, boutique hotels, and strips of fashionable restaurants. Durban formed the coastal hub of the British Colony of Natal, declared in 1843 after the annexation of the former Boer Republic of Natalia. In 1910 Natal combined with three other colonies to form the Union of South Africa. One of the most sought-after addresses in the upscale Berea suburb is Musgrave Road. Tree-lined avenues feature luxury homes and apartment blocks interspersed with parks, schools, and sports clubs. The Musgrave Centre shopping hub is a major drawing card.

TOP ATTRACTIONS

Campbell Collections. Amid bustling, suburban Berea, Muckleneuk is a tranquil Cape Dutch home in a leafy garden. It was built in 1914 upon the retirement of Sir Marshall Campbell, a wealthy sugar baron and philanthropist who lived here with his wife, Ellen, and daughter, Killie. Today it is administered as a museum by the University of KwaZulu-Natal, and is furnished in similar style to when the Campbells lived here, with some excellent pieces of the family's Cape Dutch furniture. In addition to the **William Campbell Furniture Museum** (William was the son of Sir Marshall) there is an extensive collection of works by early European traveler artists, such as Angas, and paintings by prominent 20th-century black South African artists, including Gerard Bhengu, Daniel Rakgoathe, and Trevor Makhoba. The **Mashu Museum of Ethnology** displays the best collection of traditional Zulu glass beadwork in the country, plus African utensils, like tightly woven wicker beer pots, carvings, masks, pottery, and musical instruments. There are also weapons dating from the Bambatha Uprising of 1906, during which blacks in Natal rebelled against a poll tax and were brutally put down. Paintings of African tribespeople in traditional dress by artist Barbara Tyrrell, who traveled around South Africa from the 1940s to 1960s gathering valuable anthropological data, add vitality to the collection. The **Killie Campbell Africana Library,** open to the public, is a treasure trove of historical information on KwaZulu-Natal. It includes the papers of James Stuart, a magistrate and explorer during the early 20th century; the recorded oral tradition of hundreds of Zulus; a collection of pamphlets produced by the Colenso family in their struggle for the recognition of the rights of the Zulu people; and a good collection of 19th-century works relating to game hunting. ⊠ *220 Gladys Mazibuko [Marriott] Rd., at Stephen Dlamini [Essenwood] Rd., Berea* ☎ *031/207–3432, 031/260–1722* ⊕ *campbell.ukzn.ac.za* ✉ *Muckleneuk daily tours R20 (reservations essential); library free.*

WORTH NOTING

FAMILY **Durban Botanic Gardens.** Opposite the Greyville Racecourse, Africa's oldest surviving botanical garden is a delightful 150-year-old oasis of greenery interlaced with walking paths, fountains, and ponds. The gardens' orchid house and collection of rare cycads are renowned. The Garden of the Senses caters to the blind, and there's a lovely tea garden where you can take a load off your feet and settle back with a cup of hot tea and cakes—crumpets with "the works" are the best in town. On weekends it's a popular place for wedding photographs. During the Music at the Lake events, which happen on some Sundays, various musical acts perform in the gardens (additional fee) and people take along picnics. ⊠ *70 St. Thomas Rd., Berea* ☎ *031/309–9240* ⊕ *www.durbanbotanicgardens.org.za* ✉ *Free.*

INDIAN QUARTER

It's said that the largest Indian population outside of India resides in Durban, and the influence on the city is much in evidence, from the architecture to the cuisine. Under apartheid's Group Areas Act that designated where various race groups could live and own businesses, Indian traders set up shop on Dr. Yusuf Dadoo Street (Grey Street]. Here, at the Indian Quarter known in recent times as the Grey Street Casbah you can eat vegetarian curry, bargain for goods, buy fabrics, or just browse shops whose ownership spans generations, and soak up the Eastern vibe. ■**TIP→ You can find inexpensive freshly baked goods at street corners made by local bakers. Look out for filled doughnuts, queen cakes, and Madeira slices.** In addition, this part of town can be quite grubby, and in the midday summer heat it can get unpleasantly humid.

TOP ATTRACTIONS

Jumah Mosque. Built in 1927 in a style that combines Islamic and colonial features, this is the largest mosque in the Southern Hemisphere. Its colonnaded verandas, gold-domed minaret, and turrets give the surrounding streets much of their character. Tours (the only way to visit) are free and can be arranged through the Islamic Propagation Center, in a room at the entrance of the mosque, or through the Durban Tourism offices at Tourist Junction. ■**TIP→ If you plan to go inside, dress modestly: women should bring scarves to cover their heads and shoulders and skirts should extend to the ankles; men should not wear shorts.** It's a good idea to keep a *kikoi* (a lightweight African sarong readily available in local markets) in your bag to use as a skirt or scarf. Men can use them, too, to cover bare legs. You'll have to take off your shoes as you enter, so wear socks if you don't want to go barefoot. No tours are offered during Islamic holidays, including Ramadan, which varies but lasts a whole month in the latter part of the year. ⊠ *Dr Yusaf Dadoo [Grey] St. at Denis Hurley [Queen] St., Indian District* ☎ *031/304–1518* ✆ *Free.*

Madressa Arcade. There's a Kiplingesque quality to this thoroughfare, recalling the bazaars of the East. Built in 1927, it's little more than a narrow, winding alley perfumed by spices and thronged with traders plying a mishmash of drab goods. You can buy everything from cheap plastic trinkets to household utensils and recordings of Indian music. Bursts of color—from bright yellow fabric to dark red spices—create a refreshing and photogenic sight. You can buy striking costume jewelry that would cost three times as much at major shopping centers. Leave large bags and valuables at your hotel to browse unencumbered. ⊠ *Entrances on Denis Hurley [Queen] and Cathedral Sts., Indian District.*

Fodor's Choice **Muti Market.** For a uniquely African experience, hire a guide through
★ Durban Tourism at Tourist Junction or book a comprehensive tour that includes the adjacent markets with Markets of Warwick to take you to southern Africa's largest and most extensive *muti* (traditional medicine, pronounced moo-tee) market. Expect to find trestle tables filled with bunches of fresh and dried herbs, plant matter, and (controversially) animal bones, skin, and other parts, possibly including endangered species. The market also serves as a distinctive traditional-medicine facility, where *sangomas* (traditional healers) offer consultations to locals in a bustling, urban atmosphere. If you're feeling bold, you might wish to consult a sangoma on matters of health, wealth, or personal problems. ■ TIP→ Respect the traders and don't take photographs of people or the goods for sale, particularly any animal matter. If you are with a guide, ask them to negotiate picture-taking on your behalf, if you must— there's no guarantee though. ⊠ *Warwick Junction, Julius Nyerere Ave.*

Victoria Street Market. Masses of enormous fish and prawns lie tightly packed on beds of ice while vendors competing for your attention shout their respective prices. In the meat section, goat and sheep heads are stacked into neat piles (a spectacle for those with iron stomachs), and butchers slice and dice every cut of meat imaginable. The noise is deafening. In an adjacent building—where all the tour buses pull up—you'll discover a number of curio shops whose proprietors are willing to bargain over wood and stone carvings, beadwork, and basketry. You'll also find shops selling spices with creative names like Mother-in-Law's Revenge and Exterminator, recordings of African music, and Indian fabrics. The current structures stand on the site of an original, much-loved market, a ramshackle collection of wooden shacks that burned down during the years of Nationalist rule. ■ TIP→ Make a visit to Joe's Corner or to much-loved RA Moodley spice store, where Sanusha Moodliar, the shop's charismatic heir, will prepare you the freshest spice packs to take home. It's not cheap, but it's worth it. ⊠ *Denis Hurley [Queen] St. at Jospeh Nduli [Russell] St., Indian District* ☎ *031/306–4021.*

7

VICTORIA EMBANKMENT

Margaret Mncadi Avenue (formerly Victoria Embankment or the Esplanade) skirts Durban harbor from Maydon Wharf with its sugar terminal in the west, past Wilson's Wharf and the yacht mall to the docksides in the east.

TOP ATTRACTIONS

BAT Centre. This vibrant center (buoyed by a current contemporary revival) is abuzz with artists and musicians. Most days—and some nights—you can watch sculptors and painters at work, hear poetry readings, and see Africology (African teachings and traditions) dancers and musicians. The center is home to several small galleries that showcase the work of local artists. The center contains a coffee bar overlooking the bay and shops that sell an excellent selection of high-quality African crafts, including fabrics and ceramics. ⊠ *Small Craft Harbour, 45 Maritime Pl., Victoria Embankment* ☎ *031/332–0451* ⊕ *www.batcentre.co.za* ⊠ *Free.*

NEED A BREAK

Walk over to Wilson's Wharf in the nearby Maydon Wharf neighborhood, where you can have a cool cocktail or a meal on a deck overlooking the harbor at one of several restaurants ranging from an oyster bar to fast-food outlets.

GREYVILLE

Between the foot of the Berea ridge and the beachfront, this suburb of older homes and apartment blocks is dominated by the legendary Greyville Racecourse, where Durban's social highlight, the Durban July horse race, takes place. Greyville is bounded in the south by the Botanical Gardens and in the north by Morningside.

WORTH NOTING

Kendra Hall and Ekta Mandir. One of the most easily accessible and opulent temples in the city, the Kendra, next to the Durban Botanic Gardens, opened in 2001 after two years of intricate work by sculptors in India. The structure is unmistakably Eastern, with golden domes that tower above a palm tree supported by ornately decorated columns and arches that give the temple an East-meets-West look. Inside are two halls: a small one on the ground level and a larger one upstairs, which is a popular venue for weddings and leads to the temple. Huge statues of Hindu gods, notably Ganesha, Krishna, and Rama, are garlanded and clothed in exquisite Indian fabric. You can join an early morning or evening prayer daily at 6:30 am and 6:30 pm. ⊠ *5 John Zikhali [Sydenham] Rd., Greyville* ☎ *031/309–1824* ⊠ *Free.*

MAYDON WHARF

Maydon Wharf is an extensive cargo handling section of Durban's harbor, sandwiched between the suburb of Congella and the ocean. Its northern section features the Wilson's Wharf entertainment node, with a number of restaurants and the Catalina Theatre.

WORTH NOTING

S. A. Sugar Terminal. Much of Durban's early economy was built on the sugar industry and the backs of forced labor, both local and indentured, and even today the hills and fields around the city and along the north and south coasts are covered with sugarcane. It's not surprising then that Durban's Sugar Terminal is the largest in southern Africa and one

Bunny Chow

Contrary to what you may think, bunny chow is not about lettuce and carrots. This Durban specialty, prevalent in the Indian Quarter and around town, is a hollowed-out loaf of bread traditionally filled with bean, vegetable, chicken, or mutton curry. Though historical sources can't confirm it, the dish is said to have been popularized in the late 1930s and 1940s during apartheid, when blacks were prohibited from entering a restaurant or lingering at the tables. Many credit Kapitan's Restaurant, in the city center, as the first to sell a bunny chow, though Patel's Vegetarian Refreshment Room may contest that. Another theory supports the story that bunny chow is derived from the term "Bania" or "Baniya," used to describe the Gujarati merchants who ran the Indian shops like Kapitans and Patels. Others postulate that the bunny chow was a convenience meal already developed by home cooks, and made popular by the traders who sold it cheaply. Whatever the true history, the bunny chow has found a permanent and loving home in Durban.

Good bunnies can be found at several eateries across the city. Try **Hollywood Bets** for outstanding broad beans and mutton curry bunnies. Ignore the betting environment—there's an air-conditioned interior, covered deck, and Bunny Bar for takeaways. **Patel Vegetarian**

Refreshment Room, which has been satisfying customers since 1912; and **Capsicum at Britannia Hotel**, an incredibly busy restaurant and take-away business supported by locals.

Capsicum at Britannia Hotel. The tables are somewhat grimy and the red interior is unattractive, yet the clientele here remains loyal. You can get a wide range of curries and "exotic" bunnies, with curry fillings like tripe, trotters, and the more regular sugar beans, mutton, and chicken curries. ✉ *Britannia Hotel, 1299 Umgeni Rd.* ☎ *031/303–2266* ⊕ *www. hotelbrits.co.za.*

Hollywood Bets. Though you'll be surrounded by big screens broadcasting live horse races and games, don't be put off. The air-conditioned restaurant, with a large covered deck and dedicated Bunny Bar for take-out, serves up some of the best bunny chow in Durban. ✉ *126 Intersite Ave.* ☎ *031/263–2073* ⊕ *www.hollywoodbets.net.*

Patel's Vegetarian Refreshment Room. Founded in 1912, this place has built a family legacy of good traditional Indian food. Serving only vegetarian dishes in the form of curries, the restaurant is run by Mr Manilal Patel, now in his late 70s, who lives in the apartment above the shop, and gets up around 2 am each day to start the day's prep. ✉ *202 Dr Yusuf Dadoo St.* ☎ *031/306–1774.*

7

of the most advanced in the world. A short video presentation provides background to the sugar industry, and then you'll be taken on an educational tour of the terminal. Together, the tour and video presentation take 45 minutes. It's extraordinary to see the terminal's three enormous silos piled high to the domed ceiling with tons of raw sugar. The architectural design of the silos has been patented and used in other parts of the world. ✉ *25 Leuchars Rd., Maydon Wharf* ☎ *031/365–8100, 031/365–8100* ⊒ *R20* ⚓ *Reservations essential.*

Zack's. This popular spot overlooks the Durban harbor and often hosts live music. It serves breakfast until late, as well as lunch and dinner. ⊠ *Wilson's Wharf, 14 Boatman's Rd., Shop 23, Maydon Wharf* ☎ *031/305–1677.*

Wilson's Wharf. On the edge of the harbor, this pleasant, privately developed section of waterfront is a lovely place to while away a few hours, soaking up the atmosphere, admiring the harbor view, and maybe having a meal or drink at one of the open-air restaurants on the expansive wooden deck. In addition to restaurants and fast-food outlets, there are boat rentals, sightseeing cruises, and a market with stands selling local crafts or cheaper trinkets from India and China. ⊠ *Boatman's Rd., Maydon Wharf* ☎ *031/907–8968.*

CHATSWORTH

The predominantly Indian inner-city suburb of Chatsworth is a vibrant, cosmopolitan mix of old and new architecture complemented by myriad home-based businesses and a couple of large shopping malls. It comprises seven residential wards along the Higginson Highway, bounded to the north by the Umhlatuzana River and to the south by the Umlaas River. It's home to one of South Africa's most spectacular Hare Krishna temples.

WORTH NOTING

Hare Krishna Temple of Understanding. This magnificent lotus-shaped temple, opened in 1985, is at the heart of activities run by the city's International Society for Krishna Consciousness. Gold-tinted windows add a glow to the interior, floored with imported Italian marble and intricate artwork. Colorful laser drawings depicting the life of the Hindu god Krishna cover the ceiling, and statues of Krishna and his consort Radha are elaborately dressed in traditional Indian attire. Love fests and traditional singing and dancing take place on Sunday (1:30–5) and all are welcome. You need to remove your shoes when entering the temple. ⊠ *50 Bhaktivedanta Swami Circle, Unit 5, Chatsworth* ☎ *031/403–3328* ⊕ *www.iskcondurban.net* ⊠ *Free.*

Govinda's Pure Vegetarian Restaurant. This is an inexpensive yet excellent vegetarian restaurant catering to Hare Krishna devotees, who do not use onions, garlic, or mushrooms in their food. The traditional Indian rice dish biryani (breyani as it's known locally) is a favorite. ⊠ *Hare Krishna Temple of Understanding, 50 Bhaktivedanta Swami Circle, Unit 5, Chatsworth* ☎ *031/403–4600.*

DURBAN NORTH AND GLENASHLEY

Along the eastern coastline north of the Umgeni River, you'll find the well-established middle- to upper-income suburb of Durban North, the highlight of which is the superb Umgeni River Bird Park. One of the city's older suburbs, Glenashley sits between Durban North and La Lucia. Palatial properties line its beachfront, whereas more modest yet upscale homes fill the inland area. The Ruth First Highway (M4) connects these suburbs southward to the city and northward to the more upscale Umhlanga Rocks region.

TOP ATTRACTIONS

FAMILY **Umgeni River Bird Park.** Ranked among the world's best, this bird park shelters beneath high cliffs next to the Umgeni River and has various walk-through aviaries containing more than 800 birds. The variety of birds, both exotic and indigenous, is astonishing. You'll be able to take close-up photographs of macaws, giant Asian hornbills, toucans, pheasants, flamingos, and three crane species, including the blue crane, South Africa's national bird. Try to time your visit to take in the free-flight bird show, which is a delight for both children and adults. Drinks and light lunches are available at the park's kiosk. ⊠ *490 Riverside Rd., off the M4, Durban North* ☎ *031/579–4600* ⊕ *www.umgeniriverbirdpark.co.za* ⊠ *R55.*

GLENWOOD

Dotted with parks, schools, churches, and sports clubs, Glenwood is a quiet family suburb. Helen Joseph Road is the social hub, where restaurants, bistros, pubs, and clubs attract hordes of partygoers on weekends.

WORTH NOTING

Fodor's Choice **KwaZulu-Natal Society of Arts Gallery.** This arts complex, known as
★ KZNSA, houses four exhibition areas, in addition to a crafts shop, the Durban Center for Photography, and a classy open-air restaurant. The center does not have a particular focus but is committed to promoting emerging talent in the province. Exhibition media ranges from photos and paintings to video installations. The center's clean architectural lines and leafy setting, with ever-changing colorful murals on the exterior, make this a popular venue with Durban's trendy set, and it's a lovely place to cool off after a hot morning touring the town. The gallery and crafts shop support and promote local art, so it's worth seeking out for tasteful souvenirs. Local musicians are given a platform fairly regularly on Friday nights. The daytime-only restaurant is a wonderful child-friendly pit stop. ⊠ *166 Bulwer Rd., Glenwood* ☎ *031/277–1700* ⊕ *www.kznsagallery.co.za* ⊠ *Free.*

CATO MANOR

This neighborhood came about when black South Africans settled in the area during the 1920s, renting land from Indian landlords. The area saw race riots in the 1950s and 1960s when squatters and police clashed, but since the 1980s new infrastructure and urban development has created a more formal, working-class suburb with schools, a market, and a community center.

WORTH NOTING

Umbilo Shree Ambalavaanar Alayam Temple. One of Durban's most spectacular Hindu shrines is in Cato Manor. The temple's facade is adorned with brightly painted representations of the Hindu gods, notably Ganesha, Shiva, and Vishnu. The magnificent doors leading to the cellar were salvaged from a temple built in 1875 on the banks of the Umbilo River and subsequently destroyed by floods. The culmination of a long fast results in the carrying of "kavadi," a sacrifice in honor of Lord Murugan, held annually in March, where unshod fire walkers cross beds of burning, glowing coals. There are no set visiting hours. The kavadi-carrying devotees, often adorned in pins and needles walking in a deeply meditative state known as "trance," draw huge crowds of spectators and well-wishers. If the temple is open you'll be welcome to go inside; if not, the exterior of the building is still worth seeing. ⊠ *890 Bellair Rd., Cato Manor ⚓ Take the M13 (from Leopold St.) out of the city; at the major fork in road after Westridge Park and the high school, veer left onto Bellair Rd.* ☎ *031/261–6509* ✉ *Free.*

UMHLANGA

Umhlanga's sophisticated charm and lovely beaches have entrenched it as one of the most sought-after vacation destinations for locals and foreigners, and it has many of Durban's top hotels. Also known as Umhlanga Rocks (meaning "Place of the Reeds"), this area used to be a small vacation village, but Durban's northward sprawl has incorporated it into a popular and upscale residential and business suburb, much like Sandton is to downtown Johannesburg. To the north are the nicest sea views; to the south is Umhlanga's lighthouse.

TOP ATTRACTIONS

FAMILY **Gateway Theatre of Shopping.** The largest mall in the Southern Hemisphere, Gateway has been designed to let in natural light and is surprisingly easy to navigate. Shopping ranges from surfing paraphernalia and imported and local fashions to electronics, Indian spices, and designer wedding frocks. Gateway also has a large variety of entertainment options including an IMAX theater and the art-nouveau Barnyard Theatre, which hosts live music compilation shows in an informal "barn" environment. The Wave House has various levels of artificially generated waves for surfing and waterslides, and there's a funfair, karting track, and sports arena. ⊠ *New Town Centre, 1 Palm Bd., Umhlanga* ☎ *031/514–0500* ⊕ *www.gatewayworld.co.za.*

FAMILY **KwaZulu-Natal Sharks Board.** Most of the popular bathing beaches in KwaZulu-Natal are protected by shark nets maintained by this shark-research institute, the world's foremost. Each day, weather permitting, crews in ski boats check the nets, releasing healthy sharks back into the ocean and bringing dead ones back to the institute, where they are dissected and studied. One-hour tours are offered, including a shark dissection (sharks' stomachs have included such surprising objects as a boot, a tin can, and a car license plate!) and an enjoyable and fascinating audiovisual presentation on sharks and shark nets. An exhibit area and good curio shop are also here. You can join the early morning trip from Durban harbor to watch the staff service the shark nets off Durban's Golden Mile. Depending on the season, you will more than likely see dolphins and whales close at hand. Booking is essential for trips to the shark nets, and a minimum of six people is required; no one under age six is allowed. ■TIP→ **Book well in advance for this—it may turn out to be a highlight of your trip.** ⊠ *1a Herrwood Dr., Umhlanga* ☎ *031/566–0400* ⊕ *www.shark.co.za* ✉ *Presentation R50, boat trips R350.*

WORTH NOTING

Hawaan Forest. This 114-acre coastal forest grows on a dune that dates back 18,000 years and has 175 species of indigenous trees, fungi (during wet months), and various species of birds. Guided walks take two to three hours and are conducted on the first Saturday of every month (except in January or February), but if you call ahead you may be

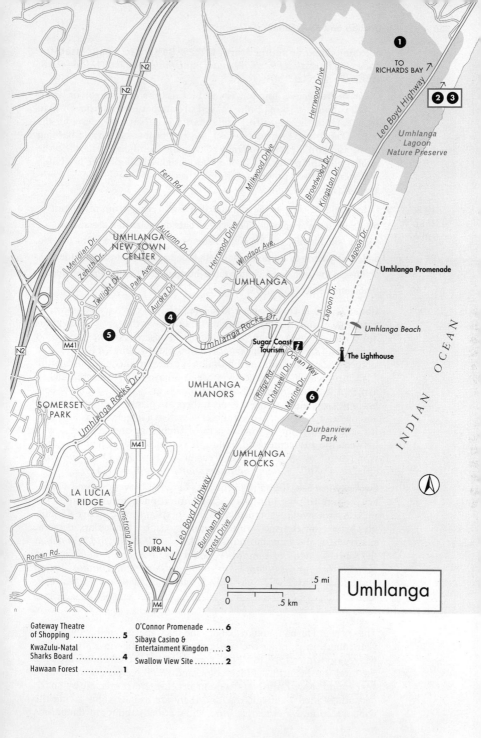

TO
RICHARDS BAY

1

2 3

Leo Boyd Highway

Umhlanga
Lagoon
Nature Preserve

Herwood Drive

Broadwood Dr.

Kingston Dr.

Milkwood Drive

Fern Rd.

Autumn Dr.

Herwood Drive

Windsor Ave.

Lagoon Dr.

Umhlanga Promenade

Meridian Dr.
Zenith Dr.
Twilight Dr.
Park Ave.
Aurora Dr.

UMHLANGA
NEW TOWN
CENTER

UMHLANGA

Lagoon Dr.

4

5

Umhlanga Rocks Dr.

⚓ *Umhlanga Beach*

Sugar Coast
Tourism 🛈

Ridge Rd.
Chartwell Dr.
Ocean Way

🗼 **The Lighthouse**

Marine Dr.

6

M41

Umhlanga Rocks Dr.

UMHLANGA
MANORS

Durbanview
Park

I N D I A N   O C E A N

SOMERSET
PARK

N2

M41

UMHLANGA
ROCKS

LA LUCIA
RIDGE

Armstrong Ave.

Leo Boyd Highway

Burnham Drive

Forest Drive

Ronan Rd.

TO
DURBAN

M4

0		.5 mi
0		.5 km

Umhlanga

accommodated at another time. ■**TIP→ Be sure to wear closed-toe shoes.** ✉ *Portland Dr. at Herald Dr., Umhlanga* ☎ *031/566–4018, 083/275–2216* ▨ *R30.*

FAMILY **O'Connor Promenade.** Join tourists and locals for a gentle stroll or vigorous run along the 3-km (2-mile) paved stretch that reaches from Durban View Park in the south to Umhlanga Lagoon Nature Reserve in the north. This is a great way to check out the local coastline and bathing areas, and you'll pass Umhlanga's landmark lighthouse (closed to the public) and the pier, with steel arches designed to look like a whale's skeleton. It's also known as the Umlhanga Rocks Promenade. ✉ *Umhlanga Beach, Umhlanga.*

NEED A BREAK

La Spiaggia. As close to the Indian Ocean as you can get, this restaurant overlooking the main bathing beach has outside tables that are always packed with families sipping milk shakes or friends sharing a bottle of wine and having a bite to eat off a menu with broad appeal. Not the best food on offer in the area, but an unbeatable location. ✉ *O'Connor Promenade, Umhlanga* ☎ *031/561–6499.*

Sibaya Casino & Entertainment Kingdom. Sibaya is expansive—in size, appearance, and number of activities—but is worth seeing for its grandiose, Zulu-themed design. The buildings themselves, for example, echo a giant and opulent Zulu *kraal* (compound/dwelling). Huge bronze statues of Zulu warriors and buffaloes at the entrance provide a truly African welcome. Wherever you are at Sibaya—all 48 hectares (119 acres) of it—a breathtaking view of the ocean is only a window or a balcony away. As you might expect, there are plenty of dining options, and there's a 36-room, five-star hotel as well as a lodge with 118 rooms. It's quite a way out of town, north of Umhlanga and about halfway between the city center and Ballito. If you have only a few days, you won't want to spent them at a casino. ✉ *1 Sibaya Dr., Umhlanga* ☎ *031/580–5000* ⊕ *www.suninternational.com/sibaya* ▨ *Free.*

FAMILY **Swallow View Site.** If you're in the area between November and February, be sure to take in this amazing natural phenomenon that sees 3 million barn swallows returning to their nests at sunset. Arrive 45 minutes before sunset armed with something to sit on, binoculars, camera, sundowners, and some mosquito repellent. ✉ *Mt. Moreland, Umhlanga* ✛ *From N2 take the Umdloti/Verulam off-ramp and follow signs to Verulam Dr. for less than 1 km (600 yards), turn at Umdloti Estate and follow signs* ☎ *031/568–1557* ⊕ *www.barnswallow.co.za* ▨ *R10.*

BEACHES

The sea near Durban, unlike that around the Cape, is comfortably warm year-round: in summer the water temperature can top 27°C (80°F), whereas in winter 19°C (65°F) it's considered cold. The beaches are safe, the sand is a beautiful golden color, and you'll see people swimming year-round. KwaZulu-Natal's main beaches are protected by shark nets and staffed by lifeguards, and there are usually signs giving the wind direction, water temperature, and warnings about any dangerous swimming conditions. Directly in front of uShaka Marine World, **uShaka Beach** is an attractive public beach. The **Golden Mile,** stretching from South Beach all the way to Snake Park Beach, is packed with people who enjoy the waterslides, singles' bars, and fast-food joints. A little farther north are the **Umhlanga beaches,** and on the opposite side of the bay are the less commercialized but also less accessible and safe beaches on **Durban's Bluff.** Another pretty beach and coastal walk, just north of the **Umhlanga Lagoon,** leads to miles of near-empty beaches backed by virgin bush. You should not walk alone on deserted beaches or carry jewelry, phones, or cameras, and never walk the beaches at night.

■TIP➜ A great way to see Durban's beaches is by bicycle.

BEREA
Bluff Beaches. South of Durban's harbor, these beaches offer a less crowded alternative to the more central city beaches, although it can get rough at times, with big waves. Brighton Beach and Anstey's Beach are popular surf spots, with southerly surf swells breaking on the rocky reef below. Cave Rock at low tide is a paradise for anyone who enjoys exploring rock pools; at high tide it's a wave ride for the fearless. **Amenities:** lifeguards. **Best for:** surfing; swimming. ⊠ *Marine Dr., Berea.*

UMHALANGA
Umhlanga Beaches. Some of the country's finest beaches are on this stretch of the coast, and they can be less crowded than those in central Durban. Safe and clean—Umhlanga Rocks beach has a Blue Flag award—the beaches are easily accessed via pathways from parking lots down to a promenade skirting the busy beachfront. Vacation apartments and premier hotels like the Oyster Box, Cabanas, and Beverly Hills line this paved walkway southward to Umhlanga's famous lighthouse. If you're driving here, arrive early at peak times so you'll have a better chance of finding a parking spot. **Amenities:** food and drink; parking. **Best for:** jogging; sunrise; surfing; swimming; walking. ⊠ *Lighthouse Rd. or Marine Dr., Umhlanga.*

BEACHFRONT
Golden Mile. From Vetch's Pier in the south to Suncoast in the north, the Golden Mile is a series of golden, sandy beaches divided by piers. Beaches are cleaned regularly, and each has a beach report board warning of bluebottles, jellyfish, strong currents, or dangerous conditions. Bodyboarders favor North Beach, and New Pier and Bay are preferred surfing spots. Swimmers should remain between the flags or beacons and away from the sides of piers, where strong currents wash straight out to sea. Chairs and umbrellas can be rented. Just off the sand, popular beachfront hotels like the Edward, Blue Waters, Elangeni, Belaire, Tropicana, and Garden Court jostle for visitors' favor. Rent a bicycle, Segway, or go-kart from a few points along the beachfront and fully enjoy the promenade when you tire of sunbathing. **Amenities:** food and drink; lifeguards; parking; showers; toilets. **Best for:** surfing; swimming. ⊠ *O. R. Tambo Parade, Beachfront.*

uShaka Beach. In front of uShaka Marine World aquarium and water theme park this beach has small waves and calm conditions, making it great for families. Sand sculptors are often here, too, creating intricate

7

artwork. Grassy banks offer an alternative to the sand (which isn't always as clean as the more central beaches), and the local surf school is busy all year round. A block inland, in the rejuvenated Point area, is the trendy Docklands hotel. **Amenities:** parking. **Best for:** swimming; walking. ✉ *Escombe Terr., Beachfront.*

WHERE TO EAT

The dining scene in Durban is small but on par with global trends, so expect to find a little of everything at a very good price. Durban offers some superb dining options, provided you eat to its strengths. Thanks to a huge Indian population, it has some of the best curry restaurants in the country, and the Italian food options are numerous at various price points.

Durbanites eat lunch and dinner relatively early because they're early risers, particularly in summer, when it's light soon after 4. They're also generally casual dressers—you'll rarely need a jacket and tie, and jeans and tanks are de rigueur. ■ **TIP→ Durban North's Mackeurtan Avenue has transformed into a restaurant strip that gives the famed Florida Road a run for its money.**

For more information on South Africa food, see Flavors of South Africa in Chapter 1.

CITY CENTER

$$$ AFRICAN

🍴 **Big Easy Wine bar + Grill Durban by Ernie Els.** Inside the dramatically revamped Hilton Hotel in Durban's CBD, this wine bar and grill is frequented by suited business folk and vacationers who choose to stay centrally. A distinctly South African menu—think smoked snoek (a local barracuda) and corn cakes, oxtail marrow fritters, duck curry, and a *braai* (barbecue) sharing platter—and a masterful wine list, including Ernie Els's signature wines, round the offering. **Known for:** business traveler vibe; elegant setting; comprehensive wine list. [$] *Average main: R200* ✉ *12–14 Walnut Rd.* ☎ *031/336–8166* 🌐 *www.bigeasydurban.co.za.*

$$$ ITALIAN

🍴 **Roma Revolving.** In business since 1973, this slowly revolving restaurant, which takes about an hour to do one full rotation, offers what has to be the most spectacular views of the city, especially the harbor. It's run by the original Italian owners, and the extensive menu runs the gamut from pasta to seafood. **Known for:** kitschy setting; old-school vibe; special-occasion dinners. [$] *Average main: R190* ✉ *John Ross House, Margaret Mncadi Ave., 32nd fl., City Centre* ☎ *031/337–6707* 🌐 *www.roma.co.za* ⏲ *Closed Sun. No lunch Mon.–Thurs.*

MORNINGSIDE

$$ SOUTH INDIAN

Fodor's Choice ★

🍴 **Mali's Indian Restaurant.** An unexpected find within a residential section of the Morningside neighborhood, Mali's is loved by chefs and locals for its broad Indian menu serving specialities from the North and South, like steamed idli with sambar, masala dosai, and vadai—dishes you'll be hard-pressed to find in many Indian eateries. While the biryanis and tandoori dishes are very good in this homey restaurant with its cozy dining room, the Chinese-influenced offerings like the deep-fried mushroom Manchurian and Szechuan chicken noodles have a loyal following.

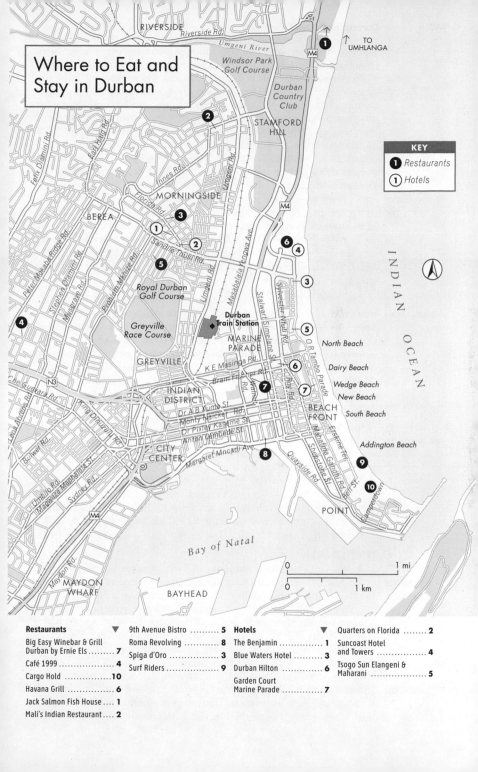

Where to Eat and Stay in Durban

KEY

🔵 *Restaurants*
① *Hotels*

Restaurants ▼

Big Easy Winebar & Grill
Durban by Ernie Els **7**
Café 1999 .... **4**
Cargo Hold **10**
Havana Grill **6**
Jack Salmon Fish House **1**
Mali's Indian Restaurant **2**

9th Avenue Bistro **5**
Roma Revolving **8**
Spiga d'Oro **3**
Surf Riders **9**

Hotels ▼

The Benjamin **1**
Blue Waters Hotel **3**
Durban Hilton **6**
Garden Court
Marine Parade **7**

Quarters on Florida **2**
Suncoast Hotel
and Towers **4**
Tsogo Sun Elangeni &
Maharani **5**

Known for: Chettinad chicken; unique Indian flavors; mango lassi. [$] *Average main: R100* ✉ *77 Smiso Nkwanyana Rd.* ☎ *031/312–8535.*

$$$ ECLECTIC
🍴 **9th Avenue Bistro.** This is one of few upmarket restaurants in the city to indulge in a six-course tasting menu, though the à la carte options are plentiful, too. Think gin-cured salmon, creamy shellfish orzo, and roast lamb rump—classics with a twist, done perfectly. **Known for:** international and local wine list; loyal customers; fine dining. [$] *Average main: R175* ✉ *Avonmore Centre, Shop 2, 9th Ave., Morningside* ☎ *031/312–9134* 🌐 *www.9thavenuebistro.co.za* 🕒 *Closed Sun. No lunch Mon. and Sat.*

$ ITALIAN Fodor's Choice ★
🍴 **Spiga d'Oro.** On the ever-popular Florida Road, Spiga is something of a Durban institution, and it certainly represents the attitude and overall feeling of Durban—unpretentious with an animated atmosphere that makes diners feel part of the crowd. The Italian menu is not always classical in its interpretation, but you can count on it being delicious and a good value (pasta dishes come in medium or large portions). **Known for:** buzzy atmosphere; bruschetta di pomodoro; seafood pasta. [$] *Average main: R80* ✉ *200 Florida Rd., Morningside* ☎ *031/303–9511* 🌐 *www.spiga.co.za.*

BEREA

$$$ MEDITERRANEAN
🍴 **Café 1999.** Trendy as this restaurant may be, the food is infinitely more memorable than the shopping center setting. Let your fork and fingers wander between dishes like duck and date samosas; plum-glazed duck breast with pancetta, pea risotto, and white truffle oil; or the slow-roasted tomato tart. **Known for:** tapas-style meals; triple chocolate brownies. [$] *Average main: R170* ✉ *Silvervause Centre, Shop 2, 117 Vause Rd., Musgrave* ☎ *031/202–3406* 🌐 *www.cafe1999.co.za* 🕒 *Closed Sun. No lunch Sat.*

DURBAN NORTH AND GLENASHLEY

$$ SOUTH AFRICAN
🍴 **Jack Salmon Fish House.** A short drive north of the city, the small suburb of Glenashley has an elevated position that offers diners a pleasant sea view, but this restaurant's fresh seafood, prepared in unique and traditional ways, is the drawing card, with excellent service keeping the place busy during lunch and dinner. For starters, opt for the sushi or the Falkland Island calamari tubes stuffed with prawns and peri-peri dressing and then char-grilled. **Known for:** fresh seafood; excellent view; panna cotta. [$] *Average main: R110* ✉ *Glenore Centre, Shop 15, 1 Aubrey Dr., Glenashley* ☎ *031/572–3664* 🌐 *www.jacksalmon.co.za.*

UMHLANGA

$$$ FRENCH Fodor's Choice ★
🍴 **Ile Maurice.** This restaurant is one of Umhlanga's culinary gems, with a soft-hued interior and pretty veranda that overlooks the Umhlanga beach. On the menu you'll find classic French Mauritian fare such as soupe de poisson à la Mauricienne and Creole-style octopus curry. **Known for:** excellent wine list; fresh seafood; French-inspired island cuisine. [$] *Average main: R200* ✉ *9 McCausland Crescent, Umhlanga* ☎ *031/561–7609* 🌐 *www.ilemauricerestaurant.co.za* 🕒 *Closed Mon. (but open Mon. in Dec.)* 👔 *Jacket required.*

$$ STEAKHOUSE
🍴 **Little Havana.** This award-winning steak house has a modern dining room—expect well-dressed diners on romantic dates or small business teams strategizing over lunch. The steaks are unmissable (try the chimichurri sirloin), though the line fish with coconut and lime and the

caponata gnocchi will satisfy those without carnivorous tastes. **Known for:** local wine list; Cuban vibe; excellent steaks. $ *Average main: R150* ⊠ *Granada Sq., 16 Chartwell Dr.* ☎ *031/561–7589, 081/393–8205* ⊕ *www.littlehavana.co.za.*

$$
ITALIAN
Fodor'sChoice
★

✕ **Old Town Italy.** This chic outpost of Old Town Italy is a cleaned-up, thoroughly modern version of an old-fashioned Italian delicatessen, with a restaurant serving simple, wholesome fare, that seats patrons indoors and outside on the pavement—a favorite in warm weather. Order a platter of the finest Italian salumi or cheeses; heartier appetites may look to the lemon caper chicken or steak Florentine. **Known for:** Italian wines; inviting decor. $ *Average main: R150* ⊠ *Meridian Park, 39 Meridian Dr.* ☎ *031/566–5008* ⊕ *www.oldtown.co.za.*

$$
MEDITERRANEAN

✕ **Olive & Oil.** You can't go wrong with the fantastic and well-priced Mediterranean-inspired fare here. The best way to start your meal is with a meze platter to share before moving on to main courses like calamari, steaks, pastas with Sicilian and Moroccan flavors, and the easy-on-the-budget pizzas. **Known for:** outdoor seating; family-friendly setting; excellent value. $ *Average main: R150* ⊠ *Chartwell Centre, Shop 19, 15 Chartwell Dr., Umhlanga* ☎ *031/561–2618* ⊕ *oliveandoil. co.za/branches/umhlanga.*

$$
TAPAS

✕ **Pintxada.** This fun, modern space with eye-catching retro tiles and splashes of yellow has a custom grill brought from France that churns out succulent rotisserie chicken and chorizo. Try the *boquerones* (white anchovies) and roasted peppers on crostini, the de-boned pork ribs, and the *churrasco* (sirloin steak). **Known for:** jovial atmosphere; excellent cocktails; Mediterranean fare. $ *Average main: R150* ⊠ *Granada Sq. (above Little Havana), 16 Chartwell Dr.* ☎ *082/688–1310 They use whatsapp for reservations; add them to your contacts first* ⊕ *www. pintxada.co.za.*

BEACHFRONT

$$$
SEAFOOD

✕ **Cargo Hold.** You might need to book several weeks in advance to secure a table next to the shark tank here, but if you do it'll be one of your most memorable dining experiences. Enjoy a carpaccio of smoked ostrich or tomato veloute—while massive ragged-tooth sharks drift right by your table and sand sharks stir up the sandy bottom. **Known for:** unique setting; shipwreck decor; tourists. $ *Average main: R165* ⊠ *uShaka Marine World, 1 Bell St., Beachfront* ☎ *031/328–8065* ⊕ *www.ushakamarineworld.co.za/restaurants/cargo-hold-promenade.*

$$$
SOUTH AFRICAN

✕ **Havana Grill.** Attention to detail and freshly prepared, quality food combine to make this one of Durban's finest restaurants serving steak—prepared and aged in the in-house butchery—and seafood. It offers spectacular sea vistas (ask for a table with a view when making your reservation) and a chic interior, with white leather-upholstered chairs, wall-length couches, and antelope horns on the walls. **Known for:** fresh seafood; local wine list. $ *Average main: R180* ⊠ *Suncoast Casino & Entertainment World, Shop 42, 20 Suncoast Blvd., Beachfront* ☎ *031/337–1305* ⊕ *www.havanagrill.co.za* ☞ *Parents with young children are requested to make sure little ones are on their best behavior.*

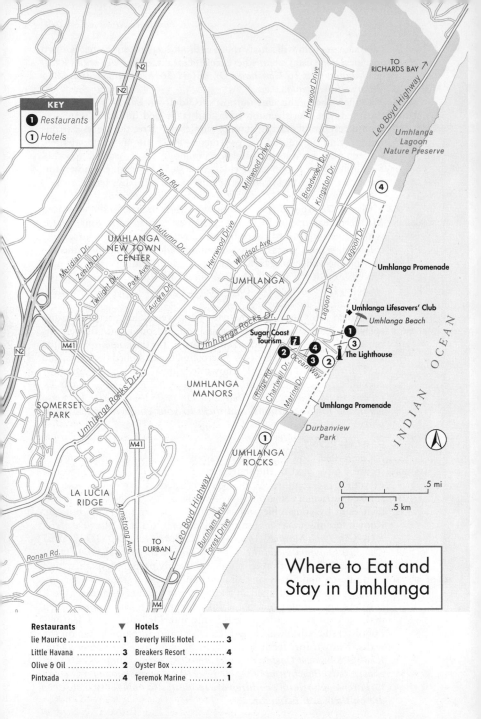

Where to Eat and Stay in Umhlanga

$ ✕ **Surf Riders.** Surf Riders is a welcome, fun addition to the beachfront
BURGER   serving a solid menu of all-day breakfasts (they close around 5 pm),
FAMILY   burgers, and freshly pressed juices. Try the sunrise smoothie with orange
Fodor's Choice   juice, mint, plain yogurt, and honey and one of several eggs Benedict
★   combos—portions are small, made with high-quality ingredients, and
hit the spot. **Known for:** long lines on weekends; laid-back vibe. $ *Average main: R80* ⊠ *South Beach, 17 Erskine Terr.* ☎ *031/825–8528, 062/747–7037.*

WHERE TO STAY

Many of Durban's main hotels lie along the Golden Mile, but there are some wonderful boutique hotels and bed-and-breakfasts (especially in Berea, Morningside, and Umhlanga) that offer a more personalized experience.

■**TIP**→ **Prices, especially along the coast, tend to rise with the summer heat.**

CITY CENTER

$ 🏨 **Durban Hilton.** This massive luxury hotel adjacent to the International
HOTEL   Convention Centre, that underwent a multimillion-rand face-lift in
Fodor's Choice   2016, is a short taxi ride from the city center and beachfront and is
★   favored by businesspeople and conference-goers. **Pros:** close to convention center; good gym; newly refurbished with luxurious touches. **Cons:** not within walking distance of restaurants; large and formal; no personal service. $ *Rooms from: R1480* ⊠ *12–14 Walnut Rd., City Centre* ☎ *031/336–8100* ⊕ *www.hilton.com* ⇆ *343 rooms* ⦿ *Breakfast.*

MORNINGSIDE

$$ 🏨 **The Benjamin.** In one of Durban's transformed historic buildings, this
HOTEL   small hotel offers excellent value, and its location on trendy Florida Road is ideal for restaurants and nightlife and only a short distance from the city center and beaches. **Pros:** within walking distance to restaurants; covered swimming pool; approximately five minutes from beaches and city center. **Cons:** limited secure parking; no on-site restaurant for lunch or dinner; no elevator. $ *Rooms from: R1655* ⊠ *141 Florida Rd., Morningside* ☎ *031/303–4233* ⊕ *www.benjamin.co.za* ⇆ *41 rooms* ⦿ *Breakfast.*

$$ 🏨 **Quarters on Florida.** Four converted Victorian homes comprise the city's
HOTEL   most intimate boutique hotel, a contemporary European-style property that's been reinvented with a colonial African makeover. **Pros:** tasteful rooms; on-site restaurants; close to restaurants and nightlife of Florida Road. **Cons:** despite efforts, street-facing rooms are noisy; no pool; limited off-street parking. $ *Rooms from: R1750* ⊠ *101 Florida Rd., Morningside* ☎ *031/303–5246* ⊕ *www.quarters.co.za* ⇆ *25 rooms* ⦿ *Breakfast.*

UMHLANGA

$$$$ 🏨 **Beverly Hills Hotel.** In a high-rise building right on the beach, this
HOTEL   upscale hotel is popular with both vacationers and businesspeople and has a long-standing reputation for gracious hospitality. **Pros:** unbeatable sea views; hotel has its own demarcated piece of beach with lounge chairs; every room gets a free bottle of wine and snacks. **Cons:** some

7

rooms and many of the bathrooms are smaller than you might expect; prices increase in-season; a dedicated local crowd may give this hotel a cliquey feel. $ *Rooms from: R4580* ✉ *2 Lighthouse Rd., Umhlanga* ☎ *031/561–2211* ⊕ *www.tsogosunhotels.com/deluxe/beverly-hills-hotel* � *89 rooms* ❍ *Breakfast.*

$$
RESORT
FAMILY
⛱ **Breakers Resort.** This property enjoys an enviable position at the northern tip of Umhlanga, surrounded by the wilds of the Hawaan Forest and overlooking the unspoiled wetlands of Umhlanga Lagoon. **Pros:** sprawling gardens; great pool; family-friendly. **Cons:** taxi is required to get to local restaurants, especially at night; overrun with families in-season; furniture is basic. $ *Rooms from: R1775* ✉ *88 Lagoon Dr., Umhlanga* ☎ *031/561–2271* ⊕ *www.breakersresort.co.za* ➚ *80 rooms* ❍ *No meals.*

$$$$
HOTEL
Fodor's Choice
★
⛱ **Oyster Box.** The iconic multi-award-winning Oyster Box hotel has achieved a perfect marriage between old colonial and African contemporary style in its luxurious accommodations and offers an eye-popping range of services and complimentary extras. **Pros:** fabulous food and service; award-winning spa includes complimentary healthful buffet; free shuttle to Gateway Shopping Centre. **Cons:** rooms are small; the resident vervet monkeys can make a nuisance of themselves—lock your room doors; public areas fill up with nonresidents attending various events in the hotel; Colonial decor is off-putting. $ *Rooms from: R4850* ✉ *2 Lighthouse Rd., Umhlanga* ☎ *031/514–5000* ⊕ *www.oysterboxhotel.com* ➚ *86 rooms* ❍ *Breakfast.*

$$$$
HOTEL
Fodor's Choice
★
⛱ **Teremok Marine.** Translated from Russian as "little hideaway," this delightful boutique lodge has eight huge individually styled rooms, each offering a different sensory experience—its own specific body-product fragrance, mood CD, candy—and the three rooms at the top have beautiful ocean views. **Pros:** close to Umhlanga village and one block from the sea; personalized service; free transfers to village. **Cons:** 1 km (½ mile) from nearest restaurants; open-plan bathrooms in all but one room; no minibars in the room. $ *Rooms from: R3800* ✉ *49 Marine Dr., Umhlanga* ☎ *031/561–5848* ⊕ *www.teremok.co.za* ➚ *8 rooms* ❍ *Breakfast.*

BEACHFRONT

$
HOTEL
⛱ **Blue Waters Hotel.** Ideally located on North Beach, 250 meters from the Suncoast Entertainment Complex, the Blue Waters Hotel is an excellent value. **Pros:** enviable location; front-facing rooms have balconies and sea views; parking available. **Cons:** elevators are slow and always full; children can be noisy. $ *Rooms from: R900* ✉ *175 Tambo [Snell] Parade* ☎ *031/327–7000* ⊕ *www.bluewatershotel.co.za* ➚ *92 rooms* ❍ *Breakfast.*

$
HOTEL
⛱ **Garden Court Marine Parade.** You can't beat the location of this pleasant hotel midway between South and North beaches and only a five-minute drive from the city center. **Pros:** central location on Golden Mile; sea views; friendly staff. **Cons:** hotel lobby and bar area lack atmosphere; recommended restaurants a taxi ride away; inadvisable to walk in area after dark. $ *Rooms from: R1405* ✉ *167 Tambo (Marine) Parade, Beachfront* ☎ *031/337–3341* ⊕ *www.tsogosun.com/garden-court-marine-parade* ➚ *352 rooms* ❍ *Breakfast.*

$$$ HOTEL [H] **Suncoast Hotel and Towers.** This hotel mostly attracts businesspeople and gamblers, but it's a stone's throw from the beach and has some great sea views. **Pros:** closest hotel to Moses Mabhida Stadium; has a good spa; access to beach. **Cons:** smallish rooms; like with all Golden Mile hotels, it gets filled with participants during major sporting events; open-plan bathrooms aren't for everyone. [$] *Rooms from: R2590* ✉ *20 Battery Beach Rd., Beachfront* ☎ *031/314–7878* 🌐 *www.tsogosun.com/suncoast-towers* 🛏 *201 rooms* 🍴 *Breakfast.*

$$ HOTEL [H] **Tsogo Sun Elangeni & Maharani.** Overlooking North Beach along the Golden Mile, this combination of two adjacent high-rise hotels is a two-minute drive from the city center and attracts a mix of business, conference, and leisure travelers. **Pros:** helpful tour and travel desk; business center; sea views; discounted rates on weekends. **Cons:** not for those who prefer an intimate hotel experience; breakfast not included in price during peak times; minimum stay requirements in peak season. [$] *Rooms from: R1800* ✉ *63 Tambo [Snell] Parade, Beachfront* ☎ *031/362–1300* 🌐 *www.tsogosun.com/southern-sun-elangeni-maharani* 🛏 *753 suites* 🍴 *No meals.*

NIGHTLIFE

What's On in Durban, a free bimonthly publication put out by the tourism office and distributed at popular sites, lists upcoming events.

DURBAN CENTRAL - POINT WATERFRONT

The Chairman. The Chairman is a sophisticated jazz bar (you'll have to dress the part and leave the Durban uniform of tank top and flip-flops in the hotel room) with an achingly cool industrial feel—think upholstered leather seats, exposed brickwork, vases of gorgeous blooms, low lighting, and contemporary art. It's anything but stuffy. This live jazz bar (check the website for new listings) and restaurant attracts a diverse and politically aware crowd—possibly the best place to mingle with a range of Durban's hip, professional set. They encourage reservations, especially for groups of six or more. ✉ *146 Mahatma Gandhi Rd.* ☎ *031/368–2133* 🌐 *www.thechairmanlive.com* 🎫 *R150, will be deducted from your bill.*

MORNINGSIDE

Drop Kick Murphy's. A modern take on an Irish pub, this bar, right in the heart of Florida Road's lively center, offers a range of craft beers, signature cocktails, and comfort food like the local classic chicken livers panfried in peri-peri (hot sauce made from bird's eye chili), Philly Chili Steaks, deep-fried chicken wings, and a salad with homemade fish cakes. Happy Hour from 5 to 6 each day offers half-price on drinks and cocktails and 25% off burgers, craft beers, and draughts. A late-night (9:30–midnight) food menu keeps the hungry fed, and friends gather here to watch rugby matches and contribute to the festive atmosphere. Expect loud Irish singing at times. ✉ *219 Florida Rd., Windermere* ☎ *031/825–1858* 🌐 *www.dropkickmurphys.co.za.*

Velvet Lounge. African-Indian cuisine teamed with white-and-gold interior design sets the style in this bar/lounge, a see-and-be-seen place for local movers and shakers. ✉ *178 Florida Rd., Morningside* ☎ *031/312–0864, 031/561–6505.*

7

SPORTS AND THE OUTDOORS

BOATING

It's easy to charter all manner of boats, from a paddleboat (a flat fiberglass board that you paddle) for a few rand to a deep-sea fishing vessel for a few thousand. Inexpensive harbor tours lasting a half hour, booze cruises, and dinner cruises can all be booked from the quayside at Wilson's Wharf. Shop around to find something that suits your budget, taste, and time frame.

DOLPHIN-WATCHING AND DIVING

FAMILY **Calypso Dive and Adventure Centre.** This PADI five-star Instructor Development Center, located inside uShaka Village Walk, organizes boat and aquarium dives, sardine run adventures, and equipment rentals. ⊠ *Shop K8 uShaka Village Walk, 1 King Shaka Ave.* ☎ *031/332–0905, 082/976–6018* ⊕ *www.calypsoushaka.co.za.*

FISHING

Deep-sea fishing is a popular activity, as there's almost always something biting. Summer (November–May) brings game fish like barracuda, marlin, sailfish, and dorado, whereas winter is better for the bottom fishes, like mussel crackers, salmon, and rock cod.

Fodor's Choice **Aqua Nautical Adventures.** With daily departures at 6 am, this company
★ deploys luxury 30- and 48-foot catamarans and a 30-foot Lee Cat, equipped with electric flush loos, a covered cabin for respite from the sun, and a even a bed if you're worn out from fighting a mahimahi (dorado). They provide all equipment and professional staff will barbecue lunch on board for R80, or you could bring your own meat and braai (barbecue) it yourself in South African fashion. Half-day and full-day tours for game fish deep-sea and harbor fishing, with stunning views of Durban city, start at R8,000 for a maximum of six. The company operates on a strict catch-and-release policy for all billfish (such as marlin) with a limited number of catch allowed per customer for other fish. ⊠ *Wilson's Wharf, 18 Boatmans Rd.* ☎ *082/410–7116* ⊕ *www.aquanautical.co.za.*

Casea Charters. Trips on a ski boat depart from Granny's Pool, in front of Umhlanga's Cabana Beach. Various trips are available, ranging from one to six hours. The popular three- and four-hour trips are priced per person at R600 and R700 respectively; otherwise you need to get a group together and hire the whole boat (R2,500–R4,700 depending on the length of time you want). Fish for dorado, yellowfin tuna, king and queen mackerel, garrick, rock cod, salmon, and other species. Bait and equipment are supplied, but bring your own food and drinks. You can keep the fish you catch. Booking is essential, and you need to obtain a fishing license (from any post office) in advance of the trip. ⊠ *1 Lighthouse Rd.* ☎ *031/561–7381, 083/690–2511* ⊕ *www.caseacharters.co.za.*

Lynski Charters. Deep-sea fishing trips for barracuda, sailfish, marlin, shark, and reef fish head out from Durban's harbor at 5 am in a 30-foot game-fish boat, returning at 2 pm. They charge a set fee for up to 6 people fishing for a day trip, although the boat can take 12 people. The price includes equipment, tackle, and bait. Bring your own refreshments. ⊠ *Durban Harbor, Off Maritime Pl.* ☎ *031/539–3338, 082/445–6600* ⊕ *www.lynski.com.*

GOLF

Durban is a great destination for golfers, with a number of internationally acclaimed courses in subtropical settings. Lush, forest-fringed fairways make for a scenic and challenging golfing experience, and thanks to Durban's sunshine and perennially warm climate, golf can be enjoyed throughout the year.

Beachwood Country Club. The layout is challenging to the links-course golfer, with most fairways running parallel in a N-NE/S-SW direction. The 6th and 9th fairways feature doglegs, and 74 bunkers lure wayward shots. Four holes have water features and tree-lined fairways. Set high in the dunes, the par-4 6th is a hugely demanding hole at 448 yards from the back tee. The hole doglegs left, with a stream, bush, and water hazard to be negotiated before reaching the green. ⊠ *Beachwood Pl., off Fairway* 🕾 *031/564–4257* ⊕ *www.durbancountryclub.co.za/home/golf/durban-country-club/beachwood* ⌨*R375 day rate* 🏌*18 holes, 6016 yards, par 71.*

Fodor's Choice
★

Durban Country Club. Durban Country Club was the first public course on the African continent to be rated in the Top 100 Golf Courses of the World by *Golf Magazine USA*. Lush subtropical vegetation, sand dunes, and elevated views of the Indian Ocean and the striking Moses Mabhida Stadium lend this course its unique and challenging appeal. Classic features include large undulating fairways on the 5th, 8th, and 17th, and massive sand dunes that form part of the design. The 1535-foot par 5 3rd hole—high tee-off to a narrow fairway with dense vegetation and a left-hand fairway bunker—is rated among the world's best. ⊠ *Walter Gilbert Rd.* 🕾 *031/313–1777* ⊕ *www.durbancountryclub.co.za/home/golf/durban-country-club* ⌨*R600 day rate* 🏌*18 holes, 6683 yards, par 72.*

Mount Edgecombe Country Club. This two-course championship estate—Mount Edgecombe One and Mount Edgecombe Two—is set in rolling hills inland from Umhlanga. Designed by Sid Brews in 1936, Course One was upgraded in 1992 and modernized by Hugh Baiocchi to meet USGA specifications. Both feature indigenous vegetation that attracts a variety of birdlife. Course One's water features and multi-tiered greens demand accurate play, whereas Course Two has more undulating terrain that tests the serious golfer and hones the amateur's skill. Signature holes are the 13th to 16th, referred to by locals as "Amen corner." ⊠ *Golf Course Dr., Gate 2, Mount Edgecombe* 🕾 *031/502–1010* ⊕ *www.mountedgecombe.com* ⌨*Rate: Mon. and Tues. R200, Wed.–Fri. R300, weekends R400. Gold cart hire: Mon and Tues: R200, Wed.–Fri. R300, weekends R400* 🏌*18 holes, 6302 yards, par 71.*

Royal Durban Golf Club. Tucked in the center of the Greyville Racecourse, the Royal Durban Golf Club course, built in 1898, appears deceptively easy. However there's no wind protection, so hitting narrow fairways is difficult, and subtle green breaks are challenging. On the plus side, it's centrally located, surroundings are attractive, the course is flat, and trees are minimal. The par-4 7th is the most difficult with palm trees punishing a sliced or blocked tee shot. First tee-off is at 6:30 am. ⊠ *16 Mitchell Crescent, Gate 15, Greyville* 🕾 *031/309–1373* ⊕ *www.royal-durban.co.za* ⌨*Day rate: R275 all wk* 🏌*18 holes, 6444 yards, par 73.*

7

Umhlali Country Club. This Peter Matkovich–designed golf course is a premier golf destination on the North Coast. It features sweeping greens, exotic palms, and manicured fairways that offer an easy walk for golfers of all abilities. Strategically positioned tee boxes and seven water holes test the mettle of competitive golfers, and longer handicappers can take advantage of front markers. The 4th and 8th present more of a challenge, with greens surrounded by water. ✉ *Compensation Rd., Ballito* ☎ *032/947–1181* ⊕ *www.umhlaliclub.co.za/sports/golf* 🖃 *R310 weekdays, R405 weekends* ⚑ *18 holes, 6228 yards, par 72.*

Zimbali Country Club. This prestigious eco-friendly course, 1.2 km (¾ mile) from Ballito, embraces one of the region's few remaining natural forests. It holds a five-star Golf Experience Award from *Complete Golfer*, reflecting its standards of service, the quality of its clubhouse facilities, and the condition of the course. Designed by Tom Weiskopf, the course lies amid sand dunes above a secluded beach, natural springs, and a lake. Weiskopf's philosophy of "presenting a fair challenge to any level of play" is seen at Zimbali. The club's Crowned Eagle Restaurant serves breakfasts and lunches. ✉ *Zimbali Estate, M4, Ballito* ☎ *032/538–1041* ⊕ *zimbali. com/hole-by-hole* 🖃 *R800 weekdays, R860 weekends (includes compulsory golf cart rental)* ⚑ *18 holes, 6618 yards, par 72.*

HELICOPTER TOURS

JNC Helicopters. Flips (a short flight on a helicopter) are undertaken with up to three people leaving from Virgina Airport. Take a scenic trip to Umhlanga (10 minutes), Umdloti (14 minutes), Durban harbor (14 minutes), or to Ballito (25 minutes). Seeing the coast from the air is quite breathtaking. ✉ *Virgina Airport, Hangar 1, 220 Fairway, Umhlanga* ☎ *031/563–9513* ⊕ *www.jncheli.co.za* 🖃 *12 mins, Durban harbor R1,150 for 3 people; 20 mins, harbor plus Umhlanga R2,550 for 3 people; 30 mins, Ballito R3,550 for 3 people.*

SURFING

Surfing has a fanatical following in Durban, and several local and international tournaments are staged on the city's beaches, at nearby Umhlanga, Ballito, or on the Bluff. Crowds of more than 10,000 are not unusual for night surfing competitions or the annual Ballito Pro championship (formerly the Gunston 500), a top World Qualifying Series event on the world surfing circuit. When the conditions are right, New Pier is one of the best beach breaks in the world.

Just on the other side of Durban's protected bay, Cave Rock, on the Bluff, offers a seething right-hander that can handle big swell. It can be a tough paddle and is not for amateurs. Farther down the South Coast, surfers head for Scottburgh, Green Point, Park Rynie, or Southbroom. North of Durban, popular spots include Umhlanga, Ballito, Richard's Bay, and Sodwana Bay.

The more popular spots can get crowded, and locals are known to be territorial about certain sections. Be sure to obey the laws of surfing etiquette. Usually the best waves are found at dawn and dusk. If the southwester blows, the Durban beaches are your best bet. In the winter months look out for an early-morning land breeze to set up good waves along the whole coastline.

Surfing lessons are offered at uShaka Beach, where experienced coaches supply boards and advice. Surf shops along the beachfront will put you in touch with surf coaches, including professional surfers and body-boarders who offer one-on-one coaching and group lessons. You can also rent surfing equipment from the surf shops, by the hour or by the day, at nominal rates during peak vacation season.

Learn2Surf. Run by a surfer-lifeguard, this surf school just north of uShaka Beach at Addington Beach caters to beginners and improvers, for individuals or groups—and can even organize surf parties. Equipment is supplied. Prices depend on your individual requirements. ⊠ *Erskine Terr., Beachfront* ☎ *083/414–0567 SMS hotline* ⊕ *www.learn2surf. co.za* ⊠ *R500 per lesson, per person; various rates apply.*

Ocean Ventures. Based on the beachfront at uShaka Marine World, this company offers surf instruction suitable for beginners for R200 per hour as well as ocean kayaking. You can rent surfboards and bodyboards here, too. ⊠ *uShaka Marine World, 1 Bell St., South Beach, Beachfront* ☎ *031/332–9949, 0861/100–1138 toll-free in South Africa* ⊕ *www. oceanventures.co.za* ⊠ *R200 per hr, per person for private surf lesson.*

SHOPPING

Durban offers a great array of shopping experiences, from the Beach-front, where you can buy cheap beadwork and baskets, to enormous shopping malls such as Gateway in Umhlanga. In general, bargaining is not expected, though you might try it at the Beachfront or with hawkers anywhere. Look out for goods indigenous to the province: colorful Zulu beadwork and tightly handwoven baskets.

MORNINGSIDE

African Art Centre. An outstanding collection of art and crafts from local artisans is on offer at this nonprofit center dedicated to promoting their work. Purchases can be shipped overseas. ⊠ *94 Florida Rd., Morningside* ☎ *031/312–3804* ⊕ *www.afriart.org.za.*

Cécile & Boyd's. Super-stylish interiors here cleverly combine the best of African and colonial design in a contemporary space. ⊠ *253 Florida Rd., Morningside* ☎ *031/303–1005* ⊕ *www.cecileandboyds.com.*

Elizabeth Gordon Gallery. This small gallery in a cozy Edwardian house carries a wide selection of work—including prints—by local and international artists and photographers. ⊠ *120 Florida Rd., Morningside* ☎ *031/303–8133* ⊕ *www.elizabethgordon.co.za.*

WESTVILLE

Fodor's Choice ★ **The Space.** Since 2000, when The Space launched its first stand-alone store in Durban, it has provided a showcase for local young South African designers to display their talent. Michelle Ludek, Amanda Laird Cherry, Ruff Tung, and Colleen Eitzen have all earned theirs stripes here. A handful of stores have spread across the country, with Space-Man offering the latest in local men's fashion. Expect a combination of classic, contemporary, and exceptionally affordable pieces that are well tailored and crafted by respected local designers. ⊠ *The Pavilion, 5 Jack Martens Dr.* ☎ *031/265–1292.*

BEREA

FAMILY **The Morning Trade Market.** Founded by Anna Savage, who established the
Fodor's Choice popular I Heart Market at the Moses Mabhida Stadium, this market
★ is a showcase of organic and wholesome food and local produce in the
city's most hip creative hub, The Station Drive Precinct. It's a great way
to gather with the locals and pick up excellent bread, cheese, yogurt,
freshly squeezed juices, and farm-fresh veggies while sipping on a great
coffee. Open Sundays from 8 to 1. ⊠ *5–15 Station Dr., off Umgeni Rd.*
⊕ *www.themorningtrade.co.za.*

NEWMARKET

The Stables Lifestyle Market. Although the market, next to the Mr Price
Rugby Stadium, carries cheap imports from the East, these are offset
by an interesting selection of local crafts, antiques, collectibles, wooden
masks, beaded and leather goods, and more. Add-ons include live entertainment and varied food stalls. ⊠ *Newmarket horse stables, 9 Jacko
Jackson Dr.* ☏ *031/312–3058* ⊕ *www.stableslifestylemarket.co.za.*

INDIAN QUARTER

FAMILY **Victoria Street Market** (*Indian Market*). The most vibrant cross-cultural
market in the city is a century-old trading area where more than 150
vendors sell everything from recordings of African music to rolls of
fabric, curios, brass ornaments, Chinese goods, incense, and curry
spices. Bargaining is expected here, much as it is in India, though
not for spices. Also known among locals as the Indian market, it's
worth booking a tour of this and the adjacent markets with Markets of Warwick (⊕ *www.marketsofwarwick.co.za*). ⊠ *Denis Hurley
[Queen] St. at Bertha Mkhize St., Indian District* ☏ *031/306–4021*
⊕ *www.indianmarket.co.za.*

SIDE TRIPS FROM DURBAN

VALLEY OF A THOUSAND HILLS

45 km (27 miles) northwest of Durban.

In the early part of the 19th century, before cars were introduced, wagons traveled from the port of Durban up along the ridge of this region of
plunging gorges, hills, and valleys into the hinterland, where the mining
industry was burgeoning. Today the Old Main Road (M103) still runs
between Durban and Pietermaritzburg, winding through a number of
villages and offering stunning views of hills and valleys dotted with
traditional Zulu homesteads. It is along this route that the Comrades
Marathon—South Africa's most famous road race—is run.

For purposes of exploring, the area has been organized into routes by
the local tourism office. A favorite with Durbanites, the routes wind
through villages and past coffee shops, art galleries, restaurants, quaint
pubs, small inns, farms, and nature reserves. There are a number of
excellent B&Bs, small inns, and lodges in the area, often with fantastic
views of the gorges.

GETTING HERE AND AROUND

The main route—the T1, or Comrades Route—follows the M13 out of Durban, up Field's Hill, through the village of Kloof, and past Everton, Gillits, and Winston Park; it then joins the Old Main Road (M103) at Hillcrest. A number of small shopping centers along the M103 sell a variety of goods, from crafts to old furniture, and there are some excellent coffee shops, restaurants, and small hotels as well as cultural attractions. At the end of the M103 is the small town of Monteseel, known for its climbing routes. Drive along the dirt roads to the signposted overlook for one of the best uninterrupted views of the Thousand Hills. Other well-marked routes in the area are the T2 Kranzkloof Route, T3 Assagay Alverstone Route, T4 Isithumba Route, and T5 and T6 Shongweni Shuffle, all of which make for scenic drives.

VISITOR INFORMATION

Contacts 1000 Hills Tourism Association. ⊠ *47 Old Main Rd., Botha's Hill* ☎ *031/322–2855* ⊕ *www.1000hillstourism.co.za.*

EXPLORING

FAMILY **PheZulu Safari Park.** Popular with big tour buses, PheZulu is the equivalent of fast-food tourism, good for people who want a quick-fix African experience. A tour of the cultural village, in collaboration with the Gasa clan, with its traditional beehive huts gives some insight into African traditions, and there are performances of traditional Zulu dancing, but the operation is not as vibrant or professional as the cultural villages up north in Zululand. An old-fashioned crocodile farm and snake park is fairly interesting, if a little tacky. The curio shop is enormous; you can probably get just about any type of African memento or booklet imaginable. Impala and zebra are frequently spotted on the hour-long game drive (additional fee). ⊠ *Old Main Rd., Drummond* ☎ *031/777–1205* ⊕ *www.phezulusafaripark.co.za* 🖘 *Village tour and Zulu dancing R120, game drive R240, reptile park tour R55* 🖙 *Accommodations available here, book online.*

WHERE TO EAT

$ ✕ **Treat Cafe.** Tucked away from the road, this café with its fresh
CAFÉ palette and friendly service welcomes guests with fresh food, hearty
FAMILY breakfasts, and healthy lunches. Opt for a seat outdoors overlooking the Alverstone Valley. **Known for:** good coffee and light meals in a relaxing setting; beautiful local gifts; on-site spa. 🖼 *Average main: R65* ⊠ *61 Old Main Rd.* ☎ *031/777–1586* ⊕ *www.talloula.co.za/treat-cafe-at-talloula-restaurants-in-hillcrest-bothas-hill.*

SHOPPING

FAMILY **The Puzzle Place.** With quirky wooden puzzles for the young and young-at-heart, this small shop provides a selection of locally themed puzzles, including brainteasers and 3-D puzzles. Consider the various well-crafted Africa and Big Five–shaped puzzles as unusual curios to take back home. ⊠ *1000 Hills Village, 138 Old Main Rd.* ☎ *072/986–1168* ⊕ *www.puzzleplace.co.za.*

DOLPHIN COAST

48 km (30 miles) northwest of Durban.

About an hour north of Durban, the Dolphin Coast (North Coast) lies along the warm waters of the Indian Ocean, with lifeguards and shark-netted beaches making it a popular vacation choice. Bordered by the Tugela River in the north and Zimbali in the south, it includes Ballito, Chaka's Rock, Salt Rock, Sheffield Beach, Blythedale, and Zinkwazi. Four excellent golf courses, a crocodile farm, cultural villages, and historical Indian, British, and Zulu sites are easily accessible at KwaDukuza, Shakaskraal, and Sheffield.

Large shopping malls straddle the entry into Ballito, and the Gateway Theatre of Shopping and La Lucia malls are just a 15-minute drive away. All types of accommodations are covered, from hotels to camping, and a host of restaurants are available.

Culture and history form an integral part of life on the Dolphin Coast. Indian, Zulu, and colonial cultures can all be explored on one estate at The Kingdom in Sheffield. You can visit the King Shaka Memorial in KwaDukuza/Stanger, the Dukuza Museum, or the grave and home of Nobel Peace Prize winner Chief Albert Luthuli in Groutville. There are also many temples and mosques in the Shakaskraal and KwaDukuza/Stanger area.

GETTING HERE AND AROUND
A rental vehicle will afford you the flexibility needed to visit select destinations. You can take the N2, but the M4 north is a more scenic option. King Shaka International Airport lies 22 km (14 miles) north.

VISITOR INFORMATION
Contacts North Coast Tourism. ⊠ *Ithala Trade Center, 29 Canal Quay Rd.* ☎ *031/366–7500* ⊕ *www.zulu.org.za/destinations/northcoast.*

WHERE TO EAT
$$
AFRICAN
FAMILY
✕ **Mo-zam-bik.** Sample the authentic tastes of Mozambique without ever crossing the border at this funky, vibrant restaurant. The eatery's rustic charm extends from the interior design to the service to the food. **Known for:** specialty seafood dishes; lively atmosphere. $ *Average main: R150* ⊠ *Boulevard Centre, Shops 4 and 5, Compensation Rd., Ballito* ☎ *032/946–0979* ⊕ *www.mozambik.co.za.*

$$$
ECLECTIC
Fodor's Choice
★
✕ **Two Shrimps.** Smack-dab against the ocean with the sound of waves tumbling just outside, Two Shrimps at The Canelands Beach Club & Spa, a converted former luxury beach house, offers incredible views and contemporary classics. This is the place for seafood, so splurge on the seafood platter for two, the peri-peri prawns, or the saffron-infused poached crayfish. **Known for:** seafood; views; proximity to the ocean. $ *Average main: R200* ⊠ *2 Shrimp La., Salt Rock* ☎ *032/525–2300.*

WHERE TO STAY
$$$$
HOTEL
🛏 **Fairmont Zimbali Resort.** Zimbali's tranquil 700-hectare (1,730-acre) setting is in one of the few remaining coastal forests in the province with direct access to the beach, and the award-winning resort is a stylish

mix of African and Balinese, with lots of glass, dark wood, and rough woven fabrics. **Pros:** access to unspoiled beach; professional service; good golf course. **Cons:** overly formal for some; a little tired; too large to offer intimate service. [$] *Rooms from: R4000* ✉ *M4, Ballito* ✥ *20 km (12 miles) north of Umhlanga* ☎ *032/538–5000* 🌐 *www.fairmont.com* 🛏 *172 rooms* 🍴 *Breakfast.*

SOUTH COAST

60 km (37 miles) southwest of Durban.

Vacation towns like Scottburgh, Margate, Ramsgate, Trafalgar, and Palm Beach dot KwaZulu-Natal's southern coast, which stretches for more than 200 km (125 miles) from Durban in the north to Port Edward in the south. The area has some of the country's best beaches, set against a tropical background of natural coastal jungle and palm trees. In fact, Blue Flag status has been conferred on Alkantstrand, Lucien, Marina (San Lameer), Ramsgate, Southport, Trafalgar, and Umzumbe beaches.

The South Coast is also famous for the annual sardine run, dubbed the Greatest Shoal on Earth, which usually occurs in June or July. Colder currents in Antarctica at this time bring millions of sardines to local waters, and they often wash right up on the beach. Dolphins, seabirds, sharks, and whales follow in a feeding frenzy. Paddle into the sea and collect your own lunch in a bucket.

7

GETTING HERE AND AROUND

The best and really only way to explore this area is with your own transportation. Main roads (the N2 and R61) are easy to navigate, and following the coastal road (turn off the R61 toward the coast) is picturesque.

If you're looking to explore the South Coast, Sapphire Coast Tourism and Tourism South Coast can provide relevant information. It's also worth checking out the *Southern Explorer* magazine and its website (🌐 *southernexplorer.co.za*), which includes maps of the various tourist routes, along with details of restaurants, sights, and accommodations.

VISITOR INFORMATION

Contacts Tourism South Coast. ✉ *16 Bisset St., Port Shepstone* ☎ *039/682–7944* 🌐 *www.tourismsouthcoast.co.za.*

EXPLORING

FAMILY
Fodor's Choice ★

Beaver Creek Coffee. Coffee grown in the seaside town of Port Edward? You best believe it! At Beaver Creek, four coffee trees have grown since 1984 to more than 60,000 today. Family-run (three generations have worked here), this coffee plantation and roastery is open to the public for daily 40-minute tours of the estate called Crop to Cup (R55 per person) to better understand the process, outlining the flavors you can expect from the different coffee regions and what goes into creating a meticulous hand-harvested cup of coffee. The Estate Café (8 am–4 pm) brews freshly roasted coffee and serves light meals. Buy bags of beans or ground coffee as a unique souvenir from this region. You can also book a three-hour barista course to learn to make a great cup at home using various brewing methods—by appointment only. ✉ *Izingolweni Rd., Port Edward, Durban* ☎ *039/311–2347* 🌐 *www.beavercreek.co.za.*

WHERE TO STAY

$$$$ RENTAL FAMILY 🏨 **San Lameer Villas.** The vacation rental properties in this exclusive resort between Ramsgate and Palm Beach offer a great getaway for a group of friends or a family, and golfers are drawn by the on-site championship course. **Pros:** on a Blue Flag beach; championship golf course on-site; lively atmosphere. **Cons:** estate is very large; it's a car ride away from off-site restaurants; busy in-season. [$] *Rooms from: R3600* ✉ *Lower South Coast Main Rd., San Lameer* ☎ *039/313–0450* 🌐 *www.sanlameer.com* 🛏 *62 rooms* 🍴 *No meals.*

THE KWAZULU-NATAL MIDLANDS

104 km (65 miles) northwest of Durban.

Set amid the rolling green foothills of the Drakensberg, the Midlands encompass waterfalls, lakes, reservoirs, forests, fields, Zulu villages, game reserves, and battle sites. The climate is pleasant most of the year, though summers tend to be hot, with a brief afternoon thunderstorms. Nights in the mountains can get bitterly cold, even in summer. The area has long been an enclave for craftspeople—weavers, potters, woodcrafters, metalworkers, cheese makers, and beer brewers—who escaped the cities.

As a way to draw customers to the area, the crafters created a growing number of routes, called the Midlands Meander, in 1985, which include more than 160 shops, galleries, cultural activities, restaurants, and accommodations. Running through the towns of Curry's Post and Howick in the northeast and the little village of Nottingham Road, Mooi River, Balgowan, the Dargyle District, Lion's River, and Midmar in the southwest, the routes provide a great opportunity to shop for authentic, high-quality South African arts and crafts while enjoying the tranquility and beauty of the countryside. The area is filled with top accommodations and dining options.

The most popular time to do the Meander is in the autumn (March to May), when it's not too hot or too cold. Many South Africans love the winters here; it often snows, particularly on the higher ground, and many establishments burn fires. Don't be surprised to experience four seasons in one day! No matter what time of year you visit, though, there's always something to see and do, most of which involves shopping for local crafts or indulging in artisanal produce.

GETTING HERE AND AROUND

The only way to explore this area is in your own transportation. Roads are easy to navigate, and all establishments are well marked. The N3 is the quickest route between places, but the R103 is a scenic route that passes through all areas.

VISITOR INFORMATION

If you plan to explore the area, contact the Midlands Meander Association for its magazine that includes maps of the routes and details of the various establishments. Members of the association also stock the magazine for sale or for free if you are a paying guest at one of the accommodation establishments. ■TIP➔ **More-remote artisans may follow their own schedules**

Contact Midlands Meander Association. ☎ *033/330–8195* ⊕ *www. midlandsmeander.co.za.*

EXPLORING

Howick Falls. Although this area in the heart of the KwaZulu-Natal Midlands is mainly about dining, shopping, and the arts, this lovely waterfall is definitely worth a stop. In the town of Howick, the Umgeni River plunges an impressive 300 feet into a deep pool in the gorge. Local people and sangomas (traditional Zulu healers) believe the waterfall is inhabited by ancestral spirits and has mystical powers. Take photographs from the viewing platform, or if you have more time, there are numerous hikes of varying difficulty that provide different vantages of the falls. Contact or visit the Howick Tourism Office, which is just a few hundred yards from the falls, for information. ⊠ *Falls Dr., Howick.*

FAMILY

Fodor'sChoice

★

Nelson Mandela Capture Site. In 2012, on the 50th anniversary of Nelson's Mandela's capture, this breathtakingly dramatic steel sculpture was unveiled and the visitor center opened. You will never have seen anything quite like this—don't miss it. The magnitude of what happened here is remarkable: on August 5, 1962, after 17 months on the run, Nelson Mandela, disguised as a chauffeur, was arrested at this very spot on his way from Durban to Johannesburg. He was convicted of incitement and illegally leaving the country and was sentenced to 5 years in jail before being prosecuted in the Rivonia Trials that led to his 27-year incarceration, most of it served on Robben Island. The on-site museum and craft shop is open daily 9–4; the Truth Café, also on-site, is open Friday and Saturday 8–4. ⊠ *R103, Howick* ✢ *From the N3 take the Tweedie Interchange and get onto the R103; the monument is just outside Howick* ⊕ *www.thecapturesite.co.za* 🗐 *Free* ◷ *Café closed Mon.–Thurs.*

Nottingham Road Brewery. On the same premises as Rawdon's Hotel, this rustic microbrewery has developed a cult following. With names like Pickled Pig Porter, Whistling Weasel Pale Ale, Pye-Eyed Possum Pilsner, and Wobbling Wombat Summer Ale, you may have a tough time choosing which brew to taste first, so order a tasting paddle in the hotel's pub to sample them all. Call ahead if you would like to do a tour of the small brewery; otherwise just pop into the shop to stock up on beer, accessories, and clever merchandising. Guaranteed you'll head home with a "pickled as a pig" or "I'm as possed as a pye-eyed pissum" T-shirt. ⊠ *Rawdons Estate, R103, Nottingham Road* ☎ *033/266–6728* ⊕ *www.rawdons.co.za.*

FAMILY

Swissland Cheese. Expect to be greeted by white free-roaming Saanen goats grazing happily in luscious green pastures when you visit this family-owned-and-run cheesery. In the Swiss-chalet-style tasting room, you can sample a range of goat cheeses including *chevin*—similar to a cream cheese but a little crumblier—and a mild blue cheese, and learn about the cheese-making practices that Fran Isaac and her family have been following here for more than two decades. Relax on the lawn with a picnic hamper you can choose at the deli or at the restaurant next door. If you're here between

August and May, you can watch the daily goat-milking between 3 and 4:30 pm. ✉ *R103 Old Main Rd., Balgowan* ☎ *082/418–3440* 🌐 *www.swisslandcheese.net* ⏲ *Closed Tues.–Thurs., Christmas, and New Year's Day.*

WHERE TO EAT

$ GREEK FUSION FAMILY

🍴 **Blue Cow Deli at Gourmet Greek.** The producer of arguably the best small-batch double-cream yogurt in the country, Blue Cow Deli at Gourmet Greek, situated on a small estate in the heart of the Meander, offers a café-style menu of Greek-inspired items and you can take tubs of yogurt and wedges of cow's milk cheese home. You won't find these products outside the province, so indulge while you can. **Known for:** yogurt and cheese; dairy tours. [$] *Average main: R60* ✉ *No. 10 D369, Lions River* ☎ *033/234–4338* 🌐 *www.thegourmetgreek.com.*

WHERE TO STAY

$$ HOTEL FAMILY

🏨 **Brahman Hills Hotel & Spa.** Brahman Hills is a contemporary slick country hotel with serviced self-catering cottages ideal for couples or families. **Pros:** self-catering cottages offer solitude; set on a nature reserve with zebra and buck roaming; good food and coffee at the main building. **Cons:** hotel rooms are small and close to each other; focused on weddings and functions; lacks the typical Midlands intimacy. [$] *Rooms from: R1875* ✉ *Old Curry's Post Rd., Mount West* ☎ *033/266–6965* 🛏 *42 rooms* 🍽 *Breakfast.*

$$ HOTEL

🏨 **Fordoun Hotel and Spa.** In the heart of a lush dairy farm that dates back to the 1800s, original stone buildings have been converted into a five-star luxury hotel and spa. **Pros:** complimentary sauna, steam room, and gym; tranquil country setting; wholesome country fare at the restaurant. **Cons:** not all suites face mountains or dam; spa is a little way out from some cottages; can get cold at night in rooms, though fireplaces and electric blankets are provided. [$] *Rooms from: R2080* ✉ *R103, Nottingham Road* ✣ *3 km (2 miles) off N3* ☎ *033/266–6217* 🌐 *www.fordoun.com* 🛏 *22 suites* 🍽 *Breakfast.*

$$ B&B/INN Fodor's Choice ★

🏨 **Granny Mouse Country House.** One of the best-loved and oldest hotels on the Meander, Granny Mouse has cozy thatch rooms, all slightly different, with a bush view, fireplace, and homey, though upmarket, atmosphere. **Pros:** lovely setting in rolling green countryside; highly regarded restaurant; on-site spa run by Camelot. **Cons:** popular wedding venue so can be noisy; country feel isn't for everyone; smaller rooms may be considered expensive. [$] *Rooms from: R2333* ✉ *R103, Balgowan* ✣ *25 km (15½ miles) south of Nottingham Rd. exit off N3* ☎ *033/234–4071, 033/234–4071* 🌐 *www.grannymouse.co.za* 🛏 *32 rooms* 🍽 *Breakfast.*

$$$ B&B/INN Fodor's Choice ★

🏨 **Hartford House.** Deliciously luxurious, if rather formal, this 1875 inn, high up on the Meander in the foothills of the Drakensberg, is steeped in history and misty beauty. **Pros:** gourmet getaway; beautiful English-styled garden; all suites are thoughtfully appointed. **Cons:** dinner is served at 7:30 on the dot for all guests; can feel a little formal; service exceedingly polite. [$] *Rooms from: R3020* ✉ *Hlatikulu Rd., off road to Giant's Castle, Mooi River* ☎ *033/263–2713* 🌐 *www.hartford.co.za* 🛏 *15 rooms* 🍽 *Breakfast.*

SPORTS AND THE OUTDOORS

ZIPLINES

Karkloof Canopy Tours. Zip along steel cables through the treetops of the Karkloof Forest, the second-largest indigenous forest in South Africa. The 1,800-foot-long *foefie* (zip) course is divided into 10 slides—the longest an exhilarating 656 feet long—that are interspersed with wooden platforms. Designed by a civil engineer, safety is paramount, and two trained guides (well versed in the forest and ecology) accompany each group; group size ranges from one to eight people. Tours (R595) take two hours and leave every hour in most weather conditions; call ahead to reserve your spot. Anyone from the ages of 7 to 70 can participate, but there's a weight limit of 130 kg (286 pounds). Light refreshments, lunch, and a 4x4 trip up the mountain are included. ⊠ *Karkloof Rd., Howick* ✛ *From Howick, take Karkloof Rd. for 19 km (12 miles) and follow signs to Canopy Tours for another 2 km (1¼ miles)* ☎ *033/330–3415* ⊕ *www.karkloofcanopytour.co.za* ⌑ *R595.*

SHOPPING

Though on the whole the route is known for its quality, you can also find some establishments that are not quite up to standards of others. If you've only a limited time, head for the concentration of crafts shops on the R103 between Nottingham Road and Lion's River. Or visit the one-stop Piggly Wiggly Country Village, which showcases the work of many of the Meander members. If you have a couple of days, base yourself at one of the hotels and explore the Meander using the large-format, free guide available at most Meander stops. Many of the better establishments offer shipping services for those unusual items large and small.

ART AND CRAFTS

Fodor's Choice ★ **Ardmore Ceramics.** Ardmore Ceramics, known for its exquisite and elaborate pieces, was established on the Ardmore farm in 1985 by ceramic artist Fée Halsted who was soon joined by the now late Bonnie Ntshalintshali, 18 years old at the time. The on-site museum dedicated to Bonnie is testament to her role in making Ardmore the brand it is today, with exhibitions in top galleries and private homes around the world, including a collaboration with Hermès and auctions by Christie's of London. There are glorious luxury fabrics with Ardmore prints for sale, too. None of the ceramics are below R1,000 and some go up to an eye-watering R500,000. They offer tours of the site with artists busy at work, too—call in advance to arrange ⊠ *Caversham Rd., Lidgetton* ☎ *033/940–0034* ⊕ *www.ardmoreceramics.co.za.*

FAMILY **Culamoya Chimes.** As you enter the gardens of Culamoya Chimes, in the Dargyle District, your ears will be gently assailed with harmonious chimes of every description. There's a 13-foot chime in the garden as well as other chimes inside the shop that mimic the sounds of Big Ben and St. Paul's Cathedral down to gentle tinkles of fairy magic. The chimes are handmade and can be shipped to your home. ⊠ *Lidgetton* ✛ *3 km (2 miles) off R103* ☎ *033/234–4503* ⊕ *www.culamoyachimes.co.za* ◷ *Closed Mon.*

7

FAMILY **Piggly Wiggly Country Village.** If you're short on time, but still want to experience some of the best of the Midland Meander's arts and crafts, drop in at the one-stop Piggly Wiggly, where a wide range of shops—all representing Meander destinations and selling their products—are clustered round a central green with a Piggly putt-putt course. There are fast-food outlets serving pizza and hamburgers, but be sure to sample the award-winning cappuccino and a slice of freshly baked cheesecake at Piggly Wiggly's famous coffee shop. ⊠ *1 Dargle Rd., Lions River* ☎ *033/234–2911, 072/077–5917* ⊕ *www.pigglywiggly.co.za.*

Woodturner. Andrew Early specializes in making elegant wooden bowls, modern wood sculptures, and one-of-a-kind furniture pieces using salvaged, exotic woods like jacaranda and local varieties like African mahogany and stinkwood. The pieces are often snapped up by studios in New York and elsewhere. Ask if you can visit the delightful studio behind the sprawling farmhouse, which you'll find 6 km (4 miles) from Rosewood, down Dargyle Road. ⊠ *Dargyle Rd., Lions River* ☎ *072/365–6270* ⊕ *www.andrew-early.com* ⊙ *Closed holidays.*

CLOTHING

FAMILY **Spiral Blue.** Here you'll find a veritable Aladdin's cave of colorful cotton, silk, and tie-dye garments and scarves, leather slippers, silver jewelry with precious and semiprecious stones, homewares, and esoteric gifts. Candles, incense, curtains, chimes, unusual door knobs, and even hammocks will keep you amused and browsing this fun space. Few things say "Midlands arts and crafts" like this iconic store. There's a garden outdoors if the kids get restless. ⊠ *Lions River, R103, Shop No. 407, Lions River* ☎ *033/234–4799* ⊕ *www.spiralblue.co.za* ⊙ *Closed Christmas Day.*

FOOD AND CANDY

FAMILY **Peel's Honey.** Established in 1924, Peel's Honey is the oldest honey label in the country. Snack on peanut honey brittle, or other tasty treats, or take a jar of creamed honey with you for *padkos* (the popular South African word for "road food," to munch as you drive). It's on the N3 below the Midmar Dam. ⊠ *1 Boston Rd., Merrivale* ☎ *033/330–3762* ⊕ *www.peelshoney.co.za.*

SHOES, LUGGAGE, AND LEATHER GOODS

FAMILY
Fodor's Choice
★
Tsonga. Makers of gorgeous handcrafted handbags and leather shoes for men, women, and children, Tsonga has its roots and inspiration in Lidgetton, where the iconic hand-stitching detail, a skill of the local women, originates. Inspired by the people he grew up around, founder Peter Maree created an African-influenced collection that provided valuable skills to this impoverished community. The Thread of Hope farm has become a training center where the motto is a hand up, not a hand out. Tsonga's shoes are based on a wide, ultra-cushioned sole and are supremely comfortable. With stores in South Africa, Australia, and France, you'd do well to visit the original outpost. Note, this isn't a factory store selling bargains, though you can occasionally find items on sale. ⊠ *R103, Lidgetton, Lions River* ☎ *33/387–9221* ⊕ *www.tsonga.com.*

THE DRAKENSBERG

240 km (150 miles) northwest of Durban.

Afrikaners call them the Drakensberg: the Dragon Mountains. To Zulus they are uKhahlamba (pronounced Ooka-hlamba)—"Barrier of Spears." Both are apt descriptions for this wall of rock that rises from the Natal grasslands, forming a natural fortress protecting the mountain kingdom of Lesotho. Although you don't come here for big game, or much game at all, it's well worth visiting this World Heritage Site, the first in South Africa to be recognized for both its natural and cultural attractions, with some of the finest rock art in the world.

If possible plan your visit to the Berg during the spring (September and October) or late autumn (late April–June), because although summer sees the Berg at its greenest, it's also the hottest and wettest time of the year. Vicious afternoon thunderstorms and hailstorms are an almost-daily occurrence. In winter the mountains lose their lush overcoat and turn brown and sere. Winter days in the valleys, sites of most resorts, are usually sunny and pleasant, although there can be cold snaps, sometimes accompanied by overcast, windy conditions. Nights are chilly, however, and you should pack plenty of warm clothing if you plan to hike high up into the mountains or camp overnight. Snow is common at higher elevations.

GETTING HERE AND AROUND

The main resort area of the Drakensberg is almost a direct shot along the N3 from Durban. A car is not strictly necessary for a trip to the Berg, although it is certainly a convenience, and though a 4x4 would be an advantage, it, too, is not a necessity. Gas stations can be found in Bergville, Winterton, and at the foot of Champagne Castle. Driving in this area is time consuming. Trucks often slow up traffic, and you should watch for animals on and attempting to cross the road.

VISITOR INFORMATION

Ezemvelo KZN Wildlife. For more information on viewing rock-art sites, contact Ezemvelo KZN Wildlife, the province's official conservation organization. ☎ *033/845–1999* ⊕ *www.kznwildlife.com.*

EXPLORING

The Natal Drakensberg is not conducive to traditional touring because of the nature of the attractions and the limited road system. It's best to check into a hotel or resort for two or three days and use it as a base for hiking and exploring the immediate area. If you decide to stay at one of the self-catering camps, do your shopping in one of the bigger towns, such as Winterton or Harrismith for Tendele, and Bergville or Estcourt for Giant's Castle, Kamberg, and Injasuti. For more information on touring the area, visit the Drakensberg Tourism Association website (⊕ *www.drakensberg.org.za*).

The Drakensberg. The Drakensberg is the highest range in southern Africa and has some of the most spectacular scenery in the country. The blue-tinted mountains seem to infuse the landscape, cooling the "champagne air," as the locals refer to the heady, sparkling breezes that blow around the precipices and pinnacles. It's a hiker's dream, and you could easily spend several days here on the gentle and challenging slopes, just soaking up the awesome views.

The Drakensberg is not a typical mountain range—it's actually an escarpment separating a high interior plateau from the coastal lowlands of Natal. It's a continuation of the same escarpment that divides the Transvaal Highveld from the hot malarial zones of the lowveld in Mpumalanga. However, the Natal Drakensberg, or Berg, as it is commonly known, is far wilder and more spectacular than its Transvaal counterpart. Many of the peaks—some of which top 10,000 feet—are the source of crystalline streams and mighty rivers that have carved out myriad valleys and dramatic gorges. The Berg is a natural watershed, with two of South Africa's major rivers, the Tugela and the Orange, rising from these mountains. In this untamed wilderness you can hike for days and not meet a soul, and the mountains retain a wild majesty missing in the commercially forested peaks of Mpumalanga. ☎ *036/448–1557 Drakensberg Tourism Association* 🌐 *www.drakensberg.org.za.*

WHERE TO STAY

$$$ HOTEL FAMILY 🏨 **Cathedral Peak Hotel.** You'll get breathtaking views from almost every spot in this friendly, delightful hotel nestled among the mountains, 43 km (18 miles) from Winterton. **Pros:** well-organized activities make it ideal for families; good horse trails around; views are wonderful. **Cons:** crowded in season; can get loud with bands of children running about; decor and rooms a little tired. [$] *Rooms from: R2990* ✉ *Cathedral Peak Rd., Winterton* ☎ *036/488–1888, 036/488–1889* 🌐 *www.cathedralpeak.co.za* 🛏 *105 rooms* 🍴 *Some meals.*

$$$$ B&B/INN Fodor's Choice ★ 🏨 **Cleopatra Mountain Farmhouse.** This truly enchanting hideaway tucked away at the foot of the Drakensberg Range near Rosetta overlooks a trout-filled lake encircled by mountains and old trees. **Pros:** exclusive yet modish accommodations; gourmet breakfasts and dinners—come hungry; excellent service. **Cons:** stay away if you're on a diet; if you're a fan of minimalistic decor, you'll have a hard time here; there's a formula—guests gather for a drink and dine at one set time, so you can't come and go as you please. [$] *Rooms from: R4590* ✉ *Highmoor Rd., off Kamberg Rd., Kamberg* ☎ *033/267–7243* 🌐 *www.cleomountain.com* 🛏 *11 rooms* 🍴 *Some meals.*

$$ RESORT FAMILY 🏨 **Thendele Hutted Camp.** Smack in the middle of Royal Natal National Park west of Bergville, amid some of the most spectacular mountain scenery in the Drakensberg, this very affordable popular camp makes a great base for hikes into the mountains. **Pros:** great views from every room; superb launch pad for hiking; family-friendly. **Cons:** not for urban party animals; no luxury amenities nearby; supplies are limited. [$] *Rooms from: R2400* ✉ *Royal Natal National Park* ☎ *031/208–3684* 🌐 *www.royalnatal.info* 🛏 *29 rooms* 🍴 *Some meals.*

CLOSE UP

San Paintings

Besides the hiking opportunities and the sheer beauty of the mountains, the other great attraction of the Berg is the San (Bushman) paintings. The San are a hunter-gatherer people who once roamed the entire country from 8,000 years ago to the 1800s. With the arrival of the Nguni peoples from the north and white settlers from the southwest in the 18th century, the San were driven out of their traditional hunting lands and retreated into the remote fastnesses of the Drakensberg and the Kalahari Desert. San cattle raiding in Natal in the late 19th century occasioned harsh punitive expeditions by white settlers and local Bantu tribes, and by 1880 the last San had disappeared from the Berg. Today only a few clans remain in the very heart of the Kalahari Desert. More than 40,000 of their paintings enliven scores of caves and rock overhangs throughout the Berg in more than 550 known San rock-art sites—one of the finest collection of rock paintings not only in the country, but also in the world. They tell the stories of bygone hunts, dances, and ceremonies as well as relating and representing spiritual beliefs and practices. Images of spiritual leaders in a trance state, their visions, and their transformation of themselves into animals have now been studied and written about, although some of the meanings are still not fully understood. ■ TIP→ **Be sure to bring binoculars and a cotton shirt and hat to cover up from the sun.**

7

ZULULAND AND THE BATTLEFIELDS

Zululand stretches north from the Tugela River all the way to the border of Mozambique. It's a region of rolling grasslands, gorgeous beaches, and classic African bush. It has also seen more than its share of bloodshed and death. Modern South Africa was forged in the fiery crucible of Zululand and northern Natal. Here Boers battled Zulus, Zulus battled Britons, and Britons battled Boers. Some of the most interesting historic sites, however, involve the battles against the Zulus. Names like Isandlwana, Rorke's Drift, and Blood River have taken their place in the roll of legendary military encounters.

No African tribe has captured the Western imagination quite like the Zulus. A host of books and movies have explored their warrior culture and extolled their martial valor. Until the early 19th century the Zulus were a small, unheralded group, part of the Nguni peoples who migrated to southern Africa from the north. King Shaka (1787–1828) changed all that. In less than a decade Shaka created a military machine unrivaled in Africa. By the time of his assassination in 1828, Shaka had destroyed 300 tribes and extended Zulu power for 800 km (500 miles) through the north, south, and west. It remains a pity that the majority of sites and guides, many of them of English origin, adopt a British sympathy with scant knowledge available from the Zulu perspective.

Fifty years after Shaka's death, the British still considered the Zulus a major threat to their planned federation of white states in South Africa. The British solution, in 1879, was to instigate a war to destroy the

Zulu kingdom. They employed a similar tactic 20 years later to bring the Boer republics to heel and the rich goldfields of the Witwatersrand into their own hands.

Interest in the battlefields continues to grow, particularly since the Boer and Zulu War centenary celebrations in 2000. If you're not a history buff, the best way to tour the battlefields is with an expert guide, who can bring the history to life, because many of the battle sites are little more than open grassland graced with the occasional memorial stone.

GETTING HERE AND AROUND

Unless you're on a tour, it's almost impossible to see this part of the country without your own car. Your best bet is to rent a car in Durban and perhaps combine a trip to the battlefields with a self-driving tour of KwaZulu-Natal's game reserves. Roads are in good condition, although some of the access roads to the battlefields require more careful and slower driving, as dirt roads can be bumpy and muddy when wet.

TOURS

The visitor information offices at Dundee's Talana Museum and in Ladysmith have lists of registered battlefield guides. Information about battlefield guides and guides specializing in authentic Zulu culture can be obtained at any information center or tourism office.

Fodor's Choice **Lindizwe (Dalton) Ngobese.** The resident guide at Isandlwana Lodge leads
★ the lodge's flagship daily tours to Isandlwana and Rorke's Drift. Mentored by the late Rob Gerrard, who was a Fellow of the Royal Geographical Society, Dalton brings the Zulu perspective to life, dramatically playing out the history of the Anglo-Zulu War on the actual battlefields of Isandlwana and Rorke's Drift. Dalton also takes guests to local villages, otherwise unaccustomed to foreigners for a day (or half day) of respectful cultural exchange and for a variety of battlefield tours including right up to the Zulu kingdom's capital, Ulundi. Reservations for tours can be booked through your travel operator or direct with the lodge. ⊠ *Off R68, Isandlwana* ☎ *034/271–8301* ⊕ *www.isandlwana.co.za* ⊠ *R600.*

Pat Rundgren. An official registered guide, Pat Rundgren offers 68 battlefield tours dealing with the Anglo-Zulu and Anglo-Boer wars. He will tailor tours to your requirements, but his most popular day tour is Isandlwana and Rorke's Drift for the Zulu War, or Spioenkop/Ladysmith for the Boer War. He has also introduced a three-day tour which includes a visit to Nambiti, a Big Five game reserve. Prices range according to length of trip and type of accommodations. Pat also offers "novelty" tours to coincide with annual reenactments of battles at Isandlwana in January and Talana in October. He operates via the Talana Museum in Dundee. ☎ *034/212–4560, 082/690–7812* ⊠ *From R1,500 for day trip (not including site entrance fee and lunch).*

VISITOR INFORMATION

Battlefields Route is a good source for information on the battlefields. For a good overview covering this area, go to Tourism KwaZulu-Natal's website.

Contacts Battlefields Route. ☎ *082/801–0551* ⊕ *www.battlefieldsroute.co.za.*
Tourism KwaZulu-Natal (Tourist Junction). ⊠ *160 Monty Naicker Rd., Durban* ☎ *031/322–4164, 031/305–6693* ⊕ *www.zulu.org.za.*

LADYSMITH

160 km (99 miles) northwest of Pietermaritzburg.

Ladysmith, dating back to the middle of the 19th century, became famous around the world during the South African War, when it outlasted a Boer siege for 118 days. Nearly 20,000 people were caught in the town when the Boers attacked on November 2, 1899. Much of the early part of the war revolved around British attempts to end the siege. The incompetence of British general Sir Redvers Buller became apparent during repeated attempts to smash the Boer lines, resulting in heavy British losses at Spioenkop, Vaalkrans, and Colenso. Finally, the sheer weight of numbers made possible the British defeat of the Boers in the epic 10-day Battle of Tugela Heights and ended the siege of Ladysmith on February 28, 1900.

Today Ladysmith is a small provincial town with a haphazard mix of old colonial and newer buildings and the same inhospitable climate (scorchingly hot in summer, freezing in winter). Seek out the elegant, historic Town Hall built in 1893 and visit the gleaming white Soofie Mosque on the banks of the Klip River—this national monument is regarded as one of the most beautiful mosques in the Southern Hemisphere. On Murchison Street (the main street) is Surat House, a shop built in the 1890s, where Gandhi used to shop on his way through Ladysmith. On the same street is the Siege Museum, and in its courtyard stands a replica of a Long Tom, the 6-inch Creusot gun used by the Boers during the siege to terrify the inhabitants of Ladysmith. In front of the town hall are two howitzers used by the British and christened Castor and Pollux.

GETTING HERE AND AROUND

There are only two ways to get around the battlefields: with your own rental car or with an organized tour.

VISITOR INFORMATION

Contacts Emnambithi/Ladysmith Information Bureau. ⊠ *Siege Museum, Town Hall, 151 Murchison St.* ☎ *036/637–2231.*

EXPLORING

Ladysmith Siege Museum. Formerly an 1884 market house, this is regarded as the best South African (Anglo-Boer) War Museum in South Africa. Step back into history and into the siege itself with electronic mapping, old uniforms, memorabilia, artifacts from the period, and black-and-white photos. The museum can arrange guided tours, but it also sells two pamphlets that outline self-guided tours: the Siege Town Walkabout and the Siege Town Drive-About. ⊠ *151 Murchison St.* ☎ *036/637–2992* ⊕ *www.battlefieldsroute.co.za/place/ladysmith-siege-museum* ⊠ *R11* ⊘ *Closed Sun.*

WHERE TO STAY

$$ 🏨 **Royal Hotel.** This historic South African country hotel shares much
HOTEL of Ladysmith's tumultuous past—it was built in 1880, just 19 years before the town was attacked by the Boers during the South Africa (Anglo-Boer) War. Expect small rooms, although TVs and air-conditioning are standard features. **Pros:** convenient, central location; great 1800s facade and front door; steeped in South African (Anglo-Boer)

Boers, Brits, and Battlefields

The Second Anglo-Boer War (1899–1902), now referred to as the South African War, was the longest, bloodiest, and costliest war fought by Britain for nearly 100 years. The Brits and the Boers, Afrikaner descendants of 17th-century Dutch settlers fighting for independence from Britain, engaged in numerous battles in which the little guys (the Boers) often made mincemeat of the great British colonial army sent out to defeat them. Britain marched into South Africa in the spring of 1899, confident that it would all be over by Christmas. However, the comparatively small bands of volunteers from the republics of the Transvaal and the Orange Free State were to give Queen Victoria's proud British army, as Kipling wrote, "no end of a lesson." Today history has also revealed the part played by hundreds of thousands of black South Africans in the war as messengers, scouts, interpreters, and laborers— hence the renaming of the war.

The most famous—or infamous—battle was fought on top of Spioenkop, in KwaZulu-Natal, where the mass grave of hundreds of British soldiers stretches from one side of the hill to the other. Of interest is that three men who were to change the course of world history were there on that fateful day: war correspondent Winston Churchill (who wrote "The shallow trenches were choked with dead and wounded"), Mahatma Gandhi (who was a stretcher bearer), and Louis Botha, the first prime minister of the Union of South Africa.

—Kate Turkington

War history. **Cons:** undistinguished, bland rooms; roadside rooms are noisy; kitschy bed linens. $ *Rooms from: R2100* ⊠ *140 Murchison St.* ☎ *036/637–2176* ⊕ *www.royalhotel.co.za* ⇥ *71 rooms* ⑩ *Breakfast.*

SPIOENKOP

38 km (24 miles) southwest of Ladysmith.

The Second Anglo-Boer War (1899–1902), now called South African War, was the biggest, the longest, the costliest, the bloodiest, and the most humiliating war that Great Britain had ever fought. The **Battle of Spioenkop** near Ladysmith was a focal point, where the Boers trounced the British, who suffered 243 fatalities during the battle; many were buried in the trenches where they fell.

WHERE TO STAY

$$$$
RESORT

⊞ **Spionkop Lodge.** This lovely secluded lodge, with the spectacular Drakensberg Mountains as a backdrop, lies in a 700-hectare (1,730-acre) nature reserve and is a perfect base for touring the battlefields, discovering the mountains and rock art, birding, or looking for big game. **Pros:** superb location; knowledgeable and friendly hosts; warm hospitality. **Cons:** cold winters; expensive for what you get; interior of rooms could do with some minor renovation. $ *Rooms from: R4340* ⊠ *On R600 between Ladysmith and Winterton, Ladysmith* ☎ *036/488–1404* ⊕ *www.spionkop.co.za* ⇥ *10 rooms* ⑩ *All meals.*

$$$$ RESORT FAMILY **Fodor's Choice** ★ [hotel] **Three Trees Lodge.** This quaint little Victorian lodge is run by a safari- and mountain-guide couple who follow Fair Trade, sustainability, and social ethics, and also offer guided walks and activities. **Pros:** superb hosts; fabulous tours, including game walks and rhino tracking; excellent food. **Cons:** bleak in winter; pricey, as with all properties in the area; drinks not included in price. [$] *Rooms from: R5400* ✉ *D564, Ladysmith* ✣ *25 km (16 miles) northeast of Bergville* ☎ *036/448–1171* 🌐 *www.threetreehill.co.za* 🛏 *8 rooms* 🍴 *All meals.*

DUNDEE

74 km (46 miles) northeast of Ladysmith.

Once a busy coal-mining town, Dundee still has straight roads wide enough for the ox wagons of pioneer days to turn in, but today it's just a small commercial center in an area of subdued farming activity.

GETTING HERE AND AROUND

To get to Dundee from Ladysmith, take the N11 north and then the R68 east. For a more scenic route, take the R602 toward Elandslaagte from the N11 and then go east on the R68.

VISITOR INFORMATION

Tourist Offices Dundee Tourism. ✉ *Civic Gardens, Victoria St.* ☎ *034/212–2121* 🌐 *www.tourdundee.co.za.*

EXPLORING

Battle of Blood River Site. One of the most influential events in the history of South Africa with long-reaching tragic consequences for the original inhabitants of the land, this battle, fought between the Boers and the Zulus in 1838, predates the Anglo-Zulu War by more than 40 years. After the murder of Piet Retief and his men at Mgungundlovu in February 1838, Dingane dispatched Zulu impis to kill all the white settlers in Natal. But by November Andries Pretorius's new group of 464 men and 64 wagons moved to challenge the Zulus and took a vow that should God grant them victory, they would forever remember that day as a holy day. On December 16 an enormous Zulu force armed only with spears attacked the armed Boers. At the end of the battle 3,000 Zulus lay dead, but it's said not a single Boer had fallen. The long-term effects of the battle were dramatic. The intensely religious Voortrekkers saw their great victory as a confirmation of their role as God's chosen people which led to the apartheid system that surfaced more than a century later. Two powerful monuments—one to the Boers, the other to the Zulus—today commemorate the battle. ✉ *Dundee* ✣ *Approach site via a gravel road, off R33 between Vryheid and Dundee* ☎ *034/632–1695, 087/808–2964* 🌐 *www.bloedrivier.org.za* 🎟 *R40.*

FAMILY **Talana Museum.** The first-rate Talana Museum, set in an 8-hectare (20-acre) heritage park, on the outskirts of Dundee, is well worth a visit. Fascinating exhibits, spread over 17 buildings, trace the history of the area, from the early San hunter-gatherers to the rise of the Zulu nation, the extermination of the cannibal tribes of the Biggarsberg, and, finally, the vicious battles of the South African (Anglo-Boer) War. The museum stands on the site of the Battle of Talana (October 20, 1899), the opening

7

skirmish in the war, and two of the museum buildings were used by the British as medical stations during the battle. The military museum here is an excellent starting point for the Battlefields Route, where Zulus, Brits, and Boers battled it out for territory and glory. Reenactments, living history, and special events are regular features. ⊠ *R33* ✛ *2 km (1 mile) east of Dundee* ☎ *034/212–2654, 034/212–2376* ⊕ *www.talana. co.za* ✉ *R30 (cash only).*

NEED A BREAK?

Miners' Rest Tea Shop. In a delightfully restored pre-1913 miner's cottage at the Talana Museum, the tea shop serves light refreshments as well as more substantial home-cooked meals. The food is excellent and the atmosphere most welcoming. **Known for:** Sunday buffet; quality meals; friendly service. ⊠ *Talana Museum* ☎ *034/212–1704* ⊕ *www. talana.co.za.*

RORKE'S DRIFT

35 km (22 miles) southwest of Dundee.

From the British perspective the Battle of Rorke's Drift was the most glorious battle of the Anglo-Zulu War, all the more so because it took place just hours after the British humiliation at Isandlwana on January 22, 1879. For 12 hours, a British force numbering just 140 men, many of them wounded in the previous battle, fought off and ultimately repelled more than 3,000 Zulu warriors. The 1964 movie *Zulu* brought the story to the masses.

GETTING HERE AND AROUND
Rorke's Drift is southwest of Dundee on the R68.

EXPLORING
Fugitives' Drift. This drift (ford) was where, on 22 January 1879, the British survivors of the Battle of Isandlwana crossed the Buffalo River, and it was here that Lieutenants Melvill and Coghill were killed as they tried to save the Queen's Colour. They are buried on the hillside above the drift, which is now on the grounds of what is now the Fugitives' Drift Lodge, part of a nature reserve. The Queen's Colour was later recovered and, now restored, hangs in Brecon Cathedral in Wales. ■ **TIP→ There's no information on-site, so read up about it before your visit, or hire a an accredited battlefields guide.** ⊠ *Rorke's Drift Rd.* ☎ *034/271–8051, 034/271–8053* ⊕ *www.fugitivesdrift.com.*

Shiyane/Rorke's Drift. This is by far the best of the Zulu War battlefields to see without a guide. An excellent small museum and orientation center retells the story of the battle from the British perspective, with electronic diagrams, battle sounds, and dioramas. The British force at Rorke's Drift consisted of just 140 men, of whom 35 were ailing or wounded. They occupied a Swedish mission church and house, which had been converted into a storehouse and hospital. The Zulu forces numbered some 3,000–4,000 men, composed of the reserve regiments from the earlier battle of Isandlwana. When a survivor from Isandlwana sounded the warning at 3:15 pm, the tiny British force hastily erected a stockade of flour bags and biscuit boxes around the mission. The Zulus attacked 75 minutes later, and the fighting raged for 12 hours before the Zulus faltered and retreated. A record number of 11 Victoria Crosses (Britain's highest military honor) were awarded at Rorke's Drift. There's a small tuck shop and craft shop selling rugs and craft work on-site. ✉ *Rorke's Drift Rd., off R68* ☎ *034/642–1687* 🎫 *R35* 🕒 *Closed Christmas and Good Friday.*

WHERE TO STAY

$$$$ RESORT 🏨 **Fugitives' Drift Lodge.** Set in a 5,000-acre natural heritage site, this attractive lodge lies just a couple of miles from the famous battle site of Rorke's Drift and overlooks the drift where survivors of the British defeat at Isandlwana fled across the Buffalo River. **Pros:** lovely garden settings; you'll be contributing to the local communities through the David Rattray Foundation; knowledgeable hosts. **Cons:** pricey; can be full of groups of old military gentlemen; harks back to a colonial era. [$] *Rooms from: R8500* ✉ *Rorke's Drift Rd., Dundee* ☎ *034/642–1843* 🌐 *www.fugitivesdrift.com* 🛏 *9 rooms* 🍴 *All meals.*

$$$$ HOTEL 🏨 **iSibindi Zulu Lodge.** This lodge within the iSibindi Eco Reserve, 9 km (4 miles) from Rorke's Drift, combines game-viewing and Zulu cultural experiences with battlefield tours led by excellent local guides and historians. **Pros:** lovely eco-reserve with game (not predators); refreshing small infinity pool with glorious views; lots of local design elements immerse you in local culture. **Cons:** very hot in summer; no air-conditioning, but does have ceiling fan; pricey. [$] *Rooms from: R5100* ✉ *iSibindi Eco Reserve, Dundee* ☎ *035/474–1473, 035/474–1490* 🌐 *www.isibindizululodge.co.za* 🛏 *6 rooms* 🍴 *Some meals.*

SHOPPING

Rorke's Drift ELC Art and Craft Centre. Rorke's Drift is still a mission station, run by the Evangelical Lutheran Church, and this center at the mission sells handmade bags, handwoven rugs, curios, and beadwork, all created by local artists. It's a good one to support. ✉ *Rorke's Drift Rd., off R68, Dundee* ☎ *034/642–1627* 🌐 *www.centre-rorkesdrift.com* 🕒 *Closed Christmas Day, Boxing Day, and New Year's Day.*

ISANDLWANA

35 km (22 miles) northeast of Rorke's Drift on R68.

The name of Isandlwana went down in British military history on January 22, 1879, when the then mighty British Empire suffered a resounding defeat at the hands of the 20,000-strong Zulu army. Today, the site remains a poignant reminder, dotted with memorials to the fallen—about 1,000 Zulus and 1,329 British soldiers.

GETTING HERE AND AROUND

The site of the Battle of Isandlwana is halfway between Dundee and Babanango, just off the R68.

EXPLORING

Isandlwana. The Battle of Isandlwana, on January 22, 1879, was a major defeat for the British army. Coming as it did at the very beginning of the Zulu War, the humiliating defeat shocked Imperial Britain. Lt. Gen.

Lord Chelmsford was in charge of one of three invasion columns that were supposed to sweep into Zululand and converge on King Cetshwayo's capital at Ulundi. On January 20 Chelmsford crossed the Buffalo River into Zululand, leaving behind a small force at Rorke's Drift to guard the column's supplies.

Unknown to Chelmsford, the heart of the Zulu army—20,000 men—had taken up a position just 5 km (3 miles) away. Using Shaka's classic chest-and-horns formation, the Zulus swept toward the British positions. The battle hung in the balance until the Zulus' left horn outflanked the British. The fighting continued for two hours before the British fled the field, with the Zulus in triumphant pursuit. About 1,000 Zulus perished in the attack, as did 1,329 British troops. Today the battlefield is scattered with whitewashed stone cairns and memorials marking the resting places of fallen soldiers. ■TIP→ **The visitor center houses a small but excellent museum of mementos and artifacts, following the course of the battle in marvelous detail—a good place to start if you're here without a guide. Allow at least two or three hours for a visit.** ✉ *Off R68, Dundee* ☎ *034/271–0634* 💲 *R35* ⊙ *Closed Christmas Day and Good Friday.*

WHERE TO STAY

$$$$
HOTEL
Fodor's Choice
★

📷 **Isandlwana Lodge.** It's said that on January 22, 1879, during the Battle of Isandlwana, which was a major defeat for the British army, the chief of the Zulu army stood on Nyoni Rock where this lodge is now built. **Pros:** amazing views; battle tours start on-site; beautiful rooms. **Cons:** area a bit bleak if the weather's bad; remote location; food served, while very good, depends on what's delivered and portions aren't big. 💲 *Rooms from: R7200* ✉ *Off R68* ☎ *034/271–8301* ⊕ *www.isandlwana.co.za* 🍴 *13 rooms* 🍽 *All meals.*

SHAKALAND

13 km (8 miles) north of Eshowe; 96 km (59 miles) southeast of Babanango.

If you're interested in learning more about the fierce warrior Shaka Zulu or the Zulu people, this living history museum will give you a glimpse into this amazing culture, its social structure, ceremonies, and crafts.

EXPLORING

FAMILY **Shakaland.** A living museum of Zulu culture, Shakaland is one of the most popular tourist stops in the region. Originally the movie set for *Shaka Zulu* (1987), it consists of a traditional 19th-century Zulu kraal, with thatch beehive huts arranged in a circle around a central cattle enclosure. Watch traditionally dressed Zulus making beer, forging spears, and crafting beadwork. Opt for a three-hour day tour with lunch or spend the night. A Zulu cultural adviser leads you through the kraal, explaining the significance of the layout and the roles played by men and women in traditional Zulu society. A highlight is a performance of traditional Zulu dances. This is undoubtedly an excellent introduction to Zulu culture, but some critics have labeled it Zulu Disneyland. ✉ *Normanhurst Farm, Off R66, Nkwalini ✦ 13 km (8 miles) north of Eshowe* ☎ *035/460–0912, 087/740–9292 central reservations, 086/865–3992 central reservations* ⊕ *www.shakaland.com* ✉ *R560.*

WHERE TO STAY

$$ ⊡ **Shakaland.** For a more in-depth exploration of Shakaland, stay the
HOTEL night at the 55-room Shakaland. **Pros:** warm, friendly staff; one-off
FAMILY experience; good variety and quality of food. **Cons:** fake but fun; can
get noisy at dinner and during the shows—all part of the vibe; touristy.
⑨ *Rooms from: R2200* ✉ *Normanhurst Farm, Off R66 ✦ 13 km (8 miles) north of Eshowe* ☎ *035/460–0912, 087/740–9292 central reservations* ⊕ *www.shakaland.com* ⤳ *55 rooms* ⦿ *All meals.*

THE ELEPHANT COAST

The Elephant Coast is bordered in the northwest by the Ubombo Mountains, in the east by the Indian Ocean, and in the south by the iMfolozi River, which is just below the St. Lucia Estuary. The estuary is part of the iSimangaliso Wetland Park (Greater St. Lucia Wetland Park), South Africa's very first World Heritage Site. Although the area is only 200 km (124 miles) long and 70 km (43 miles) wide, its eco-diversity offers some of South Africa's most varied and gorgeous scenery: pristine coastal bird-rich forests, floodplains and inland lakes, unspoiled miles-long beaches, deep rivers, and unique sand forests. It's an outdoor lover's paradise, where you can swim (with sharks!), snorkel, surf, watch turtles, go hiking, mountain biking, deep-sea fishing or diving, check out the Big Five, or see hippos, dolphins and whales.

KwaZulu-Natal's best private lodges lie in northern Zululand and Maputaland, a remote region close to Mozambique. With one exception, the lodges reviewed here do not offer the Big Five. However, they are sufficiently close to one another and to the Hluhluwe-iMfolozi Game Reserve to allow you to put together a bush experience that delivers the Big Five and a great deal more, including superb bird-watching opportunities and an unrivaled beach paradise. Malaria does pose a problem, however, and antimalarial drugs are essential. Summers are hot, hot, hot. If you can't take heat and humidity, then autumn and winter are probably the best time to visit.

WHEN TO GO

This area is hot and humid in summer, but if you can stand the heat, it's a great time to visit, because the scenery is at its greenest and most spectacular. Want to see turtles or whales? November through March is turtle-tracking time, and July through December is whale-watching time. Witnessing these magnificent creatures leaping or breaching above the waves is an unforgettable sight. From July to September you can spot humpback whales, and occasionally see Southern Right whales moving north to their breeding grounds off Mozambique; in September and November you can spot them on their way back to their Antarctic feeding grounds.

GETTING HERE AND AROUND

The Richards Bay airport is the closest to the Hluhluwe-iMfolozi area—about 100 km (60 miles) south of Hluhluwe-iMfolozi and about 224 km (140 miles) south of Ithala.

There are daily flights from Johannesburg to Richards Bay; flight time is about an hour. Private lodges will arrange your transfers for you.

If you're traveling to Hluhluwe-iMfolozi from Durban, drive north on the N2 to Mtubatuba, then cut west on the R618 to Mambeni Gate. Otherwise, continue up the N2 to the Hluhluwe exit and follow the signs to the park and Memorial Gate. The whole trip takes about three hours, but watch out for potholes.

If you're headed to Ithala from Durban, drive north on the N2 to Empangeni, and then head west on the R34 to Vryheid. From here cut east on the R69 to Louwsburg. The reserve is immediately northwest of the village, from which there are clear signs. The journey from Durban takes around 5 hours and from Hluhluwe-iMfolozi about 2½ hours. Roads are good, and there are plenty of gas stations along the way.

Contacts Richards Bay Airport. ⊠ *30 Fish Eagle Flight, Birdswood, Richards Bay* ☎ *035/789-9630.*

TOURS

umHluhluwe Safaris. By far the largest tour operator in Zululand, this company offers a full range of three- and six-hour game drives in Hluhluwe-iMfolozi, as well as night drives and bush walks. The company also leads game drives into the Mkuze Game Reserve and guided tours to the bird-rich wetlands and beaches of St. Lucia. ☎ *035/562–0519, 082/964–2547 cell* ⊕ *www.hluhluwesafaris.co.za* ☒ *3-hr game drive R533, 6-hr game drive R715 (minimum of 4 people).*

VISITOR INFORMATION

Ezemvelo KZN Wildlife can provide information about the Hluhluwe-iMfolozi and Ithala game reserves and can help you book hikes on wilderness trails.

The Elephant Coast's website has information about dining and lodging, as well as attractions, towns you'll pass through, sports facilities, and much more. If you're visiting the Hluhluwe-iMfolozi Park, all activities can be booked through the website of the province's official conservation organization, Ezemvelo KZN Wildlife.

Contacts Elephant Coast. ⊠ *Elephant Coast, 1020 Main Rd., Hluhluwe* ☎ *035/562–0966, 086/690-6157* ⊕ *www.elephantcoast.kzn.org.za.* **Ezemvelo KZN Wildlife.** ☎ *033/845–1000, 033/845–1001* ⊕ *www.kznwildlife.com.*

RICHARDS BAY

177 km (110 miles) northeast of Durban.

Founded in the 1880s during the Anglo-Zulu colonial wars, Richards Bay was named after British Rear Admiral Sir Frederick William Richards, who landed a naval force here. An early claim to fame came in 1891, when colonial adventurer John Dunn killed a 22-foot crocodile in the estuary—still one of the largest ever documented—but the town remained a backwater with a population of less than 200 people until as recently as 1968. Today, Richards Bay is the major port in the region and is adjacent to significant mineral deposits, which have contributed to the town's massive growth. Visitors may be more interested in what awaits beyond in the hinterland. Richards Bay is the gateway to the land of the Zulu, one of Africa's most fascinating indigenous peoples, and from here you have easy access to some of the world's finest wildlife game parks, including the Hluhluwe-iMfolozi Game Reserve, which protects the highest concentration of white rhino left in Africa.

EXPLORING

Richards Bay Game Reserve. Just south of town, the lagoon formed by the confluence of the Mzingazi and Mhlatuzi rivers has populations of hippos, crocodiles, monkeys, fish, and eagles. In 1935, 1,198 hectares (2,961 acres) of the lagoon was saved from development and named the Richards Bay Game Reserve. It is particularly important as a bird habitat, with more than 300 documented species, and offers permanent hides from which you can watch wading birds on the tidal flats and swamp wetlands. ✉ *Richards Bay* 🌐 *www.sa-venues.com/game-reserves/kzn_richardsbay.htm* 🎟 *Small entrance fee.*

7

WHERE TO EAT

$$ INTERNATIONAL 🍴 **Elephant & I.** The question is what *won't* you find to eat at this popular restaurant in the Boardwalk Inkwazi shopping center. You name it, they've got it: from burgers, wraps, salads, bagel sandwiches, and paninis, to a jumble of international dinner dishes, like moussaka, lasagna, quiche, shepherd's pie, or stir-fry, topped off with dessert. **Known for:** variety; breakfasts; burgers and salads. [$] *Average main: R100* ✉ *Shop L26, Boardwalk Centre* ☎ *035/789–7269* 🌐 *www.elephant-and-i.co.za.*

$$ PORTUGUESE 🍴 **Portuguese on the Bay.** This casual eatery draws families and groups for the local Portuguese grub with Mozambican flare—peri-peri (or piri-piri) chili sauce is king here. Start with the flaming chouriço (chorizo) and you can't go wrong with the grilled peri-peri chicken or prawns for mains. **Known for:** generous portions; groups of friends and family dining; Afro-Portuguese flavor. [$] *Average main: R135* ✉ *Tuzi Gazi Bay Waterfront, Richards Bay* ☎ *035/788–0022.*

WHERE TO STAY

$ B&B/INN FAMILY 🏨 **Aristo Manor Guesthouse.** Minutes from the airport and close to Richard's Bay and Lake Mzingazi, this elegant seven-room guesthouse combines all the personalized service of a bed-and-breakfast with the amenities of an inn or small hotel. **Pros:** owners go out of their way to be accommodating; plenty of privacy; parking. **Cons:** not in the city center; many antiques and collectibles around—it's not everyone's taste; feels like someone's home. [$] *Rooms from: R1050* ✉ *16 Whydah Wing* ☎ *035/786–1212* 🌐 *www.aristomanor.com* 🛏 *7 rooms* 🍽 *Some meals.*

$ B&B/INN FAMILY Fodor's Choice ★ **Imvubu Lodge.** An unexpected city find surrounded by lush forests, this romantic hotel has luxurious touches like deep stone baths and separate living rooms with views of scenic Menywa Lake and the Indian Ocean. **Pros:** privacy; proximity to the ocean; good value. **Cons:** the monkeys can be ruthless—don't leave doors and windows open; furniture is a little old; food options at restaurant aren't too exciting. [$] *Rooms from: R1100* ✉ *Corner Krewelkring at Hibberd Dr., Meer en See* ☎ *035/753–4120* 🌐 *www.imvubulodge.co.za* 🛏 *50 rooms* 🍴 *Breakfast.*

$ HOTEL **Protea Hotel Waterfront Richards Bay.** Views are not an issue at this modern hotel right on the bay, as all of the rooms face the water (some on the second and third floors also have balconies). **Pros:** close to the beach; great views; everything provided on-site. **Cons:** service spotty; can feel impersonal; mediocre breakfast. [$] *Rooms from: R1483* ✉ *Pioneer Rd. at Bridgetown Rd., TuziGazi Waterfront* ☎ *35/788–0448* 🌐 *www.marriott.com/hotels/travel/rcbwa-protea-hotel-richards-bay-waterfront* 🛏 *75 rooms* 🍴 *Breakfast.*

SHOPPING

Zulu art and handicrafts are the must-have souvenirs from a visit to Richards Bay. The beadwork objects are of particular interest because the traditional colors and patterns on the belts and bands were developed as secret coded messages from the Zulu women who made them, telling of love, jealousy, and loneliness. Needless to say, these days most pieces produced for the tourist market are simply pleasing to the eye rather than having any symbolic significance. Other handcrafted objects include pottery, used as everyday utensils, and carved wooden spears and shields once carried into battle by the Zulu warriors. The skill of carving is also put to good, and less bloody, use to produce statues of warriors and African animals (make sure that any wooden artifacts you buy have been treated against termites). Zulu handicrafts are best bought directly from the artisans at tribal villages, but they can also be found in craft markets and street stalls throughout the region. In Richards Bay, the Tuzi Gazi Waterfront shopping mall has a range of shops and, with its restaurants, boardwalk, and leisure marina, is a great place for strolling and browsing.

Boardwalk Inkwazi Shopping Centre. Richards Bay's most popular shopping mall has the kinds of chain stores you'd expect, plus some surprises. There's also a large selection of fast food and a movie theater. ✉ *Kruger Rand Rd.* ☎ *35/789–7251* 🌐 *www.boardwalkinkwazi.co.za.*

HLUHLUWE-IMFOLOZI PARK

264 km (165 miles) northeast of Durban.

Renowned for its conservation successes—most notably with white rhinos—this reserve is a wonderful place to view the Big Five and many other species. Until 1989 it consisted of two separate parks, Hluhluwe in the north and iMfolozi in the south, separated by a fenced corridor. Although a road (R618) still runs through this corridor, the fences have been removed, and the parks now operate as a single entity. Hluhluwe and the corridor are the most scenic areas of the park, notable for their bush-covered hills and knockout views, whereas iMfolozi is better known for its broad plains.

EXPLORING

FAMILY **Hluhluwe-iMfolozi Park.** Reputedly King Shaka's favorite hunting ground, Zululand's Hluhluwe-iMfolozi (pronounced shloo- *shloo*-ee im-fuh-*low*-zee) incorporates two of Africa's oldest reserves: Hluhluwe and iMfolozi, both founded in 1895. These days the reserves are abbreviated as HIP. In an area of just 906 square km (350 square miles), Hluhluwe-iMfolozi delivers the Big Five plus all the plains game and species like nyala and red duiker that are rare in other parts of the country. Equally important, it encompasses one of the most biologically diverse habitats on the planet, with a unique mix of forest, woodland, savanna, and grassland. You'll find about 1,250 species of plants and trees here—more than in some entire countries.

The park is administered by Ezemvelo KZN Wildlife, the province's official conservation organization, which looks after all the large game reserves and parks as well as many nature reserves. Thanks to its conservation efforts and those of its predecessor, the highly regarded Natal Parks Board, the park can take credit for saving the white rhino from extinction. So successful was the park at increasing white rhino numbers that in 1960 it established its now famous Rhino Capture Unit to relocate rhinos to other reserves in Africa. The park is currently trying to do for the black rhino what it did for its white cousins. Poaching in the past nearly decimated Africa's black rhino population, but as a result of the park's remarkable conservation program, 20% of Africa's remaining black rhinos now live in this reserve—and you won't get a better chance of seeing them in the wild than here. ⊠ *Hluhluwe iMfolozi* ☎ *035/562–0848* ⊕ *www.kznwildlife.com* ✉ *R220 international guests, R110 South Africans.*

ACTIVITIES

BUSH WALKS

Armed rangers lead groups of eight on two- to three-hour bush walks departing from Hilltop or Mpila Camp. You may not spot much game on these walks, but you do see plenty of birds, and you learn a great deal about the area's ecology and tips on how to recognize the signs of the bush, including animal spoor (tracks). Walks depart daily at 5:30 am and 3:30 pm (6 and 3 in winter) and cost R350. Reserve a few days in advance at **Hilltop Camp reception** (☎ *031/208–3684*).

GAME DRIVES

A great way to see the park is on game drives led by rangers. These drives (R1,900 for three hours, four people maximum) hold several advantages over driving through the park yourself: you sit high up in an open-air vehicle with a good view and the wind in your face, a ranger explains the finer points of animal behavior and ecology, and your guide has a good idea where to find animals like leopards, cheetahs, and lions. Your guide will also take you to a picnic spot or for lunch if you're on a longer drive. Game drives leave daily at 5:30 am in summer, 6:30 am in winter. The park also offers three-hour night drives, during which you search with powerful spotlights for nocturnal animals. These three-hour drives depart at 7, and you should make advance reservations at **Hilltop Camp reception** (☎ *031/208–3684*).

WILDERNESS TRAILS

The park's **Wilderness Trails** are every bit as popular as Kruger's, but they tend to be tougher and more rustic. You should be fit enough to walk up to 16 km (10 miles) a day for a period of three days and four nights. An armed ranger leads the hikes, and all equipment, food, and baggage are carried by donkeys. The first and last nights are spent at Mndindini, a permanent tented camp. The other two are spent under canvas in the bush. While in the bush, hikers bathe in the iMfolozi River or have a hot bucket shower; toilet facilities consist of a spade and toilet-paper roll. Trails, open March–October, are limited to eight people and should be reserved a year in advance (R3,450 per person per trail).

Fully catered two- or three-night **Short Wilderness Trails** (R2,250 per person) involve stays at a satellite camp in the wilderness area. You'll sleep in a dome tent, and although there's hot water from a bucket shower, your toilet is a spade.

If that sounds too easy, you can always opt for the four-night **Primitive Trail.** On this trek hikers carry their own packs and sleep out under the stars, although there are lightweight tents for inclement weather. A campfire burns all night to scare off animals, and each participant is expected to sit a 90-minute watch. A ranger acts as guide. The cost is R2,400 per person.

A less rugged wilderness experience can be had on the **Base Camp Trail,** based out of the tented Mndindini camp, where you're guaranteed a bed and some creature comforts. The idea behind these trails is to instill in the participants an appreciation for the beauty of the untamed bush. You can also join the Mpila night drive if you wish. Participation is limited to eight people and costs about R3,900 per person.

The Explorer Trail, two nights and three days, combines the most comfortable Base Camp trail with the Primitive Trail. On this trail you sleep out under the stars at a different spot each night. The cost is R2,350 per person.

WHERE TO STAY

Hluhluwe-iMfolozi offers a range of accommodations in government-run rest camps, with an emphasis on self-catering (only Hilltop has a restaurant). The park also has secluded bush lodges and camps, but most foreign visitors can't avail themselves of these lodgings, as each must be reserved in a block, and the smallest accommodates at least eight people. Conservation levies are R80 per person.

$$
RESORT
FAMILY

⌖ **Hilltop Camp.** This delightful lodge in the Hluhluwe half of the park matches some of South Africa's best private lodges. **Pros:** floodlit water hole; warm, friendly staff; incredible views. **Cons:** watch out for marauding monkeys; outdoor grill area not covered and is dimly lit at night; bathrooms can smell a little moldy. Ⓢ *Rooms from: R2188* ✉ *Hluhluwe* ☎ *031/208–3684* ⊕ *www.hilltopcamp.co.za* ↝ *70 rooms* ⏹ *Breakfast.*

$$$
HOTEL
FAMILY

⌖ **Hluhluwe River Lodge.** Overlooking False Bay lake and the Hluhluwe River floodplain—follow signs from Hluhluwe village—this fantastic-value, family-owned lodge is the ideal base for visiting the game reserves and the iSimangaliso Wetland Park. **Pros:** only 25 minutes from Hluhluwe-iMfolozi; great for families; excellent food. **Cons:** lots of kids in holiday times; activities cost extra; four-wheel drive recommended. [$] *Rooms from: R2700* ✉ *Hluhluwe* ☎ *031/208–3684* 🌐 *www.hluhluwe.co.za* 🛏 *13 rooms* 🍴 *All-inclusive.*

$$ RENTAL FAMILY 🏨 **Mpila Camp.** In the central iMfolozi section of the park, Mpila is reminiscent of some of Kruger's older camps. **Pros:** free-roaming game; lovely location; good value for money compared to other parks up north. **Cons:** needs a refurb; watch out for hyenas stealing your braai meat; little privacy. [$] *Rooms from: R1640* ✉ *Hluhluwe iMfolozi* ☎ *033/845–1000, 031/208–3684* 🌐 *www.mpilacamp.co.za* 🛏 *40 rooms* 🍴 *No meals.*

$$ HOTEL FAMILY 🏨 **Ubizane Zululand Tree Lodge.** About 16 km (10 miles) from Hluhluwe-iMfolozi Park, this lodge lies in a forest of fever trees on the 3,700-acre Ubizane Game Reserve and makes a great base from which to explore Hluhluwe, Mkuze, and St. Lucia. **Pros:** bird's-eye views over lovely surroundings; friendly staff; mosquito nets on all beds. **Cons:** crocodiles in pool near dining area are off-putting; bathrooms need attention; dinner buffet a little expensive for what you get. [$] *Rooms from: R2234* ✉ *1020 Main Rd., Hluhluwe* ☎ *035/562–1020* 🌐 *www.ubizane.co.za* 🛏 *49 rooms* 🍴 *Breakfast.*

UMKHUZE KZN PARK

48 km (30 miles) northeast of Hluhluwe-iMfolozi.

Wildlife—and amazing birdlife—abounds in this 400-square-km (154-square-mile) reserve in the shadow of the Ubombo Mountains. Lying between the uMkhuze and Msunduzi rivers, it makes up the northwestern spur of the iSimangaliso Wetland Park, a World Heritage Site. It has been a protected area since 1912.

EXPLORING

OFF THE BEATEN PATH

Jozini Dam. It may be off the main tourist routes, but if you have time head for the huge, beautiful 160-square-km (62-square-mile) Jozini Dam (or Lake Jozini), that lies in northern KwaZulu-Natal and borders Swaziland. Easily accessible from Gauteng, it's approximately five hours southeast by road from Johannesburg, via Pongola, and approximately three hours northeast from Durban. The dam is lined by the Pongola Game Reserve—one of South Africa's oldest reserves (proclaimed in 1894)—so all sorts of game meanders along the banks, from black and white rhinos to elephants and hippos. If you're a birder you'll be in avian heaven, as the dam is a magnet for waterbirds of every description. **TIP→ The dam has the best tiger fishing in South Africa (in season), but if you don't catch and release a tiger, maybe you'll hook a yellowfish, carp, or tilapia.** ✉ *Mkuze.*

uMkhuze KZN Park. If you're a birder, then you'll find yourself in seventh heaven in this reserve, 48 km (30 miles) north of Hluhluwe-iMfolozi, which is famous for its birds: more than 420 bird species have been spotted here, including myriad waterfowl drawn to the park's shallow pans in summer. Several blinds, particularly those overlooking Nsumo Pan, offer superb views. Don't miss out on the amazing 3-km (2-mile) walk through a spectacular rare forest of towering, ancient fig trees.

This is a good place to spot rhinos and elephants, although lions, cheetah, and leopards are much harder to find. However, there's is plenty of other game, including hippos, zebras, giraffes, kudus, and nyalas. **■ TIP→ There are variant spellings of Mkuze in the area; you may also see Mkuzi or Mkhuzi.** ✉ *Off N2, Mkuze* ☎ *035/573–9004* 🌐 *www.kznwildlife.com* 🎟 *R40 per vehicle plus R40 per person.*

SELF-GUIDED TRAILS

An unusual feature of Ithala is its self-guided walking trails, in the mountainside above Ntshondwe Camp. The trails give you a chance to stretch your limbs if you've just spent hours cooped up in a car. They also let you get really close to the euphorbias, acacias, and other fascinating indigenous vegetation that festoon the hills. Ask at the camp reception for further information.

WHERE TO STAY

$$ B&B/INN 🏨 **Ghost Mountain Inn.** Swaths of scarlet bougainvillea run riot in the lush gardens of this family-owned country inn with tastefully furnished rooms that each have a small veranda. **Pros:** good value for money; generous buffet; spa on-site. **Cons:** hotel-like atmosphere; tour buses overnight here; can get noisy in peak season. [$] *Rooms from: R1675* ✉ *Fish Eagle Rd., uMkhuze* ☎ *035/573–1025* 🌐 *www.ghostmountaininn.co.za* 🛏 *50 rooms* 🍴 *Breakfast.*

$$$$ HOTEL 🏨 **Shayamanzi Houseboats.** Cabins with floor-to-ceiling windows allow you to lie on your king-size bed and view hippos, waterbirds, elephants, giraffe, zebra, crocodiles, and even an occasional rhino without even getting up. **Pros:** friendly staff; tasty food; tiger fishing in season. **Cons:** off the beaten track; very hot and humid in summer; not all rooms have a good view. [$] *Rooms from: R4900* ✉ *Jozini Tiger Lodge, 1 Main Rd., Jozini* ☎ *034/413–2299* 🌐 *www.jozinitigerlodge.co.za/shayamanzi-houseboat* 🛏 *16 rooms* 🍴 *All-inclusive.*

ITHALA GAME RESERVE

221 km (138 miles) northwest of Hluhluwe-iMfolozi.

The topography of this reserve, from mountaintop to deep river valleys, incorporates varied terrain and plant life, and makes for superior game-viewing in relation to its relatively small size. Thousands of years of human habitation have also provided archaeological and historical interest.

EXPLORING

Ithala Game Reserve. Close to the Swaziland border, Ithala (sometimes spelled "Itala"), founded in 1972 and run by KZN Wildlife, is a rugged region that drops 3,290 feet in just 15 km (9 miles) through sandstone cliffs, multicolor rocks, granite hills, ironstone outcrops, and quartz formations. Because it's a small reserve (296 square km [114 square miles]), and has no lions, it's often bypassed, even by South Africans. The other four of the Big Five are here—it's excellent for black and white rhinos—and you could spot cheetahs, hyenas, giraffes, and an array of antelopes among its 80 mammal species. It's also an excellent spot for birders. The stunning landscapes and the relaxed game-viewing make this area a breath of fresh air after the Big Five melee of Kruger. ✉ *Pongola* ☎ *033/845–1000* 🌐 *www.kznwildlife.com* 🎟 *R60.*

WHERE TO STAY

Although Ithala has several exclusive bush camps, these are booked up months in advance by South Africans, making the chalets at its main camp the only practical accommodations for foreign visitors.

$ RENTAL 🏨 **Ntshondwe Camp.** Arriving at the award-winning Ntshondwe Camp is nothing short of dramatic. **Pros:** tarred road access; game drives; self-guided walks. **Cons:** busy conference and wedding venue; you can't tick the Big Five off your list here; roads are in bad condition. [$] *Rooms from: R1360* ✉ *Ithala Game Reserve* ☎ *033/845–1000* 🌐 *www.ithala.info* 🛏 *68 rooms* 🍴 *No meals.*

PHINDA PRIVATE GAME RESERVE

134 km (83 miles) from Richards Bay; 300 km (186 miles) from Durban.

Fodor's Choice ★ Where Phinda excels is in the superb quality of its rangers, who can provide fascinating commentary on everything from local birds to frogs. It's amazing just how enthralling the love life of a dung beetle can be! There are also Phinda adventures (optional extras) down the Mzinene River for a close-up look at crocodiles, hippos, and birds; big-game fishing or scuba diving off the deserted, wildly beautiful Maputaland coast; and sightseeing flights over Phinda and the highest vegetated dunes in the world.

GETTING HERE AND AROUND

Phinda is 300 km (186 miles) from Durban by road, with a journey time of just over four hours. Before you decide to drive, bear in mind that you won't use your vehicle after you arrive at Phinda—all transportation is provided by open game-viewing vehicles. There are scheduled flights daily from Johannesburg to King Shaka International Airport and to Richards Bay Airport (check with the lodge for latest schedules). Phinda will also arrange road transfers from the airports.

EXPLORING

FAMILY Fodor's Choice ★ **Phinda Private Game Reserve.** This eco-award-winning flagship &Beyond reserve, established in 1991, is a heartening example of tourism serving the environment with panache. *Phinda* (*pin*-da) is Zulu for "return," referring to the restoration of 220 square km (85 square miles) of overgrazed ranchland in northern Zululand to bushveld. It's a triumph. Today Phinda has a stunning variety of seven healthy ecosystems including the rare sand forest (which grows on the fossil dunes of an earlier coastline), savanna, bushveld, open woodland, mountain bush, and verdant wetlands. The Big Five are all here, plus cheetahs, spotted hyenas, hippos, giraffes, impalas, and the rare, elusive, tiny Suni antelope. Birdlife is prolific and extraordinary, with some special Zululand finds: the pink-throated twin spot, the crested guinea fowl, the African broadbill, and the crowned eagle. The reserve is a little more than two hours drive from Richards Bay or four hours by road from Durban. ✉ *Phinda Game Reserve* ☎ *011/809–4300 central reservations* 🌐 *andbeyond.com.*

7

WHERE TO STAY

$$$$
RESORT
Fodor's Choice
★

⊡ **Forest Lodge.** Hidden in a rare sand forest, this fabulous lodge overlooks a small water hole where nyalas, warthogs, and baboons frequently come to drink. **Pros:** magical feeling of oneness with the surrounding bush; has all the mod cons; lovely views from the pool. **Cons:** being in a glass box could make some visitors nervous; not for traditional tastes; cell phone reception can be iffy. $ *Rooms from: R16970* ⊠ *Phinda Game Reserve* ☎ *011/809–4300 reservations* ⊕ *andbeyond. com* ⇆ *16 rooms* ⦾ *All-inclusive.*

$$$$
RESORT
FAMILY

⊡ **Mountain Lodge.** This attractive thatch lodge sits on a rocky hill overlooking miles of bushveld plains and the Ubombo Mountains. **Pros:** great mountain views; very family-friendly; guaranteed a warm welcome. **Cons:** rather bland interiors; pricey if you take the kids (pricey even if you don't take the kids); not the best choice for couples seeking solitude. $ *Rooms from: R15600* ⊠ *Phinda Game Reserve, off R22, Hluhluwe* ☎ *011/809–4300 reservations* ⊕ *andbeyond.com* ⇆ *25 rooms* ⦾ *All-inclusive.*

$$$$
RESORT

⊡ **Rock Lodge.** If you get tired of the eagle's-eye view of the deep valley below from your private veranda, you can write in your journal in your luxurious sitting room or take a late-night dip in your own plunge pool. **Pros:** personal plunge pools; amazing views; luxurious sitting rooms. **Cons:** stay away if you suffer from vertigo; not suitable for families (also, no kids under 12 allowed); not the place for a lively atmosphere. $ *Rooms from: R19500* ⊠ *Phinda Game Reserve* ☎ *011/809–4300 reservations* ⊕ *andbeyond.com* ⇆ *6 rooms* ⦾ *All-inclusive.*

$$$$
RESORT
Fodor's Choice
★

⊡ **Vlei Lodge.** Your suite at this comfortable lodge, tucked into the shade of a sand forest, is so private it's hard to believe there are other guests. **Pros:** superb views over the floodplains; intimate; Wi-Fi en suite. **Cons:** lots of mosquitoes and other flying insects; no children under 12; expensive. $ *Rooms from: R19500* ⊠ *Phinda Game Reserve* ☎ *011/809–4300* ⊕ *andbeyond.com* ⇆ *6 rooms* ⦾ *All-inclusive.*

$$$$
RESORT
FAMILY

⊡ **Zuka Lodge.** An exclusive, single-use lodge for a family or small group of friends, Zuka (*zuka* means "sixpence" in Zulu) is a couple of miles from the bigger lodges. **Pros:** exclusivity; it's like having your own private holiday retreat; gives you the feeling of immediate celebrity status. **Cons:** this exclusivity comes at a high price; entire property must be rented as a whole; choose your fellow guests carefully—you're on your own here. $ *Rooms from: R16970* ⊠ *Phinda Game Reserve* ☎ *011/809–4300 reservations* ⊕ *andbeyond.com* ⇆ *4 rooms* ⦾ *All-inclusive.*

THANDA PRIVATE GAME RESERVE

23 km (14 miles) northeast of Hluhluwe; 400 km (248 miles) north of Durban.

One of KwaZulu-Natal's newer game reserves, Thanda offers a more intimate nature experience than some. Game may sometimes be elusive, but the highly experienced and enthusiastic rangers work hard to find the Big Five and other wildlife. Enjoyable cultural interactions with local people are a highlight of any visit.

GETTING HERE AND AROUND

Road transfers from Richards Bay and Durban airports can be arranged with the reserve.

EXPLORING

Thanda Private Game Reserve. In wild, beautiful northern Zululand, the multi-award-winning 150-square-km (60-square-mile) Thanda reserve, continues to restore former farmlands and hunting grounds to their previous pristine state, thanks to a joint venture with local communities and the king of the Zulus, Goodwill Zweletini, who donated some of his royal hunting grounds to the project. Game that used to roam this wilderness centuries ago has been reestablished, including the Big Five. *Thanda* (*tan*-da) is Zulu for "love," and its philosophy echoes just that: "for the love of nature, wildlife, and dear ones." There's a main lodge, a private villa, and a small tented camp and opportunities to interact with the local people. ✉ *D242, off N2, Hluhluwe* ☎ *032/586–0149 reservations* 🌐 *www.thanda.com.*

WHERE TO STAY

$$$$ RESORT FAMILY 🏨 **Thanda Safari Lodge.** This exquisite lodge blends elements of royal Zulu with an eclectic pan-African feel. **Pros:** luxurious; private plunge pool; unique dwelling in Zulu beehive hut. **Cons:** some might say it's Hollywood in the bush; wild animals do roam close; furniture could do with a refurb. [$] *Rooms from: R15400* ✉ *Off N2 and D242, Hluhluwe* ☎ *032/586–0149 reservations* 🌐 *www.thanda.com* 🛏 *9 rooms* 🍴 *All-inclusive.*

$$$$ RESORT FAMILY 🏨 **Thanda Tented Camp.** Perfect for a family or friends' reunion (although it's great for individual travelers, too), this intimate and luxurious eco-forward camp deep in the bush brings you into close contact with your surroundings. **Pros:** five-star luxury; eco-friendly. **Cons:** not for the nervous type; no air-conditioning; no children under eight. [$] *Rooms from: R8080* ✉ *Off N2 and D242, Hluhluwe* ☎ *032/586–0149 reservations* 🌐 *www.thanda.co.za* 🛏 *15 rooms* 🍴 *All-inclusive.*

7

AMAZULU PRIVATE GAME RESERVE AND AMAKHOSI LODGE

155 km (14 miles) northwest of Hluhluwe; 400 km (248 miles) northeast of Durban.

Amazulu Private Game Reserve incorporates mountains, wetlands, and savanna and, in addition to the Big Five, many other mammals and hundreds of bird species make their home here. Zululand has more frog species than the whole of Europe, and to go on a frogging safari at Amakhosi is a unique and unforgettable experience.

GETTING HERE AND AROUND

Roads are good here, so you can drive yourself. The nearest airport is Richards Bay, which has scheduled flights from all major cities. If necessary, AmaKhosi Lodge does road transfers from Richards Bay.

EXPLORING

AmaZulu Game Reserve and AmaKhosi Lodge. More than 100 square km (39 square miles) of pristine wilderness on the perennial Mkhuze River are the attraction at this private reserve, where habitats range from rocky hillsides to thick bushveld, tamboti forests to broad wetlands. AmaKhosi has all of the Big Five, in addition to wildebeests, zebras, giraffes, and a variety of antelopes, including the shy nyala. Most animals have been reintroduced, with the exception of leopards, which remain secretive and very difficult to spot. Hundreds of birds, however, are much easier to see. ■ **TIP→ Try something really special—after a day spotting big game, join a guided frogging safari at night. Armed with a lighted miner's helmet, you'll discover a whole new exciting amphibian world. The reserve is 40 km (21 miles) south of Pongola.** ✉ *Pongola* ☎ *034/414–1157* 🌐 *www.amakhosi.com.*

WHERE TO STAY

$$$$ RESORT

🏨 **AmaKhosi Lodge.** This spectacular lodge overlooks the Mkhuze River in the heart of northern KwaZulu-Natal, where birdlife is abundant and the Big Five are all present. **Pros:** unique nighttime frogging expeditions; outstanding game drives; top-notch service. **Cons:** off the beaten track; no lunch option, though breakfast and high tea are substantial; if there's a family with a rowdy child, it can ruin the atmosphere. [$] *Rooms from: R5570* ✉ *Off N2, Pongola* ☎ *034/414–1157* 🌐 *www.amakhosi.com* 🛏 *9 rooms* 🍴 *All meals.*

MAPUTALAND COASTAL FOREST RESERVE

300 km (186 miles) from Richards Bay.

Expect great swaths of pale, creamy sand stretching to far-off rocky headlands, a shimmering, undulating horizon where whales blow. Watch out for pods of dolphins leaping and dancing in the morning sun. If you're here in season (November to early March), one of nature's greatest and most spiritually uplifting experiences is waiting for you—turtle tracking.

GETTING HERE AND AROUND

Visitors fly into Richards Bay from Johannesburg and are picked up by the lodge's transportation—they will make all the flight and pickup arrangements, and if you'd like to travel by road instead of air, they can arrange a car service to get you to and from Johannesburg. You could drive yourself, but it's really an unnecessary waste of time and car-rental fees, as you won't be able to use the vehicle once you're on the property. Plus, you'd need to rent a 4x4, because the last part of the road is very bumpy and muddy.

WHEN TO GO

The loggerhead and leatherback turtle egg-laying season goes from November through early March. During these months rangers lead after-dinner drives and walks down the beach to look for turtles, and you can expect to cover as much as 16 km (10 miles) in a night. From a weather standpoint, the best times to visit the lodge are probably spring (September–October) and autumn (March–May). In summer the temperature regularly soars past 38°C (100°F), but this is when the turtles come ashore to dig their nests and lay their eggs—an awesome spectacle. Swimming during winter is a brisk proposition, and August is the windiest month.

EXPLORING

Fodor's Choice ★ **iSimangaliso Wetland Park.** Declared a UNESCO World Heritage Site (South Africa's first) in 1999, the iSimangaliso Wetland encompasses a number of disparate natural African environments including the iMfolozi Swamp forest and the Maputaland Marine Reserve, an important nesting site for endangered loggerhead and leatherback turtles. The most carefree way to enjoy the reserve is on a boat trip, where you'll be able to get close to hippos and immense Nile crocodiles and try to spot some of the more than 500 species of birds that call the park home. Two-hour trips run by the park on a rustic covered barge with a guide (R240/person) leave daily every two hours, and require a minimum of six people. The park protects myriad river and coastal environments, including the estuary of the St. Lucia River, coral reefs, sandy beaches, coastal dunes, inland and tidal lakes, swamps, mangrove forests, and papyrus wetlands. **■TIP→ There's a nondescript arts and crafts center at the boat landing, filled with authentic Zulu woven baskets, storage vessels, place mats, and beaded and wooden crafts made by local women. Prices vary according to the artist and are extremely good value for excellent quality. Shop away.** ☎ *035/590–1633* 🌐 *www.isimangaliso.com* 🎟 *R240.*

7

Maputaland Coastal Forest Reserve. The highlight of a visit here, if it's timed right, is to view the loggerhead and leatherback turtles. Nothing—not photographs, not wildlife documentaries—prepares you for the size of these creatures. On any given night, you might see a huge, humbling leatherback, 6 feet long and weighing up to 500 kg (1,100 pounds), drag her great body up through the surf to the high-water mark at the back of the beach. There she will dig a deep hole and lay up to a 120 gleaming white eggs, bigger than a golf ball but smaller than a tennis ball. It will have taken her many, many years to achieve this moment of fruition, a voyage through time and across the great oceans of the world—a long, solitary journey in the cold black depths of the sea, meeting and mating only once every seven years, and always coming back to within about 300 feet of the spot on the beach where she herself had been born. And if your luck holds, you might even observe the miracle of the hatchlings, when perfect bonsai leatherback turtles dig themselves out of their deep, sandy nest and rush pell-mell toward the sea under a star-studded sky. ✉ *Off Hwy. 2, south of Mtunzini.*

WHERE TO STAY

$$$$ RESORT FAMILY 🏨 **Rocktail Beach Camp.** Tucked away in the Maputaland Coastal Forest, with glorious unspoiled beaches, this lovely lodge is perfect for families, though it's great for individual travelers and honeymooners, too. **Pros:** pristine reefs; loggerhead and leatherback turtle nesting sites. **Cons:** 20- to 30-minute walk to beach; difficult to access. [$] *Rooms from: R7110* ✉ *D1850* ☎ *011/257–5000 reservations* 🌐 *www.wilderness-safaris.com/camps/rocktail-beach-camp* 🛏 *17 rooms* 🍴 *All meals.*

$$$$ RESORT Fodor's Choice ★ **Thonga Beach Lodge.** Dramatically sited, this lovely beach lodge a stone's throw from the sea has air-conditioned, thatch suites decorated in chic Robinson Crusoe style with wooden floors, reed interior walls, cane and wooden furniture, gorgeous bathrooms with sea views, and personal decks looking out over rolling coastal dunes and the blue Indian Ocean. **Pros:** Robinson Crusoe deluxe; turtle tracking; spa treatments. **Cons:** difficult to get to; expensive; booked up frequently. [$] *Rooms from: R11380* ✉ *Maputaland Coastal Forest Reserve* ☎ *035/474–1490, 035/474–1473 reservations* 🌐 *www.thongabeachlodge.co.za* 🛏 *24 rooms* 🍴 *All meals.*

JOHANNESBURG

Updated by
Barbara Noe
Kennedy

Johannesburg, Jo'burg, Egoli ("City of Gold"), or Jozi, as it is affectionately known by locals, is the commercial heart of South Africa and the primary gateway for international visitors. Historically, it is where money is made and fortunes are found. The city has an unfair reputation for being an ugly, dangerous place you ought to avoid on any trip to South Africa. On the contrary, much of Johannesburg is quite pretty, largely because of the millions of trees that cover it (it has, purportedly, the largest human-planted forest in the world), and statistically speaking it is less dangerous than Cape Town.

Johannesburg is South Africa's most-visited city by far, and it's well worth a stopover of at least two or three days. There's plenty to see here, including the Apartheid Museum and Constitution Hill in the city, not to mention the nearby city of Soweto, and the Cradle of Humankind World Heritage Site about 90 minutes away. All the attractions listed *in this chapter*, including areas like Sandton, Rosebank, Greenside, and Parkhurst, are perfectly safe to visit on your own.

Ask a *jol* (lively party) of Jo'burgers what they love about their hometown, and they may point to its high-paced energy; its opportunity; afternoon thunderstorms in the summer; the Pirates versus Chiefs derby (the Orlando Pirates and Kaizer Chiefs are South Africa's most loved—and hated—soccer teams); spectacular sunsets; jacaranda blooms carpeting the city in purple in October and November; a great climate; the dog walks around Emmarentia Dam; the fast-paced lifestyle; the can-do attitude; the down-to-earth nature of its people; and the city's rich history.

Johannesburg's origins lie in the discovery of gold. The city sits at the center of a vast urban industrial complex that covers most of the province of Gauteng (the *g* is pronounced like the *ch* in Chanukah), which means "Place Where the Gold Is" in the Sotho language and is home to the world's deepest gold mines (more than 3.9 km [2.4 miles] deep). More than 100 years ago it was just a rocky piece of unwanted highveld land. But in 1886 an Australian, George Harrison, officially discovered gold, catapulting Johannesburg into a modern metropolis that still helps to power the country's economy (though gold mining has been winding down in recent years).

With a population between 8 and 10.5 million—if you include the surrounding cities like Soweto, the East Rand, and the West Rand—greater Jo'burg is a fairly populous city by world standards (bigger than Paris but smaller than Tokyo) and is by far the country's largest city. Despite its industrial past, Jozi remains a green city, with more than 10 million trees and many beautiful parks and nature reserves, which is all the

TOP REASONS TO GO

History in Your Lifetime: Do a self-guided tour of the Constitutional Court, built on the site of a prison whose inmates included Mahatma Gandhi and Nelson Mandela. The Apartheid Museum takes a holistic look at South Africa's road to democracy.

Iconic Soweto: Visit the site of some dramatic antiapartheid struggles, including the Hector Pieterson Museum, as well as former homes of Nobel Peace Prize laureates Nelson Mandela and Archbishop Desmond Tutu.

African Arts and Crafts: The Rosebank Art and Craft Market showcases ornaments, masks, and fabrics from across Africa, ranging from the cheap and cheerful to one-off collector's items.

Cradle of Humankind: Visit the Sterkfontein Caves and Maropeng Visitor Centre at this World Heritage Site, about 90 minutes from Johannesburg, to view humankind's evolutionary pathway, fossils, and paleontology, presented in a fun, kid-friendly manner.

more exceptional considering it is the largest city in the world not built on a river or near a significant water source.

In addition, an extensive public transportation system serves the local working population and tourists alike. This includes the Gautrain rapid rail system that connects Johannesburg with Pretoria and the O. R. Tambo International Airport, moving Jo'burg steadily toward its goal of being—as the city's government is eager to brand it—"a world-class African city."

8

ORIENTATION AND PLANNING

GETTING ORIENTED

South Africa's biggest city is in the middle of Gauteng, South Africa's smallest but wealthiest province. The greater metropolitan area is a massive 1,645 square km (635 square miles), most of which is made up of suburban sprawl. The M1, a major highway, runs centrally through the city and its suburbs. Two adjoining highways circle the city: the N3 to the east and the N1 to the west; the M1 bisects this circle.

Johannesburg City Center. Jo'burg was born as a mining camp, and its downtown area—the oldest part—is a jumbled grid of one-way streets heading in opposite directions, reflecting its hasty start to life. A number of important attractions, such as Constitution Hill, are found here. The city center is beginning to experience a rebirth, with trendy restaurants, boutiques, and hotels.

Soweto and the South. About 20 km (12 miles) south of downtown Johannesburg, the vast township of Soweto is where the 1976 antiapartheid student uprisings began; Soweto is now officially part of greater Johannesburg, though during apartheid, they were regarded as poles apart. Take a full- or half-day township tour and visit the Hector Pieterson

Memorial and Museum and former home of Nelson Mandela. City Sightseeing also offers a Soweto add-on.

Northern Suburbs. Most of the city's good hotels and major malls are in the northern suburbs: notably Sandton, the new financial center of South Africa, and Rosebank, a chic commercial center. Greenside and Parkhurst, close to Rosebank, are popular for eating out.

PLANNING

WHEN TO GO
Jo'burgers boast that they enjoy the best climate in the world: not too hot in summer (mid-September–mid-April), not too cold in winter (mid-April–mid-September), and not prone to sudden temperature changes. Summer (especially during December and January) may have the edge, though: it's when the gardens and open spaces are at their most beautiful.

GETTING HERE AND AROUND
It's difficult but not impossible to see the Johannesburg area without a car. A good bet is to rent one, decide what you want to see, and get a good road map or rent a GPS navigator. If you're reluctant to drive yourself, book a couple of full-day or half-day tours that will pick you up from your hotel or a central landmark. The City Sightseeing bus can give you an excellent overview of the city and enable you to hop on and off at most of Johannesburg's attractions. Spend a half day or a full day doing this.

AIR TRAVEL
O. R. Tambo International Airport is about 19 km (12 miles) from the Johannesburg city center and is linked to the city by a fast highway, which is always busy but especially before 9 am and between 4 and 7 pm. The best way to travel to and from it is via the Gautrain, a high-speed train that connects Sandton, Johannesburg, and Pretoria directly with O. R. Tambo. It takes about 30 minutes to travel from the airport to Sandton. The train runs from between 5 or 5:30 am and 9 or 9:30 pm every day, depending on the station.

Alternatively, Magic Bus offers private transfers to all major Sandton hotels (R675 per vehicle for one or two people, R740 for three people, R780 for four to seven people). The journey takes 30 minutes to an hour.

Airport Link will ferry you anywhere in the central Johannesburg area for R580 for one person, R635 for two people, R690 for three people, plus R55 per additional person up to seven.

In addition, scores of licensed taxis line up outside the airport terminal. By law they must have a working meter. Expect to pay about R500 for a trip to Sandton. Negotiate a price before you get into a taxi.

Lines at the airport can be long: plan to arrive two to three hours before an international departure and at least an hour before domestic departures. The airport has its own police station, but luggage theft has been a problem in recent years. Keep your belongings close to you at all times.

If your hotel or guesthouse does not have a shuttle, ask a staff member to arrange for your transportation with a reliable company. Most lodgings have a regular service they use, so you should have no problem arranging this in advance.

Prices vary, depending on where you are staying, but plan on R400–R500 for a ride from your hotel or guesthouse in Sandton, Rosebank, or the city center to the airport. Some companies charge per head, whereas others charge per trip, so be sure to check that in advance. The Gautrain is less expensive, quick, and safe, but you'll have to handle your own luggage. Most guesthouses or hotels will be able to drop you at the closest Gautrain station.

For airline contact information, see Air Travel in Travel Smart.

Airport Contacts O. R. Tambo International Airport. ☎ 086/727–7888, 011/921–6262 *information desk* ⊕ www.acsa.co.za.

Airport Transfers Airport Link. ☎ 011/794–8300, 083/625–5090 ⊕ www.airportlink.co.za. **Gautrain.** ☎ 0800/428–87246 ⊕ www.gautrain.co.za. **Legend Tours and Transfers.** ☎ 021/704–9140 ⊕ www.legendtours.co.za. **Magic Transfers.** ☎ 011/548–0800 ⊕ www.magictransfers.co.za/us.

BUS TRAVEL

Intercity buses depart from Park station in Braamfontein in the Johannesburg city center. Greyhound, TransLux, and Intercape Mainliner operate extensive routes around the country. The Baz Bus operates a hop-on, hop-off door-to-door service, stopping at backpackers' hostels between Johannesburg and Durban and Cape Town via the Drakensberg. You can buy Greyhound, Intercape Mainliner, and TransLux bus tickets through Computicket. Airfares with budget airlines in South Africa, such as Mango or Kulula *(see Air Travel in Travel Smart)* are more expensive than bus fares, but traveling by plane is much more efficient and comfortable, because the distances in South Africa can be vast. Be sure to book as far in advance as you can if you are going to fly or go by bus, as tickets can get more expensive as you approach the date of travel, and during peak holiday times (especially over Easter in April and December/January) tickets can sell out. *For more information, see Bus Travel in Travel Smart.*

CAR TRAVEL

Traveling by car is the easiest way to get around Johannesburg, as the city's public transportation is not that reliable or extensive, though this is changing (the Gautrain, for example, is incredibly reliable). Speed limits recently have been changed. The general speed limit for city streets is now 40 kph (24 mph); for rural streets it's 80 km (50 mph), and for highways it's 100 kph (62 mph). Be warned that Johannesburg drivers are known as the most aggressive in the country, and minibus taxis are famous for ignoring the rules of the road, often stopping for passengers with little or no warning. Most city roads and main countryside roads are in good condition, with plenty of signage. City street names are sometimes visible only on the curb, however. Avoid driving in rush hours, 7 to 8:30 am and 4 to 6:30 pm, as the main roads become terribly congested. Gas stations are plentiful in most areas. (Don't pump your own gas, though; stations employ operators to do that for you.) And remember, South Africans drive on the left side of the road.

Almost everywhere there are security guards who look after parked cars. It's customary to give these guards a small tip (R2 or R5) when you return to your car. Most big shopping centers have parking garages (about R8 per hour).

If you plan to drive yourself around, get a *good* map of the city center and northern suburbs or buy or rent a GPS (available at the airport and most car-rental agencies). MapStudio prints excellent complete street guides, available at bookstores and many gas stations and convenience stores.

Major rental agencies have offices in the northern suburbs and at the airport. *(For information, see Car Travel in Travel Smart.)*

TAXI TRAVEL

Minibus taxis form the backbone of Jo'burg's transportation for ordinary commuters, but you should avoid using them since they're often not roadworthy, drivers can be irresponsible, and it's difficult to know where they're going without consulting a local. Car taxis, though more expensive, are easier to use. They have stands at the airport and the train stations, but otherwise you must phone for one (be sure to ask how long it will take the taxi to get to you). Taxis should be licensed and have a working meter. Meters usually start at R50 (includes first 3 km [2 miles]) and are about R13 per kilometer (½ mile) thereafter. Expect to pay about R500 to the airport from town or Sandton and about R300 to the city center from Sandton. Uber is a popular, safe, and inexpensive taxi service, but it can be accessed only from an app.

Contacts Maxi Taxi. ☎ *011/648–1111, 011/648–1112* ⊕ *www.maxi-taxisa. co.za.* **Rose Taxis.** ☎ *011/403–0000, 083/255–0933* ⊕ *www.rosetaxis.com.* **Uber.** ⊕ *www.uber.com/cities/johannesburg.*

TRAIN TRAVEL

Johannesburg's train station, Park station, is in Braamfontein, at Leyds and Loveday streets. The famous, luxurious Blue Train, which makes regular runs to Cape Town, departs from here, as do Shosholoza Meyl trains to cities around the country, including the Trans-Karoo to Cape Town, the Komati to Nelspruit in Mpumalanga, and the Trans-Natal to Durban. Many of these trains have overnight service. They vary a lot in terms of comfort levels and price, and the more expensive ones such as the Blue Train are often booked up far in advance (though it's always worth a try if you want to make a reservation on short notice).

Locally, you can catch the Gautrain from O. R. Tambo, Pretoria, Sandton, or Rosebank to Park station *(see Airport Transfers in Air Travel, above).*

TOURS

Township tours (to Soweto in particular) are offered by a number of local operators. One of the best options is to do a Soweto tour with the City Sightseeing bus, which partners with local operators for tours of Soweto. Wilro Tours and JMT Tours and Safaris offer half-day and full-day tours of Johannesburg and Soweto. For more recommendations of reputable tour operators, inquire at Johannesburg Tourism.

Africa Explore. Africa Explore offers half-day, full-day, and overnight tours of sights in and around Johannesburg (and throughout South Africa), including Soweto, Pretoria, and the Rhino and Lion Park. ☎ *083/718–6065, 072/242–2281* ⊕ *www.africa-explore.co.za* ✉ *From R925.*

Fodor'sChoice
★
City Sightseeing Bus. The City Sightseeing bus is a great and very safe way to see the Johannesburg city center and all its main attractions. The bus departs from nine locations every 30 minutes from 9 to 5 every day, but the best places to catch it are either at Gold Reef City or Park station (accessible via the Gautrain). Adults and kids alike will love the experience; there's a special children's sound track, and the adult commentary is available in 15 languages. The total trip takes about 1½ hours if you don't get off (though you should consider at least getting off at the Apartheid Museum and Constitution Hill); you can get a one- or two-day pass. There is also an option to pair it with a Soweto tour, also highly recommended. You can buy your tickets at The Zone @ Rosebank (stop 1) or you can wait and buy tickets on any City Sightseeing bus, but there's a discount for purchasing them online. ✉ *Johannesburg* ☎ *0861/733–287* ⊕ *www.citysightseeing.co.za* ✉ *From R170.*

JMT Tours and Safaris. JMT Tours and Safaris can arrange tailor-made trips for small groups to a number of destinations. Prices will vary according to where you want to go and how many people are in your group. JMT Tours and Safaris specializes in tours of Soweto but also does the Cradle of Humankind and can take you farther afield. ☎ *027/233–0073* ⊕ *jmttours.com* ✉ *From R690.*

Johannesburg Heritage Foundation. Interested in checking out hundreds of heritage buildings? Most are closed to the public, but the Johannesburg Heritage Foundation organizes tours of the houses and gardens, which will give you a glimpse of turn-of-the-20th-century grandeur. Prearranged tours looking at different aspects of Johannesburg's history are arranged for most Saturdays and take about two to three hours. It's also possible to arrange a private tour if you can do it far enough in advance. ■**TIP**➔ **Departure points vary by the tour.** ✉ *Johannesburg* ☎ *011/482–3349* ⊕ *www.joburgheritage.org.za* ✉ *From R150.*

Springbok Atlas Tours & Safaris. Springbok Atlas Tours & Safaris offers a selection of half-day and full-day tours of Johannesburg, including the city center, Soweto, the Apartheid Museum, and other points of interest. Other tours explore Pretoria, Sun City, and the famous Pilanesberg Game Reserve. ☎ *021/460–4700* ⊕ *www.springbokatlas.com* ✉ *From R750.*

Wilro Tours. Wilro Tours is one of the best-known operators in Johannesburg and offers tours of Soweto, Johannesburg, and farther afield, such as Cradle of Humankind and the Pilanesberg Game Reserve. With Wilro, you hire the car and guide for a number of hours, and can mix and match attractions and activities such as shopping as you wish. Tours have a base price, so per-person rates drop dramatically the more people you have on the tour. ☎ *011/789–9688* ⊕ *www.wilrotours.co.za* ✉ *From R1300.*

8

PLANNING YOUR TIME

1 or 2 Days: If you have only one day in Jo'burg, take a tour of Soweto and visit the Apartheid Museum, then stop by Constitution Hill if you have a chance. Spend the evening having dinner at an African-style restaurant, such as Moyo. If you have a second day, focus on what interests you most: perhaps a trip to the Cradle of Humankind, where you can explore the sites of some of the world's most significant paleontological discoveries; a trip to Cullinan, where you can visit a working diamond mine; or a fun day or two at Sun City and/or the Pilanesberg Game Reserve, a 2½-hour drive west of Johannesburg.

3 to 5 Days: Spend your first day touring Soweto and visiting the Apartheid Museum and Constitution Hill, followed by an African-style dinner. The next day, leave early and do Sterkfontein Caves and Maropeng in the Cradle of Humankind, then overnight at one of the establishments in the Magaliesberg, perhaps at the luxurious Maropeng Hotel, which offers beautiful views of the Magaliesberg; the De Hoek Country House; or African Pride Mount Grace Country House & Spa. Then head out early to the Pilanesberg Game Reserve, a lovely reserve in the hills of an ancient volcano, where you're likely to see rhinos and elephants. Stay a night or two in one of the reserve's lodges, and treat yourself to an early-morning balloon ride over the reserve.

SAFETY

Johannesburg is notorious for being a dangerous city—it's common to hear about serious crimes such as armed robbery and murder. That said, it's safe for visitors who avoid dangerous areas and take reasonable precautions. Do not leave bags or valuables visible in a car, and keep the doors locked, even while driving (to minimize the risk of smash-and-grab robberies or carjackings); don't wear flashy jewelry or carry large wads of cash or expensive equipment. ■ TIP→ **Don't visit a township or squatter camp on your own.** Unemployment is rife, and foreigners are easy pickings. If you wish to see a township, check with reputable companies, which run excellent tours and know which areas to avoid. The Apartheid Museum and Constitution Hill within the city and the Cradle of Humankind just outside are perfectly safe to visit on your own.

■ TIP→ **If you drive yourself around the city, it's safest to keep your doors locked and windows up, and to not leave valuables such as bags, cameras, or phones on the seat or visible.** That said, it is safe to drive yourself around Johannesburg. If you prefer, though, you could order a car service or transportation from your hotel for trips in and around the city.

VISITOR INFORMATION

The helpful Gauteng Tourism Authority has information on the whole province, but more detailed information is often available from local tourism associations—for example, the National Accommodation Association Soweto helps find accommodations in Soweto. Joburg Tourism has a good website, with information about Johannesburg and up-to-date listings of events happening around the city.

Contacts City of Johannesburg. ⊕ *www.joburg.org.za.* **Gauteng Tourism Authority.** ☏ *011/085-2500* ⊕ *www.gauteng.net.* **Joburg Tourism.** ☏ *011/883-3525* ⊕ *www.joburgtourism.com.* **Soweto.co.za.** ☏ *083/535-4553, 071/204-5594* ⊕ *www.soweto.co.za.*

EXPLORING

Johannesburg epitomizes South Africa's paradoxical makeup—it's rich, poor, innovative, and historic all rolled into one. And it seems at times as though no one actually comes *from* Johannesburg. The city is full of immigrants: Italians, Portuguese, Chinese, Hindus, Swazis, English, Zimbabweans, Nigerians, Zulus, Xhosas. The streets are full of merchants. Traders hawk *skop* (boiled sheep's head, split open and eaten off newspaper) in front of polished glass buildings as taxis jockey for position in rush hour. *Sangomas* (traditional healers) lay out herbs and roots next to roadside barbers' tents, and you never seem to be far from women selling *vetkoek* (dollops of deep-fried dough) beneath billboards advertising investment banks or cell phones.

The Greater Johannesburg metropolitan area is massive—more than 1,600 square km (618 square miles)—incorporating the large municipalities of Randburg and Sandton to the north. Most of the sights are just north of the city center, which degenerated badly in the 1990s but is now being revamped.

To the south, in Ormonde, are the Apartheid Museum and Gold Reef City; the sprawling township of Soweto is just a little farther to the southwest. Johannesburg's northern suburbs are its most affluent. On the way to the shopping meccas of Rosebank and Sandton, you can find the superb Johannesburg Zoo and the South African Museum of Military History, in the leafy suburb of Saxonwold.

CITY CENTER

Although the city center is experiencing a revival, it's not a place everyone will choose to visit. You'll find plenty to do downtown, including a visit to the Maboneng precinct, an up-and-coming area in the inner city. Diagonal Street runs—you guessed it—diagonally through the city center. The Hillbrow Tower (now known as Telkom Tower) is 886 feet, the tallest structure in Jo'burg, and is used for telecommunications, as is the 767-foot Brixton Tower (also called Sentech Tower) in Auckland Park. The tall, round Ponte City apartment block near Hillbrow is another focal point that can be seen from almost all parts of the city.

Located in the western section of the city, Newtown, which is connected to Braamfontein via the Nelson Mandela Bridge, was once one of the city's most run-down neighborhoods. Today it is one of the city's cultural precincts, as it's the home of MuseuMAfricA, the SAB World of Beer, and the Market Theatre, among other attractions.

Braamfontein is home to Constitution Hill and the University of the Witwatersrand, one of South Africa's oldest and most respected universities. This is also where you'll find the urban-hipster Neighbourgoods Market on Saturdays, overflowing with an amazing array of specialty foods; this is where you come for mini-Mediterranean quiches, huge pans of paella, Balkan burgers, breakfast margaritas—not to mention vintage clothing, arts and crafts, jewelry, and more.

8

CLOSE UP

Posing on a Gold Mine

In 1952, Dolly Rathebe, a young black woman who was to become a jazz-singing legend, and a white German photographer, Jürgen Schadeberg, scrambled to the top of a gold-mine dump for a *Drum* magazine photo shoot. The photograph looks like it was taken on some strange beach: Rathebe smiles, posing in a bikini. They were spotted by the police and arrested under the Immorality Act, which forbade intercourse between blacks and whites. This dump was at Crown Mines, and is now the site of the Crown Mines Golf Club. Today there's a street in Newtown named after Rathebe, who died in 2004 at the age of 76. Schadeberg is still alive and lives in South Africa.

You still can see gold-mine dumps along the edge of town marching east and west along the seam of gold. Some are close to 300 feet high. Many people are fond of them—they are one of the city's defining characteristics—but those who live nearby are blinded by the dust, and little vegetation grows on the dumps. Officials are also concerned they contain radioactive uranium, which occurs naturally in reefs containing gold. Rich in minerals, they're slowly being chipped away and remined, and in years to come, they will probably be completely gone.

TOP ATTRACTIONS

Fodor's Choice **Constitution Hill.** Overlooking Jo'burg's inner city and suburbs, Constitu-
★ tion Hill houses the **Constitutional Court,** set up in 1994 with the birth of democracy, as well as the austere **Old Fort Prison Complex** (also called Number Four), where thousands of political prisoners were incarcerated, including South African Nobel Peace Prize laureates Albert Luthuli and Nelson Mandela, and iconic Indian leader Mahatma Gandhi. The court decides on the most important cases relating to human rights, much like the Supreme Court in the United States. Exhibits in the visitor center portray the country's journey to democracy. You can walk along the prison ramparts (built in the 1890s), read messages on the We the People Wall (and add your own), or view the court itself, in which large, slanting columns represent the trees under which African villagers traditionally met to discuss matters of importance. If the court isn't in session, you can walk right into the courtroom, where many of the country's landmark legal decisions have been made in recent years and where the 11 chairs of the justices are each covered in a different cowhide, representing their individuality. Group tours of the Old Fort Prison Complex are given every hour on the hour from 9 to 4 and include a visit to the Women's Jail, where there are photographs and exhibits of how women were treated in the prison system and how they contributed to the struggle against apartheid. ⊠ *Joubert St. at Kotze St., entrance on Joubert St., Braamfontein, City Center* ☎ *011/381–3100* ⊕ *www.constitutionhill.org.za* ☒ *Court free; Constitution Hill tour R65.*

Maboneng Precinct. If you need proof that Jo'burg is revitalizing, Mabo-
neng Precinct is it. Once a place to avoid, this neighborhood is now buzzing with art galleries, indie boutiques, coffee shops, restaurants,

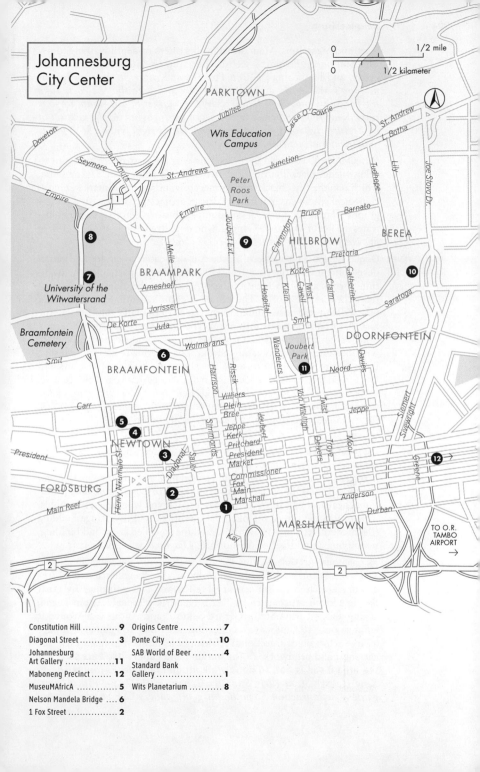

Johannesburg City Center

| | 0 | | 1/2 mile |
| | 0 | | 1/2 kilometer |

PARKTOWN

Wits Education Campus

Peter Roos Park

bars, and nightclubs. Main Street Walks offers in-depth walking tours. The Maboneng Precinct's website hosts up-to-date info on the latest events and happenings. ✉ *286 Fox St., at Kruger St.* ✛ *From Johannesburg's M1 south, go around the city and take the M2 east. Take the Joe Slovo off-ramp, followed by the Market St. off-ramp, to your right. Keep right and cross over 1 set of traffic lights. At the next set of lights, turn right on Betty St. and immediately right on Fox St.* ⊕ *www. mabonengprecinct.com.*

MuseuMAfricA. Founded in 1935, this was the first major museum to acknowledge black contributions to the city's development. The museum, which is in the city's block-long former fruit and vegetable market, houses geological specimens, paintings, African artifacts, costumes, and photographs relating to South Africa's complex history. Another display illustrates the life of Mahatma Gandhi, who once lived in Jo'burg. ✉ *121 Bree St., Newtown, City Center* ☎ *011/833–5624* ☞ *Free.*

FAMILY
Fodor'sChoice
★

Origins Centre. This modern museum is dedicated to exploring human development over the past 100,000 years, and in particular the tradition of rock art—of which southern Africa has the oldest and some of the richest in the world. The center is complementary to Maropeng, which details the past 5 million years or so of human evolution and the history of Earth since its formation. The two experiences enhance each other rather than compete. Origins is spacious and elegantly designed, with multimedia displays and photographs catering to a range of tastes, from kids to visiting professors. The shop sells high-quality crafts and hard-to-source books on rock art in southern Africa, and the center's coffee shop, Café Fino, serves good, light meals. ✉ *University of the Witwatersrand, Yale Rd., Braamfontein, City Center* ☎ *011/717–4700* ⊕ *www.wits.ac.za/origins* ☞ *R80, including audio guide.*

WORTH NOTING

Diagonal Street. On this street in the city center, among stores selling traditional African fabrics and household appliances, you'll find African herbalists' shops purveying a mind-boggling array of homeopathic and traditional cures for whatever ails you. If you're lucky, a *sangoma* (traditional healer) might throw the bones and tell you what the future holds. This is also the site of the old Johannesburg Stock Exchange building (the modern version is in Sandton) and the so-called Diamond Building, resembling a multifaceted diamond. ✉ *Diagonal St., City Center.*

Johannesburg Art Gallery. This three-story museum hosts excellent local and international exhibitions in 15 halls and has collections of 17th-century Dutch art, 18th-century French art, and paintings by great South African artists such as Jacob Hendrik Pierneef, Ezrom Legae, Walter Battiss, Irma Stern, Gerard Sekoto, and Anton van Wouw. It exhibits only 10% of its vast collection at a time. You can also admire a large selection of traditional African objects, such as headrests, tree carvings, and beadwork. ⚠ **The parking and gallery itself are safe, but the area it's in is not, so don't walk around outside.** ✉ *Joubert Park, King George St. at Klein St., City Center* ☎ *011/725–3130* ⊕ *www. gauteng.net/attractions/johannesburg_art_gallery* ☞ *Free.*

Nelson Mandela Bridge. A symbol of the renewal process going on in the city, this modern, 931-foot-long bridge with sprawling cables spans the bleak Braamfontein railway yard, connecting Constitution Hill and Braamfontein to the revamped Newtown Cultural Precinct. The bridge is especially beautiful at night (though walking across is not advised). ⊠ *Bertha St., Braamfontein, City Center* ✛ *Take Queen Elizabeth St. from Braamfontein, or follow signs from central Newtown or from M1 south.*

1 Fox Street. Part of Jo'burg's revitalization, several warehouses in the old mining district have been reborn as a trendy entertainment quarter, featuring Mad Giant microbrewery; Urbanologi, a chic Asian fusion eatery; the Good Luck Bar; the Market Shed, a collection of stands purveying artisan food and drink; and more. With live music and other events, as well as some indie boutiques, this is a buzzing place to come and hang out. ⊠ *1 Fox St.* ☎ *082/780–3595* ⊕ *www.1fox.co.za.*

Ponte City. If there's a symbol of Johannesburg, it's Ponte City, a massive, hollow 54-story cylinder of apartments perched on the edge of the central business district. Built in 1975, and standing at a height of 568 feet with a flashing cell-phone advertisement at the top, it's the tallest residential building in Africa. Once the apex of grand living, it became a slum in the 1990s as the middle class fled to the suburbs; only now is it being revitalized, with young professionals, students, and immigrants moving in. ⊠ *1 Lily Ave., Hillbrow.*

SAB World of Beer. SABMiller is Africa's largest brewing company, and its unusual museum is dedicated to that great South African favorite—beer. A guided tour takes you on an interactive, multimedia trip back in time through the origins of beer, where you'll learn about the history of beer brewing in Africa and the process of beer making, including African brewing traditions. After a 75-minute tour you can enjoy two complimentary beers in the taproom (and take home a keepsake World of Beer glass). ⊠ *15 Helen Joseph St. , Newtown, City Center* ☎ *011/836–4900* ⊕ *www.worldofbeer.co.za* ⊠ *R115.*

Standard Bank Gallery. At the home of the Standard Bank African art collection you can admire contemporary South African artwork. The gallery hosts high-quality, ever-changing local and international exhibitions, including the annual traveling World Press Photo show. Across the street, Standard Bank also hosts the entrance to a gold mine dating back to the city's earliest days; it was discovered when the headquarters was being built in the 1980s. You can take an elevator down to see it, along with a small exhibition of photos and maps. ⊠ *Frederick St. at Simmonds St., Marshalltown, City Center* ☎ *011/631–4467* ⊕ *www. sponsorships.standardbank.com* ⊠ *Free* ☉ *Closed Sun.*

FAMILY **Wits Planetarium.** This planetarium, dating from 1960, has entertaining and informative programs on the African skies and presentations that range from space travel to the planets. Phone ahead to find out what's on. ⊠ *University of the Witwatersrand, Yale Rd., Braamfontein, City Center* ☎ *011/717–1390* ⊕ *www.planetarium. co.za* ⊠ *Varies by event, average R50.*

8

SOWETO AND THE SOUTH

An acronym for *South Western Townships*, Soweto dates back to 1904, when city councilors used an outbreak of bubonic plague as an excuse to move black people outside the town. Today the suburb, which is 20 km (12 miles) south of the city, is home to about 1.5 million residents. What it lacks in infrastructure (though it's been vastly upgraded since the first democratic elections in 1994) it more than makes up for in soul, energy, and history. The largely working-class population knows how to live for today, and Soweto pulsates with people and music.

Some areas of Soweto that are worth touring include old-town neighborhood Diepkloof, just beyond Orlando West, and its neighbor, the new Diepkloof Extension, which dates from the mid-1970s, when bank loans first became available to black property owners. The difference between the two is startling: the dreary, prefabricated matchbox houses of Diepkloof next to what looks like a middle-class suburb anywhere. In nearby Dube, many of the evicted residents of Sophiatown—a freehold township (where blacks were allowed to own property) west of the city and a melting pot of music, bohemianism, crime, and multiracialism that insulted Afrikaner nationalism—were resettled in 1959, bringing an exciting vibe to the dreary, homogenous dormitory town. The area remains a vibrant suburb, with an exciting mix of people and a festive atmosphere.

Between downtown Johannesburg and Soweto lie several suburbs less affluent than their northern counterparts, including Ormonde, where Gold Reef City and the Apartheid Museum are. Both attractions are well signposted from the N1 highway going both south and north and are easy to find if you have hired a car, but many tour operators do include a stop at the Apartheid Museum in their Soweto tours.

GETTING HERE AND AROUND

Various companies offer bus tours, but we suggest hiring a private guide or joining a smaller group tour, because you'll get one-on-one attention and be able to ask any and all questions. You can also ask for a special-interest tour, such as one centered on art, traditional medicine, restaurants, nightlife, or memorials. Most tours start in Jo'burg, and you can arrange to be collected from your hotel. ■TIP→ **We strongly suggest that you take a guided tour if you decide to visit Soweto. It is a chaotic, virtually indistinguishable sprawl. Even if you found your way in, you'd struggle to find your way out—let alone around.**

TOP ATTRACTIONS

Fodor's Choice
★

Apartheid Museum. The Apartheid Museum, in Ormonde, takes you on a journey through South African apartheid history—from the entrance, where you pass through a turnstile according to your assigned skin color (black or white), to the myriad historical, brutally honest, and sometimes shocking photographs, video displays, films, documents, and other exhibits. It's an emotional, multilayered journey. As you walk chronologically through the apartheid years and eventually reach the country's first steps to freedom, with democratic elections in 1994, you

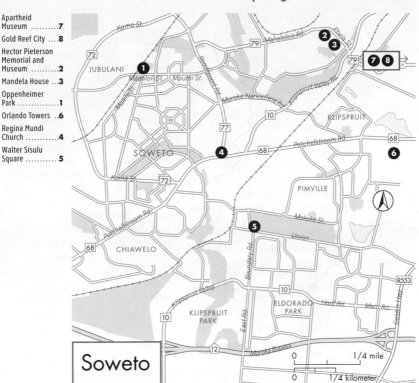

Soweto

experience a taste of the pain and suffering with which so many South Africans had to live. A room with 121 ropes with hangman's knots hanging from the ceiling—one rope for each political prisoner executed in the apartheid era—is especially chilling. ⊠ *Northern Pkwy. at Gold Reef Rd., Ormonde* ☎ *011/309–4700* ⊕ *www.apartheidmuseum.org* ✂ *R85.*

Fodor's Choice **Hector Pieterson Memorial and Museum.** Opposite Holy Cross Church, a
★ stone's throw from the former homes of Nelson Mandela and Archbishop Desmond Tutu on Vilakazi Street, the Hector Pieterson Memorial and Museum is a crucial landmark. Pieterson, a 12-year-old student, was one of the first victims of police fire on June 16, 1976, when schoolchildren rose up to protest their second-rate Bantu (black) education system. The memorial is a paved area with benches for reflection, an inscribed stone, and simple water feature; inside the museum are grainy photographs and films that bring that fateful day to life and put it into the context of the broader apartheid struggle. A total of 562 small granite blocks in the museum courtyard are a tribute to the children who died in the Soweto uprisings. ⊠ *Khumalo St. at Phela St., Orlando West* ☎ *011/536–0611* ⊕ *www.joburg.org.za* ✂ *R30.*

WORTH NOTING

FAMILY **Gold Reef City.** This theme park lets you step back in time to 1880s Johannesburg and see why it became known as the City of Gold. One of the city's most popular attractions, it has good rides that kids will enjoy and is based on the history of Jo'burg. In addition to riding the Anaconda, a scary roller coaster on which you hang under the track, feet in the air, you can (for an additional fee) descend into an old gold mine and see molten gold being poured. The reconstructed streets are lined with operating Victorian-style shops and restaurants. And for those with money to burn, the large, glitzy Gold Reef Village Casino beckons across the road. ⊠ *Northern Pkwy. at Data Crescent, Shaft 14, Ormonde ✛ 6 km (4 miles) south of city center* ☎ *011/248–6800* ⊕ *www.goldreefcity.co.za* ✉ *R190; R340 for rides and guided Jozi Story of Gold tour.*

> **FAMOUS RESIDENTS**
>
> What other place on Earth can boast of having had two Nobel Peace Prize laureates living within a block of each other? For most of his adult life Anglican Archbishop Desmond Tutu lived on Vilakazi Street, in Soweto's Orlando West neighborhood. His neighbor would have been an attorney named Nelson Mandela, had Mandela not spent most of *his* adult life incarcerated on Robben Island (*see Chapter 2, Cape Town*). The archbishop's home is a gray, two-story building that is not open to the public, but you can visit the nearby Mandela house. It became a museum in 1997 and was revamped in 2009.

Mandela House. The antiapartheid activist and former president lived in this small house for 15 years until his arrest in 1961 (and 11 days after his release), with his first wife, Evelyn Ntoko Mase, and then second wife, Winnie Madikizela-Mandela (who owns a high-security mansion in Orlando West). The house is now a museum containing Mandela memorabilia. ⊠ *8115 Vilakazi St., Orlando West* ☎ *011/936–7754* ⊕ *www.mandelahouse.com* ✉ *R60 (South African citizens R40).*

Oppenheimer Park. Named after mining magnate Ernest Oppenheimer, who established the De Beers diamond mining company as a powerful global brand, this park is one of the few green spaces in Soweto and is rich in flora and birdlife. The park is dominated by a large tower built as a tribute to Oppenheimer, who helped resettle people displaced by the apartheid government in the 1950s. Here you can also see **Khayalendaba,** a cultural village built in the 1970s by South Africa's best-known traditional healer, artist, and oral historian, Credo Mutwa. Some of his statues here portray African gods, warriors, and mythical figures, even sculptures of prehistoric African animals. ■TIP➔ **It's best to visit the park with a guide in the daytime for safety reasons.** ⊠ *991 Majoeng St., Central Western Jabavu* ⊕ *joburg.org.za* ✉ *Free.*

Orlando Towers. The brightly painted Orlando Towers complex in Soweto is a well-known landmark in Johannesburg. Originally a coal-fired power station, the site has been transformed into an adrenaline junkie's paradise, where you can do BASE and bungee jumping from the top of the 33-story structure. Afterward, go on a unique and highly memorable quad bike tour of Soweto, or relax at the popular restaurant, Chaf-Pozi, located on the premises. ⊠ *Sheffield Rd., just off*

Hector Pieterson and the Soweto Uprising

On June 16, 1976, hundreds of schoolchildren in Soweto marched to protest the use of Afrikaans as the primary language of education in the overcrowded, much neglected Bantu schools in the townships. This was a highly charged political issue. Not only was Dutch-based Afrikaans considered the language of the oppressor by blacks, but it also made it more difficult for students to learn, as most spoke an African language and, as a second language, English.

The march quickly turned nasty. The police started firing into the youthful crowd. One of the first people of 200 to 500 to die in what was the beginning of a long and protracted struggle was 12-year-old Hector Pieterson. A picture taken by photographer Sam Nzima of the dying Pieterson in the arms of a crying friend, with Pieterson's sister running alongside them, put a face on apartheid that went around the globe.

Pieterson was just a schoolboy trying to ensure a better life for himself and his friends, family, and community. He and the many students who joined the liberation movement strengthened the fight against apartheid. Eventually Afrikaans was dropped as a language of instruction, and more schools and a teaching college were built in Soweto. Today, Hector Pieterson's name graces a simple memorial and museum about the conflict, and June 16 is Youth Day, a public holiday.

Chris Hani Rd., Orlando ☏ *072/692–8159 Soweto Adventure Tours, 071/674–4343 bungee jumping* ⊕ *www.sowetooutdooradventures. co.za, www.orlandotowers.co.za* ✉ *R550 (bungee jumping).*

Regina Mundi Church. Central to the liberation struggle, this Catholic church was a refuge of peace, sanity, and steadfast moral focus for the people of Soweto through the harshest years of repression. Archbishop Desmond Tutu often delivered sermons in this massive church during the apartheid years. And it wasn't always so peaceful—you still can see bullet holes where police opened fire on students and residents seeking refuge. It has a black Madonna and Child painting and beautiful stained-glass windows, including one depicting the Annunciation. ✉ *1149 Khumalo St., Rockville* ☏ *011/986–2546* ⊕ *reginamundichurch.co.za* ✉ *R20.*

Walter Sisulu Square (*Formerly Freedom Square*). In 1955 the Freedom Charter was adopted on a dusty field here by the Congress Alliance, a gathering of political and cultural groups trying to map a way forward in the repressive 1950s. The charter, the guiding document of the African National Congress, envisaged an alternative nonracial dispensation in which "all shall be equal before the law." Its significance in South Africa is similar to that of the Declaration of Independence in the United States, and it influenced South Africa's new constitution, adopted in 1995 and widely considered one of the best and most progressive in the world. The site has been recently revamped as an open-air museum centered around the Ten Pillars of Freedom and includes shops and a four-star hotel in what is being described as South Africa's first township entertainment explosion center. ✉ *Klipspruit Valley Rd. at Union Rd., Kliptown* ⊕ *www.waltersisulusquare.co.za.*

8

NORTHERN SUBURBS

Johannesburg has dozens of northern suburbs, ranging in size from the huge and diverse Sandton, which includes the entire township of Alexandra, among other suburbs, to the smaller, leafy Saxonwold near the zoo. The northern suburbs highlighted here, in order from southernmost to northernmost, are by no means the only ones—they simply have the most attractions and are where most tourists stay.

ROSEBANK

Originally a farm known as Rosemill Orchards, today **Rosebank** is home to upmarket shopping malls, restaurants, hotels, and art galleries. It's frequented by well-to-do locals and tourists. At the Rosebank Mall you'll find all the international brands, along with the best in uniquely South African boutiques and outlets like Exclusive Books, which has an excellent range, including reference and coffee-table books on Africa. The Rosebank Mall is smaller than its larger and even swankier mall, the nearby Sandton City. The **Rosebank Art and Craft Market,** open daily, is adjacent to the Rosebank Mall and is open every day. It is popular for its curios and African art. Clubs, bars, galleries, and an art-house cinema add flavor to this trendy area.

GREENSIDE AND EMMARENTIA

Close to Rosebank, the suburb of **Greenside** is filled with popular restaurants. **Gleneagles Road** is lined with small eateries, including Italian, Indian, Portuguese, and Japanese restaurants, along with those offering a more conventional range of meats, fish, and pasta. Over the weekend, cars fill the streets and people pack the sidewalks. The adjacent suburb of **Emmarentia** is also benefiting from Greenside's popularity, with small restaurants popping up. The **Emmarentia Dam** and gardens, a popular dog-walking and picnic spot, is also a draw.

FAMILY **Johannesburg Botanical Garden and Emmarentia Dam.** Overlooking Emmarentia Dam, the large and beautiful botanical gardens here are five minutes from Greenside. This gigantic parkland, dotted with trees, statues, fountains, and ponds, is a wonderful haven. You can relax on benches beneath weeping willows surrounding the dam and lake, where canoeists and windsurfers brave the water, or wander across to the 24-acre rose and herb gardens. The gardens' flowers include an alpine collection and a cycad collection. On weekends bridal parties use the gardens as a backdrop for photographs. ✉ *Olifants Rd., Roosevelt Park* ☎ *011/375–5555, 011/712–6600* ⊕ *www.jhbcityparks.com* ✇ *Free.*

FAMILY **Melville Koppies Nature Reserve.** A 123-acre nature reserve and heritage site on the southern side of the Johannesburg Botanical Garden, Melville Koppies preserves lands as they were before the 1886 gold discovery. Two walkabout Sunday guided tours per month introduce visitors to the archaeology, history, geology, fauna, and biodiverse highveld flora. In addition, two more strenuous Sunday hikes are offered every month. The site includes a 500-year-old Iron Age furnace. ⚠ **Don't go alone, as it isn't safe to do so.** ✉ *Judith Rd., Emmarentia* ☎ *011/482–4797* ⊕ *www.mk.org.za* ✇ *R50 for guided tour; special group tours by prior arrangement.*

PARKTOWN, PARKVIEW, SAXONWOLD, AND WESTCLIFF

Perched on the Braamfontein Ridge, Parktown was once the address du jour for the city's early mining magnates. Most of the magnificent houses have since met their demise, but those that are left are worth a look, and they are all lovely areas in which to stay or to take a walk. The small but picturesque suburbs of Westcliff, Parkview, and Saxonwold are nearby.

Ditsong National Museum of Military History. In a park adjacent to the Johannesburg Zoo, this museum has two exhibition halls and a rambling outdoor display focusing on South Africa's role in the major wars of the 20th century, with an emphasis on World War II. On display are original Spitfire and Messerschmidt fighters (including what is claimed to be the only remaining ME110 jet night fighter), various tanks of English and American manufacture, and a wide array of artillery. Among the most interesting objects are the modern armaments South Africa used in its war against the Cuban-backed Angolan army during the 1980s, including French-built Mirage fighters and Russian tanks stolen by the South Africans from a ship en route to Angola. More recent exhibits include the national military art collection, memorabilia from the Anti-Conscription Campaign of apartheid days, and an exhibit on the history of Umkhonto we Sizwe (Spear of the Nation, or MK, the African National Congress's military arm). The tall, freestanding South African (Anglo-Boer) War Memorial, which looks like a statue-adorned mini Arc de Triomphe, is the most striking landmark of the northern suburbs. ⊠ *20 Erlswold Way, Saxonwold* ☎ *011/646–5513* ⊕ *www. gauteng.net/attractions/south_african_national_museum_of_military_ history* ⊠ *R30.*

FAMILY **Johannesburg Zoo.** Smaller than its Pretoria counterpart but no less impressive, the city's zoo makes for a pleasant day trip, and with plenty of lawns and shade, it's a good place to picnic. The large variety of species (more than 320) includes rare white lion and endangered white rhino. The Animals of the Amazon is an attraction that houses snakes, spiders, lizards, and frogs in a Mayan setting. Perhaps the best way to see the zoo is to take the ferry to various parts. Afterward, stroll past Zoo Lake in the large, peaceful park across the road. ⊠ *Jan Smuts Ave., opposite Zoo Lake, Parkview* ☎ *011/646–2000* ⊕ *www.jhbzoo. org.za* ⊠ *R80.*

MELROSE ARCH

Close to both Rosebank and Sandton, **Melrose Arch** is an upscale shopping, dining, and business district that features good restaurants and boutiques. This European-style lifestyle center offers pleasant accommodations, shopping, and dining in a relaxed and safe setting.

ROODEPOORT

Roodepoort is a residential suburb to the west of Johannesburg in what is known as the West Rand, a drive of about 45 minutes to an hour from the city center. Its top attraction is the Walter Sisulu National Botanical Garden, and it's also relatively close to the Cradle of Humankind World Heritage Site.

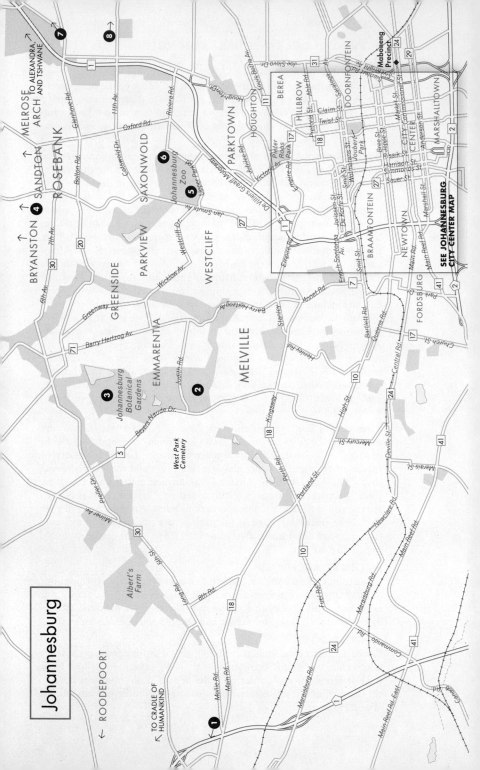

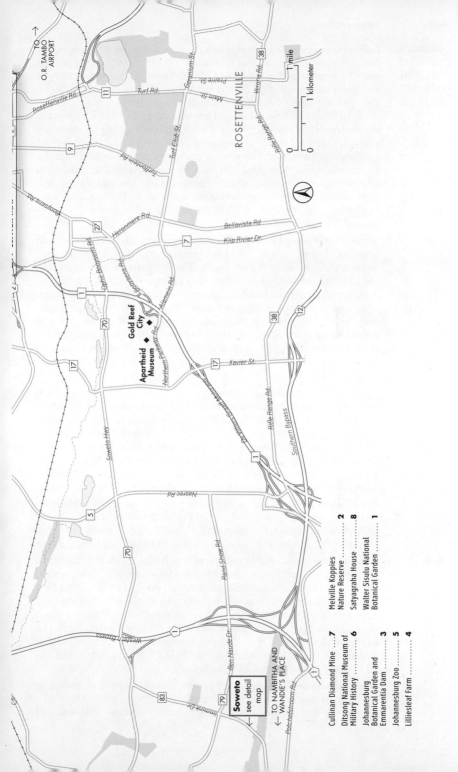

Cullinan Diamond Mine. Anyone can go to a jewelry store and bring home South African diamonds, but how many people can say they got their sparkler from an actual mine? At Cullinan Diamond Mine, you can not only buy diamonds, but get custom-made pieces from the resident jeweler, though don't expect your piece to include the world's largest diamond—the 3,106-carat Cullinan Diamond unearthed here in 1905 is now in the crown jewels in London. Ninety-minute surface tours of the mine are every day, and four-hour underground tours are offered every day but Sunday. You must reserve all tours in advance; children under 10 are not permitted on either tour. Cullinan has a series of delightful tea gardens to choose from. For pleasant outdoor dining, the Whispering Oaks Garden Café (closed Tuesday) serves breakfast, lunches, and homemade sweets. ✉ *99 Oak Ave., Cullinan* ☎ *012/734–0081* ⊕ *www.diamondtourscullinan.co.za* ✇ *Surface tours R120, underground tours R550.*

Walter Sisulu National Botanical Garden. More than 220 bird species and a variety of small mammals add to a biodiverse garden named in honor of late ANC stalwart Walter Sisulu. The Witpoortjie Falls dominate the garden, providing a backdrop to a succulent rockery, cycads, an arboretum, birds and butterfly garden, wildflowers, a children's section, and more. The garden is famous for a pair of Verreaux eagles that breed in early spring (August/September). Most of the garden is accessible by wheelchair, and there are refreshment facilities. Guided tours are offered (R170). ✉ *End of Malcolm Rd., Poortview, Roodepoort* ☎ *086/100–1278* ⊕ *www.sanbi.org/gardens/walter-sisulu* ✇ *R45.*

SANDTON

Originally a residential area, **Sandton** is now home to the Johannesburg Stock Exchange and the enormous Sandton Convention Centre, which hosts large conferences and concerts. In the large and expensive **Sandton City Shopping Centre** and adjacent open-air **Nelson Mandela Square** (also known as Sandton Square), you'll find trendy restaurants selling good but pricey food. There's also a small theater, Theatre on the Square, which favors short, lightweight productions such as stand-up comedy. The convention center is next to the square.

But Sandton is not all glitz and glamour—a few miles from the Sandton City Shopping Centre and part of the large suburb is the township of **Alexandra,** home to an estimated 500,000 people, mostly living in overcrowded, squalid conditions in shacks and rented run-down houses.

Fodor's Choice
★

Lilliesleaf Farm. An award-winning national heritage site, this unassuming farm in the leafy Rivonia neighborhood is where ANC leaders plotted to violently overthrow the government, only to be thwarted by a police raid in 1963 that resulted in their incarceration. Nelson Mandela lived here, disguised as a domestic worker; though he wasn't here when the raid took place, he was implicated in the ensuing Rivonia Trial. The exhibits are extremely well done, with original video, images, audio, and text. ✉ *7 George Ave.* ☎ *011/803–7882* ⊕ *www.liliesleaf.co.za* ✇ *R65 self-guided tour, R110 guided tour.*

Satyagraha House. A young Gandhi spent 10 years in Jo'burg, including one year at this house in the residential neighborhood of Orchards. Today, it's been transformed into a small museum and tranquil guesthouse, infused with his peaceful spirit. You can stop by to see exhibits (call ahead), or indulge in a night of mindfulness. Vegetarian meals are served, sourced from the garden. ⊠ *15 Pine Rd.* ☎ *011/485–5928* ⊕ *www.satyagrahahouse.com.*

BRYANSTON
Bryanston is an old, treed residential suburb that is farther north (toward Fourways) of the city center than suburbs like Rosebank and Sandton. It's one of Johannesburg's wealthier suburbs, and is characterized by tree-lined streets and homes with large gardens. The Bryanston Organic Market at 40 Culross Road is open Thursday and Saturday between 9 and 3.

FOUR WAYS
Fourways is one of Johannesburg's fast-growing suburbs, in the far north of the city. It's home to many upscale housing estates, as well as good shopping centers and places to stay. The Bungee SkyBar is exactly what it sounds like: a bungee-jump tower with a cocktail bar, rising above a shopping center. It's a journey of at least 30 minutes to an hour into Sandton or Johannesburg from Fourways.

WHERE TO EAT

Jo'burgers love eating out, and there are hundreds of restaurants throughout the city to satisfy them. Some notable destinations for food include Melrose Arch, Parkhurst, Sandton, and Greenside. Smart-casual dress is a good bet. Many establishments are closed on Sunday night and Monday.

There's no way to do justice to the sheer scope and variety of Johannesburg's restaurants in a few examples. What follows is a (necessarily subjective) list of some of the best. Try asking locals what they recommend; eating out is the most popular form of entertainment in Johannesburg, and everyone has a list of favorite spots, which changes often.

For more information on South Africa food, see Flavors of South Africa, in Chapter 1. Restaurant reviews have been shortened. For full information, visit Fodors.com.

WHAT IT COSTS IN SOUTH AFRICAN RAND			
$	**$$**	**$$$**	**$$$$**
Restaurants	under R100	R100–R150	R151–R200	over R200

Restaurant prices are the average cost of a main course at dinner or, if dinner is not served, at lunch.

OAKLANDS

Oaklands is an old residential suburb not far from Rosebank and Melrose. It's known for its wide streets, large homes (most often behind high walls), and trees. The whole area seems to turn purple when the jacarandas bloom in October and November.

$$ ITALIAN Fodor's Choice ★ 🍴 **Tortellino d'Oro.** This small and unpretentious restaurant and deli has legendary food, especially the pasta. Try the Parma ham and melon as an antipasto, and then get a pasta for your main course, such as the tortellini, which is filled with a mixture of ham, mortadella sausage, chicken, and Parmesan cheese, then served with mushroom cream, or butter and sage sauce. **Known for:** outstanding service; excellent wine list; authentic pasta. [$] *Average main: R150* ✉ *Oaklands Shopping Centre, Pretoria St. at Victoria St., Oaklands* ☎ *011/483–1249* 🌐 *www.tortellino.co.za* 🕒 *No dinner Sun.*

SOWETO AND THE SOUTH

$$ AFRICAN 🍴 **Nambitha.** Nambitha has evolved from a township restaurant catering only to African tastes into a more versatile establishment, serving mutton curry, *mogodu* (tripe), and marinated traditional chicken, lamb shank, and oxtail. The restaurant plays an eclectic selection of music—soul, jazz, R&B, and more traditional African—and is constantly buzzing with people. **Known for:** local vibe; cheap eats; traditional flavors. [$] *Average main: R120* ✉ *6877 Vilakazi St., Orlando West* ☎ *011/936–9128* 🌐 *www.nambitharestaurant.co.za.*

$$ AFRICAN 🍴 **Wandie's Place.** Wandie's Place isn't the only good township restaurant, but it's the best known and one of the most popular spots in Jo'burg. The waiters are smartly dressed in ties, and the food is truly African, with meat stews, sweet potatoes, beans, corn porridge, traditionally cooked pumpkin, chicken, and tripe laid out in a buffet of pots and containers. **Known for:** eclectic decor; tour groups. [$] *Average main: R150* ✉ *618 Makhalamele St., Dube* ☎ *081/420–6051* 🌐 *www.wandiesplace.co.za.*

NORTHERN SUBURBS

ILLOVO AND MELROSE ARCH

Illovo and Melrose Arch are two small suburbs between the trendy suburbs of Rosebank and Sandton. Illovo is home to several shopping centers, office parks, and small restaurants; Melrose Arch is a smaller development with shops, offices, and restaurants. Both are popular with locals and very safe to visit.

$$ ITALIAN 🍴 **Bellinis.** This small, friendly restaurant offers both memorable food and quick and professional service. The atmosphere can be quite noisy and energy-packed, as friends catch up over lunch and businesspeople chat animatedly about work over a plate of legendary potato rostis: try one with smoked salmon or a pepper fillet. **Known for:** good wine list; local favorite. [$] *Average main: R129* ✉ *18 Chaplin Rd., Illovo* ☎ *011/880–9168/9* 🌐 *www.bellinis.co.za* 🕒 *Closed Sun.*

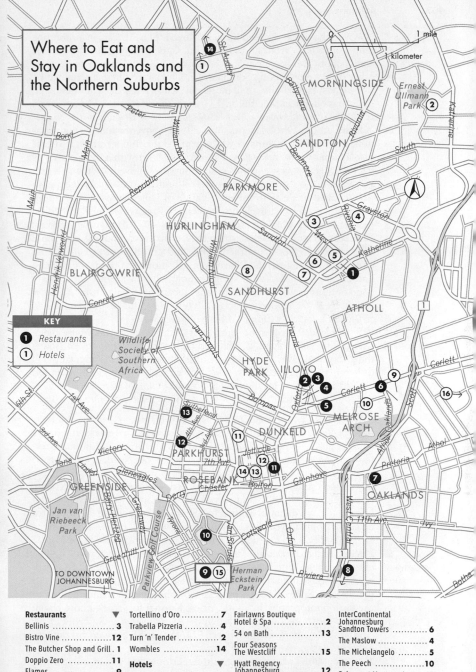

Where to Eat and Stay in Oaklands and the Northern Suburbs

KEY
- **1** *Restaurants*
- **1** *Hotels*

$$$ AFRICAN Fodor's Choice ★ 🍴 **Moyo.** The rich and varied menu at Moyo is pan-African, incorporating tandoori cookery from northern Africa, Cape Malay influences such as lentil bobotie, Moroccan-influenced tasty *tagines*, and ostrich burgers and other dishes representing South Africa. Diners are often entertained by storytellers, face painters, and musicians. **Known for:** live entertainment; African food, music, and decor. [$] *Average main: R180* ✉ *Melrose Arch, High St., Shop 5, Melrose Arch* ☎ *011/684–1477* 🌐 *www.moyo.co.za.*

$$ GREEK 🍴 **Parea.** At this Greek taverna, music floats above the buzz of conversation, a souvlaki spit turns slowly near the door, and a refrigerated case displays an array of *meze* (small appetizers). Start with a meze platter of souvlaki, feta, olives, cucumber, and tomato, followed by the line fish, grilled on an open flame with olive oil and lemon, or *kleftiko* (lamb slow-cooked in a clay oven) and a carafe of wine. **Known for:** outdoor dining; belly dancers; lively atmosphere. [$] *Average main: R150* ✉ *3D Corlett Dr., at Oxford Rd., Illovo* ☎ *011/788–8777* 🌐 *www.parea.co.za.*

$ ITALIAN 🍴 **Trabella Pizzeria.** Trabella's strength is its pizza, some of the best you'll ever taste, whether it's with the Brie and cranberry topping; Parma ham, rocket (arugula), and Parmesan; or smoked salmon, sour cream, and caviar, sprinkled with spring onion. The pasta and gnocchi are good options as well. **Known for:** busy location; Italian cuisine. [$] *Average main: R80* ✉ *Illovo Junction, Oxford Rd. 3, at Corlett Dr., Illovo* ☎ *011/442–0413* 🕒 *Closed Mon. No lunch Sun.*

$$$ STEAKHOUSE 🍴 **Turn 'n Tender.** Meat is the specialty at this upmarket steak-house chain, with a wide range of steaks, ribs, and burgers to choose from. For something very South African—and yet a little different from the popular oxtail dish—try the lamb steak slow-cooked in a rich brown gravy. **Known for:** relaxed atmosphere; local meats. [$] *Average main: R160* ✉ *Thrupps Center, 204 Oxford Rd., Illovo* ☎ *011/268–2107* 🌐 *www.turnntender.co.za.*

PARKHURST AND PARKTOWN NORTH

$$ FRENCH 🍴 **Bistro Vine.** On one of the best-known streets for restaurants in the country and with only a dozen or so tables, this small and intimate restaurant on Parkhurst's famous 4th Avenue can be crowded, but the food is good and the service is excellent. Try the *moules frites,* fresh Saldhana bay mussels simmered in their own stock, dry white wine, lemon, cream, leeks, celery, and herbs, and served with deliciously crunchy fries and homemade mayonnaise. **Known for:** South African wines; French bistro cuisine; sophisticated flavors. [$] *Average main: R135* ✉ *24 4th Ave., Parkhurst* ☎ *011/327–4558* 🌐 *www.bistrovine.co.za* 🕒 *Closed Mon.*

$$ STEAKHOUSE FAMILY 🍴 **Mike's Kitchen, Parktown.** At Mike's Kitchen in Parktown, you'll find an extensive menu with hearty fare and a convivial atmosphere. The steak house is housed in an old mansion called Eikenlaan, which was built in 1903 for James Goch, a professional photographer and the first to use flash photography in South Africa. **Known for:** steak-house chain; historic location; outdoor garden. [$] *Average main: R129* ✉ *15 St. Andrew's Rd., Parktown North* ☎ *011/484–2688* 🌐 *www.mikeskitchenparktown.co.za.*

$ CAFÉ 🍴 **Nice on 4th.** This easygoing, unpretentious café serves only breakfast, lunch, and tea, but is always busy, mostly because the food is so fresh and good. Breakfast is a specialty, with wholesome breakfast baskets made from toast and piled with succulent tomatoes, bacon, and a poached egg. **Known for:** fresh ingredients; healthy breakfasts; busy atmosphere. [$] *Average main: R80* ✉ *37 4th Ave., at 14th St., Parkhurst* ☎ *011/788–6286* 🌐 *www.niceon4th.co.za* ⏲ *Closed Mon. No dinner.*

$$$$ STEAKHOUSE Fodor's Choice ★ 🍴 **Wombles.** Wombles is an upmarket steak house with a warm, yet rather formal atmosphere and generous portions. If you want to try something very South African, go for the springbok shank with savory green peppercorn sauce and stewed fruit on the side. **Known for:** rosewater ice cream; impeccable service. [$] *Average main: R400* ✉ *Hobart Grove Shopping Centre, 88 Hobart Rd., Bryanston* ☎ *011/880–2470* 🌐 *www.wombles.co.za* ⏲ *Closed Sun. No lunch Sat.* 👔 *Jacket required.*

PARKTOWN, PARKVIEW, SAXONWOLD, AND WESTCLIFF

$$ AFRICAN Fodor's Choice ★ 🍴 **Moyo.** The second Moyo location in Johannesburg, this Parkview branch is the nicest during the day, as you can dine with a view of the lake and take a stroll or a ride in a rowboat afterward. The branch retains the quintessential Moyo vibe, with pan-African cuisine, decor, and live performances. **Known for:** lush garden setting; leisurely lunch spot. [$] *Average main: R150* ✉ *Zoo Lake Park, 1 Prince of Wales Dr., Parkview* ☎ *011/646–0058* 🌐 *www.moyo.co.za.*

SANDTON

$$$ STEAKHOUSE 🍴 **The Butcher Shop and Grill.** This is a good place for hungry meat lovers, specializing in prime South African meat aged to perfection by Alan Pick, the butcher-owner. Kudu, springbok, ostrich, and other game are often on the specials list, and only the most tender cuts are served. **Known for:** in-house butcher shop; excellent wine cellar; custard pudding. [$] *Average main: R190* ✉ *Nelson Mandela Sq., Shop 30, Sandton* ☎ *011/784–8676* 🌐 *www.thebutchershop.co.za.*

$$$$ EUROPEAN 🍴 **Flames.** A golf cart whisks you up the hill to this chic establishment overlooking Johannesburg Zoo and the city, with the best sunset views in town. The menu showcases seasonal regional cuisine, with South African braai, Karoo lamb chops prepared with thyme and garlic, and the ostrich tournedos, including French beans, corn, pap balls, and rosemary sauce. **Known for:** sundowners; high-end dining at the Four Seasons Hotel; Wagyu beef burger. [$] *Average main: R250* ✉ *Four Seasons Hotel The Westcliff, 67 Jan Smuts Ave., Saxonwold* ☎ *011/481–6000* 🌐 *www.flamesrestaurant.co.za.*

ROSEBANK

$$ MEDITERRANEAN 🍴 **Doppio Zero.** Doppio Zero serves wholesome, tasty Mediterranean-inspired meals with ingredients like grilled halloumi, fresh tomato, arugula, avocado, and salmon. More substantial meals such as pastas and pizzas are also on the menu. **Known for:** outdoor seating; nearby shopping district. [$] *Average main: R110* ✉ *The Firs Shopping Centre, Cradock St. at Bierman St., Rosebank* ☎ *011/447–9538* 🌐 *www.doppio.co.za.*

8

WHERE TO STAY

You can find just about every type of lodging in Johannesburg, from the stately and classic Saxon to the fun and funky Ten Bompas or The Peech. Although these varied options are all worthy places to lay your head, the truth is that most travelers stop here only for an overnight or two before they head out to their safari destination. With that in mind, we have compiled a list of places that are easy to get to from the airport and are in well-secured areas so that you will feel safe and comfortable.

Most of the good hotels are in the northern suburbs, though some are found elsewhere, including the revitalized central city. Many are linked to nearby malls and are well policed. Boutique hotels have sprung up everywhere, as have bed-and-breakfasts from Melville to Soweto. Hotels are quieter in December and January, when many locals take their annual vacations and rates are often cheaper. But beware: if there's a major conference, some of the smaller hotels can be booked months in advance.

All the hotels we list offer no-smoking rooms, and many have no-smoking floors.

Hotel reviews have been shortened. For full information, visit Fodors.com.

WHAT IT COSTS IN SOUTH AFRICAN RAND				
	$	$$	$$$	$$$$
Hotels	under R1,500	R1,500–R2,500	R2,501–R3,500	over R3,500

Prices are the lowest price for a standard double room in high season.

CITY CENTER

$
HOTEL
Reef Hotel. Jo'burg was founded on gold-mining, and this hotel in the city center commemorates those early beginnings. **Pros:** convenient downtown location; great breakfast buffet; open-air rooftop pool and bar. **Cons:** charge for some shuttle service; noise from downtown. $ *Rooms from: R1065* ⊠ *56 Anderson Rd.* ☎ *011/689–1000* ⊕ *www. reefhotel.co.za* ↗ *120 rooms* ⫶◯⫶ *Breakfast.*

NORTHERN SUBURBS

KEMPTON PARK

$$$$
HOTEL
InterContinental Johannesburg O.R. Tambo Airport. A few paces from international arrivals and adjacent to the car-rental companies and bus terminal, this is a good choice for those who have a one-night layover. **Pros:** ideal for those who don't need to go into Johannesburg or who have a layover before a connecting flight; free Wi-Fi; free meet-and-greet service with escort to the hotel. **Cons:** large and impersonal; you won't see much of Johannesburg without leaving the hotel. $ *Rooms from: R3850* ⊠ *O.R. Tambo Airport, Kempton Park* ☎ *011/961–5400, 877/859–5095* ⊕ *www.ihg.com* ↗ *140 rooms* ⫶◯⫶ *Breakfast.*

ROSEBANK

$$ HOTEL 🏨 **Clico Boutique Hotel.** This small, upmarket boutique hotel in central Rosebank is a renovated Cape Dutch house with a gracious garden that offers good value in an area known for expensive accommodations. **Pros:** 24-hour manned security and CCTV cameras; free Wi-Fi throughout the hotel; central location near Rosebank Mall. **Cons:** neighborhood not safe to walk at night; noise from the pool activity can travel to the suites; stairs might be difficult to navigate. [$] *Rooms from: R1685* ✉ *27 Sturdee Ave., at Jellicoe Ave., Rosebank* ☎ *011/252–3300* 🌐 *www.clicohotel.com* 🛏 *9 suites* 🍴 *Breakfast.*

$$ HOTEL 🏨 **Crowne Plaza Johannesburg–The Rosebank.** Notable for its quirky public spaces—Louis XVI reproduction armchairs, white shaggy rugs, and the very popular Circle Bar with its beaded booths—The Rosebank Crowne Plaza has standard rooms that are small but perfectly formed, with white vinyl armchairs and side tables. **Pros:** hip nightspot; great spa and gym; excellent location near Rosebank Mall. **Cons:** popular with partying locals; bathrooms in deluxe suites lack privacy; standard rooms are on the small side. [$] *Rooms from: R1700* ✉ *Tyrwhitt Ave. at Sturdee Ave., Rosebank* ☎ *011/448–3600* 🌐 *www.therosebank.co.za* 🛏 *318 rooms* 🍴 *Breakfast.*

$$$ HOTEL 🏨 **54 on Bath.** Most of the visitors to 54 on Bath are international business travelers and foreign tourists drawn to the modern yet intimate elegance behind the towering brick facade and Doric columns, though the Champagne bar is popular with locals. **Pros:** free Wi-Fi for guests throughout the hotel; direct access to malls via sky bridge; friendly staff. **Cons:** construction in the area can be noisy; not on airport shuttle route, although the hotel will arrange transport from the airport for a fee; the hotel is looking a little dated. [$] *Rooms from: R3200* ✉ *54 Bath Ave., Rosebank* ☎ *011/344–8500* 🌐 *www.tsogosun.com/54-on-bath* 🛏 *90 rooms* 🍴 *Breakfast.*

$$$ HOTEL 🏨 **Hyatt Regency Johannesburg.** This Hyatt Regency hotel is trendy and opulent, with lots of black, gold, and glass and enormous picture windows revealing stunning views of the northern suburbs. **Pros:** direct basement access to the adjoining malls; very cosmopolitan atmosphere; bustling lobby area is frequently used for meetings. **Cons:** busy area with lots of traffic; an expensive option for the area; decor somewhat generic. [$] *Rooms from: R3300* ✉ *191 Oxford Rd., Rosebank* ☎ *011/280–1234* 🌐 *johannesburg.regency.hyatt.com* 🛏 *259 rooms* 🍴 *Breakfast.*

$$ HOTEL 🏨 **The Peech.** This upscale boutique hotel has uncluttered but comfortable interiors and quality dining options. **Pros:** fabulous rain showerheads and Molton Brown toiletries in every bathroom; free Wi-Fi throughout the hotel and iPod docking stations in every room; every room has a private outdoor space. **Cons:** rooms and the neighboring gym overlook the pool; fee to use the gym; not great for families. [$] *Rooms from: R2500* ✉ *61 North St., Rosebank* ☎ *011/537–9797* 🌐 *www.thepeech.co.za* 🛏 *19 rooms* 🍴 *Breakfast.*

MELROSE ARCH

$$ HOTEL 🏨 **African Pride Melrose Arch Hotel.** Primarily catering to business travelers, this ultramodern hotel is within the Melrose Arch shopping, dining, and residential enclave. **Pros:** Melrose Arch is a high-security gated community with good dining and shopping options within safe walking distance; the Library bar is a favorite with well-heeled executives; swimming pool

(with drinks and light food). **Cons:** hipster decor might not appeal to everyone; some might find it hard to relax in a high-energy environment; no on-site gym but day pass for the nearby Virgin Active Gym available for a small fee. $ *Rooms from: R1600* ⊠ *1 Melrose Sq., Melrose Arch* ☎ *011/214–6666* ⊕ *protea.marriott.com* ⟿ *119 rooms* ⏐◯⏐ *Breakfast.*

SANDTON

$$$$ 🗆 **Fairlawns Boutique Hotel & Spa.** In a residential area, this gracious
HOTEL boutique hotel was once a private home owned by the Oppenheimer family. **Pros:** well-stocked library; complimentary shuttle service to Sandton City mall; recently renovated. **Cons:** service can be slow; not great for families; Wi-Fi can be sluggish. $ *Rooms from: R4870* ⊠ *Morningside Manor, 1 Alma Rd., Sandton* ☎ *011/804–2540* ⊕ *www.fairlawns.co.za* ⟿ *40 rooms* ⏐◯⏐ *Breakfast.*

$$ 🗆 **InterContinental Johannesburg Sandton Towers.** Directly connected to
HOTEL Sandton City via a sky bridge, this hotel is particularly attractive to keen shoppers and businesspeople who value proximity and easy access to Johannesburg's premier mall and meeting venues. **Pros:** free Wi-Fi throughout the hotel; free morning newspaper; international adapters provided in the rooms; room windows open; great location. **Cons:** large and not as personal as a smaller hotel; public areas used extensively by locals for meetings; not great for a romantic getaway. $ *Rooms from: R2300* ⊠ *Maude St. at 5th St., Sandton* ☎ *011/780–5555* ⊕ *www.tsogosun.com* ⟿ *248 rooms* ⏐◯⏐ *Breakfast.*

$$ 🗆 **The Maslow.** Conveniently situated in the heart of bustling Sandton,
HOTEL the Maslow is a case study in modern, seamless sophistication. **Pros:** one of the best business-orientated hotels in the province; stellar attention to detail; great location. **Cons:** people have complained that the breakfast buffet does not reflect the high standard of the hotel; not great for families; can feel crowded due to its popularity. $ *Rooms from: R1975* ⊠ *146 Rivonia Rd., Sandton* ☎ *010/226–4600, 011/780–7855* ⊕ *www.suninternational.com/maslow* ⟿ *281 rooms* ⏐◯⏐ *Breakfast.*

$$$$ 🗆 **The Michelangelo.** As though taken from a street in Florence, this hotel
HOTEL forms the northern facade of much-touted piazza-inspired Nelson Mandela Square, also called Sandton Square. **Pros:** great shopping (especially for designer labels and high-fashion items from Gucci and Louis Vuitton) in the Square and adjoining Sandton Sun Mall; high security is omnipresent; perfect for a romantic getaway. **Cons:** Nelson Mandela Square is very popular and never quiet; service can be inattentive at times; outdated gym equipment. $ *Rooms from: R3510* ⊠ *135 West St., Nelson Mandela Sq., Sandton* ☎ *011/282–7000* ⊕ *www.legacyhotels.co.za* ⟿ *242 rooms* ⏐◯⏐ *Breakfast.*

$$ 🗆 **Radisson Blu Gautrain.** Located just across the road from the Sand-
HOTEL ton Gautrain station, the Radisson Blu Gautrain hotel is a popular destination for both international travelers and city locals. **Pros:** great value for money; 24-hour gym; beautiful views of surrounding Sandton. **Cons:** no free parking; not child-friendly; not for a romantic getaway. $ *Rooms from: R1850* ⊠ *Rivonia Rd. at West St., Sandton* ☎ *011/286–1000* ⊕ *www.radissonblu.com/hotelsandton-johannesburg* ⟿ *222 rooms* ⏐◯⏐ *Breakfast.*

$$$
HOTEL

Sandton Sun. One of the first luxury hotels to open in Sandton, the Sun has a very upmarket designer African feel. **Pros:** linked to Sandton City, Johannesburg's premier mall, by a first-floor sky bridge; business suites have home-automation technology and video conferencing; excellent restaurants are within easy walking distance. **Cons:** shopping's the name of the game here; if conspicuous consumption bothers you, stay elsewhere; pricey. $ *Rooms from: R3300* ✉ *Sandton City, 5th St. at Alice La., Sandton* ☎ *011/780–5000* ⊕ *www.tsogosun.com/sandton-sun-hotel* ⤳ *334 rooms* ❘⊙❘ *Breakfast.*

SANDHURST

$$$$
HOTEL
Fodor's Choice
★

The Saxon Hotel, Village & Spa. In the exclusive suburb of Sandhurst, the luxurious, exclusive, and impeccably designed Saxon Hotel has repeatedly received awards for its excellence. **Pros:** possibly the most exclusive address in Gauteng; exceptional spa on-site; good for business travelers or high-profile folk who'd rather not see anyone else in the corridors. **Cons:** some might find the atmosphere a bit snooty; children under 14 not welcome in restaurant; pricey. $ *Rooms from: R6600* ✉ *36 Saxon Rd., Sandhurst* ☎ *011/292–6000* ⊕ *www.saxon. co.za* ⤳ *53 rooms* ❘⊙❘ *Breakfast.*

WESTCLIFF

$$$$
HOTEL
Fodor's Choice
★

Four Seasons The Westcliff. The iconic Westcliff, now under the Four Seasons banner and with a $56-million revamp, has been transformed into the paragon of a luxurious urban resort. **Pros:** great location; spectacular views over Johannesburg; impeccable service. **Cons:** all this luxury and service comes at a high cost; rather formal atmosphere, which may not be to everyone's liking; rooms spread out along a steep hill, sometimes requiring a shuttle. $ *Rooms from: R3600* ✉ *67 Jan Smuts Ave., Westcliff* ☎ *011/481–6000* ⊕ *www.fourseasons.com/johannesburg* ⤳ *153 rooms* ❘⊙❘ *Breakfast.*

FOURWAYS

$$
HOTEL

Palazzo at Montecasino. Built in the style of a Tuscan villa, the hotel is set among formal herb gardens in a location far north of Johannesburg that's good for shopping but somewhat distant from most of the city's sights and the business center of Sandton and the city center itself. **Pros:** neighboring casino complex has malls, cinemas, and major theater; the hotel's grounds contain great gardens and a pool; service is impeccable. **Cons:** gridlocked traffic in the area means longer than usual traffic jams; as in the casino, the decor is faux-Tuscan; Fourways feels remote from Johannesburg. $ *Rooms from: R2500* ✉ *Montecasino Blvd., Fourways* ☎ *011/510–3000* ⊕ *www.tsogosunhotels.com/ deluxe/the-palazzo-montecasino* ⤳ *258 rooms* ❘⊙❘ *Breakfast.*

8

NIGHTLIFE AND PERFORMING ARTS

NIGHTLIFE

Johannesburg comes alive after dark, and whether you're a rebellious punk rocker or a suave executive, there's always something to do. Rivonia and the business district of Sandton have become trendy spots for young, hip professionals and their style-conscious friends, and the old neighborhood of Greenside still has streets filled with lively little bars and restaurants and a sprinkling of clubs. The suburb of Norwood also has a central street with a good selection of small restaurants and bars. To dine and dance in one go, you should venture to one of these suburbs or visit one of the casino complexes, such as the popular Montecasino in Fourways or Emperor's Palace next to the O. R. Tambo Airport. Mabongeng Precinct in the heart of Jo'burg is one of the newest destinations, with trendy restaurants, bars, and nightclubs (plus galleries and boutiques) in a mixed-used community.

JHBLive. A useful website for event details is JHBLive. ⊠ *Johannesburg* ⊕ *www.jhblive.com.*

The Star. A good place to find out what's going on is in the "Tonight" section of *The Star*, Johannesburg's major daily. ⊠ *Johannesburg* ⊕ *www.tonight.co.za.*

BARS AND PUBS

Café Vacca Matta. Dress stylishly for Café Vacca Matta, a trendy bar and restaurant in the Montecasino complex where a sometimes-snobbish crowd dances to Top 40 hits. ⊠ *Montecasino, William Nicol Dr., Fourways* ☎ *011/511–0511.*

Capital Underground. Capital Underground is a happening dance and night club for the younger crowd. ⊠ *Tyrwhitt Ave. at Keyes Ave., Rosebank* ☎ *011/880–0033.*

CLUBS

Jo'burg's clubs are usually not too expensive. On a normal club night, you'll pay between R100 and R250 to get in, though you won't always have to pay for entrance. When dance parties or bigger events take place (or big-name DJs and musicians appear), expect to pay upward of R200. Here are just some of the city's established clubs.

Back O' the Moon. Back O' the Moon is a jazzy restaurant with a lounge showcasing live entertainment. The original Back O' the Moon was a famous 1950s shebeen in Sophiatown (a suburb destroyed during apartheid), where rich and poor alike could mingle over great music and food. ⊠ *Gold Reef City Casino, Ormonde* ☎ *011/248–5222* ⊕ *www.backofthemoon.co.za* ⊗ *Closed Mon. and Tues.*

PERFORMING ARTS

For a comprehensive guide to events, read the "Friday" section of the weekly *Mail & Guardian,* which is also available online.

CLOSE UP

Kwaito

Kwaito is a uniquely South African music genre, rooted in house, raga (a subgenre of reggae), hip-hop, and local rhythms. It emerged from the country's townships after apartheid and gets its name, some say, from township slang for "cool talk." Its hard-pumping bass beats, lightly slowed down from a house rhythm, are topped with rambled-off lyrics in a style reminiscent of American rap. It's as much a lifestyle as it is a music genre, with its own ways of dancing and dressing.

The best-selling kwaito musicians (and kwaito DJs) have superstar status in South Africa, but they have a less unsavory reputation than their American hip-hop equivalents. Though some kwaito acts stand accused of sexism and vulgar lyrics, the kwaito attitude is generally quite respectable. Lyrics are often about banning guns or respecting women, or they comment on murder, rape, AIDS, and unemployment. One kwaito star, Zola—named after an impoverished Soweto community—enjoyed a long-running TV series, in which he worked to improve people's lives. His music is featured in the 2006 Academy Award–winning movie *Tsotsi*. Other chart-topping kwaito stars include the late Mandoza, whose catchy, powerful songs earned him several awards and crossover appeal; the pop sensational duo, Mafikizolo; Mdu Masilela; the Brothers of Peace; and Mzekezeke, an enigmatic masked singer.

—Riaan Wolmarans

TICKETS

Computicket. Almost all major performances and many smaller ones can be booked through Computicket. ☎ *0861/915–8000, 011/340–8000* ⊕ *www.computicket.com.*

THEATER

Joburg Theatre. Joburg Theatre is Jo'burg's main cultural venue and the home of the Joburg Ballet Theatre. It contains the enormous Nelson Mandela Theatre and the smaller People's and Fringe theaters, plus the experimental Space.com. Many international productions are staged here, but there's also a good balance of local material, such as the annual pantomime by Janice Honeyman, which satirizes South Africans uproariously. ✉ *163 Civic Blvd., Braamfontein* ☎ *011/877–6855* ⊕ *www.joburgtheatre.com.*

Teatro at Montecasino. The Teatro opened in 2007 at the Montecasino leisure and casino complex in northern Jo'burg, introducing patrons to a world-class theater facility with its debut production, *The Lion King.* Since then, it's staged dozens of world-class productions, including shows as diverse as *Phantom of the Opera, War Horse*, and *Swan Lake.* Although it seats more than 1,800, no seat is more than 33 meters (100 feet) from the action—and there's plenty of that. Expect large-scale music productions, cirque arts, drama performances, stand-up comedy, and National Theatre productions. Teatro is one of the world's 10 largest lyric theaters. ✉ *Montecasino, Blvd. Fourways, Fourways* ☎ *011/510–7472 management offices, 011/510–7366 box office* ⊕ *www.montecasino.co.za.*

8

Theatre on the Square. Located on Nelson Mandela Square in Sandton, this intimate, 200-seater theater has hosted hundreds of shows since it opened in 1997. An extensive repertoire includes comedy shows, cultural celebrations, author interviews, jazz concerts, plays, and music recitals. Friday lunchtime concerts are a boon to Sandton-based workers. ✉ *Nelson Mandela Sq., Sandton* ☎ *011/883–8606* ⊕ *www.theatreonthesquare.co.za.*

SHOPPING

Whether you're after designer clothes, the latest books or DVDs, high-quality African art, or glamorous gifts, Johannesburg offers outstanding shopping opportunities. In fact, many people, particularly from other African countries, come here with the express aim of shopping. Dozens of malls, galleries, and curio shops are scattered throughout the city, often selling the same goods at widely different prices. It's best to shop around.

NORTHERN SUBURBS

ROSEBANK

AFRICAN ARTS AND CRAFTS

Everard Read Johannesburg. The Everard Read Gallery, established in 1913, is one of the largest privately owned galleries in the world. It acts as an agent for several important South African artists. The gallery specializes in wildlife paintings and sculpture. ✉ *2 and 6 Jellicoe Ave., Rosebank* ☎ *011/788–4805* ⊕ *www.everard-read.co.za* ☉ *Closed Sun.*

MARKETS

At the city's several markets, bargaining can get you a great price. At the Rosebank Art and Craft Market, in particular, bargain hard by offering half the asking price, and then work your way up to about two-thirds of the price if you're interested in the item. Take your time before you buy anything, as you will see similar crafts at different stalls, and the prices may vary considerably.

Fodor's Choice ★ **Rosebank Art and Craft Market.** The Rosebank Art and Craft Market, between the Rosebank Mall and the Zone, has a huge variety of African crafts from Cape to Cairo, all displayed to the background beat of traditional African music. Drive a hard bargain here—the vendors expect you to! If you want to save your shopping until the end of your trip, then this should be your destination. It's the best place in Jo'burg to buy African crafts, and it's an entertaining place to visit as well. ✉ *Mall of Rosebank, Cradock Ave., Rosebank* ☎ *072/614–5506* ⊕ *www.rosebankartandcraftmarket.co.za.*

Rosebank Sunday Market. The Rosebank Sunday Market, on the rooftop of Rosebank Mall, has become a Sunday tradition in the city. More than 600 stalls sell African and Western crafts by local artisans, antiques, original clothing, and more. It's also a great place to fill your picnic basket, with tempting specialties from Greek wraps to Thai spring rolls to gourmet cupcakes. Frequently, African musicians, dancers, and other entertainers delight the crowds. ✉ *The Mall of Rosebank, Level 4, Bath St. at Baker St., Rosebank* ☎ *072/243–8582* ⊕ *www.rosebanksundaymarket.co.za.*

BRYANSTON
MARKETS
Bryanston Organic and Natural Market. If you're into healthful living, visit the Bryanston Organic and Natural Market. More than 140 stalls feature artisanal, organic, and naturally sourced fresh produce. There's a dairy section, delicatessen and bakery, choice of five coffee shops, flowers, crafts in wood, leather, glass and metal, handmade clothes and shoes, and many other products clamoring for your clean-living attention. ⊠ *Michael Mount Waldorf School, 40 Culross Rd., off Main Rd., Bryanston* ☎ *011/706–3671* ⊕ *www.bryanstonorganicmarket.co.za.*

PARKTOWN, PARKVIEW, SAXONWOLD, AND WESTCLIFF
AFRICAN ARTS AND CRAFTS
Art Africa. Art Africa brings together a dazzling selection of ethnic arts, crafts, and artifacts from across the continent and also sells funky items, such as tin lizards and wooden animals, that are produced in community empowerment projects that uplift and benefit the craftsmen and their communities. ⊠ *62 Tyrone Ave., Parkview* ☎ *011/486–2052.*

Goodman Gallery. The highly successful, five-plus-decade-old Goodman Gallery presents exciting monthly exhibitions by the stars of contemporary African and African diaspora art, including William Kentridge, David Goldblatt, and Kudzanai Chiurai. ⊠ *163 Jan Smuts Ave., Parkwood* ☎ *011/788–1113* ⊕ *www.goodman-gallery.com* ☉ *Closed Mon.*

SANDTON
GOLD AND DIAMONDS
Krugerrands, which carry images of President Paul Kruger and a springbok on either side, are among the most famous gold coins minted today. They lost some of their luster during the apartheid years, when they were banned internationally. Krugerrands are sold individually or in sets containing coins of 1 ounce, ½ ounce, ¼ ounce, and 1/10 ounce of pure gold. You can buy Krugerrands through most city banks, and at reputable coin shops such as the Scoin chain of shops, which you'll find in upmarket malls. The most convenient branches are in the Sandton City Shopping Centre and Rosebank Mall.

Charles Greig. Charles Greig is a reputable jeweler with a long-standing record, and a reputation for excellence, making this shop a good choice if you wish to buy a special South African piece, such as a ring or necklace containing diamonds. There's also an outlet at Michelangelo in Sandton, on Nelson Mandela Square. ⊠ *Hyde Park Corner, Jan Smuts Ave., Hyde Park* ☎ *011/325–4477* ⊕ *www.charlesgreig.co.za.*

Mynhardts Diamonds. Mynhardts Diamonds sells diamonds and jewelry, and specializes in women's and men's rings, especially engagement and wedding rings. The company makes up the rings from loose stones on demand and even offers a 3-D rendering so you can see how your ring will look. An appointment is required. ⊠ *27 Ridge Rd., Parktown* ☎ *079/525–8969, 083/663–3207* ⊕ *www.mynhardts.com.*

8

SIDE TRIPS FROM JOHANNESBURG

About an hour north of Johannesburg (depending on the traffic—on a bad day it can take more than two hours), Pretoria, the country's capital, is within the larger metropolitan area of Tshwane (pronounced *chwa*-ah-neh). About an hour and a half from Johannesburg is the Cradle of Humankind, declared a World Heritage Site for its rich fossil record reflecting the history of humanity over the past 3.5 million years or so. To the north of Johannesburg, not far from the Cradle of Humankind, lies the Magaliesberg (pronounced muh- *xuh*-lees-berg, where the first g is pronounced like the *ch* in *Chanukah*), a gentle, ancient mountain range and leisure area, where you can get a restful break amid lovely mountain scenery, farmlands, and quiet country roads. Sun City, a multifaceted entertainment and casino complex comprising hotels, championship golf courses, and a water park, and the adjacent Pilanesberg Game Reserve are about a three-hour drive from Johannesburg—well worth a visit if you have the time.

PRETORIA

48 km (30 miles) north of Johannesburg.

The city of Pretoria lies within the greater Tshwane metropolitan area, which was formed in 2000 when Pretoria and its surrounding areas—Centurion, the townships of Atteridgeville, Mamelodi, and Shoshanguve, and neighboring areas—merged under a single municipal authority. The country's administrative capital and home to many senior politicians and diplomats, Pretoria is a pleasant city, with historic buildings and a city center that is easily explored on foot.

Founded in 1855, the city was named after Afrikaner leader Andries Pretorius, one of the Voortrekkers (pronounced *fooer*-trekka) who moved from the Cape to escape British rule. In 1860 it became the capital of the independent Transvaal Voortrekker Republic. After the South African War of 1899–1902 (the Second Anglo-Boer War), the city became the capital of the then British colony, and in 1910 it was named the administrative capital of the Union of South Africa. In 1948, when the National Party came to power, Pretoria became the seat of the apartheid government. In 1964 the Rivonia Treason Trial (named for the Johannesburg suburb where 19 ANC leaders were arrested in 1963) was held here, and Nelson Mandela and seven of his colleagues were sentenced to life in prison.

GETTING HERE AND AROUND

There are a few options for getting to Pretoria. The Gautrain offers a safe, convenient, and high-speed connection between O. R. Tambo International Airport, Johannesburg, and Pretoria. Alternatively, a rental car gives you the flexibility to explore the city at your leisure, and private transfers are offered by all of O. R. Tambo's airport transfer companies *(see Air Travel, in Planning, at the beginning of the chapter)*. It takes at least an hour to travel from Johannesburg to Pretoria in the Tshwane metropolitan area on the N1 (two hours if the traffic is bad, which happens quite regularly, especially between about 7 and 9 am and 4 and 7 pm).

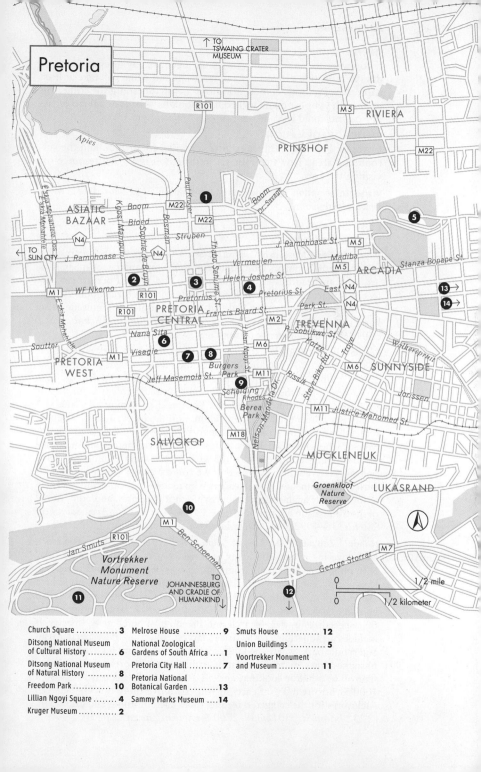

Pretoria

TIMING AND PRECAUTIONS

If you want to see everything, schedule an entire day or even couple of days here. A side trip to the Cullinan Diamond Mine will take at least half a day. Pretoria is not as notorious as Johannesburg for crime, but drive with your car doors locked, and don't have bags or valuables visible or you could become a target of a "hit-and-grab."

VISITOR INFORMATION

Covering Pretoria, Centurion, Atteridgeville, Mamelodi, and the surrounding area, Tshwane Tourism Information is a good resource for visiting the area.

Visitor Information Tshwane Tourist Information. ☎ *012/841–4212* ⊕ *www. tshwanetourism.com.*

EXPLORING

TOP ATTRACTIONS

Ditsong National Museum of Cultural History. This museum offers an insightful look at the country's indigenous cultures. You can marvel at San rock art, African headdresses, clay sculptures, and several permanent collections of archaeological material dealing with Pretoria, South Africa, and the many people who call this country home. The museum also has a restaurant. ⊠ *149 Visagie St., between Bosman and Schubart Sts.* ☎ *012/324–6082* ⊕ *www.ditsong.org.za* ⊠ *R35.*

Freedom Park. Opened in 2013, the 129-acre Freedom Park is dedicated to the struggle for freedom and humanity, as well as other aspects of South African heritage, including human evolution. At Salvokop, a prominent hill at the entrance to Pretoria on the highway from Johannesburg, and within view of the Voortrekker Monument, the site comprises a memorial, interactive museum, archives, and a garden of remembrance. The park was launched in 2002 by President Thabo Mbeki, who said, "We dedicate this day to all the heroes and heroines in this country and the rest of the world who sacrificed in many ways and surrendered their lives so that we could be free." Individual South African, African, and global leaders who made significant contributions to the struggle against oppression, exploitation, racism, and other forms of discrimination are honored here. ⊠ *Koch Ave. at 7th Ave., Salvokop* ☎ *012/336–4092* ⊕ *www.freedompark.co.za* ⊠ *R50.*

FAMILY
Fodor's Choice
★

National Zoological Gardens of South Africa (*Pretoria Zoo*). The city's zoo, covering nearly 200 acres, is considered one of the world's best, with about 9,000 animals from almost every continent (including rare Komodo dragons, the world's largest lizards). The animal enclosures here are much larger than those of most zoos. Like any modern zoo worth its name, this is just the public facade for a much larger organization that specializes in the research and breeding of endangered species. It includes an aquarium (with Africa's largest collection of freshwater fish) and reptile park, where the king crocodiles and the impressive collection of snakes don't fail to intimidate. A cable car transports you high above the zoo to a hilltop lookout, and it's a fun, worthwhile ride. It's also a good idea to rent a golf cart, so you can move more quickly between enclosures for the staggered feeding times each morning and afternoon. ⊠ *232 Boom St.* ☎ *012/339–2700* ⊕ *www.nzg.ac.za* ⊠ *R110.*

WORTH NOTING

Church Square. Anton van Wouw's statue of President Paul Kruger, surrounded by sentries, dominates this pleasant square, which is flanked by some of the city's most historic buildings: the Old Raadsaal (Council Chamber), designed by Dutch architect Sytze Wierda; the Palace of Justice (used as a military hospital during the South African War), built in early Italian Renaissance style; and the modern Provincial Administration Building. On Wednesday mornings you can watch a ceremonial military parade and flag-raising. ⊠ *Bordered by Paul Kruger and Church Sts.*

NEED A BREAK?

Café Riche. In a building dating from 1905, Café Riche is one of the better coffee shops in the center of town. It also serves *tramezzini* (toasted sandwiches) and salads. ⊠ *2 Church Sq.* ☎ *012/328–3173.*

Ditsong National Museum of Natural History. This massive natural-history museum has an extensive collection of land and marine animals from around the world, with an emphasis on African wildlife. The beautiful building also contains the most comprehensive display of taxidermied African birds in southern Africa. Of particular interest are the Genesis exhibits, tracing the evolution of life on Earth, and the geology section, with displays of weird and wonderful rocks and minerals. Mrs. Ples, the famous Australopithecus skull found at the Sterkfontein Caves in the Cradle of Humankind, resides here. ⊠ *432 Paul Kruger St., across from City Hall* ☎ *012/322–7632* ⊕ *www.ditsong.org.za* ⊠ *R35, tours additional R5.*

Kruger Museum. This was once the residence of Paul Kruger, president of the South African republic between 1883 and 1902 and one of the most revered figures in South African history. The home, still fully furnished, is humble and somber, befitting this deeply religious leader who loved to sit on the front *stoep* (veranda) and watch the world go by. Exhibits in the adjoining museum trace Kruger's career, culminating in his exile by the British and eventual death in Switzerland in 1904. Of particular interest are the letters of support that Kruger received from all over the world, including the United States, when Britain instigated the South African War (1899–1902), also known as the Anglo-Boer War. Across the road is the Dutch Reformed Church, where Kruger's wife is buried. ⊠ *60 WF Nkomo St.* ☎ *012/000–0010* ⊕ *www.ditsong.org.za* ⊠ *R65 for international visitors, R45 for domestic visitors.*

Lillian Ngoyi Square. This square, once called the J. G. Strijdom Square, was in apartheid times dominated by a huge bust of former pro-apartheid prime minister J. G. Strijdom. However, on May 31, 2001—exactly 40 years to the day after the government declared South Africa a republic—the supporting structure of the whole edifice crumbled, and Strijdom fell unceremoniously into the parking garage under the square. The public square has since been renamed the Lillian Ngoyi Square for the prominent antiapartheid activist. The Living Women's Monument was inaugurated here in 2016, honoring Ngoyi and other anti-apartheid leaders, including Helen Joseph, Rahima Moosa, and Sophie de Bruyn. ⊠ *Church St. at van der Walt St.*

Melrose House. Built in 1886, this opulent structure is one of South Africa's most beautiful and best-preserved Victorian homes, furnished in period style. It has marble columns, mosaic floors, lovely stained-glass windows, ornate ceilings, porcelain ornaments, and richly colored

8

carpets. On May 31, 1902, the Treaty of Vereeniging was signed in the dining room, ending the South African War. You can view a permanent exhibit on the war or arrange for a guided tour. ⊠ *275 Jeff Masemola St.* ☎ *012/322–0420* 🖾 *R25, guided tour R160 per hr* ⊙ *Closed Mon. and certain public holidays.*

Pretoria City Hall. This imposing structure, inaugurated in 1935, has an Italianate style that borrows freely from classical architecture. A tympanum on the front, by Coert Steynberg, one of South Africa's most famous sculptors, symbolizes the growth and development of the city. Statues of Andries Pretorius, the city's founder, and his son Marthinus, stand in the square fronting the building, and relief panels depict the founding in 1855. ⊠ *Visagie St. at Paul Kruger St.* ☎ *012/326–5012* 🖾 *Free.*

FAMILY **Pretoria National Botanical Garden.** Natural grassland and lawns fringed by indigenous flowers provide a welcome contrast to city life in Pretoria. Within the main garden a succulent garden, cycad garden, and dassie trail provide added interest, and more than 200 bird species have been recorded. Look out for hawks, falcons, kestrels, and Verreaux's eagle. An Enabling Garden near the entrance is dedicated to the physically challenged. ⊠ *2 Cussonia Ave., off Church St.* ☎ *012/843–5071* ⊕ *www.sanbi.org/gardens/pretoria* 🖾 *R33 (free Tues.).*

OFF THE
BEATEN
PATH

Sammy Marks Museum. About 23 km (14 miles) east of Pretoria's city center, this furnished, 48-room Victorian mansion, in a mixture of grand styles, and its outbuildings, surrounded by gardens, were built in 1884 for mining and industrial magnate Sammy Marks. Guided tours take place every hour on weekends; every 90 minutes on weekdays; and there are ghost tours at night by appointment. A restaurant is on-site, and you can picnic on the grounds. ⊠ *Off N4, Old Bronkhorstspruit Rd.,* ✛ *Exit at Solomon Mahlangu Dr./M10 and follow the signs* ☎ *012/755–9542* ⊕ *www.ditsong. org.za* 🖾 *R65 for international visitors, R45 for domestic visitors.*

Smuts House. This small wood-and-iron country house in Irene, an outlying suburb of Pretoria, was the residence of three-time South African prime minister Jan Christian Smuts, who played active roles in the South African War and World Wars I and II and was instrumental in setting up the League of Nations (forerunner of the United Nations). Despite his military background, he was committed to working for peace and remains one of South Africa's most interesting historical characters. His home illustrates the simple manner in which he lived until his death in 1950. There's a tea garden on the large grounds, an adjacent campsite, and easy trails up a nearby hill. A crafts market takes place on the grounds on certain weekends (visit ⊕ *ireneatsmuts.co.za* for upcoming dates). ⊠ *Off Nelmapius Rd., Jan Smuts Ave., Irene* ☎ *012/670–9016* ⊕ *www.smutshouse.co.za* 🖾 *R20.*

Union Buildings. Built in 1901, this impressive cream-sandstone complex—home to the administrative branch of government—was designed by Sir Herbert Baker, one of South Africa's most revered architects. It is his masterpiece and closely resembles the Parliament Buildings in New Delhi, where he went on to work. The complex incorporates a hodgepodge of styles—an Italian tile roof, wooden shutters inspired by Cape Dutch architecture, and Renaissance columns—that somehow works beautifully.

Expansive formal gardens step down the hillside in terraces, which are dotted with war memorials and statues of former prime ministers. There's no public access to the building, but the gardens are perfect for a picnic lunch. ⊠ *Near Church Sq., Government Ave.* ☎ *012/300–5200.*

Voortrekker Monument and Museum. This famous national heritage site is regarded as a symbol of Afrikaner nationalism and independence. Completed in 1949, the monument honors the Voortrekkers, who rejected colonial rule and trekked into the hinterland to found their own nation. The Hall of Heroes traces in its marble frieze their momentous Great Trek, culminating in the Battle of Blood River (December 16, 1838), when a small force of Boers defeated a large Zulu army without losing a single life. The Voortrekkers considered this victory a covenant with God. An adjoining museum displays scenes and artifacts of daily Voortrekker life, as well as the Voortrekker Tapestries, 15 pictorial weavings that trace the historical high points of the Great Trek. The monument is in a nature reserve, which has a picnic area and hiking and biking trails. You can dine in the restaurant and tea garden if you don't like to rough it. Also on-site is **Fort Schanskop,** the best preserved of four area forts commissioned by President Paul Kruger in about 1897. The fort houses a South African (Anglo-Boer) War museum and gift shop. ⊠ *Eeufees Rd.* ☎ *012/326–6770, 012/325–7885* ⊕ *www.vtm.org.za* ⊠ *R55.*

WHERE TO STAY

$$$
HOTEL
Fodor's Choice
★

🏨 **The Orient Hotel.** This exquisite, Asian-themed boutique hotel is aimed at the discerning traveler who is looking for an unusual and memorable experience and wants to be out of the center of the Johannesburg business district. **Pros:** superb cuisine; majestic surroundings; extraordinary service. **Cons:** not great for families; stairs can be a hindrance; need a car to get around. $ *Rooms from: R3000* ⊠ *Francolin Conservancy, Crocodile River Valley* ☎ *012/371–2902* ⊕ *www.the-orient.net* ⤴ *10 rooms* ⍝ *Breakfast.*

8

CRADLE OF HUMANKIND

72 km (45 miles) northwest of Johannesburg.

This World Heritage Site stretches over an area of about 470 square km (181 square miles), with about 300 caves. Inside these caves, paleoanthropologists have discovered thousands of fossils of hominids and other animals, dating back some 3.5 million years. The most famous of these fossils are Mrs. Ples, a skull more than 2 million years old, and Little Foot, a skeleton more than 3 million years old. Although the Cradle does not have the world's oldest hominid fossils, it has the most complete fossil record of human evolution of anywhere on Earth, has produced more hominid fossils than anywhere else, and has been designated a UNESCO World Heritage Site.

Archaeological finds at the Cradle of Humankind include 1.7-million-year-old stone tools, the oldest recorded in southern Africa. At Swartkrans, near Sterkfontein, a collection of burned bones tells us that our ancestors could manage fire more than a million years ago.

Not all the fossil sites in the Cradle are open to the public, but a tour of the Sterkfontein Caves and the visitor center provides an

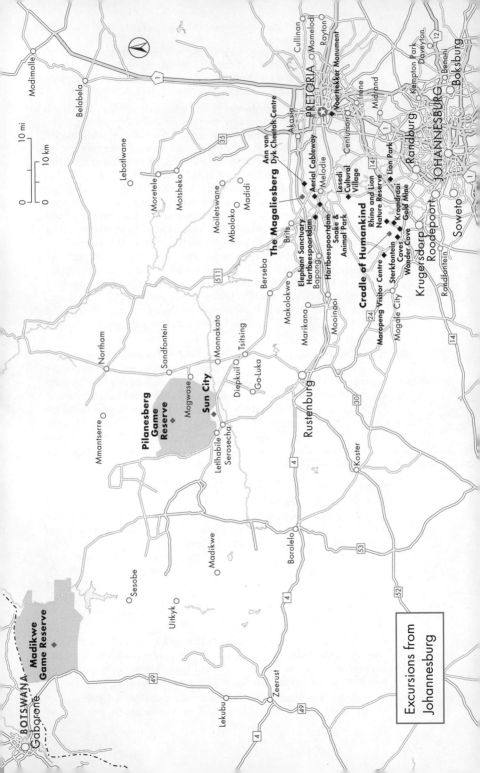

Excursions from Johannesburg

excellent overview of the paleontological work in progress, and a trip to Maropeng, a much larger visitor center 10 km (6 miles) from the Sterkfontein Caves, provides even more background.

GETTING HERE AND AROUND

Public transportation to the Cradle of Humankind area is limited, so using a rental car or taking an organized tour is best. Some hotels in the area will arrange transportation on request. The Cradle of Humankind is about a 90-minute drive from Johannesburg or Pretoria, but isn't well signposted, so use a GPS or download instructions on how to get there from the Maropeng website if you don't visit on a guided tour.

VISITOR INFORMATION

The Maropeng Visitor Centre provides information about the various sites in the Cradle of Humankind, and you can pick up many different promotional pamphlets here about things to do and see in the area. *(See Exploring.)*

EXPLORING

Kromdraai Gold Mine. For more recent history of South Africa's Gold Rush era (as opposed to the ancient history of humanity you'll find in the Cradle of Humankind like Maropeng and the Sterkfontein Caves), tour the small but fascinating Kromdraai Gold Mine, one of the country's oldest mines begun in 1881. Frankly, it's a little spooky. You don a miner's helmet and wander into the mine's murky depths on one-hour guided tours. It's not a difficult walk, and if you're lucky, you'll see bats roosting. ⊠ *Ibis Ridge Farm, Kromdraai Rd., Kromdraai ✢ Entrance on the R540 between Sterkfontein Caves and the Rhino and Lion Nature Reserve* ☎ *082/259–2162, 073/147–8417* ⊕ *www.gauteng.net* ☜ *R150.*

Lion Park. This highly rated drive-through safari park offers a rare chance to get up close with Africa's iconic predator. And while the experience might be trumped by seeing lions in more natural, expansive settings like the Kruger National Park, the opportunity to interact with a lion cub, take a guided walk with a cheetah, or feed a giraffe is not to be passed up. A leisurely drive around the small park will also guarantee sights of lions and other carnivores roaming through grassland, but try visit when it's a little cooler (early evening is a good time), as they tend to seek shady refuge during hot days. You can self-drive, or take one of the several tours on offer, including the guided lion and wild dog tour and the safari tour. ⊠ *R512, Lanseria Rd., Broederstroom, Pretoria* ☎ *087/150–0100* ⊕ *www.lionandsafaripark.com* ☜ *R165, more for tours.*

FAMILY
Fodor'sChoice
★

Maropeng Visitor Centre. Maropeng is the official visitor center of the Cradle of Humankind World Heritage Site and offers much more than information about the region: it's a modern, interactive museum dedicated to the history of humanity. It provides information about the various fossil sites in the area. About a 90-minute drive from either Johannesburg or Pretoria, it's one of the area's top attractions. It's best visited in parallel with the nearby fossil site of Sterkfontein Caves (about 5 km/3 miles away), but to visit both you'll need to set aside at least half a day. ⊠ *Off R563 (Hekpoort Rd.), Sterkfontein* ☎ *014/577–9000* ⊕ *www.maropeng. co.za* ☜ *R120 (combo ticket with Sterkfontein Caves for R190).*

8

FAMILY **Rhino and Lion Nature Reserve.** Rhinos, lions, wild dogs, cheetahs, hippos, and crocodiles are among the animals you can see at the Rhino and Lion Nature Reserve. You can spot about 650 head of game; visit the lion, wild dog, and cheetah enclosures (be careful of lions approaching vehicles) or vulture hide, or be thrilled by live snake shows every day but Monday and Friday. You can also visit the endangered-species breeding center and the magnificent white lions or cuddle a baby animal at the nursery for an additional charge of R40. In addition to the self-driving tour, you can book an escorted game drive or guided walk. There's a small swimming pool, four restaurants, and a curio shop, as well as rustic chalets and fully equipped cabins for overnights. ✉ *Cradle of Humankind, 520 Kromdraai Rd., Kromdraai* ☎ *011/957–0106* 🌐 *www.rhinolion.co.za* 🎫 *R160* 🕒 *Closed most Mon.*

FAMILY Fodor's Choice ★ **Sterkfontein Caves.** It was in the Sterkfontein Caves, in 1947, that Dr. Robert Broom discovered the now famous Mrs. Ples, as she is popularly known—a skull of an adult *Australopithecus africanus* that is more than 2 million years old. The find reinforced the discovery of a skull of an *Australopithecus* child, the Taung Skull, by Professor Raymond Dart in 1924, which was the first hominid ever found. At the time, Dart was ostracized for claiming the skull belonged to an early human ancestor. Scientists in Europe and the United States simply didn't believe that humanity could have originated in Africa. Today, few disagree with this theory. Another important find was the discovery in the 1990s of Little Foot, a near-complete skeleton of an *Australopithecus*, embedded in rock deep inside the caves. Guided tours of the excavations and caves last an hour and are not advisable if you are claustrophobic. Wear comfortable shoes. Start with the excellent museum, which has exhibits depicting the origins of the Earth, life, and humanity. A small on-site restaurant is open daily. ✉ *Sterkfontein Caves Rd., off R563, Sterkfontein* ☎ *014/577–9000* 🌐 *www.maropeng.co.za* 🎫 *R165 (combo ticket with Maropeng Visitor Centre for R190).*

FAMILY **Wonder Cave.** Wonder Cave is a huge single-chamber cave with a number of intact stalagmites and stalactites and formations up to 50 feet high. Steep stairs and a elevator take regular guided tours all the way down, but if you're feeling adventurous you can rappel down (by prior arrangement only). Groups of 20 or more may book evening tours. ✉ *Lion and Rhino Nature Preserve, 520 Kromdraai Rd., Kromdraai* ☎ *011/957–0106, 011/957–0109* 🌐 *www.rhinolion.co.za/wonder-cave-index* 🎫 *R100* 🕒 *Closed Mon.*

WHERE TO EAT

$$$$ AFRICAN 🍴 **The Carnivore.** Don't come expecting a quiet romantic dinner, as the huge space lends itself to a loud and sometimes frenetic scene. Game meat such as warthog, impala, and crocodile vies with tamer fare such as pork and mutton for space around an enormous open fire in the center of the restaurant. **Known for:** churrascaria-style service; vegetarian options. [$] *Average main: R285* ✉ *Misty Hills Country Hotel, 69 Drift Blvd., Muldersdrift* ☎ *011/950–6000* 🌐 *www.carnivore.co.za.*

WHERE TO STAY

$$$$ HOTEL **Forum Homini.** This boutique hotel in a game estate within the Cradle of Humankind aptly alludes to the mysterious and fascinating story of the development of humanity in every bit of its decor and can be a good option if you want to spend some time outside but near Johannesburg. **Pros:** luxury accommodations; daily changing menu; unique decor that blends into natural surroundings. **Cons:** hotel can be overwhelmed with wedding parties on weekends; not suitable for children; some rooms feel closed in. [$] *Rooms from: R4450* ✉ *Letamo Game Estate, R540 (off N14), Kromdraai, Mogale City* ☎ *011/668–7000* 🌐 *www.forumhomini.com* 🛏 *14 rooms* 🍴 *All-inclusive.*

$ HOTEL **Maropeng Hotel.** The Maropeng Hotel offers peace and tranquility with magnificent views of the Magaliesberg and Witwatersberg mountain ranges just 90 minutes from Johannesburg. **Pros:** attentive service; easy access to the Maropeng Visitor Centre and Cradle of Humankind; delicious, fresh food. **Cons:** rooms on the small side; difficult to access without a car; some rooms can be noisy. [$] *Rooms from: R1289* ✉ *R400, off the R563 Hekpoort Rd., Kromdraai* ☎ *014/577–9100* 🌐 *www.maropeng.co.za* 🛏 *24 rooms* 🍴 *Some meals.*

$$ HOTEL **Toadbury Hall.** This small, upscale country hotel is well located for trips into the Cradle of Humankind World Heritage Site, with elegant rooms and a neutral palette. **Pros:** luxurious spa facilities; fresh, tasty cuisine at the in-house restaurant; romantic setting. **Cons:** difficult to reach without a car; not a family destination. [$] *Rooms from: R2300* ✉ *Beyers Naude Dr. Extension, Plot 64, Elandsdrift* ☎ *010/593–7523* 🌐 *www.toadburyhall.co.za* 🛏 *10 rooms* 🍴 *Breakfast.*

THE MAGALIESBERG

The Magaliesberg are about 100 km (62 miles) northwest of Johannesburg.

The Magaliesberg Mountains (actually rolling hills) stretch 120 km (74 miles) between Pretoria and the town of Rustenburg. The South African War once raged here, and the remains of British blockhouses can still be seen. The region is most remarkable, however, for its natural beauty—grassy slopes, streams running through the ferns, waterfalls plunging into pools, and dramatic rock formations. It's an outdoor lover's paradise: go hiking, mountain biking, zip lining, or horseback riding; swim in crystal streams; picnic in one of the natural hideaways; or take a balloon flight at dawn followed by a Champagne breakfast. It's also home to the large Hartbeespoort Dam, a water-sports hot spot. You can get a great view of the Magaliesberg from atop them by riding up in the Hartbeespoort Aerial Cableway, a highly recommended attraction.

GETTING HERE AND AROUND

About a 90-minute drive northwest of Johannesburg, the region is fairly isolated, requiring a rental car or private transfer. Some of the hotels and lodges in the area can arrange transfers on request.

TIMING AND PRECAUTIONS

The main areas and attractions become crowded on weekends. On Friday evenings and Sunday afternoons there's always a wait—sometimes half an hour or more—to cross the one-way bridge over the Hartbeesport Dam. The area is relatively small, and two to three days is more than enough time to spend exploring.

VISITOR INFORMATION

Magalies Reservations covers accommodations and attractions in the Magaliesberg area.

EXPLORING

Fodor's Choice
★

Ann van Dyk Cheetah Centre. The Ann van Dyk Cheetah Centre (formerly the De Wildt Cheetah Centre, it has been renamed after its founder) is respected for its conservation and breeding programs. It offers a variety of different tours, including three-hour guided tours in vehicles (included in the price of admission); at an additional cost you can witness a cheetah run. No children under six are permitted. Visits to the center must be booked in advance. The center is in an area of the Magaliesberg called De Wildt, near Harbeespoort, about a 90-minute drive from Johannesburg. ⊠ *Pretoria North Rd., entrance to the farm at No. 22, Magaliesberg* ✣ *Take R513; the center is near Hartbeespoort Dam* ☎ *012/504–9906* ⊕ *www.dewildt.co.za* ☞ *R250, R350 with a cheetah run* ⊗ *Closed Mon.*

Elephant Sanctuary Hartbeespoortdam. The Elephant Sanctuary has three refuges across South Africa, including this one in the Magaliesberg Mountains. Five of the rescued mammals live here, including Amarula, a bull that spent most of his life in zoos; and Khuma, the matriarch. Visits must be prearranged and include interactive educational sessions. As part of the session, you can groom and feed the elephants; learn about their habits, personalities, and anatomy; and (for an additional fee) ride one of Africa's largest mammals. A small on-site lodge sleeps up to 12. This is a good option if you're spending a day in the Hartbeespoort area (do the Ann van Dyk Cheetah Centre and the Hartbeespoort Aerial Cableway on the same day), or visit it on the way to Pilanesberg or Madikwe if you're headed there. ⊠ *Hartbeespoort* ✣ *R104, about 2 km (1 mile) from Hartbeespoort Dam* ☎ *012/258–9904* ⊕ *www.elephant-sanctuary.co.za* ☞ *R695; elephant rides are an extra R525.*

Hartbeespoort Dam Snake and Animal Park. The Hartbeespoort Dam Snake and Animal Park is not big (you can walk through in less than two hours), but it has lions, tigers, pumas, jaguars, hyenas, many primate species, and birds of prey. Its selection of reptiles is overwhelming. Snake cages line the walkways, containing anything from harmless little garden snakes to poisonous cobras and giant pythons. Keep an eye out for snake shows, especially on weekends. The park offers a ferry boat cruise and a tea garden. ⊠ *1 Scott St., Hartbeespoort* ☎ *012/253–1162* ⊕ *www.hartbeespoortsnakeanimalpark.co.za* ☞ *R100.*

Lesedi Cultural Village. This is not just a place to stay and eat (although you can stay here in a very comfortable hut); it's a place to learn about the cultures and history of South Africa's Basotho, Ndebele, Pedi, Xhosa, and Zulu nations. Daily shows of dancing and singing, tours of traditional homesteads, and a crafts market complement the dining, lodging, and conference facilities. The large Nyama Choma restaurant serves food from all over the continent so you can taste North African fare, East African cuisine, or opt for a South African barbecue. Dishes include roast meats, porridge, and vegetables, often cooked in traditional African three-legged iron pots. Packages can include breakfast, dinner, and the tours, but most people just come for a day visit and a meal. If you do decide to stay, you have your choice of one of five traditional homesteads. ✉ *Kalkheuwel, R512 (Pelindaba Rd.), Broederstroom* ☎ *087/741–2696 general info, 087/740–9292 central reservations* 🌐 *aha.co.za/lesedi* 🎫 *R500 with lunch, R310 without lunch* 🛏 *38 rooms* 🍴 *Some meals.*

WHERE TO STAY

Although it's an hour drive from the city center, Hartbeespoort is these days almost a suburb of Johannesburg. You might choose to stay here for the night if you're en route from O. R. Tambo International (or the even-closer domestic airport of Lanseria) to a game reserve like the Pilanesberg or Madikwe, rather than staying in Johannesburg itself. It's on the way, after all, and has a pleasant, relaxed atmosphere, and you could more easily squeeze in a trip up the cableway, which is well worth doing. There are loads of bed-and-breakfasts and guesthouses to choose from.

$$$ HOTEL 🏨 **African Pride Mount Grace Country House & Spa.** One of South Africa's largest hotel spas, this retreat near Magaliesburg sits in the midst of beautiful gardens with drop-dead gorgeous views of the Magaliesberg Mountains. **Pros:** luxury accommodations; top-rated spa facilities; activity club specially for kids. **Cons:** some guests say the decor is a little tired; pricey; some say TV reception is poor. [$] *Rooms from: R2900* ✉ *Old Rustenburg Rd.* ✣ *Take the R24 to Hekpoort, near Magaliesburg* ☎ *014/577–5600* 🌐 *www.mountgracecountryhouseandspa.com* 🛏 *121 rooms* 🍴 *Some meals.*

$$$ HOTEL 🏨 **Budmarsh Country Lodge.** Surrounded by a lush garden in the heart of the Magaliesberg, this lodge has rooms with beautiful antique furniture and is a good place to base yourself if you just want to get into the country for a river ramble or a mountain hike. **Pros:** relaxing setting; peaceful library; rooms have Jacuzzis and outdoor showers. **Cons:** can be busy on weekends; inaccessible without a car; odors from the neighboring cows sometimes drift through the hotel—a reality for any country-based hotel. [$] *Rooms from: R3200* ✉ *T1, Magalies Meander Rd., R96* ✣ *Magaliesburg* ☎ *011/728–1800* 🌐 *www.budmarsh.co.za* 🛏 *18 rooms* 🍴 *Some meals.*

$$$$ HOTEL 🏨 **De Hoek Country House.** In France this exclusive establishment would be called an *auberge*—a small destination hotel with a great restaurant suitable for an overnight or weekend jaunt—and the two-story, sandstone building along the river would not be out of place in Provence. **Pros:** plenty of activities; attentive service; lovely setting; fabulous food. **Cons:** difficult to access with public transport; pricey; children under 12 not welcome. [$] *Rooms from: R3535* ✉ *Off R24, north of Magaliesberg, adjacent to Bekker School* ☎ *014/577–9600* 🌐 *www.dehoek.com* 🛏 *28 suites* 🍴 *All-inclusive.*

8

$ B&B/INN 🏨 **Jameson Country Cottages.** These pretty, well-appointed, self-catering cottages can sleep four or six people and have stoves, refrigerators, TVs, and a good selection of culinary appliances. **Pros:** fully equipped with modern amenities; facilities to keep the kids entertained; pet-friendly. **Cons:** additional cost for folding beds; difficult to reach without a car; some cottages don't have fireplaces. [$] *Rooms from: R700* ✉ *Farm Vlakfontein, R509 (Koster Rd.)* ✣ *10 km (6 miles) from Magaliesburg* ☎ *076/773–0275* 🌐 *www.jamesoncottages.com* 🛏 *6 cottages* 🍴 *No meals.*

$ RESORT 🏨 **Mountain Sanctuary Park.** This wilderness retreat offers campsites, rustic huts, and comfortable self-catering cabins and chalets with electricity, hot water, and cooking facilities. **Pros:** inexpensive; peaceful, rural setting; unspoiled nature reserve. **Cons:** rustic accommodations; it's just a self-catering experience, so not good if you don't like to do it yourself; some trails not marked very well, so it's easy to get lost. [$] *Rooms from: R530* ✉ *Magaliesberg* ✣ *40 km (25 miles) from Magaliesburg on dirt road, 15 km (9 miles) south of N4* ☎ *014/534–0114, 082/707–5538* 🌐 *www.mountain-sanctuary.co.za* 🛏 *19 rooms* 🍴 *No meals* ☞ *Bedding and towels not included with huts.*

$$$ HOTEL 🏨 **Valley Lodge & Spa.** Although it's too big to be called a hideaway, this beautiful lodge on a 250-acre nature reserve with a stream running through it also has a bird sanctuary. **Pros:** excellent food and good wine list; peaceful surroundings; spacious accommodations. **Cons:** can get busy with conference groups; pricey; anyone expecting country charm will be disappointed by the urban corporate decor. [$] *Rooms from: R2650* ✉ *13 Jennings St.* ☎ *014/577–1301, 014/577–1305* 🌐 *www.valleylodge.co.za* 🛏 *76 rooms* 🍴 *Breakfast.*

SPORTS AND THE OUTDOORS

BALLOONING

Fodor's Choice ★ **Bill Harrop's "Original" Balloon Safaris.** A fun and fascinating way to start the day is with an early-morning balloon ride. Bill Harrop's "Original" Balloon Safaris flies daily at sunrise, weather permitting, over beautiful green valleys, mountains, and glassy lakes, with views taking in the Cradle of Humankind, the sparkling Hartbeespoort waterways, and the Johannesburg skyline. A one-hour flight costs R2,570, including breakfast and sparkling wine. Bill Harrop's will pick you up from Johannesburg at an additional price, if necessary. ✉ *R560, near Skeerpoort Rd.* ☎ *011/705–3201* 🌐 *www.balloon.co.za.*

Flying Pictures. Flying Pictures offers daily (though dependent on good conditions) hot-air balloon trips at sunrise over the Magaliesberg and Cradle of Humankind, and are a reputable operator, having been in business for many years. The flight costs approximately R1,900, lasts about an hour, and includes sparkling wine and a full English breakfast on landing. You can be picked up from any hotel in the Magaliesberg. The company also partners with Airtrackers, which operate daily flights over the Pilanesberg Game Reerve. ✉ *Magaliesberg* ☎ *082/990–6924* 🌐 *www.flyingpictures.co.za.*

SHOPPING

Chameleon Village. The Chameleon Village is a lively African market with more than 200 vendors offering jewlery, home products, and artwork, as well as four restaurants with live music on weekends. There's also the Lion and Tiger Park (R100) and the Reptile and Snake Park (R100). ✉ *Hartbeespoort Dam, Hartbeespoort ✢ 2 km (1.2 miles) west from Hartbeespoort Dam Wall* ☎ *012/253–1454* ⊕ *www.chameleonvillage.co.za.*

Welwitschia Country Market. The Welwitschia Country Market sells arts and crafts among other goodies at dozens of shops and stalls in the shade of giant trees. There are three restaurants and live music on Wednesday, Friday, Saturday, and Sunday; it's especially bustling on weekends. ✉ *Rustenburg Rd., Hartbeespoort ✢ R104, 2 km (1 mile) from Hartbeespoort Dam, at Damdoryn 4-way stop* ☎ *083/302–8085* ⊕ *www.countrymarket.co.za* ☷ *Closed Mon.*

SUN CITY

177 km (110 miles) northwest of Johannesburg.

A huge entertainment-and-resort complex in the middle of dry bushveld in the North West Province, Sun City is popular with golfers and families—and with South Africans and foreign tourists alike. Sun City's appeal is vastly enhanced by the Pilanesberg Game Reserve, which is only a few miles from the resort, and by a full round of outdoor sports and activities, including two Gary Player–designed world-class golf courses. Developed by the same company that built the elaborate Atlantis resorts in the Bahamas and Dubai, this is a real destination resort.

Sun City was built in 1979, in the rocky wilds of Pilanesberg Mountain, the remains of an ancient volcano. The area was in the then Bantustan of Bophuthatswana—one of several semi–self-governed areas during apartheid set aside for black ethnic groups. As such, it was exempt from South Africa's then strict anti-gambling laws. Today Sun City comprises four luxurious hotels; one casino with slot machines, card tables, and roulette wheels; major amphitheaters that host international stars; and an array of outdoor attractions. The complex is split into two parts: the original Sun City, where the focus is on entertainment and gambling, and the Lost City, anchored by the magnificent Palace Hotel, which offers guests an opportunity to enjoy outdoor adventure at the Valley of the Waves.

In addition to its casinos, the original Sun City also stages rock concerts, major boxing bouts, the annual Nedbank Golf Challenge, and many major conferences. At the Lost City, painted wild animals march across the ceilings, imitation star-spangled skies glitter even by day, lush jungles decorate the halls, and stone lions and elephants keep watch over it all. The Lost City has hosted a long list of celebrities, including Michael Jackson, Frank Sinatra, and Oprah.

8

GETTING HERE AND AROUND

Ingelosi, the official Sun City shuttle, travels between Johannesburg (pickups are in various locations, including O. R. Tambo) and Sun City twice daily, and once a day from Pretoria. The tickets cost R1,250 one-way for one or two people, though the per-person price drops quickly with a larger group. Otherwise, to get to the area you'll need to arrange a private transfer or a rental car.

Within the Sun City complex are shuttle buses that ferry visitors between the entertainment complex and the various hotels, and the Sky Train monorail transports day visitors from the parking lot to the resort's entertainment complex.

TIMING AND PRECAUTIONS

There is plenty to keep you entertained in the area, so a few days are needed to do justice to the entertainment complex and adjacent Pilanesberg Game Reserve.

VISITOR INFORMATION

Covering the entire North West Province (including Hartbeespoort Dam, Sun City, and the Pilanesberg Game Reserve), the North West Tourism Information website offers plenty of useful information on what to do and where to stay in the province. The Sun International website also offers useful information on Sun City.

Visitor Information North West Province Tourism Information. ☎ *086/111–1866* 🌐 *www.tourismnorthwest.co.za.* **Sun International.** ☎ *011/780–7855* 🌐 *www.suninternational.com.*

WHERE TO STAY

There's a wide variety of dining options in and near Sun City (mostly pricey), from upmarket and glitzy to poolside cafés selling light meals like toasted sandwiches.

$$$$ RESORT FAMILY 🏨 **The Cabanas.** Paths thread through pleasant gardens to rooms in these small apartment blocks overlooking a man-made lake. **Pros:** great for kids; more affordable than other Sun City accommodations; access to activities. **Cons:** not a particularly tranquil setting; smallish rooms; need to hop a shuttle for dining options. [$] *Rooms from: R3790* ✉ *Sun City Resort* ☎ *014/557–1000, 011/780–7800 reservations* 🌐 *www.suninternational.com/sun-city/cabanas* 🛏 *380 rooms* 🍴 *Breakfast.*

$$$$ HOTEL 🏨 **Palace of the Lost City.** You might think a hotel based on the concept of a lost African palace would suffer from theme-park syndrome, but happily that's not the case here. **Pros:** luxury accommodations; impeccable service; great activities in surrounding area. **Cons:** pricey; some would find it unbearably ostentatious; some say the decor is showing its age. [$] *Rooms from: R5930* ✉ *Sun City Resort* ☎ *014/557–3131, 011/780–7800 reservations* 🌐 *www.sun-city-south-africa.com/palace.asp* 🛏 *338 rooms* 🍴 *Breakfast.*

$$$$ HOTEL 🏨 **Soho Hotel.** This is the original Sun City hotel, housing spacious and comfortable rooms in the complex that houses the resort's gaming casino, banks of slot machines, and other gaming activities. **Pros:** classic turndown and chocolate-on-the-pillow service; easy access to all the entertainment facilities; top-notch restaurants. **Cons:** casino can be noisy; crowded

during high season; expensive food and drink. $Rooms from: R4000* ⊠ *Sun City Resort* ☎ *014/557–5370, 011/780–7800 reservations* ⊕ *www. sun-city-south-africa.com/suncity.asp* ⤳ *340 rooms* ⦿❘ *Breakfast.*

PILANESBERG GAME RESERVE

200 km (124 miles) northwest of Johannesburg.

The 150,000-acre Pilanesberg Game Reserve is often called the Pilanesberg National Park. It isn't actually a South African national park these days, though it was one in the days when Bophutatswana was independent Bantustan. The game reserve is centered on the caldera of an extinct volcano dating back 1.3 billion years that may well have once been Africa's highest peak. Concentric rings of mountains surround a lake filled with crocodiles and hippos. Open grassland, rocky crags, and densely forested gorges provide ideal habitats for a wide range of plains and woodland game, including rare brown hyenas and cheetahs, and wildebeests and zebras, which are abundant in this reserve. Since the introduction of lions in 1993, Pilanesberg (pronounced pee- *luns-* berg) can boast the Big Five. One of the best places in the country to see rhinos, it's also a bird-watcher's paradise, with a vast range of grassland species, waterbirds, and birds of prey. It's also malaria-free and an excellent choice for game-viewing if you're short on time and can't make it all the way to Kruger National Park, for instance. You can drive around the park in your own vehicle or join a guided safari. The entertainment and resort complex of Sun City is nearby.

GETTING HERE AND AROUND

To get to the Pilanesberg from Johannesburg, get on the N4 highway to Krugersdorp and take the R556 off-ramp and follow the signs. The drive is about 2½ to 3 hours. There is a shuttle from Johannesburg to Sun City, just outside the park, but public transportation in and around the park is limited, so you'll need to rent a car or hire a transfer company.

TOURS

Several major tour operators in Johannesburg offer trips to Pilanesberg, including Springbok Atlas and Wilro Tours *(see Tours in Planning)*.

Booking these tours ahead of time is essential.

EXPLORING

Pilanesberg Game Reserve. The 150,000-acre Pilanesberg Game Reserve is centered on the caldera of an extinct volcano. Concentric rings of mountains surround a lake filled with crocodiles and hippos. Open grassland, rocky crags, and forested gorges provide ideal habitats for a wide range of plains and woodland game, especially wildebeests and zebras, which are plentiful here. The Pilanesberg (pronounced pee- *luns-* berg) can boast the Big Five (you have a great chance of seeing elephants and rhinos here on almost any single drive) and is malaria-free. It's a bird-watcher's paradise, with a vast range of grassland species, waterbirds, and birds of prey. The entertainment and resort complex of Sun City is nearby. ⊠ *Pilanesberg Game Reserve, Sun City* ☎ *014/555–1600, 018/397–1500 North West Parks Board* ⊕ *www.pilanesbergnational-park.org* ⧉ *R40 per vehicle, R80 per person.*

WHERE TO STAY

$$$$ HOTEL 🏨 **Bakubung Bush Lodge.** Abutting Pilanesberg, this lodge sits at the head of a long valley with terrific views of a hippo pool that forms the lodge's central attraction—it's not unusual to have hippos grazing 100 feet from the terrace restaurant. **Pros:** malaria-free; resident hippos; cheerful atmosphere. **Cons:** close to a main gate; always crowded; feels vaguely institutional. [$] *Rooms from: R4380* ✉ *Bakubung* ☎ *014/552–6000 lodge, 014/552–4006 reservations* 🌐 *www.legacyhotels.co.za* 🛏 *142 rooms* 🍴 *Some meals.*

$$$$ HOTEL FAMILY 🏨 **Kwa Maritane Bush Lodge.** The greatest asset of this hotel, primarily a time-share resort, is its location: in a bowl of rocky hills on the edge of the national park. **Pros:** malaria-free; you've got the best of both worlds—bushveld on your doorstep and Sun City only 20 minutes away by free shuttle bus; lovely swimming pools. **Cons:** you can't get away from the hotel feel; busy during school holidays; it gets noisy around reception, pool, and dining areas. [$] *Rooms from: R5316* ✉ *Kwa Maritane* ☎ *014/552–5100* 🌐 *www.legacyhotels.co.za* 🛏 *90 rooms* 🍴 *Some meals.*

$$ RESORT 🏨 **Manyane.** In a thinly wooded savanna east of Pilanesberg's volcanic ridges, this resort offers affordable accommodations in the Sun City area for those travelers who want to experience the region but can't pay five-star prices. **Pros:** accommodations are very basic but a good value; there is a good restaurant if you want a break from self-catering; lovely pool, which is a delight on a hot day. **Cons:** more downmarket than other options in the area; can be full of noisy campers and late-night revelers; there's a lot of dust. [$] *Rooms from: R1800* ✉ *Manyane* ☎ *014/555–1000 reservations, 072/746–9013 reception* 🌐 *www.manyaneresort-pilanesberg.com* 🛏 *24 rooms* 🍴 *No meals.*

$$$$ HOTEL 🏨 **Tshukudu Bush Lodge.** Tshukudu Bush Lodge is built into the side of a steep, rocky hill and overlooks open grassland and a large water hole where elephants bathe. **Pros:** malaria-free; luxurious and secluded accommodations; high on a hill with great views. **Cons:** it's a 132-step climb to the main lodge from the parking area, so may not be suitable for guests with disabilities or who get winded easily; game good, but not as abundant as Kruger; no children under 12 permitted. [$] *Rooms from: R9960* ✉ *Tshukudu* ☎ *014/552–6255* 🌐 *www.legacyhotels.co.za* 🛏 *10 rooms* 🍴 *All-inclusive.*

MADIKWE GAME RESERVE

300 km (186 miles) northwest of Johannesburg (or farther, depending on which gate you enter).

Just as leopards and Sabi Sand Game Reserve are synonymous, think of Madikwe Game Reserve and wild dogs in the same way. This is probably your best chance in South Africa to have an almost guaranteed sighting of the "painted wolves."

More than 25 years ago the 765-square-km (475-square-mile) area bordering Botswana was a wasteland of abandoned cattle farms, overgrown bush, and rusting fences. A brilliant and unique collaboration between the North West Parks Board, private enterprise, and local communities changed all that when Operation Phoenix—one of the most ambitious game relocation programs in the world—relocated more than 8,000 animals of 27 different species to Madikwe. Soon after, it became one of the fastest-growing safari destinations in South Africa.

Madikwe today is teeming with game. Spot the Big Five, plus resident breeding packs of the endangered painted wolves—the wild dogs of Africa. On your morning, evening, or night game drive, you also might spot cheetahs, hippos, lions, elephants, and buffalo, but you'll certainly see zebras, wildebeests, and several kinds of antelope (South Africans refer to all antelope generically as buck, whether they're male or female). Birders can spot more than 350 birds. Be dazzled by the crimson-breasted shrike, the lilac-breasted roller, yellow-billed and red-billed hornbills, blue waxbills, and many more.

GETTING HERE AND AROUND

Madikwe is an easy drive on good roads from Johannesburg. Go to Sun City via Hartbeespoort Dam and follow the signs to Madikwe, which is about an hour's drive from Sun City (though your trip could be an hour longer if your lodge is in the north of the park). Ask at your lodge for detailed instructions. You'll be driven around in an open game vehicle by a staff member of your lodge; guided bush walks are also available. No day visitors are allowed.

EXPLORING

Madikwe Game Reserve. This 187,500-acre game reserve in the North West Province (about 3½ hours from Johannesburg and Pretoria) close to the Botswana border is open only to overnight visitors, who can choose from 18 luxury lodges to stay. The reserve is famous for its wild dog population, but is also known for cheetah, the Big Five, and its general game, such as zebra, wildebeest, giraffe, and impala. It was established in 1991 and is fast becoming one of the most popular private reserves in the country, because of its abundance of game, promixity to Johannesburg, and the fact that it is malaria-free (so is very safe for children). ✉ *Madikwe Game Reserve* 🌐 *www.madikwegamereserve.co.za* 🎫 *R180 gate fee.*

8

WHERE TO STAY

In the south, choose between the ultraluxurious Tuningi Lodge, where a 300-year-old fig tree stands sentinel over a busy water hole, or either of Jaci's delightful lodges. Madikwe Safari Lodge, managed by the More family of Mpumalanga's Lion Sands, is another example of this company's high standards of luxury, service, and game-viewing.

Always check for special offers at any of the Madikwe lodges. You can often get very affordable rates, especially off-season.

$$$$
ALL-INCLUSIVE
FAMILY

🏨 **Jaci's Lodges.** The two lodges that make up Jaci's Lodges are family owned and have a longstanding reputation for friendliness, superb game drives, and comfortable accommodations that has made them synonymous with the name Madikwe Game Reserve. **Pros:** friendly, welcoming atmosphere; great children's activities and facilities; great game-viewing. **Cons:** if children aren't your thing, stay away from Jaci's Safari Lodge; pricey. [$] *Rooms from: R16990* ✉ *Madikwe Game Reserve* ☎ *083/700–2071 reservations, 083/303–0885 Jaci's Safari Lodge manager, 083/276–2387 Jaci's Tree Lodge manager* 🌐 *www.jacislodges.co.za* 🛏 *10 rooms* 🍴 *All meals.*

$$$$
RESORT
FAMILY

Ⓣ **Madikwe Safari Lodge.** This stunning five-star lodge in the central eastern region of the park is managed by the More family of Lion Sands, and their attention to detail, reputation for fine food and excellent service, and thrilling game drives are readily apparent. **Pros:** malaria-free; superb accommodations; great food; excellent game-viewing. **Cons:** not as scenically beautiful as the Mpumalanga and KwaZulu-Natal reserves; long walks between suites. Ⓢ *Rooms from: R9010 ⊠ Madikwe Game Reserve ☎ 018/350–9902 ⊕ www.madikwesafarilodge. co.za ⟿ 20 suites ⎮◎⎮ All meals.*

$$$$
ALL-INCLUSIVE

Ⓣ **Thakadu River Camp.** This gorgeous community-based tented safari camp is built of stone, wood, and canvas. **Pros:** drop-dead luxury; gorgeous views; full-on community involvement. **Cons:** you'll be sharing the reserve with lots of other vehicles (although only three allowed around a predator sighting); pricey; can be cold in winter. Ⓢ *Rooms from: R6260 ⊠ Thakadu ☎ 018/365–9912 general inquiries, 087/740– 9292 reservations ⊕ aha.co.za/thakadu ⟿ 12 rooms ⎮◎⎮ All meals.*

$$$$
RESORT

Ⓣ **Tuningi Safari Lodge.** A 300-year-old fig tree dominates the ultraluxurious Tuningi Lodge overlooking a busy water hole that will keep you entranced all day. **Pros:** superb accommodations; excellent Big Five game-viewing; designed with families in mind, including a children's program. **Cons:** pricey, but watch for special offers particularly in the off-season; additional fee per child per night. Ⓢ *Rooms from: R7000 ⊠ Madikwe Game Reserve ☎ 011/781–5384 ⊕ www.tuningi.com ⟿ 6 rooms ⎮◎⎮ All meals ⟃ Rate includes accommodations, 3 meals daily, 2 game drives daily, tea/coffee.*

MPUMALANGA AND KRUGER NATIONAL PARK

Updated by
Barbara Noe
Kennedy

In many ways Mpumalanga ("where the sun rises") is South Africa's wildest and most exciting province. Its local history is action packed: local wars, international battles, and a gold rush every bit as raucous and wild as those in California and the Klondike. Kruger National Park and the private game reserves abutting its western borders provide the country's best and most fulfilling game experience; in fact, it's highly probable that you will see all of the Big Five (lion, elephant, Cape buffalo, leopard, rhinoceros) during an average two- to three-night stay at one of the private reserves.

If you look at a map of South Africa, Mpumalanga is in the top right just below Limpopo. It spreads east from Gauteng to the border of Mozambique. The 1,125-km (700-mile) Drakensberg, part of the Great Escarpment, separates the high, interior plateau from a low-lying subtropical belt that stretches to Mozambique and the Indian Ocean. These lowlands, called the lowveld, are classic Africa, with as much heat, dust, untamed bush, and big game as you can take in. This is where you find Kruger National Park, covering a 320-km (200-mile) swath of wilderness and undoubtedly one of the world's finest game parks. Apart from its ease of access (there are nine entry gates along its western border), there are plenty of excellent accommodations ranging from bushveld and tented camps to luxury lodges. Mbombela (Nelspruit), south of Kruger, is the nearest big town.

The Drakensberg area rises to the west of Kruger and provides a marked contrast to the lowveld; it's a mountainous area of trout streams and waterfalls, endless views, and giant plantations of pine and eucalyptus. The escarpment region has some of South Africa's most spectacular scenery, including the Blyde River (Motlatse) canyon—one of the world's largest canyons and one of its greenest because of its luxuriant subtropical foliage—waterfalls, amazing vistas, great hiking, and river rafting. People come to the escarpment to unwind, soak up its beauty, and get away from the summer heat of the lowveld. Touring the area by car is easy and rewarding—the 156-km (97-mile) Panorama Route winds along the lip of the escarpment—and you can reach many of the best lookouts without stepping far from your car. You'd miss fabulous sightseeing opportunities if you failed to stop on the way to or from Kruger to take in some of Mpumalanga's fantastic sightseeing opportunities.

ORIENTATION AND PLANNING

ORIENTATION

In a nutshell: imagine the province of Mpumalanga as a large horizontally squashed ball in the northeast of South Africa with Limpopo to the north, Gauteng to the west, and Swaziland and KwaZulu-Natal to the south. The Drakensberg, where you'll find the Blyde River [Motlatse] canyon and more stunning scenery, divides the high plateaus of the South African interior from the low, lush, subtropical lowveld, home of Kruger National Park and other smaller game reserves, all teeming with wildlife.

Mpumalanga. Mpumalanga (Mm-puma-langa) Province has activities galore, from poking around cultural villages and hiking on mountain trails to driving through game reserves. The best way to get around Mpumalanga is by car, either from Johannesburg or from the airports at Mbombela (Nelspruit), Hoedspruit, Skukuza, or Phalaborwa (if you're going into the central section of Kruger). Plan your road trip with booked-in-advance accommodations (there are superb options all over the province), and visit at least one of the farm stalls that dot country roads for fresh fruit and veggies (in season), nuts, and creamy farm milk.

Kruger National Park. Larger than Israel and approximately the same size as Wales, Kruger National Park encompasses diverse terrain ranging from rivers filled with crocodiles and hippos to rocky outcrops where leopards lurk and thick thorn scrub shelters lions and buffalo. Roaming this slice of quintessential Africa are animals in numbers large enough to make a conservationist squeal with delight: in all, there are nearly 150 mammal species and more than 500 species of birds.

Sabi Sand Game Reserve. Named after the Sabie and Sand rivers that flow through it, and situated adjacent to Kruger's western boundary at its southern end (no fences separate the two), South Africa's oldest private reserve is famous for its abundant game and world-famous luxury lodges. You'll find the Big Five here, including the best opportunities in South Africa of spotting leopards, plus hundreds of birds. It's easily accessible by road and air.

West of Kruger. Manyeleti, Timbavati, Thornybush, and Kapama game reserves all lie north of Sabi Sand Game Reserve, but also border Kruger's western boundary. Although the reserves are less well known than Sabi Sand, they offer much the same game experiences, often at more affordable prices.

PLANNING

Where you stay on the escarpment may well dictate the kind of weather you get. High up, around Pilgrim's Rest and Sabie, the weather can be chilly, even in summer. Pack a sweater whatever the season. At these elevations fog and mist can be a hazard, especially while driving. On the other hand, the lowveld, especially in summer, is downright sultry.

TOP REASONS TO GO

Classic Africa: Apart from the tarred roads and rest camps, Kruger National Park is legendary Africa, where countless wild animals, birds, insects, and reptiles freely roam the plains, rivers, and forests.

Discovery Channel Comes Alive: From grasses and flowers to trees and shrubs, from comical dung beetles to gaudy butterflies, from tiny colorful lizards to huge dozing crocodiles, from dainty bushbuck to giant giraffes, from leaping bush babies to languorous lions, you'll marvel at them all.

A Total Escape: When you're steeped in the bush, watching that approaching elephant or pod of harrumphing hippos, you'll forget all the pressures of today's living.

Safari Opulence: Stay for a couple of nights at one of Sabi Sand's private game reserves. You're guaranteed luxury accommodations, impeccable service, and probably Big Five sightings. Kids are usually welcome, but check before you book.

Blyde River Canyon: The gigantic rocks, deep gorges, and high mountains of the Three Rondawels create one of South Africa's great scenic highlights.

WHEN TO GO

Kruger National Park is hellishly hot in midsummer (November to March), with afternoon rain a good possibility, though mostly in the form of heavy short showers that don't interfere with game-viewing for long. If you plan your drives in the early morning (when the gates first open) or in the late afternoon, you will manage even if you are extremely heat sensitive. ■TIP→ **Don't drive with the windows up and the air conditioner on—you'll cocoon yourself from the reason you're there.** In summer the bush is green, the animals are sleek and glossy, and the birdlife is prolific, but high grasses and dense foliage make spotting animals more difficult. Also, because there's plenty of surface water about, animals don't need to drink at water holes and rivers, where it's easy to see them. There are also more mosquitoes around then, but you'll need to take malaria prophylactics whatever time of year you visit.

In winter (May through September), the bush is at its dullest, driest, and most colorless, but the game is much easier to spot, as many trees are bare, grasses are low, and animals congregate around the few available permanent water sources. Besides, watching a lion or leopard pad across an arid but starkly beautiful landscape could be the highlight of your trip. It gets very cold in winter (temperatures can drop to almost freezing at night and in the very early morning), so wear layers of warm clothes you can shed as the day gets hotter. Lodges often drop their rates during winter (except July), because many foreign tourists prefer to visit in the South African summer months, which coincide with the Northern Hemisphere winter.

Spring (September and October) and autumn (March to early May) are a happy compromise. The weather is very pleasant—warm and sunny but not too hot—and there are fewer people around. In October migratory birds will have arrived, and in November many animals give birth. In April some migrating birds are still around, and the annual rutting season will have begun, when males compete for females and are often more visible and active.

PLANNING YOUR TIME

If you have more than a handful of days in the area, split them between the mountain scenery of the escarpment and wildlife-viewing in the lowveld. You could complete a tour of the Drakensberg Escarpment area in two days, but you're better off budgeting three or more if you plan to linger anywhere. To take in parts of Kruger National Park or one of the private game lodges, which are simply a must, add another three days or more.

3 Days: One of the prime reasons for visiting Mpumalanga is for big game, so fly into the airport nearest your destination and either rent a vehicle and take off into Kruger or get picked up by the private game lodge of your choice. Driving anywhere else in such a short time is not really an option.

5 Days: Your biggest decision will be how much time to spend wildlife-watching and how much to spend exploring the escarpment and its historic towns. A good suggestion is two days for the mountains and three in Kruger. Driving from Johannesburg, plan an overnight in Sabie after driving the awesome Long Tom Pass. The next day, head to the former mining town of Pilgrim's Rest and soak up some of the colorful local history. Spend the night there or at one of the friendly and superb value-for-the-money bed-and-breakfasts in the area, and start out early the next morning for Blyde River (Motlatse) canyon, with its hiking trails and magnificent escarpment scenery. Then it's off to Kruger, Sabi Sand, Manyeleti, Timbavati, Thornybush, or any of the other game reserves adjacent to Kruger, but make sure you get to Kruger or your private lodge in time for the afternoon game drive.

GETTING HERE AND AROUND
AIR TRAVEL

Two airlines—SA Airlink and SA Express—link Johannesburg to KMIA (Kruger Mpumalanga International Airport), at Mbombela (Nelspruit), which is equipped to handle the largest and most modern aircraft. KMIA has a restaurant, curio shops, banking facilities, car-rental agencies, VIP lounges, information desks, and shaded parking. Mbombela (Nelspruit) is good for accessing southern Kruger, but if you need to reach other areas, SA Express also flies directly to MalaMala airstrip, which serves the Sabi Sand lodges; Hoedspruit Airport, close to Kruger's Orpen Gate and serving Timbavati Game Reserve, and Skukuza Airport, in the middle of Kruger. SA Airlink also flies to Phalaborwa (Hendrik Van Eck) Airport, near Kruger's Phalaborwa Gate. *For information on airlines, see Air Travel in Travel Smart.*

Charter flights between parks and lodges are usually booked by tour operators as part of the tour package.

Contacts Hoedspruit Airport (*HDS*). ✉ *Eastgate Airport, Hoedspruit* ☎ *015/793-3681* ⊕ *www.eastgateairport.co.za.* **Kruger Mpumalanga**

International Airport (KMIA). ☎ 013/753–7500 ⊕ www.kmiairport.co.za.
Phalaborwa Airport (PHW, Hendrik Van Eck Airport). ✉ Off R71, near
Phalaborwa Gate, Access Rd., Phalaborwa ☎ 015/781–5823. **Skukuza Airport**
(SZK). ☎ 013/735–5074 ⊕ www.skukuzaairport.com.

BUS TRAVEL

Greyhound runs daily between Johannesburg and Mbombela (Nelspruit). The direct trip takes five to six hours, but there are also buses that stop along the way. A one-way ticket starts at R200. Mbombela (Nelspruit) is 50 km (31 miles) from Kruger's Numbi Gate and 64 km (40 miles) from Kruger's Malelane Gate.

Public bus service is limited or nonexistent within Mpumalanga. If you don't have your own car, you're dependent on one of the tour companies to get around the escarpment and into the game reserves. Many of these companies also operate shuttle services that transfer guests between the various lodges and to the airport. It's usually possible to hire these chauffeured minibuses at an hourly or daily rate.

Only tour-company buses actually go through Kruger, but they're not recommended. Being in a big tour bus in the park is like being in an air-conditioned bubble, totally divorced from the bush. Also, the big tour buses aren't allowed on many of Kruger's dirt roads and have to stick to the main paved roads. *For information on buses, see Bus Travel in Travel Smart.*

CAR TRAVEL

The road system in Mpumalanga is excellent, making it a great place to travel by car. Three principal routes—the N4, N11, and R40—link every destination in the province. From Johannesburg drive north on the N1, and then head east on the N4 to Mbombela (Nelspruit), which is close to many of Kruger's well-marked gates. It's best to arm yourself in advance with up-to-date maps, available at most large gas stations or bookstores, and plan your route accordingly.

The N4 is a toll road (approximately R139 for the one-way trip between Johannesburg and Kruger). International credit cards are not accepted at the toll booths; if you don't have a South African credit card, you will have to pay cash. Though it's a very good, well-maintained road, always look out for the ubiquitous, often reckless taxi drivers in their overcrowded *combis* (vans). Traffic jams are common on weekends and at the beginning and end of school vacations. Secondary roads are also well maintained, but watch out for goats and donkeys that stray from the villages.

The best places to pick up rental cars are at the KMIA, Hoedspruit, and Phalaborwa airports. Avis, Budget, and Europcar all have desks at KMIA and Phalaborwa, whereas Hoedspruit offers Avis and Budget. Rental cars are also available at Skukuza. *For information on car-rental agencies, see Car Travel in Travel Smart.* Maps of Kruger are available at all the park gates and in the camp stores, and gas stations are available at the park gates and at the major camps. Once in the park, observe the speed-limit signs carefully (there are speed traps): 50 kph (31 mph) on paved roads, 40 kph (25 mph) on dirt roads. Leave your vehicle only at designated picnic and view sites, and if you do find animals on the road, allow them to pass before moving on. Sometimes you have to be very patient, especially if a breeding herd of elephants is blocking your way. ■TIP→ **Animals always have the right-of-way.** Always be cautious. Kruger is not a zoo; you are entering the territory of wild animals, even though many may be habituated to the sights and sounds of vehicles.

If you are planning to go into Kruger, it's worth renting an eight-seater combi (van) or SUV. Though more expensive than a car, they provide more legroom and you'll probably spot more game and see it better from your lofty perch. It's best to reserve well in advance, particularly if you want a bigger vehicle. Opt for the "supercover" insurance; it's not that much more expensive, but if you do get bumped by an elephant, you'll be covered.

TRAIN TRAVEL

If you really like train journeys, the Shosholoza Meyl/Spoornet's *Komati* train travels between Johannesburg and Mbombela (Nelspruit) via Tshwane (Pretoria) on Wednesday and Friday, and although it's comfortable and has a dining car, it's very slow (10 hours). It departs from Johannesburg at 6 pm and arrives in Mbombela (Nelspruit) at 4:02 am, so make sure there's somebody to meet you at that early hour. A one-way, first-class ticket costs R230, round-trip R460. But don't expect the Orient Express. *For information on trains, see Train Travel in Travel Smart.*

HOTELS

You may be in wildest Africa, but you'll be amazed by the very high standards you'll encounter for both service and accommodations. The private camps and lodges in the private reserves bordering the national park are renowned for offering the ultimate in luxury. With glossy-magazine decor, spa treatments, private plunge pools, and five-course meals served beneath the stars, you may forget you're in the bush until an elephant strolls past.

For the more budget-minded, the park offers self-catering huts and more pricey (but worth it) self-catering cottages in the more remote and exclusive bushveld (*bushveld* is the generic term for the wild indigenous vegetation of the lowveld) camps. There are also private concessions that step up the pampering. Visit the South African National Parks website (⊕ *www.sanparks.org*) to get information and book accommodations. It's essential to note that there are no elevators in any lodging facility in Mpumalanga or in Kruger. ■TIP→ **Make sure you book well in advance and, if possible, avoid July, August, and December, which are South African school vacations.**

That said, there are plenty of hotels, B&Bs, self-catering cottages, and other lodgings available just outside the park, in and around, for example, the towns of Hazyview and White River. Remember, you can still go on a game drive even if you're staying in a chain hotel, and you'll pay much, much less (you'll need to book the game drives separately through an outfitter).

If you're here to experience Mpumalanga beyond Kruger, including the Drakensberg, there are plenty of historic towns with charming inns and chain hotels, including Sabie and Pilgrim's Rest. If you stay in Hazyview or White River, you could feasibly experience both Kruger and the Drakensberg. *Hotel reviews have been shortened. For full information, visit Fodors.com.*

RESTAURANTS

Because Mpumalanga is a sought-after tourist destination, its culinary scene keeps getting better and better, both in *larney* (South African slang for "posh") restaurants and attractive cafés. Cuisines range from Mediterranean to pan-African, and many places serve local delicacies such as fresh trout, venison, Cape Malay favorites such as *bobotie* (a spicy meat-and-egg dish), and curries.

Food is cheap and cheerful in Kruger's cafeterias and restaurants, and usually excellent in the private game lodges. Dinner is eaten 7:30-ish, and it's unlikely you'll get a meal in a restaurant after 9. The more expensive the restaurant, the more formal the dress, with "smart casual" the norm. In Kruger you might put on clean clothes for an evening meal in a restaurant, but that's how formal it gets. After an exciting night game drive in a private reserve, you'll want to change or at least freshen up, but keep the clothes very casual. Wear long sleeves and long pants because of mosquitoes. Many higher-end restaurants close on Monday, and it's always advisable to make reservations at these in advance. *Restaurant reviews have been shortened. For full information, visit Fodors.com.*

	WHAT IT COSTS IN SOUTH AFRICAN RAND			
	$	$$	$$$	$$$$
Restaurants	under R100	R100–R150	R151–R200	over R200
Hotels	under R1,500	R1,500–R2,500	R2,501–R3,500	over R3,500

Restaurant prices are the average cost of a main course at dinner or, if dinner is not served, at lunch. Hotel prices are the lowest cost of a standard double room in high season.

SAFETY

The lowveld area, which stretches from Malelane (east of Mbombela/Nelspruit) to Komatipoort, on the Mozambique border, and up throughout Kruger National Park, is a malarial zone, and you should take antimalarial drugs. Note: malaria prophylactics may be unsuitable for children under six. Consult your doctor about the best options when planning your trip. ■TIP→ **Prevention is the best medicine: at dawn and dusk, smother yourself with insect repellent, and wear long sleeves, long pants, socks, and covered shoes. The private camps all have mosquito (mozzie) nets, but not Kruger, so spray yourself again before you go to sleep.**

TOUR OPTIONS

The easiest way to visit this region is to sign up with an outfitter to organize your stay. They will take care of your accommodations and game-viewing trips into Kruger National Park and the private reserves, as well as add on a visit to the Panorama Route; they will also shuttle you from one point to another, so you don't need to hire a car. Springbok Atlas, Trips SA, Welcome Tours, and Shinzelle Safaris are just some of the many operators that lead trips in the area.

Shinzelle Safaris. Full-day and overnight safari experiences in Kruger National Park, as well as day trips along the Panorama Route, are offered by this small but impressive company that offers a personal touch. It's run by a husband-and-wife team—he's the guide, she's the amazing chef. You're in good hands, guaranteed. ⊠ *White River* ☎ *013/750–0815, 079/517–2232* ⊕ *www.shinzellesafaris.co.za.*

Springbok Atlas Tours and Safaris. An assortment of tours and excursions that cover game-viewing trips into Kruger National Park and the private reserves, as well as the Panorama Route, which links the major escarpment sights, is offered through Springbok Atlas. ⊠ *Head Office, 17 Chiappini St., Woodstock* ☎ *021/460–4700 head office* ⊕ *www.springbokatlas.com.*

Trips SA. As with most of the tour companies in the area, Trips SA offers an excellent variety of trips and tours that cover the game-viewing trips into Kruger National Park and the private game reserves, as well as the spectacularly scenic Panorama Route, which links the major escarpment sights. ⊠ *90 Main St., Sabie* ☎ *013/764–1177* ⊕ *www.sabie.co.za.*

Welcome Tours. The highly respected Welcome Tours has more than 30 years' service under its belt and offers a wide range of trips and tours ranging from self-drive to fully escorted tours throughout Mpumalanga along the Panorama Route, to Kruger National Park, the private game reserves, and beyond. They will tailor a personal itinerary or you can choose from scheduled day or weekly trips. ⊠ *Norwich Pl. W, 2 Norwich Close, 4th fl., Sandton* ☎ *011/676–3300* ⊕ *www.welcome.co.za.*

VISITOR INFORMATION

The Mpumalanga Tourism and Parks Authority has a host of information. There are also tourist information offices for Hoedspruit, Mbombela (Nelspruit), and White River. The towns of Sabie and Hazyview have websites for additional information.

In Kruger there are information centers at the Letaba, Skukuza, and Berg-en-Dal rest camps.

Contacts Hazyview tourist information. ☎ *013/764–1177* ⊕ *www. hazyviewinfo.co.za.* **Hoedspruit tourist information.** ⊕ *www.hoedspruit. co.za.* **Mpumalanga Tourism Authority.** ⊠ *Hall's Gateway, N4 National Hwy., Mbombela (Nelspruit)* ☎ *013/759–5300, 013/755–3928* ⊕ *www.mpumalanga. com.* **Nelspruit (Mbombela) tourist information.** ⊠ *„ Mbombela (Nelspruit)* ☎ *013/759–5300, 044/873–4595* ⊕ *www.nelspruit-info.co.za.* **SA-Venues.** ⊕ *www.sa-venues.com.* **Sabie tourist information.** ☎ *013/764–1177, 013/767–1886* ⊕ *www.sabie.co.za.* **White River tourist information.** ☎ *013/759–5300* ⊕ *www.white-river-info.co.za.*

9

MPUMALANGA

In addition to Cape Town and the Winelands, Mpumalanga should be high on any South African list. Nowhere else in the country can you spend one day seeing spectacular wildlife, the next climbing or gazing over the escarpment, and a third poking around some of the country's most historic towns—all within proximity of each other. The local history is fascinating. In the late 1800s, skirmishes and pitched battles pitted the local Pedi against the Boers (the original Dutch farmers who moved here from the Cape to escape British oppression), as well as the Brits against the Boers (in the First South African War). At the turn of the 20th century, the Brits and Boers fought again (the Second South African War) when England's Queen Victoria brought some of her finest troops from all corners of the British Empire to South Africa, hoping for a final victory over the Boers. Gold and diamonds had been discovered in South Africa, and there was more at stake than political games. The Pilgrim's Rest gold strike of 1873 was minor compared with those in and around Johannesburg, but it nevertheless provided inducement for gold-hungry settlers.

These early gold-mining days have been immortalized by Sir Percy Fitzpatrick in *Jock of the Bushveld,* a classic of South African literature. Jock was a Staffordshire terrier whose master, Percy (he was later knighted by the British crown), worked as a transport rider during the gold rush. Sir Percy entertained his children with tales of his and Jock's adventures braving leopards, savage baboons, and all manner of dangers. Rudyard Kipling, who wandered this wilderness as a reporter covering the First South African War in the early 1880s, encouraged Fitzpatrick to write down the stories. Jock is still a household name in South Africa today. You'll see lots of Jock of the Bushveld signs all over Mpumalanga, seemingly wherever he cocked a leg.

SABIE

355 km (220 miles) east of Johannesburg on the N12.

As you descend Long Tom Pass, the town of Sabie (sah-bee) comes into view far below, in a bowl formed by the surrounding mountains. It's by far the pleasantest and most enjoyable town in the region, with restaurants, shops, and bars. The name Sabie is derived from the Shangaan word *uluSaba,* which described the "fearful river," home to many crocodiles. Today it makes a great base for exploring.

In the 1900s gold provided the community's livelihood, but today it's been replaced by timber, and Sabie sits in the heart of one of the world's largest human-made forests—more than a million acres of exotic pine and eucalyptus. The first forests were planted in 1876 to provide the area's mines with posts and supports. Today you'll find both pine and eucalyptus forests (neither of which is indigenous to the region), with the timber being used for pulp and cardboard, mining timber, and telephone poles, as well as veneer and furniture.

Sabie itself is a busy little town with a farming feel. It boasts some of the biggest traffic humps in South Africa, ensuring that farmers' and visitors' tractors and cars drive slowly through the broad, shady, tree-lined streets. It's easy to walk from one end of the central part of town to the other, taking in sights like **Market Square,** the commercial hub of Sabie in its early days. Here St. Peter's Anglican Church, designed by the famous architect Sir Herbert Baker and built by Italians in 1913, stands in its own pleasant gardens. Also in the square is a Jock of the Bushveld sign, said to commemorate Jock and Percy's arrival in 1885.

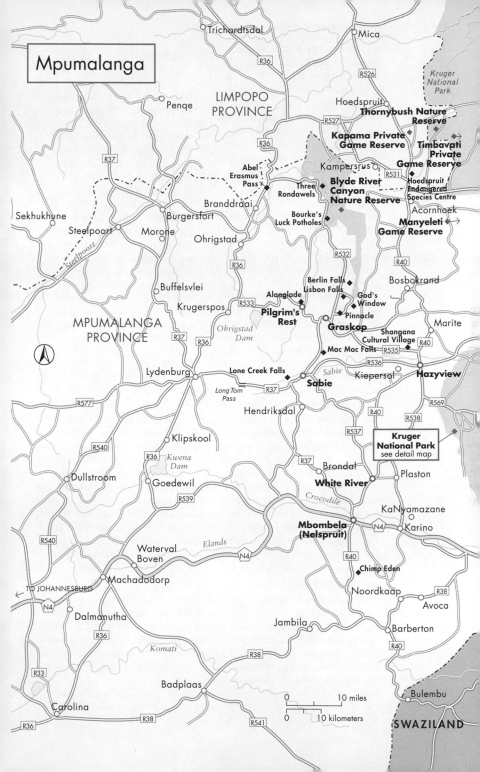

Mpumalanga

Trichardtsdal

Mica

R36

Kruger National Park

Penqe

LIMPOPO PROVINCE

R526

Hoedspruit

R527

Thornybush Nature Reserve

Kapama Private Game Reserve

Timbavati Private Game Reserve

R36

Kampersrus

R531

Blyde River Canyon Nature Reserve

Hoedspruit Endangered Species Centre

Abel Erasmus Pass

Three Rondawels

Acornhoek

Branddraai

Bourke's Luck Potholes

Manyeleti Game Reserve

Sekhukhune

Burgersfort

R37

Steelpoort

Morone

Ohrigstad

R36

R532

R40

Buffelsvlei

Berlin Falls

Bosbokrand

Lisbon Falls

God's Window

MPUMALANGA PROVINCE

Krugerspos

R533

Alanglade

Pinnacle

Marite

Ohrigstad Dam

Pilgrim's Rest

Graskop

Shangana Cultural Village

R37

R36

Mac Mac Falls

R535

R40

Lone Creek Falls

R536

Lydenburg

Sabie

Kiepersol

Hazyview

Long Tom Pass

R37

Sabie

R569

R577

Hendriksdal

R40

R538

Klipskool

R537

Kruger National Park
see detail map

R540

R36

Kwena Dam

Brondal

Plaston

Dullstroom

Goedewil

White River

R539

Crocodile

KaNyamazane

Waterval Boven

Elands

N4

Mbombela (Nelspruit)

Karino

R540

N4

R40

Machadodorp

Chimp Eden

TO JOHANNESBURG

Noordkaap

R38

N4

Avoca

Dalmanutha

Barberton

R36

Jambila

R40

Komati

R38

R33

Badplaas

R541

Bulembu

Carolina

R36

R38

0   10 miles

0   10 kilometers

SWAZILAND

GETTING HERE AND AROUND

Travel 355 km (220 miles) east of Johannesburg on the N12. You'll drive on good roads through lovely scenery. Plan to explore the tiny town on foot after parking your vehicle near the main square.

> **THE MPUMALANGA GOLD RUSH**
>
> On November 6, 1872, a prospector located deposits of gold in a creek on the Hendriksdal farm, now a small hamlet about 16 km (10 miles) from Sabie. Sabie itself owes its origins to an altogether luckier strike. In 1895 Henry Glynn, a local farmer, hosted a picnic at the Klein Sabie Falls. After a few drinks, his guests started taking potshots at empty bottles on a rock ledge. The flying bullets chipped off shards of rock, revealing traces of gold. Fifty-five years later, when mining operations closed down, more than 1 million ounces of gold had been taken from the Klein Sabie Falls.

EXPLORING

Lone Creek Falls. This is the prettiest, most peaceful, and last of three local waterfalls on a dead-end road (the others are Bridal Veil Falls and Horseshoe Falls). An easy paved walkway leads to the falls, which plunge 225 feet from the center of a high, broad rock face framed by vines and creepers. The path crosses the Sabie River on a wooden bridge and loops through the forest back to the parking lot. If you're feeling energetic, follow the steep steps leading up to the top of the falls. Lone Creek is accessible to the elderly and those with disabilities because of its easy approach. ✉ *Old Lydenburg Rd.* ✥ *6½ km (4 miles) down Old Lydenburg Rd., off Main Rd.* ☎ *013/764–2580 Sabie tourism* 🌐 *www.sabie.co.za* 🎟 *R12.*

Mac Mac Falls. Set in an amphitheater of towering cliffs, the Mac Mac Falls—a national treasure—is arguably the most famous waterfall in Mpumalanga. The water plunges 215 feet into the gorge as rainbows dance in the billowing spray. A small entry fee gets you through the gate for a closer look. At the gate a number of peddlers sell very well-priced curios. In 1873, President Thomas Burger named the falls after the area's Scottish miners who panned for gold. You can't swim at the falls themselves, but you can at the Mac Mac Pools, about 2 km (1 mile) before you reach the falls. It's worth the small fee to use the picnic and braai facilities there. ✉ *R532, 15 km (9 miles) northeast of Sabie* ☎ *013/764–2580 Sabie tourism* 🌐 *www.southafrica.net* 🎟 *R5.*

WHERE TO EAT

$$ ECLECTIC 🍴 **Wild Fig Tree Restaurant.** This excellent, casual eatery, in the shade of a wild fig tree, is open daily from 8:30 am to 9 pm for breakfast, light lunches, and dinner. Although the emphasis is on local specialties ranging from biltong pâté to impala kebabs, try the local trout dishes or a homemade burger. **Known for:** local meats; cozy bar; lovely patio. [$] *Average main: R150* ✉ *Main St. at Louis Trichardt St.* ☎ *013/764–2239* 🕒 *Closed Sun.*

WHERE TO STAY

$ B&B/INN FAMILY [HOTEL] **Sabie Town House.** Built of local Sabie stone, this charming bed-and-breakfast is the perfect base for exploring Mpumalanga's scenic attractions. **Pros:** excellent value for money; near Panorama Route; friendly. **Cons:** bar can get noisy at weekends; the road leading to the hotel is not in good condition; creaky doors. [$] *Rooms from: R1250* ✉ *25 Malieveld St.* ☎ *013/764–2292 office, 082/556–7895 cell* 🌐 *www.sabietownhouse.co.za* 🛏 *17 rooms* 🍴 *Breakfast.*

PILGRIM'S REST

16 km (10 miles) north of Sabie on R533.

The charming (although very touristy) village of Pilgrim's Rest—also a national monument—dates back to the 1870s gold-rush days when it was the first proper gold-mining town in South Africa. Alec "Wheelbarrow" Patterson abandoned the overcrowded Mac Mac diggings and, carting all his belongings in a wheelbarrow, left to search elsewhere for gold. He found it in Pilgrim's Creek, setting off a new gold rush in 1873. Rumors about the richness of the strike spread quickly around the world, bringing miners from California, Australia, and Europe. Within a year 1,500 diggers, living in tents and huts, had moved to the area. Most of the alluvial gold was found by individuals who recovered more than R2 million worth of gold dust and nuggets using pans, sluice boxes, and cradles. It wasn't until about 1876 that most of the tents were replaced by buildings. Most of the beautifully restored houses seen in the village today are from the more staid and elegant period of the early 1900s. It's worth walking up to the cemetery, as the old graves provide an instant history of the village.

GETTING HERE AND AROUND

Pilgrim's Rest is on the R533, 15 km (9 miles) northwest of Graskop. You'll need a vehicle to tour the area, but plan to explore the village on foot, as most of the attractions are on Main Street. There's a great five-hour walking tour through the village with the Friends of Pilgrim's Rest, but this should be booked in advance.

VISITOR INFORMATION

Your first stop should be the Pilgrim's Rest Information Centre, in the middle of town, opposite the Victorian-era Royal Hotel, which is the town's focal point and well worth a visit for its history. The friendly staff at the center will advise you on what to do and what tours to take, such as panning for gold and the Prospector's Hiking Trail, as well as provide maps and tickets for all the museums in the village.

Contacts Pilgrim's Rest Information Centre. ✉ *Main St., Uptown* ☎ *013/768–1060 reception* 🌐 *www.pilgrims-rest.co.za.*

EXPLORING

TOP ATTRACTIONS

Alanglade. Guided tours, including refreshments, are offered at Alanglade, the former beautiful home of the Transvaal Gold Mining Estates' mine manager, set in a forested grove 2 km (1 mile) north of town. The huge house was built in 1916 for Richard Barry and his family, and it

9

is furnished with pieces dating from 1900 to 1930. Look carefully at the largest pieces—you will see that they are segmented, so they could be taken apart and carried on ox wagons. Tour tickets are available at the information center and should be reserved 30 minutes in advance. ⊠ *Main St.* ☏ *013/768–1060 Pilgrim's Rest Information Centre* ⊕ *www. pilgrims-rest.co.za/sightsee/#alanglade* ☙ *Tours R20.*

The Diggings. To see how the whole valley looked during gold-rush days, visit the Diggings just outside the village. In the creek where the gold was originally panned, you'll find authentic displays of a water-driven stamp battery, the Gold Commissioner's hut, a transport wagon, a waterwheel, a steam engine, a sluice box, a prison tent, and wattle-and-daub huts typical of the early gold-rush years. The tour lasts about an hour, and you'll watch a gold-panning demonstration (you can even try your own hand at gold-panning). The retired prospector who conducts the tours adds to the atmosphere with yarns about the old days. Tickets are available at the information center. ⊠ *R533* ✢ *3 km (2 miles) south of Pilgrim's Rest* ☏ *013/768/1060 Pilgrim's Rest Information Centre* ⊕ *www.pilgrims-rest.co.za* ☙ *R12.*

Dredzen Shop and House Museum. Experience life after the heady gold-rush days, and relive the '30s and '40s, when 16 general stores lined the streets of Pilgrim's Rest. By 1950 mine production had taken a nosedive, and most of the businesses had shut down. The Dredzen Shop and House Museum re-creates the look of a general store during those lean years, with shelves displaying authentic items that would have been on sale, from jams and preserves to candles and matches. The attached house belonged to the shopkeeper and re-creates the life of a middle-class family of the period. ⊠ *Main St., Uptown* ✢ *After you come down the hill from the cemetery, turn left on Main St.* ☏ *013/768–1060 Pilgrim's Rest Information Centre* ⊕ *www.pilgrims-rest.co.za* ☙ *R12.*

House Museum. Originally a doctor's house, the House Museum, across and up the street from the Royal Hotel, re-creates the way of life of a middle-class family in the early part of the 20th century. The house was built in 1913 of corrugated iron and wood and is typical of buildings erected at the time. Check out the late Victorian furnishings, kitchen utensils, and the very grand carved wooden commode (precurser to the toilet). Purchase tour tickets at the information center. ⊠ *Main St., Uptown* ☏ *013/764–1177 Pilgrim's Rest Information Centre* ⊕ *www. pilgrims-rest.co.za* ☙ *R12.*

Pilgrim's and Sabie News Printing Museum. The tiny Pilgrim's and Sabie News Printing Museum is full of displays of antique printing presses and old photos. The building, constructed in the late 19th century as a residence, later served as the offices of the weekly *Pilgrim's and Sabie News.* The first newspaper in Pilgrim's Rest was the *Gold News,* published in 1874 and notable for its libelous gossip. The editor, an Irishman by the name of Phelan, felt obliged to keep a pair of loaded pistols on his desk. Purchase tour tickets at the information center. ⊠ *Main St., Uptown* ☏ *013/768–1060 Pilgrim's Rest Information Centre* ⊕ *www. pilgrims-rest.co.za* ☙ *R12.*

Pilgrim's Rest Cemetery. The Pilgrim's Rest Cemetery sits high on the hill above Main Street. The fascinating tombstone inscriptions evoke the dangers and hardship of life in Mpumalanga a century ago. Tellingly, most of the dead were young people from Wales, Scotland, and England. The cemetery owes its improbable setting to the Robber's Grave, the only grave that lies in a north–south direction. It contains the body of a thief banished from Pilgrim's Rest for stealing gold from a tent, after which he was tarred and feathered and chased out of town; he later foolishly returned and was shot dead. Buried where he fell, the area around his grave became the town's unofficial cemetery. ✉ *Pilgrim's Rest* ✣ *Follow the steep path that starts next to the picnic area, near the post office* ☎ *013/768–1060 Pilgrim's Rest Information Centre* 🌐 *www.pilgrims-rest.co.za.*

WHERE TO EAT

$ SOUTH AFRICAN 🍴 **Vine Restaurant and Pub.** In a former trading store dating from 1910, the Vine uses antique sideboards, sepia photos, and country-style wooden furniture to recapture that heady 1800s gold rush–era feeling. The food is straightforward and hearty, like traditional South African *bobotie* (curried ground beef topped with egg), *potjiekos* (lamb stew), digger's stew (beef and veggies) served in a digger's gold-prospecting pan, or *samp* (corn porridge). **Known for:** South African pub fare; people-watching. [$] *Average main: R80* ✉ *Main St., Downtown* ☎ *013/768–1080* 🌐 *www.thevinerest.co.za.*

WHERE TO STAY

$ HOTEL 🏨 **Royal Hotel.** Established in 1873, this hotel dates from the very beginning of the gold rush in Pilgrim's Rest—you'll see its corrugated-iron facade in sepia photos all over town. **Pros:** step-back-in-time ambience; friendly staff; good value. **Cons:** restaurant food unimaginative; popular with bus tours, so can be overcrowded with tourists; rooms can be cold. [$] *Rooms from: R1200* ✉ *Main St., Uptown* ☎ *013/768–1044* 🌐 *www.pilgrims-rest.co.za* 🛏 *50 rooms* 🍽 *Breakfast.*

GRASKOP

25 km (16 miles) northeast of Sabie; 15 km (9 miles) southeast of Pilgrim's Rest.

Graskop (translation: "grass head") was so named because of the abundance of grassveld and few trees. Like so many of the little towns in this area, it started as a gold-mining camp in the 1880s, on a farm called Graskop that was owned by Abel Erasmus, who later became the local magistrate. After the gold mines closed down, the town served as a major rail link for the timber industry. Today the main features of this rather featureless little town are its curio shops and eateries. Perched on the edge of the Drakensberg/Mpumalanga Escarpment, Graskop considers itself the window on the lowveld, and several nearby lookouts do have stunning views over the edge of the escarpment. It's an ideal base for visiting scenic hot spots, including Mac Mac Falls and the beauties in and around the Blyde River (Motlatse) Canyon Nature Reserve.

Traveling east toward Hazyview, you enter the lovely Koewyns Pass, named for a local Pedi chief. Unfortunately, there are few scenic overlooks, but you'll still get sweeping views of the Graskop gorge. Look for the turnoff to Graskopkloof on your left as you leave town, and stop to get a closer view into this deep, surprisingly spectacular gorge, where in the rainy season two waterfalls plunge to the river below.

GETTING HERE AND AROUND

It's best to approach Graskop from Mbombela (Nelspruit), the biggest town in the area. It's a pleasant drive (a vehicle is essential) via White River and Hazyview. But don't hold your breath: the town is hardly memorable. Still, it's a good base for exploring the region.

WHERE TO STAY

$$

B&B/INN

🖼 **West Lodge Bed & Breakfast.** This attractive Victorian-style B&B is set in a delightful garden bursting with roses. **Pros:** a wide choice of eateries and the town center are only minutes away; friendly; great breakfast. **Cons:** Graskop is not the prettiest town; a tad pricey for the area; some say the dinners were merely average. $ *Rooms from: R2100* ⊠ *12 Hugenote St.* ☎ *013/767–1390* ⊕ *www.westlodge.co.za* ⤴ *6 rooms* ⃝⃝ *Breakfast.*

BLYDE RIVER CANYON NATURE RESERVE

15 km (9 miles) northeast of Graskop.

Also known as the Motlatse Canyon Nature Reserve, this breathtakingly beautiful 71,660 acres of red sandstone mountains, gorges, and grassland stretches 60 km (37 miles) north of Graskop, to the Abel Erasmus Pass. Its spectacular main feature is the canyon itself. Carved out of almost 2½ km (1½ miles) of red sandstone, Blyde River canyon is the world's third biggest—and is often described as the world's greenest, on account of its lush evergreen vegetation. But there are other stunning natural spectacles to see as well, including Bourke's Luck Potholes, God's Window, Three Rondawels, and several waterfalls. All are connected by the Panorama Route north of Graskop (the R532).

GETTING HERE AND AROUND

Situated on the scenic Panorama Route, the Blyde River (Motlatse) Canyon Nature Reserve is easily accessible from Mbombela (Nelspruit), Sabie, and Graskop, and from the west of Kruger. A vehicle is essential, but if you're keen on hiking, it's hiking heaven.

EXPLORING

TOP ATTRACTIONS

Blyde River Canyon. Starting just below the point where the Blyde (joy) River and Treur (sorrow) River converge, the world's third-largest canyon is also South Africa's second-most-visited natural attraction (after Table Mountain). Discover spectacular scenery of red cliffs jutting up from the canyon base, quirky geological formations, indigenous rare Afromontane forest, cascading waterfalls, and an abundance of birds, small animals, and biodiversity. You can also try your hand at all sorts of adventure activities, from white-water rafting and abseiling to mountain biking and hiking. ⊠ *Along R532, Bourke's Luck* ☎ *013/767–1886 Graskop Tourism* ⊕ *www.mtpa.co.za, www.graskop.co.za* ☞ *Individual fees at different access points.*

Bourke's Luck Potholes. The amazing Bourke's Luck Potholes are 27 km (17 miles) north of Berlin Falls. Named after a gold prospector, the cylindrical and rather alien-looking deep potholes filled with green water are carved into the rock by whirlpools where the Treur (sorrow) and Blyde (joy) rivers converge—and where the canyon begins. Several long canyon hiking trails start from here, as do shorter walks and trails. A three-hour walk, for example, could take you down into the bottom of the canyon, where you follow a trail marked by rocks painted with animal or bird symbols as the gorge towers above you. Be sure to stop by the Blyde River Canyon Nature Reserve visitor center at the entrance to the site, where interesting exhibits describe the canyon's flora, fauna, and geology. ⊠ *Graskop* ✛ *27 km (17 miles) north of Berlin Falls on R532* ☎ *013/755–3928 Mpumalanga Tourism and Parks Agency* ⊕ *www.mtpa.co.za, www.graskop. co.za* ☞ *R50 per person, plus R5 per car.*

God's Window. God's Window is the most famous of the lowveld lookouts along the Panorama Route. It got its name because of the rock "window" that looks out at the sublime view below. Gaze out into seeming infinity from the edge of the escarpment (which drops away almost vertically). Geared to tourists, it has toilet facilities, paved parking areas, curio vendors, and paved, marked walking trails leading to various lookouts. The God's Window lookout has a view back along the escarpment framed between towering cliffs. For a broader panorama, make a 10-minute climb along the paved track through the rain forest to a small area with sweeping views of the entire lowveld. The altitude here is 5,700 feet, just a little lower than Johannesburg. ⊠ *Off R534, Graskop* ☎ *013/759–5300 Mpumalanga Tourism and Parks Agency* ⊕ *www.graskop.co.za, www.mtpa.co.za* ☞ *R20 per person.*

Three Rondawels. This is one of the most spectacular vistas in South Africa—you'll find it in almost every travel brochure. Here the Blyde River, hemmed in by towering buttresses of red rock, snakes through the bottom of the Blyde River canyon. The Three Rondawels are rock formations that bear a vague similarity to the round, thatch African dwellings of the same name. Before Europeans moved into the area, the indigenous local people named the formations the Chief and His Three Wives. The flat-top peak to the right is Mapjaneng (the Chief), named in honor of a Mapulana chief, Maripe Mashile, who routed invading Swazi at the battle of Moholoholo ("the very great one"). The three "wives," in descending order from right to left, are Maseroto, Mogoladikwe, and Magabolle. ⊠ *R536, Graskop* ☎ *013/759–5300 Mpumalanga Tourism and Parks Agency* ⊕ *www.mpumalanga.com, www.graskop.co.za* ☞ *R20 per person.*

WORTH NOTING

Berlin Falls. A small stream, Waterfall Spruit, runs through a broad expanse of grassland to Berlin Falls. A short walk takes you to a platform overlooking the cascade, shaped like a candle. It starts off as a thin stream that drops through a narrow sluice (this looks like the candlewick), and then widens out to fall 150 feet into a deep-green pool surrounded by tall pines. If the weather's good, plan to swim and picnic here. Why the not-very-local name? The German miners who came here during the gold rush named it nostalgically after their home country. ⊠ *Off R532, Graskop ⊕ 10 km (6 miles) north of Graskop* ☎ *013/759–5300 Mpumalanga Tourism and Parks Agency* ⊕ *www. mpumalanga.com, www.graskop.co.za* ⊠ *R10 per car.*

Lisbon Falls. You'll find more gorgeous waterfalls clustered on the Panorama Route than anywhere else in southern Africa. Just north of Graskop, the dramatic falls are set in a bowl between hills just outside the Blyde (Motlatse) Canyon Nature Reserve, sending cascades 120 feet onto rocks below, throwing up spray over a deep pool. Named nostalgically by European miners who came here looking for gold in the late 1800s, this is a good kick-off point for the whole Panorama Route. Hike down to the pool on a path from the parking area, and enjoy a picnic. ⊠ *Off R532, Graskop ⊕ A few km north of Graskop; watch for signs* ☎ *013/759–5300 Mpumalanga Tourism and Parks Agency* ⊕ *www. mpumalanga.com, www.graskop.co.za* ⊠ *R10 per car.*

Pinnacle. Pinnacle is a 100-foot-high quartzite "needle" that rises dramatically out of the surrounding fern-clad ravine, as it has for countless millennia. Way down below, beneath and to the right of the viewing platform, you can see the plateau beneath the escarpment. The watercourse drops down some 1,475 feet in a series of alternating falls and cascades. Stay away from the edge if you suffer from vertigo. ⊠ *Graskop ⊕ 6 km (3.7 miles) north of Graskop off R532, on R534* ☎ *013/759–5300 Mpumalanga Tourism and Parks Agency* ⊕ *www. mpumalanga.com, www.graskop.co.za* ⊠ *R20 per person.*

SPORTS AND THE OUTDOORS
HIKING

Blyde River Canyon Hiking Trail. This breathtakingly scenic 60-km (37-mile) five-day hike runs from God's Window right along the edge of the escarpment. Accommodations range from comfortable cottages to sleeping under the stars. You can also take shorter two-day and three-day trails. The mountain scenery is spectacular, making it one of the most popular trails in the country. You'll need to stop—not just to catch your breath—but to drink in the glorious scenery. Several shorter trails explore the canyon from trailheads at Bourke's Luck Potholes. The number of hikers on the multi-day trails is controlled, so it's essential to reserve far in advance (contact the nature reserve). There is also a recently developed circular 2-km (almost 1-mile) trail for disabled visitors. ⊠ *Off R534, Graskop* ☎ *013/759–5300 Mpumalanga Tourism Authority* ⊕ *www.mtpa.co.za.*

■ EN ROUTE

Abel Erasmus Pass. The descent out of the nature reserve, down the escarpment, and through Abel Erasmus Pass is breathtaking. (From the Three Rondawels, take the R532 to a T, and turn right onto the R36.) Be careful as you drive this pass. Locals graze their cattle and goats on the verges, and you may be surprised by animals on the tarmac as you round a bend. The J. G. Strijdom Tunnel serves as the gateway to the lowveld. At the mouth of the tunnel are stands where you can buy clay pots, African masks, wooden giraffes, curios of many kinds and subtropical fruit. As you emerge from the dark mouth of the tunnel, the lowveld spreads out below, and the views of both it and the mountains are stunning. On the left, the Olifants River snakes through the bushveld, lined to some extent by African subsistence farms. ✉ *Graskop* ☎ *013/759–5300 Mpumalanga Tourism Authority, 015/293–3600 Limpopo Tourism Authority* 🌐 *www.mtpa.co.za.*

HAZYVIEW

45 km (28 miles) east of Sabie.

Named for the heat haze that drifts up from the fruit plantations and bush in the surrounding area, Hazyview is a bustling little town. Situated in the center of the prime tourist attractions, it's also another gateway to Kruger through the nearby Phabeni, Numbi, and Kruger gates. There are plenty of good places to stay and eat, and Hazyview is also the adventure mecca of the region. Here you can try your hand at horseback riding, helicopter trips, river rafting, hiking, ballooning, quad biking, golf, and game-viewing safaris.

GETTING HERE AND AROUND

Hazyview is easily accessible from Mbombela (Nelspruit) on good, well-signposted roads. From here, it's a comfortable drive to the major attractions of the Panorama Route, including God's Window, Bourke's Luck Potholes, and the spectacular Blyde River (Motlatse) canyon.

EXPLORING

FAMILY **Shangana Cultural Village.** The Shangana Cultural Village is a genuine Shangaan village that's presided over by the incumbent chief, whose family have lived here for decades. An hour-long tour of the *kraal* (traditional rural village) includes a meeting with the chief and a visit to the *sangoma* (traditional healer who'll throw the bones to predict your future). Enjoy a traditional lunch or a light meal in the tea garden after visiting the Marula Market, where you can stock up on a great variety of good-quality handcrafted items (some made on-site). Don't miss the memorable evening firelight song-and-dance performance hosted by the chief portraying the history of the Shangaan people. A traditional dinner is included. Booking for the performance (5:15 pm in summer, 5 pm in winter) is essential. ✉ *Graskop Rd.* ✣ *R535, 5 km (3 miles) northwest of Hazyview* ☎ *013/737–5804, 086/653–3452* 🌐 *www.shangana.co.za* 🎫 *Day tour R150, midday tour and meal R325, evening festival R525.*

WHERE TO STAY

$$ B&B/INN 🏨 **Rissington Inn.** This lovely reasonably priced lodge offers fine food, superb hospitality, and all the facilities you'd expect at a top lodge. **Pros:** superb value for money; fine food; great base for Kruger. **Cons:** always busy; book well in advance; as beautiful as it is, not for anyone looking for the luxurious perks of a five-star (i.e., no bathrobes or slippers). [$] *Rooms from: R1900* ✉ *Off R40* ✣ *1 km (¾ mile) from Hazyview and down a dirt road* ☎ *013/737–7700, 086/246–1370* 🌐 *www.rissington.co.za* 🛏 *16 rooms* 🍴 *Breakfast.*

9

CLOSE UP

Rock Art

An important key to understanding humankind's past, rock art is a fascinating aspect of the South African and world's heritage. Engravings (made by scratching into the rock surface), paintings, and finger paintings proliferate throughout the province and carry an air of mystery, since relatively little is known about them. Although some archaeologists have attributed the origins of rock art to ancient Egyptians, Phoenicians, and even extraterrestrial races, the rock art found here was created by ancestors of the San. Materials came from the immediate environment. Ocher (red iron-oxide clay) was used to obtain red, charcoal for black, and white clay for white. Blood, egg, and plant juices were used for binding, creating a paint with obvious staying power.

Most rock art illustrates the activities and experiences of the African medicine people, or shamans. Religious rituals, such as those for making rain and healing the sick, involved trances and inspired visions, from which rock-art images were created. The images included large animals, such as the highly regarded eland and rhino, which were believed to possess supernatural power. Half-animal, half-human representations and geometric patterns and grids are also featured. The shamans believed that when an image was drawn, power was transferred to the people and the land.

WHITE RIVER

35 km (22 miles) southeast of Sabie.

This pleasant little town is set amid nut and tropical-fruit plantations and is one of the gateways to the escarpment's major sights, as well as to Kruger National Park. Settled by retired British army officers in the early 20th century, it still retains some of its colonial feel, but it's now much more representative of the "new" South Africa, crowded with people of all backgrounds. Casterbridge is an attractive shopping center, and because White River is home to a resident esoteric community, those who feel like a bit of alternative therapy will find holistic healing hands.

GETTING HERE AND AROUND

White River is very conveniently situated on good, well-signposted roads between Mbombela (Nelspruit) and Kruger National Park. You'll need wheels to tour the area, and be sure to shop for fresh fruit and produce at the numerous roadside stalls.

EXPLORING

Sabie Valley Coffee. From the moment you enter Sabie Valley Coffee, recently moved from Hazyview to White River, the delicious smell of freshly roasted beans lures you in. A fascinating coffee tour, led by owner Tim Buckland, takes you through the whole coffee-making process—from orchards to roasting to packaging. Find out about a coffee grower's life, and the different kinds of beans that produce different tastes, which is why there are so many (often bewildering) coffees available today. Challenge your taste buds with a tasting of homegrown, 100% pure Arabica specialty coffees, before sampling some of the coffee-related goodies for sale: coffee liqueur, cake, and candies. Reservations are essential. ✉ *Casterbridge LIfestyle Centre, R40, corner of Hazyview and Numbi Rds.* ☎ *013/737–8169, 082/751–3400 reservations* 🌐 *www.sabievalleycoffee.com* 🎟 *Tours with tastings R70.*

White River History & Motor Museum. If you're into automobiles and their history, travel to the Casterbridge Lifestyle Centre for the White River History & Motor Museum. It has an impressive collection of more than 60 vehicles, dating from as early as 1911, including a 1936 Jaguar SS100, one of only 314 ever built. ✉ *Casterbridge Lifestyle Centre, R40 at Numbi Rd.* ☎ *013/751–1540* 🌐 *www.casterbridge.co.za* 🎟 *Free.*

WHERE TO STAY

$$$ HOTEL 🏨 **Casterbridge Hollow Boutique Hotel.** Mpumalnga's first green hotel has contemporary and stylish rooms with balconies and verandas overlooking the pool and flourishing gardens. **Pros:** friendly service; spacious rooms; good location if you want a single base to visit both Panorama Route and Kruger. **Cons:** some rooms can be noisy; Kruger's Phabeni Gate is about an hour's drive away; popular with weddings on weekends so could be crowded. [$] *Rooms from: R3400* ✉ *Casterbridge Lifestyle Centre, R40* ☎ *013/751–3088* 🌐 *www.seasonsinafrica.com/hotels-in-south-africa/lowveld-hotels/casterbridge-hollow-boutique-hotel* 🛏 *30 rooms* 🍴 *Breakfast.*

$$$ B&B/INN 🏨 **Oliver's Restaurant and Lodge.** This large, white-walled, red-roofed country house situated among pine trees and lush forest overlooks lovely gardens and the 1st hole of the White River Golf Course. **Pros:** gorgeous setting; great food; excellent and friendly service. **Cons:** quite formal; about an hour from Kruger for those entering at Phabeni. [$] *Rooms from: R2800* ✉ *R40, between Hazyview and White River* ☎ *013/750–0479* 🌐 *www.olivers.co.za* 🛏 *14 rooms* 🍴 *Breakfast.*

SHOPPING

Casterbridge Lifestyle Centre. If you need some classy retail therapy, stop off at this upmarket lifestyle center. Once a rambling mango estate, it's now home to art galleries, pottery and sculpture studios, and quirky boutiques selling designer clothes, jewelry, and much more, all set in lovely manicured gardens. The White River Art Gallery always has interesting local and national exhibitions, and when you've shopped till you dropped, tuck into a good meal at one of the eateries that serve everything from tasty pub fare and fine dining to wood-oven pizza. If wheels are your thing, pop into the vintage White River History & Motor Museum and feast your eyes on immaculately restored past motoring beauties. You'll even find Mpumalanga's first green hotel here, the Cambridge Hollow Boutique Hotel. ✉ *R40 at Numbi Rd.* ☎ *013/751–1540 information* 🌐 *www.casterbridge.co.za.*

MBOMBELA (NELSPRUIT)

19 km (12 miles) southwest of White River on the R40.

Mbombela (formerly Nelspruit), the capital of Mpumalanga and home of the provincial government, is a modern, vibrant subtropical city of some 56,000 people. Known as the gateway to Kruger and the lowveld, it's also a notable stop on the main route between Gauteng and Maputo, Mozambique. The compact town sits in the middle of a prosperous agricultural community, which farms citrus (a third of South Africa's citrus exports come from here), subtropical fruit, tobacco, and vegetables. It has an international airport, excellent hospitals, great restaurants, superb botanical gardens, and the Riverside Mall, Mpumalanga's biggest shopping center. Nearby is the Jane Goodall Institute's Chimpanzee Eden.

GETTING HERE AND AROUND

Approximately a five-hour drive from Johannesburg, Mbombela (Nelspruit) is easily accessible by road. The Kruger Mpumalanga International Airport (KMIA) is 22 km (13 miles) northeast of the town.

EXPLORING

Chimp Eden. Jane Goodall Institute's Chimp Eden provides sanctuary to chimpanzees that have been uprooted from their homes. Established in 2006, it's located on 1,000 hectares (2,500 acres) of wild lands just outside Mbombela (Nelspruit). Visitors can observe the chimps from several viewpoints overlooking the forest. You can also take a one-hour tour where you'll learn all about the chimps and the sanctuary, and a small restaurant provides refreshments. ⊠ *R40 (Baberton Rd.)* ✛ *Off N4, about 12 km (7½ miles) from Mbombela (Nelspruit)* ☎ *079/777–1514 tours* ⊕ *www.chimpeden.com* 🖻 *R190 for chimp tour.*

FAMILY **Lowveld National Botanical Gardens.** The gorgeous Lowveld National Botanical Gardens, just outside Mbombela (Nelspruit), is the only one in the province. It's a must-see if you are at all interested in plant life. Apart from its collection of more than 2,000 species of plants, it has the largest collection of cycads in Africa. Take great photos from the wooden suspension bridge over a tumbling waterfall where the Crocodile and Nel rivers (which flow through the gardens) join together. In spring and summer, when many of the indigenous plants are flowering, you'll see lots of iridescent sunbirds feasting on the blossoms. But at any time of year, don't miss the lush man-made African rain forest that gives the gardens its "evergreen" moniker. The gardens are wheelchair-friendly. ⊠ *White River Rd.* ✛ *3 km (2 miles) outside Mbombela (Nelspruit)* ☎ *013/752–5531* ⊕ *www.sanbi.org/gardens/lowveld* 🖻 *R24* ↻ *Book guided tours 2 wks in advance.*

KRUGER NATIONAL PARK

561 km (348 miles) from Johannesburg.

Kruger National Park is undoubtedly one of the world's best game parks, where teeming game roams freely over an area the size of Wales or Israel. Visiting Kruger is likely to be one of the greatest experiences of your life, truly providing ultimate "Wow!" moments. You'll be amazed at the diversity of life forms—the tallest (the giraffe), the biggest (the elephant), the funkiest (the dung beetle), the toothiest (the crocodile), and the glitziest (the lilac-breasted roller).

But it's not all game and safari. If you're into ancient human history, there are also major archaeological sites and fascinating San (Bushman) rock paintings. (There is ample evidence that prehistoric humans— *Homo erectus*—roamed the area between 500,000 and 100,000 years ago.) Founded in 1898 by Paul Kruger, president of what was then the Transvaal Republic, the park is a place to safari at your own pace, whether with a guide in a safari jeep or driving your own car.

Kruger lies in the hot lowveld, a subtropical section of Mpumalanga and Limpopo provinces that abuts Mozambique. The park cuts a swath 80 km (50 miles) wide and 320 km (200 miles) long from Zimbabwe and the Limpopo River in the north to the Crocodile River in the south. It is divided into 16 macro eco-zones, each supporting a great variety of plants, birds, and animals, including 150 mammal species and more than 500 species of birds, some of which are not found elsewhere in South Africa. In 2002 a treaty was signed between South Africa, Zimbabwe, and Mozambique to form a giant conservation area, the Great Limpopo Transfrontier Park. It's a complex ongoing process, but once all the fences between Kruger, the Gonarezhou National Park in Mozambique, and the Limpopo National Park in Zimbabwe are finally removed, the Peace Park will be the largest conservation area in the world.

GETTING HERE AND AROUND

You can fly to Kruger Mpumalanga International Airport (KMIA), at Mbombela (Nelspruit); Skukuza Airport in Kruger itself; Hoedspruit Airport, close to Kruger's Orpen Gate; or Phalaborwa Airport (if you're going to the north of Kruger) from either Johannesburg or Cape Town. *(See Air Travel in Travel Smart.)* You can also drive to Kruger from Johannesburg in about six hours.

MONEY MATTERS

Kruger accepts credit cards, which are also useful for big purchases, but you should always have some small change for staff tips (tip your cleaning person R20 per hut per day) and for drinks and snacks at the camp shops, although camp shops also accept credit cards. Some camps, including Skukuza and Letaba, have cash machines.

TIMING

How and where you tackle Kruger will depend on your time frame. If you can spend a week here, start in the north at the very top of the park at the Punda Maria Camp, where there are always fewer people. Then make your way leisurely south to the very bottom at Crocodile Bridge Gate or Malelane Gate. With only three days or fewer, stick to the south or central sections of the park and just plan to explore those areas. No matter where you go in Kruger, be sure to plan your route and accommodations in advance (advance booking is essential). And be sure to take at least one guided sunset drive; you won't likely forget the thrill of catching a nocturnal animal in the spotlight.

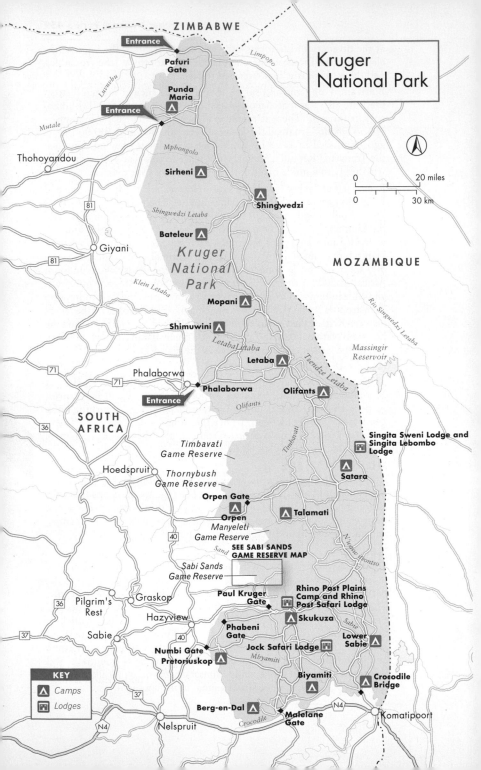

EXPLORING

The main reason you come to Kruger, of course, is to see the amazing wildlife. Game-spotting isn't an exact science: you might see all the Big Five plus hundreds of other animals, but you could see much less. Old Africa hands claim that the very early morning, when the camp gates open, is the best time for game-viewing, but it's all quite random—you could see a leopard drinking at noon, a breeding herd of elephants mid-morning, or a lion pride dozing under a tree in the middle of the afternoon. You could also head out at dawn and find very little wildlife.

The southern and central sections of the park are the best for sightings because riverine forests, thorny thickets, and large, grassy plains studded with knobthorn and marula trees, typical vegetation of this region, make ideal habitats for a variety of animals, including black and white rhinos, leopards, giraffes, hyenas, numerous kinds of antelope, lions, and the rare "painted wolf"—a wild dog.

As you head north to Olifants, Letaba, and Shingwedzi, you enter major elephant country, although you're likely to spot lots of other game, too, including lions and cheetahs. North of Letaba, however, the landscape becomes a monotonous blur of mopane trees, the result of nutrient-poor land that supports smaller numbers of animals, although the lugubrious-looking *tsessebe* (sess-a-bee) antelope and the magnificent and uncommon roan antelope, with its twisty horns, thrive here. Elephants love mopane, and you'll certainly see plenty of them. The Shingwedzi River Drive towards the Kanniedood Dam is one of the park's most rewarding drives, with elephants, leopards, giraffes, and other game. Park your vehicle underneath the lovely hide on this drive, then sit upstairs and take in life on the river, including waterbirds, hippos, and basking crocs.

To experience the full richness of the northern Kruger, visit the Pafuri Picnic Site (hot water and braais available), where ancient massive leadwood and jackalberry trees lean over the often dry Luvuvhu River, the haunt of the scarlet-and-green Narina trogon (a bird) and the much-sought-after Pel's fishing owl. But don't leave your picnic unattended while you look for more special birds, such as the wattle-eyed flycatcher, because the vervet monkeys will have it in a flash.

Wherever you go, **don't get out of your vehicle** except at certain well-marked picnic sites or view sites, unless you want to make an international headline.

FodorsChoice **Kruger National Park.** There are nine entrance gates to Kruger, namely
★ (counterclockwise from the north) Pafuri, Punda Maria, Phalaborwa, Orpen, Paul Kruger, Phabeni, Numbi, Malelane, and Crocodile Bridge. National access roads to all the entrance gates are paved. If you're staying at one of the park's lodges or camps, you can arrange for a late-entry escort until 9 pm for the following gates (and their nearby camps): Paul Kruger (Skukuza), Numba (Pretoriuskop), Malelane (Berg-en-Dal and Malelane), Crocodile Bridge (Brocodile Bridge), Punda Maria (Punda Maria), and Orpen (Orpen).

With excellent roads and accommodations, Kruger is a great place to drive around yourself. Though first-timers may want to think again about getting behind the wheel, since not everyone knows what to do when an enormous elephant with wavering ears is standing in front of your vehicle, blocking the road. Travel times in the park are tough to estimate, in addition, and a hefty fine is levied if you don't make it out of the gates on time.

An affordable solution is to join a game drive with a park ranger, who will drive you around in an open-sided four-wheel-drive. All the major rest camps offer ranger-led bush drives in open-air vehicles (minimum of two people), and, if you're not staying in the park itself, you can still join a tour led by ranger; your option for this are the Park & Ride tours, which leave from the park's entrance gates. There are also plenty of outfitters who will arrange a safari for you (as well as accommodations). Most drives depart in the early morning for either a half day or full day.

There are also bush walks on offer, something else you can't do on your own.

Whatever you do, don't miss out on a ranger-led night drive, when the park is closed to regular visitors. You'll sit in a large open-air vehicle, scanning the bush with the ranger, who uses a powerful spotlight to pick out animals, including nocturnal creatures that you would never see otherwise. You might see bush babies (enchanting furry, big-eared, big-eyed little primates that leap from bush to bush), servals (mini-leopard-looking felines), civets (black-and-white possum look-alikes), genets (spotted catlike creatures with bushy tails), or an aardvark ambling along in the moonlight. Scrutinize branches of big trees for the giant eagle owl, with its pink eyelids, or a leopard chewing on its kill. Night is also the time when hyenas and lions hunt. These opportunities alone make a night drive an unforgettable experience. The three- to four-hour trip leaves the rest camps half an hour before the gates close.
■TIP→ **Book as far in advance as possible.** Don't forget your binoculars, a snack or drink, and a warm jacket whatever the season.

Game drives start at R230 per adult. Book drives at least two weeks in advance or when you make your park reservations.

You'll have to pay a daily conservation fee of R304 per adult per day, but Wild Cards, available at the gates or online, are more economical for stays of more than a few days.

Check the SANParks' website (⊕ *www.sanparks.org*) for more details. ⊠ *Kruger National Park* ☎ *012/428–9111 reservations* ⊕ *www.sanparks.org.*

WHERE TO STAY

You have your choice of rest camps, bushveld camps, and private game lodges within the confines of Kruger National Park. And within those options your choices include cottages, safari tents, campsites, and guest lodges that are ideal for families. It's impossible to recommend just one place to stay. One person might prefer the intimacy of Kruger's oldest rest camp, Punda Maria, with its whitewashed thatch cottages;

WALKING KRUGER

You can take a morning or afternoon bush walk along one of Kruger's seven wilderness trails, which is no doubt an amazing experience. But for those with the time (and courage), Kruger's seven walking trails also offer the chance to experience a three-day, two-night hike. Led by an armed ranger and local tracker, you walk in the mornings and evenings, with an afternoon siesta, approximately 19 km (12 miles) a day.

These trails encourage a sense of companionship among the group, which decides together on speed and length of walks, but this isn't about pushing endurance records. Many hikers can recount face-to-face encounters with everything from rhinos to lions. No one under 12 is allowed; those over 60 must have a doctor's certificate. Hikers sleep in rustic two-bed huts and share a bathroom (flush toilets, bucket showers). Meals are simple (stews and barbecues); you bring your own drinks. Summer is uncomfortably hot (and trails are cheaper), but nights can be freezing in winter—bring warm clothes and an extra blanket. Reserve 13 months ahead. The cost is about R4,000 per person per trail.

Bushmans Trail. In the southwestern corner of the park, this trail takes its name from the San rock paintings and sites found here; the camp is in a secluded valley. Watch for white rhinos, elephants, and buffalo. Check in at Berg-en-Dal.

Metsi Metsi Trail. The permanent water of the nearby N'waswitsontso River makes this one of the best trails for winter game-viewing. Midway between Skukuza and Satara, the trail camp is in the lee of a mountain in an area of gorges, cliffs, and rolling savanna. Check in at Skukuza.

Napi Trail. White rhino sightings are common on this trail, which runs through mixed bushveld between Pretoriuskop and Skukuza. Other possibilities are black rhinos, cheetahs, leopards, elephants, and, if you're lucky, nomadic wild dogs. The camp is tucked into dense riverine forest at the confluence of the Napi and Biyamiti rivers. Check in at Pretoriuskop.

Nyalaland Trail. In the far north, this trail camp sits among ancient baobab trees near the Luvuvhu River and has the best birding in the park. Walk at the foot of huge rocky gorges and in dense forest. Hippos, crocs, elephants, buffalo, and the nyala antelope are almost a sure thing. Check in at Punda Maria.

Olifants Trail. This spectacularly sited camp sits on a high bluff overlooking the Olifants River and affords regular sightings of elephants, lions, buffalo, and hippos. The landscape varies from riverine forest to the rocky foothills of the Lebombo Mountains. Check in at Letaba.

Sweni Trail. East of Satara, this trail camp overlooks the Sweni Spruit and savanna. The area attracts large herds of zebras, wildebeests, and buffalo with their attendant predators: lions, spotted hyenas, and wild dogs. Check in at Satara.

Wolhuter Trail. You just might come face-to-face with a white rhino on this trail through undulating bushveld, interspersed with rocky kopjes, midway between Berg-en-Dal and Pretoriuskop. Elephants, buffalo, and lions are also likely. Check in at Berg-en-Dal.

9

another might favor big, bustling Skukuza. The bushveld camps are more expensive than the regular camps, but offer much more privacy and exclusivity—but no shops, restaurants, or pools. If you seek the ultimate in luxury, stay at one of the private luxury lodges in the private concession areas, some of which also have walking trails. A great way to experience the park is to stay in as many of the camps as possible. The SANParks website has a comprehensive overview of the different camps. The private game lodges include safaris and meals in the price, whereas the rest camps and bushveld camps are self-catering, and you'll need to book your drives and walks.

Reservations for park-operated accommodations should be made through **South African National Parks.** *(For SANParks contact information, see Visitor Information in Travel Smart.)* If air-conditioning is a must for you, be sure to check the website to confirm its availability in the accommodation of your choice. ■TIP➔ **Book your guided game drives and walks when you check in. Opt for the sunset drive. You'll get to see the animals coming to drink plus a thrilling night drive.**

Another option is to stay in one of the luxury camps located within one of the private reserves bordering Kruger, with Sabi Sand Private Game Reserve being the most renowned and most exclusive; dozens of private lodges here will take care of all your safari and dining and relaxing needs.

Or you can opt for a hotel or self-catering lodging in one of the communities just outside the park, such as Hazyview or White River, and either self-drive through the park, join a "Park & Drive" game drive at one of the gates, or make arrangements with one of the region's many outfitters. Elephant Herd Tours & Safaris (⊕ *elephantherd.co.za*) and Shinezelle Sararis (⊕ *shinzellesafaris.co.za)* are recommended. ⊕ *Safaribookings.com* is one of the many online marketplaces that compares tour operators and safari tours.

TYPES OF LODGINGS WITHIN THE PARK
BUSHVELD CAMPS
Smaller, more intimate, more luxurious, and consequently more expensive than regular rest camps, Kruger's bushveld camps are in remote wilderness areas of the park that are often off-limits to regular visitors. Access is limited to guests only. As a result you get far more bush and fewer fellow travelers. Night drives and day excursions are available in most of the camps. There are no restaurants, gas pumps, or grocery stores, so bring your provisions with you (though you can buy wood for your barbecue). All accommodations have fully equipped kitchens, bathrooms, ceiling fans, and large verandas, most with air-conditioning. Cottages have tile floors, cheerful furnishings, and cane patio furniture and are sited in stands of trees or clumps of indigenous bush for maximum privacy. Many face directly onto a river or water hole. There's only a handful of one-bedroom cottages (at Biyamiti, Shimuwini, Sirheni, and Talamati), but it's worth booking a four-bed cottage and paying the extra, even for only two people. If you have a large group or are planning a special celebration, you might consider reserving one of the two bush lodges, which must be booked as a whole: **Roodewal Bush Lodge**

sleeps 18, and **Boulders Bush Lodge** sleeps 12. Reservations should be made with South African National Parks. *For SANParks contact information, see Visitor Information in Travel Smart.*

PRIVATE GAME LODGES

Kruger boasts a number of private concessions that are exclusive, uncrowded, and unfenced in prime Big Five territory (meaning animals can roam freely to and fro); each concession contains two or three luxury lodges at most, ranging in style from traditional colonial to ultramodern. They're the perfect choice for visitors not interested in roughing it—though you'll pay for that luxury. You'll enjoy good food and wine, relaxation, and plenty of game-viewing throughout the day. Singita Lombombo Lodge is the crème-de-la-crème with its super-chic lodging, wooden decks overlooking a water hole, spa treatments, and fine dining.

REST CAMPS

Kruger operates rest camps all over the park. Rest camps offer a variety of accommodations, including campsites, safari tents, bungalows, cottages, and guesthouses, and provide electricity, shop, braai, communal kitchen facilities, laundry facilities, restaurant and/or self-service cafeteria, and petrol station. Oftentimes the rest camps offer seasonal programming and evening films showcasing Kruger's wildlife. See the complete listing on the SANParks website. *For SANParks contact information, see Visitor Information in Travel Smart*

PRIVATE GAME LODGES

$$$$ RESORT Fodor's Choice ★ **Jock Safari Lodge.** This lodge, one of South Africa's loveliest, is set among 14,826 acres of private concession in southwest Kruger. **Pros:** authentic safari experience. **Cons:** busy in season. [$] *Rooms from: R15444* ✉ *Kruger National Park* ☎ *041/509–3000 reservations, 041/509–3001 reservations* 🌐 *www.jocksafarilodge.com* 🛏 *12 rooms* 🍴 *All meals.*

$$$$ RESORT **Plains Camp Tented Safari Lodge.** Overlooking a water hole amid an acacia knobthorn thicket deep in the heart of the Timbitene Plain, Plains Camp has four comfortably furnished tents with wooden decks and great views of the plains. **Pros:** right in the middle of Kruger; great game; fabulous night drives when everyone else in the Kruger camps is confined to barracks. **Cons:** surroundings a bit bleak, especially in winter; not much privacy between tents. [$] *Rooms from: R8500* ✉ *Off Marula Loop* ☎ *035/474–1473* 🌐 *www.isibindi.co.za* 🛏 *4 rooms* 🍴 *All meals.*

$$$$ RESORT **Rhino Post Safari Lodge.** Rhino Post Safari Lodge is located within the 30,000-acre Rhino Plains Concession, with eight spacious suites on stilts overlooking the Mutlumuvi riverbed. **Pros:** bang in the middle of Kruger National Park. **Cons:** canvas makes the suites very hot in summer and very cold in winter; you need to be walking-fit for this camp. [$] *Rooms from: R8400* ✉ *Kruger National Park* ☎ *035/474–1473* 🌐 *www.isibindiafrica.co.za* 🛏 *8 rooms* 🍴 *All meals.*

$$$$ RESORT **Singita Lebombo Lodge.** Named for the nearby Lebombo mountain range, the breathtakingly beautiful Singita Lebombo—winner of numerous international accolades and eco-driven in concept—is Bauhaus in the bush, with a uniquely African feel. **Pros:** stunning avant-garde architecture; excellent game; great curio shop and spa; lovely riverside bush breakfasts. **Cons:** avoid if you prefer a traditional safari lodge; very pricey. [$] *Rooms from: R45500* ✉ *Kruger*

National Park ☎ *021/683–3424 reservations* 🌐 *www.singita.co.za* 🛏 *14 rooms* 🍴 *All-inclusive.*

$$$$ RESORT 🏨 **Singita Sweni Lodge.** Built on wooden stilts, Sweni is cradled on a low riverbank amid thick virgin bush and ancient trees. **Pros:** tiny and intimate; great location; lovely riverside bush breakfasts. **Cons:** dim lighting. [$] *Rooms from: R45500* ✉ *Kruger National Park* ☎ *021/683–3424 reservations, 013/735–5500 lodge* 🌐 *www.singita.co.za* 🛏 *7 rooms* 🍴 *All-inclusive.*

REST CAMPS

$ RESORT FAMILY Fodor's Choice ★ 🏨 **Berg-en-Dal Rest Camp.** This rest camp lies at the southern tip of the park, in a basin surrounded by rocky hills. **Pros:** you can sit on benches at the perimeter fence and watch game come and go all day; leopard and wild dog regularly seen. **Cons:** always crowded (although chalets are well spaced out). [$] *Rooms from: R1150* ✉ *Kruger National Park* ☎ *012/428–9111 reservations* 🌐 *www.sanparks.org* 🛏 *166 rooms* 🍴 *No meals.*

$ RESORT FAMILY 🏨 **Crocodile Bridge.** Situated in Kruger's southeastern corner, this award-winning small rest camp sits on the scenic Crocodile River and doubles as an entrance gate, which makes it a convenient stopover if you arrive near the park's closing time and are too late to make it to another camp. **Pros:** adjacent to one of best game roads in park; ideal for guests looking for self-catering bushveld experience; sunrise and night drives are offered. **Cons:** close proximity to the outside world of roads and farms. [$] *Rooms from: R1350* ✉ *Kruger National Park* ☎ *012/428–9111 reservations* 🌐 *www.sanparks.org* 🛏 *46 rooms* 🍴 *No meals.*

$ RESORT FAMILY 🏨 **Letaba.** Overlooking the frequently dry Letaba River, this lovely old camp sits in the middle of elephant country in the park's central section. **Pros:** camp has a real bush feel. **Cons:** far from southern entrance gates, so you'll need more traveling time. [$] *Rooms from: R1120* ✉ *Kruger National Park* ☎ *012/428–9111 reservations* 🌐 *www.sanparks.org* 🛏 *183 rooms* 🍴 *No meals.*

$ RESORT FAMILY 🏨 **Lower Sabie.** One of the most popular camps in Kruger, Lower Sabie has tremendous views over a broad sweep of the Sabie River and sits in one of the best game-viewing areas of the park (along with Skukuza and Satara). **Pros:** great location; superb game in vicinity. **Cons:** camp and restaurant always crowded. [$] *Rooms from: R1310* ✉ *Kruger National Park* ☎ *012/428–9111 reservations* 🌐 *www.sanparks.org* 🛏 *150 rooms* 🍴 *No meals.*

$ RESORT 🏨 **Mopani.** Built in the lee of a rocky kopje overlooking a dam, amid surrounding mopane woodlands, this camp in the northern section is one of Kruger's biggest. **Pros:** attractive accommodations in landscaped camp overlooking big hippo dam. **Cons:** thick mopane bush around camp and beyond not great for game-viewing although elephants love it. [$] *Rooms from: R1100* ✉ *Kruger National Park* ☎ *012/428–9111 reservations* 🌐 *www.sanparks.org* 🛏 *103 rooms* 🍴 *No meals.*

$ RESORT 🏨 **Olifants.** In the center of Kruger, Olifants has the best setting of all the camps: high atop cliffs on a rocky ridge with panoramic views of the distant hills and the Olifants River below. **Pros:** stunning location. **Cons:** huts in the middle of the camp have no privacy; high malaria area. [$] *Rooms from: R1120* ✉ *Olifants Camp Rd.* ☎ *012/428–9111 reservations* 🌐 *www.sanparks.org* 🛏 *109 rooms* 🍴 *No meals.*

$ RESORT 🏨 **Orpen.** Don't dismiss this tiny, underappreciated rest camp on Kruger's western border in the center of the park because of its proximity to the Orpen Gate. **Pros:** great game; quiet. **Cons:** close to main gate; not the most attractive camp; rustic. [$] *Rooms from: R1270* ✉ *Kruger National Park* ☎ *012/428–9111 reservations* 🌐 *www.sanparks.org* 🛏 *9 rooms* 🍴 *No meals.*

$ RESORT FAMILY 🏨 **Pretoriuskop.** This large, nostalgically old-fashioned camp, close to the Numbi Gate in southwest Kruger, makes a good overnight stop or touring base. **Pros:** good restaurant for snacks and toasted sandwiches; ideal habitat for mountain reedbuck and klipspringers; great swimming pool. **Cons:** bleak and bare in winter; barracks-style feel; lack of privacy. [$] *Rooms from: R1125* ✉ *Kruger National Park* ☎ *012/428–9111 reservations* 🌐 *www.sanparks.org* 🛏 *180 rooms* 🍴 *No meals.*

$ RESORT 🏨 **Punda Maria.** It's worth visiting this lovely little camp in Kruger's far north, because it offers one of the park's best bush experiences. **Pros:** very attractive camp; Kruger's best birding area. **Cons:** very far north; game less abundant than the south. [$] *Rooms from: R880* ✉ *Punda Maria Camp Rd.* ☎ *012/428–9111 reservations* 🌐 *www.sanparks.org* 🛏 *31 rooms* 🍴 *No meals.*

$ RESORT FAMILY 🏨 **Satara.** With some of the best guaranteed game-viewing in Kruger (especially on the N'wanetsi River Road, also known as S100), this large camp sits in the park's central section. **Pros:** good shop, restaurant, pool; great guided sunset drives; probably the most productive guided game tours in park. **Cons:** early booking essential. [$] *Rooms from: R1355* ✉ *Kruger National Park* ☎ *012/428–9111 reservations* 🌐 *www.sanparks.org* 🛏 *255 rooms* 🍴 *No meals.*

$ RESORT FAMILY 🏨 **Shingwedzi.** This attractive thatch-and-stone camp sits in northern Kruger beside the Shingwedzi River and near the Kanniedood (Never Die) Dam. Consequently there's more game around this camp than anywhere else in the region—especially when you drive the Shingwedzi River Road early in the morning or just before the camp closes at night. **Pros:** game-busy river road; in winter, gorgeous bright pink impala lilies. **Cons:** some accommodations are grouped in a circle around a big bare open space that affords little individual privacy; more rustic than most; lack of modern technology (which some might consider a good thing). [$] *Rooms from: R880* ✉ *Kruger National Park* ☎ *012/428–9111 reservations* 🌐 *www.sanparks.org* 🛏 *130 rooms* 🍴 *No meals.*

$ RESORT FAMILY 🏨 **Skukuza.** Skukuza is highly popular because it lies in an area teeming with game, including lions, cheetahs, and hyenas, and sits on a bank of the crocodile-filled Sabie River, with good views of dozing hippos, elephants, and grazing waterbuck. **Pros:** in middle of the park's best game areas; great river location. **Cons:** usually crowded with regular visitors and busloads of day-trippers. [$] *Rooms from: R1135* ✉ *Kruger National Park* ☎ *012/428–9111 reservations* 🌐 *www.sanparks.org* 🛏 *309 rooms* 🍴 *No meals.*

BUSHVELD CAMPS

$$ RESORT 🏨 **Bateleur.** Hidden in the northern reaches of the park, this tiny camp, the oldest of the bushveld camps, is one of Kruger's most remote destinations. **Pros:** private and intimate; guests see a lot at the camp's hide; no traffic jams. **Cons:** long distance to travel; there's a TV, which can be a pro or a con depending on your point of view. [$] *Rooms from:*

R1930 ✉ *Kruger National Park* ☎ *012/428–9111 reservations* 🌐 *www.sanparks.org* 🛏 *7 rooms* 🍴 *No meals.*

$ RESORT 🏨 **Biyamiti.** Close to the park gate at Crocodile Bridge, this larger-than-average, beautiful, sought-after bush camp overlooks the normally dry sands of the Biyamiti River. **Pros:** easily accessible; lots of game; variety of drives in area. **Cons:** difficult to book because of its popularity. [$] *Rooms from: R1375* ✉ *Biyamiti Camp Rd.* ☎ *012/428–9111 reservations* 🌐 *www.sanparks.org* 🛏 *15 rooms* 🍴 *No meals.*

$ RESORT 🏨 **Shimuwini.** Birders descend in droves on this peaceful bushveld camp set on a lovely dam on the Letaba River. **Pros:** lovely situation overlooking permanent lake. **Cons:** only one access road, so coming and going gets monotonous; game can be sparse. [$] *Rooms from: R1200* ✉ *Shimuwini Camp Rd.* ☎ *012/428–9111 reservations* 🌐 *www.sanparks.org* 🛏 *15 rooms* 🍴 *No meals.*

$ RESORT 🏨 **Sirheni.** Remote and lovely, Sirheni lies on the edge of the Sirheni Dam in an isolated wilderness area in Kruger's far north. **Pros:** permanent water hole; superb bird-watching. **Cons:** high malaria area; no electrical plug points; no cell-phone reception (which can be a pro or con). [$] *Rooms from: R1150* ✉ *Sirheni Camp Rd.* ☎ *012/428–9111 reservations* 🌐 *www.sanparks.org* 🛏 *15 cottages* 🍴 *No meals.*

$ RESORT 🏨 **Talamati.** On the banks of the normally dry N'waswitsontso River in Kruger's central section, this peaceful camp in the middle of a wide, open valley has excellent game-viewing. **Pros:** peaceful; good plains game; couple of good picnic spots in vicinity; bigger camps near enough to stock up on supplies. **Cons:** a bit bland. [$] *Rooms from: R1200* ✉ *Talamati-camp Rd.* ☎ *012/428–9111 reservations* 🌐 *www.sanparks.org* 🛏 *15 rooms* 🍴 *No meals.*

SABI SAND GAME RESERVE

The Sabi Sand Game Reserve, more commonly referred to as the Sabi Sands, is a grouping of private game reserves located on 153,000 acres along the border of Kruger National Park, each one featuring private lodges that offer the ultimate safari experience. This is where you'll find the world-famous MalaMala and Londolozi, among scores of other lodges that pamper their guests. Not only will you be treated to luxury accommodations—the kind you see in the glossy travel magazines—your rate includes safaris, chef-produced meals, and lots of personal touches.

As nice as it is to be pampered, you're here to see the wildlife. And Sabi Sands fully deserves its exalted reputation, boasting perhaps the highest game density of any private reserve in southern Africa. With an average of 20 vehicles watching for game and communicating by radio, you're bound to see an enormous amount of game and almost certainly the Big Five; since only three vehicles are allowed at a sighting at a time, you can be assured of a grandstand seat. Sabi Sands is the best area for leopard sightings. It's a memorable experience to see this beautiful, powerful, and often elusive cat padding purposefully through the bush at night, illuminated in your ranger's spotlight. There are many lion prides, and occasionally the increasingly rare wild dogs will migrate from Kruger to den in Sabi Sands. You'll also see white and black rhinos, zebras, giraffes, wildebeests, and most of the antelope species, plus birds galore. The daily program at each of Sabi Sands' lodges rarely deviates from a pattern, starting with tea, coffee, and muffins or rusks (Boer biscuits) before an early-morning game drive (usually starting at dawn, later in winter). You return to the lodge around 10 am, at which point you dine on an extensive hot breakfast or brunch. You can then choose to go on a bush walk with an armed ranger, where you learn about some of the minutiae of the bush (including the Little Five), although you could also happen on giraffes, antelopes, or any one of the Big Five. But don't worry—you'll be well briefed in advance on what you should do if you come face-to-face with, say, a lion. The rest of the day, until the late-afternoon game drive, is spent at leisure—reading up on the bush in the camp library, snoozing, swimming, or having a spa treatment. A sumptuous afternoon tea is served at 3:30 or 4 before you head back into the bush for your night drive. During the drive, your ranger will find a peaceful spot for sundowners (cocktails), and you can sip the drink of your choice and nibble snacks as you watch one of Africa's spectacular sunsets. As darkness falls, your ranger will switch on the spotlight so you can spy nocturnal animals: lions, leopards, jackals, porcupines, servals (small spotted cats like bonsai leopards), civets, and the enchanting little bush babies. You'll return to the lodge around 7:30, in time to freshen up before a three- or five-course dinner, with at least one dinner in a *boma* (open-air dining area) around a blazing fire. Often the camp staff entertains after dinner with local songs and dances—an unforgettable experience. Children under 12 aren't allowed at some of the camps; others have great kids' programs.

GETTING HERE AND AROUND

Kruger Mpumalanga International Airport (KMIA), at Mbombela (Nelspruit), Skukuza Airport, and Hoedspruit Airport, close to Kruger's Orpen Gate, serve Sabi Sand Game Reserve. You can also drive yourself to the reserve and park at your lodge. Most lodges offer charter flights to and from Johannesburg.

VISITOR INFORMATION

Contacts Sabi Sand Game Reserve. ☎ *013/735–5102* ⊕ *www.sabisand.co.za.*

DJUMA PRIVATE GAME RESERVE

504 km (329 miles) from Johannesburg, via N12.

This 17,297-acre reserve sits right up against Kruger within the northeast corner of the world-famous Sabi Sand Game Reserve. Expect classic bushveld terrain—dams, rivers, ancient riverine trees, grassland, and plains. And because no fences separate Kruger from Sabi Sand—and therefore from Djuma as well—game wanders freely back and forth, offering you some of South Africa's best game-viewing. The Big Five are all here, plus hundreds of birds. You'll find none of the formality that sometimes prevails at the larger camps. For example, members of the staff eat all meals with you and join you around the nighttime fire. In fact, Djuma prides itself on its personal service and feeling of intimacy.

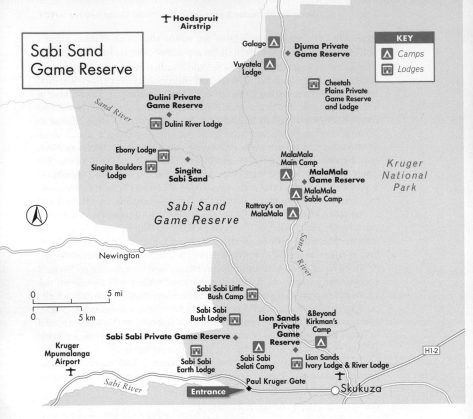

Sabi Sand
Game Reserve

Hoedspruit
Airstrip

Galago △

Vuyatela △
Lodge

Djuma Private
Game Reserve

KEY
△ Camps
▣ Lodges

Dulini Private
Game Reserve

Sand River

▣ Dulini River Lodge

Cheetah
Plains Private
Game Reserve
and Lodge

Ebony Lodge ▣

Singita Boulders ▣
Lodge

Singita
Sabi Sand

MalaMala
Main Camp △

MalaMala △
Game Reserve

MalaMala △
Sable Camp

Kruger
National
Park

Sabi Sand
Game Reserve

Rattray's on
MalaMala △

Sand River

Newington

0   5 mi
0   5 km

Sabi Sabi Little
Bush Camp ▣

Sabi Sabi
Bush Lodge ▣

Lion Sands
Private
Game
Reserve △

&Beyond
Kirkman's
Camp

Sabi Sabi Private Game Reserve

Kruger
Mpumalanga
Airport

▣
Sabi Sabi
Earth Lodge

Sabi Sabi △
Selati Camp

Lion Sands ▣
Ivory Lodge & River Lodge

H1-2

Sabi River

Paul Kruger Gate

Entrance ◆   ○ Skukuza

GETTING HERE AND AROUND

From Johannesburg it's approximately a seven-hour drive north to Hoedspruit via Dullstroom, Ohrigstad. and through the JG Strydom tunnel. Take the R531 to Klaserie and Acornhoek and follow the signs to Sabi Sand, Gowrie Gate. Djuma is signposted from there. You will drive yourself to the camp, and then go on safari in open game vehicles.

There are daily scheduled flights from Johannesburg to Skukuza Airport and Hoedspruit Airport, on SA Express, and Kruger Mpumalanga International Airport on SA Airlink (lodge transfers can be arranged), or you can fly in directly to one of the Sabi Sand airstrips by Fedair charter flight.

EXPLORING

FAMILY **Djuma Private Game Reserve.** Although there's a good chance of seeing the Big Five during the bush walk after breakfast and the twice-daily game drives, Djuma also caters to those with special bushveld interests, such as bird-watching or tree identification. Djuma's rangers and trackers are also adept at finding seldom-seen animals, such as wild dogs, spotted hyenas, and genets. ⊠ *Djuma Private Game Reserve* ☎ *013/735–5555 reservations* ⊕ *www.djuma.com.*

WHERE TO STAY

$$$$
RESORT

⌨ **Cheetah Plains Private Game Reserve and Lodge.** This delightfully unpretentious lodge, one of the oldest in Sabi Sands, is set among huge trees on the banks of an attractive dam that is a magnet for game—particularly elephants. **Pros:** more affordable than many other Sabi Sand lodges. **Cons:** cottages are small. $ *Rooms from: R11990* ⊠ *Sabi Sand Game Reserve* ☎ *079/694–8430* ⊕ *www.cheetahplains.com* ↬ *9 rooms* ⦿ *All meals.*

$$$$
RESORT

⌨ **Galago.** A delightful and affordable alternative to other upscale lodges, Galago, which means "lesser bush baby" in Shangaan, is a converted U-shaped farmhouse whose five rooms form an arc around a central fireplace. **Pros:** exclusive experience; luxurious. **Cons:** hire a cook or you'll spend your time working. $ *Rooms from: R12300* ⊠ *Djuma Private Game Reserve* ☎ *013/735–5555 reservations* ⊕ *www. djuma.com* ↬ *5 rooms* ⦿ *No meals.*

$$$$
RESORT
FAMILY

⌨ **Vuyatela Lodge.** Djuma's vibey, most upscale camp mixes contemporary African township culture with modern Shangaan culture, making it very different from most of the other private camps. **Pros:** amazing African art; legendary hosts; ideal for extended family or group of friends. **Cons:** funky township style (corrugated iron, recycled metals, in-your-face glitzy township feel) may not be to everyone's taste. $ *Rooms from: R16900* ⊠ *Djuma Private Game Reserve* ☎ *013/735– 5555 reservations, 013/735–5118 lodge* ⊕ *www.djuma.com* ↬ *5 rooms* ⦿ *No meals* ☞ *Rate is for entire house.*

LION SANDS PRIVATE GAME RESERVE

458 km (284 miles) from Johannesburg.

Separated from Kruger National Park by the Sabie River, this reserve has one of the best locations in the Sabi Sand Game Reserve. Purchased in 1933 by the More family as a family retreat, it was opened to the public in 1978 with two lodges and 10,000 acres of undisturbed wildlife that's available only to its guests. The family is so committed to keeping the reserve as close to its original state as possible that they employ a full-time ecologist, the only reserve in the Sabi Sands group to do so. Among its various accommodations are the ultraluxe Ivory Lodge and the relatively more economical River Lodge. There's also the once-in-a-lifetime Chalkleys Treehouse (yes, it really is a bed on a platform in a tree, but it's nothing like the treehouse in your backyard), the once-in-a-lifetime Narina Lodge, the spacious Tinga Lodge, and the 1933 Lodge, the More family's vacation home that's perfect for larger groups and comes complete with personal chef, guide, pool, gym, and wine cellar.

GETTING HERE AND AROUND

If you're coming by car from Hazyview, turn right onto the R536 toward Paul Kruger Gate (Kruger National Park). After 38 km (23 miles), turn left onto a gravel road signposted to Lion Sands, Sabi Sand. At the T-junction, turn right and enter Sabi Sand through Shaw's Gate. Then follow directions to the lodges. There's a vehicle entrance fee of R190 plus R50 per person into the Sabi Sand Reserve, payable on arrival by cash or credit card. The gates close at 10 pm. You can drive

9

yourself to the lodges, but you'll have to park your car and leave it, because while you're at the lodge, you'll be driven around in an open game vehicle.

There are daily scheduled flights from Johannesburg, Durban, and Cape Town to Skukuza Airport and Kruger Mpumalanga International Airport on SA Airlink. Lodge transfers can be arranged.

EXPLORING

Fodor's Choice ★ **Lion Sands Private Game Reserve.** All of the lodges overlook the river, which is a magnet for all kinds of game. You'll be able to peer into Kruger National Park, on the other side of the river, and watch game meander along the riverbanks among big riverine trees. You may never want to leave your personal deck, or the big viewing decks. But when you do decide to leave your perch, you have all kinds of options for activities, including game drives and walking safaris, spa treatments, and yoga beneath the African sun. ✉ *Lion Sands Private Game Reserve* ☎ *011/880–9992* 🌐 *www.lionsands.com.*

WHERE TO STAY

$$$$ RESORT Fodor's Choice ★ 🏨 **Lion Sands Ivory Lodge.** Ivory Lodge offers the ultimate in luxury, privacy, and relaxation. **Pros:** exclusivity; great views; brilliant game-viewing. **Cons:** the temptation of abundant great food; it's so decadent, you might forget to leave. [$] *Rooms from: R50900* ✉ *Lion Sands Private Game Reserve* ☎ *031/735–5000 lodge, 011/880–9992 head office and reservations* 🌐 *www.lionsands.com* 🛏 *9 rooms* 🍴 *All meals* ☞ *No children under 10 years old.*

$$$$ RESORT 🏨 **Lion Sands River Lodge.** Set on one of the longest and best stretches of river frontage in Sabi Sand, you can watch the passing animal and bird show from your deck or from the huge, tree-shaded, wooden viewing area that juts out over the riverbank facing Kruger National Park. **Pros:** fabulous river frontage; well managed. **Cons:** some chalets quite close together so not much privacy. [$] *Rooms from: R22540* ✉ *Lion Sands Private Game Reserve* ☎ *013/735–5000 lodge, 011/880–9992 head office and reservations* 🌐 *www.lionsands.com* 🛏 *20 rooms* 🍴 *All meals* ☞ *No children under 10 years old.*

LONDOLOZI GAME RESERVE

471 km (292 miles) from Johannesburg.

Established as a family farm and retreat in 1926, Londolozi today is synonymous with South Africa's finest game lodges and game experiences. (*Londolozi* is the Zulu word for "protector of all living things.") Dave and John Varty, grandsons of the original owner, Charles Varty, put the reserve on the map with glamorous marketing and a vision of style and comfort that their grandfather never could never have imagined. Now younger generation, brother-and-sister team Bronwyn and Boyd Varty are carrying on their family's quest to honor the animal kingdom. Game abounds; the Big Five are all here, and the leopards of Londolozi are world-famous. There are five camps, each representing a different element in nature: Pioneer Camp (water), Tree Camp (wood), Granite Suites (rock), Varty Camp (fire), and Founders Camp (earth).

Each is totally private, hidden in dense riverine forest on the banks of the Sand River. The Varty family lives on the property, and their friendliness and personal attention, along with the many staff who have been here for decades, will make you feel part of the family immediately. The central reception and curio shop are at Varty Camp.

GETTING HERE AND AROUND

Londolozi is an easy six-hour drive from Johannesburg on the NM12 and N4. Turn right onto R536 from Hazyview toward Paul Kruger Gate. After 37.4 km (23 miles) turn left onto a gravel road signposted "Sabi Sand Wildtuin Shaw's Gate."

There are daily scheduled flights from Johannesburg, Durban, and Cape Town to Skukuza Airport and Kruger Mpumalanga International Airport on SA Airlink (lodge transfers can be arranged), or you can fly in directly to the Londolozi airstrip by Fedair charter flight.

EXPLORING

Fodor's Choice ★ **Londolozi Game Reserve.** Each of the five camps offers unprecedented access to 34,000 acres of Africa's best Big Five game-viewing, led by renowned rangers and trackers. The camp is most famous for its leopards, with which its rangers and trackers have forged an intimate relationship over the decades. Leopard sightings are frequent. ✉ *Londolozi Reserve* ☎ *011/280–6655 reservations, 013/735–5653 lodge* 🌐 *www.londolozi.com.*

WHERE TO STAY

$$$$ RESORT FAMILY 🏨 **Founders Camp.** This inviting camp has 10 stone-and-thatch suites in individual chalets set amid thick riverine bush; some chalets are linked by interconnecting skywalks, which is great for families or groups traveling together (children six years and older are welcome). **Pros:** quick, safe access between family rooms; children over four welcome. **Cons:** lodges are in quite close proximity to one another. [$] *Rooms from: R31475* ✉ *Londolozi Reserve* ☎ *011/280–6655 reservations, 013/735–5653 lodge* 🌐 *www.londolozi.com* 🛏 *10 rooms* 🍴 *All-inclusive.*

$$$$ RESORT 🏨 **Pioneer Camp.** The most secluded of all of Londolozi's camps, Pioneer's three private suites overlook the river and are perfect for getting away from others. **Pros:** authentic romantic-safari atmosphere; only three suites; intimate atmosphere. **Cons:** with only three suites it's best if you know all other guests. [$] *Rooms from: R45400* ✉ *Londolozi Reserve* ☎ *011/280–6655 reservations, 013/735–5653 lodge* 🌐 *www.londolozi.com* 🛏 *3 rooms* 🍴 *All-inclusive* ☞ *No children under 6 years old.*

$$$$ RESORT 🏨 **Private Granite Suites.** Book all three private suites or just hide yourself away from the rest of the world like the celebrities and royals who favor this gorgeous getaway. **Pros:** one of the best locations in Sabi Sands with truly stunning views; the candelit dinner. **Cons:** pricey. [$] *Rooms from: R49500* ✉ *Londolozi Reserve* ☎ *011/280–6655 reservations, 013/735–5100 lodge* 🌐 *www.londolozi.com* 🛏 *3 rooms* 🍴 *All-inclusive* ☞ *No children under 16 years old.*

$$$$ RESORT Fodor's Choice ★ 🏨 **Tree Camp.** The first Relais & Chateaux game lodge in the world, this gorgeous camp (think leopards, lanterns, leadwoods,and leopard orchids) is tucked into the riverbank overlooking indigenous forest. **Pros:** the viewing deck; state-of-the-art designer interiors. **Cons:** stylishness nudges out coziness. [$] *Rooms from: R45400* ✉ *Londolozi Reserve*

9

☎ *011/280–6655 reservations, 013/735–5653 lodge* 🌐 *www.londolozi.com* 🛏 *6 rooms* 🍴 *All-inclusive* ☞ *Children under 16 not allowed.*

$$$$ RESORT FAMILY 🏨 **Varty Camp.** This camp's fire has been burning for more than nine decades, making Varty Camp the very soul and center of Londolozi. **Pros:** friendly atmosphere; great game; all chalets are interleading. **Cons:** lots of kids might not be for you. [$] *Rooms from: R25900* ✉ *Londolozi Reserve* ☎ *011/280–6655 reservations, 013/735–5653 lodge* 🌐 *www.londolozi.com* 🛏 *10 rooms* 🍴 *All-inclusive.*

MALAMALA GAME RESERVE

455 km (283 miles) from Johannesburg.

This legendary game reserve (designated as such in 1929) is tops in its field. MalaMala constitutes the largest privately owned Big Five game area in South Africa and includes an unfenced 30-km (19-mile) boundary with Kruger National Park, across which game crosses continuously. The first and only community-owned game reserve in Sabi Sands, it continues to be managed by the legendary Rattray family in partnership with the N'wandlamharhi Community.

You'll be delighted with incomparable personal service, superb food, and discreetly elegant, comfortable accommodations, where you'll rub shoulders with statesmen and stateswomen, aristocrats, celebrities, and returning visitors alike. Mike Rattray, a legend in his own time in South Africa's game-lodge industry, describes MalaMala as "a camp in the bush," but it's certainly more than that, although it still retains that genuine bushveld feel of bygone days. Both the outstanding hospitality and the game-viewing experience keep guests coming back.

GETTING HERE AND AROUND

MalaMala Game Reserve is approximately a six-hour drive from Johannesburg via N12 and N4. From Hazyview, take the R536 toward Skukuza and the Paul Kruger Gate. Turn left at the MalaMala Game Reserve sign onto a gravel road and follow lodge signs. There are daily scheduled flights from Johannesburg, Durban, and Cape Town to Skukuza Airport and Kruger Mpumalanga International Airport on SA Airlink (lodge transfers can be arranged), or you can fly in directly to the MalaMala airstrip by Fedair charter flight.

EXPLORING

Fodor's Choice ★ **MalaMala Private Game Reserve.** MalaMala's animal-viewing statistics are unbelievable: the Big Five are spotted almost every day, along with plenty of other amazing viewings. At one moment your ranger will fascinate you with the description of the sex life of a dung beetle, as you watch the sturdy male battling his way along the road pushing his perfectly round ball of dung with wife-to-be perched perilously on top; at another, your adrenaline will flow as you follow a leopard stalking impala in the gathering gloom. Along with the local Shangaan trackers, whose eyesight rivals that of the animals they are tracking, the top-class rangers ensure that your game experience is unforgettable. ✉ *Mala Mala Game Reserve* ☎ *011/442–2267 reservations* 🌐 *www.malamala.com.*

WHERE TO STAY

$$$$ RESORT FAMILY **MalaMala Main Camp.** Stone and thatch air-conditioned rondavels with separate his-and-her bathrooms are decorated in creams and browns and furnished with cane armchairs, colorful handwoven tapestries and rugs, terra-cotta floors, and original artwork. **Pros:** authentic; sweeping wilderness views; amazing game-viewing. **Cons:** rondavels are a bit old-fashioned, but that goes with the ambience. [$] *Rooms from: R21418* ✉ *Mala Mala Game Reserve* ☎ *011/442–2267 reservations, 013/735–9200 MalaMala Main Camp* 🌐 *www.malamala.com* 🛏 *17 rooms* 🍴 *All-inclusive.*

$$$$ RESORT Fodor's Choice ★ **MalaMala Sable Camp.** This fully air-conditioned, exclusive camp with six ultra-luxurious suites lies at the southern end of Main Camp and overlooks the Sand River and surrounding bushveld. **Pros:** small and intimate; privacy guaranteed; unparalleled game-viewing. **Cons:** you might like it so much you never want to leave. [$] *Rooms from: R124812* ✉ *Mala Mala Game Reserve* ☎ *011/442–2267 reservations, 013/735–9200 MalaMala Sable Camp* 🌐 *www.malamala.com* 🛏 *6 rooms* 🍴 *All-inclusive.*

$$$$ RESORT Fodor's Choice ★ **Rattray's on MalaMala.** The breathtakingly beautiful Rattray's merges original bushveld style with daring contemporary ideas. **Pros:** superb game-viewing; tantalizing views over the river. **Cons:** Tuscan villas in the bush may not be your idea of Africa; though this may be a pro for some, no children under 16. [$] *Rooms from: R15018* ✉ *Mala Mala Game Reserve* ☎ *011/442–2267 reservations, 013/735–3000 Rattray's on MalaMala* 🌐 *www.malamala.com* 🛏 *8 rooms* 🍴 *All-inclusive.*

SABI SABI PRIVATE GAME RESERVE

500 km (310 miles) from Johannesburg.

Founded in 1978 at the southern end of Sabi Sand, the multi-award-winning Sabi Sabi Private Game Reserve was one of the first reserves to offer photo safaris and to link ecotourism, conservation, and community. Superb accommodations and abundant game lure guests back to Sabi Sabi in large numbers. There are four very different lodges, each individually remarkable: Bush Lodge, famous for its friendly hospitality and ever-busy water hole; Little Bush Camp, an intimate, back-to-nature tented camp; Selati, haunt of celebs and royalty, themed on an old Kruger National Park railway line; and the daringly innovative Earth Lodge.

GETTING HERE AND AROUND

Sabi Sabi is an easy six-hour drive from Johannesburg on the N4 and N12. Turn right onto R536 from Hazyview toward Paul Kruger Gate. After 37.4 km (23 miles) turn left onto a gravel road signposted "Sabi Sand Wildtuin Shaw's Gate." There are daily scheduled flights from Johannesburg, Durban, and Cape Town to Skukuza Airport and Kruger Mpumalanga International Airport on SA Airlink (lodge transfers can be arranged), or you can fly in directly to a Sabi Sand airstrip by Fedair charter flight.

EXPLORING

Fodor's Choice ★ **Sabi Sabi Private Game Reserve.** Daily game drives take place in the early morning and late afternoon. There's a strong emphasis on ecology at Sabi Sabi: guests are encouraged to look beyond the Big Five and to become aware of the birds and smaller mammals of the bush. You can also take a luxury walking safari or a specialist birding or photo safari. There's also the Amani Spa, as well as stargazing in the evenings. ✉ *Sabi Sand Game Reserve* ☎ *011/447–7172 reservations* 🌐 *www.sabisabi.com.*

WHERE TO STAY

$$$$ RESORT FAMILY 🏨 **Sabi Sabi Bush Lodge.** Bush Lodge overlooks a busy water hole (lions are frequent visitors) and the dry course of the Msuthlu River. **Pros:** always prolific game around the lodge; roomy chalets. **Cons:** big and busy might not be your idea of relaxing getaway. [$] *Rooms from: R21800* ✉ *Sabi Sand Game Reserve* ☎ *013/735–5656 reservations, 013/735–5080 lodge* 🌐 *www.sabisabi.com* 🛏 *24 rooms* 🍴 *All meals.*

$$$$ RESORT 🏨 **Sabi Sabi Earth Lodge.** This avant-garde, eco-friendly lodge was the first to break away from the traditional safari style and strive for a contemporary theme. **Pros:** stunning architecture and design. **Cons:** if you favor traditonal safari accommodations, this is not for you. [$] *Rooms from: R34500* ✉ *Sabi Sand Game Reserve* ☎ *013/735–5261 lodge, 011/447–7172 reservations* 🌐 *www.sabisabi.com* 🛏 *14 rooms* 🍴 *All-inclusive.*

$$$$ RESORT FAMILY 🏨 **Sabi Sabi Little Bush Camp.** Sabi Sabi's delightful little camp is tucked away in the bushveld on the banks of the Msuthlu River and combines spaciousness with a sense of intimacy. **Pros:** perfect for families. **Cons:** there may be other families. [$] *Rooms from: R21800* ✉ *Sabi Sand Game Reserve* ☎ *011/447–7172 reservations, 013/735–5080 lodge* 🌐 *www.sabisabi.com* 🛏 *6 rooms* 🍴 *All meals.*

$$$$ RESORT Fodor's Choice ★ 🏨 **Sabi Sabi Selati Camp.** For an *Out of Africa* experience and great game, you can't beat Selati, an intimate, stylish, colonial-style camp that was formerly the private hunting lodge of a famous South African opera singer. **Pros:** unique atmosphere; Ivory Presidential Suite superb value for money; secluded and intimate. **Cons:** some old-timers preferred the camp when it was just lantern-lit with no electricity. [$] *Rooms from: R21800* ✉ *Sabi Sand Game Reserve* ☎ *011/447–7172 reservations, 013/735–5771 lodge, 013/735–5236 lodge* 🌐 *www.sabisabi.com* 🛏 *8 rooms* 🍴 *All meals.*

SINGITA

450 km (279 miles) from Johannesburg.

The Bailes family has overseen Singita (Shangaan for "the miracle") since 1926. Located on more than 45,000 acres of private bushland in the greater Kruger area, it has no fences between the parks, so wildlife can stroll freely back and forth as they wish. Although Singita offers much of the same thrilling Sabi Sand bush and game experiences as other camps, superb service really puts it head and shoulders above many of the rest of the herd. Its two lodges, Singita Boulders and Singita Ebony, are modern and stylish, with all the rugged luxury you'll ever need. Among the perks: a resident sommelier (wine can be shipped home), a variety of public spaces (little private dining nooks to a huge viewing deck built round an ancient jackalberry tree), and an attractive poolside bar. In 1998, Singita Sabi Sand established a partnership with the local community, providing support for eduction and other programs.

GETTING HERE AND AROUND

Singita is an easy 6½-hour drive from Johannesburg on the N4 and N12. Turn right onto R536 from Hazyview toward Paul Kruger Gate. After 37.4 km (23 miles), turn left at the sign that reads "Sabi Sand Wildtuin Shaw's Gate" onto a gravel road. Follow the signs for Singita. Singita will arrange scheduled flights or private charters for your trip. All flights land at Singita's airstrip, 10 minutes from the lodge.

EXPLORING

Fodor's Choice ★ **Singita Sabi Sand.** At Singita, you'll head out during the day on your choice of game drives, then prepare to be pampered. Whether you fancy a starlit private supper, a bike ride though the bush, or just chilling alone in your megasuite, you've only to ask. Forget the usual lodge curio shop and take a ride to the on-site Trading Post where objets d'art, handmade jewelry, classy bush gear, and artifacts from all over Africa are clustered together in a series of adjoining rooms that seem more like someone's home than a shop. ✉ *Singita Sabi Sand* ☎ *021/683–3424 reservations* 🌐 *www.singita.co.za.*

WHERE TO STAY

$$$$ RESORT FAMILY 🏨 **Ebony Lodge.** If Ernest Hemingway had built his ideal home in the African bush, this would be it. **Pros:** the mother lodge of all the Singita properties; cozy library. **Cons:** the beds are very high off the ground—if you have short legs or creak a bit, ask for a stool. [$] *Rooms from: R43268* ✉ *Singita Sabi Sand* ☎ *021/683–3424 reservations, 013/735–9800 lodge* 🌐 *www.singita.co.za* 🛏 *12 rooms* 🍴 *All-inclusive.*

$$$$ RESORT Fodor's Choice ★ 🏨 **Singita Boulders Lodge.** Overlooking the beautiful Sand River, Singita Boulders Lodge intermingles the wildness of its setting among boulders with traditional Africa decor at its most luxurious. **Pros:** spacious accommodations; superb food. **Cons:** a bit of a walk from the suites to the main lodge; refuse the crackling log fire if you're at all congested. [$] *Rooms from: R43268* ✉ *Singita Sabi Sand* ☎ *021/683–3424 reservations, 013/735–9800 lodge* 🌐 *www.singita.co.za* 🛏 *12 rooms* 🍴 *All-inclusive.*

9

DULINI PRIVATE GAME RESERVE

500 km (310 miles) from Johannesburg.

Established in 1937, Dulini (formerly called Exeter), at 160,600 acres, was an original part of Sabi Sands when it was incorporated in the 1960s.

GETTING HERE AND AROUND

Dulini is about a five- to six-hour drive from Johannesburg. Charter flights from Johannesburg land at the Ulusaba Airstrip, which is near the reserve's lodges. Transfers can also be arranged from other nearby airports with regular flights. The lodges generally arrange your transportation.

WHERE TO STAY

$$$$
RESORT
FAMILY

⊞ **&Beyond Kirkman's Kamp.** You'll feel as if you've stepped back in time at this camp because rooms are strategically clustered around the original 1920s homestead, which, with its colonial furniture, historic memorabilia, and wraparound veranda, makes you feel like a family guest the moment you arrive. **Pros:** superb game-viewing. **Cons:** gets tour groups; more of a hotel feel than other lodges. Ⓢ *Rooms from: R19960* ⊠ *Exeter Private Game Reserve* ☏ *011/809–4300 reservations* ⊕ *andbeyond.com* ↙ *18 rooms* ⑩ *All-inclusive.*

$$$$
RESORT
Fodor's Choice
★

⊞ **Dulini River Lodge.** One of Sabi Sand's oldest lodges, Dulini River Lodge scores 10 out of 10 for its gorgeous location—one of the best in the whole reserve—with lush green lawns sweeping down to the Sand River. **Pros:** more affordable than many of its neighbors; genuine African-bush ambience. **Cons:** no triple rooms for guests with children. Ⓢ *Rooms from: R28000* ⊠ *Exeter Private Game Reserve* ☏ *011/792–4927 reservations* ⊕ *www.dulini.com* ↙ *6 rooms* ⑩ *All-inclusive.*

WEST OF KRUGER

Manyeleti, Timbavati, Thornybush, and Kapama, along with a couple of other smaller game reserves, all lie north of Sabi Sand Game Reserve, but also border Kruger's western boundary. Although the reserves are less well known, they offer much the same game experiences, often at more affordable prices. The best-known ones are Manyeleti and Timbavati with lovely lodges set among typical bushveld, both adjoining Kruger, so you stand a good chance of seeing the Big Five and lots more. A big bonus is that because they are less frequently visited and have fewer lodges than Sabi Sand, there are fewer people and fewer vehicles. Some lodges have no electricity, so no email or Internet, but this will free you from the pressures of everyday life.

MANYELETI PRIVATE GAME RESERVE

502 km (311 miles) from Johannesburg.

North of Sabi Sand, Manyeleti Private Game Reserve ("the place of the stars" in Shangaan) covers 59,280 acres that border Kruger, Sabi Sand, and Timbavati, but it's something of a Cinderella reserve compared with its more famous neighbors. Away from the major tourist areas, it's amazingly underused; you'll probably see very few vehicles while you're here.

GETTING HERE AND AROUND

Travel north from Johannesburg on the N12 to Ohrigstad and continue toward Hoedspruit via the Abel Erasmus Pass and the JG Strijdom Tunnel. Cross the Blyde River, and turn right at the R531 to the Orpen Gate sign. Turn left here and continue until you see the Manyeleti Reserve sign.

There are daily scheduled flights from Johannesburg to Hoedspruit Airport by SA Express. There are also daily scheduled flights from Johannesburg, Durban, and Cape Town to Skukuza Airport and Kruger Mpumalanga International Airport on SA Airlink (lodge transfers can be arranged).

EXPLORING

Manyeleti Game Reserve. The park's grassy plains and mixed woodland attract good-size herds of general game and their attendant predators. You have a strong chance of seeing the Big Five, but the Manyeleti lodges and tented camps, which are owned and operated by two separate companies (one for the lodge, one for the tented camps), focus more on providing an overall bush experience than simply rushing after big game. You'll learn about trees, birds, and bushveld ecosystems as you go on guided bush walks. ✉ *Manyeleti Game Reserve* ☎ 🌐 *www.manyeleti.com.*

WHERE TO STAY

$$$$ RESORT FAMILY 🏨 **Honeyguide Khoka Moya.** This delightful, value-priced camp owned and operated by Honeyguide is situated on both sides of a riverbed within Manyeleti Private Game Reserve. **Pros:** excellent value for money; great kids' programs. **Cons:** no air-conditioning; usually lots of kids around so if you aren't childproof, stay away. [$] *Rooms from: R9850* ✉ *Manyeleti Game Reserve* ☎ *015/793–1729 reservations* 🌐 *www.honeyguidecamp.com* 🛏 *15 rooms* 🍴 *All meals.*

$$$$ RESORT 🏨 **Honeyguide Mantobeni Camp.** This tented camp, built on wooden platforms, minimalist but with surprising luxury touches (owned and operated by Honeyguide within Manyeleti Private Game Reserve), gives you the total bush experience at half the price of some of the more upscale lodges. **Pros:** superb value for money; complimentary bar and well-stocked wine cellar; can watch wildlife from the pool deck. **Cons:** canvas structure may not be to everyone's taste; very comfortable but far from five-star. [$] *Rooms from: R9850* ✉ *Manyeleti Game Reserve* ☎ *015/793–1729 reservations* 🌐 *www.honeyguidecamp.com* 🛏 *15 rooms* 🍴 *All meals.*

$$$$ RESORT 🏨 **Tintswalo Safari Lodge.** This gorgeous ultraluxurious lodge, sited under huge jackalberry and fig trees, overlooks a seasonal river, where game come down to drink and bathe. **Pros:** drop-dead luxury; kids' program on request; suites overlook water hole. **Cons:** potentially over-attentive staff. [$] *Rooms from: R18580* ✉ *Manyeleti Game Reserve* ☎ *011/300–8888 reservations* 🌐 *www.tintswalo.com* 🛏 *9 rooms* 🍴 *All-inclusive.*

TIMBAVATI PRIVATE GAME RESERVE

515 km (320 miles) from Johannesburg.

The 185,000-acre Timbavati, the northernmost of the private reserves, is a collection of smaller private reserves managed by the Timbavati Association, a nonprofit organization that strives to conserve the biodiversity of the area. The association was established in 1956, and with the removal of fences between the member reserves and Kruger National Park, wild animals roam freely between the reserves. The name, "Timbavati," means "the place where something sacred came down to Earth from the Heavens," referring to the rare white lions that reside here. Ngala ("lion" in Tsonga) and Motswari game reserves have been amalgamated into Timbavati.

A wide selection of lodging options are available, including the popular Ngala Safari Lodge, Ngala Tented Safari Camp, and Tanda Tula Safari Camp.

GETTING HERE AND AROUND

Travel north from Johannesburg on the N12 to Ohrigstad and continue toward Hoedspruit via the Abel Erasmus Pass and the J G Strijdom Tunnel. Drive through Hoedspruit and take the R40 to Klaserie. Turn left at the Timbavati/East Gate signs. Go through the security gate, and drive straight for 17 km (10½ miles), cross the Klaserie River, and enter through the Timbavati Control Gate. Roads can be rough in the reserve, particularly in the rainy season, so a 4x4 is recommended.

There are daily scheduled flights from Johannesburg to Hoedspruit Airport by SA Express. There are also daily scheduled flights from Johannesburg, Durban, and Cape Town to Skukuza Airport and Kruger Mpumalanga International Airport on SA Airlink (lodge transfers can be arranged).

EXPLORING

Timbavati Game Reserve. Regardless of which lodge you're staying at, you'll be treated to wildlife-rich game drives with wall-to-wall game. You'll most certainly see the King of Beasts, as well as leopards, elephants, buffalo, and spotted hyenas. Rhinos are scarcer, but you might be lucky and see wild dogs, as they migrate regularly to this region from Kruger. The most amazing sighting, however, for which this reserve is famous, is the rare white lion. ⊠ *Timbavati Game Reserve* ⊕ *www.timbavati.co.za.*

WHERE TO STAY

$$$$
RESORT
FAMILY

⌗ **Ngala Safari Lodge.** Guests return again and again to this classic safari lodge with its timeless *Out of Africa* ambience. **Pros:** great kids' programs; superb game and a bird-watcher's paradise. **Cons:** always busy; kids dine with adults. Ⓢ *Rooms from: R16970* ☎ *011/809–4300 reservations* ⊕ *andbeyond.com* ⌁ *21 rooms* ⦿ *All-inclusive.*

$$$$
RESORT
Fodor's Choice
★

⌗ **Ngala Tented Safari Camp.** Marula seeds softly falling on the tents seem to be applauding this gorgeous little camp shaded by a canopy of giant trees. **Pros:** exclusivity. **Cons:** if you're nervous of too-close game, this is not for you, as hippos (and other game) wander freely around the tents; no air-conditioning. Ⓢ *Rooms from: R23300* ☎ *011/809–4300 reservations* ⊕ *andbeyond.com* ⌁ *9 rooms* ⦿ *All-inclusive.*

$$$$
RESORT

⌗ **Tanda Tula Safari Camp.** Tanda Tula has a well-deserved reputation as one of the best bush camps in Mpumalanga. **Pros:** emphasis on the whole bush experience, not just the Big Five; moonlit bush barbecues. **Cons:** if you don't like being under canvas, stay away; no air-conditioning. Ⓢ *Rooms from: R19500* ☎ *015/793–3191* ⊕ *www.tandatula.com* ⌁ *12 rooms* ⦿ *All-inclusive.*

THORNYBUSH NATURE RESERVE

504 km (313 miles) from Johannesburg.

Situated within 34,594 acres of pristine wilderness, adjacent to the Greater Kruger National Park in Limpopo, Thornybush Nature Reserve is set among classic bushveld scenery. There are eleven comfortable, unpretentious lodges offering friendly service, excellent food, and great game, including the popular Jackalberry Lodge. Thornybush was one of the first lowveld reserves to implement rhino horn treatments (injecting poison that is harmless to the rhinos) as a form of anti-poaching (some disproven but popular traditional Asian medical treatments use rhino horn), and one of the first to introduce elephant contraception as an alternative to culling.

GETTING HERE AND AROUND

Take the R40 from Hazyview to Acornhoek. Turn right after 7.4 km (4.6 miles) and take the Guernsey turnoff. Check in at the security gate, drive approximately 11 km (6.8 miles), and turn left at the T-junction. You'll find the Thornybush Nature Reserve Gate on your right after approximately 4 km (2.5 miles). There are daily scheduled flights from Johannesburg to Hoedspruit Airport by SA Express. There are also daily scheduled flights from Johannesburg, Durban, and Cape Town to Skukuza Airport and Kruger Mpumalanga International Airport on SA Airlink (lodge transfers can be arranged).

WHERE TO STAY

$$$$
RESORT
FAMILY

🏨 **Jackalberry Lodge.** This lodge offers understated luxury, excellent food, superb guiding, and the Big Five at half the price of some of the better-known lodges. **Pros:** excellent value for money; very friendly staff and super-knowledgeable rangers. **Cons:** no children under six on game drives (babysitters available, however); game not quite as prolific as at Sabi Sand and Timbavati. [$] *Rooms from: R11914* ✉ *Thornybush Game Reserve* ☎ *011/253–6500 reservations* 🌐 *www.jackalberrylodge.co.za* 🛏 *7 rooms* 🍴 *All meals.*

KAPAMA PRIVATE GAME RESERVE

481 km (315 miles) from Johannesburg on N4 and R36.

The 32,123-acre Kapama Private Game Reserve, the area's largest single-owned private reserve, boasts some high-end luxury lodges, but it lacks some of the genuine wilderness feel of other nearby reserves because of its proximity to roads and electrical towers. The reason to come here is to visit the Hoedspruit Endangered Species Centre, where rescued and endangered animals like cheetahs are to be found.

9

GETTING HERE AND AROUND

Drive north from Johannesburg on the N4 and R36 to Hoedspruit via Dullstroom and Lydenburg (Mashishing). Turn right at the R40 to Klaserie/Bushbuck Ridge. Follow signs to Kapama. Report to the gate, where your ranger will meet you.

There are daily scheduled flights from Johannesburg to Hoedspruit Airport by SA Express. There are also daily scheduled flights from Johannesburg, Durban, and Cape Town to Skukuza Airport and Kruger Mpumalanga International Airport on SA Airlink (lodge transfers can be arranged).

EXPLORING

Kapama Private Game Reserve. View wildlife, including the Big Five, against the backdrop of the majestic Drakensberg. Game drives, bush walks, and guided elephant interactions are available. ☎ *012/368–0600 reservations* 🌐 *www.kapama.com.*

FAMILY **Hoedspruit Endangered Species Centre.** This center, which cares for, breeds, and protects endangered species, is in the Kapama Private Game Reserve, outside the little Limpopo town of Hoedspruit. It started in a small way, when South African Lente Roode, who owns the reserve, decided to dedicate herself to saving cheetahs—a highly endangered species. The center quickly gained credibility and fame when other animals and birds were brought to her, nursed back to health, and returned to the wild (when possible). It now has a state-of-the-art veterinary center, a highly respected research program, outreach programs for schools, international volunteer programs, a restaurant, and a shop, and is a great day destination. You'll meet Little G, a white rhino found in 2014 beside his mother, who had been brutally slaughtered for her horn. You can also watch wild vultures feast at a vulture restaurant or see wild dogs being fed. You can take a standard tour, or join a dawn or dusk tour; a cheetah-focused tour is also available. The center also rents out two three-bedroom, self-catering cottages on the grounds, and the staff can help you arrange guided game drives; alternatively, you can visit and do things on your own. ✉ *R40, just outside of Hoedspruit* ☎ *015/793–1633* 🌐 *www.hesc.co.za* 🎟 *R150.*

WHERE TO STAY

$$$$ RESORT 🏨 **Camp Jabulani.** This sumptuous Relais & Châteaux lodge, a cross between a Hollywood set designer's and an Arab prince's idea of colonial Africa, sits in the 32,123-acre Kapama Private Game Reserve, only 40 km (25 miles) from Kruger. **Pros:** ultraluxurious accommodations. **Cons:** all this opulence could be excessive. [$] *Rooms from: R28400* ✉ *R40* ☎ *015/793–1265 lodge, 012/460–5605 reservations* 🌐 *www.campjabulani.com* 🛏 *7 rooms* 🍴 *All-inclusive.*

$$$$ RENTAL 🏨 **Khula's Cottage.** Built round a weeping boer-bean tree, Khula's Cottage, just 40 km (25 miles) from Kruger's Orpen Gate, is a delightful self-catering three-bedroom wooden house on the grounds of the Hoedspruit Endangered Species Centre (HESC). **Pros:** exclusive; no other properties near by. **Cons:** could be cold in winter and very hot in summer as no air-conditioning and minimal heating. [$] *Rooms from: R3600* ✉ *Hoedspruit Endangered Species Centre, R40* ☎ *015/793–1633* 🌐 *hesc.co.za* 🛏 *3 rooms* 🍴 *No meals.*

SAFARI PRIMER

Updated by Claire Baranowski

A safari is one of the biggest travel adventures you can have. Planning well is crucial to ensure you get the most out of it. Even a basic question like "What should I wear?" is extremely important. In this safari section, we'll cover all the special considerations and lingo you'll need, with plenty of insider tips along the way.

Most people start planning a safari six to nine months in advance, but it's never too soon to start planning your trip. In fact, planning your trip 12 months in advance isn't unreasonable, especially if you want to travel during peak season—November through February in South Africa, July through October elsewhere—and have your heart set on a particular lodge.

If you're keen to see big game, particularly the Big Five, then your best bets for success will be in East Africa and South Africa. In South Africa, Kruger National Park and the private Sabi Sand game reserve just outside of Kruger *(Chapter 9)* are ideal places to observe the Big Five as well as hundreds of other species. In Kruger alone, there are an estimated 1,200 species of flora and fauna. You'll see the African elephant everywhere in the park, with lions more abundant in the central and eastern regions; rhinos and buffalo make their home in the woods of southwest Kruger.

Deciding where you want to go and choosing the right safari operator are the most important things you need to do. Start planning for your safari the way you would any trip. Read travel books about the areas that most interest you. Talk to people who have been on a similar trip; word-of-mouth advice can be invaluable. Surf the 'net. Get inspired. Line up your priorities. And find someone you trust to help plan your trip.

GETTING STARTED

AIR TRAVEL

Traveling by plane is the best and most viable means of transportation to most safari destinations. If you're visiting a game lodge deep in the bush, you'll be arriving by light plane—and you really will be restricted in what you can bring. Excess luggage can usually be stored with the operator until your return. Don't just gloss over this: charter operators take weight very seriously, and some will charge you for an extra ticket if you insist on bringing excess baggage.

CHARTER FLIGHTS

Charter flights are a common mode of transportation when getting to safari lodges and remote destinations throughout South and East Africa. These aircraft are well maintained and are almost always booked by your lodge or travel agent.

On-demand flights, those made at times other than those scheduled, are very expensive for independent travelers, as they require minimum passenger loads. If it's just two passengers, you'll be charged for the vacant seats. Keep in mind that you probably won't get to choose the charter company you fly with. The aircraft you get depends on the number of passengers flying and can vary from very small (you'll sit in the copilot's seat) to a much more comfortable commuter plane. Those with a severe fear of small planes might consider road travel instead.

CUSTOMS AND DUTIES

Visitors traveling to South Africa or other Southern Africa Customs Union (SACU) countries (Botswana, Lesotho, Namibia, and Swaziland) may bring in new or used gifts and souvenirs up to a total value of R3,000 (in South African rand, $280 at this writing) duty-free. For additional goods (new or used) up to a value of R12,000, a fee of 25% is levied. In addition, each person may bring up to 200 cigarettes, 20 cigars, 250 grams of tobacco, two liters of wine, one liter of spirits, 50 ml of perfume, and 250 ml of eau de toilette. The tobacco and alcohol allowance applies only to people 18 and over. If you enter a SACU country from or through another in the union, you aren't liable for any duties. You will, however, need to complete a form listing items imported.

The United States is a signatory to CITES, a wildlife protection treaty, and therefore doesn't allow the importation of living or dead endangered animals, or their body parts, such as rhino horns or ivory. If you purchase an antique that's made partly or wholly of ivory, you must obtain a CITES preconvention certificate that clearly states the item is at least 100 years old. The import of zebra skin or other tourist products also requires a CITES permit.

MONEY MATTERS

Most safaris are paid in advance, so you need money only to cover personal purchases and gratuities. (The cash you take should include small denominations, like $1, $5, and $10, for tips.) If you're self-driving, note that many places prefer to be paid in the local currency, so make sure you change money where you can. MasterCard and Visa are accepted almost everywhere. Neither Diners Club nor Discover is recognized in most African countries. ■TIP→ It's a good idea to notify your credit-card company that you'll be traveling to Africa so that unusual-looking transactions aren't denied.

10

FIGURING YOUR BUDGET

Consider three things: your flight, the actual safari costs, and extras. You can have a low-budget self-catering trip in a national park or spend a great deal for a small, exclusive camp. Almost every market has high-priced options as well as some economical ones.

Besides airfare and safari costs, make sure you budget for visas, tips, medications, and other sundries such as souvenirs. You'll likely stay at a hotel in your arrival/departure city on your first and last nights in Africa. Rates range from $50 for basic accommodations to $750 a night in the most luxurious hotels. If you do splurge on your safari, but want to keep costs down elsewhere, look for special offers—sometimes South African lodges will throw in a free night's accommodation in Cape Town, for example.

Plan to spend $15–$25 a day per traveler on gratuities *(see Tipping below)*. In South Africa tips are on the higher end of this range and usually are paid in rand; you may also use U.S. dollars for tips, however. Elsewhere in southern Africa, U.S. currency is preferred.

SAFARIS ON A SHOESTRING BUDGET

Don't let a tight budget deter you. There are many opportunities for great big-game experiences without going over the top. And, you won't have to completely abandon the idea of comfort and style either. Here are some money-saving tips that every budget can appreciate.

Drive yourself and/or self-cater. The least expensive option is to choose a public game park—Kruger National Park in South Africa, for example— where you drive yourself and self-cater (shop for and prepare all meals yourself). Most South Africans travel this way. The price of this type of trip is approximately a tenth of that for private, fully inclusive lodges.

Driving yourself can be enjoyable, but keep in mind that you'll have to identify all the animals yourself, and you can't go off-road. Hire a guide from the main office of the park or opt for a game drive in a national park vehicle if you're in South Africa; it's inexpensive and will add a great deal to your experience.

Stay in accommodations outside the park or in a nearby town. This cuts down on the "mark-ups" that you may experience for the convenience of staying inside a park, and you can come into the park on day trips, so you won't miss anything.

Stick to one park or visit a lesser-known one, and keep your trip short. The high-end safari-goer may visit up to four different parks in different terrains and areas of the country, but the budget traveler would do well to stick to just one. Lesser-known parks can be just as good as famous ones, and sometimes being far from the madding crowds is a luxury in itself. Many travelers tack a two- or three-day safari onto the end of a beach holiday; this is enough time to see the Big Five and get a good understanding of the animals you'll encounter.

Consider mobile-camping safaris. Travel is by 4x4 (often something that looks like a bus), and you sleep in tents at public or private campsites. There are different levels of comfort and service, and the price varies accordingly: at the lower end, you'll pitch your own tent and help with cooking; but with a full-service mobile-camping safari, your driver/ guide and a cook will do all the setup. The cost will also vary according to the number of people on the tour. You'll really feel at one with nature and the wildlife if you take this option, but you'll need to be able to put up with a certain level of roughing it. A full-service safari costs in the region of $200–$500 a day, depending on the comfort level.

Book a private lodge in the off-season. Many lodges—South Africa's Sabi Sands area, for example—cost about $800 per person per night during the high season but can drop to about $500 a night during the slower months of July and August; on average savings can be 30%–40%. In the rainy season, however, roads may be impassable in some areas and the wildlife hard to spot, so do your research beforehand. Sometimes, the high season merely correlates with the European long vacation. In South Africa, the low season is from May to September, mostly because

Cape Town is cold and wet during this time. Regions north of the country, such as Kruger, are excellent for game-viewing during this time, as the winter is the dry season and grasses are short. Early morning and nighttime can get cold, but the daytime is usually dry and sunny. You'll also have the benefit of fewer crowds, although if you're very social, you may find the off-season too quiet. If you're a honeymooner, it's perfect.

Cheap flights are out there, but you'll have to work for them. Aggregators such as Skyscanner.net and ebookers.com can help you search for the best fares that meet your requirements. American travelers can sometimes save money by flying through Europe. Book a flight to a regional hub like Nairobi or Johannesburg, and then catch a connecting flight to your destination. South Africa's budget airline, Kulula Airlines (⊕ *www. kulula.com*), flies from South Africa to Kenya, Namibia, Zambia, and Zimbabwe. For flights to South Africa, look into flying via Dubai or Doha. You'll add extra time to your flight, but you could save big. Always book at least two months in advance, especially during the high season.

Budget for all aspects of your trip and watch out for hidden extras. Most safaris are all-inclusive, so you don't think about the cost of your sundowner drink, snacks on your game drive, or cocktails at mealtime. However, some lodges charge extra for drinks and excursions. You can keep your costs down by going to a place where things are à la carte and pay only for the things you deem important. ■TIP→ **Local beer is usually cheap, but wines are often imported (outside of South Africa) and are quite expensive.**

Book your trip locally, or at the last minute. Last-minute deals can offer massive discounts, as long as you're prepared to be flexible about everything to do with your trip. Alternatively, book a trip locally once you're at your destination. You can also gather a group of people at your lodging and do a group booking. This way you'll have the benefit of a guide, too, with the cost shared among a number of people. You can also save money by booking with a tour operator that is based in the country you are visiting, as you will be cutting out the commission charged by an American agent. Make sure that you thoroughly research your prospective tour operator first, however, to ensure they have a consistently good reputation.

10

TIPPING

Ranger/Guide: About $20 per person, per day.

General staff: Roughly $15 a day (per couple) into the general tip box, and $15 each to your tracker and butler (if applicable), and $15 per trip for a vehicle transfer. (Note that some safari operators, such as Micato, include tips in their price, so you don't have to worry about carrying around the correct denominations.)

It's also nice if you bring thank-you cards from home to include with the tip as a personal touch. Fodor's Forum member atravelynn adds, "Put bills in an envelope for your guide and in a separate envelope with your name on it for the camp staff. Sometimes the camps have envelopes, but bringing some from home is also a good idea."

PASSPORTS AND VISAS

A valid passport is a must for travel to any African country. ■TIP→ Certain countries, such as South Africa, won't let you enter with a soon-to-expire passport; also, you need two blank pages in your passport to enter South Africa. If you don't have a passport, apply immediately, because the process takes approximately five to six weeks. For a greatly increased fee, the application process can be shortened to as little as one week, but leaving this detail to the last minute can be stressful. If you have a passport, check the expiration date. If it's due to expire within six months of your return date, you need to renew it at once.

TRAVEL INSURANCE

You may want to consider a comprehensive travel-insurance policy in addition to any primary insurance you already have. Travel insurance incorporates trip cancellation; trip interruption or travel delay; loss or theft of, or damage to, baggage; baggage delay; medical expenses; emergency medical transportation; and collision damage waiver if renting a car. These policies are offered by most travel-insurance companies in one comprehensive policy and vary in price based on both your total trip cost and your age.

It's important to note that travel insurance doesn't always include coverage for threats of a terrorist incident or for any war-related activity. It's important that you speak with your operator before you book to find out how they would handle such occurrences. For example, would you be fully refunded if your trip was canceled because of war or a threat of a terrorist incident? Would your trip be postponed at no additional cost to you?

■TIP→ Purchase travel insurance within seven days of paying your initial trip deposit. For most policies this will not only ensure your trip deposit, but also cover you for any preexisting medical conditions.

Many travel agents and tour operators stipulate that travel insurance is mandatory if you book your trip through them. This coverage isn't only for your financial protection in the event of a cancellation but also for coverage of medical emergencies and medical evacuations due to injury or illness, which often involve use of jet aircraft with hospital equipment and doctors on board and can amount to many thousands of dollars.

Consider signing up with a medical-evacuation assistance company. A membership in one of these companies gets you doctor referrals, emergency evacuation or repatriation, 24-hour hotlines for medical consultation, and other assistance. International SOS and AirMed International provide evacuation services and medical referrals. MedjetAssist offers medical evacuation.

VACCINATIONS

The Centers for Disease Control, or CDC, has an extremely helpful and informative website where you can find out country by country what you'll need. Remember that the CDC is going to be extremely conservative, so it's a good idea to meet with a trusted health-care professional to decide what you'll really need, which will be determined by your itinerary.

Keep in mind that there's a time frame for vaccines. You should see your health provider four to six weeks before you leave for your trip. Also keep in mind that vaccines and prescriptions could run you anywhere from $1,000 to $2,000. It's important to factor this into your budget when planning, especially if your plans include a large group.

You must be up-to-date with all of your routine shots such as the measles/mumps/rubella (MMR) vaccine, and diphtheria/pertussis/tetanus (DPT) vaccine. If you're not up-to-date, usually a simple booster shot will bring you up to par. If you're traveling to northern Kenya December through June, don't be surprised if your doctor advises you to get inoculated against meningitis, as this part of the continent tends to see an outbreak during this time.

We can't stress enough the importance of taking malaria prophylactics. But be warned that all malaria medications aren't equal. Chloroquine is *not* an effective antimalarial drug. And halofantrine (marketed as Halfan), which is widely used overseas to treat malaria, has serious heart-related side effects, including death. The CDC recommend that you do *not* use halofantrine. Their website has a comprehensive list of the different malaria medications available, and which are recommended for each country. *For more information on malaria, or other health issues while on safari, see Health below.*

HEPATITIS A AND B AND OTHER BOOSTERS

Hepatitis A can be transmitted via contaminated seafood, water, or fruits and vegetables. According to the CDC, hepatitis A is the most common vaccine-preventable disease in travelers. Immunization consists of a series of two shots received six months apart. You only need to have received the first one before you travel. This should be given at least four weeks before your trip.

The CDC recommends vaccination for hepatitis B only if you might be exposed to blood (if you're a health-care worker, for example), have sexual contact with the local population, stay longer than six months, or risk exposure during medical treatment. As needed, you should receive booster shots for tetanus-diphtheria (every 10 years), measles (you're usually immunized as a child), and polio (you're usually immunized as a child).

YELLOW FEVER

Some countries will require you to present a valid yellow-fever inoculation certificate if prior to arrival you traveled to a region infected with yellow fever.

10

PACKING

You'll be allowed one duffel-type bag, approximately 36 inches by 18 inches and a maximum of 26 kilos (57 pounds)—less on some airlines, so it's essential you check ahead—so that it can be easily packed into the baggage pods of a small plane. A personal-effects bag can go on your lap. Keep all your documents and money in this personal bag.

■ TIP→ **At O.R. Tambo International Airport in Johannesburg and Cape Town International Airport you can store your bags at Bagport (www. bagport.co.za).** The cost is approximately $8 per bag per day, and the facility is open 24 hours a day, seven days a week. Many travelers also pay to have their luggage wrapped in shrinkwrap, but locking your suitcase should be sufficient.

BINOCULARS

Binoculars are essential and come in many types and sizes. You get what you pay for, so avoid buying a cheap pair—the optics will be poor and the lenses usually don't stay aligned for long, especially if they get bumped, which they will on safari. Whatever strength you choose, pick the most lightweight pair, otherwise you'll be in for neck and shoulder strain. Take them with you on a night drive; you'll get great visuals of nocturnal animals and birds by the light of the tracker's spotlight. Many people find that when they start using binoculars and stop documenting each trip detail on film, they have a much better safari experience.

CLOTHING

You should need only three changes of clothing for an entire trip; almost all safaris include laundry as part of the package. If you're self-driving you can carry more, but washing is still easy, especially if you use drip-dry fabrics that need no ironing. On mobile safaris you can wear tops and bottoms more than once, and either bring enough underwear to last a week between lodges, or wash as you go in the bathroom sink. Unless there's continual rain (unlikely), clothes dry overnight in the hot, dry African air.

■TIP→ **In certain countries—Botswana and Tanzania, for example—the staff won't wash undergarments because it's against cultural custom.**

For game walks, pack sturdy but light walking shoes or boots—in most cases durable sneakers suffice for this option. For a walking-based safari, you need sturdy, lightweight boots. Buy them well in advance of your trip so you can break them in. If possible, isolate the clothes used on your walk from the remainder of the clean garments in your bag. Bring a couple of large white plastic garbage bags for dirty laundry.

ELECTRICITY

Most of southern Africa is on 220/240-volt alternating current (AC). The plug points are round. However, there are both large 15-amp three-prong sockets (with a ground connection) and smaller 5-amp two-prong sockets. Most lodges have adapter plugs, especially for recharging camera batteries; check before you go, or purchase a universal plug adapter before you leave home.

Safari hotels in the Serengeti, the private reserve areas outside Kruger National Park, and the less rustic private lodges in South Africa are likely to provide you with plug points and plugs, and some offer hair dryers and electric-razor sockets as well (check this before you go). Lodges on limited generator and solar power are usually able to charge cameras, as long as you have the right plug.

TOILETRIES AND SUNDRIES

Most hotels and game lodges provide toiletries such as soap, shampoo, and insect repellent, so you don't need to overpack these items. In the larger lodges in South Africa's national parks and private game reserves, stores and gift shops are fairly well stocked with clothing and guidebooks; in self-drive and self-catering areas, shops also carry food and drink. Many lodges have small shops with a selection of books, clothing, and curios.

ON SAFARI

Your safari will be one of the most memorable trips you'll ever take, and it's essential that your African experience matches the one you've always imagined. Nothing should be left to chance, and that includes where you'll stay and how you'll get around.

The whos, whats, and hows still need to come into focus. If you have questions like, "Where's the best place to sit in a game-drive vehicle? Can you get near a honey badger? Where do you go to the bathroom in the bush?," then read on.

By the way, "bush" is a term used to describe the natural setting of your safari—be it in forests, plains, or on riverbanks. The expression "going to the bush" means going away from urban areas and into the wilderness.

ACCOMMODATIONS

The days are long gone when legendary 19th-century explorer Dr. David Livingstone pitched his travel-stained tent under a tree and ate his sparse rations. But whether you go simple in a basic safari tent with an adjacent bucket shower and long-drop toilet, choose ultracomfort in a megatent or canvas-and-thatch chalet, or go totally over the top in a glass-walled aerie-cum-penthouse with a state-of-the-art designer interior, you'll still feel very much part of the bush.

LUXURY LODGES

Some would say that using the word "luxury" with "safari lodge" is redundant, as all such lodges fall into this category. But there's luxurious, and then there's *luxurious*. Options in the latter category range from *Out of Africa*–type accommodations with antique furniture, crystal, and wrought-iron chandeliers to thatch-roofed stone chalets, Tuscan villas, and suites that wouldn't seem out of place in midtown Manhattan. In nearly all, you can expect to find air-conditioning; in many there will be a small library, a spa, a gift shop, and Internet service—often in a "business center" (a computer in the main lodge) or Wi-Fi. You may even have your own plunge pool.

PERMANENT TENTED CAMPS

Think luxurious, oh-so-comfortable, and spacious ... in a tent. This is no ordinary tent, though. Each has its own bathroom, usually with an outdoor shower; a wooden deck with table and chairs that overlooks the bush; carpet or wooden floors; big "windows"; and an inviting four-poster (usually) bed with puffy pillows and fluffy blankets (for those cold winter months). The public space will comprise a bar, a lounge, dining areas, viewing decks, usually a pool, and a curio shop. Some will have Wi-Fi, air-conditioning, and private plunge pools.

MOBILE TENTED CAMPS

This option varies enormously. You could have the original, roomy walk-in dome tent (complete with canvas bedrolls, crisp cotton bedding on G.I. stretchers, open-air flush toilets, and bucket showers) that's ready and waiting for you at day's end. Or you could have luxury tents (with crystal chandeliers, antique rugs, and shining silver) that stay in one place for a few months during peak seasons. They're all fully serviced (the staff travels with the tents), and you'll dine under the stars or sip coffee as the sun rises.

10

NATIONAL PARK ACCOMMODATIONS

What you'll get in this category depends on which park you're in and what type of lodgings you're looking for. Accommodations can vary from campsites to simple one-room rondavels, or round huts, with en suite bathrooms; safari tents to two- to four-bed cottages; or possibly a top-of-the-range guesthouse that sleeps eight people. With the exception of some camping sites, and some places in South Africa, all national-park accommodations are fully serviced with staff to look after you.

CHILDREN ON SAFARI

Most safari operators and private game reserves don't accept children under a certain age, usually under 8, but sometimes the age limit is as high as 12. This age limit is largely for safety reasons. Animals often respond, not in a positive manner, to something that is younger, slower, or smaller than they are. And even though you might think your six- or seven-year-old adores all sorts of animals and bugs, you'd be surprised how overwhelmed kids can become, out of the comfort of their home and backyard, by the size and multitude of African insects and wildlife.

Take into account, also, that when you're following a strange schedule (with jet lag) and getting in and out of small planes, safari vehicles, boats, and the like with other people whom you probably won't know, there often is no time to deal with recalcitrant children—and fussing will, you can be guaranteed, annoy the other people in your plane or lodge, who have spent a great deal of money for what may be a once-in-a-lifetime safari trip.

One option, if you can afford it, is to book a private safari where no other people are involved and you dictate the schedule. Many private lodges will rent you the entire property for the length of your stay; this is often the only way these camps allow children under age eight on safari. At the very least, a camp will require that you pay for a private safari vehicle and guide if you have children under 12. Be advised that, even if you're renting the whole camp, babies and toddlers still aren't allowed out on game-viewing trips.

Another great family option is to stay with &Beyond, a safari operator with children's programs at several of its upscale camps throughout South and East Africa. While you follow your own program, your kids pursue their own wilderness activities; and you all meet up later for meals and other activities.

A much cheaper alternative is also one of the most enjoyable for a safari as a family: a self-driving trip where you stay at national parks. No destination is better in this regard than Kruger National Park in South Africa, where there are comfortable accommodations and lots of other families around. You'll be able to set your own schedule, rent a cottage large enough for the entire family, and buy and prepare food you know your children will eat.

It's best not to visit malarial areas with children under age 10. Young kidneys are especially vulnerable to both the effects of malaria and the side effects of malaria prophylactics. You might opt to practice stringent nonchemical preventive measures, but know the risks: malaria's effects on young children are much worse than they are on older people.

COMMUNICATIONS

You will notice that pretty much everyone in Africa has a cell phone, and areas with 3G reception are increasing rapidly and can include remote areas. Don't count on it, though. This is Africa, and networks can be down. If you urgently need to get in touch with home, most camps have a radio or satellite phone.

GAME DRIVES

In most regions the best time to find game is in the early morning and early evening, when the animals are most active, although old Africa hands will tell you that you can come across good game at any time of day. Stick to the philosophy "you never know what's around the next corner," and keep your eyes and ears wide open all the time. If your rest camp offers guided night drives on open vehicles with spotlights—go for it. You'll rarely be disappointed, seeing not only big game but also a lot of fascinating little critters that surface only at night. Book your night drive in advance or as soon as you get to camp.

Arm yourself with specialized books on mammals and birds rather than a more general one that tries to cover too much. Airports, lodges, and camp shops stock a good range, but try to bring one with you and do a bit of boning up in advance. Any bird guide by Ken Newman (Struik Publishers) and the *Sasol Guide to Birds* are recommended.

Many national parks have reception areas with charts that show the most recent sightings of wildlife in the area. To be sure you see everything you want to, stop at the nearest reception and ask about a spotting chart, or just chat with the other drivers, rangers, and tourists you may encounter there, who can tell you what they've seen and where.

BATHROOM BREAKS

On your game drive you'll very likely be pointed to a nearby bush (which the ranger checks out before you use it). Tissues and toilet paper are usually available in the vehicle (but you may want to make sure). Sometimes there might be a toilet—well, actually, it'll very likely be a hole in the ground below a toilet seat—called drop toilets. Bury any paper you use. If you have an emergency, ask your ranger to stop the vehicle and he or she will scout a suitable spot.

GAME RANGERS AND TRACKERS

Game rangers (sometimes referred to as guides) tend to be of two types: those who've come to conservation by way of hunting and those who are professional conservationists. In both cases they have vast experience with and knowledge of the bush and the animals that inhabit it. Rangers often work in conjunction with trackers, who spot animals, and advise the rangers where to go. Often a tracker will be busy searching out animal tracks, spoor, and other clues to nearby wildlife while the ranger drives and discusses the animals and their environment. Rangers often communicate with each other via radio when there's been a good sighting.

The quality of your bush experience depends heavily on your guide or game ranger and tracker. A ranger wears many hats while on safari: he's there to entertain you, protect you, and put you as close to the wilderness as possible while serving as bush mechanic, first-aid specialist, and host. He'll often eat meals with you, will explain animal habits

10

and behavior while out in the bush, and, if you're on foot, will keep you alive in the presence of an excitable elephant, buffalo, hippo, or lion. This is no small feat, and each ranger has his particular strengths. Because of the intensity of the safari experience, with its exposure to potentially dangerous animals and tricky situations, your relationship with your guide or ranger is one of trust, friendliness, and respect. Misunderstandings may sometimes occur, but you're one step closer to ensuring that all goes well if you know the protocols and expectations.

VEHICLES ON GAME DRIVES

Your safari transportation is determined by your destination and could range from custom-made game-viewing vehicles (full-service safari) to a combi or minivan (basic safari or self-drive). There shouldn't be more than six people per vehicle. To make sure you experience every view, suggest to your ranger that visitors rotate seats for each drive. Be warned if you're going it alone: roads in Africa range from superb to bone crunching. Plan your route carefully, arm yourself with reliable maps, and get up-to-date road conditions before you go.

In closed vehicles, which are used by private touring companies operating in Kruger National Park, sit as close to the driver-guide as possible so you can get in and out of the vehicle more easily and get the best views.

HEALTH

The Travel Health Online website is a good source to check out before you travel because it compiles primarily health and some safety information from a variety of official sources, and was created by a medical publishing company. The CDC has information on health risks associated with almost every country on the planet, as well as what precautions to take. The World Health Organization (WHO) is the health arm of the United Nations and has information by topic and by country. Its clear, well-written publication *International Travel and Health,* which you can download from the website, covers everything you need to know about staying healthy abroad.

DEHYDRATION AND OVERHEATING

The African sun is hot and the air is dry, and sweat evaporates quickly in these conditions. You might not realize how much bodily fluid you're losing as a result. Wear a hat, lightweight clothing, and sunscreen—all of which will help your body cope with high temperatures. If you're prone to low blood sugar or have a sensitive stomach, consider bringing along rehydration salts, available at camping stores, to balance your body's fluids and keep you going when you feel listless.

Drink at least two to three quarts of water a day, and in extreme heat conditions as much as three to four quarts of water or juice. Drink more if you're exerting yourself physically. Alcohol is dehydrating, so try to limit consumption on hot or long travel days. If you do overdo it at dinner with wine or spirits, or even caffeine, you need to drink even more water to recover the fluid lost as your body processes the alcohol. Antimalarial medications are also very dehydrating, so it's important to drink water while you're taking this medicine.

Don't rely on thirst to tell you when to drink; people often don't feel thirsty until they're a little dehydrated. At the first sign of dry mouth, exhaustion, or headache, drink water, because dehydration is the likely culprit. ■**TIP→ To test for dehydration, pinch the skin on the back of your hand and see if it stays in a peak; if it does, you're dehydrated.** Drink a solution of ½ teaspoon salt and 4 tablespoons sugar dissolved in a quart of water to replace electrolytes.

Heat cramps stem from a low salt level due to excessive sweating. These muscle pains usually occur in the abdomen, arms, or legs. When a child says he can't take another step, ask if he has cramps. When cramps occur, stop all activity and sit quietly in a cool spot and drink water. Don't do anything strenuous for a few hours after the cramps subside. If heat cramps persist for more than an hour, seek medical assistance.

INSECTS

In summer ticks may be a problem, even in open areas close to cities. If you intend to walk or hike anywhere, use a suitable insect repellent. After your walk, examine your body and clothes for ticks, looking carefully for pepper ticks, which are tiny but may cause tick-bite fever. If you're bitten, keep an eye on the bite. Most people suffer no more than an itchy bump, so don't panic. If the tick was infected, however, the bite will swell, itch, and develop a black necrotic center. This is a sure sign that you'll develop tick-bite fever, which usually hits after about 8 to 12 days. Symptoms may be mild or severe, depending on the patient. This disease isn't usually life-threatening in healthy adults, but it's horribly unpleasant. ■**TIP→ Check your boots for spiders and other crawlies and shake your clothes out before getting dressed.**

Always keep a lookout for mosquitoes. Even in nonmalarial areas they're extremely irritating. When walking anywhere in the bush, watch out for snakes. If you see one, give it a wide berth and you should be fine. Snakes really bite only when they're taken by surprise, so you don't want to step on a napping mamba.

INTESTINAL UPSET

Micro-fauna and -flora differ in every region of Africa, so if you drink unfiltered water, add ice to your soda, or eat fruit from a roadside stand, you might get traveler's diarrhea. All reputable hotels and lodges have filtered, clean tap water or provide sterilized drinking water, and nearly all camps and lodges have supplies of bottled water. If you're traveling outside organized safari camps in rural Africa or are unsure of local water, carry plenty of bottled water and follow the CDC's advice for fruits and vegetables: boil it, cook it, peel it, or forget it. If you're going on a mobile safari, ask about drinking water.

10

MALARIA

The most serious health problem facing travelers is malaria. The risk is medium at the height of the summer and very low in winter. All travelers heading into malaria-endemic regions should consult a health-care professional at least one month before departure for advice. Unfortunately, the malarial agent *Plasmodium* seems to be able to develop a hardy resistance to new prophylactic drugs quickly, so the best prevention is to avoid being bitten by mosquitoes in the first place.

After sunset, wear light-color (mosquitoes and tsetse flies are attracted to dark surfaces), loose, long-sleeve shirts, long pants, and shoes and socks, and apply mosquito repellent (containing DEET) generously. Always sleep in a mosquito-proof room or tent, and if possible, keep a fan going in your room. If you're pregnant or trying to conceive, some malaria medicines are safe to use but in general it's best to avoid malaria areas entirely.

If you've been bitten by an infected mosquito, you can expect to feel the effects anywhere from 7 to 90 days afterward. Typically you'll feel like you have the flu, with worsening high fever, chills and sweats, headache, and muscle aches. In some cases this is accompanied by abdominal pain, diarrhea, and a cough. If it's not treated you could die. It's possible to treat malaria after you've contracted it, but this shouldn't be your long-term strategy for dealing with the disease. ■TIP→ **If you feel ill even several months after you return home, tell your doctor that you've been in a malaria-infected area.**

MEDICAL CARE AND MEDICINE

As a foreigner, you'll be expected to pay in full for any medical services, so check your existing health plan to see whether you're covered while abroad, and supplement it if necessary. South African doctors are generally excellent. The equipment and training in private clinics rival the best in the world, but public hospitals tend to suffer from overcrowding and underfunding and are best avoided.

MOTION SICKNESS

If you're prone to motion sickness, be sure to examine your safari itinerary closely. Though most landing strips for chartered planes aren't paved but rather grass, earth, or gravel, landings are smooth most of the time. ■TIP→ **When you fly in small planes, take a sun hat and a pair of sunglasses.** If you sit in the front seat next to the pilot, or on the side of the sun, you'll experience harsh glare that could give you a severe headache and exacerbate motion sickness.

PEOPLE WITH DISABILITIES

Having a disability doesn't mean you can't go on safari. It's important, however, to plan carefully to ensure that your needs can be adequately met. South African lodges, especially the high-end private ones, are the easiest to navigate and have the fewest steps. MalaMala Game Reserve is completely accessible and even has specially equipped four-wheel-drive safari vehicles with harness seat belts. Many of Kruger's camps have special accommodations.

SEASONS

The seasons in sub-Saharan Africa are opposite of those in North America. Summer is December through March, autumn is April and May, winter is June through September, and spring is October and November.

HIGH SEASON/DRY SEASON

High season, also called dry season, refers to the winter months in East and South Africa when there's little to no rain at all. Days are sunny and bright, but the nights are cool. In the desert, temperatures can plummet to below freezing, but you'll be snug and warm in your tent wherever you stay. The landscape will be barren and dry (read: not very attractive), but vegetation is low and surface water is scarce, making it easier to spot game. This is the busiest tourist time.

The exception is South Africa, where high season is linked with the summer vacation schedules of South Africans (December–mid-January), and both the European summer vacations (July and August) and Christmas holidays (December and January) in the Seychelles.

LOW SEASON/RAINY SEASON

When we say "low season," we're saying that this is the rainy season. Although the rains are intermittent—often occurring in late afternoon—the bush and vegetation are high and it's more difficult to spot game. It can also get very hot and humid during this time. However, the upside is that there are far fewer tourists, lodge rates are much cheaper (often half price), and the bush is beautifully lush and green. Plus there are lots of baby animals, and if you're a birder all the migrant species are back from their winter habitats. Seychelles' low season occurs during the cusp times of February through April, October, and November, which can be the nicest times to visit in terms of both weather (especially April and November) and better prices.

SHOULDER SEASON

The shoulder season occurs between summer and winter; it's fall in the United States. The rains are just beginning, tourist numbers are decreasing, and the vegetation is starting to die off. Lodges will offer cheaper rates.

To find out exactly what the weather will be for your destination, **African Weather Forecasts** (⊕ *www.africanweather.net*) lists weather information for the entire continent.

WILDLIFE SAFETY AND RESPECT

Nature is neither kind nor sentimental. Don't be tempted to interfere with natural processes. The animals are going about the business of survival in a harsh environment, and you can unwittingly make this business more difficult. Don't get too close to the animals and don't try to help them cross some perceived obstacle; you have no idea what it's really trying to do or where it wants to go. If you're intrusive, you could drive animals away from feeding and, even worse, from drinking at water holes, where they're very skittish and vulnerable to predators. That time at the water hole may be their only opportunity to drink that day.

Never feed any wild creature. Not a cute monkey, not an inquisitive baboon, not a baby tree squirrel, or a young bird out of its nest. In some camps and lodges, however, animals have gotten used to being fed or steal food. The most common animals in this category are baboons and monkeys; in some places they sneak into huts, tents, and even occupied vehicles to snatch food. If you see primates around, keep all food out of sight, and keep your windows rolled up. (If a baboon manages to get into your vehicle, he will trash the interior as he searches for food and use the vehicle as a toilet.)

Never try to get an animal to pose with you. This is probably the biggest cause of death and injury on safaris, when visitors don't listen to or believe the warnings from their rangers or posted notices in public parks. Regardless of how cute or harmless they may look, these animals aren't tame. An herbivore hippo, giraffe, or ostrich can kill you just as easily as a lion, elephant, or buffalo can.

10

Immersion in the African safari lands is a privilege. In order to preserve this privilege for later generations, it's important that you view wildlife with minimal disturbance and avoid upsetting the delicate balance of nature at all costs. You're the visitor, so act like you would in someone else's home: respect their space. Caution is your most trusted safety measure. Keep your distance, keep quiet, and keep your hands to yourself, and you should be fine.

NIGHTTIME SAFETY

Never sleep out in the open in any area with wildlife. If you're sleeping in a tent, make sure it's fully closed as in zipped or snapped shut; if it's a small tent, place something between you and the side of the wall to prevent an opportunistic bite from the outside. Also, if you're menstruating, be sure to dispose of your toiletries somewhere other than in or near your tent. All in all, if you're in your tent and not exposed, you should be quite safe. Few people lose their lives to lions or hyenas. Malaria is a much more potent danger, so keep your tent zipped up tight at night to keep out mosquitoes.

Never walk alone. Most camps and lodges insist that an armed ranger accompany you to and from your accommodation at night, and rightly so.

TRAVEL SMART
SOUTH AFRICA

GETTING HERE AND AROUND

Countless cities, towns, streets, parks, and more have gotten or will get new monikers, both to rid the country of names that recall the apartheid era and to honor the previously unsung. The names in this book were accurate at time of writing but may still change.

■ AIR TRAVEL

Some South Africa–bound flights from U.S. cities have refueling stops en route, and sometimes those stops can be delayed. Don't plan anything on the ground too rigidly after arriving; leave yourself a cushion for a connecting flight to a game lodge. At this writing, only South African Airways and Delta provide direct service from the United States to South Africa, but flights routed through Europe may be more pleasant since they allow you a stop en route.

In peak season (midsummer, which is from December to the end of February, and South African school vacations), give yourself at least a half hour extra at the airport for domestic flights, as the check-in lines can be endless—particularly on flights to the coast at the start of vacations and back to Johannesburg's O. R. Tambo International Airport at the end.

If you are returning home with souvenirs, leave time for a V.A.T. (Value-Added Tax) inspection before you join the line for your international flight check-in. And it's always a good idea to check what you can and cannot carry onto the plane. ■TIP➜ There are fairly long distances between gates and terminals at Johannesburg's O. R. Tambo, particularly between the international and domestic terminals, so clear security before stopping for a snack or shopping, as you don't want to scramble for your flight.

The longest domestic flight within South Africa is only two hours.

If you are visiting a game lodge deep in the bush, you will be arriving by light plane—and you will be restricted in what you can bring. Excess luggage can usually be stored with the operator until your return. Don't just gloss over this: charter operators take weight very seriously, and some will charge you for an extra ticket if you insist on bringing excess baggage (see Charter Flights, below).

Airline Security Issues Transportation Security Administration. ⊕ www.tsa.gov.

AIRPORTS

Most international flights arrive at and depart from Johannesburg's O. R. Tambo International Airport, 19 km (12 miles) from the city. The country's other major airports are in Cape Town and Durban, but international flights departing from Cape Town often stop in Johannesburg. O.R. Tambo has a tourist information desk, a V.A.T. refund office, several ATMs, and a computerized accommodations service. Porters, who wear a bright-orange-and-navy-blue uniform with an Airports Company of South Africa badge, work exclusively for tips (R5 or R10 a bag). If you're leaving O. R. Tambo's international terminal (Terminal A), the domestic terminal (Terminal B) is connected by a busy and fairly long walkway. ■TIP➜ Allow 10–15 minutes' walking time between international and domestic terminals.

The Cape Town and Durban airports are much smaller and more straightforward. Cape Town International is 19 km (12 miles) southeast of the city, and King Shaka International Airport, Durban, is 35 km (22 miles) north of the city. If you are traveling to or from either Johannesburg or Cape Town airport (and, to a lesser extent, Durban) be aware of the time of day. Traffic can be horrendous between 7 and 9 in the morning and between about 3:30 and 6 in the evening.

Just 40 km (25 miles) outside Johannesburg's city center in the northern suburbs,

Lanseria International Airport is closer to Sandton than O. R. Tambo and handles executive jets, company jets, domestic scheduled flights to and from Cape Town, and some charter flights to safari camps. It has a 24-hour customs and immigration counter, a café, and a high-end flight store. It's a popular alternative for visiting dignitaries and other VIPs.

The other major cities are served by small airports that are really easy to navigate. Port Elizabeth is the main airport for the Eastern Cape, and George serves the Garden Route. Skukuza is the only airport located in Kruger National Park and is serviced by scheduled daily non-stop flights from Johannesburg and Cape Town. The next closest airports to Kruger National Park are Kruger Mpumalanga International Airport (also referred to as KMI Airport) in Mbombela (Nelspruit) and the small airports at Hoedspruit and Phalaborwa. Most airports are managed by the Airports Company of South Africa. *For more information, see individual destination chapters.*

Airport Information Airports Company of South Africa. ☎ 086/727–7888 *flight information* ⊕ *www.acsa.co.za.*

Domestic Airports Bram Fischer International Airport (*BFN*). ☎ 051/407–2200 ⊕ *www.acsa.co.za.*

International Airports Cape Town International Airport (*CPT*). ⊠ *Matroosfontein, Cape Town* ☎ 021/937–1200 ⊕ *www.capetown-airport.com.* **King Shaka International Airport** (*DUR*). ⊠ *King Shaka Dr., La Mercy* ☎ 032/436–6000 ⊕ *www.kingshakainternational.co.za.* **Lanseria International Airport** (*HLA*). ⊠ *Airport Rd., Lanseria, Johannesburg* ☎ 011/367–0300 ⊕ *www.lanseria.co.za.* **O. R. Tambo International Airport** (*JNB*). ⊠ *O. R. Tambo Airport Rd., Johannesburg* ☎ 011/921–6262 ⊕ *www.johannesburg-airport.com.*

For more information about airports and ground transportation, see Getting Here and Around in each chapter.

FLIGHTS

South Africa's international airline is South African Airways (SAA), which offers non-stop service between Johannesburg and New York–JFK (JFK) and Washington–Dulles (IAD), though some flights from Dulles make a stopover in Dakar, Senegal. Delta also offers nonstop service from the United States to South Africa. Flight times from the U.S. East Coast range from 15 hours (from Atlanta to Johannesburg on Delta) to almost 20 hours (on Delta via Amsterdam). When booking flights, check the routing carefully; some involve stopovers of an hour or two, which may change from day to day. European airlines serving South Africa are British Airways, KLM, Virgin Atlantic, Lufthansa, and Air France.

Three major domestic airlines have flights connecting South Africa's principal airports. SA Airlink and SA Express are subsidiaries of SAA, and Comair is a subsidiary of British Airways. Comair and SAA serve Livingstone, Zambia (for Victoria Falls); SAA serves Victoria Falls airport in Zimbabwe.

Recent years have seen an explosion of low-cost carriers serving popular domestic routes in South Africa with regularly scheduled flights. Kulula.com and Mango provide reasonably priced domestic air tickets if you book in advance.

Airlines Air France. ☎ 0861/340–340 in South Africa, 800/237–2747 in U.S. ⊕ www.airfrance.co.za. **British Airways.** ☎ 011/920–7525 in South Africa, 800/247–9297 in U.S. ⊕ www.britishairways.com. **Delta.** ☎ 011/408–8200 in South Africa, 800/241–4141 in U.S. ⊕ www.delta.com. **KLM.** ☎ 0860/247–747 in South Africa, 866/434–0320 in U.S. ⊕ www.klm.com. **Lufthansa.** ☎ 0861/842–538 in South Africa, 800/645–3880 in U.S. ⊕ www.lufthansa.com. **South African Airways.** ☎ 0860/003–146 in South Africa, 800/722–9675 in U.S. ⊕ www.flysaa.com. **United.** ☎ 011/463–1170 in South Africa, 800/864–8331 in U.S. ⊕ www.united.com. **Virgin Atlantic.** ☎ 011/340–3400 in South Africa, 800/862–8621 in U.S. ⊕ www.virginatlantic.com.

Domestic Airlines British Airways Comair. ☎ 011/921–0222 *in South Africa, 0860/435–922 toll-free in South Africa, 800/247–9297 in U.S.* ⊕ *www.britishairways.com.* **Kulula.** ☎ 086/158–5852 *in South Africa* ⊕ *www.kulula.com.* **Mango.** ☎ 011/086–6100 *in Johannesburg, 021/815–4100 in Cape Town, 086/101–0002 toll-free in South Africa* ⊕ *www.flymango.com.* **SA Airlink.** ☎ 011/451–7300 *in South Africa, 010/590–3170 in South Africa* ⊕ *www.flyairlink.com.* **SA Express.** ☎ 011/978–1111 *toll-free in South Africa* ⊕ *www.flyexpress.aero.*

CHARTER FLIGHTS

Charter companies are a common mode of transportation when getting to safari lodges and remote destinations throughout southern Africa. These aircraft are well maintained and are almost always booked by your lodge or travel agent. The major charter companies run daily shuttles from O. R. Tambo to popular tourism destinations, such as Kruger Park. On-demand flights are very expensive for independent travelers, as they require minimum passenger loads. If it's just two passengers, you will be charged for the vacant seats. Keep in mind that you probably won't get to choose the charter company you fly with. The aircraft you get depends on the number of passengers flying and can vary from very small (you will sit in the copilot's seat) to a much more comfortable commuter plane.

Because of the limited space and size of the aircraft, charter carriers observe strict luggage regulations: luggage must be soft-sided and weigh no more than 57 pounds (and often less); on many charter flights the weight cannot exceed 33 pounds.

African Ramble flies out of Plettenberg Bay and Port Elizabeth and will take direct bookings. **Federal Air** is the largest charter air company in South Africa; it's based at Johannesburg's O. R. Tambo International Airport and has its own efficient terminal with a gift shop, refreshments, and a unique, thatched-roof outdoor lounge. It also has branches in Cape Town, Durban, and Kruger Mpumalanga

International Airport in Mbombela (Nelspruit; near Kruger). **Wilderness Air** (previously **Sefofane**) is a Botswana-based fly-in charter company that will take you anywhere there's a landing strip from its base in Jo'burg's Lanseria Airport.

Charter Companies African Ramble. ☎ 083/375–6514, 083/375–6514 ⊕ *www.aframble.co.za.* **Federal Air.** ☎ 011/395–9000 ⊕ *www.fedair.com.* **Wilderness Air.** ⊕ *www.wilderness-air.com.*

∎ BUS TRAVEL

Greyhound, Intercape Mainliner, and Translux operate extensive bus networks that serve all major cities. The buses are comfortable, sometimes there are videos, and tea and coffee are served on board. Opt for First Class if possible. Travel times can be long; for example, Cape Town to Johannesburg takes 19 hours. Johannesburg to Durban, at about 7 hours, is less stressful. The Garden Route is less intense if you take it in stages, but the whole trip from Cape Town to Port Elizabeth takes 12 hours. Buses are usually pretty punctual. Greyhound and Intercape buses can be booked directly or through Computicket.

For travelers with a sense of adventure, a bit of time, and not too much money, the Baz Bus runs a daily hop-on/hop-off door-to-door service between backpackers' hostels around South Africa and other countries in the region. The rates are a bit higher than for the same distance on a standard bus, but you can break the journey up into a number of different legs, days or weeks apart, and the bus drops you off at some hostels so you don't need to find taxis, shuttles, or lifts. The Baz Bus offers both 7-day and 14-day unrestricted packages, an especially useful service if you're planning a long leg followed by a few short ones before returning to your starting point.

∎**TIP→** **It is illegal to smoke on buses in South Africa.**

DRIVING FROM	TO	RTE./DISTANCE
Cape Town	Port Elizabeth	769 km (478 miles)
Cape Town	Johannesburg	1,402 km (871 miles)
Johannesburg	Durban	583 km (361 miles)
Johannesburg	Kruger National Park	355 km (220 miles)
Kruger National Park	Victoria Falls, Zimbabwe	1,090 km (677 miles)
Johannesburg	Pretoria	58 km (36 miles)

Approximate one-way prices for all three major bus lines are from Cape Town to Tshwane (Pretoria) for R735; from Cape Town to Springbok for R400; Cape Town to George for R430; Cape Town to Port Elizabeth for R595; Johannesburg to Durban for R365; and Cape Town to Durban for R695. Baz Bus also runs direct routes between cities, with prices comparable to those of major bus lines.

Contacts Baz Bus. ☎ 021/422–5202, 086/122–9287 toll-free ⊕ www.bazbus.com. **Computicket.** ☎ 0861/915–8000 ⊕ www.computicket.co.za. **Greyhound.** ☎ 083/915–9000 ⊕ www.greyhound.co.za. **Intercape Mainliner.** ☎ 021/380–4400 ⊕ www.intercape.co.za. **Translux.** ☎ 0861/589–282 ⊕ www.translux.co.za.

■ CAR TRAVEL

South Africa has a superb network of multilane roads and highways, so driving can be a pleasure. Remember, though, that distances are vast, so guard against fatigue, which is an even bigger killer than alcohol. Toll roads, scattered among the main routes, charge anything from R10 to R80.

You can drive in South Africa for up to six months on any English-language license.

South Africa's Automobile Association publishes a range of maps, atlases, and travel guides, available for purchase on its website. Maps and map books are also available at all major bookstores.

The commercial website Drive South Africa has everything you need to know about driving in the country, including road safety and driving distances.

■TIP➔ Carjackings can and do occur with such frequency that certain high-risk areas are marked by permanent carjacking signs

Maps and Information Drive South Africa. ☎ 0860/000–060 ⊕ www.drivesouthafrica.co.za.

GASOLINE

Service stations (open 24 hours) are positioned at regular intervals along all major highways in South Africa. There are no self-service stations. In return, tip the attendant R5 (more if you've filled the tank). South Africa has a choice of unleaded or leaded gasoline, and many vehicles operate on diesel—be sure you get the right fuel. Gasoline is measured in liters, and the cost is higher than in the United States. When driving long distances, check your routes carefully, as the distances between towns—and hence gas stations—can be more than 100 miles.

PARKING

In the countryside, parking is mostly free, but you will almost certainly need to pay for parking in cities, which will probably run you about R10 per hour. Many towns have an official attendant (who should be wearing a vest of some sort) who will log the number of the spot you park in; you're asked to pay up front for the amount of time you expect to park. If the guard is unofficial, acknowledge them on arrival, ask them to look after your car, and pay a few rand when you return (they depend on these tips). At pay-and-display parking lots you pay in advance; other garages expect payment at the exit. Many (such as those at shopping malls and airports) require that you pay for your parking before you return to your car (at kiosks near the exits to the parking areas). Your receipt ticket allows you to exit. Just read the signs carefully.

ROAD CONDITIONS

South African roads are mostly excellent, but it's dangerous to drive at night in some rural areas, as roads are not always fenced and animals often stray onto the road. In very remote areas only the main road might be paved, whereas many secondary roads are of high-quality gravel. Traffic is often light in these areas, so be sure to bring extra water and carry a spare, a jack, and a tire iron (your rental car should come with these).

RULES OF THE ROAD

South Africans drive on the left-hand side of the road, British-style. That may be confusing at first, but having the steering wheel on the right helps to remind you that the driver should be closer to the middle of the road.

Throughout the country, the speed limit is 100 kph (60 mph) or 120 kph (about 75 mph) on the open road and usually 60 kph (35 mph) or 80 kph (about 50 mph) in towns. Of course, many people drive far faster than that. Wearing seat belts is required by law, and the legal blood-alcohol limit is 0.08 mg/100 ml, which means about one glass of wine puts you at the limit. It is illegal to talk on a handheld mobile phone while driving.

South African drivers tend to be aggressive and reckless, thinking nothing of tailgating at high speeds and passing on blind rises. Traffic accidents are a major problem.

If it's safe to do so, it's courteous for slow vehicles to move over onto the shoulder, which is separated from the road by a solid yellow line. (In built-up areas, however, road shoulders are occasionally marked by red lines. This is a strict "no-stopping" zone.) The more aggressive drivers expect this and will flash their lights at you if you don't. Where there are two lanes in each direction, remember that the right-hand lane is for passing.

In towns, minibus taxis can be quite unnerving, swerving in and out of traffic without warning to pick up customers. Stay alert at all times. Many cities use mini-traffic circles in lieu of four-way stops. These can be dangerous, particularly if you're not used to them. In theory, the first vehicle to the circle has the right-of-way; otherwise yield to the right. In practice, keep your wits about you at all times. In most cities traffic lights are on poles at the side of the street. In Johannesburg the lights are only on the far side of each intersection, so don't stop in front of the light or you'll be in the middle of the intersection.

In South African parlance, traffic lights are known as "robots," and what people refer to as the "pavement" is actually the sidewalk. Paved roads are just called roads. Gas is referred to as petrol, and gas stations are petrol stations.

RENTAL CARS

Renting a car gives you the freedom to roam freely and set your own timetable. Most of Cape Town's most popular destinations are an easy drive from the City Bowl. Many people enjoy the slow pace of exploring South Africa's Garden Route by car, or a few days meandering through the Winelands on their own.

Roads in South Africa are generally good, and rates are similar to those in the United States. Some companies charge more on weekends, so it's best to get a range of quotes before booking your car. Request car seats and extras such as GPS when you book, and ask for details on what to do if you have a mechanical problem or other emergency.

For a car with automatic transmission and air-conditioning, you'll pay slightly less for a car that doesn't have unlimited mileage. When comparing prices, make sure you're getting the same thing. Some companies quote prices without insurance, some include 80% or 90% coverage, and some quote with 100% protection. Get all terms in writing before you leave on your trip.

Most major international companies have offices in tourist cities and at international airports, and their vehicle types are the same range you'd find at home. There's no need to rent a 4x4 vehicle, as all roads are paved, including those in Kruger National Park, but for the best game-viewing, a van or 4x4 gives you a higher outlook.

Maui Motorhome Rentals offers fully equipped motor homes, camper vans, and 4x4 vehicles, many of which come totally equipped for a bush sojourn. Prices start at around R1,500 per day, not including insurance, and require a five-day minimum.

You can often save some money by booking a car through a broker, who will access the car from one of the main agencies. Smaller, local agencies often give a much better price, but the car must be returned in the same city. This is pretty popular in Cape Town but not so much in other centers.

To rent a car you need to be 23 years or older and have held a driver's license for three years. Younger international drivers can rent from some companies but will pay a penalty. You need to get special permission to take rental cars into neighboring countries (including Lesotho and Swaziland). Most companies allow additional drivers, but some charge.

Leave ample time to return your car when your trip is over. You shouldn't feel rushed when settling your bill. Be sure to get copies of your receipt.

CAR-RENTAL INSURANCE

In South Africa it's necessary to buy special insurance if you plan to cross borders into neighboring countries, but CDW and TDW (collision damage waiver and theft-damage waiver) are optional on domestic rentals. Any time you are considering crossing a border with your rental vehicle, you must inform the rental company ahead of time to fulfill any paperwork requirements and pay additional fees.

Emergency Services General emergency number. ☎ 112 from mobile phone, 10111 from landline, 107 in Cape Town only.

Local Agencies Car Mania. ☎ 021/447–3001 ⊕ www.carmania.co.za. **Maui Motorhome Rentals.** ☎ 011/230–5200, 021/385–1616 ⊕ www.maui.co.za. **Value Car Hire.** ☎ 021/386–7699 ⊕ www.valuerentalcar.com.

Major Agencies Avis. ☎ 0861/021–111, 011/387–8431 ⊕ www.avis.co.za. **Budget.** ☎ 011/387–8432 ⊕ www.budget.co.za. **Europcar.** ☎ 0861/131–000, 011/479–4000 ⊕ www.europcar.co.za. **Hertz.** ☎ 021/935–4800, 0861/600136 ⊕ www.hertz.co.za.

▎ TRAIN TRAVEL

Shosholoza Meyl operates an extensive system of passenger trains along eight routes that connect all major cities and many small towns in South Africa. Departures are usually limited to one per day, although trains covering minor routes leave less frequently. Distances are vast, so many journeys require overnight travel. The service is good and the trains are safe and well maintained, but this is far from a luxury option, except in Premier Classe, the luxury service that runs between Cape Town and Johannesburg and Port Elizabeth and between Jo'burg and Durban. In Premier Classe, sleeping compartments accommodate two to four travelers, and single compartments are also available. Compartments include air-conditioning, bedding, and limited room service (drinks only). The Jo'burg–Cape Town and Jo'burg–Durban routes have a compartment for vehicles (including 4x4s).

Tourist Class (the old First Class) has four-sleeper (bunks) and two-sleeper compartments. Don't expect air-conditioning, heat, or a shower in either class. Bathrooms are shared, compartments have a sink, and bedding can be rented. The dining car serves pretty ordinary food, but it's inexpensive.

We do not recommend Third Class or Economy Class (aka "sitter class") because that's what you do—up to 25 hours on a hard seat with up to 71 other people in the car, sharing two toilets and no shower.

You must reserve tickets in Premier Classe and Tourist Class, whereas sitter-class tickets require no advance booking. You can book up to 12 months in advance by telephone, with travel agents, at reservations offices in major cities, and at railway stations.

A fun way to see the country is on the Shongololo Express. The train is as basic as the Shosholoza Meyl trains, but while you sleep at night, it heads to a new destination. After breakfast, tour buses are loaded, and you explore the surroundings. In the evening, you reboard the train, have supper, and sleep while the train moves to the next stop. Trips include the Dune Adventure (the dunes of Namibia), the Good Hope Adventure (Cape attractions), and the Southern Cross Adventure (six African countries). Rates start at about R1,250 per person per night Johannesburg to Durban; R3,120 Johannesburg to Cape Town. By the way, a *shongololo* is a millipede.

Contacts Premier Classe. ☎ *011/774–4555* ⊕ *www.premierclasse.co.za.* **Shongololo Express.** ☎ *0861/777–014, 011/774–4555 outside South Africa* ⊕ *www.shongololo.com.* **Shosholoza Meyl.** ☎ *086/000–8888* ⊕ *www. shosholozameyl.co.za.*

LUXURY TRAIN TRIPS

South Africa's leisurely and divine luxury trains come complete with gold-and-brass-plated fixtures, oak paneling, and full silver service for every meal. The elegant Blue Train travels several routes, but the main one is between Cape Town and Tshwane (Pretoria). It departs once a week in each direction, takes 28 hours, and starts from R23,285 per person sharing one way (peak season). The fare includes all meals (extravagant three-course affairs), drinks (a full bar and great selection of South African wines), and excursions (usually a two-hour stop in Kimberley). Only caviar and French Champagne are excluded. The Blue Train

also goes to Tshwane/Hoedspruit/Tshwane from R11,595 per person sharing.

Rovos Rail's *Pride of Africa* runs from Cape Town to Tshwane every Monday (and sometimes other days). Fares are R18,950 for the 72-hour trip in Pullman Class; fancier suites cost up to R38,150. Rovos also includes all excursions, sumptuous meals, all drinks (except French Champagne), and excellent butler service, but whereas the Blue Train excels in modern luxury, the *Pride of Africa* creates an atmosphere of Victorian colonial charm (no cell phones or laptops in public spaces), and is the only luxury train in the world in which you can open the windows. Rovos also has a 9-day Cape Town–Swakopmund round-trip in April and May, and a 14-day epic Cape Town–Dar es Salaam loop in January, July, and September. Prices per person can reach R32,800 for the Royal Suite on the three-night, four-day trip from Cape Town to Victoria Falls.

All prices are for double occupancy; the single-occupancy supplement is 50%.

Contacts Blue Train. ☎ *012/334–8459 in Pretoria, 021/449–2672 in Cape Town, 973/832–4384 in U.S.* ⊕ *www.bluetrain.co.za.* **Rovos Rail.** ☎ *012/315–8242* ⊕ *www.rovos.com.*

ESSENTIALS

▌ACCOMMODATIONS

The Tourism Grading Council of South Africa is the official accreditation and grading body for accommodations in South Africa. However, you may still find some establishments clinging to other grading systems. Hotels, bed-and-breakfasts, guesthouses, and game lodges are graded on a star rating from one to five. Grading is not compulsory, and there are many excellent establishments that are not graded. Those that are given a grade are revisited annually; however, these marks are purely subjective and reflect the comfort level and quality of the surroundings.

Be warned that in southern Africa, words do not necessarily mean what you think they do. The term *lodge* is a particularly tricky one. A guest lodge or a game lodge is almost always an upmarket, full-service facility with loads of extra attractions. But the term *lodge* when applied to city hotels often indicates a minimum-service hotel, like the City and Town Lodges and Holiday Inn Garden Courts. A backpacker lodge, however, is essentially a hostel.

A *rondavel* can be a small cabin, often in a rounded shape, and its cousin, the *banda*, can be anything from a basic stand-alone structure to a Quonset hut. Think very rustic.

Be sure you understand the hotel's cancellation policy. Some places allow you to cancel without any kind of penalty—even if you prepaid to secure a discounted rate—if you cancel at least 24 hours in advance. Others require you to cancel a week in advance or penalize you the cost of one night. Small inns and B&Bs are most likely to require you to cancel far in advance. Always have written confirmation of your booking when you check in.

▌**TIP→** Most hotels allow children under a certain age to stay in their parents' room at no extra charge, but others charge for them as extra adults, and some don't allow children under 12 at all. Ask about the policy on children before checking in, and make sure you find out the cutoff age for discounts.

In South Africa, most accommodations from hotels to guesthouses do include a hearty English breakfast in the rate. Most game lodges include all meals, or they may be all-inclusive (including alcohol as well). All hotels listed have private bath unless otherwise noted.

BED-AND-BREAKFASTS

B&Bs are ubiquitous in South Africa. Many are very small and personalized. For more information, contact the Bed and Breakfast Association of South Africa (BABASA) or the Portfolio Collection, which represents more than 700 lodging options in South Africa and publishes a respected list of South Africa's best B&Bs that may also be useful; it offers a similar guide to small hotels and lodges.

Contacts BABASA. ☏ *072/947–8514, 012/480–2041* ⊕ *www.babasa.co.za.* **Portfolio Collection.** ☏ *021/701–9632* ⊕ *www. portfoliocollection.com.* **SA-Venues.** ⊕ *www. sa-venues.com.*

FARM STAYS

The Farm Stay website lists a range of farms with self-catering or bed-and-breakfast accommodations in rural areas. Activities on offer include game-viewing, bird-watching, hiking, biking, and horse riding.

Contact Farm Stay. ☏ *039/313–0770* ⊕ *www.farmstay.co.za.*

GAME LODGES

Game lodges in South Africa are often designed to fulfill your wildest wildlife fantasy. Top designers have created magical worlds in styles from African chic to throwback bush romance. At the highest end, you can enjoy dinner under starlight on your own deck, or swap stories around the boma (outdoor eating area) at night. For some people the first glimpse of their accommodations is a thrill to rival the best game-viewing.

GUESTHOUSES

The term *guesthouse* may conjure up the image of a flophouse, but in South Africa guesthouses are a cross between an inn and a B&B. Usually in residential neighborhoods, they offer an intimate experience that benefits from the proprietor's tastes and interests, often at a vast savings over hotels. A guesthouse manager might make special arrangements to drive you to an attraction, whereas a hotel might charge extra transportation fees. Long-term visitors tend to choose guesthouses, where they can meet other like-minded travelers who are interested in experiencing the country, not just checking off sites.

Contacts Guest House Accommodation of South Africa. ☎ 021/762–0880 ⊕ www. ghasa.co.za. **Sleeping Out.** ☎ 021/762–1543 ⊕ www.sleeping-out.co.za.

HOTELS

Your hotel in South Africa will be similar to one at home; the more you pay, the better the quality and amenities. As at home, peak seasons mean peak prices. There are many international chains represented in South Africa, so check with your frequent-stay program to see if you can get a better room or better rate. It might be more fun, though, to experience a local, or African, establishment.

Most hotel rates will include breakfast in the hotel's dining room, and in South Africa that means a full array of meats, cheeses, and eggs cooked to order—a little bonus that makes it easier to ease into your touring day.

▮ COMMUNICATIONS

INTERNET

Most hotels have Wi-Fi. Stores such as Woolworths, restaurants such as Wimpy, and most airports offer a countrywide Wi-Fi service called AlwaysOn that allows you 30 minutes of free Wi-Fi per day. If you need more time, you can pay for it.

If you bring your laptop or tablet, you'll have no problem finding Wi-Fi service in the cities, but it's unlikely you'll find anyone to service a Mac outside of Cape Town and Jo'burg.

Contacts Always On. ⊕ www.alwayson.co.za.

PHONES

There are toll-free numbers in South Africa. There's also something called a share-call line, for which the cost of the call is split between both parties.

The country code for South Africa is 27. When dialing from abroad, drop the initial 0 from local area codes.

CALLING WITHIN SOUTH AFRICA

Local calls (from landline to landline) are very cheap, although all calls from hotels add a hefty premium. Calls between a mobile phone and a landline are relatively expensive. Pay phones may be coin or card operated. Phone cards are available at newsstands, convenience stores, and telephone company offices.

When making a phone call in South Africa, always use the full 10-digit number, including the area code, even if you're in the same area. For directory assistance in South Africa, call 1023. For operator-assisted national long-distance calls, call 1025. For international operator assistance, dial 10903#. These numbers are free if dialed from a Telkom (landline) phone but are charged at normal cell-phone rates from a mobile—and they're busy call centers. Directory inquiries numbers are different for each cell-phone network. Vodacom is 111, MTN is 200, and Cell C is 146. These calls are charged at normal rates, but the call is timed only from when it is actually answered.

CALLING OUTSIDE SOUTH AFRICA

When dialing out from South Africa, dial 00 before the international code. So, for example, you would dial 001 for the United States, since the country code for the United States is 1.

Internet calling like Skype also works well from the United States, but it's not always functional in South Africa, unless you're on a reliable high-speed Internet connection, which isn't available everywhere. However, if you have a South African "free" cell phone (meaning you can receive calls for free; all phones using an SA SIM card do this), someone in the United States can call you from their Skype account, for reasonable per-minute charges, and you won't be charged.

Access Codes AT&T Direct. ☎ 314/925–6925 in South Africa ⊕ www.att.com. **MCI Worldwide Access.** ☎ 0800/990–011 in South Africa. **Sprint International Access.** ☎ 0800/990–001 in South Africa.

MOBILE PHONES

Cell phones are ubiquitous and have quite extensive coverage. There are four cell-phone service providers in South Africa—Cell C, MTN, Virgin Mobile, and Vodacom—and you can buy these SIM cards, as well as airtime, in supermarkets for as little as R10 for the SIM card. (If you purchase SIM cards at the airport, you will be charged much more.) Bear in mind that your U.S. cell phone may not work with the local GSM system and/or that your phone may be blocked from using SIM cards outside of your plan if your phone is not unlocked. Basic but functional GSM cell phones start at R200, and are available at the mobile carrier shops as well as major department stores like Woolworths.

Cell phones also can be rented by the day, week, or longer from the airport on your arrival, but this is an expensive option. If you plan to bring a U.S. cell phone while you're traveling, know what your own company will charge both for calls and data use. Texts cost a fraction of a call and are the handiest option for meeting up with local friends, but for calling a hotel reservations line, it's best to make the call.

Cellular Abroad rents and sells GMS phones and sells SIM cards that work in many countries, but they cost a lot more than local solutions. Mobal rents mobiles and sells GSM phones (starting at $49) that will operate in 150 countries. Per-call rates vary throughout the world. Vodacom is the country's leading cellular network.

The least complicated way to make and receive phone calls is to obtain international roaming service from your cell-phone service provider before you leave home, but this can be expensive. Any phone that you take abroad must be unlocked by your company for you to be able to use it.

Contacts Cell C. ☎ 084/140 ⊕ www.cellc.co.za. **Mobal.** ☎ 888/888–9162 in U.S. ⊕ www.mobal.com. **MTN.** ☎ 083/173 ⊕ www.mtn.co.za. **Virgin Mobile.** ☎ 0741/000–123 ⊕ www.virginmobile.co.za. **Vodacom.** ☎ 082/111 ⊕ www.vodacom.co.za.

▌CUSTOMS AND DUTIES

Visitors may bring in new or used gifts and souvenirs up to a total value of R5,000 duty-free. Duty-free allowances of tobacco and alcoholic beverages are also limited.

The United States is a signatory to CITES, a wildlife protection treaty, and therefore does not allow the importation of living or dead endangered animals, or their body parts, such as rhino horns or ivory. If you purchase an antique that is made partly or wholly of ivory, you must obtain a CITES preconvention certificate that clearly states that the item is at least 100 years old. The import of zebra skin or other tourist products also requires a CITES permit.

U.S. Information U.S. Customs and Border Protection. ⊕ www.cbp.gov. **U.S. Fish and Wildlife Service.** ⊕ www.fws.gov.

▌EATING OUT

South Africa's cities and towns are full of dining options, from chain restaurants like the popular Nando's to chic cafés. Indian food and Cape Malay dishes are regional favorites in Cape Town, and traditional smoked meats and sausages are available countrywide. Children are allowed in all restaurants, but don't expect toys and games as in American restaurants.

The restaurants we list are the cream of the crop in each price category. Price categories are based on the average cost of a main course at dinner (or at lunch if that is the only option). If you love seafood, you should make a point of visiting one of the casual West Coast beach restaurants in the Western Cape, where you sit on the beach in a makeshift structure and eat course after course of seafood cooked on an open fire.

For food-related health issues, see Health, below.

MEALS AND MEALTIMES

In South Africa dinner is eaten at night and lunch at noon. Breakfast generally consists of something eggy and hot, but many people are moving over to muesli and fruit. South Africans may eat muffins for breakfast but don't expect too many breakfast sweets. Restaurants serve breakfast until about 11:30; a few serve breakfast all day.

If you're staying at a game lodge, your mealtimes will revolve around the game drives—usually coffee and rusks (similar to biscotti) early in the morning, more coffee and probably muffins on the first game drive, a huge brunch in the late morning, no lunch, tea and something sweet in the late afternoon before the evening game drive, cocktails and snacks on the drive, and a substantial supper, or dinner, about 8 or 8:30.

If you're particularly interested in food, stay at a guesthouse selected by Good Cooks and Their Country Houses, which are noted for superior cuisine.

For a guesthouse to qualify for inclusion, the chef must be the owner (or one of them).

Unless otherwise noted, the restaurants listed in this guide are open daily for lunch and dinner.

Contacts Good Cooks and Their Country Houses. ⊕ *www.goodcooks.co.za.*

PAYING

Many restaurants accustomed to serving tourists accept credit cards, usually Visa and American Express, with MasterCard increasingly accepted.

For guidelines on tipping, see Tipping, below. For restaurant price charts, see Planning, at the beginning of each chapter.

RESERVATIONS AND DRESS

Most restaurants welcome casual dress, including jeans and sneakers. Very expensive restaurants and old-fashioned hotel restaurants (where colonial traditions die hard) may welcome nicer dress, but other than the Blue Train, few require a jacket and tie.

WINES, BEER, AND SPIRITS

You can buy wine in supermarkets and many convenience stores. Beer is available only in "bottle shops," which are licensed to sell spirits. Most restaurants are licensed to sell wine and beer, and many also sell spirits. From Saturday at 8 pm through Sunday, you can buy alcohol only in restaurants and bars. You may not take alcohol onto beaches, and it's illegal to walk down the street with an open container. You can, however, drink with a picnic or enjoy sundowners (cocktails at sunset) in almost any public place, such as Table Mountain or Kirstenbosch. The beach rule is also somewhat relaxed at sundowner time, but be careful.

For more information on food and drink, see "Flavors of South Africa," in Chapter 1.

LOCAL DO'S AND TABOOS

GREETINGS

The first words you should say to anyone in South Africa, no matter the situation, are "Hello, how are you?" It doesn't matter if you are in a hurry—African conversations begin with a greeting. To skip this and jump to the question, as we often do in the United States, is considered rude. Slow down and converse, then ask for what you need. After a few weeks you'll get used to it and miss it when you return home to instant demands.

SIGHTSEEING

South Africa, unlike the rest of the continent, is relatively casual. Aside from top-end restaurants and houses of worship, you can dress fairly casually (shorts and sandals). In national parks and by the beach, rules are even more flexible, and many people stroll into cafés right off the beach, wearing only cover-ups.

If you're visiting a house of worship, dress modestly. This is especially true at mosques, where women should bring scarves to cover their heads, wear skirts below the knees, and cover their shoulders. Some mosques prefer that non-Muslims remain outside.

OUT ON THE TOWN

When out at a restaurant or a club, behave as you would at home. Be polite to waitstaff, and don't call out.

HOUSE CALLS

If you are invited to someone's home, it's a good idea to bring a small gift. If you know your hosts' habits, you can bring a bottle of wine, chocolates, or flowers. If you've been invited to a very humble home—as can happen in rural areas—and your hosts are struggling to feed their children, they may prefer something a bit more pragmatic than a bunch of flowers. This is delicate territory, so when in doubt, ask a trustworthy, knowledgeable third party. Dress nicely and modestly when visiting homes, especially in the townships or Muslim areas.

DOING BUSINESS

Arrive on time for appointments, and hand over a business card during introductions. Handshakes are the proper form of greeting in a business setting. Gifts are not part of the business culture. Address colleagues by their titles and surnames.

It's not uncommon for business to be conducted over a meal. You may be inclined to rush proceedings along and force decisions, but this is not the African way. Slow down and relax.

Men generally wear a jacket and tie to meetings, but a suit isn't necessary, unless it's a really high-powered meeting. Women can get away with anything from a pretty floral dress to a suit, but take your cue from the general purpose of the meeting and other participants. Trousers are perfectly acceptable for women.

LANGUAGE

■TIP→ **Although many Americans consider the term coloured offensive, it's widely used in South Africa to describe South Africans who are descended from imported slaves, the San, the Khoekhoen, and European settlers. Over the years the term has lost any pejorative connotations.**

South Africa has 11 official languages: Afrikaans, English, Ndebele, North Sotho, South Sotho, Swati, Tsonga, Tswana (same as Setswana in Botswana), Venda, Xhosa, and Zulu. English is widely spoken, although road signs and other important markers often alternate between English and Afrikaans.

■ ELECTRICITY

The electrical current is 220 volts, 50 cycles alternating current (AC); wall outlets in most of the region take 15-amp plugs with three round prongs (the old British system), some take the European two narrow prongs, and a few take the straight-edged three-prong plugs, also 15 amps.

If your appliances are dual voltage, you'll need only an adapter. In remote areas (and even in some lodges) power may be solar or from a generator; this means that delivery is erratic both in voltage and supply. In even the remotest places, however, lodge staff will find a way to charge video and camera batteries, but you will receive little sympathy if you insist on using a hair dryer or electric razor.

Consider making a small investment in a universal adapter, which has several types of plugs in one lightweight, compact unit. Most laptops and mobile phone chargers are dual voltage (i.e., they operate equally well on 110 and 220 volts), so require only an adapter. These days the same is true of small appliances such as hair dryers. Always check labels and manufacturer instructions to be sure. Don't use 110-volt outlets marked "for shavers only" for high-wattage appliances such as hair dryers.

■ EMERGENCIES

The U.S. embassy is in Pretoria; there's a consulate in Johannesburg and Cape Town.

If you specifically need an ambulance, you can get one by calling the special ambulance number or through the general emergency number. If you intend to do scuba diving in South Africa, make sure you have DAN membership, which will be honored by Divers Alert Network South Africa (DANSA).

Embassies U.S. Consulate, Cape Town. ⊠ *2 Reddam Ave., Westlake* ☎ *021/702–7300 in Cape Town, 703/439–2301 in U.S.* ⊕ *za. usembassy.gov.* **U.S. Embassy to South**

Africa. ⊠ *877 Pretorius St., Pretoria* ☎ *012/431–4000.*

Emergency Contacts DANSA. ☎ *0800/020–111 emergency hotline, 27/828–106010 outside South Africa* ⊕ *www.dansa.org.* **General emergency.** ☎ *10111 from landline, 112 from mobile phone, 107 for Cape Town only.*

■ GEAR

Goods in South Africa's pharmacies and grocery stores are very similar to those in the States. If you have a favorite brand of toiletry, bring it; otherwise expect to pay average prices for items you may have left at home. Minimarts at gas stations also stock the same range of candies and sodas you would expect of a roadside shop.

Take care to bring enough prescription medicines and a copy of your prescription if you anticipate needing a refill. Ask your doctor to write down the ingredients so that a pharmacist will find a suitable substitute if necessary. Obtain your anti-malarials at home.

Incidents of theft from checked baggage in Cape Town and Johannesburg airports make luggage wrapping a popular option. For a few rand, the process of wrapping a bag in impenetrable cellophane is a great deterrent against crime. ■TIP→ **Fragile items in soft-sided bags can be crushed in the wrapping process, so remove breakable items or place them in the center of the bag to prevent their getting squeezed.** The wrapping can be removed by hand or with a knife. Security accepts wrapped bags.

In southern Africa it's possible to experience muggy heat, bone-chilling cold, torrential thunderstorms, and scorching African sun all within a couple of days. The secret is to pack lightweight clothes that you can wear in layers, and at least one lightweight fleece pullover or sweater. Take along a warm jacket, hat, and scarf, too, especially if you're going to a private game lodge. It can get mighty cold sitting in an open Land Rover at night or on an early-morning game drive. It really and truly does get very cold in almost every part of southern Africa, so don't fall into the it's-Africa-so-it-must-always-be-hot trap.

South Africans tend to dress casually. Businessmen still wear suits, but dress standards have become less rigid and more interesting since the late Nelson Mandela redefined the concept of sartorial elegance with his Madiba shirts. You can go almost anywhere in neat, clean, casual clothes, but you can still get dolled up to go to the theater or opera.

It's easy to get fried in the strong African sun, especially in mile-high Johannesburg or windy Cape Town, where the air can feel deceptively cool. Pack plenty of sunscreen (SPF 30 or higher), sunglasses, and a hat. An umbrella comes in handy during those late-afternoon thunderstorms but is almost useless in Cape Town in the winter, as it will get blown inside out. But do take a raincoat. *For more details on what to pack for a safari, see Chapter 10, Safari Primer.*

Some hotels do supply washcloths; some don't. It's always a good idea to have at least a couple of tissues in your bag, and moist towelettes, because there may not be a restroom (or toilet paper) just when you need it. Even an hour in a safari vehicle on a dry day can cover you with dust.

Make copies of all your important documents. Leave one set in one bag, another at home, and try to save them online in a PDF file, which may be the fastest way to access data if you need to replace anything. Consider carrying a small card with emergency contact numbers on it, such as the local U.S. embassy, in case things go terribly wrong.

If your luggage does get lost, your best bet for replacing staple items will be Woolworths (a high-quality brand in South Africa, with both department and food stores). Edgars and Truworths are also fine. You can find all three in most big shopping malls. Mr. Price is South Africa's Target equivalent, but with less-reliable quality. Cape Union Mart is great for safari stuff. You'll find a wide supply of toiletries in Clicks and Dis-Chem.

▌HEALTH

South Africa is a modern country, but Africa still poses certain health risks even in the most developed areas.

These days everyone is sun sensitive (and sun can be a big issue in South Africa), so pack plenty of your favorite SPF product from home, and use it generously. And drink plenty of water to avoid dehydration.

The drinking water in South Africa is treated and, except in rural areas, is absolutely safe to drink. Many people filter it, though, to get rid of the chlorine, as that aseptic status does not come free. You can eat fresh fruits and salads and have ice in your drinks.

It is always wise for travelers to have medical insurance for travel that will also help with emergency evacuation (most safari operators require emergency evacuation coverage and may ask you to pay for it along with your tour payments). If you don't want general travel insurance, many companies offer medical-only policies.

COMMON ISSUES
MALARIA
Although there are some nonmalarial safari regions in South Africa, the most serious health problem facing travelers is

malaria, which occurs in the prime South African game-viewing areas of Mpumalanga, Limpopo Province, and northern KwaZulu-Natal and in the countries farther north. The risk is medium at the height of the summer and very low in winter. All travelers heading into malaria-endemic regions should consult a health-care professional at least one month before departure for advice. Unfortunately, the malarial organism *Plasmodium sp.* seems to be able to develop a hardy resistance to new prophylactic drugs pretty quickly, so even if you are taking the newest miracle drug, the best prevention is to avoid being bitten by mosquitoes in the first place. After sunset wear light-color, loose, long-sleeve shirts, long pants, and shoes and socks, and apply mosquito repellent generously. Always sleep in a mosquito-proof room or tent, and if possible, keep a fan going in your room. If you are pregnant or trying to conceive, avoid malaria areas entirely.

Generally speaking, the risk is much lower in the dry season (May–October) and peaks immediately after the first rains, which should be in November, but El Niño has made that a lot less predictable.

BILHARZIA
Many lakes and streams, particularly east of the watershed divide (i.e., in rivers flowing toward the Indian Ocean), are infected with *bilharzia* (schistosomiasis), a parasite carried by a small freshwater snail. The microscopic fluke enters through the skin of swimmers or waders, attaches itself to the intestines or bladder, and lays eggs. Avoid wading in still waters or in areas close to reeds. If you have been wading or swimming in doubtful water, dry yourself off vigorously with a towel immediately upon exiting the water, as this may help to dislodge any flukes before they can burrow into your skin. Fast-moving water is considered safe. If you have been exposed, pop into a pharmacy

and purchase a course of treatment and take it to be safe. If your trip is ending shortly after your exposure, take the medicine home and have a checkup once you get there. Bilharzia is easily diagnosed, and it's also easily treated in the early stages.

HIV
Be aware of the dangers of becoming infected with HIV (which is a big problem in Africa) or hepatitis. Make sure you use a condom during a sexual encounter; they're sold in supermarkets, pharmacies, and most convenience stores. If you feel there's a possibility you've exposed yourself to the virus, you can get antiretroviral treatment (post-exposure prophylaxis or PEP) from private hospitals, but you must do so within 48 hours of exposure.

RABIES
Rabies is extremely rare in domesticated animals in South Africa but is more common in wild animals—one more reason you should not feed or tease them. If you are bitten by a monkey or other wild animal, seek medical attention immediately. The chance of contracting rabies is extremely small, but the consequences are so horrible that you really don't want to gamble on this one.

INSECTS AND OTHER PESTS
In summer ticks may be a problem, even in open areas close to cities. If you intend to walk or hike anywhere, use a suitable insect repellent. After your walk, examine your body and clothes for ticks, looking carefully for pepper ticks, which are tiny but may cause tick-bite fever. If you find a tick has bitten you, do not pull it off. If you do, you may pull the body off, and the head will remain embedded in your skin, causing an infection. Rather, smother the area with petroleum jelly, and the tick will eventually let go, as it will be unable to breathe; you can then scrape it off with a fingernail. If you are bitten, keep an eye on the bite. If the tick was infected, the bite will swell, itch, and

develop a black necrotic center. This is a sure sign that you will develop tick-bite fever, which usually hits after about 8 to 12 days. Symptoms may be mild or severe, depending on the patient. This disease is not usually life-threatening in healthy adults, but it's horribly unpleasant. Most people who are bitten by ticks suffer no more than an itchy bump, so don't panic.

Also, obviously, keep a lookout for mosquitoes. Even in nonmalarial areas they are extremely irritating. When walking anywhere in the bush, keep a lookout for snakes. Most will slither away when they feel you coming, but just keep your eyes peeled. If you see one, give it a wide berth and you should be fine. Snakes really bite only when they are taken by surprise, so you don't want to step on a napping puff adder. ■ TIP→ If on safari or camping, check your boots and shake your clothes out for spiders and other crawlies before getting dressed.

OVER-THE-COUNTER REMEDIES
You can buy over-the-counter medication in pharmacies and supermarkets, and you will find the more general remedies in Clicks or Dis-Chem, chain stores selling beauty products, some OTC medication, and housewares. Your body may not react the same way to the South African version of a product, even something as simple as a headache tablet, so bring your own supply for your trip and rely on pharmacies just for emergency medication.

SHOTS AND MEDICATIONS
South Africa does not require any inoculations for entry. Travelers entering South Africa within six days of leaving a country infected with yellow fever require a yellow-fever vaccination certificate. The South African travel clinics and the U.S. National Centers for Disease Control and Prevention (CDC) recommend that you be vaccinated against hepatitis A and B if you intend to travel to more isolated areas. Cholera injections are widely regarded as useless, so don't let anyone talk you into

having one, but the newer oral vaccine seems to be more effective.

If you are coming to South Africa for a safari, chances are you are heading to a malarial game reserve. Only a handful of game reserves are nonmalarial. Millions of travelers take oral prophylactic drugs before, during, and after their safaris. It's up to you to weigh the risks and benefits of the type of antimalarial drug you choose to take. If you're pregnant or traveling with small children, consider a nonmalarial region for your safari.

The CDC provides up-to-date information on health risks and recommended vaccinations and medications for travelers to southern Africa. In most of South Africa you need not worry about any of these, but if you plan to visit remote regions, check with the CDC's traveler's health line. For up-to-date, local expertise, contact Netcare Travel Clinics.

MEDICAL CARE IN SOUTH AFRICA
South African doctors are generally excellent. The equipment and training in private clinics rivals the best in the world, but public hospitals tend to suffer from overcrowding and underfunding. So if you need to seek medical treatment, ask your hotel or safari operator to get you to a private hospital. In South Africa, foreigners are expected to pay in full for any medical services, so check your existing health plan to see whether you're covered while abroad, and supplement it if necessary.

On returning home, if you experience any unusual symptoms, including fever, painful eyes, backache, diarrhea, severe headache, general lassitude, or blood in urine or stool, be sure to tell your doctor where you have been. These symptoms may indicate malaria, tick-bite fever, bilharzia, or—if you've been traveling north of South Africa's borders—some other tropical malady.

Health Warnings National Centers for Disease Control and Prevention (*CDC*). ☎ *800/232–4636 international travelers' health line* ⊕ *www.cdc.gov/travel.* **World Health Organization** (*WHO*). ⊕ *www.who.int.*

Medical-Only Insurers International Medical Group. ☎ *800/628–4664* ⊕ *www. imglobal.com.* **International SOS.** ☎ *011/541–1300 24-hr emergency,* ⊕ *www. internationalsos.com.* **Wallach & Company.** ☎ *800/237–6615* ⊕ *www.wallach.com.*

■ HOURS OF OPERATION

The most surprising aspect of South Africa's business hours, especially for tourists who come to shop, is that shopping centers, including enclosed secure indoor malls, often close by 6 pm. This is starting to change in Cape Town and Johannesburg malls, with summer hours increased until 7 or 8, but don't expect it. It's rare for a store to remain open after dinner.

Business hours in major South African cities are weekdays from about 9 to 5. Most banks close in mid-afternoon, usually about 3:30, but dedicated currency exchange offices usually stay open longer. In addition, post offices and banks are open briefly on Saturday morning from about 9, so get there early. But you'll find a handy ATM almost everywhere. In rural areas and small towns things are less rigid. Post offices often close for lunch, and in very small towns and villages, banks may have very abbreviated hours.

Most museums are open during usual business hours, including Saturday morning, but some stay open longer.

Most pharmacies close about 6, but there's generally an all-night pharmacy in towns of a reasonable size. If not, look for an emergency number posted on a pharmacy.

Many gas stations are open 24 hours, and urban gas stations have 24-hour convenience stores, some of which have an impressive range of goods.

HOLIDAYS

National holidays in South Africa are New Year's Day (January 1), Human Rights Day (March 21), Good Friday, Easter, Family Day (sometime in March or April), Freedom Day (April 27), Workers Day (May 1), Youth Day (June 16), National Women's Day (August 9), Heritage Day (September 24), Day of Reconciliation (December 16), Christmas Day (December 25), and Day of Goodwill (December 26). If a public holiday falls on a Sunday, the following Monday is also a public holiday. Election days are also public holidays, so check calendars closer to your time of travel for those, which are not on fixed dates.

In Cape Town, January 2 is also a holiday, known as *tweede nuwe jaar* (second new year). School vacations vary with the provinces, but usually comprise about 10 days over Easter, about three weeks around June or July, and then the big summer vacation from about December 10 to January 10.

■ MAIL

The mail service in South Africa is reasonably reliable, but mail can take weeks to arrive, and money and other valuables may be stolen from letters and packages. You can buy stamps at post offices, open weekdays 8:30 to 4:30 and Saturday 8 to noon. Stamps for local use only, marked "standardized post," may be purchased from newsstands in booklets of 10 stamps. PostNet franchises—a combined post office, courier service, business services center, and Internet café—are in convenient places like shopping malls and are open longer hours than post offices.

All overseas mail costs the same. At the post office a postcard is about R6.05, and a letter ranges from R5.90 to about R26.90, depending on size and weight.

ADDRESSES

Note that the first floor of a building is the one between the ground floor and the second floor. Mailing addresses are pretty straightforward. If they're not a street address, they're either a P.O. Box or a Private Bag—essentially the same, just differing in size. The only vaguely tricky variation is a postnet suite, which consists of a number, followed by a private bag and then a post office (e.g., Postnet Suite 25, Private Bag X25, name of town, postal code). Even the smallest town has its own postal code, and suburbs may have different postal codes—one for a street address and one for P.O. boxes.

SHIPPING PACKAGES

If you make a purchase, try your best to take it home on the plane with you, even if it means packing your travel clothes and items into a box and shipping those to your home, or buying a cheap piece of luggage and paying the excess weight fees. If you buy something from a store accustomed to foreign visitors, it will likely already have a system for getting your items to you, often in a surprising few weeks' time.

Federal Express and DHL offer more reliable service than regular mail, as do the new Fast Mail and Speed Courier services, yet even these "overnight" services are subject to delays. PostNet, South Africa's version of Kinko's, also offers courier services. A parcel of up to about a pound (half a kilogram) will cost around R400 to send to the United States, and a one-kilogram parcel (2.2 pounds) will cost around R790.

Express Services DHL. ☎ *0860/345-000* ⊕ *www.dhl.co.za.* **FedEx.** ☎ *87/742-8000, 080/00-3339 toll-free in South Africa* ⊕ *www. fedex.com.* **PostNet.** ☎ *0860/767-8638* ⊕ *www.postnet.co.za.*

▌ MONEY

Because of inflation and currency fluctuations, it's difficult to give exact exchange rates. It's safe to say, though, that the region is a good value, with high-quality accommodations and food at about two-thirds or half the cost they would be at home.

A bottle of good South African wine costs about the equivalent of $9 (double or triple in a restaurant), and a meal at a prestigious restaurant won't set you back more than $50 per person; an average restaurant, with wine, might be about $40 for two. Double rooms in the country's finest hotels may cost $400 a night, but $200 is more than enough to secure high-quality lodging in most cities, and charming, spotless B&Bs or guesthouses with full breakfasts can be less than $80 in many areas.

Not everything in South Africa is cheap. Expect to pay international rates and more to stay in one of the exclusive private game lodges in Mpumalanga, Limpopo Province, or KwaZulu-Natal. Expect to pay from $2,000 and $3,000 per couple per night, which could include a flight charter. Flights to South Africa are expensive, but the rash of new low-cost carriers makes popular domestic routes less expensive, with most trips less than $150 one way. Taxis are uncharacteristically expensive, compared with other vacation needs.

ATMS AND BANKS

South Africa has a modern banking system, with branches throughout the country and ubiquitous ATMs, especially at tourist attractions, in gas stations, and in shopping malls. Banks open at 9 in the morning weekdays and close at 3:30 in the afternoon; on Saturday they close at 11 in the morning, and they are closed Sunday (with the exception of Standard Bank branches in shopping malls, some of which are open on Sunday, 9:30–1). Many banks can perform foreign-exchange services or international electronic transfers, but you will always get a better exchange rate from an ATM. The major South African banks are ABSA, First National Bank, Nedbank, and Standard.

If your card gets swallowed, *stay at the ATM* and call the help line number displayed. If possible, withdraw money during the day and choose ATMs with security guards present or those inside stores.

CREDIT CARDS

MasterCard, Visa, and American Express are accepted almost everywhere, but Diners Club and Discover are not.

It's a good idea to inform your credit-card company before you travel, especially if you're going abroad and don't travel internationally very often. Otherwise, the credit-card company might put a hold on your card owing to unusual activity—not a good thing halfway through your trip. Record all your credit-card numbers—as well as the phone numbers to call if your cards are lost or stolen—in a safe place, so you're prepared should something go wrong. MasterCard, Visa, and American Express all have general numbers you can call collect if you're abroad.

If you plan to use your credit card for cash advances, you'll need to apply for a PIN at least two weeks before your trip. Although it's usually cheaper (and safer) to use a credit card abroad for large purchases (so you can cancel payments or be reimbursed if there's a problem), note that some credit-card companies *and* the banks that issue them add substantial percentages to all foreign transactions, whether they're in a foreign currency or not. Check on these fees before leaving home, so there won't be any surprises when you get the bill.

Reporting Lost Cards **American Express.**
☎ *800/528–4800 in the U.S.* ⊕ *www.american-express.com.* **Diners Club.** ☎ *0860/346–377, 011/358–8406 outside South Africa* ⊕ *www.dinersclub.com.* **MasterCard.** ☎ *800/990–418* ⊕ *www.mastercard.com.* **Visa.** ☎ *0800/990–475*

toll-free in South Africa, 1303/967–1090 collect from abroad ⊕ *www.visa.com.*

Prices throughout this guide are given for adults. Substantially reduced fees are sometimes available for children, students, and senior citizens.

CURRENCY AND EXCHANGE

The unit of currency in South Africa is the rand (R), with 100 cents (¢) equaling R1. Bills come in R10, R20, R50, R100, and R200 denominations, which are differentiated by color (beware of the similar color of the R50 and R200 notes). Coins are minted in 5¢, 10¢, 20¢, 50¢, R1, R2, and R5 denominations.

At this writing, the rand is trading at about R15.5 to $1. It's a good bargain given the quality of lodgings, which cost probably two-thirds the price of comparable facilities in the United States.

To avoid administrative hassles, keep all foreign-exchange receipts until you leave the region, as you may need them as proof when changing any unspent local currency back into your own currency. You may not take more than R25,000 or US$10,000 in cash in or out of South Africa. For more information you can contact the South African Reserve Bank.

■ TIP→ Even if a currency-exchange booth has a sign promising no commission, rest assured that there's some kind of huge, hidden fee. And as for rates, you're almost always better off getting foreign currency at an ATM or exchanging money at a bank.

Currency Conversion Oanda.com. ⊕ *www.oanda.com.* **XE.com.** ⊕ *www.xe.com.*

ITEM	AVERAGE COST
Cup of coffee	$2
Glass of beer	$1.70–$2
Quarter of roasted chicken with salad and drink at a fast-food restaurant	$5–$7
Room-service sandwich in a hotel	$5–$7
2-km (1-mile) taxi ride	$6–$8

∎ PASSPORTS

American citizens need only a valid passport to enter South Africa for visits of up to 90 days; this includes infants. Check the expiration date. If your passport will expire within six months of your return date, you need to renew it in advance, as South Africa won't let you enter with a soon-to-expire passport. ∎**TIP→ You will be denied entry to the country if you do not have two blank, facing pages in your passport.**

Before your trip, make two copies of your passport's data page (one for someone at home and another for you to carry separately). Or scan the page and email it to someone at home and/or yourself.

U.S. Passport Information U.S. Department of State. ☎ *877/487-2778* ⊕ *travel.state.gov.*

∎ RESTROOMS

All fuel complexes on the major roads have large, clean, well-maintained restrooms. In cities you can find restrooms in shopping malls, at some gas stations, and in restaurants—most of which are quite happy to allow you to use them.

∎ SAFETY

South Africa is a country in transition, and as a result experiences growing pains that reveal themselves in economic inequities, which result in high crime rates. Although the majority of visitors experience a crime-free trip to South Africa, it's essential to practice vigilance and extreme care.

Crime is a major problem in the whole region, particularly in large cities, and all visitors should take precautions to protect themselves. Do not walk alone at night, and exercise caution even during the day. Avoid wearing jewelry (even costume jewelry), don't invite attention by wearing an expensive camera around your neck, and don't flash a large wad of cash. If you are toting a handbag, wear the strap across your body; even better, wear a money belt, preferably hidden from view under your clothing. When sitting at airports or at restaurants, especially outdoor cafés, make sure to keep your bag on your lap or between your legs—otherwise it may just quietly "walk off" when you're not looking. Even better, loop the strap around your leg, or clip the strap around the table or chair.

Carjacking is another problem, with armed bandits often forcing drivers out of their vehicles at traffic lights, in driveways, or during a fake accident. Always drive with your windows closed and doors locked, don't stop for hitchhikers, and park in well-lighted places. At traffic lights, leave enough space between you and the vehicle in front so you can pull into another lane if necessary. In the unlikely event you are carjacked, don't argue, and don't look at the carjacker's face. Just get out of the car, or ask to be let out of the car. Do not try to keep any of your belongings—they are all replaceable, even that laptop with all that data on it. If you aren't given the opportunity to leave the car, try to stay calm, ostentatiously look away from the hijackers so they can be sure you can't identify them, and follow all instructions. Ask again, calmly, to be let out of the car.

Many places that are unsafe in South Africa will not bear obvious signs of danger. Make sure you know exactly where you're going. Purchase a good map and obtain comprehensive directions from your hotel, rental-car agent, or a trusted local. Taking the wrong exit off a highway into a township could lead you straight to disaster. Many cities are ringed by "no-go" areas. Learn from your hotel or the locals which areas to avoid. If you sense you have taken a wrong turn, drive toward a public area, such as a gas station, or building with an armed guard, before attempting to correct your mistake, which could just compound the problem. When parking, don't leave anything visible in the car;

stow it all in the trunk—this includes clothing or shoes. As an added measure, leave the glove box open, to show there's nothing of value inside (take the rental agreement with you).

Before setting out on foot, ask a local, such as your hotel concierge or a shopkeeper, which route to take and how far you can safely go. Walk with a purposeful stride so you look like you know where you're going, and duck into a shop or café if you need to check a map, speak on your mobile phone, or recheck the directions you've been given. ■TIP➔ **Don't walk while speaking on a cell phone.**

Lone women travelers need to be particularly vigilant about walking alone and locking their rooms. South Africa has one of the world's highest rates of rape. If you do attract someone who won't take a firm but polite *no* for an answer, appeal immediately to the hotel manager, bartender, or someone else who seems to be in charge. If you have to walk a short distance alone at night, such as from the hotel reception to your room in a dark motel compound or back from a café along a main street, have a plan, carry a whistle, and know what you'll do if you are grabbed.

For destination-specific information, see Safety in each chapter.

■ TAXES

All South African hotels pay a bed tax, which is included in quoted prices. In South Africa the Value-Added Tax (V.A.T.), which at this writing is 14%, is included in the price of most goods and services, including hotel accommodations and food. To get a V.A.T. refund, foreign visitors must present their receipts (minimum of R250) at the airport and be carrying any purchased items with them or in their luggage. You must fill out Form V.A.T. 255, available at the airport V.A.T. refund office. Whatever you buy, make sure that your receipt is an original tax

invoice, containing the vendor's name and address, V.A.T. registration number, and the words "tax invoice." Refunds are paid by check, which can be cashed immediately at an airport bank or refunded directly onto your credit card, with a small transaction fee. Be sure you visit the V.A.T. refund desk in the departures hall before you go through check-in procedures, and try to organize your receipts as you go, to make for easy viewing. Officials will go through your receipts and randomly ask to view your purchases.

Contacts V.A.T. Refund Office. ☎ 011/979–0055 ⊕ *www.taxrefunds.co.za.*

■ TIME

South Africa operates on SAST (South African Standard Time). That makes it seven hours ahead of North American Eastern Standard Time. South Africa doesn't follow any daylight saving time, so when U.S. clocks spring forward, it's only six hours ahead.

■ TIPPING

Tipping is an integral part of South African life, and it's expected that you'll tip for services that you might take for granted at home. Most notable among these is getting gas, as there are no self-service stations. If the attendant simply fills your tank, tip R5; if he or she offers to clean your windshield, checks your tires, oil, or water, and is generally helpful, tip R5–R10. In restaurants the size of the tip should depend on the quality of service, but 10% is standard, unless, of course, a service charge has already been added to the bill. Give the same percentage to bartenders, taxi drivers, and tour guides.

TIPPING GUIDELINES FOR SOUTH AFRICA	
Bartender	10% of your bill is common
Car guards	R5
Bellhop	R5 per item
Hotel concierge	Hotel managers say it's not necessary to tip a concierge. If one goes out of his way for you, getting tickets to a sold-out event, say, then anything from R70 to R175 would be appropriate.
Hotel doorman	R5, but it's not expected
Hotel maid	Tips are not expected for maids in South Africa, as hotels add service charges to the bill that are distributed to staff
Hotel room-service waiter	R5 per delivery is nice but not expected
Porter at airport or train station	R5 per bag
Skycap at airport	R5 per bag checked
Taxi driver	10%, but round up the fare to the next dollar amount.
Tour guide	10% of the cost of the tour
Valet parking attendant	R5 when you get your car
Waiter	10%; nothing additional if a service charge is added to your bill

At the end of your stay at a game lodge, you're expected to tip both the ranger and the tracker and the general staff. Different lodgings handle it differently, and checking with the management is one way to make sure you tip properly. However, a good model to follow is to factor 10% of your total room bill. Fifty percent of this figure should go to your ranger/tracker, and 50% should go to the general staff. If you have

a personal butler, factor an additional 10% (of your total tip figure). If you have your laundry done, leave R5–R10 for the laundress in a special envelope. Envelopes are usually provided in safari rooms for tipping, but it's a nice touch to bring your own note cards to write a personal message.

Informal parking attendants operate in the major cities in South Africa and even in some tourist areas. Although they often look a bit seedy, they do provide a good service, so tip them RR5 if your car is still in one piece when you return to it.

❚ TRIP INSURANCE

Comprehensive trip insurance is valuable if you're booking a very expensive or complicated trip (particularly to an isolated region) or if you're booking far in advance. Comprehensive policies typically cover trip cancellation and interruption, letting you cancel or cut your trip short because of illness, or, in some cases, acts of terrorism in your destination. Such policies might also cover evacuation and medical care. For trips abroad you should have at least medical-only coverage (*see Health, above*). Some also cover you for trip delays because of bad weather or mechanical problems as well as for lost or delayed luggage.

Another type of coverage to consider is financial default—that is, when your trip is disrupted because a tour operator, airline, or cruise line goes out of business. Generally you must buy this when you book your trip or shortly thereafter, and it's available to you only if your operator isn't on a list of excluded companies.

Always read the fine print of your policy to make sure that you're covered for the risks that most concern you. Compare several polices to be sure you're getting the best price and range of coverage available.

Comprehensive Insurers Allianz Travel Insurance. ☎ 866/884-3556 ⊕ *www.allianz-travelinsurance.com.* **CSA Travel Protection.** ☎ 877/243-4135 *toll-free in U.S., 240/330-1529 outside U.S.* ⊕ *www.csatravelprotection. com.* **HTH Worldwide.** ☎ 610/254-8700,

888/243–2358 toll-free in U.S. ⊕ *www.*
hthworldwide.com. **Travelex Insurance.**
☎ *800/228–9792* ⊕ *www.travelex-insurance.*
com. **Travel Guard.** ☎ *800/826–4919* ⊕ *www.*
travelguard.com. **Travel Insured Interna-**
tional. ☎ *800/243–3174* ⊕ *www.travelinsured.*
com.

Insurance Comparison Information Insure
My Trip. ☎ *800/487–4722* ⊕ *www.insuremy-*
trip.com. **Square Mouth.** ☎ *800/240–0369*
international customer service ⊕ *www.square-*
mouth.com.

▌ VISITOR INFORMATION

See the individual chapter Essentials sec-
tions for details on local visitor bureaus.

ONLINE TRAVEL TOOLS

All About South Africa South Africa
National Parks. ⊕ *www.sanparks.org.* **South-**
Africa.info. ⊕ *www.southafrica.info.*

Culture Artslink.co.za. ⊕ *www.artslink.co.za.*
Iziko South African Museum. ⊕ *www.iziko.*
org.za. **Mail & Guardian.** ⊕ *www.mg.co.za.*

Media Independent Newspapers. ⊕ *www.*
iol.co.za.

Visitor Information Cape Town Tourism.
⊕ *www.capetown.travel.* **South African**
Tourism. ☎⊕ *www.southafrica.net.*

INDEX

PHOTO CREDITS

Cover credit: Front cover: Four Oaks/Shutterstock [Description: Penguins at Boulders Beach, Cape Town, South Africa]. 1, Andrea Willmore / Shutterstock. 2, Miguel Sobreira/age fotostock. 4, InnaFelker / Shutterstock. 5 (top), Adstock\UIG/age fotostock. 5 (bottom), espiegle / istockphoto. 6 (top left), Frank Kahts / Alamy. 6 (top right), michaeljung / istockphoto. 6 (bottom left), Fabian von Poser/imageBROKER/age fotostock. 6 (bottom right), Ken C Moore / Shutterstock. 7 (top), Shaen Adey/age fotostock. 7 (bottom), Johan Swanepoel / Shutterstock. 8 (top left), Hel080808 I Dreamstime.com. 8 (top right), Iwan Baan/Zeitz Museum of Contemporary Art Africa. 8 (bottom), Tuxone I Dreamstime.com. Chapter One: Experience South Africa: 13, michaeljung / Shutterstock. Chapter Two: Cape Town and Peninsula: 35, David Ryznar / Shutterstock. Chapter Three: The Western Cape: 123, PhotoSky / Shutterstock. Chapter Four: The Northern Cape: 211, francesco de marco / Shutterstock. Chapter Five: The Garden Route and the Little Karoo: 245, Domossa I Dreamstime.com. Chapter Six: The Eastern Cape: 277, David Steele / Shutterstock. Chapter Seven: Durban and KwaZulu-Natal: 309, 2630ben / Shutterstock. Chapter Eight: Johannesburg: 383, Ratmandude I Dreamstime.com. Chapter Nine: Mpumalanga & Kruger National Park: 437, Delpixel / Shutterstock. Chapter Ten: Safari Primer: 483, Neil Burton / Shutterstock. Back cover (from left to right): espiegle/iStockphoto; Delpixel / Shutterstock; AnetaPics / Shutterstock. Spine: Stuporter I Dreamstime.com. About Our Writers: All photos are courtesy of the writers except for the following: Christopher Clark, courtesy of Nicola Cernik.

NOTES

NOTES

NOTES

Fodor's ESSENTIAL SOUTH AFRICA

Editorial: Douglas Stallings, *Editorial Director*; Margaret Kelly, *Senior Editor*; Alexis Kelly, Jacinta O'Halloran, and Amanda Sadlowski, *Editors*; Teddy Minford, *Content Editor*; Rachael Roth, *Content Manager*

Design: Tina Malaney, *Design and Production Director;* Jessica Gonzalez, *Production Designer*

Photography: Jennifer Arnow, *Senior Photo Editor*

Maps: Rebecca Baer, *Senior Map Editor*; David Lindroth, Mark Stroud (Moon Street Cartography), *Cartographers*

Production: Jennifer DePrima, *Editorial Production Manager*; Carrie Parker, *Senior Production Editor*; Elyse Rozelle, *Production Editor*; David Satz, *Director of Content Production*

Business & Operations: Chuck Hoover, *Chief Marketing Officer*; Joy Lai, *Vice President and General Manager*; Stephen Horowitz, *Director of Business Development and Revenue Operations;* Tara McCrillis, *Director of Publishing Operations;* Eliza D. Aceves, *Content Operations Manager and Strategist*

Public Relations and Marketing: Joe Ewaskiw, *Manager;* Esther Su, *Marketing Manager*

Writers: Claire Baranowski, Christopher Clarke, Ishay Govender-Ypma, Mary Holland, Barbara Noe Kennedy, Lee Middleton, Kate Turkington

Editor: Teddy Minford

Production Editor: Elyse Rozelle

1st Edition

ISBN 978-1-64097-014-4

ISSN 2574-3546

All details in this book are based on information supplied to us at press time. Always confirm information when it matters, especially if you're making a detour to visit a specific place. Fodor's expressly disclaims any liability, loss, or risk, personal or otherwise, that is incurred as a consequence of the use of any of the contents of this book.

SPECIAL SALES

This book is available at special discounts for bulk purchases for sales promotions or premiums. For more information, e-mail SpecialMarkets@fodors.com

PRINTED IN THE UNITED STATES OF AMERICA

10 9 8 7 6 5 4 3 2 1

ABOUT OUR WRITERS

Travel Smart updater **Claire Baranowski** spent an idyllic childhood in a small town in Zimbabwe before moving to South Africa. Today, she splits her time between London and Cape Town as a travel writer and editor. Her favorite experiences have included backpacking in Laos and beach escapes in Sri Lanka, but the most magical have been on safari in Africa.

Christopher Clark, who updated the Eastern Cape, is a freelance dreamer, writer, and wanderer based in Cape Town. Afflicted with itchy feet from a young age, he has traveled to and written from more than 50 countries across Africa and beyond. His work has been published by a number of regional and international publications including *Africa Geographic, News24, The Big Issue, Nkwazi Magazine, This Is Africa*, and more. He has twice been named as one of South Africa's best young writers by The Big Issue.

Ishay Govender-Ypma, a former lawyer, is a freelance travel photojournalist, cookbook author, and guidebook author. Her bylines appear in *Sunday Times Travel (UK), The National (UAE), Roads & Kingdoms, Marie Claire, Food 52*, and many others. She has a deep interest in cultural anthropology and what makes us human.

Mary Holland is a South African writer and editor based in New York. Mary has spent most of her life in the Western Cape, where she studied in Stellenbosch and worked in Cape Town as the digital editor of *GQ* and *Glamour, South Africa*.

Barbara Noe Kennedy left her longtime position as senior editor with NatGeo Travel Publishing in 2015 to go freelance full-time. She writes about travel for Fodor's Travel, Lonely Planet, BBC Travel, and the *Washington Post*, among others. She resides in Arlington, Virginia, but her heart is in Africa, where she volunteers at an orphanage in Zambia and spends as much time as she can exploring southern Africa.

Focusing on environment, development, and humanitarian features—and having been writing in Africa since 2005, and based in South Africa since 2006—American journalist **Lee Middleton** has written for *Time*, the *Mail & Guardian, Africa Geographic, Men's Health*, and IRIN News, among others. Having also lived in Thailand, India, and Mexico as a wildlife researcher, Himalayan adventurer, and human rights worker, her penchant for exploration now manifests in food and travel writing from across the continent, with a focus on southern and eastern Africa. She updated Cape Town dining and lodging.

Kate Turkington is one of South Africa's best known travel writers and broadcasters and updated Mpumalanga & Kruger National Park and KwaZulu-Natal for this edition. Her live Sunday night radio show, "Believe it or Not," is South Africa's longest-running radio talk show. She travels the world on a regular basis, but her heart and home are in Africa, where she lives in Johannesburg. She specializes in safari destinations, but in the last few years she has found herself at Everest Base Camp in Tibet, deep in the Amazon jungle, high in the Andes, being held up by heavily armed tribesmen in the Rift Valley, and shedding tears at Hiroshima.